mulated benefit obligation accrual basis accrued expense acid test ratio acquisition adequate disclos
tion aggregate supply amortization analog annual meeting annual
ce balloon payment bandwidth banker's acceptance bankruptcy ba
rder bleed blind pool blue chip body copy bond ratings book value bookkeeping borro g bas
aptain Coco Chanel channels of distribution charact based interface chart of accounts
ination rate comfort letter commercial paper commis sion commodity commodity future
security cooperative advertising coproduction copywriter core competencies corporate culture corr
phic segmentation demographics dependent variable depletion depreciation derivatives design capac
mer of opinion discoun e discounted cash flow discretionary income disposa
e dumping duopoly du od duration earnings report econometric demand an
icity electronic bulletin ard employee assistance program employee discharge
d rate of return expens ordinary item factoring fault tolerance federal debt
iscal year fixed assets flextime flighting float focus strategy font forced conversion forecasting foreig
future value of an annuity futures general ledger generally accepted accounting principles generic a
lization going private golden parachute goodwill government market graphical user interface green
d holding-period return home page horizontal integration hyperlink hypertext icons mage advertis
industrial goods industry-attractiveness test inflation initial public offering inputs insertion order int
ver investment banker job enrichment Steven P. Jobs joint venture junk bond kaizen Keogh plan key
ent market lead time leadership leading economic in s learning curve learnin
ngitudinal panel loss leader lot tolerance percentage low-involvement proc
dit manufacturing resource planning margin margin call markdo ket risk premium marke
pt medium-term note mega-bank megabyte metrics micromarkets microwave minimum pension liab
supply mortgage-backed bond motivation-hygiene theory multilevel marketing multitasking Ruper
York Stock Exchange new-product development news release niche marketing nondurable good no
ational research obsolescence offshore financial center oligopoly open board operating expenses op
ent outsourcing overhead pac William Paley payback period penny stocks pension plans
lant manager potential market ver preference segmentation preferred stock premium prep
ivate label private placement p ly held company pro forma product line production funct
ctus proxy statement psychographic segmentation public domain public s e an
quick ratio quota sampling random sampling random walk theory real-t roce
bank regression analysis relationship marketing reliability-centered mai e an
s John D. Rockefeller rollout market entry sale/leaseback sales promotio vag
small-issues exemption solvency span of control special item specific identification strategic plannin
on tangible asset tangible net worth target market tax haven technical specialist technology transfe
e total ret o shareholders unconsolidated subsidiary underwriting underwriting synd
red upstream utility Theodore Vail variable costing vendor financing venture capital ver
rk in process working papers workstation World Trade Organization yellow sheets yield curve zero

KNOWLEDGE EXCHANGE

BUSINESS
ENCYCLOPEDIA

Illustrated

Your Complete Business Advisor

KNOWLEDGE EXCHANGE

BUSINESS ENCYCLOPEDIA

Illustrated

EDITOR IN CHIEF
Lorraine Spurge

CHAIRMAN, EDITORIAL BOARD
Kenin M. Spivak

INTRODUCTION BY
Richard G. Hamermesh, Ph.D.

KNOWLEDGEXCHANGE
Santa Monica

Knowledge Exchange Business Encyclopedia

Editorial

Editor in Chief
Lorraine Spurge

Chairman, Editorial Board
Kenin M. Spivak

Managing Editor
Cynthia Kumagawa

Research Director
Pamela Nelson, CFA

Production Manager
David Bolhuis

Rights and Permissions
Amy McCubbin

Associate Editor
Suzanne Finne

Editorial Assistant
Gayle Pajaud

Research Associates
Scott Humphrey
Roseanne Landay
Greg Suess
Benjamin Tappan

Proofreaders
Chuck Goldman
Wendy Anderson

Design

Creative Director
Debra Valencia

Design Firm
Sussman/Prejza & Company, Inc.
   Deborah Sussman, Principal
   Yuki Nishinaka
   Paula Loh
   Armena Jehanian
   Hsin-Hsien Tsai
   Christina Brenner
   Angela Leung
   Sylvia Park

Graphic Production Support
Mark Heliger
Connie Lane
Elisa Malin
Eric M. Woodard

Cover Illustrator
Marty Gunsaullus

Legal Counsel

Neil Rosini, Esq.
Franklin, Weinrib, Rudell & Vassallo, P.C.,
New York

Knowledge Exchange, LLC
1299 Ocean Avenue, Suite 250
Santa Monica, California 90401

Copyright © 1997 Knowledge Exchange, LLC

Knowledge Exchange and the pyramid logo are trademarks of Knowledge Exchange, LLC.

Library of Congress Cataloging-in-Publication Data

Knowledge Exchange business encyclopedia / editor in chief, Lorraine Spurge;
  chairman, editorial board, Kenin M. Spivak; introduction by Richard G. Hamermesh.
     p.   cm.
   Includes bibliographical references and index.
   ISBN 1-888232-05-6 (hc : alk. paper)
   1. Business—Encyclopedias. 2. Commerce—Encyclopedias.
   3. Economics—Encyclopedias. 4. Finance—Encyclopedias.
   I. Spurge, Lorraine, 1951– . II Spivak, Kenin M., 1957– .
   III. Knowledge Exchange (Firm)
   HF1001.K52 1997
   650'.03—DC21
                                          96-52225
                                       CIP

1 2 3 4 5 6 7 8 9-VA-99 98 97
First printing April 1997
Printing: Quebecor Printing/Kingsport
Digital Prepress: Visus Group and Jokar Productions

Knowledge Exchange books are available at special discounts for bulk purchases by corporations, institutions, and other organizations. For more information, please contact Knowledge Exchange, LLC, at: **(800) 854-6239 (voice)** or **kex@kex.com (e-mail)**.

Visit Knowledge Exchange on the Internet at: **http://www.kex.com**

What the Experts Say About the *Knowledge Exchange Business Encyclopedia*

"At last! A comprehensive book of business terminology and basic information that is both entertaining and scholarly. Its scope is breathtaking, and its availability is long overdue. This exciting volume will save students and business people at all levels untold time and torture. I want all of my MBA students to read it cover to cover."

Gerald C. Meyers, Ford Distinguished Professor of Business
Graduate School of Industrial Administration, Carnegie Mellon University

"If you're too busy *doing* business to *read* about business, this is the book you've been waiting for. It compresses an awesome range of subjects into a concise, highly readable format. Absolutely indispensable for everyone involved in business, finance, or life as we race toward the 21st century."

Lynda Rae Resnick, Chairman, Teleflora
and Vice Chairman, The Franklin Mint

"This encyclopedia is an excellent source of accessible information about business concepts. In the area of Operations Management especially, there has been such a flood of new terms, ideas and techniques in the last ten years that it is hard to keep current, even for specialists. This book is a very good place to start."

Uday S. Karmarkar, Times Mirror Professor of Management Strategy and Policy
John E. Anderson Graduate School of Management, UCLA

"The *Knowledge Exchange Business Encyclopedia* is a masterful presentation of the building blocks of free enterprise and prosperity—with everything from the nitty-gritty of accounting, marketing, and management to the most advanced concepts in economics and finance. It sets a new standard for reference works, and every page is a pleasure and an education to read. Knowledge Exchange is in the forefront of making the knowledge explosion really useful."

Christopher DeMuth, President
American Enterprise Institute

"Most of us are overwhelmed by the increasing number of things we know less and less about. The *Knowledge Exchange Business Encyclopedia* is an effective way to keep up."

James C. Wetherbe, FedEx Professor of Excellence, University of Memphis
and Director of MIS Research Center, University of Minnesota

"An indispensable resource for quick business information."

Arthur Penn, Managing Director
Bankers Trust Securities/Capital Markets

"Wow! What a wonderful resource. The *Knowledge Exchange Business Encyclopedia* is a beautifully illustrated, superbly written, gentle guide through a wondrous body of business information. It is a must for all who have an interest in the world of business, and should be in every library, no matter how large or small."

Percy Sutton, Chairman Emeritus
Inner City Broadcasting

Editorial Board

Consulting Editors

Industry Profiles

Jack Grubman is managing director at Salomon Brothers Inc. He has been named to *Institutional Investor* magazine's prestigious All-American Research Team a total of 10 times, receiving the No. 2 ranking in the telecommunications industry in 1995 and 1996.

Robert A. Hageman is managing director at Oppenheimer & Co. He has been named to *Institutional Investor* magazine's All-American Research Team a total of 40 times, receiving the No. 1 ranking in the nonferrous metals industry in 1994 and 1995 and the No. 2 ranking in 1996.

Dr. John V. Kirnan is managing director at Salomon Brothers Inc. He has been named to *Institutional Investor* magazine's All-American Research Team for the last 10 years (1986–1995), receiving the No. 3 ranking in the automobile industry in 1995.

Sheri McMahon is a member of the Telecommunications team at Salomon Brothers Inc.

Gunnar T. Miller is first vice president at PaineWebber. He has covered the semiconductor capital equipment and electronics industries since 1993, and was ranked No. 1 by *Institutional Investor* magazine in 1996.

Raymond E. Neidl is managing director at Furman Selz, LLC. Mr. Neidl is the senior analyst covering the airline/transportation and casino/hotel industries for Furman Selz.

Jennifer Solomon is vice president at Salomon Brothers Inc. Ms. Solomon is the senior analyst covering the beverage industry at Salomon Brothers.

Thomas A. Thornhill is managing director at Montgomery Securities. Mr. Thornhill has been named to *Institutional Investor* magazine's All-American Research Team every year since 1986 and was ranked No. 2 in the semiconductor industry in both 1994 and 1995.

Harold L. Vogel is managing director at Cowen & Co. Mr. Vogel has been named to *Institutional Investor* magazine's All-American Research Team a total of 23 times, receiving the No. 1 ranking within the entertainment category a record 10 times.

Michael S. Worms is vice president at CS First Boston. Mr. Worms has followed the electric utilities industry throughout his 18-year career.

Reviewers

Dean Baim, Ph.D., is associate professor of economics and finance at Pepperdine University.

Gordon Klein, Ph.D., is a lecturer at the Anderson Graduate School of Management, UCLA.

Richard L. Sandor, Ph.D., is chairman and CEO of Centre Financial Products Limited.

Glenn Yago, Ph.D., is director of Capital Studies, Milken Institute.

Contents

annual report

American Stock Exchange

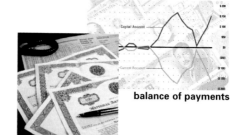

balance of payments

bond valuation

capital markets

coproduction

defined benefit
pension plan

direct marketing

Eurocurrency

efficient market theory

Federal Reserve
System

Federal Trade
Commission

gross national
product (GNP)

globalization

high-level
languages

housing starts

integrated circuits

income statement

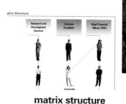

London Interbank Offered Rate (LIBOR)

labor force

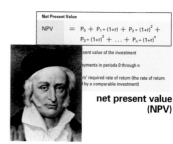

microwave

matrix structure

$$NPV = P_0 + P_1 \div (1+r) + P_2 \div (1+r)^2 + P_3 \div (1+r)^3 + \ldots + P_n \div (1+r)^n$$

net present value (NPV)

normal distribution

outdoor advertising

operating lease

Special Features

Industry Profiles

Aviation and
Air Transport

Investment and
Commercial Banks

Electric Utilities

American Dream Profiles

Percy Sutton
Inner City Broadcasting

Leadership Profiles

Chanel

Lauder

De Forest

Grove

Franklin

Smith

Mayer

Eisner

Paley

Gates

Zukor

Turner

List of Data Tables

foreign currency

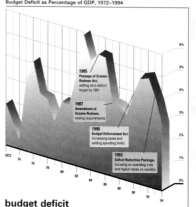

budget deficit

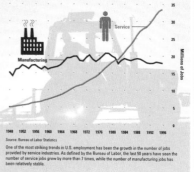

U.S. employment

List of Illustrations (Selected)

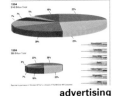

advertising

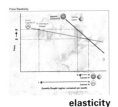

balance of trade

elasticity

European Union

See page 695 for complete list.

Others wanting to understand the world of business

This group ranges from doctors trying to cope with managed care and capitation to spouses who want to know why their mate is uptight about the possibility of a tender offer. For these people, this book will function the same way a general encyclopedia does: as a convenient place to find information.

For all of these groups, the *Knowledge Exchange Business Encyclopedia* has been designed to be as useful as possible. Each of the more than 1,200 entries begins with a concise definition. What follows, in most cases, is an extensive elaboration of what the term really means and how it is applied. For example, the definition of "break-even analysis" leads into the formula for calculating the break-even point and an example illustrating how to apply the formula.

With many items, the encyclopedia supplies other useful information. In the entry for "annual report," we learn not only what an annual report is and the various Securities and Exchange Commission requirements for what must be in it, but also the name of the electronic database where anyone with a computer and a modem can access the annual reports of publicly traded companies. Examples illustrate the entries. The "bundling" entry, for instance, discusses Microsoft's inclusion of Microsoft Network as part of Windows 95.

William Randolph Hearst

As a bonus, among the pages of this book you'll find 25 profiles of today's business leaders, each paired with a leader of yesterday. You'll learn, for example, about media tycoons Rupert Murdoch and William Randolph Hearst.

The *Knowledge Exchange Business Encyclopedia* is up-to-date and geared to the Information Age and the service economy of the future. If you read the book from cover to cover, you will be thoroughly informed on the practices of companies that are leading the way to the future and the controversies surrounding many business developments.

The inexperienced will get basic information from this book, and the experienced will come away more fully informed about the complex issues they face. And while I cannot guarantee the *Knowledge Exchange Business Encyclopedia* as a total antidote for insecurity, I can enthusiastically recommend it as the best place to start on the cure.

RICHARD G. HAMERMESH

A Note to the Reader

Scenario 1
You're on deadline. It's the night before your company's annual shareholders' meeting. You've just finished writing the Chairman's speech. You think you're done and are about ready to turn in when the boss calls. "Jones, I want you to calculate our company's **bond yields** to give some depth to my opening remarks." You're a public relations executive, not an MBA! Where do you turn?

Scenario 2
It's another working weekend. On Monday morning you have a meeting with potential investors. You're scrambling to finish your first business plan. You need to know the meaning of **accelerated cost recovery system**, **weighted-average cost**, and **capital asset pricing model**. You've spent your entire career in management, not accounting! Where do you turn?

Scenario 3
You're a summer intern at Caterpillar, and your supervisor asks you to identify some **key performance indicators** that the company can use to meet its customer service goals. You know what KPI means, but you want to find out what other companies are doing in this area. Where do you turn?

Scenario 4
You're meeting with your investment bankers and sitting in silence trying to decipher their recommendations on managing your financial assets. You're the CEO, you've managed thousands of people, and made billions of dollars for your shareholders. They're using words you barely comprehend, like **forward contracts** and **exchangeble debenture**. Where do you turn?

The answer, in all cases, is the *Knowledge Exchange Business Encyclopedia*. Created to meet your business needs, this unique reference book offers a depth and range of information not found in any other single volume.

With one in every three Americans likely to change jobs in the next three years, retraining, continuing education, and building new skill sets are essential components for job placement and job retention. This reference book is a critical tool for the American worker—novice or professional, entrepreneur or executive.

Lorraine Spurge
Editor in Chief

With case histories, real-life examples, biographies, easy-to-understand definitions, and extraordinary charts, graphs, and illustrations, the *Knowledge Exchange Business Encyclopedia* helps readers navigate through turbulent times. Whether you're starting out, at your prime, or starting over, you can no longer afford to treat business as a second language. The fundamentals of business—from program strategies to investment techniques—are key to competing and achieving success in today's global marketplace.

We hope that you will turn to the *Knowledge Exchange Business Encyclopedia* every day—to meet deadlines or just for browsing. Please turn to the next section for a guided tour of this book. Let it work for you to bridge knowledge gaps, clarify concepts, and advance your interests and career.

LORRAINE SPURGE

A Guided Tour of A *to* Z

Use this map to familiarize yourself with the myriad of elements comprising each page of the *Knowledge Exchange Business Encyclopedia*. It will help make your research and learning experience easy and effective.

① Headers

Guide you directly to the term being researched.

② Terms, Phrases, and Associations

1,225 business terms and phrases pertinent to eight critical disciplines are clearly defined and listed alphabetically. Learn about key professional associations that are responsible for education and development within specific fields. Easy to access and easy to understand, each entry adds to the wealth of essential business information that can be called on anytime.

Example: Refer to the definitions before a meeting, when preparing for an exam, or in interpreting the newspaper. *What is a current asset or liability? How do I calculate my breakeven point? Is taking a write-off good or bad? Find* your answers here.

③ Interactive Cross-Referencing

"Hot" or highlighted words indicate that a term has its own entry allowing you to "surf" from from one concept to another. Abbreviations and acronyms are included and direct you to the full definition of a term. Additional related terms are listed at the end of many definitions in a "See also…" feature.

④ Charts, Diagrams, and Formulas

Visually emphasize or expand on the definition. The charts and diagrams will help you become familiar with graphic information in general. The formulas define a term or phrase by using a mathematical rule, frequently expressed in algebraic symbols.

Example: Whether you are a student learning new concepts or an executive brushing up on time-tested theories, the formulas show you exactly how to calculate the solution you need—often with specific examples for added clarity.

EMPOWERMENT

U.S. Employment: Manufacturing and Service Jobs

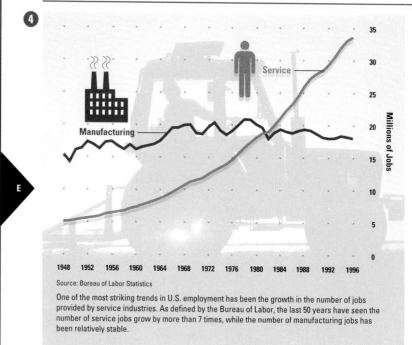

Millions of Jobs

Manufacturing

Service

1948 1952 1956 1960 1964 1968 1972 1976 1980 1984 1988 1992 1996

Source: Bureau of Labor Statistics

One of the most striking trends in U.S. employment has been the growth in the number of jobs provided by service industries. As defined by the Bureau of Labor, the last 50 years have seen the number of service jobs grow by more than 7 times, while the number of manufacturing jobs has been relatively stable.

engineering change

or businesses but did not work during the survey week because of vacation, illness, bad weather, child-care problems, and other reasons.

The number of people employed depends both on the total population aged 16 years and older and on the proportion of people who choose to work. This proportion is called the employment-population ratio. The table shows employment-population ratios and total employment over the last 40 years.

See also **unemployment rate**.

mgmt ②

empowerment   Increasing the control workers have over their own jobs.

This use of the word grew out of the **total quality management (TQM)** ③ movement, which holds that making the workers responsible for the quality of their own production will optimize their efficiency.

In addition to increasing the workers' control, empowerment boosts their sense that what they do is meaningful and has an impact on

236

5 Discipline Codes

accounting   economics

finance   management

marketing   operations

strategy   technology

Color-coded icons are a visual aid for skimming through the pages to find terms dealing with a specific area of business. Some terms may relate to multiple disciplines and have different meanings in each case.

Example: Managers need to become familiar with accounting terms and formulas, accountants need to understand marketing, operation managers need to understand technology, and so forth.

6 Frames of Reference, Quick Facts, and Breaking News

Provide historical perspective, anecdotes, insights, practical advice, and intriguing news stories that expand on a specific concept or term. Differentiated by individual icons are mini case studies that place you inside a problem and illustrate how the situation was handled.

Example: These vignettes foster new ideas on such diverse issues as how to launch a new product or service, how to manage time and efficiency, or how to maximize the value of your variable and fixed assets. Use the experience of companies that have faced similar challenges to help eliminate problems in your own business.

ENGINEERING CHANGE ORDER

6 FRAME OF REFERENCE

empowerment

Electric power producer AES Corporation does business in 35 countries and has 17,000 employees and $685 million in revenues. What it has never had in its 15-year history are corporate managers overseeing its various departments. Instead the workers handle these functions as members of volunteer teams.

Board member Robert H. Waterman, Jr., coauthor of *In Search of Excellence*, comments: "It's what I call an ad-hocracy. People can get involved however they want, without worrying about crossing boundaries." From the start, cofounders Dennis W. Bakke and Roger W. Sant shared a dissatisfaction with bureaucracy and a desire to form a company committed to their values of "integrity, fairness, social responsibility, and fun."

8

E

results. Empowerment improves morale, but that is just a small part of the payoff. Many companies have found that the workers closest to a particular process are the experts most likely to improve it if they are given the latitude to do so.

7 EXAMPLE | A midwestern toy manufacturer institutes an empowerment program that touches every aspect of the company's operations. Workers are their own bosses with the authority to hire and fire and make decisions about equipment acquisitions. The workers control everything—from budgets to marketing—and they are responsible for their results. And the results can be good: Companies that have implemented these kinds of programs have shown a much higher **return on assets**, higher sales, and payroll increases have increased at a significantly slower rate.

5 mktg oper strat

end-of-life (EOL)   Point where a product is not manufactured or sold anymore, usually because it has been edged out by a better product.

When a product approaches the EOL phase, manufacturers often find it most cost-effective to reposition the product as new and improved. For a limited time after EOL, a manufacturer will usually continue to stock spare parts and provide service either directly or through a third party.

oper

engineering change order (ECO)   Revision that the engineering department makes to a design.

The ECO corrects or alters a manufactured item, or improves a manufacturing process. The customer, the customer-service department, the quality-control department, or even manufacturing itself may request the change.

ethics

tip | 👍

Having an ethics code and putting effort into enforcing it can help blunt lawsuits and lessen fines against your company.

9

empowerment

10

It is unreasonable to expect managers to distribute power to others if they can expect to be punished when those others make mistakes. The practice of firing the coach when the team loses can be changed, but where it exists and has an entrenched history, managers will fight the process of empowering their people.

—Stephen P. Robbins,
Organizational Behavior

237

7 Examples and Sidebars

Excerpted from company annual reports and financial statements, the examples and sidebars help relate abstract concepts to the real world of business. They are snapshots of company issues that focus on the details of a business situation.

8 Photos and Illustrations

Carefully selected images, from logos and icons to photographs and cartoons, help you visualize the big picture behind a term or phrase at a glance.

9 Tips and Traps

Tips highlight how you can apply the term or concept in your business. Traps point out potential pitfalls that can be encountered when applying the term or concept. These tidbits of practical advice have been gleaned from real-life experience.

Example: Use the Tips and Traps carefully to make the best decisions for your own company.

10 Quotations

Past and present business and government leaders offer their opinions that clarify terms and crystallize relevant points.

A Guided Tour of Special Features

A Chronology of Business Time Line

This meticulously researched, beautifully designed time line brings to life critical points in our business evolution from 3000 B.C. through the 20th century. To help you grasp the role business has played in history, a supplemental time line weaves all facets of human history with that of commerce. Together they create a portrait that includes every aspect of our societies and cultures.

We should often reflect before we move forward. But simply knowing about history isn't enough. We must translate the lessons of the past into our modern-day business practices and activities.

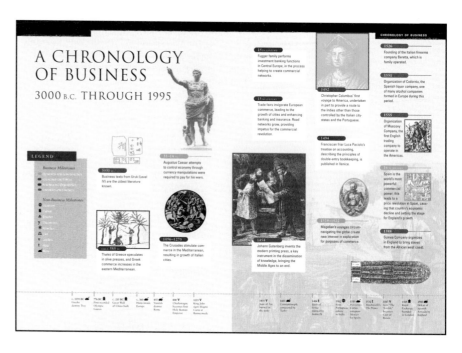

Industry Profiles

The development of fifteen of the world's leading industries and their impact on the economy and on society are chronicled. Each industry is presented in carefully researched and written profiles, which were collaborated on by ten leading brokerage firm analysts and a renowned business historian.

These profiles are useful when preparing for an interview, making a presentation to a client, or simply gaining insight on a company that you want to impress. Adding perspective is a series of mini time lines highlighting a number of the individual industries.

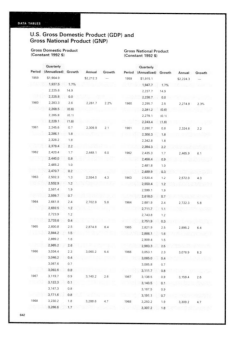

Data Tables

Twenty tables provided in the back of the book address a variety of subjects, from historical data streams of economic statistics and the securities markets to present value tables for quick reference calculating. The data tables will also be available for downloading from the Knowledge Exchange Web site for custom use in charting and personal presentations.

Leadership Profiles

This section is a compilation of 25 of the greatest business leaders of modern time paired with 25 of their notable counterparts from the past. These individuals are to be studied—not just emulated. Their stories provide building blocks of new ideas that will help you achieve your goals.

Several underlying messages have been delivered throughout this book, particularly in these fifty intimate biographies, that translate to every day life—*wealth does not necessarily mean success; management does not mean control; knowledge is not only power, but empowerment.*

American Dream Profiles

This section describes how the founders of largely diverse companies, which collectively represent our society, together with their employees and communities create the unique dynamic that enriches the global marketplace. True to the diverse origins of America itself, the American business world is composed of men and women from all cultures and races, a blend that not only creates but augments the breadth and depth of our free enterprise system.

These profiles help you understand the role that business leaders from all gender, ethnic, cultural, and religious groups have had in weaving together the fabric of society as we know it. Business binds people from disparate backgrounds in a way that few other things can do—it provides a forum for thought, intellectual stimulation, and growth. Study and use the lessons learned and passed on by our predecessors to make a difference in your business dealings now and into the future.

Indexes

Find the exact term, concept, chart, company, or other research elements by using the detailed indexes in the back of the book. Divided into three categories—Discipline, General, and Illustration—these indexes will guide you to answers you seek without wasting time.

A CHRONOLOGY OF BUSINESS

3000 B.C. THROUGH 1995

3000 BC

Business texts from Uruk (Level IV) are the oldest literature known.

31-14 BC

Augustus Caesar attempts to control economy through currency manipulations were required to pay for his wars.

CIRCA 585 BC

Thales of Greece speculates in olive presses, and Greek commerce increases in the eastern Mediterranean.

1096-1270

The Crusades stimulate commerce in the Mediterranean, resulting in growth of Italian cities.

3000 BC

1 AD

c. 1193 BC 🔫
Greeks
destroy Troy

776 BC 🏛
First recorded
Olympic
Games

c. 215 BC 🏛
Great Wall
of China built

c. 360 🔫
Huns invade
Europe

455 🔫
Vandals
destroy
Rome

800 👑
Charlemagne
becomes first
Holy Roman
Emperor

1215 👑
King John
signs Magna
Carta at
Runneymede

15TH CENTURY

Fugger family performs investment banking functions in central Europe, in the process helping to create commercial networks.

15TH CENTURY

Trade fairs invigorate European commerce, leading to the growth of cities and enhancing banking and insurance. Road networks grow, providing impetus for the commercial revolution.

1454

Johann Gutenberg invents the modern printing press, a key instrument in the dissemination of knowledge, bringing the middle ages to an end.

1492

Christopher Columbus' first voyage to America, undertaken in part to provide a route to the Indies other than those controlled by the Italian city-states and the Portuguese.

1494

Franciscan friar Luca Paciolo's treatise in accounting, describing the principles of double-entry bookkeeping, is published in Venice.

1519-1522

Magellan's voyages circum-navigating the globe create new interest in exploration for purposes of commerce.

1526

Founding of the Italian firearms company Beretta, which is family operated.

1551

Organization of Codorniu, the Spanish liquor company, one of many alcohol companies formed in Europe during this period.

1555

Organization of Muscovy Company, the first English trading company to operate in the Americas.

16TH CENTURY

Spain is the world's most powerful commercial power, this leads to a price revolution in Spain, causing that country's economic decline and setting the stage for England's growth.

1588

Guinea Company organizes in England to bring slaves from the African west coast.

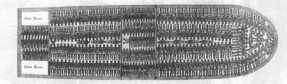

1400

1500

1599

1600

Organization of the East India Company, a major English trading company.

17TH CENTURY

The Netherlands and then France become commercial powers. The Dutch suffer from involvement in continental problems and the small size of their country, while the French are ambivalent about the importance of transoceanic commerce.

1609

London and Plymouth companies organize for colonization of North America. The English pioneer in mixed (private sector/government) capitalism, largely due to the monarchs' lack of financial resources.

1612

John Rolfe plants first successful tobacco crop in Virginia. In short order England's North American colonies become more important than South and Central America and the Caribbean islands in this key trade item.

1613

Organization of the New Netherlands Co. in Amsterdam to engage in commerce with the New World.

1639

Hugel, the French liquor company, organizes under royal charter.

1651

Passage of first Navigation Act, designed to control England's American colonies. Supplementary acts will be passed during the next century.

1682

Because of a glut of tobacco, riots break out in Virginia as planters cut production to boost prices.

1694

Chartering of Bank of England, providing England with a more stable source of currency and financing.

1698

Triangular trade begins between New England, the West Indies and West Africa, of major importance in the growing slave trade, which supported the South and Central American economies as well as that of the Caribbean, and the southern North American colonies.

CIRCA **1712**

Whaling becomes major business in Nantucket, Massachusetts and Long Island Sound, creating an important industry and expanding the business classes in this region.

1717

Mississippi Bubble in France, the first of several panics erupting from speculation in American lands and commerce.

1600

1650

 1609 Champlain founds French colony of Quebec

 1626 Dutch found colony of New Amsterdam

1644 Descartes' *Principles of Philosophy*

1661 Louis XIV begins building Versailles

1665 Great Plague in London kills 75,000

1669 The Hanseatic League, formed in 1241, has its last meeting

1683 Japan's Mitsui bank opens

1685 Chinese ports opened to foreign trade

1733

James Kay invents the flying shuttle, followed by other technological changes in the textile industry that are a major link between the commercial and industrial revolutions.

1765

James Hargreaves invents the spinning jenny, one of the most important machines in the textile industry, which helps mechanize production of cloth.

1779

Samuel Crompton invents the spinning mule, superior in the production of thread.

1735

Friendly Society for the Mutual Insurance of Houses Against Fire established in Charleston, first fire insurance company in America. This will become an important and vital industry since the nation's cities were constructed of wood; without insurance, growth would have been difficult.

1769

James Watt invents the steam engine, the crucial invention of the industrial revolution, which made possible larger and more complex factories and the railroad industry.

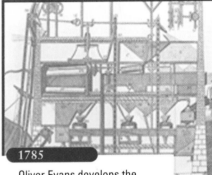

1785

Oliver Evans develops the automatic flour mill. Evans will become important in the railroad industry, and be considered one of the premier industrialists of his time.

1758

Formation of predecessor of Ciba-Geigy, dealing in pharmaceuticals from Swiss headquarters. For the next century, however, drugs were of secondary importance to dyes and spices.

1769

Nicolas Cugnot of France develops a steam-driven car, which does not gain acceptance.

1776

Publication of *Wealth of Nations* by Adam Smith, which became the manifesto and rationale for free enterprise capitalism in the 19th century.

1780s

Josiah Wedgwood's factory for producing pottery stimulates the English canal mania and becomes a landmark facility in the growth of English industrialization.

1789

1700

1745

1707
United Kingdom of Great Britain formed by England, Wales and Scotland

1709
First copyright law in Britain

1718
First bank notes in England

1732
Poor Richard's Almanack by Benjamin Franklin

1748
The Art of the Fugue J. S. Bach

1757
Beginning of British Empire in India

1762
Catherine II ("the Great") becomes czarina of Russia

1778
Captain James Cook discovers Hawaii

1789–1791

Alexander Hamilton's financial program establishes national credit and provides the framework for the development of industrial America.

1790

Moses Brown of Brown & Almy, working with Samuel Slater, produces cloth by machines in Rhode Island. Slater brought English industrial secrets to America, and his ideas soon spread throughout New England.

1791

Establishment of first Bank of the United States, which soon creates a national currency that binds the nation together and stimulates commerce.

1793

Eli Whitney invents the cotton gin at a time when the American cotton industry is starting to stagnate and the possible end of slavery seems near. However, the subsequent growth of the cotton culture will bring an increased need for slaves in America.

1797

Edmund Cartwright invents the power loom, the latest major invention in the English textile industry.

1802

Eleuthère Irénée duPont develops gunpowder mill in Delaware from which would emerge E.I. duPont, a business empire with a remarkable ability to alter itself in the face of new products and markets.

1792

Organization of the New York Stock & Exchange Board. Although there had been securities trading earlier, the Exchange indicated the growth of the investment community in New York.

1804

Richard Trevithick constructs the first steam locomotive that runs on rails.

1806

Authorization of Cumberland Road, emblematic of government/business cooperation.

1807

Robert Fulton invents the steamship, which after a slow beginning transforms oceanic commerce and creates new demand for steel and coal.

1808

John Jacob Astor, who arrived in America in 1784, founds American Fur Co. Astor would use the fortune he accumulated in fur to speculate and improve on New York real estate, a prime example of how industries fed on one another.

1790

1805

Trap Grade.

 1790
Lavoisier formulates Table of 31 Chemical Elements

 1800
Alessandro Volta produces electricity

1803
U.S. completes Louisiana Purchase from France for $15 million

1804
Napoleon proclaims himself Emperor of France

1804
Lewis and Clark begin explorations

1806
Official end of Holy Roman Empire

1807
U.S. Embargo Act against France and Britain

1808
Beethoven's *Fifth Symphony*

 1808
U.S. Congress bans importation of slaves

1810

Cornelius Vanderbilt constructs a ferry between Staten Island and Manhattan, beginning a career that will encompass steamships and railroading, and during which Vanderbilt becomes one of America's most prominent industrialists.

1817

Construction begins on the Erie Canal, which opens in 1825. First grain shipments from Chicago in 1836. The Erie drastically shortens travel time and ties New York City to the Midwest, making it the premier city in America. In addition, the Erie sparked a canal mania that lasted for two decades.

1812

First National City, which later would become Citibank, receives its charter in New York and challenges Philadelphia and Boston for commercial leadership on the East Coast.

1814

Francis Cabot Lowell organizes the first true factory under charter of Boston Mfg. Co. Lowell pioneers industrial organization, labor allocations, and the union of government and business in America.

1818

West Point Foundry is established, an important step in the creation of an American iron industry.

1819

First financial panic in America, caused by excessive land speculation. Future 19th century panics (1837, 1854, 1873, 1893) will result from speculation, monetary problems, and bank failures.

1824

Joseph Aspdin creates portland cement, a product vital for the manufacture of concrete, which would transform America's cities and highways later in the century and into the 20th century.

1825

Chesapeake & Ohio Canal Co. chartered.

1825

The Stockton and Darlington Railroad opens, becoming the first commercial railroad. Its success leads to the organization of many others in the Northeast.

1825

Establishment of Suffolk System under principle of reserve banking, which is the essential element in large-scale commercial banking.

1828

Construction begins on B & O Railroad, which will become the largest railroad of its time in the Northeast. It will use the Tom Thumb, the first locomotive built in America.

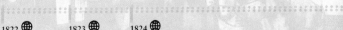

1810
New York City's population surpasses Philadelphia's

1815
Napoleon defeated at Waterloo by Wellington

1817
Simón Bolívar establishes independent Venezuela

1822
Brazil gains independence from Portugal

1823
U.S. Monroe Doctrine

1824
Mexico becomes a republic, independent of Spain

1831

Michael Faraday develops the first practical dynamo.

1832

James Gordon Bennett establishes the *Globe*, which later becomes the *New York Herald* in 1835.

1834

Cyrus McCormick patents the reaper, foundation for what would become McCormick Harvester and, later on, International Harvester. A Chicago factory opens in 1847. The reaper revolutionizes wheat farming and in the process becomes the exemplar for a good deal of American industry.

1838

Establishment of U.S. patent law, which encourages American inventors since their rights will now be protected.

1839

Charles Goodyear invents vulcanized rubber, a material of relatively minor importance for much of the century. It will become significant with the growth of the bicycle and then the automobile industries.

1832

Samuel Morse invents the electric telegraph; ready for trial in 1835 and use in 1844. While slow to gain acceptance, by the 1850s the telegraph becomes a major force in tying the country together commercially, is important in the growth of long-line railroads, and makes national companies possible.

1837

Organization of Procter & Gamble, at first a local Cincinnati soap company that allies itself with meat packing interests and in time will grow into a major diversified corporation.

1840

First regular steamer service on the Atlantic by British and Royal Mail Steam Packet Co. (forerunner of Cunard). The coming of the steamship age shortens and standardizes the travel time between Europe and America, and stimulates commerce in goods and people.

1830

1840

1830 🏛 Joseph Smith forms Mormon church

1833 🏛 Slavery abolished in British Empire

1834 ⚛ Charles Babbage invents "analytical engine," precursor of computer

1836 🌐 Texas gains independence from Mexico

1839 🔫 First Opium War between Britain and China

1841 🌐 U.S. population reaches 17 million

1843 🏛 London weekly financial paper *The Economist* founded

1844 🏛 YMCA founded in England

1844 ⚛ Wood-pulp paper invented

1845

Launching of first clipper ship; Donald McKay becomes the most important builder. While their importance has been overstated, for a brief period the clippers enable American shipping to gain prominence in the Atlantic trade.

1847

Chartering of the Pennsylvania Railroad. Fearful that New York was gaining domination of the West, Philadelphia business interests organize their own railroad with plans to extend it to Pittsburgh (completed in 1852) and, eventually, Chicago. The Pennsylvania charter also provides a model for industrial organization that affects virtually all large enterprises.

1847

Magnetic Telegraph Co. of Maryland receives charter, the first of many local telegraph companies put together to later form Western Union, the first great industrial monopoly.

1847

Formation of German firm of Telegraphenbauanstalt, Siemens & Halske to produce telegraphic equipment, predecessor of Siemens AG, a major electronics company.

1848

Alexander Stewart opens the first department store in New York.

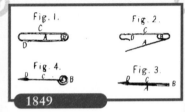

1849

Walter Hunt patents the safety pin.

1851

Isaac Singer patents his sewing machine; incorporates his company in 1863. The Singer interests revolutionize the clothing industry, providing employment for tens of thousands of women, and will become the basis for a major business. Singer becomes America's leading industrial company for a quarter of a century.

1851

William Kelly develops process for converting pig iron into steel.

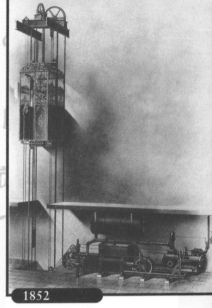

1852

Elisha Graves Otis develops his elevator, without which the modern city could not develop.

1853

Organization of the New York Central Railroad from ten short lines to compete with the Pennsylvania.

1854

Founding of W.R. Grace & Co. in Peru, which deals in raw materials, banking services, and transport, the first of the modern transnationals. Within a generation the company will be conducting business in Asia, Europe, North America, and Africa, as well as Latin America.

1845   **1850**   **1854**

1846	1847	1848	1848	1850	1851	1852	1852	1853	1854
Famine in Ireland after potato crop fails	Nitroglycerin discovered	*Communist Manifesto* by Karl Marx and Friedrich Engels	Gold discoveries in California spark gold rush	Population of New York City reaches 700,000	*New York Times* begins publication	South African Republic founded	Wells, Fargo & Co. founded in New York	Commodore Perry reaches Tokyo	U.S. Mint opens San Francisco branch

1856

Founding of Western Union by Hiram Sibley, who over time makes it a transcontinental communications company, vastly increasing the abilities of businessmen to transfer and share knowledge.

1856

Invention of the Bessemer process for making steel, lowering the price, shortening the production time, standardizing quality, and, in general, providing substantial benefits to the steel industry.

1857

Organization of Borden Co., which pioneers in the production of canned foods, starting with milk, and in the process helps create a new industry.

1857

Cyrus Field obtains grant to construct transatlantic cable; completed in 1859, provides instantaneous contacts between the United States and England.

1857

Organization of Nippon Steel, the first modern Japanese steel company.

1859

Edwin Drake drills first oil well in Titusville, PA, providing start to the petroleum industry in America.

1860

George Pullman develops the sleeping car, to be completed in 1864, which stimulates passenger transport in the United States. Pullman soon becomes the nation's largest industrial corporation.

1861

Completion of telegraph between New York City and San Francisco.

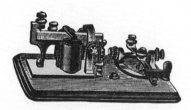

1862

Union Pacific organizes to construct transcontinental railroad; completed in 1869. This and other transcontinentals make possible national markets, which in turn stimulate the growth of American businesses.

1863

Friedrich Bayer organizes a chemical company that eventually becomes the largest firm of its kind in Europe. In the last quarter of the century, Germany challenges Great Britain for industrial leadership of Europe.

1863

Organization in London of the International Financial Society, the first known investment trust.

1865

John Wesley Hyatt receives patent for composite billiard ball, out of which comes commercial celluloid (1872) and the beginnings of the plastics industry. In time plastics will influence scores of industries, one of the first being photography.

1855

1860

 1855 Sault Ste. Marie canal opens

 1856 Banque Credit Suisse founded in Zurich

 1858 New York's Central Park opens to the public

 1859 Charles Darwin's *Origin of the Species*

 1861 U.S. Civil War begins

 1863 Perrier Water introduced commercially

 1863 World's first underground railway opens in London

1864 Geneva convention signed by 26 nations

1865

Founding of Nokia AB in Finland, a forest products company that will become the world's second largest manufacturer of cellular phones.

1866

Founding of Nestle Co. in Switzerland, which soon becomes an international marketer of foods, one of the earliest businesses to transcend national identification.

1867

Christopher Sholes invents the first practicable typewriter, patented in 1868, which will alter office work and create new opportunities for women in the workplace. Sholes sells patent rights in 1873 to Eliphalet Remington, the firearms king, who makes another fortune with the machines.

1867

Pacific Mail Steamship begins service between San Francisco and Hong Kong.

1868

Formation of what would become Armour & Co., a major meatpacker that pioneers in the use of by-products.

1868

George Westinghouse develops the air brake, which will make possible longer trains and so lower the costs of transportation.

1868

Japan develops economically during the Tokugawa shogunate (1600–1868). It is replaced by the Meiji state, during which the new government cooperates with businessmen to rapidly industrialize Japan.

1868

Abram Hewitt develops open-hearth process, enabling steel makers to use lower-quality ores.

1869

Organization of Henry J. Heinz, a large food-packing company, which will contribute to the creation of national tastes in foods and enlarge that industry.

1869

Central Pacific and Union Pacific railroads are joined in Utah, completing the first transcontinental railroad.

1869

Opening of the Suez Canal, stimulating trade between Europe and the Orient and contributing to the development of transnational economies.

1869

First Great A&P stores open in New York. Company will become an important factor in the distribution of foodstuffs to consumers, lowering costs and improving quality.

1869

Gustavus Swift further develops refrigerated railroad car, invented in 1868 by William Davis. It will make possible national markets and lower costs for meat.

1865 ❋
Stetson "10-gallon" hat created

1866 ❋
Alfred Nobel invents dynamite

1866 🏛
ASPCA founded

1867 🌐
U.S. buys Alaska for $7.2 million from Russia

1867 🏛
Karl Marx's *Das Kapital*, Volume I

1868 ❋
Rand McNally & Co. founded

1868 🏛
Badminton invented in England

1869 🐟
Mendeleev's periodic table of elements

1870

Yataro Iwasaki acquires shipbuilder Tsukumo Shokai, which becomes the foundation for Mitsubishi, one of the first industrial complexes of modern Japan.

1870

John D. Rockefeller and others organize Standard Oil; will become Standard Oil Trust in 1882. It expands production and marketing, lowers costs and prices, and provides model for national business enterprises.

1871

Organization of Thyssen AG, which will become Europe's leading steel company and the heart of a major industrial complex.

1872

Organization of Montgomery Ward, first mail-order house, which will vastly expand markets for consumer goods.

DESCRIPTIVE ILLUSTRATED PRICE LIST.
SPRING AND **No. 57.** SUMMER 1895.
Montgomery Ward & Co.
111 TO 116 MICHIGAN AVENUE, - - CHICAGO, ILL.

1872

Organization of Dai Ichi Kangyo, one of Japan's oldest banks, which finances many growing companies.

1874

Joseph Farwell Glidden receives patent for barbed wire, which will revolutionize Western settlements and make possible farming settlements in the Great Plains.

1875

Hisashige Tanaka organizes company that in time becomes Toshiba; Japan enters the electrical age.

1876

Alexander Graham Bell invents the telephone, which eventually will displace the telegraph as the primary means of business communications.

1876

Organization of L.M. Ericsson's predecessor company, which will become one of the world's leading manufacturers of telephony equipment.

1877

Founding of Tokyo University, specifically for the training of managers for rising Japanese industries.

1878

Thomas Edison starts work on the phonograph, a key invention in the coming entertainment industry. He receives patent in 1887.

1879

Edison develops the incandescent lamp.

1879

J.P. Morgan sells Vanderbilt holdings in the New York Central on the secondary market, establishing himself as a premier investment banker.

1879

Formation of Edison Electric Light Co., the first company to bring electricity into the home.

1870

1875

1871	1871	1872	1872	1873	1874	1875	1877	1877	1877	1879
Stanley meets Livingston in Africa	Great Chicago Fire	First Japanese railway opens	Yellowstone created as first national park	U.S. establishes gold standard	French "Impressionists" hold first exhibition	Electric dental drill patented	Queen Victoria proclaimed Empress of India	*Washington Post* begins publication	First Wimbledon lawn tennis championship	Saccharin discovered

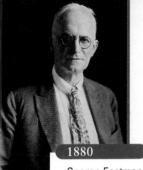

1880

George Eastman develops the first commercial camera; will be produced in 1888.

1881

Wharton School of Finance and Commerce opens at the University of Pennsylvania, initiating professional business education in the United States.

1881

C.F. Brush invents the first commercial dynamo at the Edison Works.

1882

Organization of National Cash Register, whose product was already changing retail business. In time NCR will become the world's largest business machine company, until the 1930s.

1882

Frederick Taylor, executive at Midvale Steel, presents concepts of scientific management.

1883

Joseph Pulitzer purchases *The New York World*, initiating the modern era of journalism.

1885

Gottlieb Daimler and Carl Benz form separate companies that eventually come together to produce Daimler-Benz. For a brief time Germany assumes the lead in the automobile industry.

1885

Kintaro Hattori founds Seiko in Tokyo.

1886

Invention of Coca-Cola.

1886

Ottmar Mergenthaler invents the linotype machine, the vital ingredient in creation of mass newspapers.

1888

First keystroke-recording calculating machine invented by William Burroughs.

1888

Formation of Pittsburgh Reduction; uses Hall process for producing aluminum. Out of this will come Aluminum Corp. of America (Alcoa), the world's premier aluminum company.

1889

Introduction of the modern bicycle in America, sparking a mania that results in a road-building program.

1889

Formation of New York Stock Trust, the first modern American investment trust.

1880

1885

1889

 1880 France annexes Tahiti

 **1880** Los Angeles population tops 11,000

1881 Photographic roll film patented

1883 Brooklyn Bridge opens

1883 U.S. railroads adopt standard time zone system

 1885 U.S. first-class postage doubles to 2¢

1885 Boston Pops founded

1886 Statue of Liberty dedicated

 1888 J. B. Dunlop invents pneumatic tire

 1889 *Wall Street Journal* begins publication

1890

Formation of American Tobacco by James B. Duke, one of the largest and most successful trusts.

1890–1917

International developments and the creation of a national market prompt a major consolidation movement in America, led by Wall Street, J.P. Morgan in particular.

1891

Whitcomb Judson patents the zipper, which will not be in common use for a generation.

1891

Organization of NV Philips Gloeilampenfabrieken, which soon becomes a major factor in Europe's lamp business and later expands into general electronics.

1892

Union of Edison Electric and Thomson-Houston to form General Electric, sponsored by J.P. Morgan. G.E. will become the largest producer of electrical gear in the U.S.

1892

Nikola Tesla develops the induction motor, which makes long-distance power transmission viable.

1893

Development of gasoline engine by Otto & Langen, which will improve Germany's opportunities in automobiles.

1894

Organization of Beatrice Foods, soon to become a leader in the packaged foods industry, with concentration on dairy products.

1894

Founding of Kellogg Co., which changes the nature of American breakfasts.

1895

Guglielmo Marconi invents wireless telegraphy, a major technology in itself and the progenitor of radio, a key 20th century industry.

1895

Invention of the replaceable razor blade by King Gillette.

1896

Adolph Ochs purchases the *New York Times*, which he remakes into the 20th century's newspaper of record.

1896

Appearance of the Dow Jones Industrial Average, marking a new method of interpreting stock movements.

1896

First commercial showing of motion pictures at Koster & Bial's in New York.

1899

Founding of Nippon Electric by Western Electric and Japanese investors, indicating the influence of American and European forces in Japanese industry at the time.

1899

Formation of Fiat by Giovanni Agnelli, quickly to become Italy's leading automobile company and then an industrial conglomerate.

1900

Founding of Hershey Co., soon to become the first national American candy company.

1890

1895

1890 ⚖️	1892 ❄️	1892 🏛️	1893 🏛️	1893 🏛️	1895 ☣️	1896 🏛️	1896 🏛️	1897 🌐	1897 🌐
U.S. Congress passes Sherman Antitrust Act	Diesel engine patented	U.S. "Pledge of Allegiance" first recited in schools	Wrigley introduces Juicy Fruit chewing gum	World's first Ferris wheel erected at the Chicago Fair	Wilhelm Roentgen discovers X rays	First modern Olympic Games held in Athens, Greece	Alfred Nobel establishes prizes for peace, science, and literature	U.S. annexes Hawaiian Islands	Japan adopts the gold standard

1901

Organization of U.S. Steel, the largest industrial company in the world, by J.P. Morgan.

1902

James Cash Penney opens his first store, which will further change American purchasing habits.

1902

Henry Leland demonstrates interchangeable parts in his automobiles, a major techno- logical change that will usher in the era of mass production.

1902

Organization of Minnesota Mining & Manufacturing (3M), which starts in sandpaper, goes into bonding products, and becomes the leading multi- industry company and a model for industrial organization.

1903

Wright brothers first flight. Although there had been earlier flights, the Wrights demonstrate the feasibility of aviation.

1904

Formation of Anderson Clayton, which will become the world's leading marketer of agricultural products.

1906

Organization of Shell Transport, a significant European competitor in the growing petroleum industry, which will unite in 1907 with Royal Dutch to form the first of the large binational companies.

1906

C.S. Rolls and Royce Ltd. unite to form Rolls-Royce, which becomes the leading manufac- turer of luxury autos and aircraft engines.

1906

Lee De Forest invents the vacu- um tube, a necessary compo- nent of radio transmission.

1907

Theodore Vail becomes CEO of AT&T. Under Vail's leader- ship, AT&T spreads telephony throughout the nation and provides a model for controlled competition and government/ industry cooperation.

1908

William C. Durant organizes General Motors after J.P. Morgan & Co. refuses to under- write its securities, believing that the automobile's future is chancy at best.

1908

Introduction of the Model T Ford, which will bring the automobile to the mass markets. Ford will introduce the assembly line in 1913.

1908

Glenn Curtiss produces first commer- cial airplane. Nonetheless, rapid growth of the industry will not take place for another half-century.

1908

Founding of the Harvard Graduate School of Business Administration.

1909

Organization of Kunimatsu Motor Works, first Japanese auto company. Kunimatsu becomes Tokyo Motors, which leads the small industry for a decade.

1909

Igor Sikorsky invents the first practical helicopter in Russia.

1900

1905

1909

1900	1901	1902	1902	1904	1905	1906	1907	1908	1909	1909
Sigmund Freud's *The Interpretation of Dreams*	"Instant" coffee invented	Aswan Dam opens	Cuba gains independence from Spain	New York City subway opened	First neon signs	San Francisco earthquake and fire	First canned tuna fish	Mother's Day observed for the first time	Peary reaches North Pole	DNA and RNA discovered

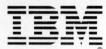

1910

Organization of Computing-Tabulating-Recording, which will become International Business Machines, the premier company in the early computer age.

1911

Dissolution of the Standard Oil Trust.

1913

Establishment of the Federal Reserve System.

1918

Konosuke Matsushita founds Matsushita Electric Housewares Manufacturing Works.

1919

Radio Corp. of America organized from American Marconi. Under the leadership of David Sarnoff, RCA will pioneer the radio and, later, television industries.

1920

KDKA, first radio broadcasting station, operates in Pittsburgh.

1920

Alfred duPont and Alfred Sloan take over at General Motors and, by the end of the decade, make it the world's leading automobile company.

1921

Sloan and duPont hire Day & Zimmerman to assist in reorganization at GM, one of the first uses of management consultants.

1922

Juan Trippe institutes his first airline. In time Trippe will create Pan American Airways, the pioneer American airline company.

1922

Founding of American Appliance, which in time will become Raytheon, a major defense electronics company.

Time Inc.

1922

Organization of Time Inc., which will greatly alter the news and information industry.

1924

Clarence Birdseye develops frozen foods, the most important innovation in foods since canning.

1924

Organization of Massachusetts Investment Trust, the first modern mutual fund.

1925

Organization of McKinsey & Co. by James McKinsey, soon to become the most prominent management consulting firm.

1927

First transmission of television signals.

1910

1915

1910 🏛 Boy Scouts of America founded	1912 ☢ *Titanic* sinks on maiden voyage	1913 ⚖ Sixteenth Amendment (income tax) adopted	1914 🌐 Panama Canal opened	1916 🌐 U.S. buys Virgin Islands from Denmark for $25 million	1919 ⚖ Eighteenth Amendment (prohibition) adopted	1920 🌐 League of Nations holds first meeting	1922 🏛 First paid radio commercials

1927

John D. Rust develops the mechanical cotton picker, prompting a large migration of blacks to the North.

1927

Formation of Merck & Co's predecessor. It will become the nation's leading pharmaceutical company.

1928

William Paley invests in CBS and starts transforming it into a major network to challenge RCA's NBC.

1929

Stock Market Crash, signaling the beginning of hard times.

1930s

Drive toward centralization and state power sweeps Western world during the Great Depression. Legitimization of state/corporate partnerships.

1930

Appearance of Geophysical Service, which will become Texas Instruments after World War II and a leader in electronics.

1930

Formation of the Fidelity Fund.

1933

Organization of Revlon, which will alter the way American women purchase and use cosmetics.

1933

Organization of Toyota Motors.

1933

Organization of Nissan (formerly Jidosha Seizo).

1936

Douglas Aviation introduces the DC-3, the first commercial passenger plane capable of flying profitably.

1937

Founding of Hewlett-Packard, which will become a pioneering electronics company; the following year the company produces its first product, an audio-oscillator.

1937

Founding of Polaroid to exploit new developments in instant photography.

1937

British inventor Frank Whittle develops the first jet engine.

1939

DuPont introduces nylon, the most important artificial fabric.

1939

Heinkel, a German aircraft manufacturer, flies the first jet-powered airplane, developed by Hans von Ohain.

1925

1930

1939

1926 Hemingway's *The Sun Also Rises*	**1927** *The Jazz Singer,* first talking motion picture	**1927** Charles Lindbergh flies nonstop from New York to Paris	**1928** Alexander Fleming discovers penicillin	**1930** Planet Pluto discovered	**1931** *Star Spangled Banner* becomes U.S. national anthem	**1933** Hitler appointed German Chancellor	**1936** Spanish Civil War begins	**1936** Boulder Dam completed	**1937** Golden Gate Bridge opens	**1938** First patent for ballpoint pen

1943

Penicillin is produced in the United States. The first of the antibiotics, penicillin and other drugs will revolutionize the pharmaceutical industry.

1945

Production of ENIAC computer, the first of its kind.

1946

Formation of Tokyo Tele-communications Engineering, which in time becomes Sony, emblematic of Japan's post–World War II resurgence and emergence as a major industrial power.

1947

William Shockley and others at Bell Laboratories invent the transistor, from which will come the microprocessor and other building blocks of the new industrial revolution.

1948

Founding of Xerox; in 1949 xerography is perfected for commercial use.

1951

First bank credit card introduced by Franklin National Bank.

1952

Introduction of the de Havilland Comet, the first commercial jet airliner, whose crashes two years later would put an effective end to British attempts in the field.

1952

First Holiday Inn in Memphis, which, with the highway construction program, will encourage Americans to travel long distances by automobile.

1953

First IBM computer, the 701.

1953

Organization of Litton Industries, the first of the modern electronics/defense/conglomerate corporations.

1955

Colonel Harland Sanders opens first Kentucky Fried Chicken outlet, a major firm in creating the fast-food industry.

1956

Organization of the European Common Market.

1957

The Peninsula Newspaper Group becomes the first company to set up an Employee Stock Ownership Plan (ESOP), allowing employees partial ownership of the firm's capital with the expectation that ownership would create more loyal, dependable, and efficient employees.

1957

Formation of Fairchild Semiconductor, the incubator for many high-tech companies.

1957

First production model of the Boeing 707, initiating a new era in commercial aviation.

1958

Restructuring of MCA, originally a talent agency, into a budding entertainment conglomerate centered around Universal Pictures, which will become an important model for other entertainment conglomerates.

1959

Formation of INSEAD at Fontainebleau, designed to become Europe's leading business school based on the American model.

1940

1950

1940 Estonia, Latvia, and Lithuania annexed by USSR

1942 First magnetic recording tape

1943 Income tax withholding introduced

1945 First atomic bomb

1946 First meeting of United Nations General Assembly

1949 Communist People's Republic of China proclaimed by Chairman Mao Zedong

1951 Color television introduced in U.S.

1953 Edmund Hillary and Tenzing Norkay reach top of Mount Everest

1954 Algerians begin war of independence against France

1955 AFL and CIO become one organization: AFL-CIO

1957 Russians launch *Sputnik 1*, first earth-orbiting satellite

1960s

Many leading corporate conglomerates are built through innovative financial instruments such as bond/warrant units, convertibles, and straight debt issues in exchange for common stock or assets of other companies.

1960s

The great bull stock market gives this decade the nickname the "Go-Go Years." At the end of the decade, in 1969 and 1970, the Dow Jones Industrial Average will fall 35 percent and equity investors will lose some $300 billion in market value.

1960

Ray Kroc purchases McDonald's, the emblematic company in fast food.

1968

Organization of Intel by three engineers—Robert Noyce, Gordon Moore, and Andrew Grove. Intel will become the leading firm in the creation of electronic chips.

1969

Origination of computer network ARPANET with 1,000 computers online.

1970s

New financial technologies and sources of capital are developing—major restructuring in global business, competition, and industry begins. This movement will be led principally by Michael Milken, termed the most important financial thinker of the century by *The Wall Street Journal.*

1970

Penn Central files an unexpected and dramatic bankruptcy. It is the largest corporate bankruptcy to date in America and sends shock waves throughout the financial world.

1970

Tele-Communications Inc., whose origins go back to 1952, becomes a publicly owned company led by John Malone. Its major expansion program begins in the late 1980s.

1970

Xerox establishes Palo Alto Research Center, from which will come important ideas regarding the personal computer and laser printer.

1971

Invention of the world's first microprocessor at Intel.

1971

Fred Smith organizes Federal Express, which will pioneer fast delivery of products and information.

1973

The price of crude oil increases 131 percent as a result of an embargo by Arab nations—the first "oil shock"—leading to severe inflation and precipitating a worldwide recession that is the worst since the Great Depression of the 1930s.

1974

A credit crunch highlights the adage "banks provide you money when you least need it" and forces corporate managers to seek alternative means of access to capital other than banks or the equity markets.

1960 · 1965 · 1974

1961	1961	1962	1963	1964	1965	1967	1969	1971	1972
East Germans erect Berlin Wall	U.S. breaks diplomatic relations with Cuba	First Wal-Mart store opens in Arkansas	Washington-Moscow "hot line" opens	U.S. gasoline prices top 30¢ per gallon	Medicare program begins	First successful human heart transplant	Human's first walk on moon	U.S. voting age lowered to 18	President Nixon visits China

1975

Formation of Microsoft as a partnership between Bill Gates and Paul Allen. The company will lead the way in altering emphasis in computers from hardware to software.

LATE 1970s

Wave of deregulation sweeps through the Western world as response to political unrest and impacts of new technologies.

1980s

The group of industrialized nations (G-7) coordinates through central bank intervention a depreciation of the U.S. dollar.

1980

Japan surpasses U.S. as leading automobile manufacturer.

1980

Interest rates in the U.S. reach their highest level this century—the prime rate tops 20 percent in December— due to the Federal Reserve's restrictive monetary policy implemented to stamp out high inflation.

1975

Apple Computers formed by Steven P. Jobs and Stephen G. Wozniak. The following year it perfects the Apple II, the premier product in the personal computer industry.

1980s

Financial managers use various creative and innovative financial instruments. Swaps, derivatives, and options allow managers to reduce risk. Options, warrants, and high-yield bonds allow financing of venture startups. Mortgage-backed securities and real estate investment trusts finance home ownership.

COMPAQ

1982

Compaq Computer Corporation founded by Rod Canion, Jim Harris, and Bill Murto, former senior managers at Texas Instruments. They produce the first clone of the IBM personal computer.

1982

Sun Microsystems founded on the premise that "the network is the computer," which revolutionizes the face of the computer industry.

1984

Breakup of AT&T under agreement with the Justice Department to resolve the 1974 antitrust suit.

ORACLE®

1977

Founding of Oracle by Larry Ellison, which becomes a major company in the software field and a key element on the information superhighway.

1975

1980

1976 Atlanta superstation WTBS founded by Ted Turner

1977 Nuclear-proliferation pact signed by 15 countries

1978 First legal casino outside Nevada opens in Atlantic City

1979 Shah leaves Iran; revolutionary forces take over

1980 Cable News Network (CNN) begins broadcasting

1981 Sandra Day O'Connor becomes first woman on Supreme Court

1982 Disney World opens EPCOT

1984 First baby born from frozen embryo

1984

Richard Branson forms Virgin Atlantic Airways, combining concepts of counterculture with corporate creation.

1986

The LTV Corp. becomes the largest company ever to file for protection under the federal bankruptcy code after purchase of its third steel company.

1987

Merger of Asea (Sweden) and Brown Boveri (Swiss) to form Asea Brown Boveri. The multi-national company's official language: English.

1987

Worldwide panic grips financial markets on October 19, "Black Monday," as the Dow Jones Industrial Average plummets 507 points after losing 150 points on the previous Friday. Investors lose $600 billion in market value in one day.

1987

The Baldrige Awards for quality management systems are established by Congress in memory of late Commerce Secretary Malcolm Baldrige. The first large companies to win are Motorola and Westinghouse led by John Malone. Its major expansion program begins in the late 1980s.

1989

The U.S. adopts the Financial Institution Reform, Recovery, and Enforcement Act (FIRREA), limiting the investment activities of savings and loans and curtailing their ability to invest in commercial real estate and corporate bonds.

1989

In the largest takeover and high-yield financing of the 1980s—$24.7 billion—Kohlberg Kravis Roberts was able to out-bid management of RJR Nabisco to take the company private.

TIME WARNER

1990

Organization of Time Warner, marking a new stage in the evolution of the media industry.

1990

Campeau Corporation seeks bankruptcy protection for its major retailing stores, Federated and Allied. It is the largest bankruptcy ever in the retailing trade.

1991

Failure of Pan Am, typical of the altering nature of American business.

1995

Walt Disney-Capital Cities merger, capping large-scale merger movement to recreate the telecommunications/ entertainment/information industries.

1985

1990

1995

A

A-B Split

to

average
collection
period

mktg

AAA   See **American Academy of Advertising**.

mktg

AAAA   See **American Association of Advertising Agencies**.

mktg

AAF   See **American Advertising Federation**.

mktg

A-B split   Way of **sampling** by contacting every other name on an alphabetical list of potential customers. The purpose is to get a true **random sample** of the **market**.

EXAMPLE   You sell automobile parts and want to experiment with a new sales strategy. You divide your list in two by moving every other name onto a second list to avoid having one list show a disproportionate number of names beginning with "A." Since many auto dealers have names that fall in that category, the A-B split helps you get a better sampling. Your results will not be skewed by having a disproportionate share of automobile companies on one list.

acct   **mgmt**

ABC   See **activity-based costing**.

acct

abnormal cost   Unusual or unexpected cost that is not likely to reoccur.

See also **extraordinary item**.

acct

ABO   See **accumulated benefit obligation**.

acct

absorption costing   Assignment of all fixed and variable costs to value of goods produced. It is the opposite of direct or marginal costing.

See also **costing**.

AAAA

A-B split

A

accelerated cost recovery system

5-Year Property Class
Cars, light and other general-purpose trucks, computers, typewriters, copiers, research equipment.

10-Year Property Class
Machinery and equipment like those used in petroleum refining and milling grain.

acct

accelerated cost recovery system (ACRS) Method of depreciating **fixed assets** for tax purposes. The most recent version is called the modified accelerated cost recovery system (MACRS).

ACRS and MACRS are forms of **accelerated depreciation**. Congress created ACRS in 1981 and MACRS in 1986. **Assets** placed in service after 1980 and before 1987 fall under ACRS; those placed in service after 1986 fall under MACRS. The purpose is to encourage investment by letting companies recover the cost of acquiring productive assets more quickly with relatively greater **depreciation** deductions early in an asset's life.

Accelerated Cost Recovery System

Property Classes

3-Year	Most small tools
5-Year	Cars, light and other general-purpose trucks, computers, typewriters, copiers, research equipment
7-Year	Office furniture and fixtures, most machinery and production equipment
10-Year	Machinery and equipment like those used in petroleum refining and milling grain
15-Year	Sewage treatment plants, telephone and electrical distribution facilities, land improvements
20-Year	Service stations and some real property
27.5-Year	Residential rental property
39-Year	Nonresidential real property

Under the ACRS system:

► Instead of basing depreciation deductions on the individual useful life of a particular asset, you can group assets into eight basic property classes. A new tool with a 4-year useful life, for example, falls into the 3-year property class.

► The **salvage value** is ignored when calculating depreciation deductions.

A

► The 3-, 5-, 7-, and 10-year property classes take a variation on the double-declining-balance depreciation method. The 15- and 20-year classes use another modification called the 150 percent declining-balance method. The remaining two property classes (depreciable over 27.5 and 39 years) must use **straight-line depreciation**. See tables for property classes and their depreciation schedules.

► A company with property in any of the classes may stretch out, rather than accelerate, depreciation by opting for *straight-line depreciation* with a feature called the half-year convention. That is, the company may deduct half the normal straight-line annual depreciation in the first year and deduct the other half in a year added at the end of the asset's economic life.

accelerated cost recovery system

27.5-Year Property Class
Residential rental property.

You would use the depreciation table (left) like this: Say you have property that falls under a 3-year classification. In the first year you would depreciate it by 33.3 percent of its cost, in the second year by 44.5 percent, and so on. Similarly, a property in the 20-year category would be depreciated by 3.8 percent the first year, 7.2 percent in the second, and so on.

Modified Accelerated Cost Recovery System (MACRS)

Depreciation Schedules (in percentages)

Year	3-Yr	5-Yr	7-Yr	10-Yr	15-Yr	20-Yr
1	33.3	20.0	14.3	10.0	5.0	3.8
2	44.5	32.0	24.5	18.0	9.5	7.2
3	14.8	19.2	17.5	14.4	8.6	6.7
4	7.4	11.5	12.5	11.5	7.7	6.2
5		11.5	8.9	9.2	6.9	5.7
6		5.8	8.9	7.4	6.2	5.3
7			8.9	6.6	5.9	4.9
8			4.5	6.6	5.9	4.5
9				6.5	5.9	4.5
10				6.5	5.9	4.5
11				3.3	5.9	4.5
12					5.9	4.5
13					5.9	4.5
14					5.9	4.5
15					5.9	4.5
16					3.0	4.4
17						4.4
18						4.4
19						4.4
20						4.4
21						2.2

A

accelerated cost recovery system

accelerated depreciation

The most common forms of accelerated depreciation are:

- The 200 percent, or double-declining-balance method

- The 150 percent declining-balance method

- The sum-of-the-years' digits method

All methods recover the same amount of depreciation over the entire life of the asset.

EXAMPLE Your automobile **assembly line**, which is putting out a new model, buys a customized steel rack to carry windshields. The rack falls under the 3-year property class and costs $6,000. Here is how its depreciation schedule would look for tax purposes under the two options available to you—**straight-line** depreciation with the half-year convention and the standard MACRS method.

Year	Straight-line (Half-year)	Cost	x	MACRS %	=	MACRS
				MACRS Method		
1	$500	$3,000	x	33.3%	=	$999
2	1,000	3,000	x	44.5	=	1,335
3	1,000	3,000	x	14.8	=	444
4	500	3,000	x	7.4	=	222
Total	$3,000			100%		$3,000

`acct`

accelerated depreciation

Accounting methods that, in comparison with the **straight-line method**, recognize greater amounts of **depreciation** in the initial years of an **asset's** life and lesser amounts as the asset ages.

These methods recognize that some assets are more efficient and productive in their early years and more costly to maintain, or even obsolete, as they age. Because accelerated depreciation gives businesses tax benefits early in an asset's life, it is sometimes used for tax reporting. For financial reporting, companies can then choose another method that suits them better.

The most common forms of accelerated depreciation are the 200 percent, or double-declining-balance method, the 150 percent declining-balance method, and the sum-of-the-years' digits method. All methods recover the same amount of depreciation over the entire life of the asset.

See also **accelerated cost recovery system (ACRS)** and **depreciation**.

`oper`

acceptance sampling

Taking random samples to decide whether or not to approve a manufactured lot you have ordered. It is a form of **statistical quality control (SQC)**.

The technique was developed in the 1920s and used extensively in producing military goods during World War II. It is still widely used, though automated techniques are rapidly making 100 percent inspections more cost-efficient.

A

acceptance sampling

Best Computer Company uses acceptance sampling for preassembled units it buys, like keyboards, monitors, mice, and printers. When receiving a shipment of monitors, say, the company takes a number for testing. If the proportion of defective monitors exceeds the maximum Best will tolerate, it takes a second random sample for testing. If that one, also, has too many defective monitors, the company will decide whether to return the whole batch to the supplier or test the remaining monitors.

To use acceptance sampling, you need to decide on two variables:

1 **Sample Size**
How many of the incoming items are you going to inspect?

2 **Acceptance Quality Level (AQL)**
Also known as **lot tolerance percentage defective (LTPD)**. What percentage of defective items are you willing to tolerate? Beyond this level, you are going to reject the entire order.

Clearly, in dealing with a **sampling**, your results will sometimes be wrong. Occasionally, you will reject a good lot because your sample happened to turn up all of the defective units; that is called a **type I error** or **producer's risk**. When you accept a bad lot because your sample showed a disproportionately small number of defects, it is called a **type II error** or **consumer's risk**. Acceptance quality levels are usually set so that 95 percent of incoming orders will be accepted and the chances of type I errors are minimized.

Acceptance sampling is not used for critical items like pacemakers and parts for space flight. And it is being used less and less in general as expectations for quality have risen. Many industry sectors (automotive, for instance) expect near-perfect quality. Companies in these sectors may not test incoming parts, moving them directly to the **assembly line**. They expect the supplier to provide the desired level of quality. This trend is a crucial aspect of **total quality management (TQM)**.

`acct` `mktg`

account   (1) In accounting, a formal record of a particular type of transaction, such as cash or sales, expressed in monetary terms and maintained in a ledger. It lists **debit** entries on the left side and **credit** entries on the right, and can be depicted most simply in the form of a **t-account**.

See also **chart of accounts**.

(2) A customer with whom you do business.

account

Chart of Accounts

100 Assets

101 Cash in bank
103 Marketable securities
105 Notes receivable
106 Accounts receivable
110 Inventory
115 Office supplies
116 Garden supplies
120 Licenses
121 Prepaid insurance
150 Land
160 Store furniture and fixtures
165 Buildings
170 Other assets

200 Liabilities

201 Accounts payable
205 Bank loan payable
210 Salaries payable
212 Interest payable
214 Taxes payable

300 Stockholders

301 Capital stock
311 Retained earnings

account

tip

The way you set up your accounts says a lot about your ability to monitor and control your business. One telephone expense account might be fine for a company with one facility. For a nationwide chain, you would want separate accounts for telephone expense at each office.

T–Account	
Left Side: Debit	**Right Side:** Credit

mktg **fin**

account executive (AE)

(1) In marketing, a midlevel employee of an **advertising agency** or **public relations** firm who looks after the interests of one or more clients.

Among the AE's duties are analyzing problems and working with the client to create an **advertising** or public relations strategy. The AE makes sure all the client's advertising or public relations activities harmonize at the agency and serves as liaison to the agency's services, such as its media, research, and creative operations.

The term has grown in use in other fields as well. A financial services firm, for instance, may have account executives looking after the interests of designated clients.

EXAMPLE | George Smith is an AE for a large advertising agency. One of his clients is a major software company that does a considerable amount of print advertising. Although the client sometimes deals directly with the people at the agency doing the creative work and developing the media plan, Smith oversees the relationship and coordinates the activities of each department to best serve the client's needs.

When Smith learns that the client is considering sponsoring a series of road races, he arranges for a presentation to the client about the agency's capabilities in promoting sports events. In addition to arranging for the presentation, Smith helps to develop the agency's strategy to best serve the client's objectives. Smith works with a creative team and an account executive in the agency's promotions division to make the presentation to the client. The client advises Smith that it has also asked its **public relations** agency to make a capabilities presentation.

(2) An AE also refers to a retail **broker** at an investment bank.

acct

accountant

Person trained in accounting.

Accountants often specialize in a particular area, like financial accounting, **cost accounting**, **managerial accounting**, taxes, or auditing. Their skill is needed both for internal analysis and for **external reporting**. An accountant's work may range from calculating company earnings and preparing monthly **financial statements** to auditing financial records and developing capital expansion plans.

A **certified public accountant (CPA)** has advanced training and must pass a rigorous certification process. A CPA usually offers a considerably higher level of service than a bookkeeper. Book-keepers usually record daily numbers such as sales, receivables, and **expenses**, while a CPA analyzes the records of these activities to determine their financial consequences for a company.

See also **audit**.

acct

accountant's responsibility   Moral and professional obligation of a public practitioner to adhere to a code of **ethics** and conduct established by the various state boards of accountancy. In general, these codes recognize that an accountant occupies a position of trust and that investors, creditors, and others rely on the accountant to provide information that truly reflects a company's economic condition.

acct   **fin**

accounting change   Switch in accounting principles, estimates, or the reporting entity.

There are three broad types of accounting changes:

1   From one generally accepted accounting principle to another, such as a change in the method of **depreciation** to **straight line** from double declining.

2   In estimates as the result of new information or additional experience, such as when collections on accounts receivable do not materialize as expected and the allowance for doubtful accounts must be increased.

3   From reporting as one type of entity to another type, such as after two companies merge.

One of the main reasons for an accounting change is when the **Financial Accounting Standards Board (FASB)** changes **generally accepted accounting principles (GAAP)**, as often happens. A new FASB standard may call for your company to make adjustments in the current year. Those adjustments have absolutely no impact on your operations or **cash flow**, but they can make an enormous difference in the year's reported results.

EXAMPLE | Until January 1, 1993, most companies accounted for the cost of retirees' health insurance when they paid out the money. Sound reasonable? Well, with an increasing number of companies offering benefits other than pensions to retirees, the FASB decided that was not good enough. The board was concerned that information about

accountant

accountant's responsibility

A

accounting change

Automakers, with a lot of employees and liberal benefits, were particularly hard hit by SFAS 106.

Breaking News

A Rude Awakening
Accounting Change
Fo
to | Boeing Sees Charge
from Accounting

EXTRA

Switch in Inventory
Accounting Method
Cited for Profit
Increase

An accounting change can mean a major headache for accountants and mass confusion for investors, so the rules for accounting discourage unnecessary changes. But, as newspaper headlines often indicate, companies do make accounting changes.

the cost and obligation of providing these benefits was missing from companies' **financial statements**. So it issued what is called **SFAS 106**—Employers' Accounting for Postretirement Benefits Other than Pensions.

Under SFAS 106, if you have employees who are entitled to post-retirement benefits like health insurance, you have to account for the expected future costs while the employees are still working for you. Now, as though figuring all that out is not tough enough, as you made the changeover, you also had to account for all the future obligations that your current and retired employees earned in the past. You either took them as a onetime charge against earnings or spread them out in equal amounts over up to 20 years.

Many companies chose to get it over with and took the onetime charge. Automakers, with a lot of employees and liberal benefits, were particularly hard hit. In 1992, General Motors reported a $23.5 billion loss, which included $20.8 billion for SFAS 106, and Ford lost $7.4 billion. Without SFAS 106, Ford would have shown a slight profit. A few other examples of the 1992 after-tax charge against earnings for implementing SFAS 106: Boeing, $1 billion; Chevron, $540 million; Hewlett-Packard, $332 million; Safeway, $11 million; and USX Corporation, $1.3 billion.

See also **cumulative effect of accounting change**.

acct

accounting control   Systems and procedures designed to maintain continuous control over business transactions. For example, a company may require dual signatures on checks of more than a certain amount.

acct **fin**

accounting equation   Formula that expresses the central relationship in accounting:

Assets = Equities

It is more commonly shown in a form that distinguishes between the equity of creditors and that of owners.

Accounting Equation		
Assets	= Liabilities	+ Owner's Equity

This equation gives rise to a system known as double-entry book-keeping. Each accounting transaction affects at least two accounts in an equal but opposite manner. Anything that changes one side of the equation has to show up on the other side as well.

EXAMPLE | You start a business with your savings of $250,000, depositing the money in a bank account.

Assets = Liabilities + Owner's Equity

$250,000 (cash) = 0 + $250,000

Then you borrow $100,000 and add it to your bank account.

$350,000 (cash) = $100,000 (debt) + $250,000

Now you buy manufacturing equipment for $200,000.

$150,000 (cash) + $200,000 (equipment) =
$100,000 (debt) + $250,000

If you incorporate your business, **owner's equity** becomes **shareholders' equity**, but the equation remains the same no matter how large and complex you become. If you make a profit, you may end up with more cash or maybe buy some more equipment. Either way, your **assets** grow, which means the other side of the equation will grow as well. Since there are no new **liabilities**, you balance the equation by increasing owner's equity.

At any given time, the accounting equation can be expressed in a **balance sheet**.

(acct)

accounting method   How you keep your books—on a cash, a modified cash, or an **accrual basis**.

Here are the different accounting methods:

► **Cash Accounting**
The simpler of the two methods. **Revenues** are reported when they are actually received; expenses are reported when they are paid.

► **Modified Cash Accounting**
Contains certain items like **accounts receivable**, **accounts payable**, **depreciation**, and so on that are added to the cash balances, but accounts for these items are not maintained on a continuous basis.

► **Accrual Accounting**
Revenues are recorded as they are earned, regardless of when you collect the money. Similarly, expenses are recorded as they are incurred, without regard to when you really pay out the money.

Many companies have to use the accrual basis at least for **external reporting**. **Generally accepted accounting principles (GAAP)** require

---

accounting equation

Anything that

changes one

side of the
has to show up
equation
on the other side

as well.

accounting method

Once you pick an accounting method for tax purposes, you cannot change it without permission from the IRS. There is, of course, a form to file asking permission. It is Form 3115, and it must be filed with the IRS no later than the 180th day of the year for which you are requesting the change.

accounting period

In 1976, the U.S. government switched its fiscal year-end from June 30th to September 30th. The three-month period between July 1, 1976, and September 30, 1976, is known as the "transition quarter."

accounts payable

A survey firm conducted market research during December 1995 that cost $25,000, but you did not get the bill until January 1996. The amount is a current liability at December 31, 1995.

---

the use of the accrual method, and the **Securities and Exchange Commission (SEC)** mandates it for publicly traded corporations. For income-tax purposes, most individual taxpayers can use the **cash basis** but not for their **inventories**. The Internal Revenue Service (IRS) has been trying to force all substantial businesses to use the accrual method.

acct **fin**

accounting period   Interval covered by a **financial statement**.

Companies typically close their books and prepare financial statements at the end of a 12-month period, although interim reports may be published more frequently, say quarterly. The 12-month period may conform to the January 1 to December 31 calendar year, or it may be a **fiscal year**, meaning it can be any continuous 12-month period, such as July 1 through June 30.

For tax purposes, owners of **sole proprietorships** and **S corporations** do not have the option of electing a fiscal year that differs from the calendar year. Some partnerships and most corporations do have the option.

Roughly two-thirds of publicly held corporations report on a calendar-year basis. One industry that frequently uses a fiscal year, however, is retailing. These corporations often select a year-end in January, a month or so after their peak holiday season.

acct

Accounting Principles Board (APB)   A forerunner of the **Financial Accounting Standards Board (FASB)** that conducted research on accounting issues and promulgated standards. The 18- to 21-member board was established in 1959 and continued its work until 1973, during which time it issued 31 opinions.

See also **generally accepted accounting principles (GAAP)**.

acct

accounts payable   Amount owed to vendors for goods and services received but not yet paid for.

An accounts payable is a **liability** to a creditor. It is listed as a current liability or a long-term liability on your **balance sheet**, depending on when the payment is due.

acct

accounts receivable   Amount that is owed to you by customers who purchase goods or services on account.

This is a **current asset**, or short-term asset, on your **balance sheet**. There may be other types of receivables, such as notes receivable.

Because an accounts receivable should reflect only what you expect to collect, **generally accepted accounting principles (GAAP)** require that you establish an allowance for doubtful accounts, money owed that you may not collect. However, you do not ordinarily show this account as a separate item on your **balance sheet**.

fin **acct** **mgmt**

accounts receivable turnover
Measure of the length of time it takes to collect on **accounts receivable**.

It is expressed as a ratio of net sales to average accounts receivable during an **accounting period**.

While the analysis varies from industry to industry, a low number—say, three—means it takes too long for you to collect money owed you. A high number means you are doing okay.

EXAMPLE | Your sales in 1995 were $6 million. At the start of the year, you had $1,000,000 in accounts receivable; at year-end, it was $800,000. To find average accounts receivable, you add $1,000,000 and $800,000 and divide by two.

($1,000,000 + $800,000) ÷ 2 = $900,000

So the accounts receivable turnover is:

$6,000,000 ÷ $900,000 = 6.6

Your average accounts receivable turned over 6.6 times during the year. Put another way, on average it took you 55 days to collect your accounts receivable (365 ÷ 6.6 = 55). That number is called your **days sales outstanding (DSO)**, which is another way of expressing the same idea.

acct

accrual basis
Method of accounting in which **revenues** are recorded as they are earned, regardless of when the money is actually received.

See also **accounting method**.

acct

accrued expense
Expense you have incurred but have not paid for by the end of your **accounting period**. Accrued expenses may also be called accrued liabilities.

See also **balance sheet**.

acct

accrued liabilities
Expenses a company has incurred but not yet paid for by the end of its **accounting period**.

See also **accrued expense** and **balance sheet**.

A

accounts receivable

EXAMPLE

After a fire in your plant in December 1995, you expect to receive a $10,000 insurance settlement in January. Since your accounting period is the calendar year, you need to show a receivable in the amount of $10,000 as of December 31, 1995.

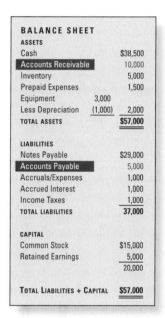

BALANCE SHEET		
ASSETS		
Cash		$38,500
Accounts Receivable		10,000
Inventory		5,000
Prepaid Expenses		1,500
Equipment	3,000	
Less Depreciation	(1,000)	2,000
TOTAL ASSETS		$57,000
LIABILITIES		
Notes Payable		$29,000
Accounts Payable		5,000
Accruals/Expenses		1,000
Accrued Interest		1,000
Income Taxes		1,000
TOTAL LIABILITIES		37,000
CAPITAL		
Common Stock		$15,000
Retained Earnings		5,000
		20,000
TOTAL LIABILITIES + CAPITAL		$57,000

accrued expense

EXAMPLE

You hired a survey firm to do market research during December 1995. The firm completes the survey and sends you a bill for $25,000, but you are not required to pay the bill until the end of January 1996. The $25,000 is an accrued expense as of December 31, 1995, and it will be classified as accrued expense payable on your balance sheet as of that date.

acid test ratio

tip |

In evaluating ratios, you really need comparable data for the industry. That way you can see how one company stacks up against others facing similar conditions.

---

acct

accrued revenue   Money earned that is neither received nor past due. It creates a receivable listed in the current asset section of the **balance sheet**.

acct

accumulated benefit obligation (ABO)   The **present value** of your company's future pension obligations accrued to date.

The ABO is based on your employees' current pay levels and amount of service rendered before a specified date. If you factor in assumptions about your employees' future service and pay levels and compute the present value, that is the **projected benefit obligation (PBO)**.

acct

accumulated depreciation   Total amount of **depreciation** taken on an **asset** or asset group based on the use of a particular method and estimates of useful lives.

The convention in accounting is to record the acquisition of plant assets in one **account** and to record and accumulate the annual depreciation charges in an offsetting account, known as a contra account.

See also **depreciation**.

mktg

ACI   See **Advertising Council, Inc.**

fin   **acct**   **mgmt**

acid test ratio   A measure of **liquidity**, or the company's ability to pay what it owes over roughly a 30-day period. Also called **quick ratio**.

Acid Test Ratio		
Acid Test Ratio	=	(Cash + Cash Equivalents + Marketable Securities + Accounts Receivable)
	÷	Current Liabilities

Different companies may give the categories slightly different names, but the numerator is cash and those things that can easily be converted to cash. The information can be found on a company's **balance sheet**.

A

EXAMPLE | In MCI's 1995 annual report, the company's balance sheet shows (in millions):

Cash and temporary investments	$ 471
Accounts receivable	2,954
Finance receivables	1,122
Total current liabilities	$4,870

We will include the *finance receivables* (interest and **dividends** due to MCI) along with accounts receivable. So the acid test ratio is:

($471 + $2,954 + $1,122) ÷ $4,870 = 0.93, or 93%

Since the ratio is close to 100 percent, MCI should have no problem meeting its current liabilities.

The Procter & Gamble 1995 annual report has these figures on its balance sheet (in millions):

Cash and cash equivalents	$2,028
Marketable securities	150
Accounts receivable	3,562
Current liabilities	$8,648

The acid test ratio is:

($2,028 + $150 + $3,562) ÷ $8,648 = 0.66, or 66%

The number is lower than MCI's, but P&G is in a different industry, one where inventories play a much larger role, and they are not included in the acid test ratio.

The rule of thumb is 1:1; that is, you should have one dollar in quick assets for each dollar of current liabilities. The acid test ratio is a more restrictive version of the **current ratio**, which includes prepaid expenses as well as inventories.

---

fin **mgmt**

acquisition When one company buys another. Usually, the acquired company gives up its independent existence; the surviving company assumes all **assets** and **liabilities**.

See also **merger/acquisition**.

---

acct

ACRS See **accelerated cost recovery system**.

---

mgmt

action research Approach to organizational change involving the systematic collection of data, with meaningful participation by the people who will be affected.

---

acid test ratio

acquisition

Quick Facts!

One of the largest acquisitions in U.S. banking history came in 1992 when BankAmerica bought the shares of Security Pacific, paying for them with BankAmerica common stock. Shareholders in Security Pacific got 0.88 of a BankAmerica share for every Security Pacific share they owned. BankAmerica then spent more than a year consolidating the new company into its own corporate structure.

No one divulges his revenues, or at least which way it comes in, but everyone publishes his acquisitions.

—Montaigne, "Of the Education of Children," *Essays,* 1580–1588

A

action research

There are five steps in action research:

1 **Diagnosis**

Initially, a consultant or a company manager studies the entire organization to determine its state of health and to offer a preliminary prognosis.

2 **Analysis**

The change agent refines the initial analysis by determining patterns of problems as well as ascertaining people's attitudes toward those problems and potential solutions.

3 **Feedback**

Action research often fails if people affected by it are not informed or allowed to participate in the change. Employees need to know what the problems are and how they can help fix them.

4 **Action**

Management seeks to implement changes prescribed by the change agents

5 **Evaluation**

Finally, managers assess the changes, comparing the new operations with those of the company as it used to be.

Action research offers significant advantages over authoritarian directives. First, because it engages employees in the process, they are less likely to resist the change. In fact, employees invited to participate in the change usually hasten its completion. Second, action research, rather than concentrating on solutions, highlights the problems and asks what those problems say about the way the company operates. Those individuals responsible for managing the change thus avoid stop-gap measures and solutions to problems that represent deep fissures in the company, which might be better filled by **business reengineering**.

You will find that demonstrating your understanding is often enough to head off trouble.

Quick Facts!

action research

Action research was the brainchild of the late social psychologist and psychoanalyst Kurt Lewin (1890–1947), who made many contributions to the behavioral sciences. He is best known for his field theory of human behavior, which looks to the social environment for behavior's roots. He developed group dynamics sessions as a form of research and founded the Research Center for Group Dynamics at the Massachusetts Institute of Technology.

A

acct   mgmt

activity-based costing (ABC)

activity-based costing (ABC)   Accountants often allocate costs to specific activities such as product development, testing, and **marketing**. Product-line costing is another name for this method.

There are three types of costs to be considered—*direct materials* (materials used to make a product), *direct labor* (employees who add value to the product), and *overhead* (such as rent, utilities, salaries, and benefits). Materials and labor costs are easily determined, but overhead is trickier. Traditional **costing** methods distribute overhead evenly among all operations at a standard rate. ABC, however, assigns overhead to each operation according to its actual cost.

With ABC, you can ascertain how much each activity contributes to your company's profits.

EXAMPLE | You own a supermarket and adopt an ABC system. With the help of a computer program designed for the purpose, your **bookkeepers** assign all of your company's expenses to the various products on your shelves. That includes each product's share of costs related to shipping, loading, warehousing, shelf-stocking, inventory-taking, cashiering, rent, insurance, and everything else that constitutes your labor, materials, and **overhead** in selling the product. The result? Not only can you see that it costs you more to sell Rice Krispies than peanut butter, you can pinpoint why. ABC helps you get a better grasp of your costs, your product margins, and, ultimately, your profits.

As manufacturing processes become more computerized, direct labor is a smaller proportion of a product's cost. That makes ABC an increasingly important tool.

fin

actual interest rate   The actual rate of interest paid on a loan, which can differ from the stated rate, depending on when the interest is paid.

See also **interest rate**.

fin

actuary   Insurance expert trained in mathematics, statistics, and probability.

Actuaries do the calculations that determine an insurance company's success or failure. Their calculations determine the **premiums** that must be charged for the insurance company to make a profit and the cash reserves that must be on hand to pay claims. Risk factors derived from the company's experience and other statistics are the tools actuaries use.

activity-based costing

tip |

By using ABC, you can determine what each activity, segment, or product line does for the company's profits.

actuary

This is a profession where it is necessary and legal to base business decisions on age. Insurance companies also have traditionally factored in gender with many of their decisions, but they are being challenged in court on that issue.

A

ad response

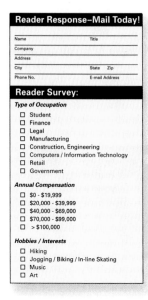

Reader Response–Mail Today!

Name		Title	
Company			
Address			
City		State	Zip
Phone No.		E-mail Address	

Reader Survey:

Type of Occupation

☐ Student
☐ Finance
☐ Legal
☐ Manufacturing
☐ Construction, Engineering
☐ Computers / Information Technology
☐ Retail
☐ Government

Annual Compensation

☐ $0 - $19,999
☐ $20,000 - $39,999
☐ $40,000 - $69,999
☐ $70,000 - $99,999
☐ > $100,000

Hobbies / Interests

☐ Hiking
☐ Jogging / Biking / In-line Skating
☐ Music
☐ Art

trap

Advertising can be highly memorable, with great reach and frequency, and still not get the response you want. To work, most advertising has to plant the brand name firmly in your customer's mind and motivate her or him to buy the product. It is a waste of money and effort if your ad gets people walking into the stores humming your jingle while buying your competitor's product.

The most familiar type of actuaries are the ones who work on life-insurance policies. They use mortality tables, **demographic** data, and the insurance company's experience to calculate life expectancies of insured individuals, premium rates, and reserves against future **liabilities**.

Actuaries also render advice to companies and governments on the administration of their pension funds.

mktg

ad response   Measure of the impact of specific **advertising** on your customer base.

One informal way of gauging advertising impact is to conduct **observational research** by asking customers where they heard about your company or product, keeping track of the responses mentioning advertising. You can make a more formal measurement by including a coded clip-out coupon in your print advertising. After the coupon is redeemed, the coding will show where it came from. You can also tailor toll-free telephone numbers to serve the same purpose, with a different number or extension listed in each ad. In **direct-mail** advertising, the responses can easily be tracked, and if you get more than one per 100 letters mailed, you can consider yourself successful.

It is much harder to track the effectiveness of an advertising campaign that does not call for an immediate, measurable response. How do you know, for example, whether the latest Nike shoe commercial worked? Finding the answer can be expensive. It involves sophisticated surveying to gauge awareness of and attitudes about the company and its products before and after the ad campaign.

Major factors that can determine ad response:

1 **Reach**
How many of the right people—what percentage of your target group—are exposed to your ad?

2 **Frequency**
How many times are people exposed to your ad? Repeating the message to deliver maximum return is the most important part of the advertising strategy.

3 **Impact**
How much do people take notice and remember? Size and color will increase the effect.

4 **Continuity**
How are you patterning the ads? Another ad should be presented before the impact of the previous ad wears off.

See also **advertising frequency**.

mgmt

ADA   See **Americans with Disabilities Act**.

acct **fin**

additional paid-in capital   Part of **shareholders' equity** on the **balance sheet** that shows what investors paid above **par value** for shares in the company.

mgmt

ADEA   See **Age Discrimination Employment Act**.

acct **mgmt**

adequate disclosure concept   Financial reporting convention requiring that, along with your **financial statements**, you give the reader whatever information is needed to understand them.

The additional information may be in notes to the financial statements or in supplementary schedules. Adequate disclosure goes hand in hand with the **materiality concept**: If it does not make much difference, you do not need to provide the details, which might overwhelm readers.

But companies court potential problems if they do not disclose information a reasonable person would consider material.

EXAMPLE | In your accounting system, some cash gets reported along with the marketable securities, and some marketable securities show up as cash. The amounts involved are small, and there is no reason for you to explain it.

See also **conservatism concept**, **consistency concept**, and **matching concept**.

mktg

ADI   See **Area of Dominant Influence**.

fin

adjustable rate   **Interest rate** that changes periodically.

The adjustments are based on a standard market rate, such as the **London interbank offered rate (LIBOR)**, the **prime rate**, or the rate on Treasury bills. Also called a **floating rate**, **increasing rate**, or **exchangeable rate**, the rate can change quarterly, monthly, or semi-annually. A floor puts a limit on how low the interest rate can fall; a ceiling limits the rise.

An adjustable rate note (also known as a resettable or exchangeable note) may be used by a company to lengthen a **bond's** maturity. In the event that the maturity date shifts out, bondholders will often have the option to sell their bonds back to the company or may receive a new "adjusted" **coupon rate**, which makes the bond trade at a certain price (usually above par). This structure may also apply to **preferred stock**.

adequate disclosure concept

Quick Facts! |

After Marriott Corp. split itself in two, creating Host Marriott from its real estate segment and Marriott International from its profitable hotel management division, some of its debt holders expressed their opinion in a lawsuit. Bond-holders of Host Marriott took the company to court claiming that Marriott and its highest-ranking officials had "withheld material facts" about the plan to restructure when they sold $400 million of bonds in April 1992. Marriott later revised its plan by shifting more debt to Marriott International.

adjustable rate

tip |

Offering adjustable-rate securities with a ceiling limits an issuing company's exposure to potentially volatile short-term rate increases, such as occurred in 1981. Companies whose issues were pegged to the prime rate watched in dismay as it soared to over 20 percent.

A

Adjustable Rates

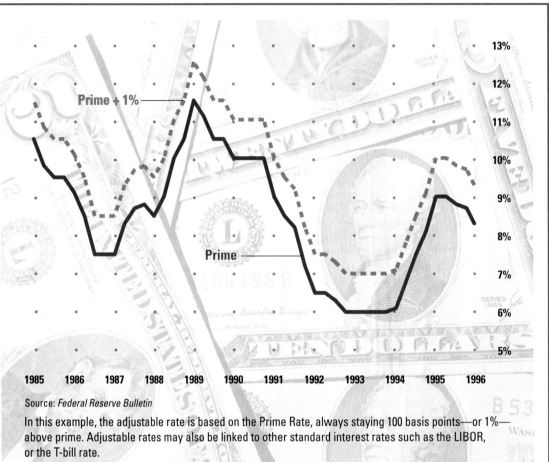

Source: *Federal Reserve Bulletin*

In this example, the adjustable rate is based on the Prime Rate, always staying 100 basis points—or 1%—above prime. Adjustable rates may also be linked to other standard interest rates such as the LIBOR, or the T-bill rate.

acct

adjusting journal entry   Addition to accounting records made at year-end to give effect to an error, an accrual, a **write-off**, an allowance for doubtful accounts, or **depreciation**.

EXAMPLE | A company must value its inventory at the lower of cost or market price. Conditions at year-end require it to reduce the value of the inventory. An adjusting journal entry would be prepared to effect the **write-down**.

acct

administrative expense   Category of expenses incurred for running an enterprise as a whole.

These are **expenses** that cannot be easily attributed to a particular function like manufacturing or **marketing**. Administrative expenses usually appear in a company's **income statement** in a line item called **selling, general, and administrative expenses.**

fin

ADR   See **American Depository Receipt**.

mktg

advertising   Paid public messages sent via any medium that are designed to attract attention and influence the attitudes and behavior of consumers.

For effectiveness, the person planning the message should consider the following six points:

1 **Mission**
What business are you in?

2 **Product**
What are you selling? Is it tangible or intangible? This may be a good, a service, an idea, or even a person.

3 **Prospect**
What is your target group? Whom are you selling to? You want to know the audiences you need to reach.

4 **Sponsor**
Whom are you selling for? Does the organization have a particular image?

5 **Means**
What medium should be used and what personality should the advertising convey?

6 **Need**
What necessity are you satisfying?

Ads are everywhere—from posters on the sides of buses to skywriting over ocean beaches. The average person receives more than 3,000 advertising messages per day. The major media are newspapers and magazines, television and radio, direct mail, billboards, and now the **Internet**. Used effectively, advertising complements other promotional tools like publicity. An automaker unveiling a new model, for example, will hold a press conference and take reporters out to the test track in addition to running ads. That way, reviews will appear in newspapers and magazines and on TV and radio around the same time as the advertising. The company might also sponsor a major sports event to keep exposing buyers to the new model name.

advertising

Quick Facts!

In 1994, McDonald's spent $1.4 billion on advertising worldwide. It segments its markets demographically by key age groupings—children, teens, young adults, and seniors.

Advertisements contain the only truths to be relied on in a newspaper.

—Thomas Jefferson

A

advertising

From 1984 to 1994, estimated advertising expenditures grew by 67 percent, a total of $149 billion.

MCI Communications Corporation has long had a reputation as a savvy marketer, and its advertising campaigns reflected that trait from the beginning. In early 1980, when MCI entered the residential market in direct competition with its giant adversary AT&T, it chose to jump into the fray with both feet by highlighting its strengths while throwing darts at AT&T's weaknesses.

Its first such TV commercial, developed by New York ad agency Ally & Gargano, called "Big Business," gave specific examples of companies that had saved hundreds of thousands of dollars using MCI's long-distance service and trumpeted its message with: "All told, 40,000 companies used us to cut their long-distance bills up to 50 percent. And starting now, you can begin saving on long distance with your own home phone." MCI's ad confronted AT&T head-on over the issue of price and probably made AT&T's ad execs see red with its final salvo, voiced as the MCI logo appeared on screen, "The nation's long-distance phone company."

Estimated Advertising Expenditures by Medium

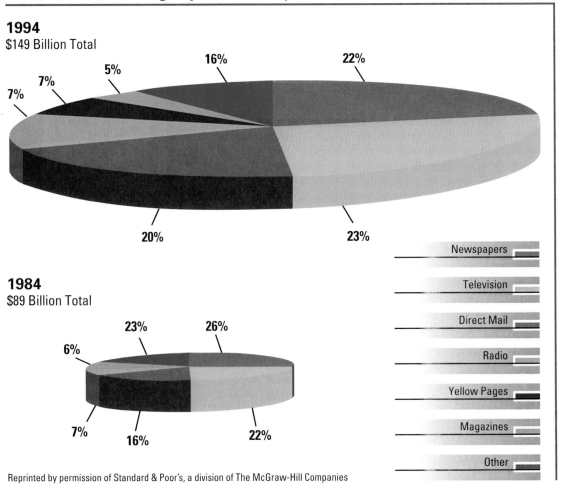

1994
$149 Billion Total

7%   7%   5%   16%   22%

20%   23%

1984
$89 Billion Total

6%   23%   26%

7%   16%   22%

Newspapers
Television
Direct Mail
Radio
Yellow Pages
Magazines
Other

Reprinted by permission of Standard & Poor's, a division of The McGraw-Hill Companies

mktg

Advertising Age
Weekly **marketing** and **advertising** trade magazine published by Crain Communications.

The magazine reports on developments in the industry, including business and government issues relating to the media, advertisers, and **advertising agencies**. It also reviews current advertising messages. It is available at newsstands and through subscriptions.

See also **Adweek**.

mktg

advertising agency
A company that helps clients improve their images and markets products or services through the use of creative ads and ad campaigns.

There are three main types of advertising agencies:

1 **Full-Service Agencies**
   Offer a wide range of services, including account management/strategic planning, creative services, media planning, media buying, research, and production. Most often, these agencies work on commission, usually 12 to 15 percent of media purchased, plus a markup of 17.65 percent on production costs. Larger, full-service firms are affiliated with public relations and promotions agencies. When a client utilizes these services, the client negotiates an additional fee.

2 **Specialty Agencies**
   Often called boutique agencies and provide limited services, sometimes within a single industry. The agencies often will provide creative services, limited market research, and media planning but virtually no media buying. They may offer other services for a fee.

3 **In-House Agencies**
   Departments usually in the marketing division of the client company, which may still use an outside agency for some projects. The Franklin Mint has one of the biggest in-house agencies in the United States, with almost 100 employees and an ad budget of more than $120 million a year.

mktg

Advertising Council, Inc. (ACI)
Organization that works with volunteer **advertising agencies** to produce and distribute national public service announcements that the media run free of charge.

Started as the War Advertising Council during World War II, the Ad Council first supported causes like war bonds and victory gardens. The council gets its funding from corporate contributions.

Advertising Age

AdvertisingAge

---

advertising agency

Quick Facts!

Young & Rubicam is one of the largest U.S.-based advertising agencies, with 1995 billings of $9.9 billion. In addition to its advertising business, Young & Rubicam's parent company owns firms that concentrate on public relations, sales promotion and direct marketing, corporate and product identity, and Hispanic and healthcare communications. The parent company and subsidiaries employ 10,000 people worldwide.

Advertising Council, Inc.

advertising frequency

tip

You need high-frequency advertising when you are fighting strong competition or weak brand loyalty, and when your message is complex.

trap

A venue with multiple advertisements can sharply reduce the probability that any single ad will make an impact, so make your ad stand out.

In mid-1995, the Ad Council announced that it would begin to focus a majority of its resources on campaigns to benefit children.

See also **American Advertising Federation (AAF)**, **American Association of Advertising Agencies (AAAA)**, and **American Marketing Association (AMA)**.

`mktg`

advertising frequency   A measure of how often a targeted audience encounters an advertisement.

EXAMPLE | You post a flyer advertising your car for sale on the bulletin board at the Laundromat. During a week in May, 100 people look at the board. Twenty people read your ad once, 30 read it twice, 30 read it three times, and 20 do not notice it. The frequency for that week is:

$$(20 \times 1) + (30 \times 2) + (30 \times 3) + (20 \times 0) \div 100 = 1.7 \text{ exposures}$$

Some research suggests that an indifferent customer or client may need almost 30 exposures to an advertising message before deciding to buy. In the Laundromat example, you can increase frequency and have a better chance of selling your car if you put several flyers at strategic locations—say, the grocery store, bus stop, and train station—where they will be seen repeatedly by the same people.

`mktg`

advertising rates   Charges for **advertising** time or space in a specific medium. Newspapers, magazines, and broadcast outlets that sell advertising describe their advertising rates in a **rate card**.

Magazines usually sell space based on page coverage, such as full page or quarter page. Ad sizes may also be measured as **bleeds**— that is, when the image extends to the edge of the page. The basic unit of measurement for newspapers is the **column inch**, with most newspapers being six columns wide. A column inch is one column wide by one inch deep, so an ad filling a space three columns wide and 10 inches deep takes up 30 column inches (3 x 10 = 30). The unit of measurement for broadcast outlets is in seconds of airtime, with most advertisements running 10, 15, 30, or 60 seconds.

Volume brings your per-ad costs down. If you agree to run a certain number of ads during the year, the broadcaster or publisher will give you a lower rate. Chains of broadcast outlets, newspapers, and magazines often offer a reduced **combination rate** to clients placing an ad in more than one outlet.

EXAMPLE | One of the most sought-after locations in the *Wall Street Journal* is Page C3, where a quarter-page ad appears every day. That is the first page of the New York Stock Exchange (NYSE) listings, and it is also opposite the "Abreast of the Market" and "Heard on the Street" columns, three of the paper's most popular features. There is a hefty premium for this space, which is usually booked many months in advance.

advertising rates

You will pay a premium for the most popular air- time for your commercial or the most strategic location for your ad.

Magazine Ad Rates

Black and White Advertising Rates

Effective October 1, 1996

Dimensions	width x height	1x	3x	6x
Spread	15 7/8″ x 10″	$5,481	$5,052	$4,625
Page	7 1/4″ x 10″	2,876	2,588	2,386
2/3	4 13/16″ x 10″	2,185	1,995	1,840
Island	4 13/16″ x 7 1/2″	1,927	1,760	1,622

Color Rates

Two-Color Process: $475 per ad

Matched Color: $600 per ad

Metallic Colors: $715 per ad

Three- or Four-Color Process: $1,225 per ad

Three- or Four-Color Process Spread: $1,950 per ad

Color Bleeds: No charge

Bleed Sizes

Gutter Bleed Spread: **17″ x 11 1/8″**

Bleed Page: **8 1/2″ x 11 1/8″**

Covers/Special Positions

Sold on a space available basis. Position surcharge is based upon black/white space costs only.

> Back Cover: +20%
>
> Inside Front Cover: +15%
>
> Inside Back Cover: +15%
>
> Special Positions: +15%

Inserts

Contact Director of Sales for pricing, (415) 555-1212.

A

advocacy advertising

Mobil Corporation was one of the pioneers of this type of corporate advocacy advertising. Mobil's ads, also called advertorials, have run every Thursday since the early 1970s on the op-ed page of the *New York Times* and on other schedules in other publications.

The ads grew out of the 1970s era of lines for gasoline and accusations of excessive profits for oil companies. Mobil took its case to the public in an attempt to avoid or weaken proposed legislation to put restrictions on the way oil companies could operate. Subjects covered by Mobil in the mid-1990s have included clean-air issues, health-insurance reform, trade agreements, and tort reform.

Adweek

---

mgmt **mktg**

advocacy advertising
Use of **advertising** to present a point of view.

We are used to seeing ads placed by noncommercial organizations or trade associations to support or oppose a bill in Congress: A group of prominent citizens pays for an open letter favoring gun control or the National Association of Manufacturers takes out a full-page ad supporting a trade agreement. TV commercials praising one candidate or ridiculing another flood the airwaves as an election approaches.

What is relatively new, though—a phenomenon of the last 25 years—is the use of advocacy advertising by individual companies.

Advocacy advertising differs from the more common image advertising (like General Electric's "We bring good things to life" or Nike's "Just do it") in that it is concerned less with people's feelings toward the company and more with their attitudes about issues.

mktg

Adweek®
Weekly trade magazine covering **advertising agencies**. *Adweek* publishes seven regional editions.

See also **Advertising Age**.

acct **fin** **mgmt**

affiliated company
(1) In strict accounting terms, this is a company owned 50 percent or less by another company.

A company more than 50 percent owned by another is a **subsidiary**. The difference to an **accountan**t is that, as a rule, only the operations of subsidiaries are consolidated into the parent company's **financial statements**.

In most cases, you account for affiliated companies using the **equity method**, as Caterpillar does. You show your percentage ownership share of the affiliate's results on your books. If your interest in the other company is small, though—say, less than 20 percent—then you use the **cost method**. Your books reflect just the cost of your investment, its value, and any **dividends** you earn.

Although the **Securities and Exchange Commission (SEC)** insists that financial statements of publicly held companies conform to **generally accepted accounting principles (GAAP)**, it does at times require disclosures beyond those set forth by GAAP. In SEC parlance, an affiliate is a company that "directly, or indirectly through one or more intermediaries, controls, or is controlled by, or is under common control with" another company. Thus, in certain SEC filings, but not **annual reports**, separate financial statements might be required for affiliates.

See also **consolidation**.

(2) In general business use, an affiliate is any company in which another company has a significant **equity** stake or a sibling company owned by the same parent.

mktg

affinity card Credit card that offers some reward for its use.

In 1995, the Memphis-based Church of God in Christ became the first religious institution to offer a nationwide affinity card. The church would get a fee from Key West Federal Savings Bank each time a church member signs up for a card or uses one. The church's 3.5 million U.S. members represent a huge potential market for the small thrift institution, which had just 100,000 credit card holders before offering this affinity card.

One of the best known is the General Motors MasterCard, initiated in 1993, which gives its users credit toward purchase of a new GM car. As financial institutions fight each other for customers, they are offering everything from contributions to a charity to frequent-flier mileage and even cash **rebates** based on the use of their cards.

affiliated company

Quick Facts!

General Electric owns 75 percent of the Japanese company GE Yokogawa Medical Systems and 100 percent of General Electric Canadian Holdings. Anywhere else but in its financial statements, where both companies must be called subsidiaries, GE might refer to either as an affiliate or a subsidiary. GE Yokogawa and GE Canadian Holdings also might refer to each other as affiliates.

affinity card

FRAME OF REFERENCE

affiliated company

Caterpillar Inc. owns 50 percent of the Japanese company Shin Caterpillar Mitsubishi Ltd. Caterpillar includes a line in its income statement called "equity in profit (loss) of affiliated companies," which includes its 50 percent share of Shin Caterpillar's results. In other places, "investments in affiliated companies" shows up as a separate line. If Caterpillar owned more than 50 percent of Shin Caterpillar, the two companies' results would be consolidated and reported as though they were a single entity. If Caterpillar owned more than 50 percent but less than 100 percent, it would consolidate 100 percent of Shin Caterpillar's income and balance sheet accounts, but there would be a line item on the liability side of the balance sheet to reflect "minority interests"—that is, the equity in the subsidiary that Caterpillar does not own.

A

affirmative action

> *The American Dream is about freedom and the fruits of freedom. It's about opportunity not just for those lucky enough to be born gripping that fabled silver spoon, but opportunity for all. It's the chance to start with nothing but an idea that makes your heart race and, with hard work, to see it happen.*
>
> —Jimmy Stewart, from *Portraits of the American Dream*

afternoon drive time

mgmt

affirmative action   Controversial set of programs affording special preferences to members of certain groups with respect to employment and admission to colleges and universities.

Employment considerations may involve new job applicants, promotions and assignments, and protection against layoffs. These programs may also include "set-asides," whereby portions of contracts or subcontracts are reserved for the designated groups.

Generally, the groups receiving these benefits are referred to as "protected classes" and include racial and ethnic minorities, such as African-Americans and individuals with Hispanic surnames, as well as women, who are considered to have been historically disadvantaged.

Affirmative action programs range from targeted recruiting and **advertising** that outline opportunities and encourage the protected classes to pursue them to special criteria used in considering members of these groups for admissions, jobs, and so on, to specific "goals" that lay out how many jobs or contracts should be reserved for women and minorities.

These programs have been the subject of numerous court challenges. In some instances, courts have ordered employers to set goals and timetables to remedy past discrimination; other courts have ordered governments to adopt specific programs. For example, seeking to increase minority representation in police and fire departments, some municipalities have then adjusted upward the test scores of applicants from protected classes, increasing the likelihood that minority applicants will be selected over other applicants with higher test scores. Still other court decisions have barred affirmative action programs, concluding that such programs discriminate against individuals who are not in the protected classes.

mktg

afternoon drive time   Hours from 2:00 P.M. to 7:00 P.M. when commuting reaches its peak and radio **advertising** rates are at a premium.

See also **drive time**.

mgmt

Age Discrimination in Employment Act (ADEA)
Federal law that protects most workers 40 and older against unfavorable treatment because of their age.

ADEA prohibits employers from making age-biased decisions, not just in hiring practices but in policies on promotions, demotions, training, layoffs, pay, and benefits as well.

When enacted in 1967, the ADEA protected job applicants and employees up to 65 years old. By 1979, the ceiling had been extended to 70, and in 1986 Congress removed the upper limit for most employees. ADEA provisions affect companies with 20 or more employees, labor unions with 25 or more members, agencies of local, state, and federal governments, as well as employment agencies. Several states have passed age-discrimination laws, with provisions that are sometimes stronger than federal ones.

In a 1987 amendment, the Equal Opportunity Commission— which enforces the ADEA—specified that the following behaviors constitute discrimination:

➤ Any implication that an employee's job performance, absenteeism rate, and health are affected by age.

➤ Any crude remark, including jokes, about one's age.

➤ Any derogatory term that refers to age.

Plaintiffs in age discrimination suits usually construct their arguments along two lines:

➤ Disparate treatment: Employees seek to show that the employer intentionally discriminated by creating different working conditions or requirements for older workers.

➤ Disparate impact: Those conditions or requirements, even if they are unintentional, had damaging effects on older employees alone.

The majority of ADEA cases seek to establish proof of disparate treatment. Employees cite any action or policy that has no bearing on one's ability to perform the work. Policies specifying a mandatory retirement age or statements that the company will not hire people past a certain age—both of which are now illegal—can be used to prove age discrimination. Citing statistical data on hiring and promoting practices, employees are sometimes successful in arguing that the company has indirectly discriminated. Indirect evidence can be inferred from comments such as "Since you are getting close to retirement, we gave the new account to Joe Johnson."

When faced with a case of age discrimination, a company may use one of these basic defenses:

➤ **Bona Fide Occupational Qualifications**
The unique requirements of the job necessitate age criteria.

➤ **A Bona Fide Seniority System**
Actions are based on an established system of on-the-job experience so that older employees may be passed over for promotion in favor of younger workers with longer service.

Age Discrimination in Employment Act

► **Good Cause**

The company makes a decision because an employee violated company policy or inadequately performed a job. "Good cause" dismissals include falsifying data, stealing, and drug dealing. Employers must show, however, that they have made a bona fide effort to discuss problems with the employee.

► **Business Necessity**

Layoffs for economic reasons or the operating conditions of particular businesses can be mitigating factors. Layoffs as part of a reorganization can fall under this category as long as workers have been assessed individually; employees cannot be singled out as a group because of their age.

mktg

agent   Intermediary that routes goods or services from a producer to consumers.

See also **distribution channel**.

econ

aggregate demand   Total quantity of goods and services that consumers, businesses, the government, and people in other countries are willing and able to buy at different possible price levels.

Aggregate Demand

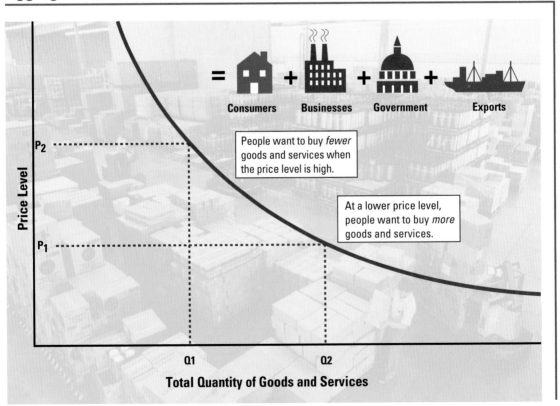

Consumers + **Businesses** + **Government** + **Exports**

People want to buy *fewer* goods and services when the price level is high.

At a lower price level, people want to buy *more* goods and services.

Price Level

P_2

P_1

Q_1 Q_2

Total Quantity of Goods and Services

People buy more total goods and services at lower price levels than at higher ones. However, aggregate demand encompasses the entire demand curve, representing what people will buy at all possible price levels in a given economy. Various factors can affect aggregate demand, including changes in government spending and taxation, the **money supply**, and foreign **exchange rates**, as well as expectations about future incomes, profits, and prices.

See also **aggregate supply**.

  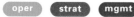

oper strat mgmt

aggregate plan   A long-term production plan that takes into account a company's ability to produce goods and meet demands at the lowest cost.

The basic idea is simple enough: Plan ahead and avoid thinking solely in the short term. Assess realistically your company's production capabilities and projected **demand**. Then develop a strategy and budget for aquiring parts, deploying workers, and planning production. An aggregate plan is a rough guideline for managing production. There will always be small deviations from the plan, but it helps you develop a strategy.

There are two broad types of aggregate plans:

1 **Level Production**
The company continues production at a constant rate without increasing or decreasing its workforce. Inventory varies with demand. Accordingly, you save on overtime but have high inventory costs. For service companies, a level-production plan means that a constant number of workers would be maintained, even if they are not always busy.

For example, your company makes plastic outdoor furniture. You aim to keep your operations steady year-round, even if it means building up your inventory during the winter.

2 **Chase Demand**
The opposite of level production, a chase-demand plan assumes the company will keep small inventories but be ready to change the workforce as demand for products increases or decreases. Inventory costs will be low, but you may have to pay more for overtime and new workers during peak seasons.

In practice, you will find elements of both level-production and chase-demand thinking in most aggregate plans.

See also **master production schedule**.

aggregate plan

An aggregate plan helps you avoid short-term thinking. Without it, you might have small shipments of materials and worker layoffs one month, followed the next by a scramble to hire workers and obtain materials.

EXAMPLE

Sunshine Toys makes dolls, indoor and outdoor games, and puzzles. Its aggregate plan considers overall projected sales and the materials and labor needed. Sunshine's managers optimize their resources by thinking of their plant as a whole.

econ

aggregate supply Total quantity of goods and services that all producers in an economy are willing and able to produce and sell at different possible price levels in a given period.

In the long run, aggregate supply depends on the production potential of the economy and is not affected by changes in **aggregate demand**. That is because changes in the price level will absorb the shock of demand changes. But in the short run, that is not the case. If labor productivity, wage rates, or nonlabor costs change, the aggregate-supply picture will change. Government tax policies may also affect the incentive to produce.

oper **tech**

AGVS See **automatic guided vehicle system**.

acct

AICPA See **American Institute of Certified Public Accountants**.

fin

alpha (α) (1) Measure of a stock's price movements in response to factors specific to the company.

To help explain alpha, we will start with **beta (ß)**. Beta is a measure of how a particular security performs in response to changes affecting the whole stock market—like shifts in the economy, interest rates, and inflation. Alpha eliminates the effect of general market fluctuations and examines how the stock would do if the market were flat—as though securities rose and fell entirely on their own

alpha

Alpha

To calculate a historical alpha (α), you need the following values:

r_j	Rate of return for the security on which you are calculating alpha
ß	The security's historical beta
r_m	Market return (such as Standard & Poor's 500 Stock Composite Index or the Dow Jones 30 Industrials)
r_f	The risk-free rate (the return on a risk-free security, such as a Treasury Bill)

The formula

$$r_j - [ß(r_m - r_f)] = \alpha$$

A

merits. These merits include such things as anticipated growth in earnings per share, management effectiveness, and labor relations. In other words, while beta measures response to the stock market's behavior, alpha responds to the company's behavior.

Let us say a company's stock had a 20 percent return last year. The stock's historical beta is 1.5, the rate of return for the market was 10 percent, and the risk-free rate was 5 percent.

$$20\% - [1.5(10\% - 5\%)] = 12.5\%$$

The stock's historical alpha is 12.5 percent.

Most alphas are historical measurements. Predicting correctly that a stock will outperform its peers in the future—which is another way of looking at alpha—is what separates the mediocre from the top performers in managing portfolios of stocks. A manager who can predict which stocks will have high or low alphas will know which stocks to keep and which to weed out to beat the average market performance.

(2) Long-established stocks on the London Stock Exchange having a solid record of paying **dividends**. In the United Kingdom, the term alpha stocks applies to stocks that in the United States might be called **blue chips**.

(3) When used in reference to mutual funds, alpha represents the relationship between a fund's performance and its beta, usually over a three-year period.

mgmt　**mktg**

AMA　See **American Management Association** and **American Marketing Association**.

alpha

t r a p | 👎

Remember that most alphas are a statistical measure based on the past. There is no guarantee they will predict the future.

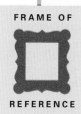

FRAME OF

REFERENCE

alpha

During 1995, the best performing stock in the Dow Jones Industrial Index was Sears Roebuck, with stock price appreciation of 68 percent versus the Dow's 33.5 percent. At the other end of the spectrum, the worst performer in the Dow was Bethlehem Steel, which dropped 23 percent.

The regression analysis equations below reflect the mathematical relationship between the performances of the two stocks and that of the Dow. The alpha of each stock, shown as the last number (or Y intercept), reflects the relative performances of the company.

Sears	Y = 0.94x + 0.53
Bethlehem Steel	Y = 1.33x − 1.15

In the equations above, Sears' alpha is 0.53, reflecting a premium return to the Dow's. (Sears' beta is 0.94.) Bethlehem Steel's alpha is −1.15, reflecting its poorer comparative performance to the Dow's. (Bethlehem Steel's beta is 1.33.)

A

American Advertising Federation

American Association of Advertising Agencies

American Depository Receipt

Breaking News

In 1994, you could get ADRs for more than 1,000 companies, a tenfold increase since 1986. Companies whose ADRs can be bought in the United States include British Telecommunications, Sony, and Volkswagen.

`mktg`

American Academy of Advertising (AAA)   Professional association striving to enhance education in **advertising**.

The membership includes primarily academicians and a few advertising practitioners.

See also **Advertising Council, Inc. (ACI)**, **American Advertising Federation (AAF)**, **American Association of Advertising Agencies (AAAA)**, and **American Marketing Association (AMA)**.

`mktg`

American Advertising Federation (AAF)   National association of some 50,000 ad industry professionals that promotes the business of **advertising**.

The AAF was established in 1967 through the merger of the Advertising Federation of America and the Advertising Association of the West. It lobbies in Washington on behalf of advertisers and promotes educational programs at universities nationwide.

See also **Advertising Council, Inc. (ACI)**, **American Academy of Advertising (AAA)**, **American Association of Advertising Agencies (AAAA)**, and **American Marketing Association (AMA)**.

`mktg`

American Association of Advertising Agencies (AAAA)   National trade association for the advertising agency business.

Founded in 1917, the AAAA acts as the industry's spokesman with government, media, and the public sector. It also provides member agencies with a wide range of informational and educational services.

See also **American Academy of Advertising (AAA)**, **American Advertising Federation (AAF)**, **Advertising Council, Inc. (ACI)**, and **American Marketing Association (AMA)**.

`fin`

American Depository Receipt (ADR)   Certificate representing stake in a foreign company held in the United States.

ADRs, also called American Depository Shares, are traded on U.S. stock exchanges and through U.S. brokers, eliminating the need for U.S. residents to deal in foreign currencies on foreign markets. Transactions are the same as for U.S. shares, although one ADR does not necessarily represent one share; it can correspond to multiple shares or fractional shares.

EXAMPLE | In the case of News Corporation Ltd., an international media company whose ordinary shares are traded on the Australian Stock Exchange, one ADR represents four ordinary shares.

Instead of receiving **dividends** in foreign currencies and reports in foreign languages directly from the company, ADR holders get dividends in U.S. dollars and reports in English. ADRs carry the same rights to dividends and voting as the shares traded in the home country.

acct

American Institute of Certified Public Accountants (AICPA)
National professional society for those who have met the requirements to be **certified public accountants (CPAs)**.

The AICPA prepares and grades the **Uniform CPA Examination**, which is given by state licensing bodies to accountants who want to be CPAs. The organization also wields considerable influence in setting accounting and auditing standards and in formulating and policing rules of ethical conduct throughout the accounting profession.

The AICPA:

► Sponsors the **Financial Accounting Foundation (FAF)**, which is the parent of and appoints the members on the **Financial Accounting Standards Board (FASB)**—the organization that establishes **generally accepted accounting principles (GAAP)**.

► Sets standards through its own Auditing Standards Board for conducting financial audits. This body of regulation is known as **generally accepted auditing standards (GAAS)**.

► Puts out publications, including the *Journal of Accountancy* and the *Tax Adviser*, that are respected voices in the industry.

► Participates in legislative activities to promote or define the role of accountancy.

Founded in 1887, the AICPA has more than 300,000 members.

See also **audit**.

mgmt

American Management Association (AMA)
Organization that trains businesspeople worldwide and publishes books, periodicals, and other material to foster professional growth.

Many large corporations have memberships in the AMA and make its resources available to employees. The AMA offers regular courses in subjects like accounting, management, and public relations at various locations in the United States and abroad. Among its publications is *Management Review*, a monthly magazine with a circulation of 85,000.

American Institute of Certified Public Accountants

American Management Association

Outside the AMA's training center in Washington, D.C., you can often spot a street vendor selling neckties. He could teach a course in identifying a target market.

A

American Stock Exchange

The American Stock Exchange moved indoors in 1921 and occupies the same quarters in New York's Wall Street area today as it did when it made the transition from the curb.

mktg

American Marketing Association (AMA)   National professional society of marketers, with 50,000 members in 92 countries.

The AMA is regarded as the leading organization for marketing professionals. Founded in 1915, it assists in the education and career development of marketing practitioners and promotes the science and ethical practices of all marketing disciplines. It publishes *Marketing Management*, *Marketing News*, *Journal of Marketing*, *Journal of Public Policy & Marketing*, and numerous other periodicals and books.

See also **American Academy of Advertising (AAA)**, **American Advertising Federation (AAF)**, **Advertising Council, Inc. (ACI)**, and **American Association of Advertising Agencies (AAAA)**.

fin

American Stock Exchange (Amex)   Smaller of New York's two stock exchanges.

Because of more lenient listing requirements than those of the **New York Stock Exchange (NYSE)**, the companies whose common shares are traded on the Amex are usually smaller. The Amex now specializes in the trading of foreign issues, **American Depository Receipts (ADRs)**, and options on many NYSE and some **over-the-counter (OTC) stocks**.

Located in downtown Manhattan, the Amex—known as the Curb Exchange until 1953—had its origins in the 1800s among traders who could not afford a place on the NYSE and so had to conduct their business of buying and selling stocks in the street. Still often called the Curb, it is dwarfed in size by both the NYSE and **The Nasdaq Stock Market**. Its 1993 dollar volume of some $52 billion ranked far behind the NYSE's $2.26 trillion and the Nasdaq's $1.35 trillion. In fact, the Amex's piece of the pie has been shrinking for decades—from a 21.3 percent share of total U.S. exchange volume in 1945 to only 5.5 percent in the early nineties.

mgmt

Americans with Disabilities Act (ADA)   Federal law, enacted in 1990, that bans discrimination against people with disabilities.

The ADA is one of the most sweeping pieces of U.S. human-rights legislation passed since the Civil Rights Act of 1964.

Barring discrimination in the private as well as the public sector, the ADA goes a step further to ensure that businesses accommodate the needs of people with disabilities and take steps to promote their economic independence. Most states also have laws protecting people with disabilities.

American Stock Exchange, 1986 and 1996

Top 10 Amex Companies by Market Value ($ billions)

1986	Market Value	1996	Market Value*
B.A.T. Industries	$10.1	B.A.T. Industries	$24.2
Imperial Oil Ltd.	$ 6.1	Viacom, Inc. (CL. B)	$13.8
The New York Times Co. (CL. A)	$ 2.9	Imperial Oil Ltd.	$ 7.9
Texaco Canada Inc.	$ 2.9	Turner Broadcasting (CL. B)	$ 5.6
The Imperial Group Plc.	$ 2.7	The New York Times Co. (CL. A)	$ 3.1
Gulf Canada Corp.	$ 2.2	Thermo Instrument Systems	$ 3.1
The Washington Post Co. (CL. B)	$ 2.0	Hasbro, Inc.	$ 3.0
Wang Laboratories, Inc. (CL. B)	$ 1.8	Courtaulds, Plc. (ADR)	$ 2.7
Courtaulds, Plc. (ADR)	$ 1.7	Telephone & Data	$ 2.6
Home Shopping Network	$ 1.6	U.S. Cellular Corp.	$ 2.5

*As of June 30, 1996

Source: American Stock Exchange

The ADA covers:

► Employment, calling for "reasonable accommodations" for employees and applicants who have disabilities.

► Public services offered by state and local governments, the most important being transportation.

► Public accommodations and services operated by private organizations, such as airports, hotels, educational institutions, recreation centers, and zoos.

► Telecommunications, mandating relay services for people with speech or hearing impairments.

See also **consumer protection legislation.**

A

analog

The hands on this clock represent analog data.

annual meeting

acct **fin**

amortization

(1) Periodic write-down of intangible **assets**, such as **patents** or **goodwill**.

The cost basis of the **assets** is gradually reduced through regular charges to income. Amortization also refers to the gradual extinction of any debt over time, such as the amortization of a mortgage.

See also **depletion** and **depreciation**.

(2) In **bond** investments, amortization is apportioning, over the life of the investment, any premium you may have paid above **par value**. In corporate financing, it means repaying a loan in installments that will cover the entire principal and interest by maturity.

tech

analog

Representing data by physical variables, the way time is shown by the hands on a clock.

A telephone turns voice vibrations into (analog) electrical vibrations that can be transmitted over phone lines. An analog signal is continuous, as opposed to a **digital** signal, which is broken up into numbers.

mgmt **fin**

annual meeting

Gathering of a corporation's shareholders where directors are elected, other key matters are voted on, and business issues are discussed.

This is a once-a-year, legally required rite for publicly held corporations. Since most of these U.S.-based corporations operate on a calendar-year basis, the season for annual meetings centers on early May, allowing time after year's end for the **annual report** and **proxy statement** to be prepared and mailed to shareholders.

While the annual meeting is necessary in its current form for various legal reasons, there is an increasing desire among corporate executives to find an alternative. Since it is common for some 90 percent of the votes to be cast by mail, the physical meeting is usually symbolic. And it is expensive, not only in costs like transportation, accommodations, and catering, but in the time that management must set aside from business operations to prepare for unpredictable questions.

The format for the annual meeting usually includes:

► A state-of-the-business speech by the top executive.

► Balloting on directors who are up for election, the firm that will perform the **audit**, any proposed changes that would involve the **capital stock** of the company, other fundamental matters, and resolutions proposed by shareholders.

► A time for comments and questions from shareholders.

In practice, only a small percentage of the outstanding stock is represented by shareholders who attend the meeting in person. Most individuals and institutions that hold the company's stock vote by proxy in advance.

fin **mktg** **mgmt**

annual percentage rate (APR)   Measurement of the true cost of credit.

The APR is more exact and higher than the stated **interest rate** for installment loans because it considers the compounding of interest during the loan period. Since 1969, federal law has required disclosure of the APR and total finance charges on all financial contracts in the United States. Essentially, the APR restates the full cost of the loan as a simple, effective annual interest rate.

There are four ways to calculate the APR for an installment loan:

▶ Actuarial Method

▶ Direct-Ratio Method

▶ Constant-Ratio Method

▶ N-ratio method

The actuarial method, generally used by lenders, gives the most accurate results but involves complicated computerized calculations. Lenders calculate interest using a fixed rate on the unpaid balance of the principal of a loan. The borrower pays an installment, the lion's share of which is applied to interest. As the loan matures, interest payments decline as those on the principal increase.

The other three methods are much less complicated but result in an APR that is slightly less accurate. The three are calculated by formulas that use the following variables:

Direct-Ratio Formula
$\text{APR} = 6tC \div [3P(n + 1) + C(n + 1)]$

t   Number of payment periods per year

C   Cash amount of total finance charges

P   Principal (the original loan amount)

n   Number of scheduled payments

annual percentage rate

tip |

Credit card companies will waive interest charges over a specified period. However, if a consumer does not pay the full balance at the end of the grace period, the company often will require the consumer to pay the interest accrued from the inception of the loan.

A

annual percentage rate

The direct-ratio formula tends to understate the APR slightly. The N-ratio formula approximates the APR more precisely than the constant-ratio or direct-ratio methods.

The constant-ratio formula tends to over-state the APR slightly.

Constant-Ratio Formula

APR	$= 2tC \div P(n + 1)$

N-Ratio Formula

APR	$= t(95n + 9)C$
	$\div \ 12n(n + 1)(4P + C)$

EXAMPLE A company borrows $1,000 at an 8 percent interest rate. The finance charge comes to $80. The company must make 12 equal payments of $90 each ($1,080 ÷12 = $90). Here is how the APR would be calculated using each of the three methods:

Direct-ratio method:

(6 x 12 x $90) ÷ [3 x $1,000(12 + 1) + $90(12 + 1)] = 0.1613, or 16.13%

Constant-ratio method:

(2 x 12 x $90) ÷ [$1,000(12 + 1)] = 0.1662, or 16.62%

N-ratio method:

(12[(95 x 12) + 9] x $90) ÷ [12 x 12 x (12 + 1)] x [4($1,000) + $90] = 0.1621, or 16.21%

 acct   fin   mgmt

annual report   Publication prepared by a company—primarily for its shareholders and bondholders—at the end of its reporting year.

Most U.S. corporations operate on a calendar-year basis, so most annual reports are prepared in January and February and distributed to security holders in late March and early April. As a rule, the annual report is mailed along with the company's **proxy statement** and **proxy card**, which enables the shareholder to vote by mail in advance of the **annual meeting**.

The **Securities and Exchange Commission (SEC)** requires distribution of the annual report, which must include the company's **income statement**, **balance sheet**, **cash flow statement**, **statement of shareholders' equity**, and the **audit** report. The **Financial Accounting Standards Board (FASB)** also requires companies to submit information about contracts and sales to foreign sources and government agencies.

A

All of this required information must be sent to shareholders before the company's annual meeting. Most publicly held corporations also include, as the front part of the annual report, a letter from the top one or two executives, an operating review focusing on the company's achievements and prospects, and photographs. In addition to the security holders, who are the primary audience for the annual report, potential shareholders, stock analysts, creditors, employees, job applicants, business associates, government officials, and others seeking information on the company may have an interest in its contents.

The SEC now requires thousands of corporations to file their annual reports electronically via a system called **EDGAR** (Electronic Data Gathering, Analysis, and Retrieval). A company's EDGAR file contains the full text of the annual report along with the tables and descriptions of photographs and other graphics. This makes it possible for individuals with computers, modems, and access to electronic research services to find out what is in an annual report without obtaining a printed copy from the company.

A small but significant number of corporations, led by Bell Atlantic, have begun to treat the annual report less as a magazine and more like a financial document. They have reduced the content to the legally required material and a letter from the chief executive, and they print the report more simply—photos and graphs are used sparingly. Bell Atlantic simplified its annual report after surveys and other feedback from shareholders, who asked for the elimination of annual-report frills.

See also **10-K**.

annual report

Right now, users often cannot find or recognize— in a reasonable time— those disclosures that affect their investment decisions.

—Ray J. Groves, retired chairman, Ernst & Young, 1977–94

FRAME OF REFERENCE

annual report

After years of rather elaborate annual reports, MCI Communications Corporation adopted the no-frills approach with its 1994 version. "This year's annual report," the company said on the first page, "reflects a more concise, cost-effective approach to reporting MCI's financial performance." There were no photos and only modest amounts of color in the text, graphs, and cover design. MCI narrowed the scope of the report to only the CEO's letter and the financial section. An annual report consultant who examined MCI's pared-down model estimated that the simplification saved the company more than a dollar a copy.

annuity

Series of equal payments, such as quarterly deposits you make into a trust account for a child's future education.

`fin` `acct`

annuity   In accounting terms, a mortgage with monthly payments qualifies as an annuity, as does a trust account into which you make quarterly deposits for a child's future education.

In general usage, though, the term annuity refers to an investment contract sold by an insurance company guaranteeing future payments to the buyer (also called the annuitant) on a monthly, quarterly, or annual basis. Annuities like these are often used to provide retirement income. When payments are made at the beginning of a specified period, it is called an **annuity due** or an annuity in advance; if payments are made at the end of the period, it is an ordinary annuity or an annuity in arrears.

Insurance companies sell two general types of annuities—fixed and variable. With a fixed annuity, all payments to the annuitant are equal. With a variable annuity, payments are determined by the value of the underlying investments. An annuity, either fixed or variable, that goes on indefinitely is called a **perpetuity**.

See also **future value of an annuity**.

`fin` `acct`

annuity due   An **annuity** in which payments are made at the beginning of a specified period rather than at the end, thus making for a larger future value. Also known as an annuity in advance.

See also **future value of an annuity**.

`mktg` `mgmt`

Antidumping Act of 1974   Federal law that prohibits the practice of **dumping**.

`mgmt` `fin` `mktg`

antitrust law   Body of laws and court precedents designed to protect citizens and companies against unfair business practices, including the formation of monopolies.

The key congressional legislation has resulted in the following:

▶ **Sherman Antitrust Act of 1890**
The first major piece of legislation designed to prevent monopolies.

▶ **Clayton Act of 1914**
Closed some of the loopholes in the Sherman Act by pinpointing specific things businesses could not do, including purchasing large quantities of a competitor's stock and using discriminatory pricing.

► **Federal Trade Commission Act of 1914**
Established a policing agency—the Federal Trade Commission (FTC)—for the increasingly complex world of big-time business. It was expected not only to track down offenders but also to counsel companies on how to avoid antitrust violations.

► **Robinson-Patman Act of 1936**
Eliminated loopholes and reduced the amount of proof required to make a case of illegal pricing. Also outlawed price discrimination.

► **Wheeler-Lea Act of 1938**
Broadened the FTC's powers to police practices, such as deceptive **advertising**, that are harmful not only to the public but to competitors as well.

► **Celler-Kefauver Act of 1950**
Forbade **mergers** through the **acquisition** of a competitor's **assets**.

Since the Celler-Kefauver Act, most of the major changes in antitrust law have evolved from court decisions. The most recent trend has been to impose fewer restraints on **vertical integration**.

APB   See **Accounting Principles Board**.

APB 15   Set of rules for accountants to use in calculating and reporting earnings per share.

The officially entitled *Accounting Principles Board Opinion No. 15*, which was issued in 1969, was so complex that the APB had to publish a 116-page interpretive booklet. Subsequently, its successor, the **Financial Accounting Standards Board (FASB)**, suspended the requirements for nonpublic enterprises.

See also **income statement**.

APB Opinions   Pronouncements on accounting issues and standards made by the **Accounting Principles Board (APB)**.

See also **generally accepted accounting principles (GAAP)**.

appreciation   (1) Increase in the value of property over time. (2) The excess of the fair value of **assets** over the **book value**.

antitrust law

Quick Facts!

The federal laws cover interstate commerce. In the last decade or so, states have passed significant antitrust laws to regulate intrastate business. In one Connecticut lawsuit, a doctor who could not gain visiting privileges at the only hospital in town sued and won. The court ruled that the hospital's power to turn away physicians unfairly jeopardized the doctor's ability to run a profitable practice.

appropriation

EXAMPLE

The federal goverment allocates specific amounts of money for national defense, housing, and other government programs. A company might appropriate specific sums in its budget for advertising and other categories of expense.

arbitrage

arbitration

tip

With the securities industry tending to prefer arbitration from the NASD or NYSE, broker agreements often specify one or the other. Investors' lawyers often would opt for the AAA if given the chance. But studies have found the outcomes are not much different.

EXAMPLE | A company may own land that has become more valuable over time. Generally, it is required to carry its assets on its books at the historical cost—what it actually paid to acquire the property. But when a business changes hands or goes through a restructuring, appreciation may be recognized by marking up book value to fair value.

acct

appropriation   Amount of money allocated for a specific purpose.

fin   **mktg**   **mgmt**

APR   See **annual percentage rate**.

fin

arbitrage   Buying a security, currency, or **commodity** on one market and simultaneously selling it (or an equivalent) at a higher price on another market.

A simple arbitrage deal might involve buying a silver contract in Chicago for $4.70 an ounce and selling an equal contract in Hong Kong for $4.72. A more complicated arbitrage strategy might involve several variables such as currency rates, **interest rates**, and **derivatives** like options. An arbitrager, for example, might buy a stock with French francs in Paris while selling an option on it in U.S. dollars in New York and **hedging** the **foreign exchange** exposure.

Because markets tend toward equal prices, arbitragers—or arbs as they are known—must act quickly to take advantage of temporary differentials. Also, because the price differences are small, arbitragers need to trade in big blocks to reap sizable profits. Some investors argue that arbitragers destabilize the markets because they trade so quickly in such large blocks. Others contend that the arbitrager's trading helps equalize the markets by pushing the price up in the weaker market and down in the stronger one.

mgmt

arbitration   Submitting a dispute for settlement by an impartial individual or panel.

When the individual arbitrator or a board of arbitration makes a decision, it is binding. That is what distinguishes arbitration from mediation, where the third party has no authority to impose a settlement.

Although commonly referred to as the alternative to litigation, arbitration preexisted the organization of court systems and was recognized 25 centuries ago by the Greeks as a means to quickly and efficiently settle disputes. Today, many business contracts, especially in the securities industry, contain provisions for arbitration. The benefits include reduced legal expenses and faster settlement than in court cases. Plus, unlike most court proceedings, arbitration is carried out in private. That means dirty linen does not get washed in public, and trade secrets are less likely to become public knowledge.

A

arbitrage

Barings PLC was England's oldest merchant bank. Founded in 1762, it became a major financial force with a list of prestigious clients that included Queen Elizabeth II, the Saudi royal family, the World Bank, and others. In 1984, the bank bought a small trading company with a staff of 15 and offices in Hong Kong, Tokyo, and London; renamed it Baring Securities; and began trading derivatives in the East Asian markets.

Barings Securities became a big source of income for its parent as the Japanese stock market boomed. When the Japanese market crashed in the early 1990s, Barings Securities nose-dived. The bank made some changes, putting a young trader in charge of futures trading in its Singapore office. Nick Leeson took considerable leeway amassing big positions arbitraging futures contracts keyed to an index of Japanese stocks. He traded them simultaneously on Singapore and Japanese markets in 1994 and early 1995, betting heavily that the Tokyo market would trade in a very narrow range. It did not. Mistakes mounted, and one Friday the tab came due for 20,000 futures contracts. The bank faced a loss of about $1 billion.

Barings went into receivership the next week before being sold to ING, a Dutch financial services group. Leeson faced charges of fraud, and several of the bank's senior managers were dismissed.

Usually, an arbitrator's award can be appealed to the courts only if there is a question over whether proper procedure was followed, not over the facts of the case.

The securities industry keeps arbitrators busy with client grievances against brokerage companies, complaints by **registered representatives** about employers, and disputes between securities companies.

EXAMPLE | Salary arbitration was the overriding issue of the 1994 baseball strike. In major league baseball, a player who has four or more years in the league can literally take his team to court for salary arbitration. The player and his agent come in with a figure, and the team makes a counter offer. An impartial judge decides the player's salary for the upcoming season based on the salaries of players with similar statistics.

In 1925, Congress enacted the Federal Arbitration Act, which enforced arbitration clauses in interstate contracts, thus providing a firm foundation for the modern form of business arbitration we know today. The following year, the American Arbitration Association was established and has since been the nation's leading full-service provider of alternative dispute resolution (ADR) services.

The association does not decide cases. Rather, it provides a forum for the hearing of disputes, rules and procedures that have broad acceptance, and a roster of impartial experts, or "neutrals," to hear and resolve cases. Recognized for their standing and expertise in their fields, their integrity, and their dispute resolution skills,

arbitration

Types of business contracts that can contain provisions for arbitration:

■ **Purchase or sales agreements**

■ **Leases**

■ **Property matters, licensing arrangements, partnerships, franchises, joint ventures, and loan agreements**

neutrals are nominated to the National Roster of Arbitrators by leaders in their industry or profession.

A not-for-profit, public service organization, the American Arbitration Association is also an information resource on the design and implementation of specialized ADR systems, which may utilize a variety of dispute resolution techniques, to address a full range of business disputes.

In 1995, more than 62,000 cases were filed with the association in a full range of matters, including but not limited to: accounting, bankruptcy, computers, construction, employment, energy, entertainment, environment, financial services, health care, labor-management, insurance-reinsurance, intellectual property, government, manufacturing, retailing, and securities.

mktg

area of dominant influence (ADI)   Counties that receive radio and television signals in a given broadcast **market**.

Each county is determined to be under the influence of one market center or another, depending primarily on the quality of reception in that county of signals from a given market. Thus, the ADI is useful for advertisers who are trying to determine which broadcasters are reaching which geographic areas. Advertisers use ADI to apportion spending and promotional efforts when creating **marketing plans**.

Arbitron, the company that defined ADI, no longer measures local television ratings, and the Nielsen Media Group uses a different designator called DMA, or Designated Market Area. Most ADIs and DMAs are similar in size and boundaries, however.

mktg

area sampling   Selecting people to be surveyed using a geographic technique.

See also **sampling**.

arm's-length transaction   A transaction where each party is able and free to act in its own best economic interest.

If both parties are fully informed, neither is under any special compulsion to complete the transaction, and both are equally capable of negotiating the transaction, the resulting price should be at fair market value.

A loan, lease, or other agreement between two parties is considered an arm's-length transaction if the terms are the same as for unrelated parties. Goods sold to a parent company by a subsidiary at cost would not be considered at arm's length. Many tax laws related to deductions and adjustments are affected by whether a transaction is deemed to be at arm's length.

---

arm's-length transaction

Quick Facts!

Multinational oil corporations conduct a lot of arm's-length transactions among their affiliates. Exxon's affiliate in France, for example, buys its crude oil from an Exxon supply company at the going market rate. If the French company exports any refined products to another Exxon affiliate, the transaction is at the market price. Exxon would lose the tax advantages of having separate affiliates if they acted as though they were integral parts of the same organization.

mktg

art director   In an **advertising agency,** the person who oversees the visual design of a client's ad or advertising campaign.

Reporting to the agency's **creative director**, the art director supervises artists and designers who create the ads. An art director will typically work with a copywriter to develop the overall theme of a campaign.

mgmt

articles of incorporation   Document individuals must file with their secretary of state to form a corporation.

The document typically gives:

- ▶ The corporation's name.
- ▶ Its officers, purposes, and **fiscal year**.
- ▶ The amount of paid-in capital; that is, how much people paid for the stock.
- ▶ Other information on the stock, such as the number of shares authorized and outstanding.

See also **bylaws** and **charter**.

tech

artificial intelligence   Computer technologies that try to mimic human mental behavior like reasoning, communicating, and sensing. Simple systems use logic that branches like tree limbs (for example, if credit limit exceeded, deny credit). More sophisticated systems can learn from mistakes and improve performance over time.

Programmers have been working on artificial intelligence systems since the mid-1960s with success in limited applications like games and **expert systems**.

oper   **tech**

AS/RS   See **automated storage/retrieval system**.

tech

assembly language   Computer programming language one step above the fundamental **machine language** the computer uses for its internal instructions. Computer programmers often write software in assembly language.

---

art director

artificial intelligence

EXAMPLE

"Ante-Up" at the Friday Night Poker Club is a computer game in which the player is matched repeatedly against other, fictitious players. The other players have names and betting personalities. So you might expect Mary to bluff infrequently, for example, whereas Bill often acts impulsively.

A

assembly line

Car manufacturer Henry Ford (1863–1947) introduced the world's first assembly line for cars in 1911. The first *moving* assembly line for the manufacture of automobiles was created in 1913 because of overwhelming demand for the Model T. After a period of experimentation by Ford and his engineers, the system completed in 1914 in Highland Park, Michigan, was able to deliver parts, subassemblies, and assemblies to a constantly moving main line.

assembly line

`oper` `tech`

assembly line   Manufacturing by a steady flow of similar work from station to station.

Each **workstation** along the path performs an operation repeatedly—welding, cutting, fitting, or fastening, for example. The process is highly interdependent: If one part breaks down, the entire process is affected.

The heyday of the assembly line came in the first half of the 20th century, when one of Henry Ford's Model Ts rolled off the line every 10 seconds. In the last decade of the century, **automation** accomplishes many high-volume, simple assembly jobs, while workers using computers and **robotics** can do other assembly tasks, especially when they are difficult, unhealthy, or dangerous. Most low-volume, complex, or delicate assembly tasks are still carried out on assembly lines. But since this work is labor-intensive, much of it has moved to countries with low labor costs.

See also **job shop** and **paced line**.

`acct`

asset   In accounting, a company's resource that has future value.

There are two broad types of assets:

1 Tangible
These assets include such things as buildings, cash, inventories, land, supplies, and vehicles.

2 Intangible
Copyrights, **goodwill**, and **patents** are examples.

Assets are reported on a company's **balance sheet** in two categories: *current* (likely to be converted to cash within one year or within the company's normal operating cycle, whichever is longer) and *fixed* (likely to have utility beyond one year).

A

fin

asset-backed security   Form of borrowing secured by **assets** and the income attached to them.

Mortgage-backed bonds may be considered a form of asset-backed security, but these have come to be regarded as a class of their own. Usually, the term asset-backed security refers to automobile loans, credit card receivables, home equity loans, and leases that have been bundled together and then sold as securities. The underlying assets will provide the cash stream to pay these instruments.

See also **securitization**.

fin

asset-based lending   Using balance-sheet assets, like **accounts receivable** or inventories, to secure a senior note.

The lender will closely monitor the company's collateral and financial data.

acct

asset depreciation range   Schedule of allowed depreciable lives published by the Internal Revenue Service. These ranges are referenced in the **modified accelerated cost recovery system (MACRS)**.

See also **accelerated cost recovery system (ACRS)**.

mgmt   **fin**   **acct**

asset turnover   Ratio showing how sales stack up against average total **assets** during an **accounting period**. Also known as the earning power of assets.

This measures the productivity of assets. To determine average total assets, add your total assets at the beginning of the year to your total assets at the end of the year and divide by two.

EXAMPLE | Your sales for 1995 were $540,000. Your total assets were $849,000 at the beginning of the year and $865,000 at the end, giving an average of $857,000. So the asset turnover ratio is:

$540,000 ÷ $857,000 = 0.63, or 63%

asset-backed security

Asset-backed securities usually refer to automobile loans, credit card receivables, home equity loans, and leases that have been bundled together and then sold as securities.

FRAME OF REFERENCE

asset-backed security

General Motors Acceptance Corporation (GMAC), which finances car and truck loans, packages a pool of these loans and sells securities in the capital markets. The payments on the securities "match," or offset, the **cash flow** of the loans.

A

As a rule, the higher your asset turnover, the better you are using your assets. But, like most ratios, the numbers vary from industry to industry. You need to compare your ratio with those of your competitors and with itself over time to determine how well you are doing.

mgmt **oper** **fin** **acct**

asset utilization   Measure of manufacturing **efficiency** based on the return you get from the resources at hand.

Since the success of an enterprise is tied closely to how well its **assets** are managed, some companies use a measure like this to evaluate their success and to determine compensation for managers.

strat

assumptions   Accepted traits of a business environment that form the starting point for **strategic planning**.

tech

asynchronous transmission   Form of data communication where only one character is transmitted or received at a time.

It is commonly used by computer modems and fax machines. Each character is preceded by a start **bit** and ended with a stop bit to let the receiving device know where a character begins and ends.

See also **synchronous transmission**.

acct

attest   To render an opinion that a company's **financial statements** are fairly presented in accordance with **generally accepted accounting principles (GAAP)**. Auditing is often referred to as the attest function.

mgmt

attribution theory   The notion that people can explain behavior by analyzing its causes.

There are two types of perceived causes for any particular personal behavior:

1 **External Causes**
Those directed by forces beyond a person's control.

2 **Internal Causes**
Those under the control of the individual.

---

attribution theory

t i p |

When judging others, people tend to overestimate the internal factors. When judging themselves, people often overestimate the internal factors for successes as well as the external factors for failures.

If, for example, a foreman yells at a line worker because the foreman's boss just told him he was being laid off, the foreman's hostility will likely be seen as externally caused. If, however, the foreman yells at all his workers every day, the latest occurrence may be seen as internally caused.

How is it that we judge behavior as externally or internally caused? We consciously or unconsciously keep track of three traits day to day:

1 **Consistency**
Does the person typically act this way? If the foreman seldom yells, an employee will probably attribute his odd outburst to external causes. If the foreman is always yelling, an employee will likely attribute the latest incident to an ongoing effect of internal causes (such as a need for control).

2 **Consensus**
How do other people behave in the same situation? If other foremen in the factory frequently yell at line workers (high consensus), an outsider will probably attribute the behavior to internal causes, such as management telling foremen they must be confrontational to keep workers in line. If one foreman yells but others do not (low consensus), an outsider will probably attribute the abrasive behavior to external causes.

3 **Distinctiveness**
Does the person behave the same way in different situations? Does the foreman yell at other foremen, too? Has he been seen in town yelling at his wife or children? Does he argue loudly with management? If so, his behavior has low distinctiveness and is likely to be internally caused. If the foreman rarely raises his voice, the unusual incident is highly distinctive and probably can be traced to an external cause.

 acct mgmt

audit   Examination of a company's books or operations.

We will deal here primarily with the **financial audit**. In performing a financial audit, an accountant must conduct his or her work in accordance with **generally accepted auditing standards (GAAS)**. These standards are promulgated by the **Auditing Standards Board**, an arm of the **American Institute of Certified Public Accountants (AICPA)**. The auditor's report or opinion will appear in the company's annual report and in its annual **10-K** filing with the **Securities and Exchange Commission (SEC)**.

attribution theory

A person's behavior toward another may be caused by external or internal factors.

audit

Quick Facts!

In our litigious society, accounting firms are taking big hits because of suits filed by shareholders of companies audited by the accounting firms. The suits usually allege a failure by the auditors to warn shareholders of a potential problem that eventually resulted in the shareholders losing money. A 1993 study by the six largest U.S.-based accounting firms found that 14.3 percent of their accounting and auditing revenue was going to judgments, settlements, and legal defense.

FRAME OF

REFERENCE

audit

The **Big Six** firms—Arthur Andersen, Coopers & Lybrand L.L.P., Deloitte & Touche, Ernst & Young, KPMG Peat Marwick, and Price Waterhouse—along with a large coalition of American corporations, have been seeking reform of liability laws. Success at the federal level was achieved with the passage of securities legislation in 1995, but state liability laws continue to be a problem. The big firms point out that many smaller accounting firms—perhaps as many as half of them—are unwilling to perform audits because of the fear of being sued. In 1990, Laventhol & Horwath, then the seventh-largest firm, declared bankruptcy in the face of mounting litigation costs.

While there is some evidence that courts are denying or reducing audit-malpractice awards, the costs to the accounting firms are still considerable.

The major types of auditors' reports are:

► **Unqualified Opinion**

The auditor finds that the **financial statements** fairly present the company's position and operations as specified by the **generally accepted accounting principles (GAAP)**. Since companies tend to work with their auditors to make sure that their procedures are sound, this is by far the most common type of audit report. It is sometimes referred to as a **clean opinion**.

► **Qualified Opinion**

The auditor includes a particular limitation: objective or independent evidence of a particular transaction or policy. The issue giving rise to the qualification must be set forth clearly in the auditor's opinion.

► **Adverse Opinion**

The auditor issues an unfavorable report. The company has not presented its financial statements according to GAAP provisions. Adverse opinions are rare, and the auditor must disclose the conditions that led to his or her conclusions in the audit report.

► **Disclaimer of Opinion**

The auditor is unable to render an opinion, usually because he or she cannot complete the audit. This might happen if records are unavailable and cannot be reconstructed.

EXAMPLE | Yes Clothing took a $4.7 million loss for its **fiscal year** ended March 31, 1995. Its auditor, Moss-Adams Accountants, announced that it would issue an unqualified opinion on the company's financial statements modified by an explanatory paragraph because of "substantial doubt" about whether the business could go on. A week after that announcement, however, clothing mogul Georges Marciano, who had already invested $6 million in Yes, agreed to pump in another $3.3 million.

Aside from financial audits, other types are:

▶ **Internal Audit**
Where an auditor within the company investigates its procedures to ensure that they meet corporate policies.

▶ **Management Audit**
Examines management's efficiency.

▶ **Compliance Audit**
Determines whether a company is following specific rules.

Auditing Standards Board   Part of the **American Institute of Certified Public Accountants (AICPA)** that establishes acceptable practices for audits.

See also **generally accepted auditing standards (GAAS)**.

augmented product   Value added to a good or service to differentiate it from the competition. These benefits give the **core product** an advantage.

Companies offering augmented products cannot compete on price with no-frills price-cutters. Occasionally, a manufacturer of an augmented product will introduce a no-frills version under a different **brand name** to compete with price-cutters, but these ventures often are not successful.

See also **market segmentation** and **tangible product**.

authority   Influence an employee has over company matters or other employees that stems from a right given by the company.

See also **power**.

authorized capital   Number of shares of stock that a corporation may issue in accordance with its **articles of incorporation** and **charter**.

automated storage/retrieval system (AS/RS)
Process that uses robotics to handle materials in a warehouse.

See also **automatic guided vehicle system (AGVS)**.

augmented product
Quick Facts!

Some hotels offer free newspapers and shoeshines, keep a bathrobe and umbrella in the closet, and send a maid around at night to check linens, turn down the bed, and leave candy and a weather forecast on the pillow. Hotels may augment their product further with a bowl of fruit, a bottle of wine, and even limousine service for regular guests.

automatic guided vehicle system

This automated guided vehicle can travel across a plant or warehouse without a human operator.

automatic merchandising

`oper` `tech`

automatic guided vehicle system (AGVS) System that moves materials without a human operator.

In an AGVS, automated guided vehicles (AGVs) travel throughout a plant or warehouse directed by wiring imbedded in the floor or by optical scanning tapes. The vehicles carry materials from one point to another in the work process. The computerized control system can be set to spread the work evenly to a number of workstations or to bypass a congested area.

Plants with an AGVS often also use an **automated storage/retrieval system (AS/RS)**, which employs **robotics** to store and retrieve material in a warehouse. This reduces labor costs and maximizes the use of warehouse space.

EXAMPLE | A large plant manufactures plastic packaging film. Polypropylene resin is fed into machines that heat and stretch it into 12-foot-wide sheets that are then cooled and wound onto giant spools. Each roll of the film weighs several tons.

When a roll is completed, an AGV picks it up and delivers it either to a cutting station if the material is needed immediately or to a storage rack to be cut later. If it is stored, an AGV will deliver it to the cutting station later. After the rolls are cut to narrower widths according to customer specifications, they are delivered by AGV to the warehouse/loading dock, where an AS/RS takes over. The AS/RS stores the completed work in optimal patterns for retrieval when it comes time to make shipment.

`mktg` `tech`

automatic merchandising Sales through vending machines.

Automatic merchandising provides retailers with continuous distribution in high-traffic places like motels, schools, offices, and hospitals. For some products, like gasoline, many customers prefer automatic purchase and payment options at the point of purchase.

`oper` `tech` `mgmt`

automation Using specialized equipment to carry out a sequence of operations with a minimum of human participation.

This is a step beyond mechanization, which usually involves just one operation. The term automation was coined by automakers when they began using machines to handle parts between operations as well as to control a series of operations. Since then, computers have taken automation to a new universe of applications, from maintaining rare-books collections to hard-rock mining.

A

Automation is described as fixed or flexible:

► In *fixed* automation, specialized machines produce a standardized product. You cannot modify them significantly to make products with different shapes and sizes. This is also known as fixed-position automation.

► In *flexible* automation, you have much more ability to produce items with different shapes and sizes. Advanced computer controls and a high level of automation can lead to a flexible manufacturing system, one that incorporates state-of-the-art technology to optimize every stage of a manufacturing process. Such systems can manufacture variations of the same product on the same assembly line.

EXAMPLE | Your plant makes sheet-metal parts for home appliances. By automating to the level of a flexible manufacturing system, you can make parts for a wide variety of uses—air conditioners, furnaces, heat pumps, hot-water heaters, and refrigerators. You start with a coil of steel on one end of your production line and end up on the other with the part you currently want to make. All it takes is one operator to feed the part's specifications into the plant's computer system.

oper **tech** **mgmt**

autonomation   Ability of an automated process to detect problems and shut itself down if necessary.

The word originated in Japan and may be a contraction of "autonomous automation." Autonomation detects conditions like defective products, a dwindling supply of needed parts, and damage to the machine. The system takes any corrective action that it can, sends out a signal seeking human help, and shuts down production if necessary.

EXAMPLE | In a highly automated book bindery, equipment with **machine vision** checks key pages as they are fed into each book on a conveyor belt. If pages are missing or upside down, the incorrectly collated book is ejected from the conveyor to a human operator. If five in a row are wrong, it is obvious that a serious problem needs attention, so the line is programmed to shut itself down.

See also **automation**.

acct **fin** **mgmt**

average collection period   Number of days it takes to collect your **accounts receivable**.

See also **days sales outstanding (DSO)**.

---

automation

t r a p |

A highly automated plant needs fewer employees, but many modern forms of automation—especially the softer ones—require educated and flexible workers. You will not get your money's worth out of your flexible manufacturing system if you do not hire and train the right people to run it.

autonomation

Aerospace and Defense

Contrary to conventional wisdom, the military-industrial complex President Eisenhower warned the nation against in his farewell address did not originate in World War II. Rather, it can be traced to the mobilization attending World War I, when President Wilson authorized creation of the Counsel of National Defense, which in turn organized the War Industries Board (WIB). Headed by Bernard Baruch, the WIB enlisted thousands of businessmen into its ranks to coordinate the production and distribution of war-related products. In the process, a link was forged that remained intact after the war.

Bernard Baruch

During much of the interwar period government procurement languished. The War Department drew up mobilization plans, which contemplated the creation of a War Resources Administration that would operate like the WIB. As war came closer in 1938, President Roosevelt sent Baruch on a fact-finding mission and learned Germany had 3,000 warplanes and the U.S.S.R. had over 1,300, while the United States had only 301.

At that point, Roosevelt mobilized a large-scale procurement program and organized the War Resources Board to coordinate efforts. Other mobilization actions followed. Appropriations were increased, and a military draft initiated. By the time of the Japanese attack on Pearl Harbor on December 7, 1941, the country was on a wartime footing.

During the war, American industry turned out 77,000 ships, 86,000 tanks, and 2.7 million machine guns. Manufacturing output increased 128 percent from 1939 to 1944 as almost all industries participated in the war effort.

Aircraft had become one of the most important parts of this new alliance between government and business; more than 300,000 aircraft were produced during the war. Some of the largest Air Force–based companies were North American, Consolidated Vultee, Douglas Aircraft, Curtiss Wright, Boeing, Lockheed, and Republic Aircraft, while Grumman Corp., Eastern Air Lines, and Chance Vought were leading Navy suppliers.

These companies had their origins in the prewar period. William Boeing was a wealthy lumberman whose fascination with flying led him to establish Boeing in 1916. Lockheed, founded by Allan and Malcolm Loughhead the

Contributing Writer: Robert Sobel
Lawrence Stessin Distinguished Professor
of Business History, Hofstra University

1916   1920   1930   1940

1916
William Boeing establishes Boeing; Allan and Malcolm Loughhead found Lockheed

1928
California-based fighter and bomber plane manufacturer North American organized

1929
Grumman starts in Leroy Grumman's garage

1938
Military expenditures total $1 billion

1944
President Roosevelt passes the Contract Settlement Act; U.S. government military expenditures reach a WW II high of $74 billion

same year, was a marginal company that went bankrupt in 1931, then reorganized and flourished during World War II. North American Aviation was a California-based manufacturer organized in 1928 that produced a variety of fighters and bombers during the war. Grumman began in 1929, in Leroy Grumman's Long Island garage.

With the coming of peace in 1945, all faced the prospect of sudden decline and possible failure. That year, the president signed the Contract Settlement Act, which provided for easing the pain when it became necessary to cancel procurement contracts. This legislation became the keystone of the government's reconversion program. National defense expenditures, which had risen from $1 billion in 1938 to $74 billion in 1944, declined to less than $11 billion in 1948. Contracts were phased out as companies returned to the products designed earlier for civilian markets.

The purely military firms were in quandaries. For example, naval cutbacks meant that Grumman had to seek other business, and it turned to the manufacture of canoes, subcontracts from other companies, and eventually buses. Others, believing that defense-oriented companies were selling for low prices and that military spending might rise once more, entered the market and made purchases. Electric Boat, an important supplier of submarines to the Navy, acquired Consolidated Vultee and renamed it Convair, while the new corporate umbrella was called General Dynamics.

The acquirers won their wager. As the Cold War began and the Korean War erupted, military purchases spiraled, rising to $44 billion in 1953 before leveling once again. From then on, expenditures traced a roller-coaster path. They declined after the Korean War and then rose

with the Vietnam War, only to dip during the early 1970s. When stories appeared in mid-decade about shortages of parts and obsolete equipment, they rose once more and continued to do so in the 1980s and into the early 1990s.

In the process, such firms as McDonnell Douglas, Lockheed, General Dynamics, and Rockwell International came to depend heavily on government procurement. Others, not ordinarily considered military, had major stakes in the business; during the 1960s, AT&T, General Electric, RCA, Chrysler, and General Motors were among the top 25 defense contractors.

Given the nature of the Cold War, the Pentagon agreed to stress airpower, which extended to outer space as well. By the time of the Vietnam War,

the industry included nuclear weapons, missiles, and a vast array of electronic supplies.

Several companies specialized in particular segments of the industry. Boeing and Rockwell received important bomber contracts. General Dynamics, McDonnell Douglas, and Grumman concentrated on fighter-aircraft. Lockheed's military transports and strategic missiles were favored by the Air Force.

But it was more complicated than that. Since there were thousands of subcontractors, prime contractors for one system might act as subcontractors for others. Moreover, rivals bidding for the same contract would agree

1960   1980   1990   1995

1957
USSR launches its Sputnik satellite

1968
North American, shattered by the failure of the Apollo program, merges with Rockwell.

1986
Challenger space shuttle explodes after takeoff

1990
Total defense spending peaks at $300 billion

1993
U.S. and Russia agree to collaborate on a space station

1995
Lockheed and Martin Marietta merge to form Lockheed Martin, the world's largest defense contractor

55

beforehand to award subcontracts to the losers. Furthermore, each bidder could count on congressional support from legislators with defense plants in their districts. The companies made sizable contributions to the campaign chests of favored congressmen and would locate new facilities in their states and districts. In this way, Eisenhower's military-industrial complex became an important part of the industrial scene and a matter for public scrutiny.

The Pentagon, Congress, and defense-oriented companies formed what one writer called "the iron triangle." Influential military officers found niches in corporations on retirement; by the late 1960s the top 10 military contractors had more than 1,000 former officers on their payrolls. Executives at companies with major contracts became key figures in Washington's defense establishment. These included Cabinet secretaries Robert McNamara (Ford), George Schultz and Caspar Weinberger (Bechtel), and David Packard (Hewlett Packard).

Defense and aerospace are monopsonistic industries in that there are many suppliers and only one buyer—the federal government (although foreign sales to other governments are important, they are marginal). Because of this, they cannot easily be compared with any other businesses. Single contracts can run more than a dozen years and involve several billions of dollars.

In such a high-stakes environment, there was bound to be waste, duplication of effort, and on occasion, even fraud. Companies that won awards often returned to request renegotiation, with the armed forces obliged to give in to obtain the needed products. Each B-1 bomber, for example, was supposed to cost $29 million, but Rockwell asked for additional funding, and

in the end the few that were delivered cost $200 million each.

Lockheed was involved with payoffs in situations that implicated Prince Bernhard of the Netherlands, Italian politicians, and a Japanese prime minister. The company was accused of overcharging the government for production of

the C-5B cargo plane. Hughes Aircraft, Boeing, Raytheon, and Teledyne pleaded guilty to charges involving bid rigging. Northrop's CEO was found guilty of making improper campaign contributions, and the company itself was indicted on criminal charges for falsifying test results. McDonnell Douglas paid a fine for violating the securities laws in connection with its accounting procedures.

The President's Private Sector Survey on Cost Control (known as the Grace Commission) was initiated by Ronald Reagan. It uncovered billions of dollars of waste, the most famous instances being $600 toilet seats. The commission discovered there were 4,000 military bases when only 312 were needed, the others kept in operation because of political considerations.

These revelations and the publicity attending them prompted reform in the way contracts were given and monitored. For a while General Dynamics, General Electric, and Litton were suspended as government contractors for shoddy billing. When Pratt & Whitney's F100 engine performed poorly, the Pentagon compelled the company to share business with General Electric. In preparing to replace the aging F-15 fighter, the government asked seven contractors to enter the bidding. The Navy required General Dynamics and McDonnell Douglas to compete for the contract to produce Tomahawk missiles, lowering their costs by one-third.

While total defense spending declined only slightly from its peak of close to $300 billion in 1990, procurement spending fell more sharply, going from more than $82 billion in 1991 to less than $70 billion in 1995. The most important reason for this was the end of the Cold War. The change had a heavy impact on the defense industries, aerospace in particular. Military sales, which had come to $40 billion in 1990, declined to $32 billion by 1995; missile sales went from $14 billion to $8 billion.

As they had done at the close of World War II, several companies merged or purchased others in the industry. North American was the prime contractor for the Apollo 1 space mission, which ended in disaster when three astronauts died on the launch pad. In 1968, its reputation shattered, the company merged with Rockwell International to form North American Rockwell. Northrop came together with Grumman, and Lockheed merged with Martin Marietta, creating Lockheed Martin. General Dynamics divested itself of several foundation businesses. Loral, on the other hand, expanded through purchases of unwanted units of divesting companies, so that in the 1990–1995 period its sales went from $2 billion to $6 billion. Missile maker Raytheon acquired another producer of corporate planes, Beech. In the late 1980s and early 1990s, it acquired British Aerospace's aircraft business and rights to produce Mitsubishi aircraft in the United States, making Raytheon the largest maker of nonmilitary aircraft.

The end of the Cold War put a damper on the space program. President Reagan's call for a "star-wars" defense, which would have cost billions of dollars, did not get far. The 1986 Challenger explosion led many to question

the wisdom of the entire effort in space, and spending on National Aeronautics and Space Administration programs was cut back.

In 1993, the United States and Russia reached an agreement to collaborate on a space station, which effected $2 billion in savings. Such cooperation, along with competitive bidding and close monitoring, reduced costs considerably, and success with these policies intensified efforts toward greater economies. Commercial companies also became a larger factor in the launch sector of the business, which may auger the privatization of several aspects of the industry.

Automobiles

There is no agreement regarding the creator of the first automobile. In 1769 Nicolas Cugnot, a French artillery officer, planned a three-wheeled contraption to be powered by a steam boiler. Richard Trevithick actually constructed such a device in 1801, and three decades later steam cars were created by inventors who dreamed of developing a rival to the railroad. But today's automobile was invented by Karl Benz and Gottfried Daimler in Germany in the 1880s.

Henry Ford

The American automobile business began when Charles and J. Frank Duryea put together a car, based on Benz's concepts, in 1893. The 1900 census reported production of 4,192 cars, of which 1,681 were steam driven, 1,575 electric, and 936 propelled by "hydrocarbon." Scores of manufacturers followed, each producing a few cars in disorganized fashion. Not until Henry Leland succeeded in creating cars with interchangeable parts in 1907 and Henry Ford perfected the assembly line in 1913 would what came to be considered mass production come into its own.

Ford produced his first car in 1896, one of the many experimental vehicles of the time. He organized an auto company in 1899. It failed, as did a second attempt in 1901. But the third firm, which appeared in 1903, succeeded. Several models were produced, as Ford experimented with turning them out on an assembly line. In 1909, when he introduced the Model T, the company manufactured just over 10,000 cars. Four years later, with the assembly line in full operation, 168,000 Model Ts were produced, and Ford alone accounted for more than one-third of the American market. America had a major automobile company. Ford instituted a program of standardization, continual improvement, and regular price reductions. With these, he dominated the industry.

General Motors (GM), organized by William C. Durant in 1908, was a seemingly random collection of several companies. Within two years GM teetered on the edge of bankruptcy. Durant was ousted, but he did not leave the industry. Instead he organized Chevrolet Motor Co. and, through it, started purchasing GM stock. Durant claimed control of GM in 1918 and merged it with Chevrolet. Two years later

Durant was again ousted and replaced by Pierre du Pont, who, together with Alfred Sloan, rationalized the random collection of car brands they had inherited.

Pierre du Pont & Alfred Sloan

Contributing Editor: Dr. John V. Kirnan
Managing Director, Salomon Brothers Inc.

1885   1900   1910   1918

1885
Automobile invented by Karl Benz and Gottfried Daimler in Germany

1893
First car assembled in the United States by Charles and J. Frank Duryea

1903
Henry Ford starts Ford Motor Company

1907
Henry Leland succeeds in creating cars with interchangeable parts

1908
General Motors organized by William C. Durant

1909
Henry Ford introduces the Model T

1913
Henry Ford perfects the assembly line for autos

1918
GM merges with Chevrolet

Out of this came the progression from Chevrolet to Pontiac to Buick to Oldsmobile to Cadillac. Unlike Ford, GM had annual model changes or modifications and many styles and car colors, and maintained prices. It financed purchases, a practice Ford rejected but eventually was forced to accept. The GM paradigm proved successful; by 1926 GM passed Ford and had 30 percent of American sales. Two years later Ford abandoned the T and retooled for the Model A. Chrysler soon followed and by 1929 was the industry's third-largest company.

There were two dozen smaller companies on the eve of the Great Depression, and most of these went out of business during the harsh times. The automakers converted to military production during World War II and returned to peacetime production in time for the 1946 model year. By then the industry was composed

of the "Big Three" plus Packard, Studebaker, Nash, Hudson, Willys, and a newcomer, Kaiser-Frazer (K-F). The smaller players were soon weeded out. After absorbing Willys, K-F ceased producing domestic cars in 1955. The union of Studebaker and Packard did not last much longer, and the combination of Nash and Hudson to form American Motors limped along for a quarter of a century until it was acquired by Chrysler in 1987.

While some foreign cars had always been sold in America, none had been sold in large numbers. After the war Austin, Hillman, Renault,

and Fiat attempted to make a dent in the small-car market that the American manufacturers had all but abandoned, but they made little progress. Then, in the early 1950s, the Volkswagen "Beetle" appeared, an unusual, well-constructed, inexpensive small car with an efficient service and dealer operation. More than 28,000 Beetles sold in 1955; five years later the figure reached 160,000, and the Beetle was looked on as the rebirth of the Model T paradigm.

Considering the Beetle acceptable to only a small portion of the population on both coasts, the Big Three at first refused to react. Then, in 1959, they reacted with "compacts" that, over time, got larger and more ornate.

In 1958, 588 Japanese vehicles were sold in the United States, most of them small trucks, but the "Japanese invasion" had begun. It picked up steam in the 1960s, as Americans bought more Toyotas and Datsuns, followed by Hondas, Subarus, and Mitsubishis. They differed from the Beetle in that they were more like conventional American cars, only smaller, less expensive, and, as it seemed to an increasing number of owners, better constructed. Still, when Americans thought of foreign models, usually the aging Beetle sprang to mind.

1926   1960   1980   1990   **1995**

1926	1950s	1958	1972	1978	1980	1982	1992	1995
GM passes Ford as the market-share leader in American car sales	Volkswagen introduces the "Beetle" in the United States	First Japanese vehicles sold in the United States	Japanese cars surpass German cars as the top import in sales	Volkswagen becomes the first foreign company to open a plant in the U.S.	Japanese auto production surpasses that of the United States for the first time	Honda begins assembling Accords in Maryland	Best-selling car in Japan is the Accord, imported from Ohio	Sport utility vehicles dominate industry sales growth

This situation changed in the 1970s as a result, in part, of a growing awareness of the qualities and values offered by Japanese cars but also because of the "oil shocks" that made Americans more aware of fuel economy. The devaluation of the American dollar, which made Japanese cars as expensive as their American counterparts, in some cases even more so, did not cut into sales. In 1972, Japanese cars, in the aggregate, passed German cars in the American market. Sales rose to 488,217 in 1977, by which time Toyota and Nissan were the world's second- and third-largest car manufacturers, behind General Motors. Toyota now led Volkswagen in the American market, while Nissan was neck-and-neck with the fading German company.

In 1980, Japanese companies produced 7 million automobiles against 6.4 million produced by the American firms. For the first time, Japan's car production surpassed that of the United States. The following year the Japanese agreed to limit car exports to the United States, a move that had unanticipated consequences.

The Japanese companies entered the higher-priced area and played down their economy cars. The Infiniti, Acura, Camry, Lexus, 929, and others now challenged the likes of BMW, Mercedes, and Jaguar, while the Honda Accord became the best-selling model for four years.

By then, the American companies realized the seriousness of the Japanese challenge and started to remake the industry. Production methods were rethought, drawing in large part on the Japanese experience. Labor relations were improved, and Detroit produced new, efficient, lower-polluting cars. The near failure of Chrysler indicated America's weaknesses,

and the transformation began in earnest. The American industry was well on the way to recovery by the 1980s, but by then it no longer could be considered a purely American industry. In the process of alteration and evolution, a world automobile industry was emerging, and it appeared fully grown in the 1990s.

In the 1970s it appeared that American and Japanese automobile companies would vie for industry domination. The situation became more complicated in the 1980s and almost bewilderingly so in the 1990s.

Other countries entered the industry; Korean firms in particular, led by Hyundai, became important players. Then, too, companies crossed national boundaries to market their cars on a worldwide basis; by 1996 GM had plants in 17 countries. This was not new; in the 1920s and afterward American firms had operations in Europe and Asia. Finally, companies formed alliances that transcended national boundaries. In the process, national companies became transnational, or to be more precise, nonnational.

Relations between American and Japanese companies became closer. Toyota and GM entered into a $300 million agreement to manufacture 200,000 Corollas a year in a shuttered GM facility in California, where GM would study Toyota techniques. GM invested another $200 million in Isuzu, importing that automaker's small sedan, and arranged for Suzuki to produce cars to be sold as the Geo in the United States. Chrysler purchased an interest in Mitsubishi and became more dependent on that company for small cars. Ford entered into close arrangements with Toyo Kogyo and, in 1996, took control at Mazda. In a related development, American companies formed alliances with non-Japanese concerns. Ford marketed a Korean car under its own nameplate, GM formed a joint venture with Daewoo, and Chrysler had similar arrangements with several companies in addition to Mitsubishi.

For their part, the foreign companies, fearing further restrictions, perceiving the growth of a "Buy American" sentiment, and realizing that

American labor costs were nearing their own, set up factories in the United States. Volkswagen was the first to arrive, opening a factory in Pennsylvania in 1978. By then, however, the company had stumbled in the American market. The goodwill earned by the Beetle was squandered by its successors, especially the trouble-plagued Rabbit. By the late 1970s, Volkswagen had declined, and continuing problems with the American-built Rabbits, compounded by labor problems, caused the company to abandon its Pennsylvania factory in 1988.

The Japanese, who by then had captured the import market, established their own American plants. Honda began assembling Accords in Maryland in 1982. Nissan went to Tennessee the following year, and most of the other Japanese companies set up their own American factories. In addition to its joint project with GM, Toyota opened a factory of its own in Kentucky, while Mitsubishi and Mazda followed suit. By 1992, the best-selling American-produced car in Japan was a Honda—manufactured in Ohio.

The Japanese were not alone in establishing American plants. In 1995 Daimler-Benz announced its intention to produce its luxury cars in the United States, and other companies indicated they would also establish "captive plants."

For their part, the American companies attempted to create "world cars," models produced in several countries and marketed locally. Ford led the way in 1976 with its Fiesta, and later its Escort was produced in three countries from components made in nine. "Global sourcing" became the buzz words, but most companies made attempts to purchase locally whenever possible.

By the mid-1990s several cars made by Japanese companies in the United States qualified as domestic models under local content rules. At the same time American companies produced cars in other countries to be marketed in the United States. GM and Ford produced cars in Mexico for the American market, and Chrysler had major installations in Canada—which, through all of this, was the country that exported more cars to the United States than any other, including Japan.

By then the Americans seemed to have learned their lessons well. This meant strong quality controls. "Lean manufacturing," operating with small inventories, and close worker-management cooperation began to displace the familiar assembly-line techniques pioneered by the American car industry. All of this was a prelude to the contest for the Asian, Latin American, and former Soviet bloc markets, a contest that will continue into the new century. By the mid-1990s most of the large companies either already had or planned to open facilities in these parts of the world, either on their own or in joint ventures. Within a few years Brazil will join Mexico as a major car manufacturer, and Indonesian companies are preparing to debut on the world scene. For reasons of economy and culture, these offerings are, and will

be, different from the world cars—smaller, more fuel efficient, and with fewer options and lower prices.

The automobile industry today is in a greater state of flux than at any time in the past three-quarters of a century. It now appears that small companies either will disappear or be gobbled up by the larger ones, and on a world scale. It is happening now, as GM has taken a major interest in Saab and Ford acquired Jaguar. The union between Renault and Volvo was abandoned, but both companies know they will either become world players or fade. Automobiles doubtless will lead the way into what has been heralded as the new global economy.

Aviation and Air Transport

Wilbur & Orville Wright

While the Wright brothers performed the first heavier-than-air flight in 1903, the United States lagged in this budding industry during the next decade as the Europeans took the lead. World War I didn't alter this situation appreciably. Aircraft was a small part of the mobilization effort. Until then, the country had produced around 200 airplanes; during the war another 1,500 were delivered to the Army, though they did not see combat service in France. Small companies grew somewhat, but no major firm was created. Instead, Wright-Martin, Curtiss Aeroplane & Motor, Dayton-Wright, and a handful of others received government contracts, along with automobile firms that entered the business, such as General Motors, Ford, and Hudson. All of this collapsed after the war.

For the next two decades, American aviation was in continual straits. Civilian demand for aircraft and air travel was low due to perceived dangers, high prices, and the attractive railroad and automobile alternatives. There were meager military sales; in only one year between 1920 and 1935 did the armed forces take more than 1,000 planes.

The one bright spot was Post Office airmail contracts. This was the beginning of the air transport industry. Walter Folger Brown, who was postmaster general in the late 1920s, established the essential industry structure, including routes, relationships with regulators, fare policies, and more. (The president under whom he served, Herbert Hoover, had performed the same task for radio.) As Secretary of Commerce, Brown established a structure that lasted into the 1980s and was a model of industry-government relations.

Charles Lindbergh's transatlantic flight stimulated interest in aviation but not enough to significantly affect civilian and military demands. There were scores of minor companies that produced a few planes, with some offering irregular transportation services, or barnstorming. Even so, the ones that eventually would become Boeing, Douglas, and Lockheed had their origins in this period. The industry was highly fluid. Mergers produced several large companies, as the smaller ones came together to survive. The most powerful of these was United Aircraft & Transport, which included Boeing Aircraft, Boeing Air Transport, Hamilton Propeller, Sikorsky Aviation, and others. United was the closest the aviation industry was to have as an all-encompassing concern. Curtiss Aeroplane & Motor joined with Wright Aeronautical to form Curtiss-Wright, which had backing from the Pennsylvania Railroad, interested in coast-to-coast transport by a combination of airplane and railroad. Aviation Corp., or AVCO, had Colonial Airways and 80 smaller companies under its umbrella. North American, organized with Curtiss-Wright as its base, included Eastern Air Transport, Sperry Gyroscope, and

---

Contributing Editor: Raymond E. Neidl
Managing Director, Furman Selz LLC

1903

					1934		1947
1903 Wright brothers first flight in Kitty Hawk, North Carolina	**1909** English aviator Henri Farman completes first 100-mile flight	**1922** Juan Trippe institutes his first airline; he would one day found Pan American Airlines	**1927** Charles Lindbergh completes first solo transatlantic flight	**1928** Amelia Earhart is first woman to fly across the Atlantic	**1934** United Aircraft and Transportation split into Boeing, United Airlines, and United Aircraft	**1936** Douglas introduces the DC-3, the first plane that was profitable on a civilian run	**1947** U.S. airplane first flies at supersonic speed

Ford Instrument. These ambitious but unwieldy enterprises were not very profitable, and they demonstrated a marked tendency to fall apart.

By the 1930s, the two major segments of the new industry had divided. Some companies would concentrate on production and others on transportation. The transport business was regulated by the government; under the terms of the Civil Aeronautics Act of 1938, the Civil Aeronautics Board (CAB) became the master of the airline industry.

Airmail contracts remained vital to the carriers. Through judicious awards, the Post Office made it possible for United, TWA, American, and Eastern to grow and prosper, and half a century later those carriers continued as the nation's principal airlines. Meanwhile, in the international field, Juan Trippe founded Pan Am and made it the nation's "chosen instrument," also with the government's support and blessings.

The creation of viable airliners was the prime task facing the manufacturers in the 1930s and the key to their futures. Two of them, Boeing and Douglas, provided aircraft that appeared satisfactory. For a while the Boeing 247 seemed an answer to the air carriers' needs. But it could not operate profitably on passenger traffic alone, so the company concentrated on trying to sell a version to the Army. Then TWA promised Douglas a large order for an econom-

ically viable airliner. From this came the DC-3, which had superior performance characteristics over the Boeing plane, and capable of carrying 14 passengers at 170 mph versus 10 passengers at 155 mph.

The DC-3, introduced in 1936, was the first plane that could be profitable on civilian runs alone. It was an immediate success, and hundreds are still in service today. Douglas received orders for some 800 of them within two years. At the time, industry insiders predicted the DC-3 would achieve for airlines what the Model T Ford did for the automobile industry—make it popular and viable.

World War II intruded before this could happen, and all the companies concentrated on warplanes. Production of fighters, bombers, and trainers for the armed forces rose from 6,000 in 1940 to just under 144,000 in 1942. Douglas became a major supplier, producing 10,000 C47s, the military version of the DC-3, and the other large firms were not far behind. In the process, the industry was remade once again. The ties between government, manufacturers, and airlines were cemented.

As a result of Washington's new interest in aviation, the leading producers always had to consider both civilian and military sales of their products. Research and development, conducted for the government, would find their ways into civilian versions of warplanes. Washington would intercede for the companies to obtain sales to foreign airlines. As for the airlines, they functioned as quasi-utilities. The government set rates to protect the weaker lines, established routes, assisted in airport construction and maintenance, and provided an air-controller system, all under the CAB umbrella. Few industries were more wedded to government than aircraft production and airlines.

The jet fighter planes designed and produced in the last stages of World War II seemed the next step in airliner construction. Jet airliners would be faster and capable of flying longer distances than the four-engine propeller planes then in service. The British were the first to develop a jet airliner, the Comet, which went into service in 1952. A series of unfortunate crashes doomed the plane and gave the Americans a chance to catch up. Boeing, Douglas, Lockheed, and others drew on their military experiences and contracts, and entered the contest.

Boeing, which already had a contract for a jet tanker, was in the lead. It entered the civilian market, attempting to translate expertise with military planes to airliners. The company planned the 707, which was energized by a $200 million order for 30 planes from American Airlines. The 707 went into service in 1958, and the following year was joined by the Douglas DC-8, while the first Convair 880s were delivered in 1960. When Boeing received an order from Pan Am for a 350-seat airliner, it produced the 747. Because of Boeing's strong lead, Convair and Lockheed were forced to cut back and eventually leave the business. Douglas, now a poor second, merged with McDonnell, a producer of fighter planes for the Air Force, and continued. Lockheed tried to reenter the business in the late 1960s with its L-1011 Tristar, which was flown by a number of airlines for several years. Ultimately, demand did not meet market projections and Lockheed discontinued production of the Tristar in 1984.

Realizing that the American companies had a duopoly in passenger planes, the British and French governments in 1962 decided to sponsor what they considered would be the first of the next generation of airliners, the Concorde, a supersonic plane capable of taking off from

Paris or London and actually beating the sun to New York, landing *earlier* than it took off.

Although the Concorde announcement set off a flurry of excitement in America, including pressures for government subsidies to make an American version possible, the support was rejected. The Concorde flights were initiated in 1977, and while considered successful, the plane proved incapable of earning back its huge development costs. Air France and British Airways were both running the Concorde in 1996, although no company is eager to take on the development costs of the next generation.

Another European venture proved more successful. British, French, West German, and Spanish governments and companies came together in 1970 to form Airbus Industries to provide competition for Boeing and McDonnell Douglas. Its first product, the A300, was successful and was followed by others. By the mid-1990s it seemed that Airbus, which had yet to show profits, and Boeing would be the primary forces in the industry, with McDonnell Douglas in third place. Likewise, in the engine business, three companies emerged as dominant forces: General Electric, Rolls-Royce, and Pratt & Whitney. (Rolls-Royce would later collapse under development cost problems with the L-1011 Tristar plane.)

Meanwhile the airlines thrived as jets made possible fast, safe flight. At one time travelers to Europe had to stop at Newfoundland to refuel; no more, as the 747 whisked them to Europe, initiating a major wave of travel. But it took time for the public to accept air travel overseas. As recently as 1953, only 8,000 passengers a week took planes to Europe; the rest went on steamers. In 1956, for the first time, airlines carried more noncommuter passengers than did the railroads.

The American airlines prospered under the regulatory umbrella, but this started to end in 1978, when, directed by CAB chief Alfred Kahn, deregulation took hold. Seeking economies of scale in this new environment, carriers started abandoning their unprofitable routes and cutting prices. But savings realized by the slimmer route structures could not compensate for losses incurred during the price wars, and 1980 brought the airline industry its first operating loss since 1947.

To effect savings, the major carriers resorted to hub-and-spoke systems, whereby flights were routed to large, central airports, where passengers transferred to planes that took them to their ultimate destinations. This system enabled the companies, along with regional and commuter lines, to use smaller planes to service less-active locations. Each major carrier had one or more central locales—Chicago and Denver for United, Atlanta for Delta, Dallas for American, and St. Louis for TWA. Freddie Laker pioneered low-priced flights to Europe with the short-lived Skytrain airline. Among the low-priced domestics were Midway, America West, Air Florida, and Southwest. The most

spectacular domestic carrier was Donald Burr's People Express, which roiled the fare schedules within the industry and set off another fare war. Economic pressures forced Burr to sell People to Texas Air, which eventually became part of Continental Airlines.

Mergers became commonplace in the 1980s. Frank Lorenzo took Texas International into the big time by acquiring Continental Airlines, Eastern Airlines, and discount airline New York before falling into another bankruptcy (Eastern would be forced into liquidation in 1991.) TWA collapsed, and so did Pan Am and Braniff. United reorganized with its employees given a major ownership stake, setting a new precedent in the industry.

In the international sphere, American companies formed alliances with European and Asian airlines. Continental had one such arrangement with Scandinavian Airlines. Delta sold stakes to Swissair and Singapore Airlines, and American formed an affiliation with British Airways. Northwest Airlines and KLM were granted antitrust immunity in 1992—a process now being used as a model by other airlines. These arrangements may lead to formal mergers, when and if the host countries agree.

The fare wars led the companies to offer many different kinds of bonuses to regular flyers. In 1981, some started frequent-flyer programs, and in time, all the majors had their versions. They also stressed use of their own reservation systems and competed with travel agents. Although these strategies were successful, it soon became evident that the airlines were facing a profitless prosperity—much higher traffic combined with lower earnings. This was a long-run phenomenon; in the early 1990s, the airlines, in the aggregate, lost more money than was made from the beginning of flight to that time.

Not until 1995 did the industry turn around and become profitable, but the veterans were not sure it would last. By then the public had become accustomed to the cycle of expansion, bankruptcy, reorganization, and, perhaps, another bankruptcy and reorganization. They learned to cope with the hub-and-spoke system and how to arrange schedules to maximize new benefits (like the recently introduced ticketless travel) and minimize costs and inconveniences.

B

baby bond

to

byte

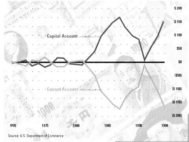

® Bell Atlantic

ANNUAL REPORT

1995

fin

baby bond   A **bond** with a **par value** of less than $1,000.

Baby bonds open the bond market to small investors but require higher administrative costs, relative to the money raised, for processing and distribution. The brokerage costs are high, too, for individuals trading them on the secondary market.

In fact, new issues of baby bonds are rare. Nevertheless, the Midwest Securities Trust Company, a subsidiary of the Chicago Stock Exchange, in the early 1990s, opened the nation's first depository service program for registered municipal and corporate baby bonds. The Baby Bond Safekeeping Program holds the certificates, keeps records, and arranges automated payment of interest and redemption money.

oper   **mgmt**

backlog   Orders for products that have not been produced yet. Also called **open orders** or the **open board**.

The backlog may exist because of earlier orders that get first priority, because of a demand surge that cannot be met, because your plant is out of needed parts, or because you do not start making your products until they are ordered. That last arrangement is common for complex, expensive products like airplanes and mainframe computers.

See also **just-in-time (JIT) inventory system**.

oper   **mgmt**

backorder   Order that cannot immediately be filled.

It usually occurs because the vendor is out of stock, and somebody misjudged consumer demand or mismanaged inventory.

strat   **mgmt**   **mktg**   **oper**

backward vertical integration   Bringing your sources of supply into your company. This can be a strategic move for a number of reasons.

EXAMPLE | Polaroid makes many of the components for its films. That way it does not have to disclose its proprietary technology to suppliers.

A product distributor can integrate backward vertically by going into the manufacturing business.

B

baby bond

backorder

B

backward vertical integration

In the 1980s MicroAge was primarily a reseller of Apple, Compaq, Hewlett-Packard, and International Business Machines computers. But at the start of the 1990s the company saw the chance to build value by assembling its own computer systems configured as its customers wanted. So it integrated backward by converting a large warehouse to a configuration facility that assembles computer systems.

`acct`

bad debt expense　Amount included as an expense on your company's **income statement** that is based on an estimate of **accounts receivable** that will not be collected. These estimates are reviewed annually in light of actual experience.

`acct`

bad debt recovery　Receivable you previously wrote off as uncollectible that you have now collected.

`acct`

balance　Sum of **debit** amounts less the sum of **credit** amounts in an **account**; also a running balance, such as when you maintain a record of deposits, checks issued, and cash available in your checking account.

`econ`

balance of payments　Record of all of a nation's economic transactions with the rest of the world over a given period.

balance of payments

 *Breaking News* |

The United States last recorded an annual surplus in its current account in 1981. The deficit for 1995 was about $148 billion. By definition, the current account will always be offset by the capital account, keeping the balance of payments at zero.

The summary consists of two major components:

1　**Current Account**
This includes exports and imports of goods and services and income received and paid on U.S. investments abroad and foreign investments in the United States. Also included are so-called unilateral transfers, which consist of U.S. government grants, pensions, and other payments.

2　**Capital Account**
This tracks investments and loans flowing into and out of the United States.

Balance on Current Account and Capital Account, 1970–1994 ($ billions)

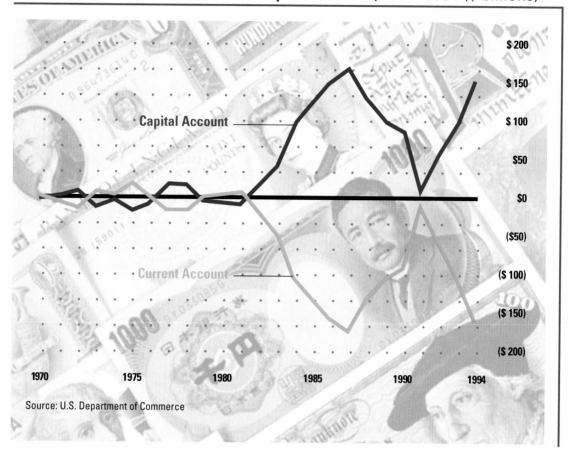

Source: U.S. Department of Commerce

Double-entry bookkeeping is used when each transaction has two equal sides—something received and something given up in exchange. And even though individually the two components may be unbalanced, they offset each other so that the overall balance of payments always balances. That is, a nation's current account deficit (more trade coming in than going out) is always matched by a corresponding surplus in its capital account (an increase in incoming foreign investment). Since all transactions cannot be precisely measured, a statistical discrepancy is included that assures the balance.

Investors, banks, businesses, and government officials keep close watch on current accounts to gauge the strength of a given country's economy and its currency. People sometimes confuse balance of payments with the current account or the merchandise account. They talk about a favorable or unfavorable balance of payments when they mean a surplus or deficit in the current account.

See also **balance of trade**.

B

balance of trade

Breaking News

The United States' merchandise trade balance was in surplus as recently as 1975; in 1995, the deficit was $152.9 billion. The U.S. surplus in services is growing, however. It reached nearly $60 billion in 1994.

There must be, not a balance of power, but a community of power; not organized rivalries, but an organized peace.

—Woodrow Wilson, address to U.S. Senate, January 22, 1917

econ

balance of trade   Difference over a given period between the market value of a country's exports and its imports of merchandise.

The balance of trade is part of the current account balance in the balance of payments. Services are not included in the balance of trade, so the measure is more correctly identified as the balance of merchandise trade.

Sometimes, however, you may see balance of trade erroneously used to include both goods and services. People also use it as a synonym for the entire balance-of-payments current account, including investment income and government payments, so it is wise to clarify how the term is being used.

U.S. Balance of Trade, 1995

Exports of Merchandise	$ 575.94
Imports of Merchandise	($ 749.36)
Balance of Trade (deficit)	**($ 173.42)**
Balance on Services (surplus)	$ 68.36
Balance on Income & Transfers	($ 43.09)
Current Account Balance	**($ 148.15)**

Source: Bureau of Economic Analysis

When a country exports more than it imports, it is said to run a favorable balance of trade, or a surplus. When the country imports more than it exports, it is said to have an unfavorable balance of trade, or a deficit. This is misleading, however, since a country's entire international economic position should be taken into account—an unfavorable balance of trade might be offset by significant service exports. By the same token, a trade deficit with one nation can be canceled by a trade surplus with another.

acct   **fin**

balance sheet   Snapshot of a company's finances at a given time, usually at the close of a fiscal quarter or year.

The balance sheet portrays the basic **accounting equation**:

$$\text{Assets} = \text{Liabilities} + \text{Owner's Equity}$$

The left side of the equation shows the company's resources (**assets**), and the right side shows the amount it owes (**liabilities**) and the amount belonging to the owners (including their capital contributions and earnings retained in the business). It is called a balance

U.S. Exports and Imports of Merchandise, 1970–1994 ($ billions)

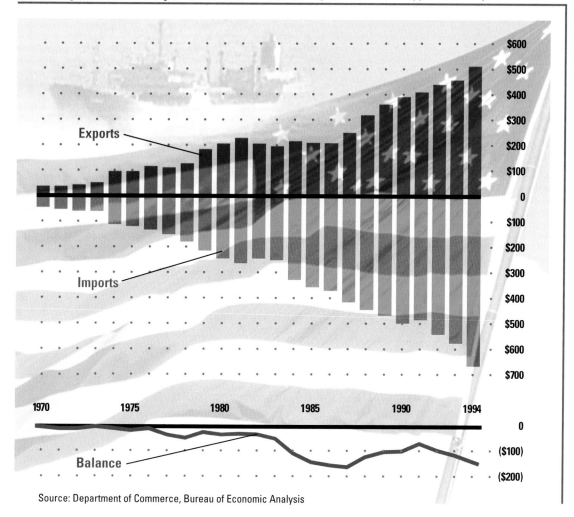

Source: Department of Commerce, Bureau of Economic Analysis

sheet because the left and right sides of the equation balance out, which is another way of saying that your company's assets equal the sources of those assets.

Because this is a corporation, **owner's equity** here is **shareholders' equity**. The only other difference between the format of this balance sheet and the accounting equation is that it is laid out vertically rather than horizontally.

Assets = Liabilities + Shareholders' Equity

$24,900,000,000 = $15,800,000,000 + $9,100,000,000

Assets are listed in the balance sheet in order of decreasing **liquidity**—that is, the speed with which a particular asset can be turned into cash should the need arise.

balance sheet

The balance sheet is divided into two sections, assets and liabilities, and is broken down into the following subsections:

1 Current assets, which will be converted into cash or used within a year or within the company's normal operating cycle, which ever is longer.

2 Fixed assets, which are not likely to be converted to cash within a year.

3 Current liabilities, or those that will be paid off within a year.

4 Noncurrent liabilities, which consist of long-term debt, other liabilities, and deferred income taxes (those that will not be paid off within a year).

5 Shareholders' equity, which in this case, represents the company's net assets.

Here is a balance sheet for a large corporation on December 31, 1995:

Balance Sheet ($ millions)	1995
Assets	
1 Current Assets	
Cash and Cash Equivalents	$ 2,300
Marketable Securities	200
Accounts Receivable	3,100
Inventories	2,800
Deferred Income Taxes	700
Prepaid Expenses and Other Current Assets	600
Total Current Assets	**9,700**
2 Properties, Plants, and Equipment	11,000
Goodwill and Other Intangible Assets	3,700
Other Assets	1,500
Total Assets	**$25,900**
Liabilties and Shareholders' Equity	
3 Current Liabilities	
Accounts Payable	$ 2,600
Accrued Liabilities	2,900
Taxes Payable	500
Short-term Debt	1,300
Total Current Liabilities	**7,300**
4 Long-term Debt	4,900
Other Liabilities	3,300
Deferred Income Taxes	300
Total Liabilities	**15,800**
5 Shareholders' Equity	
Preferred Stock	1,900
Common Stock—Shares Outstanding: 650,000,000	100
Additional Paid-in Capital	1,200
Retained Earnings	6,900
Total Shareholders' Equity	**10,100**
Total Liabilities and Shareholders' Equity	**$25,900**

Assets are divided into two types:

1 Current Assets

These will be converted into cash or used within a year or within the company's normal operating cycle, whichever is longer. Listed in order of proximity to cash, current assets typically consist of cash and cash equivalents, followed by marketable securities like government notes, banker's acceptances, and commercial paper. Next are accounts receivable, inventories, deferred income taxes, and prepaid expenses.

2 Fixed Assets

These are less liquid than current assets and not likely to be converted to cash within a year. Typically, these assets are not acquired for resale but are viewed as productive assets. They include properties, plants, and equipment; investments; and other resources, including intangibles like patents, franchises, goodwill, and exploration permits.

The second part of the balance sheet contains the right-hand side of the equation—liabilities and shareholders' equity. Like assets, liabilities are divided into current and long term, the difference being whether they will be paid off within one year.

Here is how liabilities and shareholders' equity break down:

► **Current Liabilities**

These include accounts payable, accrued liabilities (expenses incurred but not yet paid at the end of the accounting period), taxes payable, short-term debt, and the current portion of long-term debt.

► **Noncurrent Liabilities**

These consist of long-term debt (mostly loans, mortgages, and bonds), other liabilities, and deferred income taxes.

► **Shareholders' Equity**

It is shown in the following accounting equation:

Assets – Liabilities = Shareholders' Equity

Listed first under shareholders' equity is the par value of outstanding preferred stock and common stock. Next comes additional paid-in capital, which is what people paid for the stock over its par value. Retained earnings—what it takes to balance the equation—represent all the accumulated earnings of the company minus the dividends it has paid to shareholders. Taken together, the owner's equity section of a balance sheet represents the company's net assets.

See also **income statement** and **statement of financial position**.

B

balance sheet

B

bankruptcy

Some investment managers specialize in investments in Chapter 11 companies. Although every company's experience is different, many point to the fact that a company's securities (stocks and bonds) tend to bottom out during the 30-day period surrounding its Chapter 11 filing date and then reach a short-term high once a reorganization plan is announced, thus presenting a potentially successful investment opportunity for the timely investor.

bandwidth

Bank for International Settlements

fin

balloon payment   A payment on a loan that is particularly large relative to any other payments. A balloon payment is usually the last payment on a loan and usually retires the balance of the loan.

tech

bandwidth   Range of frequency available for a communications channel.

A channel with greater bandwidth can transmit more information. Voice transmission requires little bandwidth; video transmission requires a great deal.

A fiber-optic cable has greater bandwidth than a coaxial cable.

econ   **fin**

Bank for International Settlements (BIS)   Consortium of central banks.

The BIS, with headquarters in Basel, Switzerland, holds monthly meetings of its board, which is made up of members of the central banks of Belgium, France, Germany, Italy, the Netherlands, Sweden, Switzerland, and the United Kingdom. Representatives of other countries, including the United States, Canada, and Japan, also attend the meetings.

Its original function was to administer German reparations after World War I. But today the BIS acts as a sort of central bank for central banks and as a sounding board, although the **International Monetary Fund (IMF)** plays a more prominent role. In 1988, the BIS issued minimum standards for the capital reserves needed by banks with significant international operations. These were recognized throughout the world and took effect in 1993. The bank also collects and publishes information on **macroeconomic** and international monetary topics.

fin

banker's acceptance
A draft drawn on and accepted by a bank that orders payment to a third party at a later date.

Banker's acceptances are a common method of financing import and export transactions. That is because backing by the bank assures the seller that the funds for payment will be available.

fin **mgmt**

bankruptcy
When an individual or a company is insolvent; that is, unable to pay debts as they come due.

A court-appointed trustee liquidates the debtor's assets under **Chapter 7**. In **Chapter 11**, a company attempts to reorganize while the courts provide some protection from creditors.

tech **oper** **mktg**

bar code
System of coding involving lines of various thicknesses to represent letters and numbers.

Optical scanners can easily read this type of code, even on a moving object. A common example is the **universal product code (UPC)** you see on supermarket items. Bar codes are used in inventory management. They are also used in **marketing** to track the purchasing behavior of consumers, because the best way to determine what consumers will buy is to know what they bought.

strat **mgmt**

barriers to entry
Whatever keeps a company from entering an industry or **market**.

Barriers to entry can be crucial components in the design of a company's competitive strategy. If you have an established company, they protect your market share. If you are the newcomer, the barriers are a real hindrance and expense.

bankruptcy

> *A company may decline for any number of reasons. Now technology can make its products and markets obsolete. Management errors or changes in the economic environment may also be the cause.*
>
> —Professor Robert Sobel, from *Portraits of the American Dream*, 1991

B

FRAME OF

REFERENCE

bar code

A cashier in a department store scans the bar code on a coffeemaker being purchased by a customer. A computer determines exactly what is being bought and enters the price into the cash register as it also removes the item from an inventory **database**. In a factory, all parts are bar-coded and entered into a database when they are received. They are **cycle-counted** periodically by workers with handheld optical scanners moving through the warehouse.

0 10343 81093 8

barriers to entry

FRAME OF

REFERENCE

barriers to entry

Before cable TV arrived, there were high barriers to entry for anyone who wanted to start a local television station. First, a television station had to get a license from the Federal Communications Commission (FCC). By the 1970s, however, most of the VHF frequencies (channels 2 through 13) were already licensed. The available frequencies were usually UHF stations, which had inferior technical quality.

Second, the major networks—ABC, CBS, and NBC—had affiliated with one television station in each city. The major networks were the only source of high-quality programming, thus it was difficult for any new station to obtain a large audience.

Today, of course, cable television can provide broadcasters on all frequencies with equal technical quality, and the proliferation of networks means that high-quality programming is available from many sources.

barriers to entry

barriers to exit

tip

In your strategic thinking, consider your competitor's barriers to exit. You may think that by expanding your plant and reducing your prices you will drive out the competition. But that company may not be so quick to walk away, even if you make the market unprofitable for it.

Barriers to entry can come from many sources, including:

▶ Product **differentiation**, which may create **brand loyalty** to existing products.

▶ **Economies of scale**, which can give existing companies a cost advantage.

▶ High switching costs, such as retooling equipment or retraining employees to make the new product.

▶ Access to **distribution channels**. New brands, for example, often may be hard put to get shelf space.

▶ Relationships with key suppliers.

▶ Proprietary technology.

▶ Government restrictions, such as licensing requirements.

Many companies pursue a strategy of maintaining strong barriers to entry in their markets.

See also **barriers to exit**.

strat **mgmt**

barriers to exit   Whatever discourages a company from shutting down or selling an operation.

The biggest barriers to exit are the emotional ones. Entrepreneurs and managers are reluctant to leave the enterprise they put so much work into. Other barriers to exit are the same as some of the **barriers to entry**: The large investments necessary to start up in the first place.

FRAME OF REFERENCE

barriers to exit

Giant Chemical Company spent hundreds of millions of dollars in the 1970s to establish a business in Italy. Even before it built its plant, Giant conducted studies of the market and met over and over with government officials and potential suppliers and customers. Then it engineered the plant, got all the necessary permits, and built the facility. But the European economy never grew as the company's planners thought it would, and the plant's return was inadequate, with profits almost nil.

Throughout the 1980s, Giant's board of directors kept tossing around selling or closing the Italian operation. But Giant's president argued against it. He believed that the costs of entering a country were so great that sometimes it pays to take your losses just to maintain a presence. It would cost a lot more to close up shop and then try to return. So it was not until the 1990s—when the company focused harder on its profitability—that Giant sold its Italian operations.

B

Some maintain that staying in a market just because it cost you a lot in the past is tossing good money after bad. They say the previous investments should be thought of as **sunk costs**. In other words, if an operation does not provide a desirable cash flow, write it off.

mktg **strat** **econ**

bartering   (1) Trading products or services directly for another's products or services without using money.

A company with excess inventory, for example, can obtain a needed product or service without eating up cash. In some foreign transactions, a barter arrangement in a needed **commodity** is preferable to cash payment in a **soft currency**. In other instances, agreeing to a trade is the only way a company can finalize a transaction because of a country's restrictions on exporting currency. A company agrees to take goods or commodities produced in that country and then sells them in other markets.

A more complicated form of barter is sometimes arranged by smaller companies within the United States that cannot get needed credit. These agreements with suppliers and others may involve directly reciprocal trade or complex three- or four-party transactions.

See also **parallel trade**.

(2) In advertising, trading products or services for advertising time or space.

bartering

Quick Facts!

Bartering is an ancient way of doing business that is still around today, with around $300 billion of goods and services bartered annually.

fin **acct** **mgmt**

base case   Basic set of **assumptions** about **revenue**, expenses, taxes, and **discount rates** used to estimate **cash flow**.

Making small changes in the assumptions in the base case will determine the sensitivity of the cash flow.

B

fin

basis point   Measure of **yield** or interest rate that is equal to .01 percent.

If a bond's yield moves from 8.25 percent to 8.50 percent, it has moved 25 basis points.

oper

batch process   Manufacturing procedure involving quantity production of one product—or part of a product—at a time.

> **EXAMPLE** | Your factory makes consumer glass cookware. You produce a batch of two-quart pots for two days until you reach the desired output. Then you change the molds on the forming machines and restart the process for three-quart ware. Your production goes into inventory for shipment over time into the **distribution channels**.

The current trend is to reduce setup costs so that a "batch size of one" becomes economic. But most products are still made in batches.

tech

BBS   See **bulletin board system**.

fin

bearer bond   A **bond** not registered to a specific holder.

Rather, these securities have coupons attached, and each interest payment is made to the person presenting the coupon for that payment. Today, most bonds are registered bonds. If you own a registered bond, the interest payments will likely go to your bank or broker (as your nominee), who then forwards them to you. Bearer bonds, with their coupons, were once so common that a bond's stated interest rate even now can be called its **coupon rate**.

mktg

behavioral response   Ways in which potential customers react to marketing activities.

Savvy marketers study the cultural, social, personal, and psychological factors influencing potential consumers to determine the style of **marketing** that will achieve the hoped-for response.

Usually, the hoped-for response involves more than having the customer make a purchase. Most marketers want the consumer to feel positive toward the company and to buy its products again. Sometimes, a marketing approach that used to leave customers well disposed has to be changed because of demographic or cultural shifts.

batch process
Quick Facts!

Batch processing is used when it is not economic to make one item at a time.

FRAME OF REFERENCE

behavioral response

Neil Rackham, president and founder of Huthwaite, Inc.—a training company serving IBM, Kodak, Xerox, and other major corporations—is a psychologist who spent 12 years researching behavioral response in large-account selling. He found that techniques focusing on client behavior and developing long-term relationships with clients consistently produced higher success rates than those based on single-sale techniques. He spun his findings into a popular book called *SPIN Selling*.

B

EXAMPLE | The home selling parties made popular by companies like Tupperware have become an annoyance to working people with little time at home. So the equivalent sales technique has become office selling parties held during lunch and coffee breaks.

See also **market segmentation**.

mktg

behavioral segmentation Subdividing a market according to what motivates customers to buy a product.

See also **market segmentation**.

fin

bellwether Security whose price is widely viewed as an indicator of a market's direction.

There are almost as many bellwether stocks as there are analysts and commentators on the stock market, but IBM is one that has carried the label many times over the years. Microsoft and Intel have been considered bellwethers in the 1990s. In the **bond** market, the 20-year U.S. Treasury bond is widely viewed as the bellwether. (See charts on the following page.)

mgmt   **strat**

benchmarking Systematic approach to comparing your company with others in an effort to learn the best ways of conducting your business.

While it has always been common for managers to ask what the competition does before making a decision on changing a business practice, the concept that has gained popularity rapidly in the 1990s involves:

➤ A continual search for the companies with the **best practices**.

➤ An effort to understand how the best-practice company gets the job done with fewer people.

➤ An attempt to adapt the best-practice company's procedures to your company.

bellwether

Quick Facts!

The term comes from sheep farming: Shepherds used to put a bell on the neck of the animal that led the flock so they would always know which direction the flock was heading. The wether, or lead sheep, would wear the bell.

Changing Bellwethers: IBM and Microsoft

Microsoft®

IBM vs. S&P 500 (Indexed, 1973 = 100)

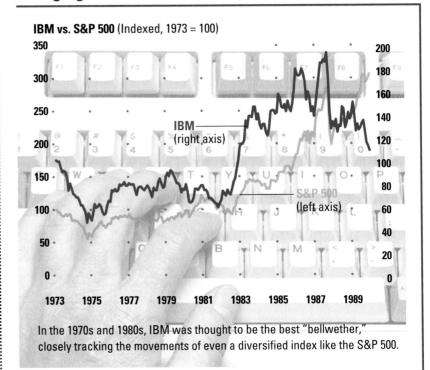

IBM
(right axis)

S&P 500
(left axis)

In the 1970s and 1980s, IBM was thought to be the best "bellwether," closely tracking the movements of even a diversified index like the S&P 500.

Microsoft vs. S&P 500 (Indexed, 1990 = 100)

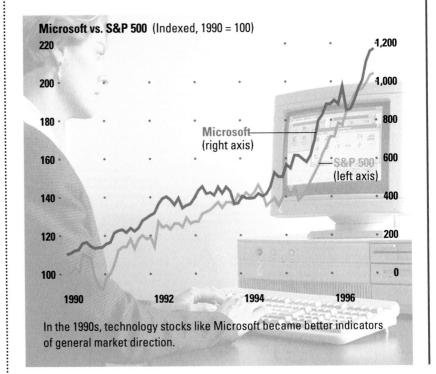

Microsoft
(right axis)

S&P 500
(left axis)

In the 1990s, technology stocks like Microsoft became better indicators of general market direction.

EXAMPLE | In 1994, Amoco Corporation began supplying accounting and other staff support through a **shared services center**, a concept for efficiency that appeals to other large decentralized companies. It is less clear that this is a best practice for public relations. General Electric's lean and effective public-relations staff may provide a better bet for comparison. A company rethinking its staff services might benchmark against Amoco for accounting and GE for public relations.

To work, benchmarking must involve both quantitative and qualitative analysis—measurements to determine exceptional performance and then an understanding of what practices led to the performance. These practices are called enablers.

Here is a four-step description of how a benchmarking study might work:

1 Select the process or processes to be studied, establish the measures of performance, evaluate how your own company stacks up, determine which other companies will be studied.

2 Study public records—annual reports, **Securities and Exchange Commission (SEC)** filings, and published articles—on the companies selected. Then make direct contact via telephone surveys, written questionnaires, or site visits.

3 Evaluate the data and reach conclusions about: (1) the differences in performance between your company and others that were studied and (2) what enabled the leading companies to perform as they did.

4 Adapt the practices of the leading companies in ways that make sense for your company and implement those improvements.

There are several problems with benchmarking:

► To the extent that you are focused on what others have done, you may be held back from the kind of innovative thinking that is really needed.

► You may not get an accurate sense of what really goes on at the best-practice company. While there is a surprising amount of information available in public documents, they will never paint a complete picture of what the business processes are like. For that, you need access to the company and frank answers, which may not be forthcoming.

► Take this question as an example: "How much time does your chairman spend writing his or her own speeches and how much is done by staff?" Since people are reluctant to portray their chairman as dependent on others for his or her own communications, you can assume that they will exaggerate the chairman's involvement and understate staff support.

benchmarking

tip |

If you are reorganizing all of your staff support services, for example, you will need to find different best-practice companies to benchmark performance for each of the various functions.

trap |

A company with the best approach to supplying accounting services may lag when it comes to other staff services, like public relations.

B

B

FRAME OF REFERENCE

benchmarking

Xerox is considered a pioneer in U.S.-based benchmarking because of its 1979 effort to understand how Japanese manufacturers were selling copiers in the United States below Xerox's production cost. A Xerox team conducted a study, obtaining most of its information from a Xerox joint venture in Japan that was familiar with competitive practices there. After learning that the Japanese manufacturers were much more efficient, Xerox could identify the areas that needed improvement and embark on programs to catch up.

THE DOCUMENT COMPANY
XEROX

---

mktg **mgmt**

Berne Convention   International agreement dating back to 1886 that protects the **intellectual property** of creators of literary and artistic works.

Some 80 countries have signed the Berne Convention. It, the **Geneva Phonograms Convention**, and (since 1995) the **General Agreement on Tariffs and Trade (GATT)** make up the major international protections of **copyrights**. The convention is administered by the **World Intellectual Property Organization (WIPO)**.

fin

best effort   When an **investment banker** takes on the sale of a new security without committing its capital or resources to complete the total amount of the issue.

In some offerings, investment bankers form a pool and underwrite, or buy, the entire issue. The underwriters then sell the securities to the public. Now and then when an investment banking company takes an issue on a best-effort basis, it tries to sell the securities but does not promise to buy the entire issue from the client. The banker can also sell a partial offering or increase the offering if demand permits and the client agrees.

After the investment banker determines how much it can sell, it either buys the securities from the client or cancels the deal, forgoing its fee. Although common in the past and in some other countries, in the United States today best-effort arrangements generally apply only to the more speculative securities of new companies.

mgmt **strat**

best practices   Phrase used in **benchmarking** to represent the most efficient way to perform a particular function or process.

best practices

tip |

Best practices are relevant only if found in a company whose circumstances are similar to yours.

FRAME OF REFERENCE

best practices

You are representing a large multinational corporation with many subsidiaries in a complex technical business, and your company wants to benchmark headquarters staffing. You might look to companies like Exxon, General Electric, Halliburton, Hitachi, Royal Dutch Shell, Toshiba, and Westinghouse as possibilities. You would not look at Wal-Mart or Starbucks. While both of those companies have practices worthy of emulation, neither is in a business as complex as yours, so their practices might not work in reorganizing your headquarters support services.

When your benchmarking research shows that your chosen benchmark operates with a complete staff of only 150 employees in its London headquarters, you might investigate further to see how it is done. If you decide that its headquarters organization and business processes make sense for your company, then that company would become your best-practice model.

fin

beta (β)   Measure of a security's volatility, or how much its price moves in relation to the average performance of the stock market.

The factors that influence the overall market include the economy, **interest rates**, **inflation**, and general investor confidence. Beta coefficients for actively traded stocks can be obtained from published sources, such as the *Value Line Investment Survey*, or through brokerage firms. You can calculate beta by comparing a security's historical price movements with the movements of the overall market as measured by an index, usually the Standard & Poor's 500. A security with a beta of 1.0 carries no more or less risk than the market in general. When the market rises 4 percent, a stock with a beta of 1.0 is expected to rise 4 percent as well. When the market falls 4 percent, such a stock ought to fall to the same degree. With a beta of 2.0, a security should rise 10 percent whenever the market increases 5 percent and fall 10 percent whenever the market dips 5 percent. A stock with a beta of less than 1.0 rises or falls less sharply than the overall market.

You can also use beta to measure the price movements of your portfolio or of the holdings of a mutual fund versus the market.

Beta looks at what is called **systematic risk**, or **market risk**. A related measurement, **alpha (α)**, considers internal risk factors that relate to the individual company and its unique business risk.

beta (β)

The factors that influence the overall economy, market include the interest rates, the inflation, and general investor confidence.

beta (β)

trap 👎

Remember that beta is a statistical measure based on the past. There is no guarantee it will predict the future.

β

Beta

To calculate beta (ß), you need the following values:

r_m	Historical market return (such as Standard & Poor's 500 Stock Composite Index or the Dow Jones 30 Industrials) for each year of your calculation
r_f	The risk-free rate (the return on a risk-free security, like a Treasury bill)
r_j	Historical rate of return for the security on which you are calculating beta, for each year of your calculation
M	$(r_m - r_f)$, or the market's performance compared with the risk-free rate for each year of the calculation
K	$(r_j - r_f)$, or the stock's return compared with the risk-free rate for each year of the calculation
n	Number of years
$\overline{M}$	Average of M
$\overline{K}$	Average of K
$ß$	Beta
$\sum$	The sum of

The formula

$$(\sum MK - n\overline{M}\,\overline{K}) \div (\sum M^2 - n\overline{M}^2) = ß$$

EXAMPLE | Consider the following historical rates of return for stock ABC:

Year	r_j(%)	r_m(%)
1991	3	12
1992	6	10
1993	9	14
1994	12	22
1995	14	17

Assume that the risk-free rate (r_f) comes to 7 percent. The following table can then be created:

Year	r_j	r_m	r_f	K $(r_j - r_f)$	M $(r_m - r_f)$	M^2	MK
1991	0.03	0.12	0.07	(0.10)	0.05	0.0025	(0.0050)
1992	0.06	0.10	0.07	(0.01)	0.03	0.0009	(0.0003)
1993	0.09	0.14	0.07	0.02	0.07	0.0049	0.0014
1994	0.12	0.22	0.07	0.05	0.15	0.0225	0.0075
1995	0.14	0.17	0.07	0.07	0.10	0.0100	0.0070
Total				0.03	0.40	0.0408	0.0106

$$\overline{K} = 0.006, \quad \overline{M} = 0.08, \quad n = 5$$

So the beta for stock ABC is:

$$[0.0106 - (5)(0.08)(0.006)] \div [0.0408 - (5)(0.08)^2] = 0.93$$

The beta of 0.93 means the stock should move at 93 percent of the market rate. If the market rate of return is 10 percent, then the stock should be expected to return 9.3 percent.

strat **tech**

beta-tester
One who tries out a new product with potential consumers before it is sold to the general public, looking for problems that the producer should fix.

See also **bug**.

strat **mgmt**

better-off test
When you are considering buying a new business unit, this test will assess its impact on overall strategy.

In a better-off test, ask yourself whether the purchase will do one of the following:

► Improve the new unit's competitive advantage.

► Improve your company's competitive advantage.

See also **cost-of-entry test** and **industry-attractiveness test**.

beta-tester

B

better-off test

In buying Lotus, IBM captured the high ground in the war for the high-potential groupware market. The software product Lotus Notes has the biggest market

share of that market, which may also mean an advantage for other products designed for the networked systems that are replacing both personal computers and mainframes in offices. So Lotus gives IBM a competitive advantage. It may also gain a competitive advantage from IBM's financial strength.

Big Six

acct

Big Six   The major accounting firms in the United States as measured by revenues.

These are the names you see under the audit report of just about every publicly traded **Fortune 500** corporation. Each has offices throughout the world. In addition to auditing, these firms perform tax services for their clients, **Securities and Exchange Commission (SEC)** reviews, and consulting services.

The Big Six firms are:

▶ Arthur Andersen

▶ Coopers & Lybrand

▶ Deloitte & Touche

▶ Ernst & Young

▶ KPMG Peat Marwick

▶ Price Waterhouse

Once known as the "Big Eight," mergers among the eight consolidated the list to six. In 1989, Deloitte, Haskins, & Sells merged with Touche Ross to form Deloitte & Touche, and Ernst & Whinney joined with Arthur Young to create Ernst & Young.

oper **mktg** **mgmt**

bill of lading   Document issued by a carrier, such as a railroad, acknowledging receipt of goods and terms of delivery.

oper

bill of material (BOM)   Quantitative list of all the materials needed for production of a product.

A BOM is an important part of **materials-requirement planning (MRP)**.

Bill of Lading

Name of Claimant

Telephone #

Current Address

Former Address

Name of Carrier

Loading Date

Delivery Date

Address of Carrier

Was shipment in storage?

Where?

Inventory Number	Description of Item and Nature of Claim	Acquired Date	Original Cost	Amount Claimed

I warrant that I am the true and lawful owner of the items listed above. The above claim is true and correct to the best of my knowledge. All claims for loss or damage incurred during the transport or storage. No pertinent information was withheld and the above constitute my entire claim against the Carrier.

Any person knowingly and with intent to defraud any insurance company, files statements of claim containing any materials, false information, conceals for the purpose of misleading, information concerning fact material thereto, commits a fraudulent insurance act, which is a crime.

The actual cash value of my shipment was:

$ _____

Signature

Notary

Date

---

econ **fin**

BIS   See **Bank for International Settlements**.

---

tech

bit (binary digit)   The basic unit of information stored or processed in a computer.

A bit is represented in the computer's code as a one or zero. A computer uses these binary bits to represent all numbers, letters, and forms of data in its memory and processing units.

See also **byte**.

bit

Bitmap Graphic

Vector Graphic

B

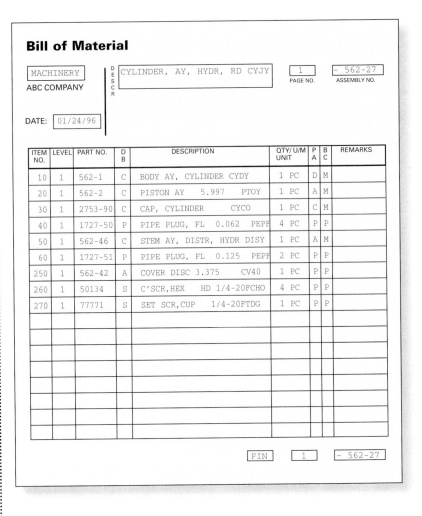

Bill of Material

MACHINERY				
ABC COMPANY		D E S C R	CYLINDER, AY, HYDR, RD CYJY	1 PAGE NO.	- 562-27 ASSEMBLY NO.

DATE: 01/24/96

ITEM NO.	LEVEL	PART NO.	D B	DESCRIPTION	QTY/ U/M UNIT	P A	B C	REMARKS
10	1	562-1	C	BODY AY, CYLINDER CYDY	1 PC	D	M	
20	1	562-2	C	PISTON AY 5.997 PTOY	1 PC	A	M	
30	1	2753-90	C	CAP, CYLINDER CYCO	1 PC	C	M	
40	1	1727-50	P	PIPE PLUG, FL 0.062 PEPF	4 PC	P	P	
50	1	562-46	C	STEM AY, DISTR, HYDR DISY	1 PC	A	M	
60	1	1727-51	P	PIPE PLUG, FL 0.125 PEPF	2 PC	P	P	
250	1	562-42	A	COVER DISC 3.375 CV40	1 PC	P	P	
260	1	50134	S	C'SCR,HEX HD 1/4-20FCHO	4 PC	P	P	
270	1	77771	S	SET SCR,CUP 1/4-20FTDG	1 PC	P	P	

FIN	1	- 562-27

fin

Black-Scholes options pricing model   A complex but manageable method of gauging whether **options** contracts are fairly valued.

Developed by Fischer Black and Myron Scholes, the mathematical formula was first published in 1973, the same year the **Chicago Board Options Exchange (CBOE)** opened its doors. It includes factors such as the volatility of a security's return, interest-rate levels, the relationship of the underlying stock's price to the strike price of the option, and the time remaining until the option expires.

The model has been often misunderstood, and its improper use by many portfolio insurers may have been a factor in the 1987 stock-market crash.

oper **mktg** **mgmt**

blanket purchase order   Contract to buy a quantity of goods or services from a supplier, with delivery to be made over time.

Because of the commitment to buy in quantity, blanket purchase orders may involve a discounted price. They also eliminate the need for a new purchase order for each transaction or delivery.

mktg

bleed   Reproducing a photograph or other artwork so there is no margin.

The image can be full bleed, taking up the entire page, or it can bleed off one or more edges of the page. Most magazines charge more for printing advertisements that bleed, because they require larger printing plates. **Art directors** like to use bleeds because they attract attention.

fin

blind pool   An offering by a company or **limited partnership** that does not list the specific properties the managers or general partner intends to acquire although usually indicating the industry, such as oil and gas, real estate, or technology.

Blind-pool ventures (1) are often set up to buy equity stakes in small, private companies, and (2) may have high risks because the investor doesn't know what the manager of the money pool is going to do with the money raised. Because of this additional risk, investors usually charge a premium to the issuing company. However, they provide a way to invest in small, potentially profitable companies that need financing to develop their product or distribution. Investors can evaluate these ventures on the track record of the general partner or chief executive and the potential for the targeted industry.

fin

blue chip   Considered to be the most tried-and-true performers among stocks. In the U.K., blue chips are called alpha stocks.

Blue chips are not necessarily the most expensive stocks on the market or the fastest short-term earners. That distinction goes to whatever industry group is hottest at the moment. But blue chips are not cheap, either. (See related story on the following page.)

mktg

body copy   Basic text of a print advertisement other than features like headlines and logos.

The body copy will usually include the import and force of the message. The **copywriter** will try to keep it short and informal, often using the tone of an individual chatting with another.

B

blind pool

t i p |

A key assessment to make before investing in a blind pool is your feeling about the manager. Do you have confidence in his or her track record? And if the idea is to buy controlling interests, what about his/her financial management skills? A blind pool will be only as successful as the people managing it.

body copy

t i p |

Since body copy tends to be read less often than other parts of an ad—85 percent of those exposed to a print ad do not read the body copy—the headline becomes extremely important in capturing the consumer's awareness.

Quarterly Price Change, 1980–1995: IBM vs. S&P 500

B

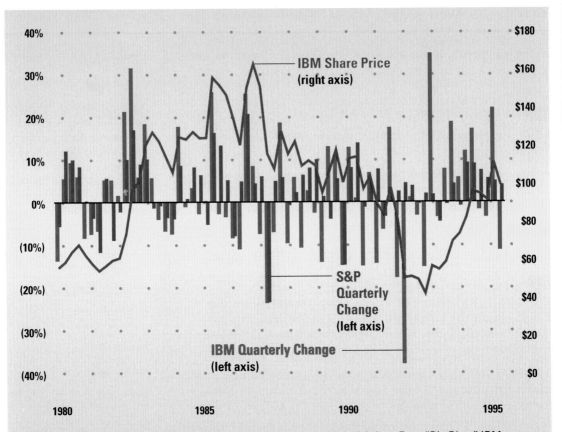

Just because a stock is considered to be blue chip does not mean it is risk-free. Even "Big Blue," IBM, comes with no guarantees. From 1980 through 1995, IBM lost value in 31 of the 64 quarters, or 48% of the time. By comparison, the S&P 500 index declined in 21 quarters, for a 33% loss ratio.

FRAME OF

REFERENCE

blue chip

The nickname comes from the gambling chip having the highest value. These are companies with a long history of sustained earnings and uninterrupted dividends. They have been around long enough to show a good track record, but they are not over the hill. Their top-drawer management and well-regarded products and services hold out the potential for continued growth.

The ranks of the blue chips change over time, of course, but some old stalwarts are U.S. Steel, now USX Corporation; Standard Oil of New Jersey, now Exxon; General Electric; and General Motors. A newer member of the club is McDonald's.

Investing with the conventional wisdom is usually the path of least resistance, but it can often lead to subpar results. In the early 1970s, the "nifty-fifty," a group of rapidly growing companies whose stocks were selling at high-price earnings ratios, were commonly believed to be the key to superior investment performance. Those issues performed well for several years but then faltered throughout most of the 1970s. From the end of 1972 (near their peak) to the end of 1981, 90 percent of them showed a negative real rate of return, with an average inflation-adjusted return of –48 percent. Considering that the nifty-fifty began the period with $100–120 billion in market value, the loss translates into at least $48 billion of lost stock market worth.

fin

boilerplate   Standard wording in a document, particularly in legal contracts.

Most boilerplate consists of important words, phrases, and clauses that have survived many years of close inspection by lawyers. They save everyone's time since the lengthy texts do not need rewriting.

EXAMPLE | Investment bankers often use boilerplate to describe the legal aspects of a bond offering in the **prospectus**.

Office supply companies, such as Office Depot and Office Max, sell standard (boilerplate) rental agreements, bills of sale, and other everyday legal documents where you simply fill in the blanks. Software is also available now that provides a wide range of fill-in-the-blank legal documents, including leases, corporate minutes and resolutions, and **copyright** and **trademark** agreements.

oper

BOM   See **bill of material**.

fin

bond   Debt security issued by a corporation or government entity, usually in multiples of $1,000, obligating the issuer to pay bondholders a fixed amount of interest at specific intervals, usually semiannually, and to repay the principal of the loan at maturity.

Since bondholders are creditors, not stockholders, they have no ownership privileges, such as voting, but they do have a senior claim to **assets** in the event of a firm's liquidation or **bankruptcy**.

See also **bond ratings, bond valuation, bond yield, convertible security, debenture, high-grade bonds,** and **high-yield bonds**.

fin

bond ratings   Classifying bonds by sizing up their risk of default. Also called **quality ratings**.

Several organizations publish bond ratings, most prominently Moody's Investors Service and **Standard & Poor's (S&P)**. Other rating agencies include Fitch Investors Service, Duff & Phelps, and McCarthy, Crisanti & Maffei. Bonds considered **high-grade**, or **investment-grade**, have ratings of Aaa through Baa3 in the Moody's system; in the S&P rankings, they have AAA through BBB–. Bonds with ratings below those are considered non–investment grade, or **high-yield bonds**.

boilerplate

t r a p |

While do-it-yourself boilerplate documents may save you legal expenses, they may miss some of the fine points of your transaction. It is safer to consult with a lawyer, even though he or she will use boilerplate for a large part of the work.

bond

Quick Facts! |

Wall Street has come a long way from the original straight bond, using new financial technologies to tailor securities to just about any investor type or issuer need. The list of new fixed-income innovations now includes floating-rate bonds, convertible bonds, bonds with warrant units, exchangeable resettable bonds, zero-coupon bonds, pay-in-kind (PIK) bonds, commodity-indexed bonds, and equipment trust certificates, to name a few.

Bond Ratings

Investment-Grade		Non–Investment Grade	
Moody's	Standard & Poor's	Moody's	Standard & Poor's
Aaa	AAA	Ba1	BB+
Aa1	AA+	Ba2	BB
Aa2	AA	Ba3	BB–
Aa3	AA–	B1	B+
A1	A+	B2	B
A2	A	B3	B–
A3	A–		CCC+
Baa	BBB+	Caa	CCC
Baa2	BBB		CCC–
Baa3	BBB–	Ca	CC
		C	C
			CI
			D

FRAME OF REFERENCE

bond ratings

Both Moody's and **S&P** point out that their ratings are not a recommendation to buy, sell, or hold a particular security. In fact, since much of the ratings decision depends on historical financial information about the issuing company, changes in ratings could lag investors' more forward-looking perceptions.

In fact, entire industries are sometimes misperceived by the rating agencies. These tend to be newer, rapidly growing industries—like cable television, cellular, or technology. Clearly, it is difficult to predict that **acquisitions** or **mergers** that affect credit quality may be under consideration by management. And in other cases where a company is successfully implementing its business plan— but not lobbying the agencies for an upgrade—the market's assessment of credit quality may be at odds with the ratings.

bond valuation   Calculation to figure out the current price of a **bond**.

Bond valuation looks at the **present value** of all the bond's anticipated **cash flow** to tell you how much it is worth today. If you know the current yield of similar bonds, this calculation establishes the price a buyer will pay or a seller will get.

Bond valuation requires five key pieces of information:

▶ The number of interest payments in one year—most bonds pay semiannually, but some pay quarterly or annually.

▶ The dollar amount of each periodic interest payment.

▶ The face value of the bond—how much you will get when it matures.

▶ The date the bond matures.

▶ The interest rate currently being paid for bonds of similar risk and similar maturity.

Adding the present value of the bond's future interest payments and the present value of the money you will receive at maturity gives you the bond's value today. The money you will get at maturity, the bond's face value, is usually $1,000.

Bond Value

$$V_b = I_{pv} + F_{pv}$$

V_b The bond's value

I_{pv} The present value of future interest payments

F_{pv} The present value of the bond's face value at maturity

---

bond valuation

tip |

Many business calculators can determine present value, which can also be drawn from published tables. Calculating the present value of the interest payments is like finding the present value of an annuity.

EXAMPLE | You hold a bond in XYZ Corporation that matures in five years and has a 9 percent stated interest rate, or **coupon rate**. The face value is $1,000, so the bond pays $90 a year. The interest rate currently being paid on the five-year bonds of companies with XYZ's credit rating is 8 percent.

So, using an 8 percent interest rate, the present value of $90 a year for five years is $359.34, and the present value of the $1,000 principal to be received in five years is $680.58.

$359.34 + $680.58 = $1,039.92

The value of the bond is $1,039.92.

See also **bond yield**.

bond/warrant unit

t i p

The higher cost of straight debt (vs. convertible debt) can be offset by attaching an option that enables bond-holders to participate in share price increases.

bond/warrant unit   Security in which a **bond** and a set number of equity **warrants** are sold as a unit. Sometimes called a **synthetic convertible**.

In accounting for these units, the issuer records the bond as debt and the warrants as equity. In contrast, traditional convertible bonds are recorded entirely as debt until exchanged. The bond portion can be used as currency—generally at par—to exercise the warrants.

Unlike conventional **convertible securities**, the debt (bond) and equity (warrant) can be traded separately.

fin

bond yield   Return an investor gets on a **bond** investment, expressed as an annual percentage.

Usually, when a bond is issued, its **interest rate** is based on market conditions, and it sells at or very close to its **par value**, or face value. If the bond sells at par, its yield is the same as its stated interest rate, or **coupon rate**. But during the bond's life, market interest rates will rise and fall. If you want to resell a bond, you will have to price it so that it yields the prevailing interest rate.

EXAMPLE   You paid $1,000 two years ago for a long-term bond with a coupon rate of 5 percent. So it pays $50 a year. You want to sell it, but interest rates are now 6 percent. You will need to set a price lower than $1,000 so that the $50 annual interest equals 6 percent. You will have to settle for about $833. For the purchaser, the yield—in this case called the **current yield** or simple yield—on the bond is now 6 percent. If market rates had fallen to 4 percent, on the other hand, you would have raised your price to about $1,250, where the $50 interest would equal 4 percent of the buyer's investment. In both of these cases, the nominal, or **coupon, rate** on the bond remains 5 percent, but the yield grows or shrinks.

Current Bond Yield

Coupon Rate: 5% ($50 yearly coupon payments)

Interest Rates at 5% (at purchase)	Bond Price: $1,000 Current Yield: 5%	$\dfrac{\$50}{\$1000} = 5\%$
Interest Rates Fall to 4% ↓ 🙂	Bond Price ↑ $1,250 Current Yield: 4%	$\dfrac{\$50}{\$1250} = 4\%$
Interest Rates Rise to 6% ↑ ☹	Bond Price ↓ $833.33 Current Yield: 6%	$\dfrac{\$50}{\$833.33} = 6\%$

When interest rates rise, bond prices fall to make the current yields improve. When interest rates decline, bond prices rise so the yields are smaller. When a bond is selling below par value, it is referred to as selling at a discount; above par is called selling at a **premium**.

So far, we have been talking about current yield. But there is another element to the bond's overall return. If a bond has sold at a discount, an allowance must be made for the principal that will be recovered at maturity. This gets important as the maturity date nears. Likewise, if the bond is sold at a premium, an allowance must be made for the money lost at maturity. This type of bond yield is called **yield to maturity (YTM)**, and it can be more important than current yield.

EXAMPLE | Let us say you were the buyer of the bonds in the example above, rather than the seller. If you bought a bond for $833.33 with a 5 percent coupon, your current yield is 6 percent. But if there are 15 years left to the bond's term, its yield to maturity is 6.8 percent; with 10 years left, the figure is 7.4 percent. If you bought a bond with a 5 percent coupon at $1,250, the current yield is 4 percent, but the yield to maturity is 2.9 percent for a 15-year term and 2.2 percent for 10 years.

The bond market tables in the *Wall Street Journal* and other newspapers usually list the current yield as well as the coupon rate. Here is the formula for current yield:

Current Bond Yield	= ÷	Annual Coupon Payment Bond Price

Since calculating a bond's yield to maturity is complex and involves trial and error, it is done by computer. Essentially, the yield to maturity is the **discount rate** in a **present value (PV)** calculation where the PV is the bond's current price. The future **cash flows** are both the bond's interest payments and its value at maturity.

bond yield

 acct   fin

book value   (1) In accounting, the original cost of an **asset** (plant or equipment) less its **accumulated depreciation**, or the total of all **depreciation** taken to date.

More generally, it is the dollar figure of an asset that appears on the **balance sheet**. It is sometimes called the carrying amount.

(2) In securities analysis, the per-share valuation of the equity that holders of **common stock** have in a company. Also called book value per share.

It is calculated by deducting from **shareholders' equity** the liquidation value of any **preferred stock** and any preferred dividends that are owed, then dividing the result by the number of common shares outstanding.

B

book value

During the 1980s, Exxon decided to use excess **cash flow** to buy back its common stock—some $16 billion worth. It also took advantage of lower interest rates, doubling its long-term debt to more than $8 billion. Meanwhile, Exxon's equity market value rose by almost $40 billion, to $63 billion, or 10 times the extra debt. Looking only at book values, one would have mistakenly concluded that Exxon was a more leveraged company at the end of the decade.

book value

tip

Book value can give you some sense of the value of your investment or prospective investment. The relationship between stock price and book value can help you decide whether the market is undervaluing or overvaluing the shares. Some investors look especially for stocks selling under their book value.

trap

Remember that book value reflects accounting conventions, which do not usually tell you the economic value of the assets on the market. There is a trend toward using the market value of assets in financial analysis.

EXAMPLE | We will determine the book value for a company based on the following information:

Total shareholders' equity = $22,000,000

Preferred stock has a 12 percent dividend rate, $30 par value, $35 liquidation value, 300,000 shares outstanding

Liquidation value of preferred stock (300,000 x $35) = $10,500,000

Common stock has $52 par value, 500,000 shares outstanding

Preferred dividend:

Par value of preferred stock ($300,000 x $30) = $9,000,000

Preferred dividend rate: 12%

Preferred dividend: $1,080,000

The book value per share is:

$22,000,000 − ($10,500,000 + $1,080,000) ÷ 500,000 = $20.84

Book Value per Share		
Book Value per Share	**=**	[Total Shareholders' Equity – (Liquidation Value of Preferred Stocks + Preferred Dividends Owed)]
	÷	Common Shares Outstanding

acct

bookkeeping   Recording daily transactions in an accounting system.

To keep track of transactions, bookkeepers use a general journal, which is a chronological listing of transactions showing **debits** and **credits** to particular **accounts**. Most businesses use special journals as well, determined largely by the specific transactions of the business involved.

Three common types of bookkeeping systems are:

1 **Cash Payments Journal**
   Listing entries for all cash paid out.

2 **Cash Receipts Journal**
   Where all cash received by the business is recorded.

3 **Sales Journal**
   Which contains entries for all sales of merchandise on account. (Sales of merchandise for cash are listed in the cash receipts journal.)

tech   **fin**

boot   (1) To start a computer system.

A cold boot involves turning the power on, sometimes immediately after turning it off; a **warm boot** can be performed on many computers by pressing a button or series of buttons without turning the power off. Warm boots may be required when a system stops functioning because of a software **bug**; sometimes even that will not work and you will need a cold boot to get out of hot water.

(2) Cash consideration added to even out the exchange of similar properties.

EXAMPLE | George Roberts exchanges a three-acre country building parcel valued at $150,000 for Hal Smith's house on an in-town, quarter-acre plot. Smith's property is valued at $200,000, so Roberts also pays $50,000 in cash to equalize the transaction. The $50,000 in cash is the boot.

fin   **acct**

borrowing base   Receivables and inventory that banks will make short-term loans of cash against to use in a company's operations.

mgmt

boundaryless   Environment stripped of the hierarchical and functional hurdles that inhibit communication and the free flow of information.

B

bookkeeping

boot

boundaryless

brainstorming

**Electrical engineers join
in a brainstorming session
as they try to correct a
design flaw, while down
the hall advertising copywriters may brainstorm in
search of a theme for a
new ad campaign.**

The term has been attributed to General Electric CEO Jack Welch, whose objective is to "get everyone in the game." That means that in a boundaryless organization you will not find the traditional vertical barriers that keep your employees from mentioning their ideas about product effectiveness or operating efficiency to higher-ups. Nor will your staff be reluctant to bypass horizontal barriers, to go to another department or outside the confines of the company— say to a customer, a supplier, or even a competitor—to get ideas and information.

More radical even than the promotion of free-flowing information is the idea that boundaryless can mean a lack of clearly defined roles and specialization.

EXAMPLE | At a GE factory in Auburn, Maine, employees are cross-trained to perform all the jobs on the floor. A computer system tells workers about the priority and status of each order and fills them in on the availability of materials and quality requirements. Employees then decide where they want to work.

The transition to such an environment will not necessarily be easy for your company. Employees may balk at moving away from the less flexible—and, out of habit, more comfortable—confines of traditional supervision. But the dividends can be enormous, including increased productivity, greater customer satisfaction, and fewer worker complaints and less discontent.

See also **empowerment** and **workout**.

mgmt

brainstorming   Way of coming up with ideas to spur variety and creativity and avoid making judgments.

This technique is most commonly used early in an attempt at problem-solving. Typically, a half-dozen or so employees meet in a brainstorming session and are encouraged to freely offer ideas in an uncritical setting. Ideas are welcomed by group leaders even if they sound silly or impractical, and all participants refrain from criticism. Each idea is recorded for analysis and possible testing. The technique is used in technical disciplines as well as in more creative ones.

mktg

brand   A product feature, such as a name or design, that identifies it with a particular company.

The **American Marketing Association** defines the **brand name** as the written part and the **brand mark** as the symbol or pictorial part of the brand. A brand may be registered as a **trademark** and identified by a ® (registered) or ™ (trademark) symbol. But the 1946 **Lanham Act** will not let you hijack ordinary terms. You cannot, for example, register *pencil* as your brand name for a writing instrument with lead in it or *telephone* for the object with buttons and a handset that lets you talk to people far away. You might be able to register *pencil* as a brand of telephone and vice versa, but who would want to do that?

FRAME OF REFERENCE

brand

Betty Crocker has gone through seven transformations since she entered the cooking scene in 1921 as part of General Mills' effort to keep up with the changing self-image of its target market. The latest rendition of Betty is a compilation of features from 75 women from around the United States.

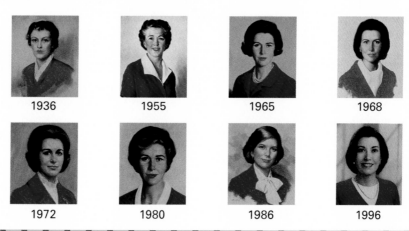

| 1936 | 1955 | 1965 | 1968 |

| 1972 | 1980 | 1986 | 1996 |

B

One struggle to protect a brand name that has become just a little too popular is being waged by Rollerblade, Inc. If it is not made by that company, it is called an *inline skate*, and the activity is inline skating.

But sometimes it is a losing battle. How often do you hear someone ask for an "adhesive bandage" instead of a Band-Aid? The Johnson & Johnson product carries a registered trademark, but that has not stopped the world from appropriating it for everyday use.

Old brand names or symbols may be updated to appeal to ever-changing tastes. For example, General Mills has updated the image of Betty Crocker seven times since she was created in 1921 to stay in step with consumers.

Although unbranded products gain popularity in tough times when people are watching their pennies, most products are branded. A well-known brand gives buyers a sense that they can count on the level of quality.

See also **brand equity**, **brand extension**, **branding**, **brand licensing**, and **private label**.

mktg

brand awareness
Consumers' recognition of a product by its name alone.

See also **branding**.

brand

Quick Facts!

Companies with popular brand names—like Kleenex or Xerox—run the risk of losing their valuable intellectual property if the words become part of everyday language. So publications get letters from Kimberly-Clark or Xerox if they use "kleenex" to mean any facial tissue or "xerox" for any form of copying. And competitors who use the terms may get served with legal papers.

tip

You want a brand name that is easy to pronounce and that conveys the benefits of your product or service—like DieHard batteries or Comfort Inns.

B

brand equity

tip |

Consumers do not buy products or services; they buy what a product or service can do for them. When designing a brand, pay attention to the benefits of the product based on consumer perception. Achieving brand equity is money in the bank.

Quick Facts!

In 1995, *Financial World* magazine ranked Coca-Cola as the most valuable brand worldwide and Marlboro as the second, with estimated worths of $39.1 billion and $38.7 billion, respectively.

brand extension

Quick Facts!

Procter & Gamble successfully extended its Ivory brand—long famous for bath soap—to a dish detergent. You can buy Mars ice cream as well as candy bars. When Mobil Chemical introduced a line of disposable dinnerware, it named the line Hefty after its popular trash bags. A notable failure came after Bic bought a line of pantyhose and called it "Bic." The name worked for disposable pens but did not survive the leap to clothing.

---

mktg

brand equity   The value of a **brand** in itself apart from **product attributes**.

Factors going into brand equity are:

▶ **Brand Awareness**
   Are people aware of the brand name? Has it been properly positioned in the mind of the consumer?

▶ **Perceived Quality**
   Do people think it is good? Are customers aware of the benefits they receive from the product or service?

▶ **Brand Association**
   Do people associate your brand name with the product itself, like Kleenex, Xerox, and Rollerblade?

If you are successful in marketing your product, it may get **brand preference**, where customers select your product over a competitor's. Ultimately, your product may benefit from **brand loyalty**, where customers go out of their way to buy it.

Some companies have **brand managers** who oversee the brand's image and help ensure the consistency of the products and services appearing under its name.

mktg   **strat**

brand extension   Using a well-known **brand** name to help launch a new or modified product in a different category.

See also **brand equity, branding, licensing,** and **private label**.

mktg

brand licensing   Rights allowing one company to use the **brand name** of another company on its own products.

See also **licensing**.

mktg

brand loyalty   Behavior where customers go out of their way to purchase only a certain **brand** of a given item.

See also **brand equity** and **brand preference**.

mktg

brand manager   Employee who oversees the work related to maintaining a **brand's** image and product quality.

See also **brand equity**.

mktg

brand mark   Picture or symbol that identifies a **brand**.

mktg

brand name   Wording that identifies a **brand**.

mktg

brand preference   Behavior where customers select your **brand** over those of competitors.

See also **brand equity** and **brand loyalty**.

mktg   **strat**

branding   Establishing a product with a **brand name** and an individual identity.

Branding gives the marketer something distinct to advertise and promote, thus building customers' **brand awareness**—often the first step in making a sale.

EXAMPLE | When U.S. Robotics began marketing modems for the home PC market under its own name, its first goal was to make the brand known. It targeted key groups like information services employees and salespeople at computer retail chains, selling them modems at a discount and offering free training. This approach ensured that those who influence sales would play an important part in developing the brand name with knowledgeable computer retailers.

Developing brand identity is expensive, requiring huge outlays for **pretesting** as well as **advertising** and promotion. And it is a difficult undertaking when a product has few **differentiating** features, like cigarettes. The 500 brands currently marketed consist of basically the same three ingredients: tobacco, paper, and a filter. So marketers try to distinguish a brand by focusing on image—such as the macho image of the Marlboro Man or the thin, professional woman who smokes Virginia Slims.

See also **brand**, **brand equity**, **brand extension**, and **licensing**.

acct   **oper**   **econ**   **mgmt**

break-even analysis   The determination of that point where your sales revenue covers all your costs.

At the break-even point, expressed as the number of units sold, there is no profit or loss. The calculation requires knowing both the **fixed costs** and the average **variable costs** of making a product. Fixed costs are those that do not change when the level of production changes such as rent and salaried payroll. Variable costs, by comparison, rise and fall, reflecting increases and decreases in the number of units produced. Such costs include raw materials or hourly payroll.

B

brand loyalty

branding

break-even analysis

You can calculate the break-even point with the following formula:

Break-Even Point	
U	$= (NP + FC) \div (P - VC)$

U	Number of units required to break even
NP	Net profit (set at zero for break-even analysis)
FC	Fixed costs
P	Selling price
VC	Variable costs per unit

As long as NP is set at zero, the formula will yield the break-even point.

EXAMPLE | You are opening a plant to manufacture storage boxes for compact disks. You estimate that your fixed costs (mostly rent) during the first year of operation will be $300,000. Your average variable costs (chiefly parts and labor) will come to around $1 per storage box, and the price will be $2 per box. Here is your break-even analysis:

$$0 + \$300{,}000 \div (\$2 - \$1) = 300{,}000$$

Your break-even point for your first year of operation is 300,000 units.

broadband channel

tech

broadband channel   High-speed, high-capacity channel on coaxial cable or optical fiber that has a wider **bandwidth** than a conventional telephone line.

It can carry voice, video, and data simultaneously.

mktg   **fin**

broker   (1) Intermediary that routes goods or services from a producer to consumers.

See also **distribution channel**.

(2) In finance, the salesperson who deals with a brokerage firm's customers.

Top 10 Brokerage Firms, 1984 and 1994, Ranked by Total Capital ($ billions)

1984	1994
1 Merrill Lynch	1 Merrill Lynch
2 Shearson Lehman Brothers	2 Salomon Brothers
3 Salomon Brothers	3 Goldman Sachs
4 Dean Witter Financial Services	4 Lehman Brothers
5 The E. F. Hutton Group	5 Morgan Stanley
6 Goldman Sachs	6 Bear Stearns
7 First Boston	7 CS First Boston
8 Prudential Bache Securities	8 Paine Webber
9 Paine Webber Group	9 Smith Barney
10 Drexel Burnham Lambert Group	10 Donaldson, Lufkin, Jenrette (DLJ)

In the ten years from 1984 to 1994, the top players in the brokerage industry underwent significant changes. Of the ten companies on the 1984 list, six had major changes in their ownership structure, although they may have survived in a different form. (For example, Shearson Lehman became Lehman Brothers when it spun off its retail operation, and First Boston was bought by Credit Suisse.) Only one company, Drexel Burnham Lambert, disappeared. (Drexel declared bankruptcy in 1990.)

Source: *Standard & Poor's Industry Surveys*

mgmt

brown-paper exercise   Consulting practice technique that originally involved lining the walls with brown paper to diagram the way things are done in a company.

The technique has been attributed to the Alexander Proudfoot Co., which originated the practice in the 1940s. The idea is to make a flow chart of all the steps of whatever process is being studied and the information flow (the reports and paperwork) used to control the process. Today, flip charts and computer-generated graphics are being used instead of brown paper.

Consulting companies using this technique today include Coopers & Lybrand Consulting, Gemini Consulting, and McKinsey & Co.

budget deficit

acct   mgmt

budget   Statement of expected **revenues** and expenditures for a certain period. It also serves as a preliminary financial plan.

econ

budget deficit   Amount the government spends over what it receives in a given period, usually a year.

The U.S. government has outspent its receipts every year since 1969, and a **budget surplus** is not likely in the forseeable future. As annual deficits pile up, the total **federal debt** mounts. Political pressure to cut the budget deficit is increasing. Here is the yearly budget deficit from 1990 to 1995, expressed also as a percentage of annual **gross domestic product (GDP)**. (See related graphs on pages 105 and 106.)

U.S. Budget Deficit

Year	U.S. Budget Deficit ($ billions)	Percentage of GDP
1990	$ 221.4	4.0%
1991	$ 269.2	4.6%
1992	$ 290.4	4.7%
1993	$ 255.1	3.9%
1994	$ 203.2	2.9%
1995	$ 192.5	2.7% *

Source: U.S. Office of Management and Budget, Bureau of Economic Analysis
* Based on Third-Quarter Annualized GDP

Comparison of International Deficits and Debts

	1995 Deficit as Percentage of GDP	1995 Debt as Percentage of GDP
Britain	5.1%	52.5%
France	5.0%	51.5%
Germany	2.9%	58.8%
Italy	7.4%	124.9%
United States	2.0%	69.2%

Source: *Standard & Poor's Industry Surveys*

Federal Budget: Receipts, Outlays, and Deficit ($ billions)

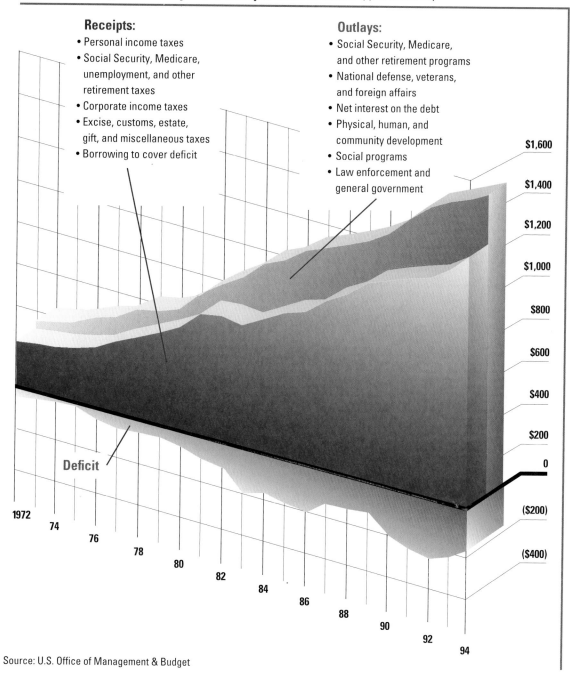

Receipts:
- Personal income taxes
- Social Security, Medicare, unemployment, and other retirement taxes
- Corporate income taxes
- Excise, customs, estate, gift, and miscellaneous taxes
- Borrowing to cover deficit

Outlays:
- Social Security, Medicare, and other retirement programs
- National defense, veterans, and foreign affairs
- Net interest on the debt
- Physical, human, and community development
- Social programs
- Law enforcement and general government

B

$1,600
$1,400
$1,200
$1,000
$800
$600
$400
$200
0
($200)
($400)

Deficit

1972 74 76 78 80 82 84 86 88 90 92 94

Source: U.S. Office of Management & Budget

econ

budget surplus   When spending is less than income over a particular period, either because outlays fall short of the amount established in the budget or because **revenues** exceed expectations.

See also **budget deficit**.

Budget Deficit as Percentage of GDP, 1972–1994

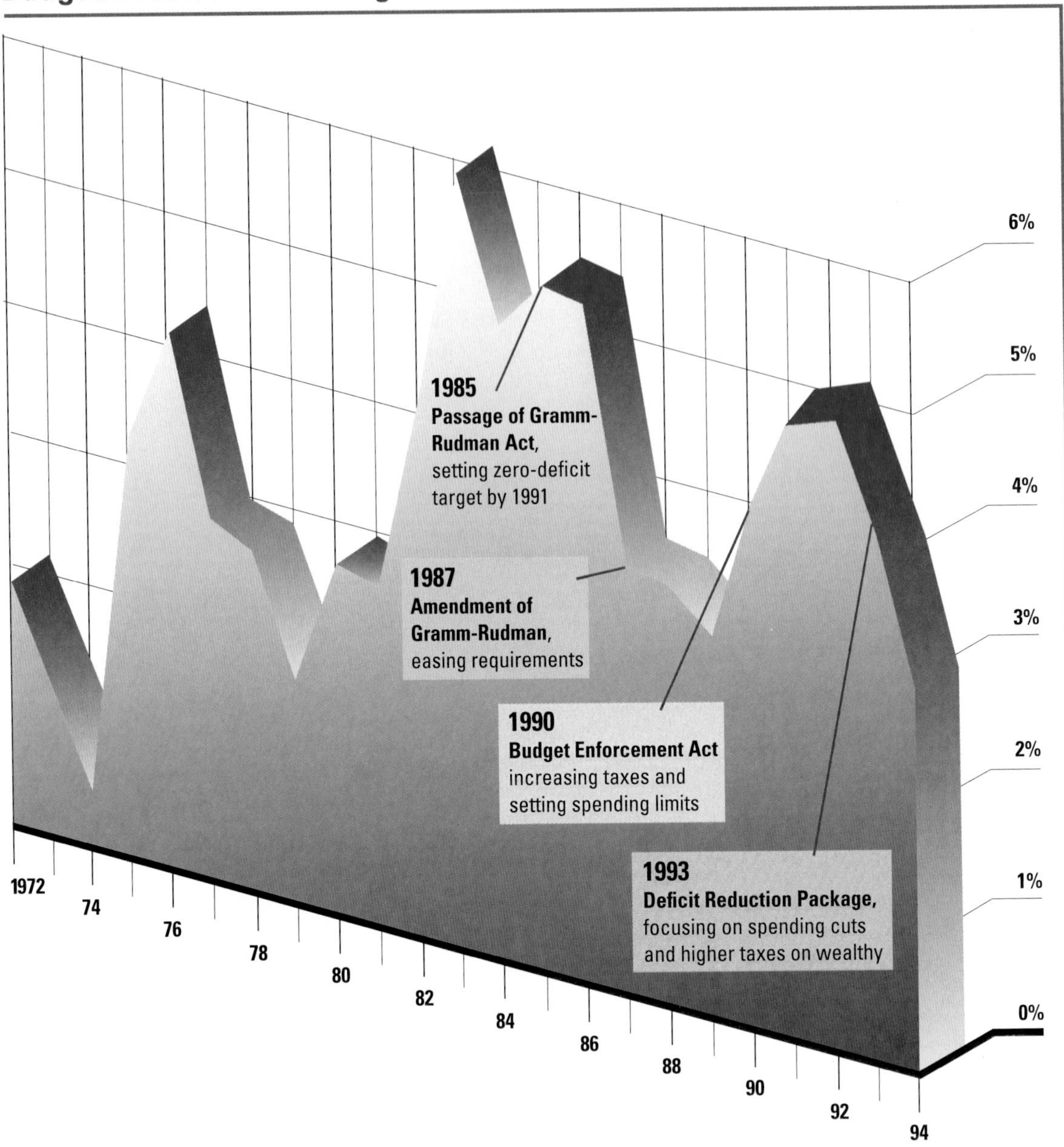

B

1985
Passage of Gramm-Rudman Act,
setting zero-deficit target by 1991

1987
Amendment of Gramm-Rudman,
easing requirements

1990
Budget Enforcement Act
increasing taxes and setting spending limits

1993
Deficit Reduction Package,
focusing on spending cuts and higher taxes on wealthy

6%

5%

4%

3%

2%

1%

0%

1972 74 76 78 80 82 84 86 88 90 92 94

Source: U.S. Office of Management & Budget, Bureau of Economic Analysis

FRAME OF

REFERENCE

budget deficit

The relationship between Social Security revenue and federal budget figures is sparking controversy. Legislation passed in 1983 set the stage for huge surpluses in the Social Security Trust Fund to ensure its solvency when the baby boomers—people born in record numbers between 1946 and 1964—begin to retire and collect benefits in the next century. When the surpluses are included in federal budget calculations for the year in which they are collected (as seen in the earlier tables), they disguise the size of the deficit.

In the mid-1990s, this accounting procedure reduced figures for the budget deficit by tens of billions of dollars a year. Social Security surpluses are expected to reach $100 billion annually later in the decade.

tech

bug Glitch in software.

Software is a complex web to develop. Before a new program is released, it is often given out to **beta-testers** who use it and identify bugs—errors to be fixed. Even so, the early versions of any program are likely to have many bugs. You will know one when you see one because, very likely, odd things will occur; your screen may freeze up as you are working furiously to get something done (that was probably due yesterday), and you will have to **boot** your computer again.

Once identified, bugs are eliminated in subsequent versions of the software. It is rare, though, for any program to be totally bug-free. Do not confuse bugs with **viruses**, though: The best medicine for those is preventive.

tech

bulletin board system (BBS) Messages posted and read by people using computers linked by a telecommunications **network**.

See also **electronic bulletin board**.

mktg **strat**

bundling Selling a package of products for one total price.

For example, travel services offer a variety of packages for Walt Disney World that might include, in addition to airfare, admission to the park, lodging, some meals, and shuttle service.

If your price is competitive and is used as an enticement, bundling becomes important in marketing the product because it provides extras that the customer might not get from a competitor at the same price. Increasingly, bundling has been used in the computer hardware and software industries to make products more attractive.

A Packard Bell computer, for instance, may come bundled with a monitor, a fax modem, an operating system, Windows, and several software applications. Operating systems themselves come bundled with applications. The Department of Justice (DOJ) has investigated whether software bundling gives one company an unfair advantage. One example was the case of whether the bundling of Microsoft Network software with Windows 95 was unfair to other information services like America Online, CompuServe, and Prodigy. The Microsoft/Windows package did not take off, however, and the investigation was never completed.

See also **cherry picking** and **pricing**.

tech

bus One or more conductors in a **digital** system that connects a related group of devices.

A bus may connect a computer processor and memory to units that control communications, a disk, a printer, and so on. A bus always connects several devices in a grouping.

bundling

t i p

Bundling can help you increase sales of the bundled products and cover the expense of attracting new customers by spreading the cost. It also means the buyer will find it unattractive to buy items separately and have a tough time making item-by-item price comparisons.

t r a p |

A competitor can zero in on one key item in the package and market it on a lower-cost basis.

B

business cycle

Quick Facts! |

For the economy as a whole, some economists think business cycle is the wrong term. The short-term fluctuations of the U.S. economy have been more like a roller-coaster ride. In fact, we have taken the ride—from business peak to contraction to recessionary trough to expansion and back to business peak—20 times between 1900 and 1995. A number of economists, however, believe that the ride from peak to trough is getting smoother.

In the chart below, which plots the GDP's annual change since 1980, we see relatively long stretches of sustained growth interrupted by two short recessions in 1980 and 1981–82.

econ   fin

business cycle   Short-term fluctuations of the aggregate economy around its long-run growth path.

Various indicators such as **gross domestic product (GDP)**, **employment**, and **housing starts** are used to gauge business cycles.

Recurring patterns of expansion and contraction also occur in particular industries and in regional economies.

EXAMPLE | The petrochemical industry repeatedly goes through periods when good profit margins attract new investment in plants. Within a few years, plants in operation are turning out more petrochemicals than the market can absorb, and profit margins sink. It then takes a few more years for a shakeout in which underperforming facilities close and demand overtakes supply. That starts the process of new investment all over again.

The business cycle of an industry will, of course, have an effect on the overall economy, but the industry and the larger economy do not always move in the same direction. When crude-oil prices dip modestly, oil companies slump, but the overall economy gets a boost from cheaper energy prices. A more severe drop in crude prices, though, cuts oil-company profits so sharply that the companies reduce spending, pinching the overall economy.

To plan for a company's future—its financing, pricing, and employment policies—it is necessary to understand both an industry's and the overall economy's cycles and how they will likely impact sales, **inflation**, labor availability, **interest rates**, and so on.

Business Cycle

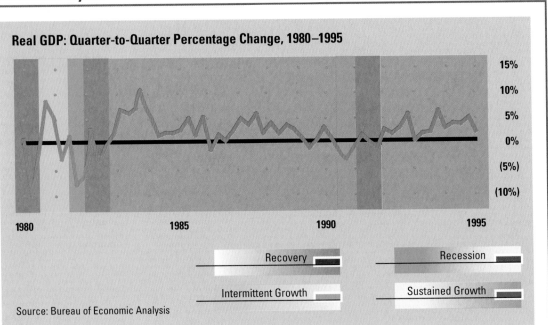

Real GDP: Quarter-to-Quarter Percentage Change, 1980–1995

Recovery   Recession   Intermittent Growth   Sustained Growth

Source: Bureau of Economic Analysis

mgmt

business ethics   Standards of right and wrong applied in the corporate environment.

See also **ethics**.

mktg

business market   All the people and organizations that buy your goods or services except for the final consumers.

See also **industrial market**.

mgmt

business reengineering   Fundamental and drastic redesign of an organization's business processes to achieve improvement in performance. Also called business process reengineering.

This term is most closely identified with Michael Hammer and James Champy whose 1993 book *Reengineering the Corporation* became a best seller and made **reengineering** a household word. (See related story on following page.)

The idea behind reengineering is not simply to improve the efficiency of an existing process but to ask whether it needs to be done at all, to ask whether each part of the process contributes to making a good product, supplying it at a competitive price, and providing quality service. Viewing processes in this light can help an organization fundamentally rethink underlying premises and redesign the way its work is done.

This sort of fundamental rethinking is key to business reengineering. What has happened since the 1993 book, however, is that reengineering has become a buzzword in danger of losing its meaning. It is often misused as a euphemism for firing workers. Misunderstood reengineering may start with an arbitrary cost-cutting goal of eliminating a percentage of the workforce from a particular function. Thus, the benefit of rethinking the process is lost. The result is fewer people struggling to do the old work.

In the name of reengineering, one large corporation eliminated many of the jobs in its U.S. computer services group in 1995 only to discover that it could not get its work done. Within weeks, it rehired a number of the terminated workers. It is likely that some of the work could have been rethought and eliminated, but that never happened because demands on the department had not changed.

strat   **mgmt**

business strategy   Totality of a company's approach to developing and selling its goods and services.

---

business reengineering

We found that many tasks that employees performed had nothing at all to do with meeting customer needs—that is, fair price, and providing excellent service. Many tasks were done simply to satisfy the internal demands of the company's own organization.

—Michael Hammer & James Champy, *Reengineering the Corporation*

B

FRAME OF

REFERENCE

business reengineering

By redesigning its annual report to eliminate all photographs and most text that is not legally required, Bell Atlantic was doing more than reducing printing costs. The company eliminated the staff time formerly required to select and obtain photos, write captions, and review those decisions at the appropriate corporate level. Bell Atlantic concluded those activities did not contribute enough—or at all—to its business.

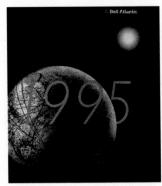

Several other companies have rethought the process and formed different conclusions. General Motors, for instance, has reduced the number of color photographs in its annual report but does use a few, printed on glossy paper, showing new-model cars. The automaker obviously feels that this chance to show its products to shareholders and others interested in GM is worth the cost.

Another example of reengineering cited by Hammer and Champy is Ford Motor Company's look at why it needed so much staff in Accounts Payable. The culprit turned out to be the difficulty in reconciling discrepancies between purchase orders for parts, what suppliers actually delivered, and the suppliers'

invoice. While only a few shipments involved discrepancies, reconciliation was extremely time-consuming. The solution was not to redesign Accounts Payable but to rethink the whole process of purchasing, delivery, and payment.

Now, when a buyer orders parts, he or she enters the order and price in a database. When the supplier makes delivery, a clerk at the receiving dock uses a computer terminal to check the database and see whether the order was properly filled. If it was, the clerk enters an acknowledgment that the shipment has been received, and the vendor is paid automatically. If the shipment does not match what was ordered, the clerk rejects it.

---

mgmt **fin**

Business Week 1000 Annual roster of America's most valuable companies published by *Business Week* magazine. The largest public companies are ranked according to their **market value**.

fin

buy-side analyst Person who analyzes and recommends securities for a company that buys them for its own account, usually **institutional investors** like mutual funds, insurance companies, **pension funds**, banks, and so on.

Among the more highly anticipated events in the brokerage community each year is the analyst-ranking survey published each October in *Institutional Investor* magazine. Each year, the magazine polls the industry to compile its "All-Star" teams of analysts in different industries. While the "sell-side" ranking is most widely followed, *Institutional Investor* also published a "buy-side" listing up to 1994.

See also **sell-side analyst**.

fin   **acct**   **mgmt**

buyback   Company's purchase of its own securities.

A company might decide to buy back some of its **common stock** if it thinks that the price is too low and that a return of capital to shareholders is the most efficient use of its money. A buyback sends a signal to existing and prospective shareholders that management thinks the securities are undervalued and tends to boost the price by reducing the supply of shares on the market while increasing the demand for them. The repurchased shares become **treasury stock** or are retired and are no longer used in calculating per-share figures, such as earnings. So the buyback improves per-share measures of the company's performance.

Companies sometimes buy back their bonds on the open market. They may be motivated to do this when they have spare cash and rising **interest rates** have reduced the market price of the bonds significantly below their face value.

See also **call feature** and **capital stock**.

Business Week 1000

Reprinted from March 25, 1996, issue of *Business Week* by special permission. Copyright © by The McGraw-Hill Companies, Inc.

FRAME OF REFERENCE

buyback

Shareholders of Mirage Resorts have ample reason to applaud their company's buyback program. Over an approximately 20-year span, the hotel and gaming company bought back more than 54 million shares at a cost of $442 million, averaging a little more than $8 a share. Over the same period, Mirage sold 29 million shares for some $443 million, an average of more than $15 a share.

The net effect of this buying and selling? Twenty-five million shares were retired at no cost whatsoever to the company. In fact, based on the more than $32-per-share price prevailing when the buybacks were completed, the net gain to shareholders amounted to over $600 million.

B

fin **mktg**

buyer credit A credit extended to buyers, either directly by the seller or through a third party.

See also **trade credit**.

mktg

buyer-decision process Steps a buyer goes through before and after a purchase.

They include need recognition, information search, weighing alternatives, actual purchase decisions, and after-purchase behavior.

See also **purchase-decision process**.

mktg **strat**

buyer power Ability of customers to force price reductions.

buyer power

trap

When you get selective about your customers, you may unknowingly be pumping up the power of those that remain. With fewer of them, they may be able to get you over a barrel.

Buyer power tends to be high when:

▶ Buyers are sparse.

▶ Buyers see that alternative products can fill their needs.

▶ Buyers can easily use alternative products at minimum cost.

▶ Buyers can design their own alternative products.

▶ The product constitutes a large part of the buyers' costs.

▶ Sellers in the market compete on price.

▶ A seller has open capacity or is in financial need.

▶ Business activity is depressed.

Ways to decrease buyer power:

▶Bundle your products into a package your customers need.

▶ Differentiate your product—for instance, by building in useful new features.

▶ Finance the product for your customers.

▶ Use **relationship marketing** to build a customer base.

▶ Partner your company with your customer.

See also **backward vertical integration**, **bundling**, **differentiation**, and **supplier power**.

mgmt

bylaws   Rules for governing a corporation or other organization.

A corporation's bylaws spell out such things as how directors are elected, how board committees are formed, what the officers' duties are, and how, when, and on what issues shareholders get to vote. The bylaws will conform to the laws of the state where the company is incorporated.

See also **articles of incorporation** and **charter**.

tech

byte   Unit of eight **bits**, which often represents a single character or letter—the common unit of computer memory storage.

A **kilobyte** is 1,024 bytes, and a **megabyte** is 1,048,576 bytes.

byte

Broadcasting and Cable

Radio emerged from the wireless industry in the 1920s. David Sarnoff, then general manager at Radio Corporation of America, realized that the technology that earlier had been considered a competitor to the telegraph might become an entertainment and education medium. In essence, Sarnoff suggested that instead of the "narrowcasting" for which wireless originally had been intended, radio could be used for "broadcasting."

The idea caught on, and several companies, among them the parents of RCA—AT&T, Westinghouse, and General Electric—and RCA itself, entered the field with "networks" of radio stations. Receiver manufacturers proliferated, led by the Atwater Kent Company, Crosley Corp., Philco Corp., and Zenith Radio (later Zenith Electronics). But RCA was the clear leader, controlling many of the important patents. In 1921, there were 12 million receivers sold; by 1926, the number was 207 million.

Secretary of Commerce Herbert Hoover objected when the stations started to air commercials. In the 1920s, Hoover organized several conferences to discuss regulating the new industry; these led to the formation of the Federal Radio Commission in 1927. In 1934, the FRC became the Federal Communications Commission (FCC), whose duty was guiding the industry to make certain it served the public interest.

By then, RCA had organized the National Broadcasting System, which had two networks, the Red and the Blue. William Paley created the Columbia Broadcasting System. Prodded by antitrust considerations, RCA sold the Blue network to Edward Noble, who eventually established the American Broadcasting Company. Additionally, there were hundreds of independents and some smaller chains.

Music programs dominated the early days of radio and were joined by comedy and drama in the 1930s. Newscasts and analysis were downplayed until World War II, when all three networks developed impressive news-gathering and analysis teams.

For a period in the 1930s and 1940s, it appeared radio might be reinvented in the form of frequency modulation (FM), a superior, static-free technology. FM would require listeners to have another radio, though, in time, radios were

Contributing Editor: Harold L. Vogel
Managing Director, Cowen & Co.

1919   1920   1930   1940

1919
RCA organized by David Sarnoff

1920
KDKA, the first radio broadcasting system, operates in Pittsburgh

1927
First transmission of television signals

1928
William Paley invests in CBS and starts transforming it into a major network

1934
The Federal Radio Commission becomes the FCC

1945
RCA wins FCC approval to begin broadcasting through television

capable of receiving both FM and AM. A more serious drawback was that FM used radio frequencies needed for an even more important advance in the industry—television.

Initially it appeared television might be developed in one of two ways: It could become radio with pictures or motion pictures in the home. In the post–World War II period, the motion-picture industry was under attack for antitrust violations, so its leaders were diverted from the television challenge. Sarnoff once again took the lead and steered television into the radio model.

RCA experimented with television in the 1930s and in 1945 won FCC approval to start broadcasting. NBC, CBS, and ABC quickly entered the field, along with some short-lived networks and many independent stations.

The networks transferred radio shows to television with much success. Some stars, whose careers seemed over or faded, became television luminaries: Hopalong Cassidy, Lucille Ball, Jackie Gleason, and Milton Berle, to name a few. Sports became a television staple. News programs were slow to develop before the advent of videotape cameras. Some of the motion-picture studios sold their old films to television, believing them worth very little. But the motion-picture industry declined to come to terms with television, forbade its

stars to appear on the "tube," and except for Disney, refused to produce programs for television—a situation that did not change until the mid-1960s.

As had been the case with radio, RCA was the largest factor in the industry, but it was hardly alone. By 1947 there were 14 receiver manufacturers and more than 80 by 1950. The smaller ones were soon winnowed out, leaving RCA, Zenith, GE, Motorola, Sylvania, and Magnavox to lead the field. Set production rose from 10,000 in 1946 to 7.3 million in 1953.

RCA and CBS engaged in a bitter struggle over color television, developing rival systems. RCA won the fight in 1953, largely because its version was compatible with the monochrome sets then in use, while the CBS system would have required different receivers for color and monochrome.

During the late 1950s and 1960s, some American receiver manufacturers expanded into other fields—Motorola into electronics, RCA and GE into computers—and behaved as though the television-set business was mature and no longer required extensive research and development. That was not the case.

Lucille Ball

It was then that the Japanese companies started to move into the American market. Sony purchased the right to manufacture transistors from Bell Labs in 1949 and produced small radios for the American market. By the 1960s, Sony, Toshiba, Hitachi, and other Japanese firms were shipping transistorized television receivers to the United States at a time when the Americans were still making sets based on vacuum tubes. Likewise, Ampex licensed its videotape patents to Sony, which sold its recorders and players in the United States.

1947		1970	1980				1996
1947 Transistor invented at Bell Laboratories	**1949** Sony purchases the right to manufacture transistors from Bell Labs, which allows them to produce small radios for the U.S. market	**1972** Time Inc. creates Home Box Office (HBO)	**1984** Cable Communications Policy Act	**1985** Rupert Murdoch organizes Fox network	**1994** DirecTV begins direct-to-home satellite distribution service		**1996** Microsoft and NBC begin airing MSNBC, an all-news station

In 1963, when RCA refused to permit Sears Roebuck to sell RCA-produced color televisions under the Sears Roebuck label, Sanyo accepted the terms. Then RCA sold technology licenses to Japanese firms. As a result, the Japanese share of the consumer electronics market rose from 7 percent in 1963 to 40 percent in 1974, with the Japanese controlling 20 percent of the color television market. That year no American firm manufactured radios or monochrome televisions.

RCA, along with Ampex, pioneered videotape technology and fell behind Japanese manufacturers as well. By the late 1980s, Japanese and other foreign firms controlled the American consumer electronics market. Moreover, the Japanese industry continued to innovate and, in the mid-1990s, led by Toshiba, came up with a new product, the digital video disc, which has sufficient capacity to record a full-length movie and allows the viewer to rewind or fast forward more rapidly than the current VCRs.

Japanese firms started purchasing entertainment companies as well. Sony acquired Columbia and Matsushita took over at MCA, which owned Universal. Japanese companies were experimenting with high-definition television (HDTV), which seemed capable of transforming the industry once again. The future for the American industry appeared bleak.

Unlike radio signals, which follow the curvature of the earth, television signals travel in a straight line. For this reason it appeared in the late 1940s that cable television, known then as "community antennas," had a bright future. At the same time Zenith Electronics experimented with "phonevision," scrambled signals of commercial-free movies that could be unscrambled in homes for a fee, over the community antennas, thus reviving thoughts of television being used as a form of motion pictures in the home.

In the early 1970s, with the approval of the FCC, pay services made their appearance. In

1972, Time Inc. created Home Box Office (HBO) for the company's New York cable system, and it was taken up by other cable operators hoping to woo new customers. In 1975, HBO switched to less-expensive and more efficient satellite transmission, even though the receivers were still wired.

The concept of using satellites to transmit signals inspired Ted Turner to transform his Atlanta outlet into a "superstation" whose signals were offered to cable systems throughout the country. When he instituted Cable News Network (CNN), Turner not only achieved great success but created a leading global news source.

While cable was popular, its momentum slowed in the mid-1980s. Several problems, not realized earlier, surfaced and put the future of the industry temporarily on hold. The economics of cable were also troublesome. While the marginal costs of providing service were low and profits high, the initial installation was quite expensive. Thus, rapidly growing cable systems had an almost insatiable hunger for capital. Customers objected to higher charges, and as a regulated industry, the cable companies had to apply for rate boosts, which were increasingly denied by the regulators.

Two new wireless systems also threatened the fixed nature of the cable industry: direct broadcasting systems that beamed programs from satellites into homes and multipoint distribution, which was the transmission of signals to special rooftop antennas.

Even more threatening were "pirates," who used illegal converters to steal signals from pay services, a problem that cost the operators an estimated $500 million a year in the early 1980s. Some consumers purchased "dishes," which took signals from the satellites, attempting to avoid fees in this way. By the late 1980s, however, the dishes, capable of receiving more than 150 stations and expanding regularly, were incorporated into the paying sector and provided a new source of revenue for the companies.

By then the industry had resumed its expansion. Help came from government in the form of the Cable Communications Policy Act of 1984, which ended many regulations as of 1987. In 1985, the cable operators were permitted to convert more channels to pay status. Also, rate regulations were cut back, freeing the companies to adjust them to meet market conditions. Now pay-per-view, an improved version of the old phonevision, became more popular along with special-interest channels dealing with nature, business, ethnic affairs, court trials, and a host of other subjects.

The plethora of channels created problems as well as possibilities. As viewing became more fractionalized, audiences spread out, and so advertisers, who were charged by the size of the audience, paid lower rates. This set off bidding wars for such programs as the Academy Awards, the Olympics, and popular sporting events. The 1995–96 O.J. Simpson murder trial focused attention on programs following the story, and the stations vied with one another for coverage. Pressures were placed on the networks to develop popular programs, and stars and their writers were richly remunerated.

By 1995, the networks were in turmoil. That year, CBS was sold to Westinghouse, and ABC, which had recently merged with Capital Cities, was acquired by Disney. Since RCA, which owned NBC, earlier had been purchased by General Electric, all three networks' parents

were companies outside the broadcasting industry. Ironically, GE and Westinghouse, two of the pioneers of radio, emerged as major forces once more. The "Big 3" networks had also been shaken up by the arrival of Fox Broadcasting, the fourth network introduced by Rupert Murdoch's News Corp. in the 1980s.

While television and cable provided the glamour for broadcasting, radio underwent an unexpected renaissance. It was still an important source for news, and music remained a staple. And somewhat surprisingly, talk radio became a big draw as call-in shows proliferated.

Both television and radio were further roiled by the regulatory movement of the 1980s and 1990s. Legislation passed in 1996 lifted many of the remaining restrictions previously imposed on the industry. Additionally, the legislation permitted telephone companies to purchase some cable franchises and the cable companies in turn to enter telephony.

This appeared to open the way for a melding of telecommunications, electronics, software, and cable television. Microsoft entered into a relationship with NBC to form an all-news station, MSNBC, made possible by electronics and telecommunications developments. Time Warner gained control of Turner, while Tele-Communications owned a substantial interest in Turner. In essence, all three companies came together, a marriage made possible—even necessary—by developments in electronics, which today is central to all of these industries.

C

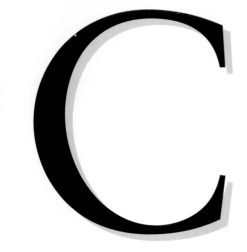

to

cycle counting

call feature

call feature

Provision of a **bond** agreement that allows the issuer to repurchase the bond before it matures.

The price an issuer pays to redeem a bond is the call price, which is usually higher than the bond's face value. The call **premium** is the difference between a bond's call price and its face value. Companies or other bond issuers may exercise their call features when interest rates have fallen. They repurchase their high-interest bonds and issue new ones at lower interest rates. The call feature also gives management flexibility in controlling its capital structure.

The document below is the prospectus page from an MCI **convertible bond** issue. It includes a general description of the bond's features, including total amount, maturity, and the call schedule set by the company.

RATIO OF EARNINGS TO FIXED CHARGES

Year ended December 31,

1981	1982	1983	1984	1985
2.7	3.6	2.7	1.1	1.5

The ratio of earnings to fixed charges is computed by adding interest expense to income before income taxes and extraordinary item and dividing that by the sum of interest expense and capitalized interest costs. If the ratio were computed by adding interest expense to income before income taxes, extraordinary item and nonrecurring items and dividing that by the sum of interest expense and capitalized interest costs, the ratios for 1984 and 1985 would be 1.3 and 1.2, respectively.

DESCRIPTION OF DEBENTURES

General. The statements under this caption relating to the Debentures and the Indenture pursuant to which they are to be issued are a summary of such instruments and do not purport to be complete. Such summary makes use of terms defined in the Indenture and is qualified in its entirety by express reference to the Indenture, a copy of which has been filed with the Commission. For purposes of this summary, "MCI" refers to MCI Communications Corporation, a Delaware corporation, the issuer of the Debentures.

The Debentures are to be issued under an Indenture to be dated as of April 1, 1986 (the "Indenture") between MCI and Bankers Trust Company (the "Trustee"). The Debentures will be limited to $575 million aggregate principal amount and will be unsecured, subordinated obligations of MCI.

The Debentures are issuable only as fully registered debentures without coupons in denominations of $1,000 and integral multiples of $1,000 and as otherwise authorized by MCI. All Debentures must bear a certificate of authentication executed by the Trustee. The Debentures will be transferable at the principal trust office or agency of the Trustee in the City of New York. Unless MCI otherwise determines, the Trustee will act as the paying agent and registrar for the Debentures.

MCI's assets consist principally of the stock in its subsidiaries. Therefore, its rights and the rights of its creditors, including the holders of the Debentures, to participate in the assets of any subsidiary upon the latter's liquidation or recapitalization or otherwise will be subject to the prior claims of the subsidiary's creditors, except to the extent that claims of MCI itself as a creditor of the subsidiary may be recognized. See "Subordination of Debentures."

Maturity and Interest. The Debentures will mature on April 1, 2011, and will bear interest from April 14, 1986, at the rate shown on the cover page hereof, payable semi-annually on April 1, and October 1 of each year, commencing on October 1, 1986. Interest on the Debentures is payable to the persons in whose names the Debentures are registered at the close of business on the preceding March 15 or September 15. The Debentures are payable as to principal and interest at the principal trust office or agency of the Trustee in the City of New York, provided that, at MCI's option, payment of interest may be made by check mailed to the registered Debentureholders entitled thereto at their addresses as they appear on the registry books for the Debentures.

Redemption Provisions. The Debentures are to be redeemable at any time on and after April 1, 1991, at the option of MCI, as a whole or from time to time in part (except that no redemption at the option of MCI may be carried out prior to April 1, 1996, directly or indirectly from the proceeds of, or in anticipation of, money borrowed at an interest cost, computed in accordance with generally accepted financial practice, of less than 10% per annum), on not less than 15 days' nor more than 60 days' prior notice by mail, at the redemption prices set forth below (expressed in percentages of the principal amount) plus accrued interest to the redemption date:

If redeemed during the twelve-month period beginning April 1,

1991	110%	1996	105%
1992	109%	1997	104%
1993	108%	1998	103%
1994	107%	1999	102%
1995	106%	2000	101%
		2001 and thereafter	100%

5

---

call feature

The call premium a company pays to retire bonds generally declines over time as the bond approaches its maturity. When MCI issued this callable bond in 1986, it used the call price schedule shown to the left. MCI agreed to a $1,100 call price if they called the bond as early as 1991 but only $1,000 (or par) by 2001 or later.

call option

Let's say that you've been following Disney stock. You see that it closed the day* at $59-3/8, and you think it has a good chance of going higher over the next few weeks. You decide to buy a call option. This screen from Bloomberg (right) lists various types of call options on Walt Disney stock.

Line 6 shows an option with a $60 *strike price*, expiring in October 1996 that will cost you $1-15/16, or $1.9375 (the *asking price*) per share. This gives you the right to buy Disney stock for $60 until October 1996, although you won't make money—barring transaction costs—unless Disney stock moves above $61.9375 (*strike price* + what you paid for the option). Because option contracts trade in 100-share blocks, you would pay $193.75 for the contract, which gives you the option to buy 100 shares of Disney stock at $60 per share.

**As of August 26, 1996.*

---

fin

call option   Gives the holder of a stock the right to buy an asset at a particular price before a certain date. A European option would allow the option to be exercised only on the expiration date.

See also **derivatives**.

Call Option

```
OPTION   BID  ASK  MONITOR
Exch: Comp              Time      Current
D I S   U S             16:11      59³⁄₈
THE WALT DISNEY CO.
                C A L L S
```

DIS	SEP 96	Bid	Ask	Last	Volume
1) IJ	50	$9\frac{1}{4}$	$9\frac{3}{4}$	$8\frac{1}{2}$ y	
2) IK	55	$4\frac{1}{2}$	$4\frac{7}{8}$	$4\frac{5}{8}$ y	15
3) IL	60	1	$1\frac{3}{16}$	$1\frac{1}{16}$ y	412
DIS	OCT 96				
4) JJ	50	$9\frac{5}{8}$	10	$8\frac{3}{4}$ y	
5) JK	55	5	$5\frac{3}{8}$	$4\frac{1}{2}$ y	2
6) JL	60	$1\frac{13}{16}$	$1\frac{15}{16}$	$1\frac{3}{4}$ y	117
7) JM	65	$\frac{5}{16}$	$\frac{7}{16}$	$\frac{3}{8}$ y	22
8) JN	70	$\frac{1}{16}$	$\frac{1}{8}$	$\frac{1}{8}$ y	6
9) JO	75		$\frac{1}{8}$	$\frac{1}{16}$ y	
DIS	JAN 97				
10) AF	30	$29\frac{1}{2}$	$30\frac{1}{4}$	$26\frac{1}{2}$ y	
11) AH	40	$19\frac{5}{8}$	$20\frac{3}{8}$	$19\frac{1}{8}$ y	3
12) AJ	50	$10\frac{1}{2}$	$11\frac{1}{4}$	10y	
13) AK	55	$6\frac{5}{8}$	$7\frac{1}{8}$	$6\frac{7}{8}$ y	25
14) AL	60	$3\frac{1}{2}$	$3\frac{3}{4}$	$3\frac{3}{8}$ y	29
15) AM	65	$1\frac{1}{2}$	$1\frac{3}{4}$	$1\frac{1}{2}$ y	72

Source: Bloomberg Financial Markets

---

fin **mgmt**

call provision   Provision of a **bond** agreement that allows the issuer to repurchase the bond before it matures. Also referred to as a **call feature**.

---

mktg

camera ready   Text or images prepared for reproduction by a printing process.

In modern printing, the type and graphics for a page are laid out and then photographed in the first step toward making printing plates. When an advertisement or other part of a layout is camera ready, the type and graphics are crisp and clean and suitable for photography.

mktg

canned approach
A predetermined sales pitch and strategy to try to hook a new customer. It is often used in **cold calling**.

mktg

cannibalization
When a new product takes away sales from an existing one made by the same company.

Although cannibalization usually is undesirable, the profits from your new product may more than make up for the costs of its development and the other product's lost sales.

A company may actually seek to cannibalize its own sales if it believes that it must introduce a superior new product to fend off competitors. Trying to preempt the competition may not bring in any new customers and may, in fact, hurt sales of the existing product, but, in the long run, the company will keep its customers from switching to the competition.

oper

capacity cushion
Excess production capacity that gives a manufacturer the ability to hit the ground running to meet unexpected demand for a product or products.

The cushion can be achieved in several ways, including:

▶ Designing plant and processes so that capacity exceeds anticipated market demand by some percentage.

▶ Maintaining inventories.

▶ Keeping dedicated cash reserves to meet unexpected requirements for rapid plant expansion.

econ

capital account
Measure of investments and loans flowing into and out of a country in a period of time. It is one component of the **balance of payments**.

fin **mgmt**

capital asset pricing model (CAPM)
Way of balancing the **market risk** of a security, or a portfolio of securities, and its return.

CAPM is based on this principle: The required **rate of return** on a security equals the return required for securities that have no risk (like U.S. Treasury bills), plus a **risk premium**. You can determine the premium by the amount of market risk, as indicated by the security's **beta (ß)**, a measure of how its price moves against a market index like the **Dow Jones** 30 Industrials or **Standard & Poor's 500**. The higher the risk, the higher the required premium.

cannibalization

One new product with great potential is the digital videodisc. Market analysts are predicting worldwide videodisc sales approaching $5 billion a year by 2000. But they put net new sales at less than half that number. That is because they expect videocassette sales to fall by around $2.5 billion a year.

capital account

C

121

Managers sometimes use CAPM internally to calculate the rate of return they will strive to achieve for shareholders.

EXAMPLE | If the return on risk-free U.S. Treasury bills (r_f) equals 6 percent, the market return (r_m) comes to 9 percent, and the beta (ß) for stock X is 1.75, the required return for that stock is:

0.06 + 1.75 (0.09 - .1125) = .1125, or 11.25%

In other words, to compensate for stock X's market risk, investors need to collect a return of 11.25 percent. The risk premium, then, equals 5.25 percentage points—the amount over the risk-free rate (6 percent) that must be paid to investors for assuming the stock's market risk.

capital asset pricing model

tip

This model considers only market risk—what happens to the security in response to moves of the overall market. No allowance is made for factors specific to the company, like the development of a new product or an anticipated management shake-up or labor problem.

C

Capital Asset Pricing Model (CAPM)

$$r_j \quad = \quad r_f + ß(r_m - r_f)$$

r_j The required return on security j

r_f The risk-free rate (the return on a risk-free security, such as a U.S. Treasury bill)

ß   Beta, a measure of the security's risk vs. overall market risk

r_m Expected market return, as measured by the Dow Jones 30 Industrials or Standard & Poor's 500 Stock Composite Index

---

`acct` **`fin`**

capital lease   Lease that, in accounting, is treated as an installment purchase. Also called **financing lease**.

That means, among other things, that the item leased becomes an **asset**, and the future payments are a **liability**, on the **balance sheet**.

A lease is considered a capital lease if any of the following four conditions are met:

1   The **present value** of the minimum lease payments exceeds 90 percent of the fair market value of the asset.

2   The lessee owns the asset at the end of the lease term.

3   The lease term is equal to 75 percent or more of the asset's estimated economic life.

4   The lessee has the option at the end of the lease of acquiring the asset for a price significantly lower than its expected fair value.

If a lease meets none of these conditions, it is an operating lease. In which case it is not recorded on the company's balance sheet but may be disclosed in a footnote to the **financial statements**.

fin **econ**

capital markets All the markets where securities are traded, including both debt and equity, for corporations, government entities, and municipalities. The primary market involves the sale of new debt and equity issues; the secondary market is for trading previously issued securities. The organized secondary markets in the United States include the **New York Stock Exchange (NYSE)**, the **Nasdaq Stock Market**, the **American Stock Exchange (Amex)**, the **Chicago Board Options Exchange (CBOE)**, and regional exchanges.

When businesses want funds for start-up or expansion, they can try to attract savers' money by issuing new debt, such as corporate **bonds**, or new equity, such as **common stock**. Governments also participate in the capital markets when issuing new debt securities to fund their expenditures.

See also **money markets**.

capital markets

C

Total U.S. Underwritings, 1970–1995 ($ billions)

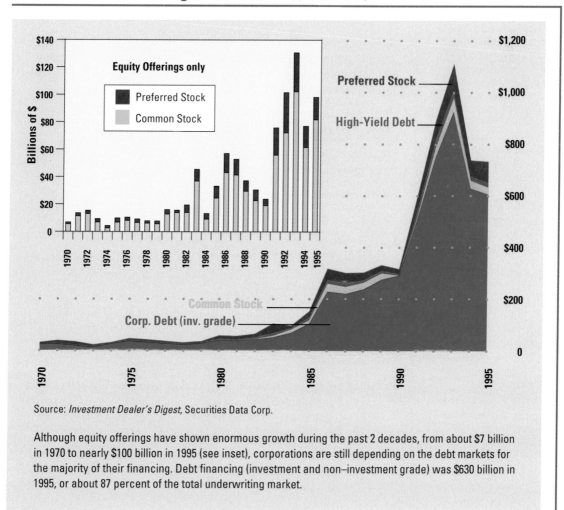

Source: *Investment Dealer's Digest*, Securities Data Corp.

Although equity offerings have shown enormous growth during the past 2 decades, from about $7 billion in 1970 to nearly $100 billion in 1995 (see inset), corporations are still depending on the debt markets for the majority of their financing. Debt financing (investment and non–investment grade) was $630 billion in 1995, or about 87 percent of the total underwriting market.

C

capital markets

Companies have raised as much as $1 trillion a year in primary capital markets in the United States. For the past quarter-century, the federal government has sold billions of dollars a year of government securities to finance its deficit, which stood at about $200 billion in 1995.

capital structure

Managing a capital structure is as important to a company's survival as managing its business. I believe that capital structure is a continuum–it should be constantly changed and adjusted to match what is occurring in a company's basic business, the abilities of its human capital, the strength of its competition's financial condition, and the current state of the economic and regulatory environment.

—Michael Milken

capitalization ratio

There's only one mistake in business, everything else you can recover from, but if you run out of cash, they take you out of the game.

—Harold Geneen, former
Chairman of ITT Corporation

---

fin **econ** **acct**

capital stock   (1) **Common** or **preferred stock** that represent ownership, authorized by a company. A company's **articles of incorporation** specify a set number of authorized shares. When stock is sold, it is called issued capital stock. As long as it remains in the hands of stockholders, it is outstanding. If it's bought back by the company, it becomes treasury stock.

As a rule, an owner of capital stock may claim the following:

1 A percentage of the company profits in the form of **dividends**—although these are paid out at management's discretion.

2 A claim (subordinated) on the assets if the company goes out of business.

3 The right to vote on membership of the board of directors and on fundamental company changes.

4 The right to maintain the same proportion of ownership should additional stock be issued.

Unlike partners or **sole proprietors** of a business, holders of capital stock have no liability beyond the price they paid to buy their shares.

(2) In economics, all durable **assets** that people have created that produce a stream of future goods and services, including plant and equipment of private businesses, residences of households, buildings and equipment of government, and durable goods of consumers.

acct **fin**

capital structure   Mix of stocks and bonds in a company's financial makeup. (See chart on following page.)

See also **capitalize**.

acct **fin**

capitalization ratio   Proportions of **common stock**, **preferred stock**, other securities, and debt that make up a company's capital structure.

The ratio is used in evaluating the relative risk that faces holders of each security. If there is a high proportion of preferred stock and debt, holders of common stock have less security.

EXAMPLE | Your company has total debt of $500 million, preferred stock valued on the **balance sheet** at $150 million, and common stock valued at $350 million. So its capitalization ratio is 50 percent debt, 15 percent preferred stock, and 35 percent common stock.

Capital Structure

Senior Secured Debt

Senior Debt

Subordinated Debt

Preferred Stock

Common Stock

One of the more important concepts behind capital structure is that of stakeholder priority—that is, the precedence of claims on a company's assets in the event of bankruptcy. This idea can be illustrated as drawers in a safe, which can be opened only in descending order from the top. In this example, senior secured debt holders will be paid first, then senior debt holders, and so on. Equity holders are always at the bottom of the priority scale, with preferred stockholders—as the name might imply—taking precedence over common stockholders.

acct   **fin**

capitalize   (1) To treat a cost that is expected to provide a future benefit as an **asset** on your **balance sheet**, rather than deducting it all as a current **expense** on your **income statement**. The asset is then usually subject to **depreciation** or **amortization**.

EXAMPLE | Your company, Hot Shot, decides in 1995 to upgrade its warehouse facilities to improve efficiency. You pay out $500,000 in design and construction fees to accomplish that. Those costs have to be capitalized. That is because you will feel the benefit of them over many years, so it is not fair to attribute all the expense to 1995. You put the $500,000 on the books as an asset and depreciate it.

(2) In a corporation's **charter**, to set the size of the capital structure (its stocks and **bonds**). Also, to issue stock as a **dividend** (turning some retained earnings into capital).

C

fin **econ** **acct**

CAPM   See **capital asset pricing model**.

acct

carrying amount   The amount at which an **asset** is listed on the **balance sheet**.

See also **book value**.

acct **fin** **mgmt**

carrying charges   Any ongoing charge that results from asset ownership, such as charges for warehousing goods or interest charged by **brokers** on margin accounts.

One effective way to minimize your carrying costs is to control inventory. By reducing inventory, you can reduce the cost of storage, insurance, and interest.

econ **strat** **mktg**

cartel   Group of companies, governments, or other entities that try to control the supply and price of a product. Although cartels are illegal in the United States, they are legal in world markets.

cartel

EXAMPLE | The best-known current cartel is the **Organization of Petroleum Exporting Countries (OPEC)**, which meets regularly to set crude-oil prices and production quotas for its member nations. OPEC wielded considerable power in the 1970s, but its loss of influence since then is a prime example of the difficulty cartels have overcoming market forces in the long run.

By the early 1980s—after oil prices reached more than 10 times their 1970 level—individuals, companies, and other energy users were all finding ways to conserve fuel and switch to alternatives like coal and natural gas. Non-OPEC oil production was developed in places like the British and Norwegian North Sea. As demand softened and production capacity swelled, OPEC found it harder to enforce discipline on its members. OPEC has never regained its clout, and crude-oil prices in the mid-1990s were less than half their early-1980s peak.

acct

cash basis   Accounting method that recognizes revenue when it is actually received.

See also **accrual basis**.

fin **mgmt** **strat**

cash cow
Company or product that generates plenty of cash with little effort or additional investment.

Coined by The Boston Consulting Group in the early 1970s as an element in its **growth share matrix**, the term has come into common use.

EXAMPLE | *TV Guide* magazine was for many years a cash cow for Walter Annenberg's Triangle Publications. Rupert Murdoch's News Corporation bought Triangle from Annenberg in 1988, a purchase that did not work out well overall. Although *TV Guide* continues to fill the milk buckets for News Corporation as it did for Triangle, Murdoch eventually sold all of Triangle's other magazines. The presence of *TV Guide* has helped both parent companies maintain and work with less profitable ventures.

Cash cows usually have dominant **market share** as well as a profitable product. In a mature market (like *TV Guide*'s), where aggressive promotion for the product is no longer needed, the cash cow's profits can be directed to dividends, to finance research and development for new products, or to cover debt.

acct **fin**

cash flow
Amount of net cash earned by a business or an investment during a specific period.

On a company's income statement, noncash charges like **depreciation** are deducted from revenues along with other expenses to arrive at net income. So to determine cash flow from operations, you add back the noncash charges.

Cash flow is the lifeblood of any business and may be considered its most important financial statistic. In the **mergers** and **acquisitions** of the 1980s and early 1990s, companies with substantial cash flow have been prime targets for takeovers. The people looking for takeover candidates are aware that the cash coming in can be used to help pay the cost of the acquisition.

fin

cash flow coverage
Ratio of a company's cash flow to its outstanding debt.

It is used as a measure of **bond** safety. Companies with a AAA rating from Standard & Poor's tend to have more than three times as much cash flow as they do long-term debt. The cash flow of companies rated A tends to be around 75 percent of their long-term debt.

cash cow

tip

Just because you have a cash cow, do not let your guard down. Even in a mature market, competition may develop, and your cow may run dry.

C

cash flow coverage

cash flow statement

The cash flow statement consists of three parts:

1 Operating activities, which is cash received and spent.

2 Investing activities, which is the buying and selling of long-term assets.

3 Financing activities, which are the transactions between the company and its owners and other investors.

C

Cash Flow Statement ($ millions)   1995

1 **Cash Flow from Operating Activities**

Net Income (loss)	**$706.1**

Adjustments to reconcile net income (loss) to net cash provided by operating activities:

Provision for doubtful receivables	39.6
Provision for depreciation	283.1
Undistributed earnings of unconsolidated subsidiaries and affiliates	(9.2)
Provision (credit) for deferred income taxes	75.5

Changes in assets and liabilities:

Receivables	(355.4)
Inventories	(17.0)
Accounts payable and accrued expenses	8.9
Insurance and health care claims and reserves	38.0
Other	69.8
Net cash provided by operating activities	**$839.4**

2 **Cash Flow from Investing Activities**

Collections of credit receivables	3,409.9
Proceeds from sales of credit receivables	837.3
Proceeds from maturities and sales of marketable securities	181.2
Proceeds from sales of equipment on oper. leases	45.5
Proceeds from sales of businesses	90.5
Cost of credit receivables acquired	(5,147.7)
Purchases of marketable securities	(194.1)
Purchases of property and equipment	(262.4)
Cost of operating leases acquired	(120.8)
Other	(35.2)
Net cash provided by (used for) investing activities	**($1,195.8)**

3 **Cash Flow from Financing Activities**

Increase (decrease) in short-term borrowings	490.1
Proceeds from long-term borrowings	775.0
Principal payments on one-term borrowings	(636.7)
Proceeds from issuance of common stock	43.6
Dividends paid	(190.5)
Other	(8.2)
Net cash provided by (used for) financing activities	**$473.3**

Effect of Exchange Rate Changes on Cash	**1.4**
Net Increase (Decrease) in Cash and Cash Equivalents	**118.3**
Cash and Cash Equivalents at Beginning of Year	**245.4**
Cash and Cash Equivalents at End of Year	**$363.7**

cash flow statement Document that focuses on cash—coming in and going out—over an **accounting period**.

Let us look at Deere & Company's statement of consolidated cash flows for its **fiscal year** ended October 31, 1995, on the previous page. As you can see, the cash flow statement is divided into three sections:

1 **Operating Activities**
Cash you received and what you spent in the normal course of your business. This differs from the net earnings in your income statement for several reasons—chiefly that depreciation is eliminated and cash is reflected when you get it and when you spend it, rather than when it is earned and when the expenses are incurred. Major companies start with net earnings and then adjust for items like accounts payable, accounts receivable, deferred income taxes, and depreciation.

2 **Investing Activities**
Buying and selling long-term assets like plants and equipment.

3 **Financing Activities**
Transactions between the company and its owners (shareholders) and other investors, such as bondholders. This shows dividends paid, borrowings, and repayments of debt, as well as the proceeds of securities issued.

See also **accounting method**.

fin **mgmt**

cash management systems In corporate finance, methods for determining the optimal amount of cash that a company should have on hand.

The systems look at the company's **cash flow**, returns on short-term investments, the cost involved in making those investments, and the **opportunity cost** of maintaining any cash balances that do not pay interest.

strat **mktg**

cause-related marketing A **marketing strategy** focusing on a particular social issue that is endorsed by the target audience for your product.

EXAMPLE | In 1994, The Dannon Company, Inc., introduced Dannon Danimals®, a line of yogurt specially developed for children. The packaging features wild animals, and Dannon donates 1.5 percent of the sales revenue to the National Wildlife Federation. One year after Danimals was introduced, the company donated more than $450,000 to the wildlife organization.

See also **image advertising**.

cause-related marketing

t r a p | 👎

If the cause has nothing to do with the product, the association will be lost and the customer will be confused. Little benefit will be derived from the strategy.

The Dannon Company donates 1.5 percent of Danimals sales to the National Wildlife Federation.

CD-ROM

tech

CD-ROM (compact disk–read only memory)   Optical storage medium popular for use with computers. Data are represented as microscopic **bits** on a plastic disk and are read by a laser.

econ   **fin**

central bank   Government authority that has a monopoly on providing a nation's currency, thereby regulating its **money supply** and financial institutions and markets.

A central bank typically requires commercial banks to hold on reserve with it a certain percentage of their deposits, giving the central bank considerable control over the nation's money stock.

Most countries, including all of the developed nations, have central banks. The central bank for the United States is the **Federal Reserve System (Fed)**.

mgmt

CERCLA   See **Comprehensive Environmental Response, Compensation, and Liability Act** and **superfund**.

Certainty Equivalents

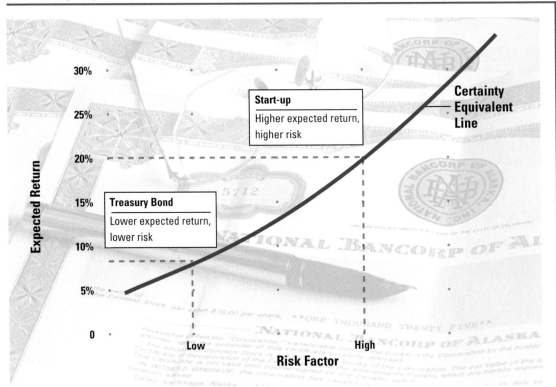

Understanding Risk

An investor feels that buying a five-year U.S. Treasury bond yielding 8 percent is about as attractive as investing in a start-up company with an expected return, if things work out, of 20 percent a year. The two options are certainty equivalents.

fin

certainty equivalents   Method of determining when an investor with a low-paying, safe investment will be willing to opt for a higher-paying, more risky investment.

acct

certified management accountant (CMA)   Designation given to someone who has passed a test and met other requirements of the **Institute of Certified Management Accountants**.

acct

certified public accountant (CPA)   An **accountant** who has met her or his state's licensing requirements.

A CPA's requirements usually include:

▶ Passing the **Uniform CPA Examination**, which is prepared and graded by the **American Institute of Certified Public Accountants (AICPA)**.

▶ Practicing as an accountant within the state for a period, often two years.

The **Securities and Exchange Commission (SEC)** requires that an independent CPA **audits** the **financial statements** of every publicly held corporation.

strat   **mgmt**   **mktg**

channel captain   Dominant manufacturer among others in a single product-supply chain.

See also **keiretsu**.

mktg

channels of distribution   Various routes that goods or services take in moving from producers to consumers.

See also **distribution channel**.

fin   **mgmt**

Chapter 7   Most common form of **bankruptcy** for individuals and privately owned companies.

Also referred to as straight bankruptcy. In Chapter 7, either there is no attempt at a reorganization or one has been attempted and failed. A court-appointed trustee gathers and liquidates all **assets** that are not exempt from a bankruptcy order, then distributes any proceeds (after fees and expenses) to the creditors. With few exceptions, all remaining debts are discharged: The debtor is not required to pay them.

central bank

The Federal Reserve Board, Washington, D.C.

certainty equivalents

t i p   👍

This perspective can help you see how big a return investors will require from your company. You can ask yourself what it would take to compete with a risk-free investment.

C

Chapter 11

Quick Facts!

- Some major companies have used the protection of Chapter 11 to gain time and bargaining power, especially when faced with big legal actions. Perhaps one of the most successful reorganizations ever was Texaco's after it lost a $10 billion court judgment to Penzoil in 1985.

  Penzoil eventually settled for $3 billion, hardly a puny sum but one that left Texaco a little room to breathe, reshuffle its assets, and emerge from bankruptcy protection. Texaco's 1994 profits were more than $900 million. (Penzoil, by the way, had a loss of almost $300 million.)

- When Orange County filed for bankruptcy in 1994, it filed under Chapter 9, which is the public sector equivalent to Chapter 11.

For a company or individual to file under Chapter 7, debts usually exceed assets. So it is almost certain that the liquidation proceeds will not cover all debts. Common shareholders of a bankrupt corporation, who are last in line to be paid, normally receive nothing. That is sometimes true also for preferred shareholders, who rank just ahead of common shareholders.

A business will file Chapter 7 when it sees no possibility of salvaging its assets and operations. If it believes a reorganization is possible, the company will use Chapter 11.

See also **common stock** and **preferred stock**.

fin   **mgmt**

Chapter 11   Bankruptcy filing involving an attempt to reorganize.

This is the most common form of bankruptcy filing for larger companies. When a business has substantial **assets**, it is likely to try a Chapter 11 reorganization rather than a **Chapter 7** bankruptcy.

In a Chapter 11 proceeding, the business may continue to operate—in most cases, without a trustee—while senior managers negotiate a financial reorganization and payment plan. Usually, the terms of debt repayment will be extended over a longer period. Creditors accept this reorganization because the eventual return is better than what would be available under the fire-sale provisions of Chapter 7. During the Chapter 11 process, the company suspends payments on

Chapter 11: Top 10 Companies Filing in 1995

By Asset Size ($ millions)

Company	Assets
Dow Corning Corp.	$ 4,093
Southwestern Life Corp. (now ICH Corp.)	$ 3,147
Trans World Airlines, Inc.	$ 2,495
Grand Union Company	$ 1,394
Rockefeller Center Properties	$ 1,250
Caldor Corporation	$ 1,136
Lomas Financial Corp.	$ 1,078
Edison Brothers Stores, Inc.	$ 894
Bradlees, Inc.	$ 885
Harrah's Jazz Co.	$ 665

Source : New Generation Research

its past debts. If the bankruptcy court decides that the company has no chance of viability as a going concern, it will order a Chapter 7 proceeding, appoint a trustee, and liquidate the business's assets.

After a decade of litigation, a U.S. Supreme Court decision in 1991 granted Chapter 11 coverage to individuals as well as businesses. Individuals may opt for Chapter 11 when they have one or more assets they want to protect from seizure and sale. The reorganization may allow them to keep those assets, sell others, and adopt a modified repayment schedule for their remaining debts.

tech

character-based interface   Computer operating system requiring the user to type in commands (as opposed to pointing to icons with a mouse, for example).

See also **graphical user interface (GUI)**.

acct

chart of accounts   Numbered list of all your company's **accounts**. It gives order and consistency to your **bookkeeping** system.

Your numbering system will reflect the order of your **balance sheet** and **income statement**. So the numbering will start with the accounts that go into current assets, the first section of your balance sheet, and end with the last category of expenses in your income statement.

character-based interface

C

Chart of Accounts (partial sample)

Category	Account	Description
Cash	1100	Cash–Operating Account
	1110	Cash–Payroll
Accounts Receivable	1200	Accounts Receivable
	1210	Allowance for Doubtful Accounts
	1220	Credit Card Receivables
Inventory	1300	Inventory–Retail / Parts
	1310	Inventory Warehouse– Retail / Parts
Prepaid Expenses	1400	Prepaid Expenses

C

chase demand

Consider the production schedule below. If you are a house painter practicing chase demand, you would focus your schedule and inventory on the "demand"—in this case probably the decorator. For example, rather than stocking up on basic paint colors, anticipating that you could use them for many jobs, you might wait to buy your paint until you know what shades the decorator has chosen.

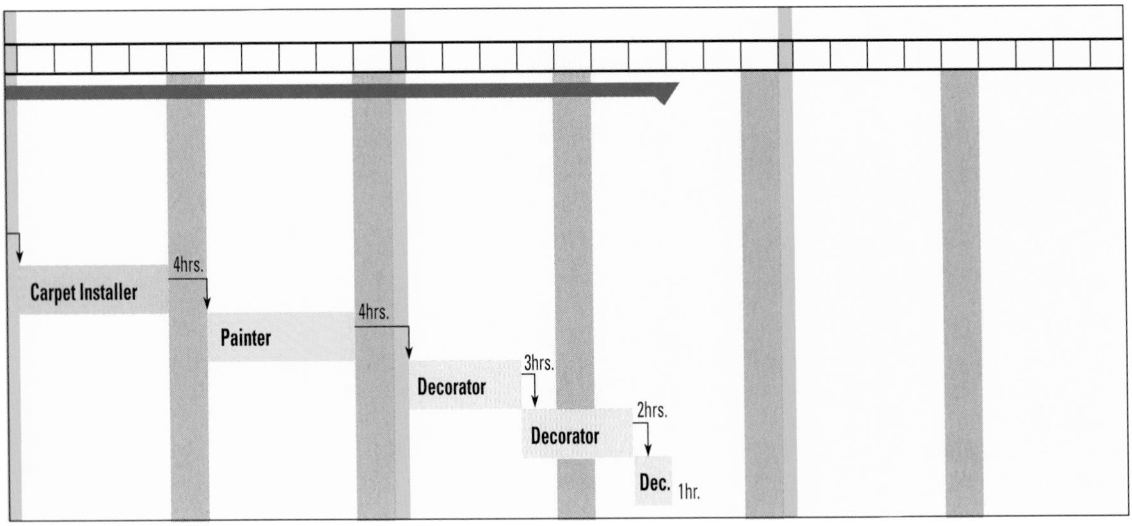

(mgmt)

charter   Comprising a certificate of incorporation issued by a state and the **articles of incorporation** filed by individuals, this legally establishes a corporation.

(oper) (strat) (mgmt)

chase demand   Manufacturing schedule that calls for small inventories and quick changes in the production rate to match demand as closely as possible.

See also **aggregate plan**.

(mktg)

cherry picking   Buyer's selection of only some items in a vendor's line. This practice is common in the computer market.

Retailers often cherry pick items from different manufacturers to create packages that offer the features and prices consumers want. On the other hand, a manufacturer may bundle its products, offering a complete system at a discounted price.

Another form of cherry picking occurs when HMOs enroll only the healthiest individuals, allowing the HMOs to remain profitable in a competitive market.

EXAMPLE │ In upgrading your office computer system, you buy Gateway computers and monitors, Hewlett Packard laser printers, Logitech mice, and Hayes modems.

See also **bundling**.

Carpet Installer

4hrs.

Painter

4hrs.

Decorator

3hrs.

Decorator

2hrs.

Dec. 1hr.

fin

Chicago Board Options Exchange (CBOE)
Most active options exchange in the United States.

The CBOE was founded in 1973 as the nation's first organized marketplace for trading **options** contracts. Before that time, options were traded through a limited number of securities firms that specialized in them.

See also **derivatives**.

fin

Chicago Mercantile Exchange (CME)
National marketplace, established in 1919, for the organized trading of **futures** contracts in numerous agricultural commodities, such as hogs, cattle, and lumber. In addition, the CME's **International Monetary Market (IMM)** division, which was organized in 1972, trades financial instruments, such as futures in foreign currencies, U.S. Treasury bills, and **Eurodollars**.

See also **derivatives**.

mktg   **mgmt**

Child Protection Act of 1966
Outlaws the sale of dangerous toys.

See also **consumer protection legislation**.

mktg

Children's Television Act of 1990
Limits the amount of advertising during children's programs to 10.5 minutes an hour on weekends and 12 minutes an hour on weekdays.

See also **consumer protection legislation**.

fin

City-State Agency Cooperation Program
Helps small and medium-sized businesses take advantage of the services of the **Export-Import Bank**.

mgmt

classification of directors
Method for choosing a company's board that puts only part of the directors up for election each year.

See also **staggered terms**.

acct   **mgmt**

clean opinion
Positive finding by an auditor that your books fairly present the company's position.

See also **audit**.

Chicago Merchantile Exchange

CHICAGO MERCANTILE EXCHANGE®

Child Protection Act of 1966

C

clearinghouse

Breaking News

Since the Securities and Exchange Commission (SEC) decided that the industry should reduce settlement time from five days to three, it is more important than ever for brokers and dealers to know their net position right away. But with brokers, dealers, and mutual funds flashing millions of trades per day back and forth, how do they figure out what they actually owe each other at the end of each trading day?

The NSCC's Continuous Net Settlement (CNS) service is a financial accounting system that does just that—it nets out each member's transactions by security and across securities. Each day, the system also gives each company its net financial settlement position with the NSCC. On that peak day in 1994, for example, CNS was able to net out the day's 2.1 million record transactions so that only $5 billion needed to change hands, rather than $93 billion.

fin

clearinghouse (1) In securities trading, a facility that delivers certificates and payments for transactions executed by **brokers**, dealers, banks, and mutual funds. (2) In banking, an organization that settles checks between member banks.

The three major securities exchanges—the **New York Stock Exchange (NYSE)**, the **American Stock Exchange (Amex)**, and the **Nasdaq Stock Market**—clear their trades through the National Securities Clearing Corporation (NSCC), a clearinghouse they jointly own. As the industry continues to automate, the brokerage houses and exchanges have been increasingly matching buyers and sellers themselves; the clearinghouse gets the money and the certificates to where they have to go.

On an average day in 1995, the NSCC, which handles 98 percent of all U.S. securities traded, cleared 1.5 million transactions worth a total of $69 billion. One peak day in 1994, 2.1 million transactions valued at $93 billion cleared through the NSCC. It has the capacity to handle twice that peak volume.

The NSCC was created in 1976. Before that, clearing occurred broker to broker. The selling broker would send a paper bill of sale to the buying broker for each transaction, specifying the number of shares of each stock and the price. The buying broker would send its bill of sale to the seller, and at the end of the day they would compare their records. Once there was an agreement, the parties either delivered or received—physically—the securities and paid for them, mostly in check form.

During the late 1960s, this cumbersome method of handling trades led to back-office problems that contributed to the demise of several brokerage firms. With the stock market booming and share volume increasing to between 15 million and 16 million shares a day, the back offices were overwhelmed by the deluge of paper. Despite working round-the-clock, the firms could not handle all the trades. In an attempt to alleviate the backlog, the NYSE went to a four-day trading week in the summer of 1968. On January 2, 1969, the exchange resumed five-day trading but with shortened sessions—from 10 A.M. to 2 P.M. In February of that year, the first attempts at automation began, and by July the exchange was able to lengthen the trading day by 30 minutes. But regular closings (3:30 P.M. back then) did not resume until May 1970. As late as the 1970s, trades were still recorded on paper tickets on the floor of the NYSE. Today, they are all entered into computers.

Options and **futures** are settled through separate clearinghouse operations, such as the Options Clearing Corporation in Chicago. In the banking industry, the concept of clearinghouses originated in the late 1700s in Scotland, spreading to the United States in 1853. Early clearinghouses took it upon themselves to assume the role that is played today by **central banks** during banking panics—some even printing their own money and insuring deposits of member banks. Clearinghouses also started monitoring member banks, a precursor to modern banking regulation.

In the United States, most bank clearing functions are now handled by **electronic funds transfer (EFT)**.

FRAME OF REFERENCE

client/server network

Using your personal computer on a **local area network (LAN)**, you have prepared a spreadsheet using an applications program and data stored in your LAN's server, which doubles as the printer server. Now you are ready to print, so your PC (the client) lets the server know, and the server sends back a message that your job is fourth in line for the printer on your floor. You can wait or have the job run sooner on a more distant printer. You decide to wait.

tech

client/server network   Most common type of computer network.

In this arrangement, the mighty know-it-all computers are the servers. They hold many of the applications and files. The other computers in the network are clients, which ask for what they need from the servers.

A computer called a **printer server** can also manage one or more printers shared by the users of the network.

acct

close the books   Process whereby all revenue and expense **accounts** are reduced to zero, and the resultant net income or net loss is transferred to an **owner's equity** account. This procedure is done at the end of a period to prepare the accounts for the next period's transactions. Also known as the closing process.

See also **accounting period** and **fiscal year**.

acct

CMA   See **certified management accountant** and **Institute of Management Accountants (IMA)**.

mgmt

coaching   (1) Managing employees by giving advice and encouragement instead of merely making assignments. (2) Assigning employees a mentor, or coach, who helps them get comfortable with a new task.

Coaching contrasts with the other two main methods where a rookie learns needed skills—trial and error (the sink-or-swim method) and formal training. Coaching is getting thumbs up because it brings out skills that cannot be taught in a classroom.

You can use coaching informally as well as through formal mentoring programs, but either way the coach needs a lot of interpersonal skill. Unlike more authoritarian approaches to teaching new tasks, coaching encourages employees to approach problems in their own way with support from the coach. Some believe that appropriate coaching by a more experienced peer boosts the employee's self-confidence more effectively than do instructions from the boss.

coaching

The complexity inherent in today's business environment means that the autocrat is no longer in a position to make better decisions than 'subordinates' are able to make collectively, can no longer be sufficiently omniscient to monitor everything, nor omnipresent enough to take all corrective actions needed.

—Max Landsberg, in *The Tao of Coaching*

co-branding

cognitive dissonance

EXAMPLE

An employee believes that strict compliance to regulations is a given in his job. But to save money, his boss tells him to cut some corners. The employee will experience internal conflict until he either gives up his original idea or leaves to work for another, more ethical employer.

mktg

co-branding   When two or more companies sponsor a product under combined **brands**.

The term is used most often for **affinity cards**, like the General Motors MasterCard, which gives users of the card credit toward the purchase of a new GM car.

mgmt

cognitive dissonance   Emotional tension created when a person gains some knowledge that goes against his or her opinions and values. The tension arises from a person's need for consistency.

Cognitive dissonance can be used as a device to change employee attitudes. For example, if assembly line workers dislike the idea of using new automated tools, cognitive dissonance can be created by installing a few of the tools in an off-line test area. Invite the employees to try the tools. As more do, and tell their coworkers how helpful the tools actually are, employees will slowly abandon their preconceived attitudes.

econ

coincident economic indicators   Index, comprising four components, that acts like a mirror on the current state of the U.S. economy.

The four index components are:

1 Employees on nonagricultural payrolls.

2 **Personal income** minus payments such as Social Security, veterans' benefits, and welfare payments.

3 An index of **industrial production**.

4 Manufacturing and trade sales in constant dollars.

The index of coincident economic indicators is published monthly by the U.S. Commerce Department's Bureau of Economic Analysis.

See also **lagging economic indicators** and **leading economic indicators**.

mgmt   **econ**

COLA   See **cost of living adjustment**.

mktg

cold calling   Contacting a potential customer who has no previous knowledge or specific interest in your product or service.

Coincident Indicator Index

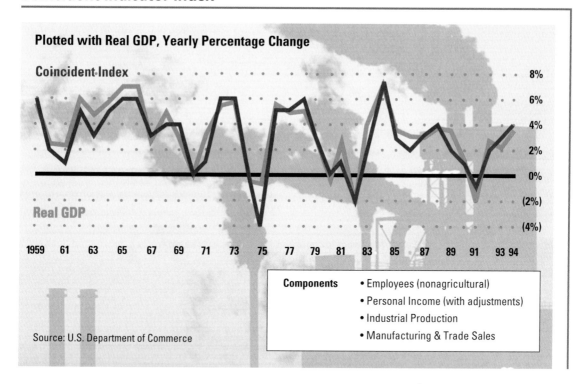

Plotted with Real GDP, Yearly Percentage Change

Coincident Index

8%
6%
4%
2%
0%
(2%)
(4%)

Real GDP

1959 61 63 65 67 69 71 73 75 77 79 81 83 85 87 89 91 93 94

Components	• Employees (nonagricultural)
	• Personal Income (with adjustments)
	• Industrial Production
	• Manufacturing & Trade Sales

Source: U.S. Department of Commerce

Both door-to-door salespeople and telemarketers employ this technique using a canned sales pitch. Of the two, telemarketing is a lot more cost-effective because one person can contact more consumers over a greater geographical area in less time. Sometimes telemarketers use **cold canvassing** to develop a list of potential customers, called leads, for salespeople to follow up on.

EXAMPLE | Smith is a financial advisor in a stock brokerage house. She hires Jones to cold canvass for her. Jones makes calls in neighborhoods where people fit the target market profile. In the cold canvassing, Jones asks about the individuals' plans to manage their retirement funds. When he identifies someone about to make a major financial move, he gives the information to Smith, who follows up.

See also **personal communications channels, purchase-decision process,** and **relationship marketing**.

mktg

cold canvassing   Developing a list of potential customers for salespeople to use in a **cold calling** sales campaign.

fin

collapsed equity test   A **covenant** on a **bond** that requires the issuer to make accelerated payments into a **sinking fund** if the company's total **shareholders' equity** on the **balance sheet** falls below a set value. Also called a **net worth requirement**.

cold calling

column inch

mktg

column inch   Basic unit of measurement that newspapers (and some magazines) use to bill for print advertisements. Also known as agate lines.

See also **advertising rates**.

Newspaper Ad Rates

			Western Region	Eastern Region
Non-Contract Rate per Column Inch			$9.00	$15.00

Contract Volume and Frequency Rates

Column Inch or	Days	Discount	Line Rate	Line Rate
3,500	26	3.5%	$9.00	$15.00
5,000	52	6.0	8.00	14.00
10,000	All issues	11.0	8.00	14.00
20,000		15.0	8.00	13.00
30,000		17.0	7.00	13.00
40,000		18.0	7.00	12.00
50,000		19.0	7.00	12.00

---

mktg

combination rate   Discount given to an advertiser for running an ad in more than one outlet owned by a newspaper, broadcast, or magazine chain.

See also **advertising rates**.

fin

comfort letter   Attachment to a securities registration or legal agreement saying that certain conditions have been or will be met.

In a securities **underwriting**, the letter comes from an independent auditor and states that the information in the registration statement and **prospectus** was correctly prepared and that there have been no material changes since its preparation. The letter does not say that the information is correct, only that there is no evidence that it is incorrect. For this reason, it is sometimes called a cold comfort letter.

In a legal agreement, a comfort letter usually specifies actions—not listed in the formal agreement—that will or will not be taken. It is also called a declaration of intent because it states what one of the parties intends to do. It is not part of the legally binding contract.

fin

commercial paper   Short-term securities sold by large corporations and other institutions.

These **unsecured** notes, with maturities of 2 to 270 days, usually provide short-term **working capital** for the issuer. Commercial paper is bought mostly by other large institutions. These investors like commercial paper because it lets them put their cash to work in a relatively secure way (it is almost always backed by a bank letter of credit) without tying it up for long.

Commercial paper is usually sold at a discount from face value; the investor receives the interest when the note is redeemed at face value. Commercial paper is rated by both Moody's Investors Service and **Standard & Poor's (S&P)**.

 mgmt   **mktg**   **fin**

commission   Incentive-based pay scale directly related to the revenue a salesperson generates.

Salespeople can be compensated by commissions only, straight salary, or a base pay plus commissions.

The advantages of commissions are:

▶ Direct financial motivation for the sales force; the more they sell, the more money they take home.

▶ Management's ability to direct sales activity by attaching higher commissions on targeted products.

The disadvantages are:

▶ Inadequate attention by salespeople to nonselling tasks—like providing customer service or completing sales reports.

▶ The potential for high-pressure sales tactics that undermine the company name.

▶ Overcompetitiveness among the salespeople, resulting in lower morale and higher turnover.

mktg   **fin**   **econ**

commodity   Product or service that is unspecialized—like corn, bricks, or nails—and in fairly steady demand.

The concern for marketers: If consumers do not perceive a difference in the same product offered by several companies, they will purchase based solely on price.

---

commercial paper
Breaking News

Most commercial paper is issued by finance companies, which may be related to banks or equipment manufacturers. In the latter case, the paper is issued to provide financing for the equipment manufacturer's customers. All three major U.S. automakers have finance companies that arrange loans for dealers and the people who buy their cars and trucks. General Motors Acceptance Corporation (GMAC) is one of the biggest issuers of commercial paper in the United States. Its commercial paper outstanding was believed to exceed $16 billion in March 1995.

commission
tip | 👍

You can restructure your sales incentive packages to include customer satisfaction indexes (CSIs). Customer satisfaction and its effect on repeat business is critical to **relationship marketing**.

C

commodity

EXAMPLE

Logitech faced the dilemma of marketing a PC mouse, which consumers basically considered a commodity product. It decided to custom-tailor a variety of mice, like a Kidz Mouse, a left-handed mouse, a cordless radio mouse, and so on. This strategy helped Logitech capture 40 percent of the global mouse market.

common stock

tip |

Issuing common stock increases a company's equity base. A good time to issue stock is when the investment community likes your company and your stock price is high.

You can do one of two things to avoid the commodization of your product:

1 Differentiate your product.

2 Provide service as a differential advantage.

EXAMPLE | Although all baby foods may be similar, one way Gerber sets itself apart is by offering a toll-free hot line around the clock, every day of the year, to answer the questions of anxious moms and dads on the care and feeding of babies and toddlers.

See also **differentiated marketing, differentiation, market segmentation,** and **undifferentiated marketing.**

 fin

commodity futures   Standardized contracts that lock in a commodities transaction at a certain price on a specific future date. These are traded on the **Chicago Mercantile Exchange**, the Chicago Board of Trade, and the New York Coffee, Sugar, and Cocoa Exchange, among others.

See also **derivatives**.

 **mktg**   **fin**   **econ**   **strat**

Common Market   Alliance of European nations.

See also **European Union (EU)**.

 acct

common-size financial statement   Comparative analysis of financial data that expresses items in a specific period as percentages of a given base. For example, the amounts listed on a company's annual **income statement** might be stated in terms of share of total revenue.

 fin

common stock   Share in a company's ownership.

Common stockholders supply equity capital and usually have voting rights and elect the board of directors. This allows majority shareholders to indirectly control the company. Shareholders may benefit from a company's success through the receipt of income (in the form of **dividends**) and through capital appreciation (a rise in the stock price). If a company declares **bankruptcy**, holders of common stock have only a residual claim to assets—behind creditors, debt holders, the IRS, and preferred shareholders—making them the last in line to collect.

See also **capital stock** and **equity**.

Stock certificate from Premiere Radio Networks

mktg

comparison advertising   Naming, or strongly suggesting, the name of a competitor in an ad.

EXAMPLE | The volleys between AT&T and MCI in the mid-1980s went so far as MCI TV commercials portraying an older woman crying over AT&T prices. In the spot, which featured a husband and wife at the dinner table, the husband tries to console his wife as she sobs uncontrollably. "Have you been talking to our son long distance again?" he asks. She manages to shake her head yes. After further questions fail to reveal what is wrong, he says, with some exasperation, "What on earth are you crying for?" Choking back more tears, the woman responds, "Have you seen our long-distance bill?"

strat   **mgmt**   **mktg**

competitive advantage   Strengths and strategies that keep a company ahead of its competitors.

It is hard to measure competitive advantage and harder to maintain it. Some competitive advantages are fleeting. The successful companies are those that leverage their competitive advantage successfully and repeatedly.

common stock

t r a p

Although issuing equity will have no ongoing effects on your cash flow (unlike interest payment on bonds), current shareholders will be diluted.

comparison advertising

t i p

Comparison advertising can work especially well when competition is fierce and you are not the market leader. If you are the dominant player, you might consider whether naming a competitor will enhance its exposure and name recognition. It is the same reasoning used by political candidates. A strong front-runner is not likely to name his or her opponent.

competitive advantage

EXAMPLE

Kodak's strong **brand equity** and long-standing **marketing** edge make it hard for competing films to get a foothold. Those familiar yellow boxes, easily recognizable to customers, line the store shelves. Another leader, De Beers, controls about 80 percent of the world's rough diamond supply, which makes it relatively easy for the company to sell half of the world's diamonds.

EXAMPLE | As the company that created the spreadsheet for PCs, Lotus led the way through much of the 1980s with its 1-2-3. But Lotus did not foresee the success that Windows would have and failed to develop a version of 1-2-3 for it until 1991. By then Microsoft's Excel had moved in to dominate the market.

A sustainable competitive advantage usually has one of three characteristics:

1 Privileged access to customers.

2 Size or momentum within the market.

3 Restraints on competition.

EXAMPLE | Visible antennas are prohibited by the covenants of many planned communities. That makes it hard for companies offering TV service via satellite. Those companies are also prohibited from offering local programming. For both of those reasons the franchise-holding cable company in any community has a competitive advantage.

acct   mgmt

compliance audit   Examination to determine if a company is following specific rules.

See also **audit**.

FRAME OF REFERENCE

competitive advantage

Microsoft Corporation is in a class by itself when it comes to exploiting competitive advantage. IBM chose Microsoft in 1980 to write the operating system for its new personal computers. Microsoft produced DOS for IBM and then licensed it to more than 100 companies turning out IBM clones. Since it knew more than anyone else about the operating system for PCs, Microsoft had a head start on applications software like word-processing and spreadsheet programs. Over the years its applications programs became leaders.

In the mid-1980s, Microsoft developed the Windows operating system, giving PCs some of the power and ease of use that had been associated with Apple computers. Microsoft continued to dominate the software industry as it built applications for Windows. But, never satisfied, in the mid-1990s the company continued to fight for two markets it did not yet dominate—information services like America Online, CompuServe, and Prodigy, and groupware like Lotus Notes, which is a type of operating system for networks. Its control over the operating system for PCs has given Microsoft an edge it does not want to lose as networks become more important.

Microsoft®

econ

composite indexes of economic indicators Tools for assessing economic activity.

See also **coincident economic indicators**, **lagging economic indicators**, and **leading economic indicators**.

mgmt

Comprehensive Environmental Response, Compensation, and Liability Act (CERCLA) Federal program that holds companies accountable for paying to clean up toxic waste sites.

See also **superfund**.

mgmt

compressed work week Way of giving workers some flexibility in setting their hours.

Businesses that use this alternative scheduling approach allow employees to put in their hours over four days instead of five. Some might try to do a week's work in three days, but usually it means working four 10-hour days rather than five 8-hour days. This arrangement gives employees three days off and cuts down on commuting time.

Business owners who have had good luck with the system say it increases morale and well-being since employees enjoy a substantial period away from work each week; during this time they can pursue other interests, spend more hours with family, or simply accomplish life's tasks at an easier pace. These employers also claim that the compressed work week can increase productivity by keeping workers fresh and help attract new employees.

See also **flextime** and **job sharing**.

oper **tech** **mgmt**

computer-integrated manufacturing (CIM) Linking a range of manufacturing processes through a computer system.

By combining some of the new computer capabilities—like computer-aided design (CAD), computer-aided engineering (CAE), and computer-aided manufacturing (CAM)—into one sophisticated system, companies can produce products more efficiently than ever before. They can also reduce a lot of the direct costs involved in the manufacturing process.

oper **mgmt**

concurrent engineering Product design performed by a team integrating several functions whose work would otherwise be carried out sequentially.

The purpose is to include inputs from manufacturing, suppliers, and marketing early in the design process, and to shorten design cycles.

---

competitive advantage

Quick Facts!

In the 1970s, Wal-Mart achieved virtual monopoly in some small Sunbelt towns by setting up shop where only one discount outlet could operate profitably. By arranging stores in rings around local distribution centers, Wal-Mart reduced its distribution costs by 50 percent. As a result, for a decade or two, competitors like Kmart found themselves excluded from some local markets—although today the dramatic growth of the Sunbelt towns and cities has restored opportunities for the competitors.

compressed work week

C

C

concurrent engineering

Rather than a sequential chain going from, say, a research group to a design group and on to manufacturing and then the customer, concurrent engineering involves a joint effort by all the groups with a stake in the outcome. The supplier can advise on the availability of materials. The customer can make her or his needs clear. Each group in the company can work for ideal conditions. In the end, concurrent engineering should reduce the cost and improve the quality of the product while bringing it to market more quickly.

EXAMPLE | In a drive to improve efficiency, GE Aircraft Engines brought concurrent engineering into its design processes. Now, it can get engines from conceptual phase to testing 17 months faster at almost half the cost.

strat **fin** **mgmt**

conglomerate   Corporation comprising a variety of companies offering different business lines.

Conglomerates were a popular form of business in the 1960s, but the complexity of managing such diverse operations has made them less appealing. Many conglomerates sold off pieces of themselves to concentrate on core businesses in the 1980s and 1990s. Litton Industries, for example, divested its subsidiaries, including Stouffer Foods and Hewitt-Robbins, so it could focus on its defense and aerospace divisions. And ITT Corp. spun off insurance and electronics divisions in 1995, leaving the parent company to concentrate on its hospitality and gambling businesses.

See also **core competencies** and **diversification**.

mgmt **mktg**

conjoint analysis   Way of sizing up how important various combinations of **product attributes** are to consumers.

This may involve surveying potential customers. You ask them to rank the importance of various attributes and to indicate which combinations of features they would be willing to buy and at what price.

Results from a conjoint analysis can tell you which features your product should include, how much of each feature it should include, and how they should be combined.

acct

conservatism concept   Idea that **accountants** are supposed to be pessimists by anticipating all losses but no gains.

Whenever there is doubt about which estimate to use in accounting, you pick the one that yields less net income or a lower **asset** value. Another way of looking at it is that you account for probable bad news as soon as you can put a number on it but recognize good news only when you have collected the money.

conglomerate
Breaking News

Procter & Gamble is one of the most well-known conglomerates in the United States, with its growth based largely on its willingness to move into entirely new industries. P&G got its first break with the introduction of Ivory Soap in the late 1800s. The company has since participated in a number of broad-based industries, varying from health care (with products like Nyquil) to cosmetics (Cover Girl, Max Factor).

Most recently, P&G has tested the waters in the entertainment industry with a new alliance in 1995 to develop television programming. Of course, this is not P&G's first experience with TV—they were the first sponsor of daytime dramas—hence the term "soap operas."

FRAME OF REFERENCE

conjoint analysis

Nikon Corporation—whose Nikonos V is the leader in high-quality underwater cameras—was mulling over introducing a new model. Technical problems make it difficult and expensive to include features like a through-the-lens viewfinder and autofocus in an underwater camera, and it was improved user-friendly attributes like these that Nikon wanted to include in its new model.

It held a series of focus groups with scuba divers who take pictures. These underwater-photo enthusiasts were asked about the features individually and in combination, and how much they would pay for various combinations. Eventually, Nikon decided to release a new model that includes many of the new features.

C

EXAMPLE | In 1995, Mobil Corporation announced a streamlining that would eliminate about 4,700 jobs. It would take a while to implement, so many of the people involved would not actually get their pink slips until 1996. But, in 1995, as soon as Mobil determined the number of jobs it was eliminating, it was obliged to take a $300 million after-tax charge to earnings. That was to cover anticipated separation pay and other expenses involved. The eventual benefits, expected to reach more than $1 billion a year, would not hit the books until they actually materialized.

See also **adequate disclosure concept**, **consistency concept**, **matching concept**, and **materiality concept**.

consignment

mktg

consignment   Arrangement where a vendor can return unsold goods.

Consignment can be from manufacturers to wholesalers or from wholesalers to retailers. The vendor may pay in advance but return any unsold goods for full credit, as with newspapers and magazines. Or the vendor may display and sell items owned by someone else, making payment only when a sale is completed. Art galleries are a common example of that arrangement.

acct

consistency concept   Idea that you use the same accounting methods year after year unless there is good reason to change, perhaps to more accurately reflect your company's performance.

The reader of your **financial statements** should be able to assume that the numbers you come up with this year are based on the same accounting procedures as last year's numbers, and so on. That is the

C

consolidation

reason for the consistency concept. If you do change an accounting method—say your way of valuing inventories—you need to disclose what you are doing and show the effects in your financial reports. Sometimes you will restate earlier years' results so that they are all consistent.

See also **adequate disclosure concept**, **conservatism concept**, **inventory valuation**, **matching concept**, and **materiality concept**.

acct　**fin**

consolidation　Reporting the **financial statements** of the parent company and its **subsidiaries** as if they were one entity in terms of **assets**, **liabilities**, and operating results.

In general, accounting principles call for consolidation when one company owns more than 50 percent of another's common stock. The precept applies even if the businesses are so dissimilar that it might seem to make more sense to report them separately. So even conglomerates like Berkshire Hathaway report their businesses on a consolidated basis. General Electric does make a separate category for General Electric Capital Services and some other units but then totals them to a consolidated number.

Consolidation does not mean that important information on a company's various businesses is obscured, however. If, among other things, a publicly held company gets 10 percent or more of its revenue from a second industry, it must make separate disclosures concerning revenues, operating profits, and assets somewhere in the **annual report**. That is called **segment reporting**.

See also **affiliated company**.

fin　**strat**

consortium　Group of companies working together and sharing resources to achieve a common objective or engage in a project that benefits all.

A consortium sometimes entails common ownership. A group of oil companies, for example, may form a consortium to explore in a high-risk frontier area like Siberia. They share the cost and agree to joint ownership of any oil that they find and can produce.

fin

Consumer Credit Protection Act of 1986　Requires lenders to disclose all terms and conditions of finance charges.

See also **consumer protection legislation**.

mgmt

Consumer Goods Pricing Act of 1975   Forbids pricing
agreements between manufacturers and resellers in interstate commerce.

See also **consumer protection legislation**.

mktg

consumer market   Buyers of goods and services for personal
or family use.

This contrasts with the **industrial market**. The U.S. consumer market
numbers well over 250 million people who spend trillions of dollars
annually. Skyrocketing in importance for American businesses is the
globalization of the consumer market.

The consumer market is distinguished by a broad array of products
and numerous (large and small) purchases over a widespread, international area that involves a huge number of buyers and sellers.

To understand consumer markets, market research looks at the
characteristics that influence the **purchase-decision process**. The
key issue is what stimuli trigger the hoped-for response—buying
your product.

See also **market**, **market segmentation**, **mass market**, and **target market**.

econ   **fin**

consumer price index (CPI)   Most common measure of **infla-
tion** in the United States, usually expressed on an annualized basis.

The Bureau of Labor Statistics computes the change in the level of
consumer prices monthly based on changes in the prices of a representative "basket" of goods and services that a typical urban
consumer is believed to buy.

Surveys are used to determine what items and how much of them
make up the basket, but the basket changes more slowly than consumers do. When prices for fresh fish rise, for example, many
consumers switch immediately to beef or chicken, but basket adjustments lag far behind. Similarly, when gasoline prices rise, people
drive less, carpool, and use more public transportation, while the
basket still includes a set quantity of gasoline.

In addition, the CPI does not account for changes in retailing, like
the huge popularity of discount stores in recent years, nor does it
assess product-quality changes or the introduction of new goods
and services. For these reasons, the CPI tends to overstate inflation,
or changes in the "cost of living."

consumer market

*You have to talk to each
demographic group indi-
vidually, and you have to
say to them, 'We under-
stand you, we understand
your lifestyle, we under-
stand your culture, and
you're important to us.'*

—David Green, Senior VP of
Marketing, McDonald's

**consumer price
index**

Consumer Price Index (CPI), Annual Change, 1950–1994

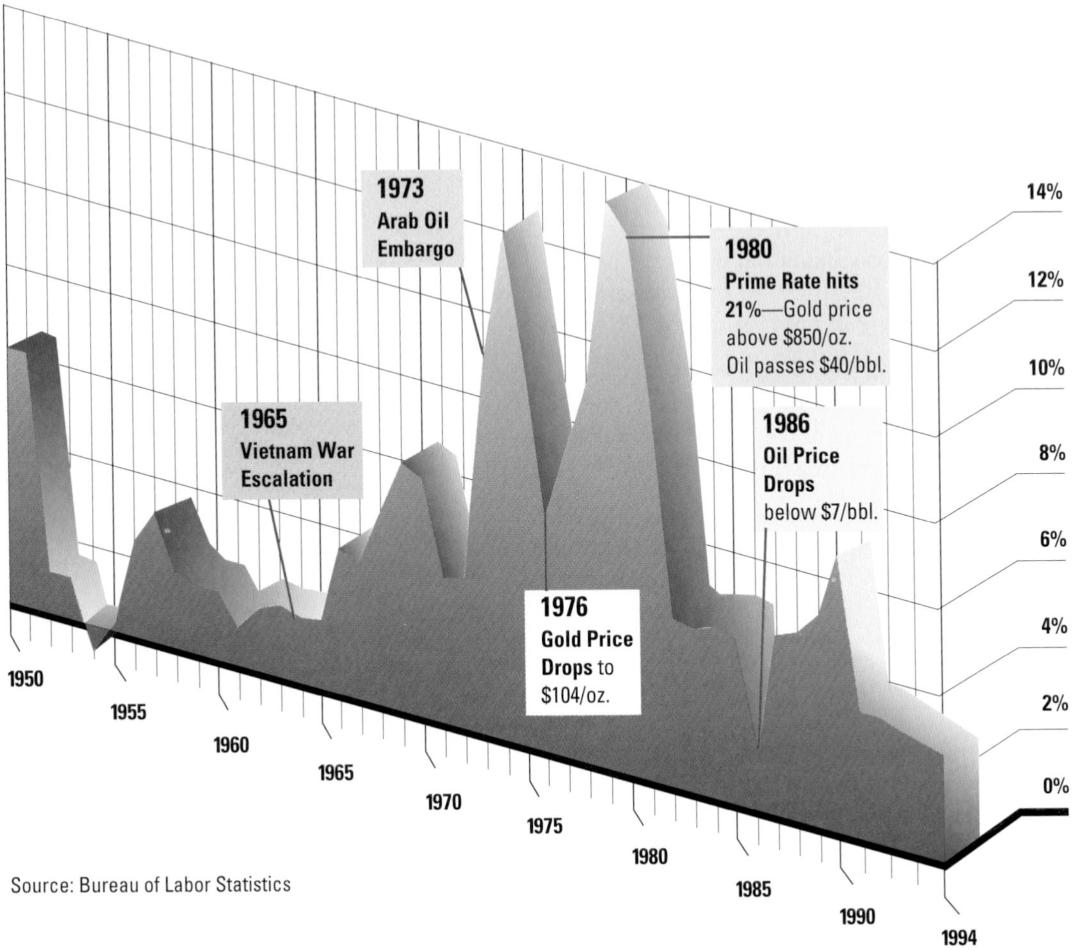

C

1973
Arab Oil
Embargo

1980
Prime Rate hits
21%—Gold price
above $850/oz.
Oil passes $40/bbl.

1965
Vietnam War
Escalation

1986
Oil Price
Drops
below $7/bbl.

1976
Gold Price
Drops to
$104/oz.

14%

12%

10%

8%

6%

4%

2%

0%

1950

1955

1960

1965

1970

1975

1980

1985

1990

1994

Source: Bureau of Labor Statistics

---

mgmt

Consumer Product Safety Act of 1972   Legislation that created the U.S. Consumer Product Safety Commission, which has the power to establish consumer product safety standards.

See also **consumer protection legislation**.

mgmt   **mktg**

consumer protection legislation   Laws designed to safeguard the consumer's well-being.

Below are some of the laws illustrating the scope of areas under which consumers are protected:

▶ **Food and Drug Act of 1906**
   Prohibiting the interstate manufacture, transport, or sale of adulterated, unsafe, or fraudulently labeled foods or drugs.

► **The Child Protection Act of 1966**
Outlawing the sale of dangerous toys, amended in 1969 to include products with electrical, mechanical, or thermal hazards.

► **Fair Packaging and Labeling Act of 1966**
Outlining basic information that must be included on the labels or packaging of most consumer products. The label gives the contents, the quantity, and the maker. Amendments passed in 1992 required the quantity's conversion into a metric measurement from 1994 on.

► **The National Environmental Policy Act (1970)**
Establishing the Environmental Protection Agency (EPA) as a watchdog over governmental policy on pollution.

► **The Consumer Product Safety Act (1972)**
Setting up the Consumer Product Safety Commission with authority to create and enforce safety standards for consumer products.

► **Magnuson-Moss Warranty / Federal Trade Commission Improvement Act (1975)**
Requiring manufacturers to clearly state the terms of their warranties. The act also requires that the warranties be displayed and available to customers in stores for all products that cost more than $25. Customers can file class-action suits over violations of the act.

► **The Consumer Goods Pricing Act (1975)**
Prohibiting manufacturers and resellers in interstate commerce from setting price agreements.

► **Toy Safety Act (1984)**
Letting the government recall dangerous toys quickly.

► **Consumer Credit Protection Act (1986)**
Requiring lenders to disclose all terms and conditions of finance charges.

► **Children's Television Act (1990)**
Limiting the amount of advertising during children's programs to 10.5 minutes an hour on weekends and 12 minutes an hour on weekdays.

► **Americans with Disabilities Act (ADA) (1991)**
Protecting the rights of people with disabilities in public accommodations, transportation, and telecommunications.

consumer protection legislation

`oper`

consumer's risk When you accept a bad lot of a manufactured item because random sample testing shows a disproportionately small number of defects.

See also **acceptance sampling** and **random sampling**.

econ

consumption tax   Tax levied on money spent rather than money earned.

Perhaps the simplest form, one in force in all but a handful of U.S. states, is the sales tax. **The value-added tax (VAT)** is another form, common outside the United States.

A tax on money earned that we are all familiar with is the income tax. In recent years, economists have debated the merits of replacing all or part of the U.S. income tax with a comprehensive consumption tax—a national sales tax, a VAT, or a third alternative: a tax on the difference between what you earn and what you add to savings each year. Some economists favor a consumption tax over an income tax because the former encourages **savings**, which boosts the supply of capital available for growing the economy. Opponents argue that a consumption tax would take a higher proportion of income from lower-income people who generally save less than do those with higher incomes.

continuous improvement

The kaizen concept is crucial to understanding the differences between the Japanese and Western approaches to managment. If asked to name the most important difference between Japanese and Western management concepts, I would unhesitatingly say, 'Japanese kaizen and its process-oriented way of thinking versus the West's innovation- and results-oriented thinking.'

—Masaaki Imai, *Kaizen: The Key to Japan's Competitive Success*

mgmt

continuous improvement   Ongoing betterment involving everyone in a company—from the top echelon all the way down the line.

The philosophy was born in Japan, where it is called **kaizen**. Continuous improvement does not focus on big innovations and breakthroughs; it is a day-to-day approach to work—the constant quest for continuous, incremental improvement on all fronts.

A lot of U.S. companies have adopted the continuous improvement philosophy, including Colgate-Palmolive, which has a director of continuous improvement at the corporate level.

Kaizen also serves as an umbrella term in Japan for **total quality management** and other current concepts like the **just-in-time (JIT) inventory system**, **robotics**, productivity improvement, customer orientation, and cooperative labor-management relations.

contribution margin

mgmt   **econ**

contribution margin (CM)   Sales revenues of a product or service less the **variable costs** (such as materials and labor).

A company analyzes contribution margins to determine if it can make a profit on a new product line or additional orders, or if it should discontinue a certain product or service as **variable costs** such as labor and materials change.

Contribution	= Sales
Margin	− Variable Costs

The contribution margin is calculated by subtracting variable costs from sales revenues since fixed costs, by definition, will not change with output.

EXAMPLE | Throughout the spring, a toy maker has been selling 50,000 units a month of a baseball bat and ball set, sold to retailers for $15. Revenue is $750,000 a month. Fixed costs are $5 a set, or $250,000, and variable costs are $8 a set, or $400,000. Thus, total cost is $650,000, for a profit of $100,000.

A major chain that has just expanded decides it will hold a nationwide grand opening sale honoring its new stores. It wants an extra 5,000 units, but at $10 a set to offset the expected sale price. The toy maker has enough idle capacity to meet the order without increasing its fixed costs. Should it accept? To decide, it calculates the contribution margin of the additional 5,000 sets:

Sales revenues	(5,000 x $10)	$50,000
Less variable costs	(5,000 x $8)	$40,000
Contribution margin		$10,000

The company concludes that it is well worth the extra variable costs to meet the order.

See also **marginal cost** and **marginal revenue**.

---

strat

control   Ability to influence your environment.

Control is a vital factor in predicting the likelihood of management's success during critical times.

---

fin

conversion price   The price at which the underlying security can be exchanged into another security, usually expressed as a dollar value. To determine how many shares a **convertible bond** would be exchangeable for, divide $1,000 by the conversion price. For example, a bond convertible at $20 means that each $1,000 **debenture** can be exchanged for 50 common shares of the issuing corporation.

If the price is not stated, you can calculate it by dividing the face value of the security by the **conversion ratio**—the number of shares you will receive.

Conversion Price	=	Face Value of Convertible Security
	÷	Conversion Ratio

---

conversion price

EXAMPLE

A $1,000 bond is convertible into 40 shares of common stock. The conversion price is:

$1,000 ÷ 40 = $25

C

conversion ratio

EXAMPLE

A $1,000 bond is convertible into common stock at a conversion price of $25 per share. The conversion ratio is:

$1,000 ÷ $25 = 40

The conversion ratio is 40:1. Each $1,000 bond can be converted into 40 shares of common stock.

convertible bond

tip

By issuing convertible rather than straight debt, a company can usually get a lower interest rate as well as a longer maturity.

trap

A convertible bond issue can also have drawbacks. If things go well, the bond becomes equity, which dilutes the ownership of the company. And if business does poorly, the bond remains as debt on the balance sheet, which can hurt a company's future financing plans.

fin

conversion ratio   Number of **common stock** shares that an investor can get in return for a **convertible security**—usually a **convertible bond** or a share of **convertible preferred stock**.

If the ratio is not stated, you can calculate it by dividing the face value of the security by the **conversion price**—the per-share value of the stock you will receive.

$$\text{Conversion Ratio} = \frac{\text{Face Value of Convertible Security}}{\text{Conversion Price}}$$

fin

convertible bond   A **bond** that can be exchanged for a specified number of shares of **common stock** usually at a predetermined price in the future.

A convertible bond is typically an **unsecured debt** obligation of a company and would rank above preferred and common stock in the event of a bankruptcy. In addition to scheduled interest payments, equity participation is offered to the investor by convertibles if the

FRAME OF REFERENCE

"Busted Converts": A Case Study of Comdisco

In April 1983, a computer leasing company called Comdisco issued $250 million of **convertible bonds** maturing May 1, 2003. At that time, Comdisco's star was rapidly rising. Its revenues had almost doubled in the previous three years, and its stock, trading at $20 in 1983, was at an all-time high. The bond was issued with an 8-percent coupon and had an exercise price of $24.33, which was 21 percent over the then-current stock price.

Later that year, the company's method of booking profits and stock sales by management was brought into question. Comdisco's stock plummeted from $26 to $15 that month and eventually traded around $8 for most of 1984.

By the middle of 1984, investors looking at the Comdisco's convertibles were unlikely to see them as a compelling equity play. Despite a clean report from the IRS, the exercise price of $24.33 looked decidedly out of reach. In July 1984, the bond was trading at 57 cents on the dollar, with a **yield** to maturity of 14.84 percent and a premium over its equity value of around 90 percent. This could be considered an example of a busted convertible bond, or a *busted convert*.

Four years later, by 1988, Comdisco was thriving. Its revenues had more than doubled and its net income was up by 159 percent. As for the convertibles issued in 1983, they traded well over par value and were finally called in March 1987, at a price of $105.60. (See also Frame of Reference on page 157).

stock price rises above the conversion price. Convertible bonds are booked as debt on the **balance sheet** unless they are converted to **equity**. Because of the **equity kicker**, the **coupon rate** is typically lower than that of a comparable straight bond of similar seniority and credit quality. Although convertible bonds can be short term, they are typically long-term obligations (i.e., 15 years or longer).

Convertible Bond New Term Sheet

Issue Description: $250,000,000 COMDISCO, INC., 8% Convertible Subordinated Debentures Due May 1, 2003 (Interest payable May 1 and November 1)

Trade Date:	April 27, 1983
Settlement Date:	May 1, 1983

Price:	$1000	**Yield to Maturity:**	8%
❶ Conversion Price:	$35-1/2	**Rating:**	Baz/BB+
❷ No. of Shares:	27.397	**Stock at Pricing:**	30-1/4
Stock Symbol:	CDO	**Listing:**	NYSE

❸ Conversion Premium: 20.66%

Stock Price at Filing: 28-3/4 (April 21, 1983)

❹ Call Feature: Two years noncall; 140% provision test

❺ Sinking Fund: 75% prior to maturity; begins May 1, 1993, and retires 18,750,000 annually

❻ Average Life: 5.9 years (March 16, 1999)

See also **conversion price, conversion ratio, convertible preferred stock, convertible security,** and **exchangeable debenture**.

---

convertible bond

In the sample term sheet to the left, the following components are the most important in a convertible bond transaction:

❶ Conversion Price
The set price at which the bonds may be converted into common stock.

❷ Number of Shares
The amount of shares that the $1,000 face value will convert into at the conversion price ($1,000 ÷ $36-1/2).

❸ Conversion Premium
The percentage by which the conversion price ($36-1/2) exceeds the stock at pricing ($30-1/4).

❹ Call Feature
The bond may not be called by the company for two years.

❺ Sinking Fund
The company is required to retire 75 percent of the $250 million issuance prior to maturity. The schedule begins in 1993, with $18.75 million to be retired each year.

❻ Average Life
A "weighted average" of the bond's life that takes into account the retirements from the sinking fund requirements.

Quick Facts!

convertible bond

Because of the equity component in convertible bonds, some investors use them in a form of **arbitrage** in which they offset a purchase of a convertible with a short sale of the underlying stock, or vice-versa. Investors may also use this approach as a way to hedge their convertible bond holdings. Let's say that you owned some IBM convertible bonds and you wanted to protect yourself from their equity risk—that is, the price swings in the convertibles that might come from movements in IBM stock. You could short-sell an appropriate number of IBM shares to effectively offset your equity risk.

fin

convertible preferred stock   A security that is similar to a convertible bond, except it represents equity in the corporation. It allows the holder to exchange it for another type, usually **common stock**.

convertible preferred stock

In the sample term sheet to the right, you should understand the following components in a convertible preferred stock offering:

❶ Offering Price
Each share of preferred stock cost $50.

❷ Dividend Rate
Annual dividend to investors is $3.625 per year.

❸ Yield
Annual yield calculated by dividing the dividend by the offering price ($3.625 ÷ $50 = 7.25%).

❹ Conversion Price
The common stock price at which the preferred stock will be converted into common.

❺ Number of Shares
The shares that each $50 preferred stock will convert into at the conversion price ($50 ÷ $60 = 0.833).

❻ Conversion Premium
The percentage by which the conversion price ($60) exceeds the stock at pricing ($48).

❼ Stock at Pricing
Share price on the day the deal was priced.

❽ Call Feature
The preferred stock may not be called by the company for three years.

❾ Sinking Fund Requirements
The amount of the preferred stock issuance the company is required to retire throughout its life (none in this case).

❿ Exchange Feature
The preferred stock can be converted into convertible bonds beginning August 15, 1989.

Convertible Preferred Stock
New Term Sheet

Issue Description:	Warner Communications, Inc., $3.625 Series A. Convertible Exchangeable Preferred Stock
Total Offering Size:	$500,000,000
❶ Offering Price:	$50.00 per share
Trade Date:	August 22, 1986
Settlement Date:	September 2, 1996

❷ Dividend Rate:	$3.625	**❸ Yield:**	7 1/4%
❹ Conversion Price:	$60.00	**❺ No. of Shares:**	0.8333
❻ Conversion Premium:	25%		
❼ Stock at Pricing:	$48	**Symbol:**	WCI
❽ Call Feature:	Three years noncall		
First Call Price:	$52.5375 scaling down to $50.00 in 1996 with 150% Provision Test for 20 out of 30 days.		
❾ Sinking Fund:	None		
❿ Exchange Feature:	Beginning August 15, 1989, preferred stock can be exchanged for 71/4% Convertible Subordinated Debentures due August 15, 2011		

The preferred shareholder receives **dividend** income while retaining the opportunity to gain from stock appreciation. For issuing corporations, dividend payments, unlike interest payments, are not tax deductible. But corporations receiving dividends can exclude at least 70 percent of the dividends from their taxable income.

EXAMPLE   Warner Communications (now Time-Warner) used convertible preferred stock to gain financial flexibility following the $592 million write-off of its Atari video game unit in the early 1980s. Warner was able to raise $500 million with convertible exchangeable preferred stock, effectively allowing it to "shore up" without resorting to untimely divestitures. The capital infusion allowed the company to maintain its leadership in film and recorded entertainment, and even to go on to purchase American Express' interest in a cable television joint venture—Warner Amex Cable Communications.

See also **conversion price**, **conversion ratio**, **convertible bond**, and **convertible security**.

fin

convertible security

A **bond** or **preferred stock** that can be exchanged at the holder's option for a specified number of shares of **common stock**.

Usually a company issues convertible rather than straight securities because it wants to obtain a lower **interest rate**. Common stock may be ruled out because of a low share price. For investors, the conversion feature offers the opportunity to benefit from a future increase in the common-stock price in return for giving up a little of the **interest rate**.

EXAMPLE

To build a new plant, the Apex Washing Machine Company needs $100 million in capital. It issues two million shares of convertible preferred stock at $50 a share to raise the money. Each share can be exchanged for two shares of Apex common stock, which is now selling at $18. So the company knows that—at some time in the future, when the common stock price rises above $25 a share ($50 ÷ 2)—it may be issuing up to four million new common shares.

Apex sets the dividends at 8 percent, or $4 a share, a little lower than what it would have to pay if the stock was nonconvertible. And the company probably will not have to issue the common stock until the plant is built and contributing to earnings. When a share of preferred stock is converted, it is removed from the balance sheet and no longer gets dividends while Apex has two more common shares outstanding.

FRAME OF REFERENCE

convertible security

Convertible securities can conceptually be divided into three classes: bonds trading with the underlying equity, bonds trading like straight bonds, and hybrids. The convertibles in the first category—those trading like straight bonds—are commonly known as "busted convertibles," reflecting a stock price that has dropped so low that the convertible price now appears virtually unreachable. (See Comdisco story on page 154). Prior to the 1987 stock market crash, "busted converts" accounted for less than 10 percent of the convertible universe. Following Black Monday, busted converts were about 30 to 40 percent of the convertible market.

What's behind these cycles in the convertible market? One theory is that convertible buyers essentially want equities with less risk. As the stock market rises and convertibles rise with them, these investors are happy and put more money into convertibles. This trend may accelerate as nervous equity investors look for downside protection in a lofty stock market. With the increased demand for convertibles, coupons tend to go down, premiums tend to go up, and the risk-reward equation shifts against the buyer. Then, if the stock market does turn, the more expensive convertibles provide less cushion than the market had assumed. (While converts typically go down less than the underlying equities, they can still be significantly impaired.) At this point, the equity-oriented buyers abandon these "busted converts"—often at distress prices—in favor of issues that appear to have better chances of rising due to their equity value.

FRAME OF REFERENCE

coproduction

In 1984, General Motors and Toyota launched a joint venture to assemble compact cars in Fremont, California. Toyota provided 35 employees and GM 18 to manage New United Motor Manufacturing Inc. (NUMMI). The cars assembled at the plant are sold as Geo Prizms and Toyota Corollas. In the mid-1990s, NUMMI also began turning out light compact trucks. The **corporate culture** is clearly different from the traditional Big Three automakers'. Workers are organized in teams of five or six led by a union member. The values stressed are mutual trust, mutual respect, and production efficiency.

new **UNITED MOTOR** MANUFACTURING

The preferred shares are not likely to be converted as soon as they are in the money (when common shares are more than $25) because their enhanced value will be recognized in the market. Owners of the preferred stock can hold them and continue to collect dividends while hoping that they will appreciate further. Or they can sell the preferred shares at a profit on the open market to others who may continue to hold them or convert them.

See also **conversion price**, **conversion ratio**, **convertible preferred stock**, and **convertible bond**.

cooperative advertising

BEEF
IT'S WHAT'S FOR DINNER.®

mktg

cooperative advertising   Ads with shared costs.

Often a manufacturer pays part of the retailers' costs for **advertising** that features the company's products. This setup is common in the music industry, for example: A record label like Virgin will pay part of the cost when a store like Tower Records features Virgin albums in an ad, especially if Tower puts those albums on sale. The National Cattlemen's Beef Association has offered rebates to grocers that feature beef in ads. Sometimes, cooperative advertising is coordinated through one **advertising agency** to keep the ads looking similar.

EXAMPLE | Digital Equipment Corporation offers cooperative advertising to companies that sell its computer **workstations** and software to businesses. The companies placing the ads work through DDB Needham Worldwide and then get billed just for their share of the cost.

strat **oper** **mgmt**

coproduction   Where two or more companies join to finance, build, or operate a facility and make products.

Coproduction can be a way to transfer management expertise or technology and to help companies from different countries establish a presence abroad.

copy   The words appearing in an ad, commercial, direct-mail piece, or any other advertising material.

In most sales material, a **copywriter** helps develop the concept and writes the copy, working closely with the **art director** for the project.

See also **body copy**.

copyright   Sole right to reproduce and sell a book, piece of music, or work of art.

A work receives copyright protection as soon as it is created; publication and registration are not required. Registration, when it is carried out, acts to serve notice of the copyright claim and carries a financial benefit if anyone challenges the copyright in court.

Copyright laws do not protect facts or ideas, but rather the presentation of those ideas. The Beatles, for example, own a copyright on the original song "Let It Be," which talks about peace in the world. Of course, that does not prevent other artists from incorporating the notion into their songs. It would, however, prevent others from using the Beatles' words as their own.

This distinction, applied to computer software, is a major issue in the 1990s. Some companies have engaged in lengthy battles over whether a particular software product was developed on its own or whether it, or a part of it, was used in violation of someone else's copyright.

FRAME OF REFERENCE

copyright

Software is both costly to develop and valuable to the end user. But the medium that holds the software—a floppy disk, a compact disk, a tape—has little intrinsic value. What users actually buy is a license, or right to use the software that is carried on the medium.

Because it is easy and inexpensive to reproduce the software, which has a high value, some potential users are tempted to copy someone else's onto their own medium. This is software piracy, about which much has been written and which costs the software industry billions of dollars each year. On a large scale, factories in some parts of the world—China, for example—make unauthorized copies of copyrighted software and sell them to the public. There has been considerable friction between China and the United States on the issue.

The latest version of the **General Agreement on Tariffs and Trade (GATT)**, ratified in 1994 and 1995, requires all countries to protect patents, copyrights, trade secrets, and trademarks. It is too early to judge how effective GATT will be in this area, but it does provide some leverage against countries with reputations for being pirates' lairs.

copyright

core competencies

tip

Core competencies do not belong to a specific business unit but rather to the whole company. Your organizational structure should make the technology of your core competencies available to all business units.

[L]eadership rests on being able to do something others cannot do at all or find difficult to do even poorly. It rests on core competencies that meld market or customer value with a special ability of the producer or supplier.

—Peter F. Drucker

EXAMPLE | In 1988, Apple Computer sued Microsoft and Hewlett-Packard, saying that two of their programs copied the "look and feel" of its Macintosh screen graphics—the little symbols, or icons, and the general appearance of the screen display. But courts have been reluctant to recognize copyright protection in the "method of operating" a program, which has been compared to the controls on a VCR. So Apple eventually lost the suit. Today, it is not at all unusual to find a number of programs in a particular application, like word processing or spreadsheets, that all have the same look and feel.

The amounts of money in software copyright cases are not trivial. In October 1994, Data General reported that it had been paid $53 million by Northrop Grumman to settle a six-year-old copyright infringement and trade-secret suit.

Copyright holders have the exclusive right to:

► Reproduce the copyrighted work.

► Distribute copies of the work.

► Perform the work publicly.

► Display the work publicly.

► Other works derived from the copyrighted work, like sheet music that is made from an original song.

When one copyrighted work is used, with permission, as part of another, both parties preserve certain rights. If, for example, a photograph is used as part of another copyrighted work like a magazine, the photographer usually maintains the rights to his or her image, but the magazine holds a copyright on the overall layout.

Copyrighted works are protected for the life of the creator plus 50 years. When the copyright expires, the work enters the public domain and can be used by anyone.

mktg

copywriter   Person who writes the wording for sales literature and advertisements.

See also **copy**.

strat   **mgmt**

core competencies   Company's key strengths—what sets it above the competition.

Understanding your company's core competencies will help you guide it to the right **markets**, alliances, and new skills. The description of this strategy is often traced to a 1990 *Harvard Business Review* article by Professors Gary Hamel of the London Business School and C. K. Prahalad of the University of Michigan. It was also developed in their 1994 book *Competing for the Future*.

EXAMPLE | Hamel and Prahalad point to a couple of Japanese companies—Honda and NEC—that grew faster than their rivals by assessing and building on their core competencies. Honda realized that its strength was in engines rather than particular vehicles, so it has become a powerhouse in cars, motorcycles, off-road vehicles, outboard motors, generators, and garden tractors.

NEC in the 1970s saw that its history pointed toward a possible leadership role in computers, communications, and the interaction of both businesses. It formed more than 100 alliances to pick up the skills and technologies it did not already have. In the 1990s, NEC was the only company among the top five worldwide in computers, telecommunications equipment, and semiconductor products.

Most companies will not have more than a few core competencies. To find them, you can look for the factors that give you access to a wide variety of markets, that please your customers, and that are hard for your competitors to duplicate.

core competencies

Honda capitalized on its core competency—the quality of their engines—rather than particular vehicles.

C

mktg

core product Basics a consumer wants or needs from a good or service.

Your core product should aim at solving the consumer's problem or providing a major benefit. For example, an airline's core product is quick transportation in reasonable comfort. The wider seats and better meals and service in the first-class section are an **augmented product**. The core product of a motion picture company is a couple of hours of entertainment. For Slim-Fast, it is easy weight loss.

See also **tangible product**.

mktg

corporate brand Product sold under a retailer's own brand.

See also **private label**.

mgmt   **strat**

corporate culture Basic style, or personality, of a company—how people work with each other.

Slogans on a wall and **mission statements** cannot make the corporate culture; it is crafted over time as employees find out what works and what does not for them in the organization. While some bottom-line-focused managers shrug off the importance of a corporate culture, others are appreciating its role in determining a company's success. In many cases, when a company undergoes a strategic change, its culture must also change.

Companies develop an upbeat corporate culture by allowing employees to take part in operations beyond their specific job descriptions. Standards committees, advisory councils, quality circles, e-mail, and electronic bulletin boards encourage participation and loyalty.

corporate culture

Quick Facts! |

When Lucio Noto became CEO of Mobil Corporation in 1994, he inherited a culture that stifled initiative. A number of seemingly small changes have begun to shift the culture, however. Noto closed the executive dining room so that the business-suited would mingle at lunchtime with the shirt-sleeved. He also declared Friday a casual-clothes day. In late 1995, it still was not a culture that encouraged people to march to their own drummers, but at least a level of formality had been relaxed. Time will tell whether that translates to more innovative thinking.

Rewards like bonuses and gifts can change or strengthen a company's culture. Many companies in recent years have introduced compensation systems that reward group results, thus encouraging teamwork.

corporate culture

> *If an executive says it's important to care about customers and then spends an hour a week on the phone with customers, the value of that time to customers may be minor, but its value to the organization is immeasurable. The hour is a symbol and a demonstration of management's personal commitment to the values by which they expect everyone to live.*
>
> —Michael Hammer & James Champy, *Reengineering the Corporation*

correlation coefficient

trap

The conditions that influence correlation can change swiftly. Normally, there is a high positive correlation between the demand for a product and its quality level. When small Japanese cars entered the American marketplace in large numbers, Volkswagen's sales began dropping despite the Beetle's reputation for high reliability and quality. The new Japanese cars were cheaper and had more features the public found enticing.

econ **strat** **mktg**

correlation coefficient
Measure of how one factor relates to another in either a positive or negative way.

EXAMPLE | The positive correlation between demand for a stock and the stock's price (as demand increases, prices rise); the negative correlation between consumer product pricing and consumer product sales levels (as prices rise, demand drops).

Statisticians express the correlation coefficient in values ranging from $+1$ (the highest level of positive correlation) to -1 (the highest level of negative correlation), with zero representing no correlation at all between the two factors.

See also **elasticity**.

acct

cost accounting
System of internal accounting designed to trace costs to products, centers, and departments.

Cost accounting is also used to allocate **overhead**. It helps management understand production processes and costs, and evaluate the profitability of various products and services. In many instances, it also serves as the foundation for pricing products and services.

See also **costing**.

mgmt **strat**

cost-benefit analysis
Assessing in advance whether returns from a particular action outweigh all the costs.

The concept seems simple on the surface. Let us say a regional restaurant chain is considering going national. It conducts a cost-benefit analysis comparing the expenses involved in establishing restaurants across the country with the likely revenue from those restaurants. If the income exceeds the costs, the chain will start adding new outlets. But life is seldom that straightforward. Some costs and benefits are not easy to measure.

EXAMPLE | An automobile manufacturer finds that one of its models has a defective part. The known cost of a full recall is substantial, probably more than settling the number of lawsuits likely to arise from the defective part. But other, intangible costs are involved—injuries to drivers and damage to the manufacturer's reputation. The manufacturer decides to undertake the recall.

See also **externality**.

C

corporate culture

In the 1970s, Digital Equipment Corp. had a culture of innovation based on "next bench" design. Since DEC's computer products were sold to engineers, and most of its employees were engineers, it developed new products and tested them based on internal feedback from its own employees.

But as top management decided DEC had to sell more to the public, this culture had to change—and it was not easy. Engineers suddenly had to pay attention to customer surveys, place much greater weight on recommendations from marketing, even test products on average consumers in shopping malls.

In 1986, when Lawrence Rawl became CEO of Exxon, he spoke of "teaching the elephant to dance," but culture change has come slowly over the years to that company. IBM recognized its need to shed the white-shirt-and-striped-tie image a little too late compared to companies like Compaq, Dell, Adobe Systems, and Novell Inc., which were not afraid to loosen up to a sports-jacket-and-slacks atmosphere.

There are many ways to develop a particular corporate culture. One intriguing technique is called symbolic action—basically, teaching by example. At DEC, when a designer wanted to discuss with a top manager the merits of a nifty new computer he had developed, the executive would call a marketing person into the meeting, much to the designer's dismay. However, after being repeated enough times, the message got through, and designers began to consult marketing directly.

Experienced managers can tell new employees about the company and its past to give them a sense of the company's history. An example is a story of extraordinary customer service by Premier Industrial Corp., a distributor of electronic parts. In 1988, it got a distress call in late afternoon from a customer, Caterpillar Inc., in Decatur, Illinois. A $10 electrical part had broken, shutting down an entire assembly line. A Premier sales rep found a replacement in Los Angeles and had it flown to Caterpillar by 10:30 that night.

---

mgmt

cost center   Section of a company for which costs can be measured, such as a production department.

See also **management control systems**.

cost leadership   Being the lowest-cost supplier of a product or service in a given market.

A company may adopt a strategy of cost leadership to boost sales and gain **market share**. This strategy is often used when a new product is introduced. But it is crucial to make sure that you can sustain your cost advantage. If you encourage customers to shop based on price and are unable to keep your costs lower than those of the competition, you will need to raise your prices and lose whatever advantage you gained. On the other hand, if you can maintain your cost leadership, you will be delighted to see customers continue to shop based on price.

cost leadership

cost of capital

EXAMPLE

QRS Corporation manufactures microprocessors. Its analysts determine that its cost of capital is 12 percent. When it evaluates the construction of a new plant, it will not undertake the venture unless it expects to get at least a 12 percent return.

EXAMPLE | Southwest Airlines has maintained a cost-leadership position since its first scheduled flights in 1971. The airline translates its no-frills approach, which includes unassigned seating and no meals, into lower fares for its customers, whose faithful patronage has contributed to 22 consecutive years of profits for the Texas-based carrier.

A company with an established brand and no intention of entering the cost-leadership game can be driven to it by competitive pressure.

EXAMPLE | At one time the name IBM meant computing, and in 1981 the company introduced the PC. But companies like Compaq Computer Corporation and Dell appeared with competitive pricing in the PC market. Soon, dozens were crowding the field with so-called IBM clones. **Margins** were driven down, and personal computers became, in effect, **commodities**. By 1994, it was believed that IBM's PC **market share** had dropped to less than 10 percent worldwide, and it was struggling to control costs and compete on price against companies like Compaq, Dell, and Packard Bell, whose products are not called IBM clones anymore.

`acct`

cost method   Method of accounting for an **affiliated company** in which you hold only a small interest.

`acct` `fin`

cost of capital   (1) In accounting, the payments that a company makes for its various sources of capital, including interest on debt and dividends on common and preferred stock. The cost of capital is calculated by using a weighted average of a company's **dividends** paid, price **appreciation** on its stock, and the interest paid on its debt.

It is also the minimum **rate of return** an investor would require to buy into a business or venture. Analysts use cost of capital in evaluating an investment or project, like building a plant or introducing a product.

(2) In corporate finance, the minimum rate of return a company would be willing to earn if it invested in another venture with equal risk.

`mgmt` `strat`

cost-of-entry test   Way to evaluate the impact of acquiring or starting up a new business.

You look at the costs of buying or starting the business to make sure they are not higher than the **present value** of the profits you will make in the future. It does not seem like rocket science, but even successful companies make some big mistakes, especially when they seek to enter a different industry.

EXAMPLE | Philip Morris greatly underestimated the difficulty of expanding into the soft drink industry when it bought 7-Up for $520 million in 1978. At that price, 7-Up's profits would have had to quadruple for Philip Morris to make money on its investment. By 1986, the tobacco company gave up and sold 7-Up at a small loss.

See also **better-off test** and **industry-attractiveness test**.

cost of goods sold   What it costs to buy or make the merchandise you sell.

See also **costing** and **income statement**.

`mgmt`   `econ`

cost of living adjustment (COLA)   Adjustment made when analysts or the government calculate economic indicators such as the **consumer price index**.

See also **indexing**.

`mktg`

cost per thousand (CPM)   Cost of reaching a thousand potential customers with an advertisement (the M stands for the Roman numeral for a thousand).

For publications, you calculate CPM like this:

CPM Publications	=	Cost of Ad
	÷	(Circulation ÷ 1,000)

For broadcast media, calculate as follows:

CPM Broadcast Media	=	Cost of Commercial
	÷	(Audience ÷ 1,000)

EXAMPLE | A full-page advertisement in a major publication costs $72,000. The magazine has a circulation of eight million, so:

$$\$72,000 \div (8,000,000 \div 1,000) = \$72,000 \div 8,000 = \$9.00$$

The cost is $9 per thousand readers, which breaks down to $.09 per person. Remember, though, that this does not indicate how many people actually see or hear your ad—just how many buy the publication or how many have their TVs or radios tuned to your station.

cost per thousand

tip |

To keep an apples-to-apples comparison, use CPM to compare different options in the same medium—say two newspapers—reaching the same target audience. You probably cannot make a fair comparison between a newspaper and a radio station, a magazine and a newspaper, and so on.

C

cost-plus pricing

tip

Price + Quality = Value. Consumers make decisions based on the relationship between an item's price and its perceived quality, which is directly related to the value received from purchasing the item.

C

mktg

cost-plus pricing   Setting a price by adding a standard markup to the cost of the product, usually expressed as a percentage of the direct out-of-pocket cost. The markup is intended to cover indirect overhead and provide a profit.

EXAMPLE | A manufacturer produces 5,000 windbreakers at a cost of $60,000 ($12 each including overhead). The manufacturer adds a markup of $4 per jacket and finds a wholesaler who will buy 4,000 jackets, at $16 apiece. The profit is $4 X 4,000 = $16,000.

Although the math is simple, the strategy is not. The manufacturer must try to predict the demand for its product at different price levels. If the clothing manufacturer decides to mark up the windbreakers to $22 each, it might have trouble finding any wholesalers at all. If the manufacturer could sell only 1,000 jackets at $22 each, it would collect a total of only $22,000—a whopping $38,000 less than the initial cost of $60,000 to make the jackets.

Before increasing the price, a manufacturer should consider the series of markups that might be added throughout the distribution chain. Once the wholesaler buys the jackets for $16 each, it may add its own markup, selling them to retailers for $20 each. The retailers, in turn, may sell them to the final customer for $40 each. Is this beyond the target customer's price range? The manufacturer should have a sense of what price the market can handle before it sets cost-plus pricing in motion.

Cost-plus pricing is also used in some contracting arrangements. An aerospace company may contract with the government to design a space satellite at cost plus the aerospace company's fee for the project. This type of contract, especially for government work, has been criticized for the lack of incentive to hold costs down.

The converse of cost-plus pricing is **perceived-value pricing**—where you price a product according to its value to the customer. If a piece of software is uniquely capable of solving a business problem, customers will pay a premium for it, as long as it remains unique. Consultants with specialized experience also command premium fees for the same reason.

acct

costing   In accounting, attributing manufacturing costs to the value of goods produced.

There are two approaches to costing:

1 **Direct Costing**
also called variable costing. Only the variable costs, such as what the company pays for materials and labor to manufacture the products, go into the cost of goods produced. If your company uses this method, it is only for internal purposes,

because it is not acceptable under **generally accepted accounting principles (GAAP)**. The other method is required for tax purposes and external financial reporting.

2 Absorption Costing

Also called the full-cost method. In addition to the variable manufacturing costs, you attribute fixed costs associated with production, like rent and insurance, to the costs of goods produced.

Does it make a difference which method you use? It sure does. Here is why:

When you attribute costs to a product, they are added to the value of the inventory on hand and are considered assets until the inventory is sold. It is like moving money from one pocket to the other. Because these costs are incorporated into inventory, they do not show up as expenses as long as the goods remain unsold.

With absorption costing, only the nonmanufacturing costs—selling and administrative expenses, for example—are treated as expenses and charged immediately against sales revenue. With direct costing, both the nonmanufacturing costs and the fixed manufacturing costs are expensed right away. In other words, while absorption costing treats both fixed and variable manufacturing costs as assets, direct costing treats variable manufacturing costs as assets and fixed manufacturing costs as expenses.

EXAMPLE | On July 1 you started a business assembling portable stereos. You spent $4,000 for parts (variable costs) and rented a workshop for $2,000 a month (fixed costs). Using all the parts you bought, you assembled 100 stereos during the month.

In absorption costing, all $6,000 of your costs are attributed to your stereos, so each one in your inventory is carried at $60 ($6,000 ÷ 100). In direct costing, the stereos in inventory are carried at only $40 each ($4,000 ÷ 100); the other $2,000 is an expense for the period. Here is another way to look at the difference: In absorption costing, you took $6,000 in cash (an asset) and put it into inventory (another asset). In direct costing, $4,000 remained as an asset and the other $2,000 became an expense.

You also had $2,800 in selling and administrative expenses—your transportation and phone calls to make sales and your clerical and bookkeeping expenses. That is treated the same way in both systems. You sold 80 stereos during July for $100 each for a total of $8,000. The other 20 stereos remained in inventory. Under which system do you think you would make more income during July? The following chart shows how your books would look if you kept them both ways.

Since you sold less than you produced, both your ending inventory and your income are higher using absorption costing than using direct costing. You had no income with direct costing, because your fixed manufacturing costs showed up as $2,000 more in expenses while you gained only $1,600 through a lower cost of goods sold. The difference is $400—equal to your income under absorption costing (and the portion of fixed manufacturing costs still in inventory).

costing

tip |

*Using both direct costing for internal analysis and the required absorption costing can give you added perspective on such things as **contribution margin**, or how much a product contributes to the recovery of fixed costs.*

The relationship between absorption and direct costing differs based on the relative sales and production volume, so that:

▶ Both methods will result in the same net income if sales and production volume are equal.

▶ Absorption costing will result in a lower ending inventory and lower net income than direct costing if sales volume exceeds production volume.

▶ Absorption costing will result in a higher ending inventory and a higher net income than direct costing if production volume exceeds sales volume.

costing

EXAMPLE

The Muncie, Indiana, plant of Borg-Warner Automotive's Power Train System Group is one of many factories that have adopted direct costing internally. It helps the plant examine performance by assigning discrete costs to product lines.

Absorption vs. Direct Costing

	Absorption Costing (Unit Cost = $60: $40 Variable, $20 Fixed)	Direct Costing (Unit Cost = $40: $40 Variable)
Sales: 70 Units @ $100	$ 7,000	$ 7,000
Cost of Goods Sold:		
Beginning Inventory	0	0
Cost of Goods Produced: 100 Units	<u>5,000</u>	<u>3,000</u>
Cost of Good Available for Sale	5,000	3,000
Less Ending Inventory: 30 Units	<u>1,500</u>	<u>900</u>
Cost of Sales	$ 3,500	$ 2,100
Gross Profit	$ 3,500	$ 4,900
Less Operating Expenses:		
Production Overhead		2,000 (100 Units X $20 Fixed Cost)
Selling, General, and Administrative	2,800	2,800
Total Operating Expenses	$ 2,800	$ 4,800
Net Income	$700	$100

fin

coupon rate The stated interest rate on a security, referred to as an annual percentage of face value.

It is called the coupon rate because **bearer bonds** carry coupons for interest payments. Each coupon entitles the bearer to a payment when a set date has been reached. Today, most bonds are registered in holders' names, and interest payments are sent to the registered holder, but the term coupon rate is still widely used.

fin

covenant A restriction, such as one placed on a company issuing debt securities.

Debt covenants are found in the agreement, known as the **indenture**, filed with the **Securities and Exchange Commission (SEC)** at the time of a debt offering. Typical covenants include restrictions on borrowing over a certain amount or from letting liquidity or operating ratios cross certain thresholds. For example, a covenant will require that a company maintain a minimum net worth, below which the company must redeem its bonds at par.

Three important covenant categories are:

1 **Net Worth Requirement**
Protects investors by requiring a minimum net worth to be maintained on a periodic (usually quarterly) basis. If a company's net worth falls significantly, the covenant usually requires the issuer to tender for a portion of its bonds at par.

2 **Limitation on Dividend and Stock Repurchase**
Specifies the maximum amount that can be used for dividends or stock buybacks. This covenant protects bondholders' priority over that of equity holders.

3 **Mergers: Sale of Assets**
Describes under what conditions a merger or substantial asset sale can occur. This covenant gives some protection against adverse impact on the bonds resulting from fundamental changes in the company.

acct

CPA See **certified public accountants**.

fin **econ**

CPI See **consumer price index**.

oper **mgmt** **mktg**

CPM See **cost per thousand** or **critical path method**.

---

coupon rate

EXAMPLE

A $1,000 bond has a coupon rate of 7 percent, so it pays $70 a year. If you buy the bond for $900, your actual current yield is 7.78 percent ($70 ÷ $900 = .0778, or 7.78%). If you buy the bond for $1,100, the current yield is 6.36 percent ($70 ÷ $1,100 = .0636, or 6.36%). In any event, the 7 percent coupon rate does not change.

C

FRAME OF REFERENCE

covenant

Investment-grade bonds have historically carried few or no covenants because investors and underwriters did not require them from "high-grade" companies. But the latter part of the 1980s proved that there was downside risk in unprotected investment-grade bonds. Once-thriving industries like energy and steel, primarily consisting of large investment-grade companies, saw their fortunes turn for the worse. Whether caused by a single precipitous event, such as the sudden decline in oil prices, or the long-term effects of increased competition, high-grade investors lost money. The fact remains that AAA, AA, or A ratings by themselves do not protect investors.

Even in healthy industries, companies have been known to decide to radically alter **capital structures** to the detriment of bondholders. Because investment-grade bonds rarely contain a covenant restricting dividend payments or stock repurchases, numerous **recapitalizations** during the mid-1980s occurred, catching investment-grade investors by surprise.

creative director

A creative director may create and combine visual images and apply them to many different contexts.

`mktg`

creative concept   Advertising term for the idea behind a product's image and its association to the consumer. For example, the Marlboro Man is an icon among creative concepts and is regarded as the premier image design.

`mktg`

creative director (CD)   Head of the creative department of an **advertising agency**.

The CD often reports to the vice president of creative services and supervises **art directors** and **copywriters**.

`acct`

credit   In accounting, an entry on the right side of an **account**. **Asset** and expense accounts are decreased on the credit side, and **liability**, **revenue**, and **capital accounts** are increased on the credit side.

See also **bookkeeping** and **debit**.

`fin` `mgmt`

credit bureau   Organization that provides information about how promptly you pay your bills.

Credit bureaus act as **clearinghouses** for businesses that want to know your payment history before they give you credit. There are three national bureaus, Equifax, TRW, and Trans-Union, as well as 750 or so local and regional bureaus to which you can write or call for your credit history. The reams of numbers you will receive will not contain any rating or summary; they will just matter-of-factly list your payment record for basic lines of credit, like your Visa card or student loan. They will not include your payment record for short-term expenses like utilities, doctors appointments, telephone bills, and such. So if you are tight on cash and want to be sure you are not damaging your credit history, give that credit card bill some priority over the dentist's bill.

In theory, the clearinghouse also taps into any public records when it does a check on you, which would uncover bankruptcies, foreclosures, tax liens, or court judgments, but the searches are not always that thorough. Federal law imposes limits on how long you can be penalized for having gone through something like a **bankruptcy**, with 10 years marking the outer range and seven years the norm.

Since studies have shown that credit reports issued to consumers do sometimes have mistakes in them, including major errors that might hurt your chances for credit, you should check your record annually. If you think the credit bureau got something wrong, contact them immediately as well as the creditor in question. Sometimes the "error" is actually a judgment call: You thought the product you bought was faulty so you refused to pay; the department store just listed your account as delinquent. If you cannot get the bureau to make a change, then exercise your right to attach a 100-word comment to your report that explains your side of the story.

 fin **mgmt**

credit history   Record of how faithfully you pay your bills.

See also **credit bureau**.

 strat

crisis   Period of extreme instability where a turning point is near. A crisis threatens the life of a business or one of its major objectives.

 oper **mgmt**

critical path method (CPM)   Visual control tool that shows the relationship among activities of a complex project, by charting the most important sequential activities as the critical path.

See also **program evaluation and review technique (PERT)**.

 econ **strat**

cross-price elasticity   Measure of how the change in one item's price affects demand for another item.

See also **elasticity**.

 acct **fin**

cumulative effect of accounting change   Item on your **income statement** that shows the catch-up cost or benefit of making an **accounting change**.

When you switch the way you do your accounting, it usually impacts not only your current period but all prior periods that are used in making comparisons. Most **annual reports** contain several years of comparable income statement and **balance sheet** data.

---

credit bureau

t i p |

A divorced woman must take special care that joint credit card accounts with her ex-husband do not translate into a good rating for the ex and no record for her. Many banks are sloppy about processing credit histories for both people listed on a card (even though they are legally obliged to do just that). Since the man's name is usually posted first, he, literally, gets all the credit.

C

Creditors are a superstitious sect, great observers of set days and times.

—Benjamin Franklin, *Poor Richard's Almanack*, 1732–57

C

EXAMPLE | In 1993, AT&T made three accounting changes in keeping with new standards issued by the **Financial Accounting Standards Board (FASB)**. The changes concerned accounting for income taxes and for the benefits of retirees and others who leave the company. So AT&T had to make an adjustment in 1993 to bring its past accounting practices up to the new standards. Making the three changes added up to a charge of more than $9.6 billion on the income statement. It turned what would have been more than $3.7 billion in **net income** into a net loss of more than $5.9 billion. Here is how it looked on AT&T's income statement:

Cumulative Accounting Changes: AT&T's Income Calculation

Dollars in Millions (except per share amounts)	1993
Income Before Cumulative Effects of Accounting Changes	**$ 3,702**
Cumulative Effects on Prior Years of Changes in Accounting for	
Postretirement Benefits: Net of Income Tax Benefit of $4,294	(7,023)
Postemployment Benefits: Net of Income Tax Benefit of $681	(1,128)
Income Taxes	(1,457)
Cumulative Effects of Accounting Changes	**(9,608)**
Net Income: Loss	**($ 5,906)**

cumulative effect of accounting change

tip |

Remember that the accounting change has no effect on the cash used in the business.

cumulative voting System of voting for elective bodies, such as boards of directors, that ensures sizable minority views or representation.

Under cumulative voting, each voter gets a number of votes equal to the number of positions to be filled and can cast all of the votes for one candidate. As a result, a voter can concentrate his voting power and may be able to elect one or more candidates. Basically, any group that holds a percentage of votes equal to the percentage of total board seats represented by one seat can elect at least one board member.

Although it's not common for **publicly held companies**, cumulative voting is often used in electing boards for private companies and organizations like condominium associations.

In recent years, shareholders have introduced proposals at the **annual meeting** of many large publicly held corporations calling for cumulative voting in the election of directors. These proposals have almost invariably been opposed by the company's management and defeated. The idea behind the proposals is that cumulative voting would make it easier to elect directors to represent a particular point of view. That's because a group—a labor union, for example, or an environmental organization—could encourage its members and sympathizers to cast all of their cumulative votes for one candidate.

Most corporate managements oppose cumulative voting because they want to avoid factionalism on the board. However, some corporations do elect their boards this way. Teledyne, Inc., is an example of a **Fortune 500** company with cumulative voting. It believes the arguments about making the board vulnerable to pressure groups are incorrect.

See also **staggered terms**.

C

FRAME OF

REFERENCE

cumulative voting

Easterly Place is a garden apartment complex made up of 120 condominiums. Sixty of the apartment owners have 100 shares each in the Easterly Place Condominium Association, and the 60 owners whose units are slightly larger have 125 shares each. The board has nine seats, with three up for election every year. At the yearly meeting, each apartment owner gets three votes per share—one for every vacant seat. So each owner with 100 shares can cast 300 votes (3 X 100 = 300), and each owner with 125 shares can cast 375 votes (3 X 125 = 375).

At this year's meeting, there are five candidates running for the three seats. The apartment owners are free to cast their votes in any way they want. Mary Jones, with 375 votes, can cast them all for one candidate, she can cast 125 votes for each of the three candidates she prefers, or she can spread her votes in any combination to as many candidates as she likes. In all, there are 40,500 votes that can be cast:

300 votes x 60 units	= 18,000 votes
375 votes x 60 units	= 22,500 votes
18,000 + 22,500	= 40,500 votes

The three candidates who get the most votes will win seats on the board. Accordingly, the smaller units could concentrate their 18,000 votes for just one candidate and guarantee the election of one board member, while the larger units could divide their votes evenly between two candidates (casting 11,250 votes for each) and elect two board members. However, if the owners of the large apartments tried to elect all three seats by splitting their votes equally for three candidates (casting 70,500 votes for each of three candidates), they could end up with only one winner if the smaller-unit owners split their votes evenly between two candidates (casting 9,000 votes for each of two winning candidates). This demonstrates that with cumulative voting, strategy is very important, and members of each group must carefully coordinate how they vote.

C

fin

currency futures   Financial instruments whose value is based on currency indexes; traded on exchanges such as the **International Monetary Market**.

See also **derivatives**.

econ

current account   Measurement of a nation's exports and imports of goods and services plus government payments; it is one component of the **balance of payments**.

acct   **fin**

current assets   **Assets** that can quickly be converted into cash or that will be used by the end of a year or within the company's normal operating cycle, whichever is longer.

See also **balance sheet**.

acct   **fin**

current ratio   Measure of **liquidity**, or the company's ability to meet currently maturing or short-term obligations.

The ratio is:

$$\text{Current Assets} \div \text{Current Liabilities}$$

The information can easily be found on a company's **balance sheet**.

Current Ratio	=	Current Assets
	÷	Current Liabilities

EXAMPLE   The AT&T 1994 annual report lists current assets of $37,611,000,000 and current liabilities of $30,930,000,000. So the current ratio is:

$37,611,000,000 \div \$30,930,000,000 = 1.22$

Procter & Gamble's 1995 annual report shows current assets of $10,842,000,000 and current liabilities of $8,648,000,000. The current ratio is:

$10,842,000,000 \div \$8,648,000,000 = 1.25$

This test is similar to the **acid test ratio** but less stringent. The acid test ratio eliminates inventory and prepaid expenses from current assets.

currency futures

current ratio

tip

In evaluating ratios, you really need comparable data for the industry. That way you can see how one company stacks up against others facing similar conditions.

current yield   Percentage return on a **bond** arrived at by dividing the dollar amount of annual interest by the market price.

See also **bond yield**.

mktg   strat

customer intimacy   Strategy to create market value by concentrating on giving specific customers what they want.

Adherents to this discipline tailor their operations to satisfy individual needs rather than aiming at a broader market.

Top Ranked Customer-Oriented Companies, 1996

	Most Customer Sensitive	Most Improved Customer Service
Communication Service	MCI Communications Corp.	AT&T
General Merchandise	Nordstrom, Inc.	Sears, Roebuck and Co.
Retail (home/hardware)	The Home Depot, Inc.	True Value
Home Delivery	Domino's Pizza, Inc.	Dial-a-Mattress
Financial Service	American Express	Citibank
Transportation Service	Delta Air Lines, Inc.	Amtrak
Chain Restaurant	Starbucks Coffee	Denny's Inc.
Automotive	Saturn Corporation	Ford Motor Co.
Catalog/Retail	Land's End, Inc.	L.L. Bean
Professional Service	Temps & Co.	ADT Security
Delivery Service	Federal Express Corp.	Airborne Express

Source: The Knowledge Exchange 1996 Customer Intimacy Survey. One hundred senior managers were surveyed nationwide and asked to list their preferred company in each category.

customer intimacy

Customer-intimate companies do not pursue one-time transactions; they cultivate relationships. They specialize in satisfying unique needs, which often only they, by virtue of their close relationship… recognize.

—Michael Treacy and Fred Wiersema, *The Discipline of Market Leaders*

C

In 1996, Knowledge Exchange established the Customer Intimacy Award, which is given to the most customer-sensitive U.S. companies in 11 industries.

FRAME OF REFERENCE

customer intimacy

In his book *Customer Intimacy,* Fred Wiersema describes the case of Nypro, Inc., of Clinton, Massachusetts: By jettisoning all but its toughest customers, the plastics-injection molder transformed itself from an undistinguished also-ran into a world leader in zero-defect production.

Nypro initially targeted cutting-edge manufacturers of health care products whose needs for product safety demanded far higher specifications than any existing injection process could deliver. It then designed new processes for each customer, sharing insights with the customer's own engineering and marketing teams to solve specific problems. Nypro even situated new plants next door to customers and integrated its new process with theirs.

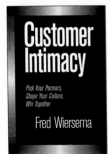

Customer Intimacy

*Pick Your Partners,
Shape Your Culture,
Win Together*

Fred Wiersema

Results? Customers got more sophisticated products at lower cost with a faster cycle time and fewer defects. Nypro saw profits rise from less than $1 million to nearly $13 million while sales more than tripled in less than a decade.

---

customer loyalty

Quick Facts!

Xerox conducted research into the buying habits of "totally satisfied," as opposed to "satisfied," customers. The very satisfied customers were up to six times more likely to buy another Xerox product.

---

customized marketing

EXAMPLE

Computerized machines in Hallmark gift shops allow customers to key in their own professional-looking messages on a selected card, instead of choosing from the traditional lines of cards with preprinted messages.

---

mktg

customer loyalty   Abiding passion among buyers for your **products**.

It starts with **customer satisfaction** and grows to a dedication that includes praising your products to friends and relatives. Burke Customers Satisfaction Associates uses a *Secure Customer Index* to rate loyalty, ranking the likelihood of repeat purchases and recommendations, along with overall product satisfaction. Such indexes, it says, give companies **marketing** material to work with "by demonstrating the ratio of secure customers to vulnerable customers."

mktg **strat**

customized marketing   A **market segmentation** strategy where the product or service is tailored to fit each customer.

It is common in **industrial markets**—such as aerospace—where planes and equipment are designed around the customer's specifications. The reupholstering, interior design, and hairstyling businesses are traditional **consumer markets** suited to customized marketing. And now the computer is helping to make it practical in other businesses.

oper

cycle   (1) Sequence of operations repeated regularly. (2) Time necessary to do a specific sequence of operations.

EXAMPLE | Every day a newspaper processes articles from around the world. After they are written, the articles go through a number of editors. Then they are converted into type, proofread, and laid out in pages, which are photographed to make printing plates. The plates are loaded onto presses, paper is fed through, and newspapers are produced, folded, bundled, and delivered. For much of the newspaper's content, the cycle time is less than 24 hours.

cycle

oper **tech**

cycle counting   Checking inventory numbers regularly by focusing on part of the stock at a time.

Cycle counting can involve a physical count or the use of computer technology and **bar codes**. It can be a supplement to or a replacement for the annual, semiannual, or quarterly wall-to-wall physical inventory tally. Cycle counts can be taken more often for fast-moving or high-value items than for slow-moving or low-value parts, products, or supplies. By tallying just part of the inventory each time, you can make inventory counting a regular activity, even incorporating it as a daily procedure.

EXAMPLE | Kinney Drugs found its daily cycle counting results so good that it eliminated the semiannual physical count that took four days. Using bar codes and scanners has given Kinney 98.5 percent accuracy on inventory numbers.

cycle counting

tip |

A number of companies have used random, unannounced cycle counts to reduce employee theft.

Computers and Software

According to some experts, the computer was invented by either Charles Babbage in the early 19th century, Percy Ludgate in the early 20th century, or Leonardo Torres y Quevedo soon after. Other scholars trace it to experiments at Bell Laboratories and RCA in the 1920s and 1930s, while a few credit English scientist Alan Turing and his colleagues, who worked on calculating devices during World War II. In addition, many support John Vincent Atanasoff's claims that, in the mid-1930s, he had the first idea for a computer.

All of this demonstrates the truism that no individual can lay claim to having produced any of the truly important inventions—the railroad, the car, the airplane, the telephone, motion pictures, and so on.

While it is not possible to attribute the computer's invention to one person, it can be said with some conviction that the industry began with the work of J. Presper Eckert and John Mauchly. Building on the accomplishments of others and their own efforts, they developed the ENIAC computer at the University of Pennsylvania during World War II. After the war they formed the Electronic Control Corp., renamed Eckert-Mauchly Computer Co. in 1947, and set about creating the UNIVAC.

The company would have folded for lack of interest were it not for financial help from American Totalizer Co., an operator of pari-mutuel machines. In 1950 American Totalizer sold its interest to Remington Rand, just in time for the UNIVAC to make its debut tallying the 1950 census and to be used in predicting the results of the 1952 presidential election.

Remington Rand was soon eclipsed by International Business Machines (IBM), then the leader in large calculators. Thomas Watson, Jr., convinced his father to make the switch to computers. IBM's first product, the 701, made for the military in 1951, was followed by the 702 for the civilian market. The machine was a huge success. By 1956, IBM had 85 percent of the market and was turning out additional machines and developing compatible software.

Thomas J. Watson, Jr. & Sr.

Contributing Editor: Thomas Thornhill
Managing Director, Montgomery Securities

1910 · 1960 · 1971

1910
Formation of Computing-Tabulating-Recording, later known as IBM

1942
First "electronic brain" developed in the U.S.

1945
Production of the ENIAC computer

1951
IBM introduces its first computer, the 701

1964
IBM releases the 360 series, a new generation of hardware

1968
Micro Instrumentation Telemetry begins experiments with "desktop" computers

1969
Completion of ARPANET, the world's first computer network

1971
Invention of the world's first microprocessor at Intel

A host of competitors were attracted to this industry. Some were established firms such as Honeywell, General Electric, RCA, NCR Corp., Burroughs Corp., and what had become Sperry Rand. Others, led by Control Data, were new to the industry. But none had IBM's success.

Recognizing these rivals were developing competitive machines, IBM released a new generation of hardware in 1964 known as the 360 series, which was another great success. By then it seemed IBM was destined to lead in this rapidly growing industry indefinitely.

There were continuing attempts to diminish IBM's dominance of the industry. Some companies were able to survive by concentrating on niches IBM ignored or by attacking them in the courts. Cray, for example, specialized in "supercomputers," a category IBM did not think held much promise. Control Data sued IBM on antitrust grounds, charging the firm with false advertising and unfair competition. IBM settled out of court in 1973, agreeing to sell its Service Bureau Corp. to Control Data at book value and pay reparations of $100 million.

Another threat to IBM came from the leasing companies, such as Mohawk, Telex, and Leasco, which purchased IBM machines and then leased them at competitive rates. Then there were designers and manufacturers of "plug compatible" machines, which functioned like their IBM counterparts but had lower price tags. This category was headed by Amdahl, founded by a former IBM scientist, who sold an interest in the firm to Fujitsu. During the 1980s there was much concern regarding

Japanese competition from firms such as Fujitsu, Hitachi, Nippon Electric, Toshiba, and Mitsubishi. The fear originated in a recognition of the success of Japanese firms in such industries as automobiles and consumer electronics. Computers seemed a natural extension of their activities. IBM competed successfully against the Japanese firms, in part because the major computer company in Japan was IBM itself.

In 1982 the FBI learned that Hitachi had purchased documents stolen from IBM, which seemed to indicate that this was the only way the Japanese could defeat the American firm. Hitachi was obliged to pay a stiff fine and reparations. IBM continued to dominate the market for large computers, which, in the view of most people, were what computers were all about.

While attention was riveted on the rivalries between IBM and its American and Japanese competitors, others were experimenting with "desktop" computers. A group of these people orga-

nized Micro Instrumentation Telemetry in 1968, which produced and sold the Altair to hobbyists in early 1975. Soon thereafter, Osborne and Kaypro achieved success with their "transportable" computers. Both bowed to a newcomer, Apple, organized by Steve Wozniak and Steve

Jobs. The Apple II and later the Macintosh, not the Kaypro, became the popular version of computers marketed to consumers, not companies.

Stephen Wozniak & Steven Jobs

1975 1980 **1993**

1975
Bill Gates and Paul Allen found Microsoft

1975
The first desktop computer, the Altair, introduced by Micro Instrumentation Telemetry

1976
Steven P. Jobs and Stephen G. Wozniak form Apple

1981
IBM introduces its own desktop computer, dubbed the PC

1982
Organization of Compaq, which produces IBM clones

1982
Sun Microsystems founded on the premise that "the network is the computer"

1993
Mosaic software introduced—Internet use explodes

IBM introduced its own desktop, the PC, in 1981, and immediately became the industry leader, setting the standard for other companies that came in with their "clones." IBM's willingness to share its technology and its encouragement of others, especially independent software companies, were major moves that helped determine the future of the computer. IBM made it possible for many rivals to enter the field by purchasing components rather than seeking permission to use its patents. In the end this approach may have resulted in a diminution of IBM's power, but the strategy led to the establishment of hundreds of new companies and transformed the industry. Clone manufacturers proliferated with the creation of Columbia and Corona first, eventually Dell and Packard Bell, and most important, Compaq in 1982. In time Japanese-, Korean-, and British-made personal computers came to market as well.

Key to the development of the personal computer market was the evolution of the silicon chip. Intel, organized in 1968 as Integrated Electronics, first concentrated on chips for large computers and later moved into microprocessor designs. IBM chose Intel's 8088 chip for its 1981 entry into to the PC market, securing Intel's future position as the industry leader.

Apple remained aloof, refusing to cooperate or license its technologies. As a result there were two standards in the young industry, but the IBM approach assured its victory. Others continued to attempt to win niches. Texas Instruments, Commodore, and Radio Shack made their bids and failed. Compaq, organized in 1982, did much better by producing a superior version of the IBM PC and assuming the lead in some areas of technology. By mid-decade it appeared that IBM and Apple would become the GM and Ford of personal computers, while IBM would continue to dominate in the category of large machines.

Several significant developments in the late 1980s scrambled the computer business, to the point where it is no longer a single industry but a web of related enterprises, with additional ones added regularly. For example, there evolved clear relationships between computers, telecommunications, electronics, entertainment, and education. Computers were being used as television sets, telephones, fax machines, learning devices, and even sound systems. They are information retrieval systems and the entry to the Internet and World Wide Web. The arrival of the Internet shook up the industry, with companies like Netscape and America Online becoming new industry forces. All of this in less than a decade.

Companies that once were major players, like Control Data and Honeywell, became minor forces or left the industry, their places taken by newcomers. Sperry Rand united with Burroughs to become Unisys. RCA no longer existed. Apple rose and declined. IBM was no longer dominant. The Japanese challenge proved not as ominous as once it seemed, but Japanese companies had strong positions in one area, laptops, a category that was transmuted into notebook computers. Software dislodged mainframes and even desktop models as the driving force in the industry when Microsoft, founded in 1975 by Bill Gates and Paul Allen, was hailed as the IBM of the future. In this area American companies had a clear lead, with more sales than the rest of the world combined. Workstations displaced some desktop computers, and Sun Microsystems became a powerhouse.

By the late 1980s it had become apparent that software would, indeed, drive the industry, and the key to software was vision. Early on, Bill Gates of Microsoft and Steve Jobs of Apple realized that PCs were only vehicles to run software, which was the paramount consideration for users. In contrast, IBM thought the machine itself was central to the sale. Gates and Jobs knew that, in time, software would become simple to understand and utilize, and that PC users would not require the kind of hand-holding IBM had provided for users of its mainframe. IBM talked of the nation becoming computer literate; Gates knew the trick was to make software so uncomplicated that such literacy would not be required.

Up until then, software was viewed as an adjunct to hardware in the personal computer area. Each company had its own operating system, so there was no industry standard. At the time this seemed as unimportant as the fact that once each typewriter brand took a different configuration of ribbon. The same was true for applications software, such as word processing. Utility software, now used to perform support tasks for the operating system, was as yet unknown. As computers moved into the home, a new market for games developed. Still, the division between desktops and computers used for games was fairly distinct. IBM and Apple were for the office and home, while Atari, Sega, and Nintendo were specifically designed for games.

The first operating system that seemed capable of becoming the PC archetype was CP/M. Microsoft purchased DOS for the bargain price of $75,000 and improved on it. When IBM decided to use DOS, that operating system quickly became the PC standard.

The 1980s were cluttered with IBM's lost opportunities. IBM was still focused on the mainframe, failing to recognize the importance of the desktop software market. The IBM-Microsoft contract permitted Microsoft to sell DOS to other suppliers, even though IBM could have insisted on a better financial arrangement. On several occasions IBM might have controlled Microsoft, which would have died without

IBM's early patronage; as late as 1986, Gates was willing to sell IBM a major interest in his company. In the early years Lotus and Borland, two important software companies, would have gone nowhere without IBM's patronage; they, too, would have sold themselves to IBM at low prices. When IBM finally purchased Lotus in late 1995, the price was exorbitant.

After the dismissal of a federal antitrust suit against IBM in 1981, IBM might have done all this with ease and today still ruled the roost.

But by the time IBM rose to the challenge and developed a rival operating system, OS/2, it was too late to defeat Microsoft.

Apple understood that its "user-friendly" operating-system performance was the key to its success. Gates undercut Apple with his creation of Windows, which went a long way to making the IBM-compatibles as easy to use as the Apples. In addition, the majority of business software was written for DOS, making it difficult for many businesses to use Apples. Ultimately, AT&T's UNIX may become a major force. In any case, despite their differences, Windows, OS/2, and UNIX share sufficient features so that true compatibility may become a reality, further marginalizing Apple.

In the area of applications software, the first word-processing systems were quite simple, in part because the early machines lacked the capacity for anything more complex. As the machines became more powerful, new systems appeared. In the mid-1980s Wordstar seemed capable of becoming an industry standard, only to be displaced by WordPerfect, created by Utah-based Novell. Then Microsoft developed Word, with a much improved Windows interface, and soon challenged WordPerfect and other systems.

Next to word processing in importance is the spreadsheet, which revolutionized business planning. The first significant spreadsheet was VisiCalc, later displaced by Lotus 1-2-3. In 1984 Lotus, which had become the leader in this sector, released Symphony, which was an attempt to present users with an advanced integrated program that proved technically difficult. Similar problems plagued Ashton-Tate, another major software house, with its dBase III. Microsoft entered the field, and Novell (later sold to Corel) tried to compete with them in the "Suite Wars" with its WordPerfect Suite. Lotus had a program of its own, as did other software vendors. New applications programs seem to appear almost weekly, and because the industry is so young and constantly evolving, solid predictions about the future are elusive.

D

to
duration

data
encryption

tech

data encryption   System for encoding and decoding computer data to protect it from unauthorized access. Data can be encrypted before it is stored or transmitted. An authorized user can then decode it when it is accessed or received using a reverse encryption procedure or a special software key.

tech

database   A collection of quantitative or descriptive information that is stored electronically.

Through the use of **database management system (DBMS)** software, the information can be accessed and manipulated in numerous ways to produce various reports.

EXAMPLE | You use a DBMS to manage your inventory in a retail business. Incoming items are entered into the system and bar-coded. At the checkout counter, an optical scanner reads the codes and enters the sale into the database as well as the cash register. You can check at any time for a report on sales of any items and the quantities you have in stock.

See also **bar code**.

tech

database management system (DBMS)   Controls the access and manipulation of information on a **database**.

acct   **fin**   **mgmt**

days sales outstanding (DSO)   Number of days it takes to collect your **accounts receivable**. Also called **average collection period**.

To find it, divide your total sales by 365 to determine average daily sales, then divide average daily sales into average accounts receivable for the year.

Days Sales Outstanding

DSO   =   (Average Accounts Receivable x 365)

÷   Period Sales

---

database

days sales outstanding

EXAMPLE

Your total sales in 1995 were $2 million. At the start of the year, you had $500,000 in accounts receivable; at year-end, it was $300,000. To find average accounts receivable, you add $500,000 and $300,000 and divide by two.

($500,000 + $300,000) ÷ 2
= $400,000

So the days sales outstanding figure is:

($400,000 x 365) ÷ 2,000,000
= 73 days

Put another way, your average accounts receivable turned over five times during the year (365 ÷ 73 = 5). That number is called accounts receivable turnover, which is another way of expressing the same idea.

D

183

D

fin

debenture   General debt obligation backed by the issuer's full faith and credit.

Typically, debentures are unsecured and do not have a lien or include a security interest in any specific asset. They are backed by a document called an **indenture,** which details the **covenants,** terms, and obligations of the issuing company. In a liquidation or **bankruptcy,** debentures rank junior to secured debt but higher than **preferred stock** or **common stock**. Debentures are by far the most common form of corporate **bond,** usually issued by large companies that have strong credit records.

Debentures often include provisions or **warrants** that permit their holders to convert the bonds or warrants for common stock under certain terms. These rights allow the debenture holders to increase returns by participating in the growth of the business.

acct

debit   Entry on the left side of an **account,** opposite the **credit** entry on the right. All asset and expense accounts are increased on the debit side ("Dr" column in general ledger below), while all **liability, revenue,** and **capital accounts** are decreased on the debit side.

See also **bookkeeping** and **credit**.

debit

General Ledger

4150-00-1050	Telephone Expense			
Date	Source	Dr	Cr	Balance
1/31/96	CD	$18		
Balance 1/31/96				$18
2/28/96	CD	$19		
Balance 2/28/96				$37
3/31/96	CD	$20		
Balance 3/31/96				$57

---

fin   **strat**

debt/equity swap   Exchanging debt for an ownership, or **equity,** stake in a company.

There are several reasons a company, government, or municipality may want to swap debt for equity. The entity may be in financial distress, and to avoid a Chapter 11 (bankruptcy) filing, which could take years to resolve, bondholders and management might be able to agree on the right portion of equity to swap for the debt issue. Another reason may be that the company wants to take advantage of its current stock market valuation, and thus change its **capital structure**—by adding more equity and reducing its debt obligations. In this case, the entity would not be in financial distress: Quite the contrary—if its equity values are strong, it could actually take advantage of the marketplace. In either case, the management has to negotiate with the bondholders. Oftentimes, the bond indenture has terms and covenants that might prevent a swap to occur without their consent.

In some debt/equity swaps, the bondholder takes a direct equity stake in the company. If a bondholder does not wish to own equity or is precluded from owning equity in the case of some financial institutions, they can sell the bond in the secondary market, and the new owner can make the swap.

Here are some examples of how debt/equity swaps might work:

▶ The government of a developing country is unable to service its debt, which is payable in U.S. dollars. The holder of a loan offers to sell it back to the government in exchange for a stake in a government-owned company that is being privatized. Or the government may offer to trade the debt for local currency, which can be used only to build local operations or invest in local companies.

▶ CBA Corporation owes $4 million to National Bank and cannot make payment. But CBA has high hopes for a product line that should take off in about two years. National agrees to accept a 15 percent interest in CBA in return for half the loan principal. CBA can handle the debt service on $2 million and National has avoided adding $4 million in nonperforming debt to its books, which, in turn, would have required the bank to raise its reserves.

▶ A chain of fast-food restaurants owes a rapidly mounting debt to its supplier of disposable cups, plates, and utensils. The supplier accepts a 10 percent stake in the chain in return for a portion of the debt. That way, the supplier has a better chance of recovering part of the debt, but moreover the deal may keep the chain in business and buying the supplier's products.

See also **recapitalization**.

debt-to-capital ratio   Measure of a company's borrowing capacity, it is used by bond-rating agencies and analysts to assess creditworthiness.

There are variations on exactly what goes into this ratio, but the most common is to divide total **liabilities** by total **assets** (equal to total liabilities plus **shareholders' equity**). If a company has minority interests in subsidiaries that are consolidated in the **balance sheet**, they need to be added to shareholders' equity.

debt/equity swap

debt-to-capital ratio

t i p

For shareholders, a high debt-to-capital ratio means less security. That is because the debt holders are paid first in any liquidation of the company.

D

debt-to-capital ratio

debt-to-equity ratio

EXAMPLE In the 1995 Chevron Corporation **annual report**, the balance sheet lists short-term debt of $3,806,000,000, long-term debt of $4,521,000,000, and total shareholders' equity of $14,355,000,000. So the debt-to-capital ratio is (in millions):

$$(\$3,806 + \$4,521) \div (\$3,806 + \$4,521 + \$14,355) = 0.367, \text{ or } 36.7\%$$

Chevron has a debt-to-capital ratio of 36.7 percent.

While you usually see the debt ratio expressed this way, you can also look at just the debt-to-equity ratio. That is

(short-term debt + long-term debt) ÷ owner's equity

Chevron's debt-to-equity ratio:

$$(\$3,806 + \$4,521) \div \$14,355 = 0.580, \text{ or } 58\%$$

Chevron has a 58 percent debt-to-equity ratio.

For this ratio, a low number indicates better financial stability than a high one does, but like all ratios, it needs to be evaluated against those of other companies in your industry and against your own company's numbers over time. When calculating the ratio, some prefer to use the **market value** of the debt and equity rather than the **book value**.

acct fin mgmt

debt-to-equity ratio   Measure of a company's borrowing capacity, calculated as follows:

(short-term debt + long-term debt) ÷ owner's equity

See also **debt-to-capital ratio**.

mgmt strat

decentralization   Dispersing of decision-making authority to various parts of a company.

Decentralization is a considerable change from the classic top-down system of **functional organizational design**, which centralizes decision making within top management.

In a functional organization, a vice president for sales, as an example, would set the policy and make the key decisions for all of the salespeople throughout the organization. This functional approach can lead to problems when a company operates in a rapidly changing **environment**.

By contrast, decentralized decisions may be inconsistent and may put the interests of an individual department or unit above the interests of the entire company. Companies whose operations can be easily broken down into individual divisions best lend themselves to decentralization.

Decentralization

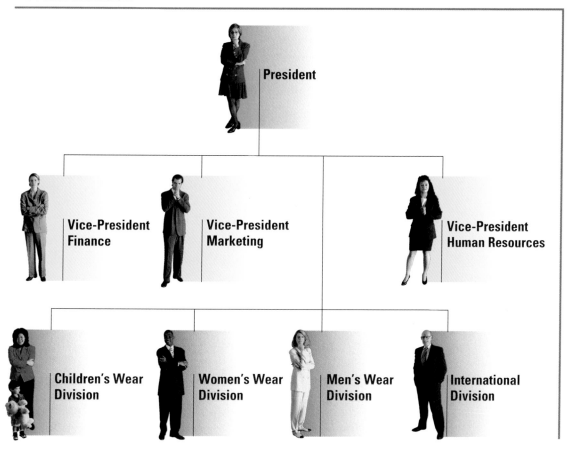

President

Vice-President Finance

Vice-President Marketing

Vice-President Human Resources

Children's Wear Division

Women's Wear Division

Men's Wear Division

International Division

D

EXAMPLE | Consider the decentralized clothing company illustrated above.

The company is organized around four product areas (Infant's, Children's, Women's, and Men's Wear) and one geographic market (international). To a large degree, each division has its own resources that enable it to perform its particular task. For example, Infant's Wear has its own production, design, testing, and marketing organizations. This lets each division concentrate on its own set of products free from the concerns facing other divisions. The International Division focuses on the special problems of doing business abroad.

The vice presidents for finance, human resources, and public affairs monitor the activities of the divisions to advise the president about what is going on, provide advice and support to the divisions, and set policy in those instances when the overall health of the company is at stake. But they do not make day-to-day operating decisions.

decentralization

In turbulent times, if lower-level managers are not free to make decisions, problems get pushed to upper management, which may become overloaded. The organization may be unable to respond to changes in time to make a difference. In such an environment, many companies have found it advantageous to decentralize their organizational structure.

There are some industries that seem to swing like a pendulum from functional to decentralized organization and back again. Integrated oil companies are an example. At any given time, some are organized

FRAME OF REFERENCE

decentralization

In 1967, *Forbes* magazine reported on various management styles. As we can see, opinions vary, but the business leaders quoted below offer comments that still resonate today: Whatever structure a company may have, the message from the top must permeate the entire organization.

In all this, although top management's job is different, it is no less important. "In the modern business," says Thompson of Textron, "the head man, No. One, is not the man who does things. He can't. If he starts being good at doing something, he's not going to be good at his job. He has got to motivate, direct, evaluate and decide when problems come to him. He's got to keep people creative or he's going to be obsolete." He is, in short, a leader, not a boss.

Says IBM's Tom Watson: "To get people to put in enough hours to accomplish something, you have to be a Billy Sunday." Says Amory Houghton, Jr., of Corning Glass: "It seems to me it doesn't really make any difference what organizational setup you have. There has to be a sense of doing something vital, which you must breathe and exude into the organization. Someone catches the rhythm and it goes all through the organization." Genesco's Hill states: "There is no such thing as the perfectly balanced executive who has everything that's needed. Basically, the man in charge of a business must be a leader above everything else."

Excerpted from *Forbes*, Fiftieth Anniversary Issue, September 15, 1967.

decentralization
Quick Facts!

Decentralization's roots date to the high-growth 1920s. Alfred Sloan, then president of General Motors, realized he could not manage it as one company any longer. Other growing companies, including DuPont and General Electric, followed suit.

functionally (with one division that finds and extracts the crude oil and another that refines and markets it), and others are decentralized, usually along geographic lines. Over time, the mix will change and Exxon and Texaco, for example, will swing from geographic to functional while Amoco and Mobil swing the other way.

See also **matrix structure** and **organizational environment**.

mgmt

decision tree   Flow chart that outlines a chain of possible decisions and their potential effects and outcomes.

The decision tree on the following page depicts the possible introduction of a new product. Management decisions appear in squares. Uncertainties appear in circles. Lines show the sequence of choices and results. A probability is assigned to each of the possible outcomes when more than one exists.

So, in our example, if the product is launched without **market** testing, the company has assigned a 45 percent probability to strong sales, a 45 percent probability to weak sales, and 10 percent to no sales. If market testing is positive, the company believes there is a 70 percent probability of strong sales, a 25 percent chance of weak sales, and a 5 percent chance of no sales. With negative market testing, there is a 5 percent probability of strong sales, a 70 percent probability of weak sales, and a 25 percent chance of no sales.

Decision Tree

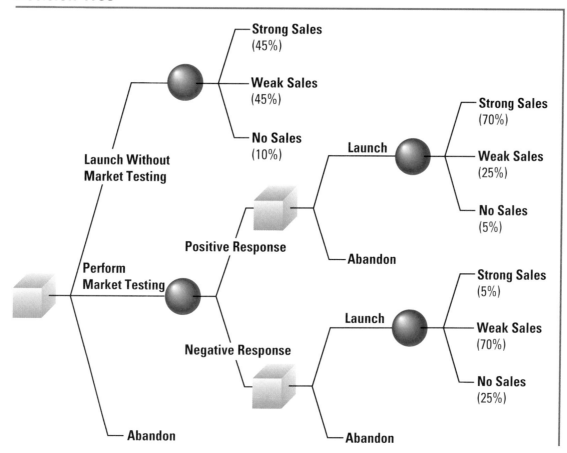

Strong Sales
(45%)

Weak Sales
(45%)

No Sales
(10%)

**Launch Without
Market Testing**

Launch

Strong Sales
(70%)

Weak Sales
(25%)

No Sales
(5%)

Positive Response

Abandon

**Perform
Market Testing**

Strong Sales
(5%)

Launch

Weak Sales
(70%)

Negative Response

No Sales
(25%)

Abandon

Abandon

Abandon

D

Of course, things are seldom as cut-and-dried as the chart suggests. Market testing, for example, may result in a positive finding with reservations. And always keep in mind that the probability forecasts may or may not be accurate. But the decision tree helps management visualize what may lie ahead.

deferred income taxes

acct

deferred income taxes   Amount to be paid or received in the future that arises from timing differences between what is reported for tax purposes and what is shown in financial reports.

Here is how deferred income taxes appear as the net amount:

► **As an Asset**
Accounting principles say you should book your expenses when they are incurred, but the IRS requires you to spread out certain expenses such as warranty expenses, thereby increasing your taxes in the near term and reducing taxes in later years. When you have booked an expense for accounting purposes but not yet deducted it from your tax returns, you have an asset.

defined benefit pension plan

D

Delphi technique

trap 👎

Even with the best of coordinators, the process is time-consuming and does not allow for the rich brew of ideas that sometimes arises from face-to-face discussion and argument.

▶ **As a Liability**

Sometimes you recognize income for accounting purposes before you have to report it to the IRS. One way that happens is in using straight-line **depreciation** for your books and **accelerated depreciation** for your taxes. But that means you "owe" taxes for the extra income on your books.

mgmt

defined benefit pension plan   Method for providing retirement income. At retirement, an employee gets payments based on his or her pay level and length of employment.

See also **pension plans**.

mgmt

defined contribution pension plan   Method for providing retirement income. At retirement, an employee gets payments based on his or her contributions to a specified retirement plan.

See also **pension plans**.

mgmt **strat**

Delphi technique   Method that lets a group make a decision without any direct contact among its members. When you use it as a forecasting tool, it is called Delphi analysis.

Members of your group, or panel, independently express their opinions and review each other's submissions without knowing the identities of the other members. This encourages members to express their opinions freely and reduces both squabbles within the group and the undue influence of one member over another. It also facilitates the development of consensus among a variety of individuals.

EXAMPLE | A computer-manufacturing company wants to forecast demand and determine its production level for the coming year. It assembles a panel of managers from within the company and outside consultants and industry experts. A coordinator submits a series of questions to each panel member, who responds with a forecast and an explanation of how it was developed.

The coordinator compiles the individual forecasts and supporting opinions, and sends the resulting document back to the panel members for comment. The panel members suggest further changes, and a new round of compilation, submission, and comment begins. The process is repeated until a consensus emerges and a decision can be made on production levels.

The technique's success depends mostly on the way information is given to the individual forecasters, the quality of the coordinator's compilations, and the panel members' ability to refine their predictions. Some organizations use **groupware** programs on computer **networks** to facilitate the Delphi technique.

FRAME OF REFERENCE

demand

Let us look at chocolate bars as an example. The biggest influence on demand will be price, but there are other factors to consider:

Current tastes and preferences
Is chocolate "in" these days?

Product quality
If I find a chocolate bar that I think tastes better than others I have had, I will definitely buy that bar.

Funds available
Do the people who want chocolate bars have the money to pay for them?

Prices of other goods
How does the price of chocolate stack up against that of other candies? If I like to eat chocolate only with milk, what is the price of milk?

Expectations about the future price
If I think the price is about to jump, I might buy more. If it is going to fall, I will put off my purchase.

demand   The quantities of a good or service that people are willing and able to buy at all possible prices. In general, at higher prices people buy less, and at lower prices they buy more.

You can measure demand for an individual or family, or even an entire economy.

See also **aggregate demand**, **shortage**, **supply**, and **surplus**.

econ   **mktg**   **strat**

demand forecasting   Educated and artful predicting of the future **demand** for a product or service under various conditions.

It can help you decide whether to enter a **market**, assess short-term needs—like supplies and overtime—to meet production schedules, and look toward long-term needs, like facilities and added staff.

You or experts you hire can forecast demand using methods based on:

1   **Qualitative Analysis**
Examples are **surveying** buyers and collecting the opinions of the sales force, marketing consultants, dealers, distributors, and trade associations.

demand forecasting

Methods for forecasting future needs:

■ Qualitative analysis

■ Observational research

■ Projection

■ Econometric analysis

demand loan

A bank is a place that will lend you money if you can prove that you don't need it.

—Bob Hope, quoted in Alan Harrington's *The Tyranny of Forms: Life in the Crystal Palace*, 1959

demographics

tip

American Demographics magazine, the "bible" of this field, publishes a useful book called The Insiders' Guide to Demographic Know-How. *One of its pointers is to find out first what demographic information is available. By adapting your search to what is available, you will avoid wasting time on a wild goose chase.*

trap

Smart marketers are cautious about relying solely on demographic correlations. Historically, demographic information has not always been a great predictor of consumer behavior.

2 **Observational Research**

The key here is **test marketing**—trying the product out on a small but representative sample of people in your target market before you make a significant investment.

3 **Projection**

Using what is called **time series analysis**, forecasters divide past sales data into the categories of trends, cycles, seasonal patterns, and random occurrences. Trends involve long-term sales patterns. **Cycles** refer to the medium-range changes caused by economic conditions and competition. Seasonal patterns are regular changes during the year. The relationship between sales volumes and each of the nonrandom categories is established using sophisticated computer modeling. Random occurrences—like a record-breaking blizzard or a clothing fad—need to be understood and then discounted in forecasting future sales.

4 **Econometric Analysis**

Using economics, statistics, and mathematics, forecasters can identify the key variables—such as price and advertising—that affect a product's sales and then make predictions based on the relationship between demand and the factors driving it.

fin

demand loan   Debt giving the lender the right to demand payment at any time.

A demand loan has no fixed maturity date. Banks and other financial institutions often require this form of lending for smaller companies and for larger ones carrying large debt burdens and showing uneven profitability.

Some demand loans carry numerous obligations on the borrower. These may specify that all business profits be applied to repay the loan, for example, or may give the lender the right to approve any actions that exceed day-to-day decision making. For example, corporate acquisitions and plant closings would be subject to review. When a demand loan is drawn up as a negotiable instrument, one that can be bought and sold, it is called a **demand note**.

fin

demand note   A **demand loan** that is drawn up as a negotiable instrument that can be bought and sold.

mktg   **econ**

demographics   Statistical profile of a population, often used to identify a market.

See also **market segmentation**.

Demographics: U. S. Population by Race (with Median Age)

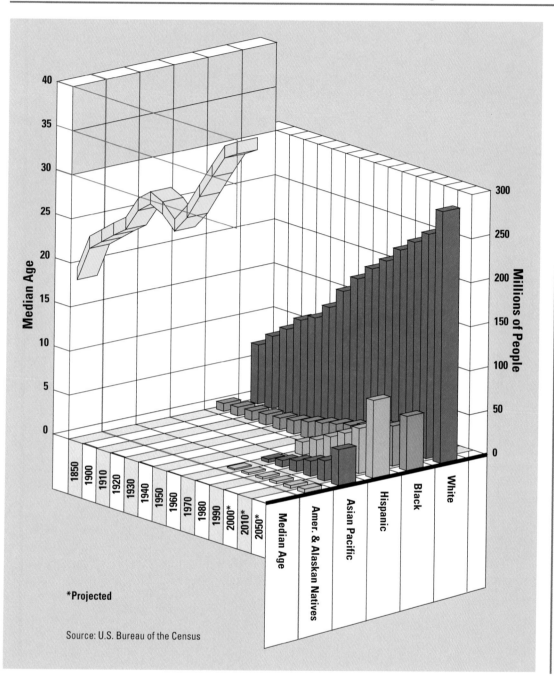

*Projected

Source: U.S. Bureau of the Census

D

mktg

demographic segmentation   Segment of a market determined
by demographic information (versus, say, customer motives).

Demographic factors include age, race, gender, income level, education, family size, and urban-versus-rural status. In population studies, demographics are often combined with social and economic factors (religion, for example) to form the so-called socioeconomic and demographic (SED) factors.

Marketing theorists often use demographic or SED analysis to forecast shopping habits and responsiveness to types of **advertising**.

See also **differentiated marketing**, **market segmentation**, and **target market**.

demographic segmentation

Demographic profiles are used to identify various markets.

mktg

dependent variable   A variable that is affected by other variables in a predictive model. For example, your company's sales may depend on a number of factors, including your prices, competitors' prices, and consumer income levels. In this framework, your sales would be the dependent variable and the other factors would be the independent variables.

See also **variable**.

acct

depletion   Accounting procedure by which the cost of a natural resource—like coal, oil, or timber—is expensed as the resource is sold.

EXAMPLE | Your company acquires the rights to mineral deposits for $5 million. Since an estimated 1 million tons of the mineral are involved, you are paying $5 a ton to acquire the rights to this natural resource. In 1995, you remove and sell 100,000 tons of the mineral, thus depleting $500,000 worth (100,000 tons x $5 per ton). So you charge an expense of $500,000 on your **income statement**, leaving a balance in the natural resource account of $4.5 million.

depletion

acct

depreciation   Extending the accounting for the cost of a tangible fixed **asset**—like a building, machinery, or equipment—over its estimated useful life.

Although accountants, engineers, and economists might each define depreciation differently, everyone can agree that most assets will inevitably lose value. So some means is needed to show, for accounting and tax purposes, that the asset's usefulness has declined. To accountants, depreciation is not so much a matter of valuation as a means of cost allocation.

For tax purposes, depreciation is determined largely by the **accelerated cost recovery system (ACRS)** and its 1986 modification. But companies cannot use these tax depreciation methods in their **financial statements** because they are not permitted under **generally accepted accounting principles (GAAP)** (nor are GAAP methods always accepted for tax purposes). The depreciation method used will have a direct impact on reported results. While depreciation does not affect a company's **cash flow**, it does reduce reported income.

When buying a fixed asset, a company has three decisions to make about depreciation:

1 Depreciation method. For financial reporting, the most common are **straight-line**, double-declining-balance, and the sum-of-the-years' digits.

2 Estimated useful life of the asset.

3 Estimated **salvage value** of the asset or estimate of what it can be sold for at the end of its useful life.

Below are the primary methods of determining depreciation:

► **Straight-Line Depreciation**
is the most commonly used method and the simplest. It assumes that the asset provides constant benefits, so the cost is spread in equal amounts over the asset's useful life. The annual amount of depreciation is calculated by subtracting the salvage value from the cost and then dividing by the useful life.

Straight-Line Depreciation	= ÷	(Cost – Salvage Value) Useful Life

► **Double-Declining-Balance Depreciation**
is a form of **accelerated depreciation** and supposes that most of the asset's value will come early in its life. The depreciation amount is calculated by using twice the straight-line rate in the first year and then continuing to use that rate against the declining balance of the asset's cost. That declining balance—the asset's cost less **accumulated depreciation**—is called **book value**, or carrying amount.

For example, a new piece of equipment for your factory costs you $100,000, and has a $10,000 salvage value and an expected useful life of 10 years, or 10 percent per annum. Salvage value is not taken into account in determining the depreciation rate, so the double-declining rate is 20 percent. Here is how the depreciation schedule would look:

depreciation

EXAMPLE

Let's say you use straight-line depreciation in your landscaping business. You buy a tractor for $15,000, and you believe you will use it for five years and then sell it for $5,000. Here is how you calculate your depreciation expense:

$15,000 – $5,000 ÷ 5 years
= $2,000

Your accounting statements will include $2,000 a year in depreciation expense for the tractor.

depreciation

Double-Declining-Balance Method

Cost	$100,000
Salvage Value	$10,000
Life (years)	10
Rate	20%

Year	Depreciation	Cumulative Depreciation	Balance
1	$ 20,000	$ 20,000	$ 80,000
2	$ 16,000	$ 36,000	$ 64,000
3	$ 12,800	$ 48,800	$ 51,200
4	$ 10,240	$ 59,040	$ 40,960
5	$ 8,192	$ 67,232	$ 32,768
6	$ 6,554	$ 73,786	$ 26,214
7	$ 5,243	$ 79,029	$ 20,971
8	$ 4,194	$ 83,223	$ 16,777
9	$ 3,355	$ 86,578	$ 13,422
10	$ 2,684	$ 89,262	$ 10,738

Under this method, if the asset is still in productive use, you can continue depreciating it but not to a point below its salvage value. Alternatively, you can switch to the straight-line method at the optimal point.

There is a variation on this method called 150%-declining-balance depreciation.

► **The Sum-of-the-Years' Digits Method** is another form of accelerated depreciation. This method assigns a number to each year of an asset's useful life— 1, 2, 3, etc. The sum of the years' digits (SYD) is the total of those numbers added together. If we call the final year "n," the shortcut formula to arrive at SYD is:

$$n (n + 1) \div 2$$

For example, an asset with an eight-year life would have 36 digits:

$$8 (8 + 1) \div 2 = 36$$

The total number of digits is divided into depreciable cost—cost less salvage value—to obtain the value of one digit. The amount of depreciation to be taken each year is based on an inverted scale of the value of the digits.

For example, you purchase a piece of equipment for $40,000 that has a salvage value of $4,000 at the end of its useful life of eight years. The depreciable cost of $36,000 is divided by 36 digits for a value of $1,000 per digit. The depreciation schedule showing the annual depreciation charges and the book value at the end of each year would look like this:

Sum-of-the-Years' Digits Method

Cost	$40,000
Salvage Value	$4,000
Life (years)	8
Depreciable Cost	$36,000

Year	Depreciation	Cumulative Depreciation	Balance
1	$ 8,000	$ 8,000	$ 32,000
2	$ 7,000	$ 15,000	$ 25,000
3	$ 6,000	$ 21,000	$ 19,000
4	$ 5,000	$ 26,000	$ 14,000
5	$ 4,000	$ 30,000	$ 10,000
6	$ 3,000	$ 33,000	$ 7,000
7	$ 2,000	$ 35,000	$ 5,000
8	$ 1,000	$ 36,000	$ 4,000

See also **amortization**.

derivatives   Financial instruments with value based on (derived from) the performance of an underlying **asset**, index, or other investment.

Examples range from **stock options** trading on major exchanges to complex private deals involving different currencies and interest rates. Many businesses use derivatives to reduce the risk to pending

depreciation
Quick Facts!

An asset can be depreciated on the books yet remain highly valuable. In 1979 Lorimar Corporation, which is now part of Warner Brothers at Time Warner, Inc., had a library of old television programming that was fully depreciated. They used depreciated, or zero-book-value, assets for financing. But the library clearly represented value to investors, since the company used its value for TV syndication as the basis for a company refinancing.

D

derivatives

tip

One way of looking at the derivatives markets is that they take risk away from those who do not want it (hedgers) and give it to those who do (speculators).

trap

D

Companies using derivatives solely for hedging are attempting to reduce their risk. But as organizations seek additional advantages from derivatives, they encounter the risks that go along with speculating. In the mid-1990s, Procter & Gamble was among the U.S. companies suffering losses on derivatives ($102 million after-tax), and Barings PLC lost more than $1 billion, both in well-publicized cases.

transactions that may arise from changes in interest or currency-exchange rates. This is called **hedging**.

> **EXAMPLE** | A company in Malaysia contracts to manufacture electrical components for a company in the United States. The Malaysian company will be paid $500,000 in about three months, once the components are made and delivered.
>
> Since payment will be made in U.S. dollars, although the manufacturer is meeting its payroll and other expenses in Malaysian currency, there is substantial risk if the dollar falls in value. So the manufacturer buys a contract giving it the right to sell $500,000 in three months at today's exchange rate. For the price of the contract, the manufacturer has eliminated any risk from currency fluctuations.

As derivatives have become more popular, companies have also begun trading them in more speculative ways to profit from swings in interest rates or the prices of commodities or currencies.

Derivatives are traded two ways:

1 On exchanges, where hedgers and speculators buy and sell standardized contracts through licensed brokers, backed by a centralized clearinghouse that requires minimum deposits, or **margins**, to cover the value of the contract. A leading exchange for currency and interest-rate futures, for example, is the **International Monetary Market (IMM)** of the **Chicago Mercantile Exchange**.

2 Through **over-the-counter (OTC)** transactions privately negotiated between two or more parties, often using a major bank as mediator. OTC deals grew about eightfold from the mid-1980s to the mid-1990s.

The use of financial derivatives has been increasing since 1971, when the United States scrapped the Bretton Woods Agreements, which for a quarter-century had pegged most currency exchange rates to the dollar, backed by gold from the U.S. Treasury. Both exporters and importers needed to find protection from swings in currency rates. The idea caught on, and hedging expanded as well for other volatile exchange markets, including those for stocks, bonds, and commodities.

Then, in the 1980s, the use of derivatives mushroomed along with the growth of both international trade and the near-instantaneous movement of capital through electronic transactions.

Derivatives fall into five basic categories:

1 **Futures**
Traded on organized exchanges, these standardized contracts lock in a transaction at a certain price on a specific future date. Futures contracts can be for (1) financial instruments, such as currencies and Eurodollars; (2) indexes, such as the S&P

500; or (3) physical commodities, such as corn and gold. The contracts change hands many times on the market where they are listed, and, at maturity, contracts to buy can offset contracts to sell. So in most cases, the underlying transaction never takes place.

2 Forwards

OTC contracts calling for delivery of a specific amount of an underlying asset on a future date at the spot price (the current cash price) or another negotiated price. Forwards differ from futures in that each agent of the contract is negotiable (grade, time, and place of delivery). Because there is no central clearinghouse spreading the risk of default across a wide pool of buyers and sellers, forwards are available primarily to large hedgers with enough collateral to satisfy an underwriting bank. Traders can use forwards to cover a futures contract. They might, for example, negotiate a forward contract to buy 50,000 bushels of corn in August because they are obligated to sell that amount then in the futures market.

3 Options

These contracts, available from organized exchanges and OTC, differ from futures and forwards in that they do not have to be exercised or offset. A **call option** gives the holder the right, but not the obligation, to buy an asset at a particular price before a certain date. If the asset does not climb to that value, or **strike** price, the option does not need to be exercised. A **put option** gives the holder the right, but not the obligation, to sell an asset at a particular price before a certain date. If the asset does not fall to the strike price, the holder will not exercise the option. Options represent two-thirds of all the derivatives trading based on equities, but trading is larger still in interest-rate options.

4 Swaps

Swaps are private agreements between two companies to exchange cash flows in the future according to a prearranged formula. For instance, firms that have branches in each other's home countries might exchange some of their **accounts receivable** to reduce costs and **foreign exchange** risk. In interest-rate swaps, traders may take responsibility for each other's loans. That makes sense when one company can get good terms on, say, a fixed-rate loan and another can do well on a floating rate. In another form of interest-rate swap, called a **yield-curve swap**, one company may trade long-term debt for another's short-term debt. **Swap** contracts last longer than most other derivatives, covering from one to 10 years.

5 Hybrids and Synthetics

These are derivative securities that combine the four basic forms of derivatives to design a complex array of hedges for meeting new situations. Options, for example, can be traded on other forms of derivatives. Synthetics allow firms to construct derivatives not covered by existing markets.

See also **arbitrage**.

derivatives

Derivatives fall into five basic categories:

1 **Futures**

2 **Forwards**

3 **Options**

4 **Swaps**

5 **Hybrids and synthetics**

D

Breaking News

Because of the risk involved in derivatives trading, a number of new policies were instituted in 1995:

- The Financial Accounting Standards Board (FASB) required publicly traded companies using derivatives to explain the risk in their annual reports.

- Major U.S. brokerage houses adopted new standards for handling derivatives.

- The Group of Thirty, an association of central banks and major financial institutions, issued recommendations for companies to monitor and direct derivatives trading more carefully.

FRAME OF REFERENCE

derivatives

After Orange County, California, filed for **bankruptcy** protection in December 1994, derivatives suddenly became known to policymakers, the media, and the general public as the "D" word—something synonymous with risk. But less well known is the fact that Orange County's losses had more to do with an unsuccessful investment strategy than its use of derivatives. In fact, the majority of Orange County's $2 billion loss was caused by its use of reverse repurchase agreements, or "reverse repos."

Robert Citron, the county treasurer, had used reverse repos to leverage his $7.5 billion fund up to $20 billion, effectively "borrowing" another $12.5 billion by using the core holding as collateral and doubling his bet that **interest rates** would remain low. He also used some of the borrowed funds to buy "inverse floaters" (derivatives), whose value declines as interest increases. When interest rates turned against him, he lost his bet: His core bonds lost value, which triggered margin calls (since the bonds were collateral on the repos). To top it off, the inverse floaters dropped in value. The problem, of course, was not with the derivatives but an optimistic "borrow short, lend long" strategy that went bad.

But the complicated nature of the strategy made it easier to refer to Orange County's "derivatives losses," and a media misconception was born. Many in the investment community tried to point out the folly of using derivatives as a scapegoat, especially since they are widely used by companies and fund managers to reduce risk. In fact, Arthur Levitt, Chairman of the SEC, testified later that "derivatives did not cause Orange County's problems; the fault lies in a failed investment strategy involving the use of borrowed money for speculation. Futhermore, it would be a grave error... to demonize derivatives and blame them for the loss. Derivatives are not inherently bad or good—they are a bit like electricity—dangerous if mishandled but bearing the potential to do tremendous good."

Alan Greenspan, chairman of the Federal Reserve, joined in the defense saying that it would be a "a serious mistake" to single out derivative instruments for special regulatory treatment in the wake of Orange County and that "it is by no means clear that these losses have been attributed solely, or even primarily, to financial instruments that would typically be called derivatives."

development bank

econ mktg

derived demand When **demand** for one product or service causes demand for something else.

Economists see labor as a form of derived demand: The demand for a person's skills depends on—is derived from—the demand for the product he or she produces.

Marketers think more about derived demand for products, such as when demand in the **industrial market** grows out of demand in the **consumer market**.

EXAMPLE | When consumers buy more ice cream, ice cream makers buy more eggs, cream, machinery, delivery trucks, and so on. If a major health study comes out implicating ice cream in heart attacks, consumer demand might suddenly plunge—affecting not only the ice cream makers but also farmers, dairies, machine manufacturers, and automakers.

Derived demand can occur within the consumer market, too.

EXAMPLE | When PC users first bought a Windows operating system, they needed more memory and disk capacity to run it. So there was derived demand for memory chips and high-capacity hard drives. Then, as they upgraded to Windows 95, they needed even more of both.

mktg

descriptive segmentation Using **demographic** and geographic factors to define a market.

See also **market segmentation**.

oper

design capacity Output level a manufacturing plant was designed to run at. Also called **nominal capacity**.

fin **econ**

development bank Institution with the primary objective of helping nonindustrialized countries.

These banks help by raising capital, providing technical assistance, and bringing in new investors. The four major development banks listed below are funded by various governments and international banks, including the World Bank.

The four major development banks are:

1 The Asian Development Bank

2 The African Development Bank and Fund

3 The Inter-American Development Bank

4 The European Bank for Reconstruction and Development (for Eastern Europe)

Small regional development banks attend to such areas as Central America. Local development banks focus on a specific country; the government of a host country may operate them in cooperation with local businesses and banks.

derived demand

In the entertainment industry today, there is an increasing demand for filmed content because of the proliferation of viewing media and channels. This, in turn, has increased the demand for scarce labor talent—such as stars and directors—involved in filmmaking.

design capacity

Quick Facts!

An oil refinery has a design capacity of 125,000 barrels of crude a day. When everything is going right and it is operating at peak levels, it may be able to process 140,000 barrels a day.

D

differentiated marketing

You have run a successful seafood restaurant in a small shopping center for several years. But over the past year, the weekend dinner and weekday lunch crowds have been declining steadily. One factor is that another (fancier and pricier) seafood restaurant has opened about a mile down the road. Another is the change in your shopping center: Big-ticket stores have closed and been replaced by low-end, family-oriented places. Your available market has changed.

So you decide to tailor some of your offerings to meet the needs of this changing market while not ignoring your loyal customers. You introduce a lunchtime and weekend bargain seafood buffet, and you add less expensive items to your menu without changing the old ones. You have differentiated your product; now you differentiate your marketing. You advertise the new offerings with coupons in the local paper. At lunchtime on weekends, you hire a clown to stand outside your restaurant giving away balloons and coupons, enticing families to stop and try the new buffet.

---

differentiated marketing

tip | 👍

Designing a segmentation strategy should be included as part of your overall marketing strategy. Only a few market leaders, like McDonald's or Wal-Mart, conduct mass marketing today.

---

oper **econ** **mktg** **acct**

differential cost   Increase (or decrease) in overall cost of production as the result of producing one more (or less) unit.

See also **marginal cost**.

---

mktg **strat**

differentiated marketing   Strategy that focuses on individual customer segment needs and designs products to address them.

You start with **market segmentation**, identify the specific **target markets** you want to reach, then tailor a **marketing mix** to fit each target. Differentiated marketing, which focuses on identifying the market, goes hand-in-hand with **differentiation**, which focuses on creating products or services tailored to the identified markets.

The upside to differentiated as opposed to **undifferentiated marketing** is that you will probably increase sales volume and your competitive position. The downside is that your costs for product development, manufacturing, and advertising will rise. Nevertheless, differentiated marketing is the trend these days except for **commodities** like steel, salt, and matches.

---

mktg **strat**

differentiation   Distinguishing a brand so that customers can perceive a difference from the competition. Also called **product differentiation**.

You can differentiate products on the basis of features like options, performance, and **warranties**.

mktg **strat**

diffusion of innovation curve Graphical plot showing patterns of acceptance of new goods and services.

See also **diffusion process**.

mktg **strat**

diffusion process Pattern of consumer acceptance of new goods and services.

Some people accept a new product as soon as it appears on the store shelves, or even earlier. Those are the people who bought pocket calculators when they sold for upwards of $100 each. Others wait until all the reviews are in and all their friends have one—and the price is down considerably. This process can take years.

A diffusion of innovation curve plots acceptance of a product in a market using the following five segments:

1 **Innovators**
The first 2.5 percent to adopt a new product (outrageous price, untried quality, and all).

2 **Early Adopters**
The next 13.5 percent of the segment—are cautious opinion leaders in the market.

3 **Early Majority**
The next 34 percent—take a long time to make up their minds but still adopt the product before most people.

4 **Late Majority**
The next 34 percent—try out new products only after they are in wide use.

diffusion process

tip |

If your strategy is to target early adopters, using an innovator in your marketing will help position your product. Early adopters admire innovators because of their foresight in selecting new products.

D

FRAME OF

REFERENCE

differentiation

Xerox achieved enormous success by differentiating themselves as the market leader in quality and customer service. For years, the company had been known for its ability to produce breakthrough products and technologies. But their competitive edge never lasted long because competitors would quickly match or improve on Xerox's products.

Xerox saved itself by instituting a program in 1983 called "Leadership through Quality," which changed the focus of the company from R & D to quality. By differentiating themselves from their powerful competitors, Xerox not only survived but actually recaptured a 4 percent market share from the Japanese. Revenues jumped from $8.7 billion in 1984 to $12.4 billion in 1989. Customer satisfaction rose 38 percent in this five-year period. In 1989, Xerox received the highest accolade for corporate quality in the United States—the Malcolm Baldrige National Quality Award.

Diffusion Process

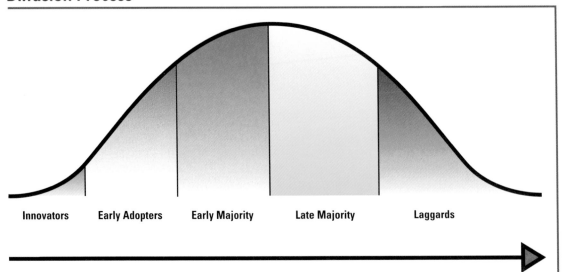

| Innovators | Early Adopters | Early Majority | Late Majority | Laggards |

Time Since Product Introduction

D

5 **Laggards**
The last 16 percent—love tradition, dislike change, and wait until the product becomes a tradition before trying it.

In the 1990s, aggressive technology companies like Intel have made an art out of introducing new, more powerful, upgraded products before the earlier versions have reached the crest of the wave.

tech

digital   Using the binary code (created from the digits 0 and 1) to represent data. The contrasting method is **analog**, which involves a continuous signal.

fin   **mgmt**

dilution   Dividing the ownership of a company among more shareholders by issuing more shares.

Dilution can result from stock offerings, the exercising of **warrants** or options, or the conversion of **preferred stock** or **bonds**.

EXAMPLE | Your corporation has 100,000 shares of **common stock** outstanding. Earnings last year were $1 million, or $10 per share ($1,000,000 ÷ 100,000 = $10). If you authorize and sell another 100,000 shares and your **earnings** do not change, per-share earnings this year will be $5 per share ($1,000,000 ÷ 200,000 = $5).

acct

direct costing   Method of attributing manufacturing costs to the value of goods produced that takes into account only **variable costs**.

See also **costing**.

digital

0 1 0 0 0 1

1011011001

1110011001

1111011111

0111011001

1100011001

0101011001

The binary code above represents data created from the digits 0 and 1.

Quick Facts!

dilution

The Flip Side

The opposite of dilution (which increases the number of shares outstanding) happens when a company buys back its shares. Investors usually see this as a positive sign because fewer shares mean higher earnings per share, by definition, or a sign of management's confidence—that their shares are a "good buy."

In 1995, many perceived the large number of shares bought back by banks as positive, contributing to big gains in those share prices. Citicorp, for instance, bought back 23 million shares of its stock during 1995 and saw its share price rise 62 percent. Similarly, Bank of America bought more than 16 million of its own shares and enjoyed an equally impressive 64 percent share price gain.

mktg

direct mail   A method of **direct marketing** using the mail that can be very effective when directed at a target audience.

mktg

direct marketing   Using a medium to stimulate consumer response without the need for direct personal contact.

Four major forms of direct marketing are catalog sales, **telemarketing**, TV selling, and electronic shopping. Direct marketing has grown rapidly in recent years. That is because of the trend toward more **market segmentation** as well as other changes—like more working women with less shopping time, traffic congestion in shopping areas, toll-free numbers, and powerful computer aids to marketers.

For a good direct marketing campaign, you should have:

▶ Understanding of the needs of the **target market**.

▶ Segmentation of the target market.

▶ Opportunity for quick customer response.

▶ Good communication, which can take place at any location.

▶ A measurable response.

EXAMPLE | Automatic Data Processing (ADP), a payroll services company, spends more than $5 million dollars a year on direct mail. ADP buys lists of prospects and sends these businesses sharp-looking personalized letters including a postcard and a toll-free number for immediate response. This direct mail is believed to yield an impressive 3 to 5 percent response rate.

See also **cold calling** and **list broker**.

direct marketing

D

D

FRAME OF

REFERENCE

discount rate

The term discount originated during the early years of the Federal Reserve, when banks used their business loans as collateral for borrowing reserves. Banks often "discounted" their loans to businesses, which meant they deducted the interest up front. If a bank later used a discounted loan as collateral for borrowing reserves, the Fed, in turn, would discount the bank's loan, deducting its interest in advance.

Today, commercial banks usually use some of their government securities as collateral when borrowing from the Fed, and interest is paid when the loan is due. Still, the term discount has survived.

direct reports

mgmt

direct reports   Number of employees a manager supervises directly.

See also **span of control**.

acct   **mgmt**

disclaimer of opinion   Indicates that an auditor cannot give an opinion, usually because the **audit** could not be completed.

acct   **mgmt**

disclosure   Giving the receiver of information—whether it be an auditor, a consumer, or an investor—everything needed to fully understand your operation or your product.

See also **adequate disclosure concept**.

fin   **econ**

discount rate   (1) Interest rate the **Federal Reserve System (Fed)** charges its member banks.

The Fed can influence **monetary policy**: Lowering the discount rate encourages banks to borrow more reserves, which they can then use to make more interest-earning loans and investments, thus expanding the **money supply**; conversely, a rise in the rate can trigger a contraction in the supply of money and credit. Despite their monetary influence, discount rate changes are usually reactive rather than proactive—that is, the Fed changes the rate to keep it in line with market **interest rates**.

(2) The interest rate used to calculate the **present value** of a series of future cash payments.

See also **internal rate of return**.

Discount Rate, 1950–1995 (Plotted with CPI*)

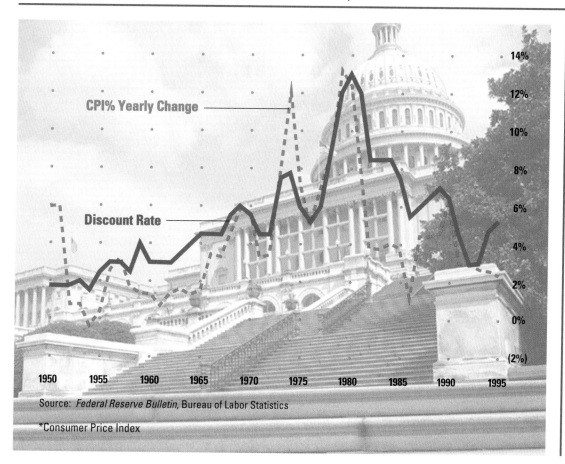

CPI% Yearly Change

Discount Rate

14%
12%
10%
8%
6%
4%
2%
0%
(2%)

1950 1955 1960 1965 1970 1975 1980 1985 1990 1995

Source: *Federal Reserve Bulletin*, Bureau of Labor Statistics

*Consumer Price Index

D

---

fin **econ** **strat** **mgmt**

discounted cash flow Current worth in dollars of an investment's future **cash flow**.

See also **net present value (NPV)**.

econ

discretionary income What is left of your **disposable income** after you have paid for essentials such as food, rent, and utilities.

See also **personal income**.

econ

disposable income What is left of your personal income after taxes are paid.

See also **personal income**.

econ

dissavings If you spend more than you earn, the negative balance is sometimes called dissavings.

See also **savings**.

discretionary income

distribution channel

Quick Facts!

Federal Express revolutionized the package delivery business when it began using fixed-cost pricing, allowing customers to accurately project shipping costs. Now FedEx uses its highly advanced information systems to offer full-fledged distribution and warehousing services, helping customers to manage their own businesses.

D

mktg

distribution channel   Integrated system of channel members that influence the movement of goods and services and have direct impact on the end consumer.

A product's distribution channel usually involves a network of interdependent organizations—like transportation companies, storage facilities, wholesalers, and retailers—needed to move the product along. What one organization adds to the process may be tangible, as when a factory converts raw material into a product, or intangible, like a wholesale distributor that handles the logistics of getting a product to retail stores.

Ownership of the product also may flow along the channel. A distributor takes title to goods and then sells them. Agents and brokers do not take ownership of what they sell. Manufacturers often promote their products to channel members as well as to consumers. The organizations between the producer and retailer are called intermediaries or middlemen. And the various layers are called channel levels.

Four forms of distribution channels are:

1 **Direct-Sales or Direct-Marketing**
Where the product goes from the producer directly to the ultimate consumer. Pitney Bowes manufactures mail processing systems and sells them to business users through its Mailing Systems Division's sales force. It also provides service through its direct sales force.

2 **One Intermediary**
Often a retailer. For example, Kmart buys TVs and other goods directly from the manufacturers and sells them to the consumer via retail stores.

3 **Multiple Intermediaries**
Typically, a wholesaler and a retailer are involved, plus in all likelihood some transportation and possibly storage companies. McKesson, a drug wholesaler and distributor, buys pharmaceuticals from manufacturers, warehouses them, and then sells to retail pharmacies, hospitals, and health care providers. Various freight companies may be involved in the transportation.

4 **Industrial Channels**
In the industrial market, the producer might sell directly to the customer. Or the producer may use intermediaries such as manufacturer's representatives or distributors.

The distribution channel, taken together, performs a variety of functions: transporting and storing goods; financing the operations; gathering information through market research and contact with the various customers; fitting the product or service to the customers' needs; promoting the product or service; identifying potential buyers, reaching them, and negotiating the transaction; and in general taking on elements of financial risk.

Distribution channels were once mainly loose collections of independent producers, wholesalers, and retailers—each member having its own way of doing business and each out to make maximum profit for itself. Recently, though, **vertical marketing systems** have been on the rise, with the elements of the channel working cooperatively.

See also **retailing**.

mktg

distributor   Company that takes title to finished goods and then sells them.

See also **distribution channels**.

fin

diversifiable risk   Potential price swings in one company's securities for reasons specific to that company (versus, say, market conditions). These swings can have a reduced effect on a portfolio's risk through **diversification**.

See also **nonmarket risk**.

strat   **fin**   **mgmt**

diversification   Strategy for spreading risk by investing in a variety of markets, industries, or types of securities.

A corporation might diversify by adding new product lines or buying other companies. A corporation that adds new companies from a variety of businesses is known as a **conglomerate**.

EXAMPLE | While Philip Morris has gotten a lot of attention recently because of its position as the No. 1 cigarette maker, this New York-based conglomerate is involved in much more than tobacco.

Consider packaged food. Brands like Jell-O, Breyer's yogurt, Claussen pickles, Oscar Mayer, and Post Raisin Bran are only a few of the items to be found in the pantry at its Kraft subsidiary, which just happens to be the largest food company in the United States. And the Miller Brewing subsidiary ranks No. 2 among beer makers with its Molson, Red Dog, Lowenbrau, and Foster's brands, among others.

Taking its diversification beyond consumer products, Philip Morris also has interests in financial services and real estate investment.

diversification
Quick Facts!

Financial experts agree that diversification works as intended for investors in the stock market. A portfolio of eight to ten stocks in different industries will reduce risk. Many investors find that a portfolio made up of 60 percent stocks and 40 percent bonds reduces risk further while keeping overall return at an acceptable level.

D

An investor should act as though he has a lifetime decision card with just 20 punches on it. With every investment decision, his card is punched, and he has one fewer available for the rest of his life.

—Warren Buffett, Chairman and CEO, Berkshire Hathaway, in *Forbes*, May 25, 1992

As a business strategy for a company, diversification often does not work as well. In some ways, diversification presents its own risks, because companies managing one business successfully may lack the ability to run a very different one. A well-publicized example of diversification gone wrong is Mobil Corporation's purchase in the 1970s of Montgomery Ward and Container Corporation of America, both of which were sold in the 1980s at a considerable loss.

The companies most successful at diversification are perhaps the ones that specialize in it, seeing themselves as holding companies looking for good investments. A notable example is Berkshire Hathaway, whose businesses include insurance; making candy, uniforms, and vacuum cleaners; publishing encyclopedias and newspapers; selling furniture; and making and distributing uniforms. General Electric has also proved adept at maintaining a successful mix of businesses.

Diversification

Cash	$	10%	
Bonds	bond	40%	– Government – High-Grade – High-Yield
Stocks	stock	50%	– Blue-Chip – Small Stocks – International Stocks

In deciding between different investments, the principal categories most investors start with are Cash, Bonds, and Stocks. But within those categories are a number of different subcategories, which may also be a part of the diversification process.

mgmt

diversity   Mixture of groupings that make up an organization.

Traditionally, diversity was thought of in terms of race, gender, and ethnic background. And it has been long recognized that the proportion of women and minorities in the workforce is on the upswing. Estimates are that by the year 2000, white males will account for only 15 percent of the growth in the total number of workers. To ensure a growing workforce, companies have aggressively recruited more women and minorities.

Companies are struggling to accommodate different groups while still promoting the interests of the organization. This effort is known as **managing diversity**. And the concept of diversity has come to

diversity

At Hoechst Celanese, we recognize the value that people from different cultures and varied experiences bring to the workplace. A diverse workforce results in better decision-making and increases the potential for extraordinary business results.

—Karl Engels, President & CEO, Hoechst Celanese, in *Forbes*, August 28, 1995

D

FRAME OF

REFERENCE

diversification

The Art of Portfolio Management

Portfolio management is not a new concept. Even the Medicis and other Renaissance financiers managed their portfolios of high-risk sovereign loans, which they had to make to conform to the political pressures of their times, by diversifying their exposure.

A diversified portfolio for an investor could include mutual funds, individual foreign and domestic stocks in several industries, corporate and government bonds, and real estate. The idea behind diversification is that a balanced mix of investments will continue to do well even when a few of them are experiencing hard times. As the saying goes: Do not put all your eggs in one basket.

---

include all people who differ from the majority. That now includes groups like single parents, gays, lesbians, the elderly, and the physically and mentally handicapped.

In the early 1990s, estimates were that 40 percent of U.S. companies had diversity-training programs.

EXAMPLE | Many companies—including Amoco, Avon, and Procter & Gamble—have diversity councils or organizations. The executive committee of Mobil Corporation's Board of Directors went on a retreat in 1994 with its diversity task force to improve the company's sensitivity. Hoechst Celanese, a leader in diversity programs, goes so far as to conduct compensation reviews to spot inequities.

See also **affirmative action**.

fin **mgmt**

dividend Payment made to shareholders.

Dividends are most often granted in cash but can take a number of forms, including additional securities. Companies that pay regular dividends traditionally issue them quarterly, but they can be granted or terminated at any interval.

Dividend policy varies greatly from company to company. If you have preferred shareholders, their dividends are already set. But if a corporation is successful enough to have decisions to make about how much to pay its common shareholders, one of the following three categories usually applies.

There are three categories used in deciding dividend policy:

1 **No Dividends**
Warren Buffett's Berkshire Hathaway. The idea is that if your company cannot make better returns for its investors than they can make for themselves, you've got no business tying up their money in the first place. The best use for your company's earnings is to plow them back into the business,

dividend

The electric utility industry has long been known for its high dividend yields—averaging close to 6%, versus 2.3% for the S&P 500 at the end of 1995. This is why they're attractive to so-called "widows and orphans" investors, who are interested in current income over share price appreciation.

The electric utility stocks have a collective "payout ratio" above 80%—meaning that they pay out more than 80% of their earnings in dividends. But recent moves toward deregulation have made the slow-and-steady earnings growth of the electrics far less certain, and many now question whether such high payouts still make sense.

dividend

Merton H. Miller, born in 1923, is a professor emeritus at the University of Chicago's Graduate School of Business, where he has been on the faculty since 1961. He was awarded a Nobel Prize in Economics in 1990 for his work in the area of corporate finance. He is best known as coauthor, along with Franco Modigliani, of a theory holding that dividends are irrelevant to the company's value.

D

I always have been a great believer in a company buying back its shares because I thought that made much more sense than paying tax on dividends. The data I've seen recently suggest that the percentage of shares repurchased compared to dividends paid out is going up annually. Apparently they're learning, but still fairly slowly.

—Merton Miller

generating growth. Besides, the company's earnings have already been taxed once. Paying them out to investors gets them taxed again.

If a company maintains a no-dividend policy and continues to grow, then any time an investor needs cash, he or she ought to be able to sell some stock profitably. Many start-up companies, of course, pay no dividends in their early growth stages but begin later.

2 Moderate Dividends

Wendy's. This approach tries to please investors who want to see profits reinvested for growth as well as those who seek some current income. The dividends represent a much smaller cash return than investors could earn in other ways, and increases in the payout are rare. Even so, companies are reluctant to reduce or eliminate a dividend because that action often sends investors fleeing.

Wendy's pays six cents a quarter (24 cents a year). Its 1994 payout ratio—the proportion of its profits used to pay the dividend—was 26 percent. With the stock price around $20, it represents a 1.2 percent return. Obviously, shareholders are counting on big increases over time in the stock price to make their investment worthwhile.

3 Steadily Growing Dividends

First Union. Many successful companies like to please their income-oriented investors with growing payouts. The most successful can pull that off and plow plenty back into growth as well. Few of the companies in this category are as regular with their dividend increases as First Union, which raised its dividend in 1995 for the 18th consecutive year. But their policy is to aim for growth in payouts.

First Union's 1994 dividends totaled $1.72, representing a payout ratio of 35 percent. At its late-1995 payout level of $2.08 a year, with the stock trading around $50 a share, it represented a 4.2 percent return. Of course, investors are hoping to see growth in the share price, too, but that 4.2 percent is a bird in the hand as they anticipate those in the bush.

Despite the differences in opinion about the wisdom of increasing dividend payments, a stock's price does tend to rise when a payout boost is announced. It is regarded as a sign that the company is confident of its outlook. If managers saw serious trouble on the horizon, they probably would not be boosting cash outlays.

An increasingly popular way for companies to reward their shareholders without increasing the dividend is via a stock **buyback**. A company that buys up its shares on the open **market** is adding value to the shares still outstanding. That is because the buyback increases demand for the stock and, by reducing the number of shares outstanding, improves all per-share calculations.

See also **stock split**.

FRAME OF REFERENCE

dividend

The railroads, divided within their own councils and unable to meet the new competition from cars, trucks, and buses, stagnated or worse; passenger traffic declined rapidly, and by 1925, the total of track miles in receivership stood at 18,000. Recklessly wooing investors by raising dividends in the face of declining earnings, the railroads fiddled while Rome burned. The New York Central earnings for 1929 were almost 10% lower than those for 1923, yet the dividend for 1923 was $5 and for 1929, $8.

Excerpted from *Forbes*, Sixtieth Anniversary Issue, September 15, 1977.

fin

dividend yield
Return on **common stock** or **preferred stock**, based on current market prices.

It is calculated by dividing the annual **dividend** distribution by the market price.

fin

DJIA
See **Dow Jones Industrial Average**.

mgmt

dotted-line relationship
On an organizational chart, an employee who reports directly to a supervisor is shown with a solid line; ancillary superiors he or she must keep informed are shown with a dotted line.

See also **matrix structure**.

fin

Dow Jones Industrial Average (DJIA)
Oldest and most commonly followed U.S. stock market index.

When people say, "The market rose 10 points today," they are usually referring to the Dow Jones Industrial Average.

The DJIA is a price-weighted average of 30 widely traded stocks on the **New York Stock Exchange (NYSE)**. The companies change from time to time, but they usually represent between 15 percent and 20 percent of the market value of all actively traded stocks on the NYSE. The DJIA is adjusted for the substitutions, mergers, stock dividends, and splits that have occurred since it was first published in 1896. Because of this 100 years of adjustments, it has more value as a measure of price movements than as a measure of absolute price levels. (See charts on the following pages.)

See also **Russell 2000 Index**, **Standard & Poor's (S&P) 500**, and **Wilshire 5000 Equity Index**.

---

dividend yield

EXAMPLE

A stock is selling at $50 a share and has been paying a dividend of 25 cents a quarter, or $1 a year. The dividend yield is 2 percent ($1 ÷ $50 = 0.02, or 2%).

D

Dow Jones Industrial Average

Quick Facts!

The only company that has been included in the DJIA during its entire history is General Electric. GE was formed in 1892 when Thomson-Houston Company and the Edison General Electric Company merged. One share of GE, bought for about $100 in 1896 at the start of the Dow, has grown to 768 shares today, with a value in 1996 of around $55,000.

Dow Jones Industrial Average

When the Dow Jones Index was first developed in 1896, it was easy to calculate: Charles Dow added the prices of the 12 stocks then in the index and divided by 12. Today, the calculation is a bit more complicated: The first step is still the simple addition to get to the numerator, but the denominator is more complicated because of adjustments for mergers, stock splits, and other events that have to be accounted for to maintain historical continuity. Because it is price-weighted, rather than market-weighted like many other indices, higher-priced stocks have a disproportionate effect on the Dow.

Dow Jones Industrial Average (Companies)

Ticker	Company
ALD	Allied-Signal Company
AA	Aluminum Company of America
AXP	American Express Company
T	American Telephone & Telegraph
BS	Bethlehem Steel
BA	The Boeing Company
CAT	Caterpillar, Inc.
CHV	Chevron
KO	Coca-Cola Company
DIS	The Walt Disney Company
DD	DuPont
EK	Eastman Kodak Company
XON	Exxon Corporation
GE	General Electric Company
GM	General Motors Corporation
GT	Goodyear Tire & Rubber Company
IBM	International Business Machines Corporation
IP	International Paper Company
JPM	J. P. Morgan & Company, Incorporated
MCD	McDonald's Corporation
MRK	Merck & Company
MMM	Minnesota Mining & Manufacturing Company
MO	Philip Morris Company
PG	Procter & Gamble Corporation
S	Sears, Roebuck and Company
TX	Texaco Incorporated
UK	Union Carbide Corporation
UTX	United Technologies Company
WX	Westinghouse Electric Corporation
Z	F. W. Woolworth & Company

Dow Jones Industrial Average (DJIA), 1970–1983

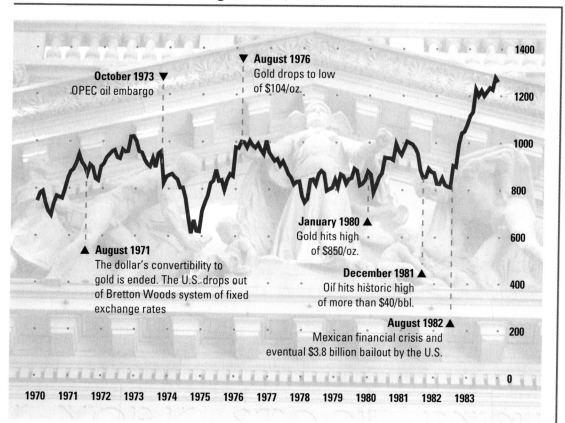

October 1973 ▼
OPEC oil embargo

▼ August 1976
Gold drops to low
of $104/oz.

▲ August 1971
The dollar's convertibility to
gold is ended. The U.S. drops out
of Bretton Woods system of fixed
exchange rates

January 1980 ▲
Gold hits high
of $850/oz.

December 1981 ▲
Oil hits historic high
of more than $40/bbl.

August 1982 ▲
Mexican financial crisis and
eventual $3.8 billion bailout by the U.S.

1400 1200 1000 800 600 400 200 0

1970 1971 1972 1973 1974 1975 1976 1977 1978 1979 1980 1981 1982 1983

Dow Jones Industrial Average (DJIA), 1984–1996

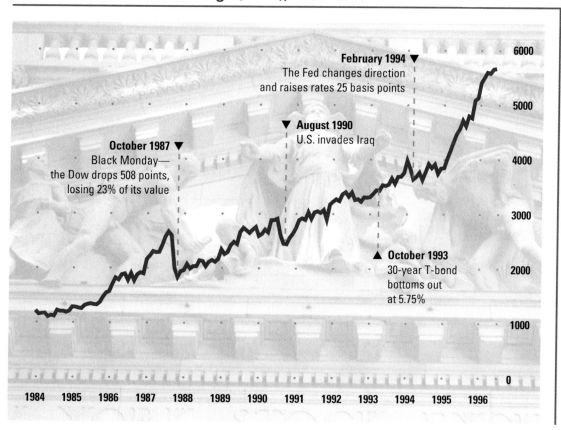

February 1994 ▼
The Fed changes direction
and raises rates 25 basis points

▼ August 1990
U.S. invades Iraq

October 1987 ▼
Black Monday—
the Dow drops 508 points,
losing 23% of its value

▲ October 1993
30-year T-bond
bottoms out
at 5.75%

6000 5000 4000 3000 2000 1000 0

1984 1985 1986 1987 1988 1989 1990 1991 1992 1993 1994 1995 1996

D

215

Dow Jones Industrial Average

Dow Jones & Company founders Charles Henry Dow (1851–1902) and Edward Jones (1856–1920) began their financial news service in 1882. Initially, the firm delivered news items by messenger to the financial institutions of Wall Street, and in 1889 began publication of the *Wall Street Journal*, of which Dow was the editor until his death. Dow is generally given credit for compiling the first average of stock prices. This average, and others he devised, evolved into what we know today as the Dow Jones stock averages.

Charles Dow   Edward Jones

D

drive time

Quick Facts!

KinderCare, the nationwide child-care centers, spent $3 million a year in the mid-1990s to advertise on drive-time radio, the time working parents would most likely be listening. On the other hand, TV ads might prove less successful for a firm like KinderCare since working moms would likely have limited TV-viewing time.

strat **mgmt** **fin**

downstream   (1) Term that refers to the divisions in a company that are further along in the manufacturing process or toward the customer. For example, a shipment of computers that has moved from basic assembly to software loading has moved further **downstream**.

(2) May also refer to the direction of financial flows or responsibilities between a parent company and a subsidiary. For example, a company might transfer a debt of obligation **downstream** to a subsidiary. When interest or dividends move from a subsidiary to a parent company, it is referred to as upstream.

See also **vertical integration**.

mktg

drive time   Prime time in radio advertising.

Morning and **afternoon drive times** are when people are trapped in their cars during rush hours, usually 7 to 10 A.M. and 2 to 7 P.M. Drive times provide advertisers with access to the largest radio audiences of the day.

acct **fin** **mgmt**

DSO   See **days sales outstanding**.

mgmt **fin** **acct**

due diligence   Gathering and verifying data before making a final commitment to a course of action.

In public offerings, due diligence includes all activities of **underwriters** to check the background and viability of the company issuing the securities and to determine how the proceeds will be used. In a **merger** or **acquisition**, due diligence calls for assembling materials that verify **financial statements**. The process might go so far as investigating potential legal or ethical problems of the other company. In banking, it involves investigating the viability of the borrower and the adequacy of the collateral.

Due diligence research may include visiting a company's headquarters, interviewing senior management, visiting plants and talking with managers, calling suppliers and creditors, and poring over financial statements (past, present, and future) with the company's auditors. As research material is often supplied by the company itself, the due diligence process should not be considered a seal of approval by the investigator.

See also **underwriting**.

mktg **mgmt**

dumping   When a company charges less than its cost for a product on the international market to gain unfair competitive advantage.

Companies dump to eliminate a surplus or gain quick **market share** in a new country or market. It is considered an unfair practice, prohibited by both the **Antidumping Act of 1974** and the latest round of the **General Agreement on Tariffs and Trade (GATT)**. If you dump, the country you are invading is likely to impose tariffs on your product.

EXAMPLE | The **European Union (EU)** keeps a watchful eye on the prices of goods imported by EU countries and frequently imposes tariffs for dumping. Even the food additive monosodium glutamate (MSG) has been a subject of controversy. In 1995, the EU imposed antidumping duties on MSG from Indonesia, South Korea, Taiwan, and Thailand.

fin **mgmt** **mktg**

Dun & Bradstreet reports   Information sold to subscribers of Dun & Bradstreet, a private credit-rating agency.

When people talk about pulling a D&B, they are referring to Dun & Bradstreet's *Business Information Report* (BIR). The BIR provides credit information to help assess the risks and opportunities involved in doing business with another company. The reports include infor-

dumping

D

FRAME OF

REFERENCE

dumping

In the 1970s and 1980s, Zenith Electronics filed a number of antidumping complaints with the U.S. government. While most of the complaints focused on Japanese TV makers, Goldstar TVs, which are made by the Korea-based LG Group, were among the products drawing Zenith's fire. In July 1995, Zenith agreed to sell a majority interest (57.7 percent) to LG. The last major U.S.-based TV maker apparently decided to join forces with its competition since it could not overcome LG because of the global nature of the TV business.

When it comes to TVs, however, even though foreign-based companies have cornered the U.S. market, they manufacture a lot of their products in the United States. Almost two-thirds of the sets bought in the United States in 1994 were manufactured domestically. And Zenith continues to be a separate publicly traded company listed on the New York Stock Exchange.

mation like credit rating, sales, net worth, number of employees, payments to suppliers, financials, suits, judgments, current debts, history, and operations. D&B also sells business-to-business marketing information.

econ

duopoly   Exclusive control by two companies of a market for particular products or services.

A duopoly can sometimes arise from legal protection, such as in the cellular communications business where the Federal Communications Commission grants only two licenses in each market. Other factors that may produce a duopoly include proprietary technology, command of supply, and control of distribution.

See also **natural monopoly**.

econ

durable good   Products such as cars, furniture, and appliances that have a useful life of more than three years.

See also **personal consumption expenditures**.

fin

duration   Calculation of the relationship between time value and a bond's interest and principal payments.

The duration of a **zero-coupon bond** is the same as its time to maturity. For other bonds, duration takes into account cash flows from interest payments as well as the final payment of principal at maturity. The longer the duration, the more sensitive the bond's price will be to interest-rate changes. Also, in general, a bond with a higher interest rate will have a shorter duration than a bond paying a lower one.

Dun & Bradstreet reports

Dun & Bradstreet Information Services

DB a company of
The Dun & Bradstreet Corporation

D

---

duopoly

EXAMPLE

Two companies currently control the cellular phone market in Tampa Bay, GTE Mobilnet and AT&T Wireless. Federal regulators divided urban areas into duopolies to encourage growth in the industry. Soon, however, new competitors will be allowed to enter the market—and the effect will most likely mean lower prices.

Duration

Time to Payment (Years)	Year	Period	Payment	Present Value of Payment*	Weight	Duration
8% Bond (Term to maturity: 2 yrs.)						
0.5	1	1	$40	$38.10	0.04	0.02
1.0		2	$40	$36.28	0.04	0.04
1.5	2	3	$40	$34.55	0.04	0.05
2.0		4	$1,040	$855.61	0.88	1.77
		Totals	$1,160	$964.54	1.00	**1.88**
Zero-Coupon Bond (Term to maturity: 2 yrs.)						
0.5	1	1	$0	$0.00	0.00	0.00
1.0		2	$0	$0.00	0.00	0.00
1.5	2	3	$0	$0.00	0.00	0.00
2.0		4	$1,000	$822.70	1.00	2.00
		Totals	$1,000	$822.70	1.00	**2.00**

*Discounted at 5% per period

In this simple example, we calculate the duration for two different bonds. In both cases we assume a half-year interest rate of 5% (for discounting). The first bond has an *8% coupon* and pays $40 semiannually. The second bond is a *zero-coupon* and pays nothing until final maturity. Because there are no coupon payments to "weight" in the duration calculation, the zero-coupon bond's duration is exactly the same as its term to maturity.

D

E

to extraordinary item

earnings before interest and taxes

fin **acct**

earnings before interest and taxes (EBIT)
Just what it says—how much a company made in an **accounting period** before it paid its income taxes and the interest on its loans.

It is usually easy to arrive at this figure from a company's **income statement**. It is sometimes listed as a separate line item. If not, just add the tax and interest figures to the one for **net earnings**. EBIT is used for various kinds of financial analyses, such as for calculating a company's ability to meet interest and principal payments on its debt.

Many analysts also use EBITDA, which simply adds depreciation and amortization to the list of items "added back" to a company's income.

fin **acct**

earnings per share
Company's **net earnings** divided by the number of shares outstanding.

See also **income statement**.

fin **acct**

earnings report
Summary of a company's income and expenses for an **accounting period**.

See also **income statement**.

fin **acct**

EBIT
See **earnings before interest and taxes**.

econ **mktg** **strat**

econometric demand analysis
Using economics, statistics, and mathematics to predict future **demand** for a product or service under various conditions.

See also **demand forecasting**.

econ

economic indexes
See **coincident economic indicators**, **lagging economic indicators**, and **leading economic indicators**.

strat **mgmt** **econ**

economic profit
(1) In economics, the measurement of profits is **revenues** less **opportunity costs**.

(2) This is slightly different in accounting, where the measure of profits is revenues less accounting costs.

The difference is that economists like to consider more than just explicit costs—they include the opportunities you give up when you make a choice. For example, an accountant may count only wages paid out when calculating your company's profits, while an economist would add in the cost of your capital and your own labor.

earnings before interest and taxes

E

221

E

economic value added

trap

Randall Tobias, CEO of Eli Lilly, points out that EVA can be misused. It can encourage companies to take on too much debt because borrowed money is usually less expensive than EVA's concept of shareholder capital. It can also encourage a short-term focus.

What you're doing is very quietly weaving into your culture a new financial management, measurement, and incentive system. Before you know it, what jumps out is a new culture that's right for times of rapid change and turmoil. People put the creation of shareholder value at the top of the pyramid, and when that happens, chances are your business will end up on top, too.

—G. Bennett Stewart III, management consultant and father of EVA, Fortune, *May 1, 1995*

mgmt fin

economic value added (EVA)   Measuring corporate performance against what shareholders could earn elsewhere.

The technique was developed by management consultant G. Bennett Stewart III. Using Stewart's approach, you depreciate investments like training and **research and development** as well as traditional ideas of capital like plants and equipment. It all goes into your capital base. Then you look at how much you are earning from that base.

In the mid-1990s, if your business entails average risk, you should be earning more than 13.5 percent. That is the 7.5 percent investors could get on long-term Treasury bonds plus the 6 percentage points they earn, on average, for the extra risk of a typical stock.

Unless you are making at least that much on your shareholders' money, Stewart would say you are doing poorly. The point is not whether you pay it out in **dividends** or reinvest it—if you are not making it, your shareholders are losing out. Says Stewart: "When you are making more money than your cost of doing business plus your cost of capital [that 13.5 percent], you are creating wealth for your shareholders."

EVA has become a yardstick many companies use to evaluate each of their business segments. Companies like AT&T and Quaker Oats have broken themselves into smaller, freestanding units whose managers get financial incentives for meeting their EVA goals. EVA is also being used to evaluate capital spending.

See also **depreciation**.

strat mgmt oper mktg econ

economies of scale   Concept that larger volumes reduce per-unit costs.

Economies of scale are generally achieved by distributing **fixed costs**—such as general and administrative expenses, **advertising**, distribution, insurance, and so on—over a larger number of products.

EXAMPLE | An orange grower grows and packs 20 million crates of oranges a year, with $100,000,000 in fixed costs. Management is considering adding a new hybrid of oranges to its line. Marketing estimates that it can sell five million crates of the new oranges, and Harvesting says it can set up the new line with minimal cost and run it with a small increase in labor. So the new product line incurs $10,000,000 more in fixed expenses. The resulting economy of scale can be represented like this:

Present fixed-cost allocation:

$100,000,000 ÷ 20,000,000 **units = $ 5.00 per crate**

Proposed fixed-cost allocation:

$110,000,000 ÷ 25,000,000 **units = $ 4.40 per crate**

The fixed costs for each orange crate will decrease by $.60.

The orange grower's economy of scale is possible because most of the infrastructure is already in place. Other economies of scale might arise from factors such as shared technology. It is important to pinpoint and understand the source of the increased **efficiency.**

There are limits, however, to expansion. At some point, size can bring inefficiencies. Employees may balk, systems may become too complex, bureaucracy may grow, management may become over-taxed, decision making may slow down, and communication may become blurred. If, in the case of our orange grower, Harvesting is wrong in its assessment and the new line leads to expensive labor grievances, per-unit fixed costs may, in fact, rise. Moreover, a company's competitive edge as a marketer of one product line may become diluted as attention is paid to introducing others. So the disadvantages of scale can quickly outweigh the advantages.

When it is cheaper for one company to produce a wide variety of related products rather than for independent firms to produce them separately, that is known as economy of scope. If our orange grower grew apples, grapefuits, and lemons, it might talk of **economies of scope.**

economies of scale

tip |

Even in industries where economies of scale are a major factor, there may be room for a small niche player to operate profitably.

E

Economies of Scale

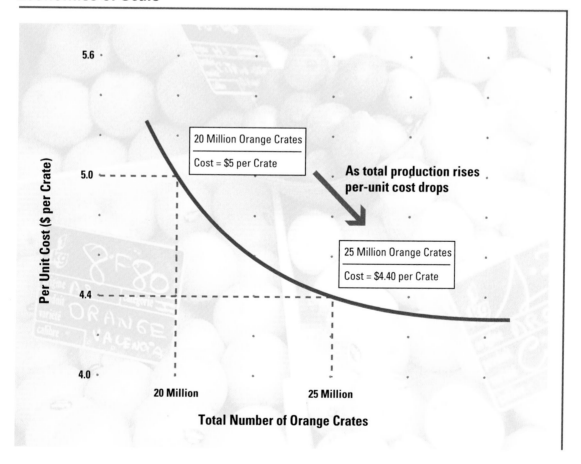

20 Million Orange Crates

Cost = $5 per Crate

As total production rises per-unit cost drops

25 Million Orange Crates

Cost = $4.40 per Crate

Per Unit Cost ($ per Crate)

5.6

5.0

4.4

4.0

20 Million   25 Million

Total Number of Orange Crates

strat **mgmt** **oper** **mktg** **econ**

economy of scope
When it is cheaper for one firm to produce multiple, related products rather than for independent companies to make them separately.

fin **acct**

EDGAR
Electronic **database** of documents filed with the **Securities and Exchange Commission (SEC)**.

Federal law requires that all publicly held corporations file an annual report, a **10-K**, a **10-Q**, **proxy statements**, and other documents, which become part of the EDGAR (Electronic Data Gathering, Analysis, and Retrieval) system. The SEC makes EDGAR available for research and inquiries. Individuals with a computer, a modem, and access to commercial online services like CompuServe and Prodigy can electronically obtain the EDGAR documents. Some organizations have also made EDGAR available free on the Internet.

fin

Edge Act
U.S. law passed in 1919 that allows U.S. banks to set up subsidiaries to conduct lending operations in foreign countries.

These subsidiaries, known as Edge Act corporations, can be chartered by states or by the federal government. They may invest in foreign companies and even own foreign banks. The Edge Act also authorized the **Federal Reserve System (Fed)** to establish reserve requirements for foreign banks doing business in the U.S. In 1978, the **International Banking Act** expanded the authority of the Fed to treat the American operations of foreign banks on an equal footing with the operations of U.S. banks.

mktg

EDLP
See **everyday low pricing**.

fin

effective interest rate
Actual percentage rate paid on borrowed money after taking into account the terms of the loan; it can differ from the stated **interest rate**.

For a bond, the effective interest rate may differ greatly from the **coupon rate**. For example, let's take a **bond** with a $1000 face value and a 10 percent coupon, which gives you $100 in coupon payments per year. If the purchase price for the bond is higher than the face value, say $12.50, your effective rate would be lower—in this case 8 percent ($100/$1,250). Of course, if the purchase price is lower than face value, your effective rate would be higher than the coupon rate. The effective rate may also take timing into account, making adjustments for time to maturity and even time between interest payments.

Edge Act

E

Quick Facts!

With California considered the gateway to the Far East, various banking organizations maintain branches of their Edge Act institutions there to cater to wealthy Asian clients. Citibank, for one, operates such branches in Los Angeles, San Francisco, and San Diego.

In 1978, the International Banking Act expanded the authority of the Federal Reserve System to treat the American operations of foreign banks on an equal footing with the operations of U.S. banks. That act also gave the Fed the authority to set reserve requirements for foreign banks doing business in the United States.

mgmt **oper**

efficiency Measure of how well a process works when it is composed of several tasks performed by different people.

Efficiency is calculated by multiplying the number of **workstations** by the time it takes for the longest component task, then expressing the total time it takes to complete one process as a percentage of that number.

Expressed as a formula, it is:

% Efficiency	=	(T × 100) ÷ (N × C)

T Total processing time actually required to make one unit

N Number of workstations

C Cycle time of process (that is, the time spent at workstations), as limited by the one that takes the longest

The higher the percentage, the more efficient the process.

EXAMPLE | A medical electronics company is assembling bedside monitors. The process can be subdivided into five tasks and five workstations:

Task		Minutes
1	Load base on assembly line	1.5
2	Insert cathode-ray tube	4.0
3	Wire major components	8.0
4	Test electronics	5.5
5	Inspect final product	2.5
Total		21.5

One complete process takes 21.5 minutes. The longest task takes 8.0 minutes for the wiring of components. With this information, we calculate the efficiency of the process.

21.5 ÷ (8.0 x 5) = 0.537, or 53.7%

efficiency

In practice, an efficiency measure between 80 and 90 percent is desirable. Any less than 80 percent and there is too much idle time.

Any more than 90 percent and the process cannot adapt to a short-term increase in demand.

E

efficient market theory

Quick Facts!

A distant relative of the efficient market theory is the proposition that if you pick stocks by throwing darts at a newspaper's financial page, you have as good a chance of outperforming the market as any professional investor. For more than five years, the *Wall Street Journal* has been testing this theory. Every month, it asks four investment professionals to each select a stock for the coming six months; then it selects four stocks by tossing darts at the stock listings.

In 61 contests, the pros outperformed the darts 36 times and had average six-month gains of 8.9 percent; the darts won 25 times, with average six-month gains of 3.7 percent. The professionals beat the Dow Jones Industrial Average 32 times and performed worse than the DJIA 29 times.

We can improve efficiency by changing workstation staffing. For example, if we hire a second person to wire components, and the work at this station gets done twice as fast, the task time falls to 4.0 minutes. The longest task time in the process would then be 5.5 minutes for testing the electronics. The new result would be:

$$21.5 \div (5.5 \times 5) = 0.78, \text{ or } 78\%$$

Quite an improvement! For some processes, efficiency can be increased through line balancing. Here is how it works: Let us say 50 of the bedside monitors must be assembled each day. We will calculate the minimum number of workstations needed for 100 percent efficiency and assign them equal cycle times. With an eight-hour (480-minute) workday and 50 instruments to process, the cycle time is 9.6 minutes (480 ÷ 50). A monitor must be assembled every 9.6 minutes. This is the optimal cycle time.

We calculate the minimum number of workstations required to do this by dividing the total process time by the optimal cycle time:

$$21.5 \div 9.6 = 2.23 \text{ workstations}$$

The number is always rounded up, so the minimum number of workstations needed is 3. We may not be able to divide the work among three workstations. Four or five may be needed. Each additional workstation reduces the efficiency of the process.

In practice, companies should strive for an efficiency measure between 80 and 90 percent. Any lower than 80 percent is an indication of too much idle time. When the measure is higher than 90 percent, the process cannot adjust to a short-term increase in demand.

See also **productivity**.

`fin`

efficient market theory   Hypothesis that **capital markets** operate so efficiently that you can assume everyone knows the same information, and that such knowledge is already reflected in the prices.

In other words, any information that exists is immediately included in the market price, so any future movements will be based on things that are unpredictable, or random. The efficient market theory suggests that there is no reason to review historical information about a security or to analyze the company's **financial statements** or business prospects because the information is already accurately reflected in the market price. Trying to reason out future events is futile because, by definition, you cannot predict the unpredictable.

See also **random walk theory**.

econ   strat

elasticity   In economics, how various elements respond to changes in others. The form of elasticity most commonly referred to is price elasticity. This measures the change in **demand** as a reaction to a change in price and is defined as the percentage change in the quantity demanded divided by the percentage change in price.

Elasticity	=	% Change in Quantity
	÷	% Change in Price

If a small price change causes a big change in demand, that is highly elastic, or responsive. If a large price change evokes only a small demand change, the demand is inelastic, or not very responsive. The biggest factor determining the degree of price elasticity is the availability of substitute products. For example, you can easily find substitutes for a type of fish, so demand is elastic, but you cannot find many substitutes for your local telephone service, so demand is inelastic.

In the example below, there are two customers, one inelastic (customer #1) and one elastic (customer #2). If the price of an apple rises from 40¢ to 50¢, their responses will be quite different.

Price Elasticity: Example

If the price of an apple went from 40¢ to 50¢ . . .

Inelastic Customer #1

Hardly Any Cutback
from 20 to 18 apples per month

Elasticity $= \dfrac{(20-18) \div 20}{(0.8-1.00) \div 0.8} = \dfrac{.10}{(.25)} = .40\ ^*$

Elastic Customer #2

Drastic Cutback
from 20 to 4 apples per month

Elasticity $= \dfrac{(20-4) \div 20}{(0.8-1.00) \div 0.8} = \dfrac{.8}{(.25)} = 3.2\ ^*$

*Negative sign eliminated by convention.

---

elasticity

tip |

A seller needs to be aware that while high prices might be enjoyed today, those prices are going to come down as supply elasticity kicks in over time.

E

Price Elasticity

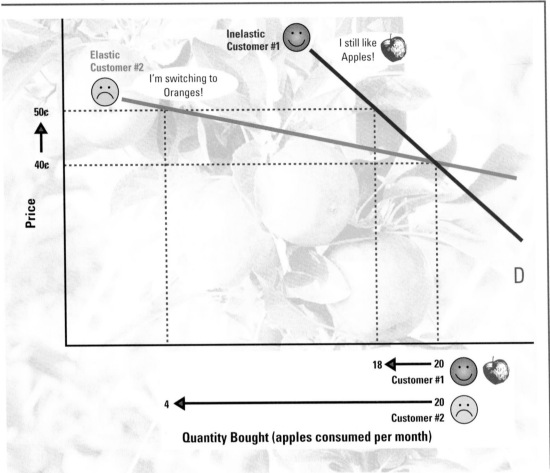

Quantity Bought (apples consumed per month)

Other forms of elasticity include:

► **Income Elasticity of Demand**

It measures how responsive demand is to a change in income. If demand rises when income rises, the good is considered a normal one. Goods with high income elasticity are considered luxuries; for example, a pay raise would prompt many beer drinkers to buy more imported beer.

If, on the contrary, demand falls when income rises, the good in question is termed inferior, and it has negative income elasticity. For example, generic brands of beer are less in demand among people whose incomes have risen.

► **Cross-Price Elasticity**

It measures how the change in one item's price affects demand for another. If cross-elasticity is positive, an increase in the price of one item sparks more demand for the other.

Take butter and margarine. Because they are substitutes, they have a positive elasticity. Cross-elasticity is negative if a price hike for one item causes less demand for another. Bread and butter, for example, would have a negative elasticity. Products with this kind of relationship are called *complements*.

FRAME OF

REFERENCE

elasticity

During the 1960s and 1970s, most economists and business planners believed that the price elasticity of demand for gasoline, diesel fuel, heating oil, and other petroleum products was relatively negative. They believed that, regardless of price, U.S. petroleum consumption would grow in step with the **gross domestic product (GDP)**. After all, Americans loved big cars, and it cost too much for industrial users to switch away from liquid fuels. All of these beliefs proved wrong.

After the 1979 Iranian crisis spiked crude-oil prices, Americans learned to like more fuel-efficient cars, industries installed equipment powered by natural gas or coal, and both individuals and businesses adopted fuel-conservation measures. Demand for petroleum products proved to be more elastic—more sensitive to price—than the experts had thought. And that is one of the reasons why oil-company profits slumped during the 1980s. The companies had invested heavily to meet demand that did not materialize.

E

► Supply Elasticity

This measures the responsiveness of producers to price changes. It indicates how much prices must change to get suppliers to increase their output by a given amount. A key factor here is the time producers have to adjust output.

For example, an increase in the price of coffee beans is not likely to get more onto the market, at least in the short run (coffee plants take many years to mature). However, if prices stay at inflated levels, the quantity supplied will eventually increase; that is, supply elasticity increases with time.

elasticity

electronic bulletin board

`tech`　`mgmt`　`mktg`　`fin`

electronic bulletin board　Messages posted and read by people using computers linked via a **network** or over phone lines. Also called **bulletin board system (BBS).**

This is a form of user-generated **database**. Once a user posts a notice, it may stay available to other users at any location indefinitely, for a set length of time, or until there has been a set number of subsequent postings.

Lotus Notes is a popular program that can set up and maintain a bulletin board on a network. As information flows to the board, Notes eliminates duplication and detects potential conflicts. Companies may use this sort of bulletin board for all their employees or for people working in a particular discipline—researchers, for example.

Many companies also use electronic bulletin boards for customers to get information and ask questions. This is especially common for software publishers.

EXAMPLE | Companies such as Borland, Microsoft, and Novell, Inc., maintain bulletin boards on the CompuServe information service. Some also maintain boards on other commercial services and on the Internet. In 1995, Pacific Gas & Electric established an electronic bulletin board with pricing information for other utilities interested in buying power from it.

electronic bulletin board

CompuServe

Master the Digital Canvas

See It to Believe It: Sight & Sound GIFs

Jam with Jimmy Buffett

Scan this Issue

? About the Cover

tech **mgmt**

electronic conferencing   Meeting via computer network where people from far-flung locations can exchange ideas, documents, drawings, and so forth.

The individuals may "talk" to each other by typing messages into their computers, and what they "say" is seen simultaneously by all the other participants; new software and hardware also permit videoconferencing between offices. The video portion of the conference appears in a window on the monitor, while the audio portion is heard on speakers built into or attached to the computer.

fin **acct**

Electronic Data Gathering, Analysis, and Retrieval
See **EDGAR**.

FRAME OF REFERENCE

electronic conferencing

You are the project manager for a multinational oil company based in Dallas that is having a large tanker built by a Japanese shipyard. The ship, which will transport crude oil, needs sophisticated navigational and safety systems that communicate with satellites and earth-based data centers. The team that is engineering these communications systems has a number of bugs to overcome, so you call an electronic conference.

You set the meeting for 7 A.M. Dallas time to make it reasonably convenient for consultants in London as well as the shipyard in Osaka. At the starting time, you use your computer to send an outline of the problem areas and an agenda for the meeting. All the other participants can see what you send, and they are free to reply.

An engineer in London asks a question about the agenda. His question is picked up by a microphone and heard by you in Dallas and the people in Osaka. Someone in Osaka adds a comment by typing into the computer, and, of course, that comment is seen by everyone instantly.

Once everyone has agreed on the agenda, you try to keep order as the electronic discussions go on. A number of suggestions are made and evaluated during the conference. Afterward, you edit the transcript to make it easier to follow, and you send electronic copies to all the participants, along with your assignments for further action.

Quick Facts!

electronic mail

- Since 1986, homes and offices have added 10,000,000 fax machines, while e-mail addresses have increased by over 26,000,000.

- Communication technology is radically changing the speed, direction, and amount of information flow, even as it alters work roles all across organizations. As a case in point, the number of secretaries is down 521,000 just since 1987.

—Rich Tetzeli, "Surviving Information Overload," *Fortune,* July 11, 1994

---

tech **mgmt**

electronic mail (e-mail)   Messages exchanged among people via computers.

The computers may be linked on a **network** or via telephone lines. There are various types of e-mail software, each with its own features. The software will usually let you store the e-mail messages you have received by date, subject matter, or sender. You can often link the replies to the original message to establish a complete record of the correspondence.

Dedicated users of e-mail extol its virtues as an efficient means of contact that saves time, effort, and paper, as well as makes communication possible virtually anytime, anywhere.

tech **mgmt**

e-mail   See **electronic mail**.

mgmt

employee assistance program (EAP)   Use of an outside agency to provide short-term counseling or psychotherapy at no cost to employees. The service is often made available to immediate relatives as well.

EXAMPLE | Smith Corporation is a large worldwide company headquartered in Smith City. With 4,000 employees in the metropolitan area, it contracts with Psychological Counseling Associates (PCA) to administer its EAP. Every Smith headquarters employee is entitled to as many as eight visits in each calendar year with a licensed psychotherapist at PCA.

Fred Jones is a Smith employee with a wife and two teenage children. His father has terminal cancer, and Fred's department is undergoing a reorganization that may result in his dismissal or demotion. Tensions are high in the Jones household. Fred calls PCA and makes an appointment for himself.

---

electronic mail

```
To:chird@faraway.com
Subject: Re: Store Ads
Author: SE: daemon@wize.net
Date: 7/31/96 11:42AM

Christy,

I will send you a list of starting
dates and locations for your review.
If you need more info right away, call
me at ext. 7284.
Best regards,

John.
```

employee assistance program

trap

Some companies have encountered difficulties over the issue of EAP confidentiality. If you have an EAP, you had better also have a policy for how to handle, say, a truck driver transporting dangerous cargo who tells his or her counselor about a drug problem.

E

employee assistance program

After one session, he is told that he may have seven more that year and up to eight the following year. He may use them himself, bring other family members with him, make sessions available to his wife and children individually, or any combination of these alternatives. He is assured that PCA will not disclose the details of the sessions to staff at Smith. If the counselor seeing the Joneses decides that any of them needs more therapy than the Smith Corporation's EAP provides, PCA will refer them to an unaffiliated psychiatrist, psychologist, or social worker who qualifies under Smith's medical insurance plan.

EAPs arose from the mounting medical costs of the 1980s and early 1990s, a large proportion of which fell into the categories of mental health and substance abuse. Since employers usually pay a large share of medical-insurance costs and must deal with absenteeism during illnesses and family emergencies, many companies introduced EAPs as a preventive measure.

mgmt

employee discharge   Firing or laying off an employee. The tradition for employee-employer relations in the United States is that either party can end the relationship at any time.

employee discharge

The most frequently used defense against wrongful-discharge suits is just cause: The employer argues that the employee was fired for a good reason, such as violating company policies, failing to perform his or her duties, or failing to meet standards of conduct.

The tradition of at-will hiring and firing is limited by:

1 **Antidiscrimination Laws**
The **Age Discrimination in Employment Act (ADEA)**, the **Americans with Disabilities Act (ADA)**, and numerous other federal civil rights laws attempt to ensure fair treatment of minorities and women in a number of situations, including termination of employment. Most states have measures that complement federal law in these areas.

2 **State and Local Employment Laws**
Other than measures taken against discrimination, there is no federal law aimed specifically at employee discharges. But many states do have employee-protection legislation that governs terminations. They may, for example, specify a **notice period**—a length of time on the job that an employee must be given after receiving his or her discharge notice. They also may spell out the basis for a possible suit on grounds of wrongful discharge.

3 **Labor-Union Contracts**
Some 16.7 million workers in the United States—15.5 percent of the 1994 workforce—were covered by contracts between unions and employers. These contracts usually specify the reasons for which an employee can be fired, the length of the notice period, and any additional compensation the employee may get.

More and more dismissed employees are initiating suits alleging discrimination or wrongful termination, and employers are becoming increasingly concerned about the potential costs of litigation. Defense fees alone for a wrongful termination suit often exceed $100,000, and juries tend to lean toward the dismissed employee. In California, for example, the average award in a wrongful-termination case exceeds $600,000.

The three most common grounds for wrongful-discharge suits under state laws are:

1 **Public Policy Violation**

When an employee is fired for refusing to do something unlawful, such as falsifying documents. In these suits, the fired employee often can seek punitive damages (which punish the employer) as well as compensatory damages (such as lost compensation). Also, an individual manager is subject to criminal action if he or she ordered an employee to break the law.

A 1980 case decided in the Supreme Court of California, Tameny v. Atlantic Richfield Co., broke ground for this sort of suit. The employee had been dismissed when he would not participate in a price-fixing plan.

2 **Breach of Good Faith**

Generally means that the discharge was based on an arbitrary or capricious factor. These suits are hard for the employee, who must establish the employer's motives and intent. As a result, few states have adopted laws that limit at-will discharges on this basis.

In those states that do have breach-of-good-faith laws, some grounds for employee legal action are the distortion of performance records, the assignment of heavy work loads that might make the employee quit, or a discharge because of such employee activities as joining a union.

3 **Breach of Contract**

When an employment contract (either written or implied) was broken. In these cases, courts examine covenants, or promises, that the employer may have expressed in writing, orally, and by implication. Usually, these covenants have created the expectation that the employee is assured of long-term employment.

An important document in these suits can be the company's handbook, which may be seen as a contract. The court may also consider such remarks as "your continued good work makes you an irreplaceable employee," as good as contracts. In several cases, the courts regarded length of service alone as an implied contract.

---

employee discharge

Breaking News

U.S. companies doing business in other countries often must adjust to a legal approach vastly different from at-will hiring and firing. In Germany, for example, important terms relating to the hiring, compensation, and working conditions of employees must be brought before a workers council for approval.

In most countries of the **European Union**, firing workers is hard, and the law mandates generous severance pay. The departure of white-collar employees is often negotiated quietly by management and presented as a decision by the employee. Firing of blue-collar workers is governed by law and by agreements with unions, which may wield considerable power within a company, and even with a national government.

E

In Pugh v. See's Candies Inc. (1981), an employee was fired after 31 years of employment. Since the employer was unable to provide an acceptable explanation for the dismissal, the court found that the length of the employee's service was equivalent to an implied contract that allowed termination only for just cause. The employee won the case.

Employers often ask a terminated employee to sign a release forgoing litigation in exchange for additional separation pay. While this may keep many cases from going to court, some states will not recognize the validity of the release. Courts are reluctant to uphold an arrangement where a person relinquishes important rights.

mgmt

Employee Retirement Income Security Act (ERISA)
Legislation passed in 1974 that regulates **pension plans**.

fin   **mgmt**

employee stock ownership plan (ESOP)
Way of giving employees an **equity** stake in their company. Occasionally the stock are regular voting shares, but often they are a special class of nonvoting stock.

An ESOP is a legal entity that receives either shares or cash donated by the company. Cash received by the ESOP is used to buy shares from the company. The shares in the ESOP are held in employees' names but cannot be sold by the employees as long as they remain in the company. Corporations receive a tax deduction for at least part of their donations to ESOPs, which also may borrow funds to buy additional shares in the company. The rules governing ESOPs change with revisions to the tax code.

employee stock ownership plan

Breaking News

Healthtrust was created in September 1987 when Hospital Corporation of America (HCA) sold 104 hospitals to employees in a $2 billion transaction. By April 1989, Healthtrust's revenues had increased and its cost structure had been lowered as a result of new marketing programs and efficiency measures. In 1995, the company was bought by Columbia/HCA for $3.3 billion in the largest hospital acquisition in history. The new company now weighs in as the nation's 10th-largest employer, operating more than 320 hospitals across 36 states.

FRAME OF REFERENCE

employee stock ownership plan

During the 1980s there was a move toward greater employee ownership, helping to create an identification between the worker and the company. By 1989, nine thousand U.S. companies had ESOPs covering nine million workers. These companies were of various sizes, ranging from 10 to 15 employees to much larger companies like Avis Rent-a-Car.

There are many reasons for the rising popularity of ESOPs. The attraction has been spurred in part by Congress, which provided ESOPs with substantial tax incentives. Restructuring companies, too, have found ESOP's to be valuable tools in providing flexibility. In the airline and steel industries, for example, employees have exchanged wage concessions for stock in the companies. Perhaps most importantly, there has been recognition on the part of management and labor that ESOPs often make good financial sense.

A study published in the *Harvard Business Review* showed that ESOPs, combined with a high level of employee participation at all levels of the decision-making process, result in an 11 to 17 percent improvement in a company's growth rates.

EXAMPLE	H.B. Fuller Company introduced an ESOP in 1992 that is targeted to reach its 6,000 employees around the world. The plan is part of the company's strategy to build employee commitment, foster a common **corporate culture**, and encourage cooperation among its far-flung operations. Company earnings are used for outright market purchases of stock, which are then distributed according to a formula involving the company's financial results and individual employee's performance appraisal results.

In addition to their salutary effects on employee motivation, ESOPs have been used for many financial situations. ESOPs financed by bank loans have facilitated employee buyouts of companies. In those cases, stock dividends are used to pay back the loans. As the debt decreases, the employee equity increases.

econ

employment   Stated simply, employment is the use of human resources to produce goods and services for exchange in the market.

Employment differs from work or labor because some work yields goods and services that are not for sale. (The substantial quantity of goods and services produced within households illustrates work or labor but not employment.)

Civilian Employment Population Ratio

Year	Total Civilian Employment	Percentage of Civilian Population
1954	60.1 million	55.5%
1964	69.3 million	55.7%
1974	86.8 million	57.8%
1984	105.0 million	59.5%
1994	123.1 million	62.5%

Source: Department of Labor, Bureau of Labor Statistics

Estimates of national employment are provided by the U.S. Department of Labor's Bureau of Labor Statistics, using survey data gathered by the Commerce Department. Using a sample of about 60,000 households, the survey determines the number of people 16 years and older who are either employed or unemployed, with employed being defined as people who, during the survey week, worked at least one hour for pay; worked in their own business, profession, or farm; or worked at least 15 hours without pay in a business operated by a family member. Employed persons also include those who had jobs

employee stock ownership plan

Quick Facts!

UAL Corporation arranged an employee buyout after suffering three straight years of losses through 1993 due partly to high labor costs. In 1994, UAL was able to negotiate $4.8 billion in wage concessions from its unions in return for an arrangement giving 53 percent of the company to the employees via an ESOP.

U.S. Employment: Manufacturing and Service Jobs

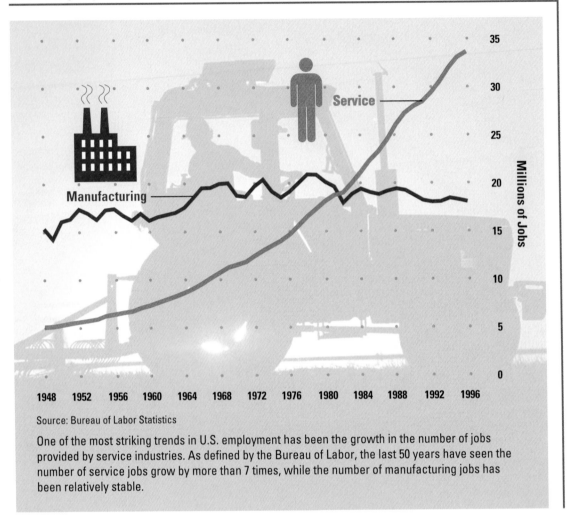

Source: Bureau of Labor Statistics

One of the most striking trends in U.S. employment has been the growth in the number of jobs provided by service industries. As defined by the Bureau of Labor, the last 50 years have seen the number of service jobs grow by more than 7 times, while the number of manufacturing jobs has been relatively stable.

empowerment

It is unreasonable to expect managers to distribute power to others if they can expect to be punished when those others make mistakes. The practice of firing the coach when the team loses can be changed, but where it exists and has an entrenched history, managers will fight the process of empowering their people.

—Stephen P. Robbins,
Organizational Behavior

or businesses but did not work during the survey week because of vacation, illness, bad weather, child-care problems, and other reasons.

The number of people employed depends both on the total population aged 16 years and older and on the proportion of people who choose to work. This proportion is called the employment-population ratio. The table shows employment-population ratios and total employment over the last 40 years.

See also **unemployment rate**.

mgmt

empowerment   Increasing the control workers have over their own jobs.

This use of the word grew out of the **total quality management (TQM)** movement, which holds that making the workers responsible for the quality of their own production will optimize their **efficiency**.

In addition to increasing the workers' control, empowerment boosts their sense that what they do is meaningful and has an impact on

empowerment

Electric power producer AES Corporation does business in 35 countries and has 17,000 employees and $685 million in revenues. What it has never had in its 15-year history are corporate managers overseeing its various departments. Instead the workers handle these functions as members of volunteer teams.

Board member Robert H. Waterman, Jr., coauthor of *In Search of Excellence*, comments: "It's what I call an ad-hocracy. People can get involved however they want, without worrying about crossing boundaries." From the start, cofounders Dennis W. Bakke and Roger W. Sant

 shared a dissatisfaction with bureaucracy and a desire to form a company committed to their values of "integrity, fairness, social responsibility, and fun."

Robert H. Waterman, Jr.

results. Empowerment improves morale, but that is just a small part of the payoff. Many companies have found that the workers closest to a particular process are the experts most likely to improve it if they are given the latitude to do so.

EXAMPLE | A midwestern toy manufacturer institutes an empowerment program that touches every aspect of the company's operations. Workers are their own bosses with the authority to hire and fire and make decisions about equipment acquisitions. The workers control everything—from budgets to marketing—and they are responsible for their results. And the results can be good: Companies that have implemented these kinds of programs have shown a much higher **return on assets**, higher sales, and payroll increases have increased at a significantly slower rate.

mktg **oper** **strat**

end-of-life (EOL)

Point where a product is not manufactured or sold anymore, usually because it has been edged out by a better product.

When a product approaches the EOL phase, manufacturers often find it most cost-effective to reposition the product as new and improved. For a limited time after EOL, a manufacturer will usually continue to stock spare parts and provide service either directly or through a third party.

oper

engineering change order (ECO)

Revision that the engineering department makes to a design.

The ECO corrects or alters a manufactured item, or improves a manufacturing process. The customer, the customer-service department, the quality-control department, or even manufacturing itself may request the change.

end-of-life

Products, like people, have a life cycle. They go through four distinct phases:

■ **Introduction**

■ **Growth**

■ **Maturity**

■ **End-of-life**

engineering change order

E

entrepreneurs

Entrepreneurs build businesses around good ideas. A spark of creativity, faith in that spark, and the ability to take it to market represent the hallmarks of entrepreneurial thinking. Some entrepreneurs, like Thomas Edison, are inventors who convert a scientific breakthrough into cash. Others, like Bill Gates, are visionaries who see existing situations in new ways and then alter the way we see the world as well. Whether inventor or visionary, however, all successful entrepreneurs share one common trait—passion for the big idea.

Among the creative thinkers who have seen their brainchild grow to transform our culture:

• Thomas Edison	The electric light
• Bill Gates	Computer-operating systems
• Aaron Montgomery Ward	Shopping by mail
• Steven P. Jobs	Computers for laypeople
• Walt Disney	Animated entertainment
• Ray Kroc	Mass-marketed hamburgers

entrepreneurs

At any given time, 3 million people are starting companies in the United States. That's more people than are getting married and more than are having children.

—Paul Reynolds, professor of entrepreneurship at Marquette University, *Inc.* magazine, August 1995

There is no secret to success here. Anyone can do it

—Howard Schultz, Chairman and CEO, Starbucks Corporation

mgmt

entrepreneurs   People who go into business for themselves, with the hope of creating wealth and lasting value.

Not long ago "entrepreneur" was a label synonymous with all sorts of derogatory appellations. Nowadays, politicians from the president on down tell us that entrepreneurial business is the engine of the economy, and what's more, they have statistics to back them up.

There is wide agreement that the overwhelming majority of jobs created in the U.S. in recent years were generated by small businesses and those considered to be non–investment grade companies. Most small business jobs are created by start-up firms. Jobs from new firms outnumber expansions by about three to one.

mgmt   **strat**

environment   Goings-on, outside a company's direct control, that can affect its performance.

The one thing companies can count on is that their environments—both the general ones and those specific to their industry—will change. Some changes come fast and others slowly. While nobody has a crystal ball on environmental change, managers must track it and try to anticipate trends. They need to follow economic data, political events, technical developments, and structural changes in their industries.

environments matrix Framework for picturing the competitive forces of a single industry.

We divide the matrix on two axes:

► **The potential size of competitive advantage**
This concept reflects the idea that companies with somewhat equal resources and capabilities will usually be able to make only marginal advances on their competitors. In other words, there is little chance that either a price cut or a premium for added value will enable a company to leap ahead. The major airlines would fall into this category. Clothing retailers, on the other hand, can make more dramatic advances by changing their **pricing** or strategy.

► **The number of potential sources of competitive advantage**
This has to do with the options for competition. In a **commodity** industry like aluminum, for example, companies usually compete on the basis of price. On the other hand, a sports gear manufacturer would have a number of ways to work toward competitive advantage.

E

Quick Facts!

environment

Changes in the environment can come from almost anywhere, anytime. They might affect a company or an industry in the following ways:

- A postage increase causes direct-mail companies like Lands' End and L.L. Bean to revamp their prices and strategy.

- Increasing public concern about caffeine drives soft-drink bottlers like Coke and Pepsi to introduce more caffeine-free product lines.

- A moratorium on offshore U.S. drilling leads multinational oil companies like Exxon, Mobil, and Texaco to invest more in foreign exploration.

- An increase in mortgage interest rates means that residential developers put off plans for new-home construction, sending shock waves on to suppliers of building materials.

- An earthquake in Southern California suspends the operations of Carter Hawley Hale Stores, which decides to give its customers in the region more time to make charge card payments.

- Changing attitudes—and in some cases laws—about tobacco use mean that many restaurants must offer smoking and nonsmoking sections.

E

environments matrix

The environments matrix classifies industries into four sectors:

1 **Volume**

In these industries, there are not many ways to compete, but the advantages of effective competition are large. Innovative measures are hard to come up with. Concentrating on a few competitive strategies—like gaining a **first mover** or **cost leadership** advantage—may be the key to gaining a lead. An example is General Electric, which parlayed its status as a pioneer in the electrical appliance industry into a commanding competitive position.

2 **Stalemate**

Companies in stalemate industries have few competitive options, and the advantages those introduce are meager. Even if the advantages are slight, you must have instant access to all required resources and skills. For example, say you are in an industry like food containers—glass jars, bottles, cans—where large-scale production is one of the few ways to establish a competitive lead. You may easily be able to raise the capital to build and staff the largest plant in the field. The advantage, however, will last only until a competitor responds with an even larger facility.

3 **Specialized**

In specialized industries, companies can gain big competitive advantages in various ways. Many companies cultivate **core competencies** like superior service or distinctive sales strategies. If you can translate these capabilities into either a price premium that adds revenue or a cost reduction that builds sales, you have created an advantage that competitors cannot easily duplicate. An example of a specialized industry is applications software.

4 **Fragmented**

These industries have many ways to gain competitive advantage but have difficulty maintaining it over time. This is typically the case when a company's success strategy is easily copied. For example, beauty salons can develop a distinct core competency, like concentrating on a particular style, which may build **market share**. But the advantage will last only until it is imitated by competitors. To build high-volume sales in a fragmented industry, you can adopt a strategy of multiple outlets, either by operating a large number of new stores directly or by franchising. Starbucks and McDonald's are examples.

fin

equity   Ownership interest in a company.

Owner's equity or **shareholders' equity** on a **balance sheet** is the company's net worth, or **assets** minus **liabilities**.

fin **mgmt**

equity kicker   Attaching an offer of an ownership position to a loan or debt instrument.

You might offer lenders an opportunity for an equity stake in your business to reduce the **interest rate** or to improve other terms of your loan.

Equity kickers attached to **bonds** may include **warrants**, **rights**, and options. The convertibility provisions for **convertible securities** are also equity kickers. In other loan agreements, a borrower may offer a lender a small ownership position in the project or acquisition that is being financed. In that case, when the property is sold, the lender is likely to get additional income.

acct

equity method   Way of accounting for an **affiliated company** in which you show your equity share of the affiliate and its results on your books.

mgmt **mktg**

ERG theory   Motivation theory pegging behavior to three groups of core needs: existence, relatedness, and growth.

ERG theory, developed by psychologist Clayton Alderfer, grew out of **Maslow's hierarchy of needs**.

The definitions for the three groups of core needs are:

1 **Existence**
   Basic material survival needs like food, water, and shelter.

2 **Relatedness**
   The drive for interpersonal and social relationships.

3 **Growth**
   The desire for personal development—to learn new skills, be creative, or master particular tasks.

Some theorists, including Abraham Maslow, believe that the relationship among these needs is linear—that existence needs must be satisfied before relatedness needs and relatedness needs before growth. Alderfer, however, maintains that a person may be motivated by two or all three needs groups at once and may seek to satisfy a higher-order need while a lower-order one is unfulfilled. You may strive for **job satisfaction** and advancement even while your salary is inadequate.

equity kicker

EXAMPLE

In 1983, MCI used an equity kicker to complete what was then the largest nonutility corporate underwriting in U.S. history. With its lead investment banker Drexel Burnham Lambert, MCI raised $1 billion by attaching warrants to 10-year bonds, securing a lower interest rate, and giving the investors a play on MCI's stock. The warrants also gave MCI a break on their balance sheet. Because $200 million of the offering was classified as equity (the warrants), MCI booked only $800 million on the balance sheet as debt.

E

ERG theory

The progression, or regression, from need to need in ERG theory is governed by desire and frustration. For example,

▶ The more difficult it is to attain a lower-level need, the more desirable it becomes: The longer you are denied a pay raise, the more important it will become to you.

▶ If you do attain a lower-level need, you will find higher-level needs increasingly attractive: Once you earn enough to sustain yourself, you will work harder for relatedness needs, perhaps starting a new course of study.

▶ If you cannot gain that higher-level need, the intensity of lower-level needs increases: After a divorce, you may focus again on getting a raise.

`mgmt`

ERISA   See **Employee Retirement Income Security Act**.

`fin` `mgmt`

ESOP   See **employee stock ownership plan**.

`fin` `mgmt` `strat`

ESOP buyout   Form of **leveraged buyout (LBO)** involving employees of the acquired company.

`mgmt`

ethics   Standards of professional conduct governing individuals and groups.

A variety of approaches to business ethics exists. At one extreme is economist Milton Friedman's argument that a business's only responsibilities are to make a profit and obey the law. At the other is Aristotle's belief that the organizations of a just society must foster the morality of its citizens.

Over the years, business ethics has become a major area of management concern. Ethical questions may arise in any number of dramatic or mundane ways, and a growing list of companies has formulated and given to employees a formal code of ethics.

EXAMPLE | National Medical Enterprises (NME), which operates hospitals, encountered serious ethical problems in its psychiatric facilities in the late 1980s and early 1990s. Among other things, the psychiatric hospitals were accused of admitting patients who did not need hospitalization and discharging patients who did, based on their insurance status. These ethical lapses resulted in numerous costly legal actions, and in 1994 NME sold its psychiatric unit. The company implemented a comprehensive ethics program company-wide. The following year, before completing its merger with American Medical Holdings (AMH), NME (since renamed Tenet Healthcare Corporation) took into consideration AMH's ethical practices as part of a three-month **due diligence** investigation.

---

ethics

t i p

Having an ethics code and putting effort into enforcing it can help blunt lawsuits and lessen fines against your company.

E

I would rather be the man who bought the Brooklyn Bridge than the man who sold it.

—Will Rogers

Ethicist Laura Nash, a fellow at Boston University's Institute for the Study of Economic Culture, has developed a series of 12 questions that can help businesspeople think through ethical issues. Nash's questions first appeared in the *Harvard Business Review*.

- ▶ Have you defined the problem accurately?

- ▶ How would you define the problem if you stood on the other side of the fence?

- ▶ How did this situation happen in the first place?

- ▶ To whom and what do you give your loyalties as a person and as a member of the corporation?

- ▶ What is your intention in making this decision?

- ▶ How does this intention compare with the likely results?

- ▶ Whom could your decision or action injure?

- ▶ Can you discuss the problem with the affected parties before you make your decision?

- ▶ Are you confident that your position will be as valid over a long time as it seems now?

- ▶ Could you disclose without qualm your decision or action to your boss, your CEO, the board of directors, your family, or society as a whole?

- ▶ What is the symbolic potential of your action if understood by others? If misunderstood?

- ▶ Under what conditions would you allow exceptions to your stand?

ethics

EXAMPLE

The clothing maker Levi Strauss & Co. implemented strict guidelines for contractors to follow and a policy of surprise inspections in 1992. Subsequently, it decided to investigate the working conditions at its contractors in foreign countries and found practices that would be considered abusive or illegal in the United States, ranging from seven-day workweeks to child labor. Levi's then implemented changes in those situations.

FRAME OF
REFERENCE

ethics

In a 1994 survey for the Ethics Resource Center, 30 percent of corporate employees said they had seen conduct that violated company policy, if not the law. But only half reported doing anything about it. In the face of statistics like those, more companies are working on ethical standards. It has been estimated that 90 percent of the largest U.S. corporations have an ethics code and an ethics officer to administer it.

The content of the codes, though, varies. Wetherill Associates' short and sweet "right-action ethic" tells employees to do what is right in every situation. The "right action" must meet three criteria: It must be "logical/workable, expedient/appropriate, and moral/honest."

Nynex, on the other hand, took almost a year of internal review and focus groups to develop its award-winning code. The Nynex ethics code covers issues specific to its business, like privacy of communications, and goes on to such things as alcohol and drug abuse, conflicts of interest, employee privacy, espionage, gifts and gratuities, nepotism, outside employment, political contributions, sabotage, safety, sexual harassment, use of competitive information, and workforce diversity.

Eurobonds

EXAMPLE

A Brazilian company has in the past sold bonds in the United States and needs to raise more capital. It issues two series of dollar-denominated Eurobonds—one in Europe and the other in Japan. This gives the company access to more investors and allows for more-favorable terms than the company could get in Brazil or by going back to the U.S. market.

Eurocurrency

fin

Eurobank   A bank that holds currency deposited from outside its nation's borders; the name comes from the common practice in Europe but applies to any bank worldwide.

See also **Eurocurrency**.

fin

Eurobonds   Corporate **bonds** denominated in one country's currency but issued in another country. Also called **international bonds**.

For example, a German company may issue Eurobonds through a U.S. investment bank, which will then be purchased by investors in many different countries.

fin

Eurocurrency   Currency deposited in a financial institution outside its home country.

The name relates to the fact that a European country is often involved, but that is not always the case. Similarly, the institution holding the money is called a **Eurobank** even if it is not in Europe.

The most common form of Eurocurrency is **Eurodollars**. These U.S. dollars deposited in banks outside the United States are often used in international business transactions. Some securities are denominated in Eurodollars, meaning that all interest, dividends, and other payments are made in dollars deposited overseas. U.S. companies sometimes find better terms for borrowing in the Eurodollar market than for borrowing at home.

fin

Eurodollars   U.S. dollars deposited in banks outside the United States.

See also **Eurocurrency**.

mktg **fin** **econ** **strat**

European Community (EC)   See **European Union (EU)**.

mktg **fin** **econ** **strat**

European Economic Community (EEC)   See **European Union (EU)**.

mktg **fin** **econ** **strat**

European Union (EU)   Alliance of 15 European nations. Formerly known as the **European Community**, the **European Economic Community**, and the Common Market.

Members are Belgium, France, Italy, Luxembourg, the Netherlands, Germany, Great Britain, Ireland, Denmark, Greece, Spain, Portugal, Austria, Finland, and Sweden.

European Union

The European Community (EC) was formed in 1967 by the merger of three organizations founded in the 1950s—the European Economic Community (EEC), the European Coal and Steel Community (ECSC), and the European Atomic Energy Community (Euratom). From the original idea of encouraging trade and coordinating energy policies among the member nations, the mission of what is now the European Union has expanded greatly. After reducing tariffs and dismantling direct trade barriers, the alliance began coordinating agricultural, banking, environmental, and other policies that affect how each country's goods and services compete against the others'.

In 1991, the EC announced a commitment to creating, in effect, a European state. The proposed union would have a common defense and foreign policy, a central bank, and a single currency. The economic plan was approved by delegates of the then 12-member group at a meeting in Maastricht, the Netherlands, in December 1991.

European Union

The European Union—originally organized in 1967—comprises 15 member nations.

E

Referendums and government actions have delayed or modified European unification, as it has come to be known, but the EU did succeed in creating the European Free Trade Zone. The free-trade zone, which began on January 1, 1993, eliminated national regulations and united more than a dozen separate markets, thus opening enormous opportunities for sellers of goods and services. It created a marketplace of more than 320 million people, a population almost a quarter larger than that of the United States.

mgmt **fin**

EVA See **economic value added**.

mktg

events marketing Strategy that uses events such as concerts, athletic competitions, or other activities to promote products to a distinct segment of the market that frequents the type of event involved.

The event should appeal to a specific **target market** and have a direct association to the product.

mktg

everyday low pricing (EDLP) System of keeping retail prices low on average, instead of maintaining higher average prices and putting items on sale.

See also **pricing**.

fin **econ** **mktg** **acct**

exchange rate Price at which one country's currency can be traded for another's.

The U.S. dollar, for example, has an exchange rate with the Mexican peso, the French franc, the Japanese yen, and every other currency. These rates are influenced by a complex set of factors and can vary daily; on any given day, the dollar may strengthen against one currency while weakening against another.

Prices of currencies are determined by **supply** and **demand**, just like prices for other goods. Factors that change the demand for or supply of a given currency will also change its world "price," or exchange rate. For example, changes in a nation's prices relative to those of other countries can influence its currency demand. If a government causes inflation by excessive increases in the nation's money supply, foreigners will demand less of its currency. At the same time, the increase in the **money supply** will make more currency available to foreigners. The combination of increased supply and reduced demand will cause the currency's price, or exchange rate, to fall.

Other factors, like **interest rates**, can produce similar effects. If interest rates rise compared with those throughout the world, foreigners are likely to demand more of the currency to buy the nation's interest-paying assets. The increased demand can then push up the currency's

price. Expectations about the future also play an important role. If people generally believe that a government is not likely to follow sound economic policies to sustain a currency's value, they will demand less of it and cause its value to fall.

Today, most exchange rates **float** in the world market, moving up or down with changes in their demand and supply. Of course, governments may try to influence their currencies' values through actions of their **central banks**, perhaps by raising domestic interest rates or directly buying a currency on the open market to prop up its price by increasing its demand.

events marketing

Foreign Currency per U.S. Dollar

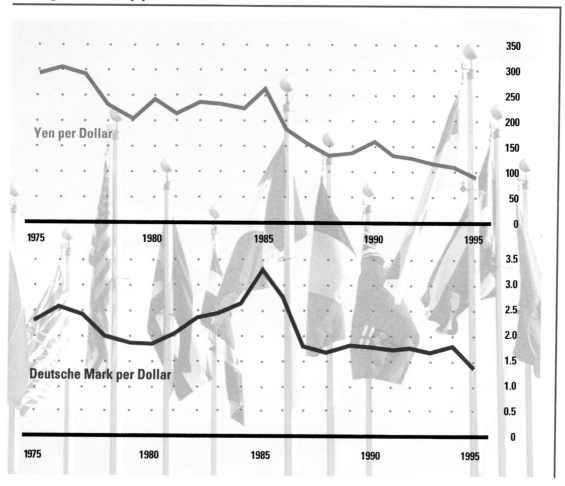

The U.S. dollar has lost considerable value against the German mark and the Japanese yen over the past 20 years. The dollar was worth about 1.5 deutsche marks in 1996—35 percent less than the 2.4 deutsche marks it was worth in 1975. And compared with the yen, the dollar holds only about one-third of its value from 1975, falling from about 300 to 100 yen over the same 20 years. Although not a positive trend at first glance, this lower exchange rate has been helpful in improving our trade balance with these countries, and in particular, Japan. A lower exchange rate makes U.S. goods more attractive on the foreign market.

Trade-Weighted Value of U.S. Dollar, 1970–1995*

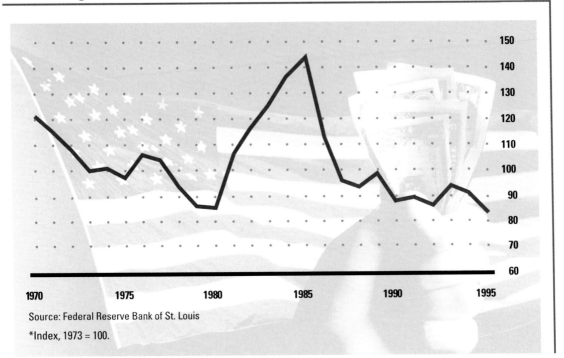

Source: Federal Reserve Bank of St. Louis

*Index, 1973 = 100.

E

As the chart above indicates, the exchange rate of the U.S. dollar has generally declined since the 1970s—except in the first half of the 1980s, when it soared. The reasons for the general decline and the upsurge during the early 1980s are debated among economists. Many argue that large federal **budget deficits** during the early 1980s pushed up U.S. interest rates, causing foreign investors to bid up the dollar's value as they demanded more dollars to make investments in the U.S. Others contend that it was the favorable investment climate brought about by efforts to reduce taxes and business regulations that made the U.S. a more attractive place for foreign investors during the early 1980s.

What is not debated, however, is that the long-term decline in the dollar has been the result of its supply increasing faster than its demand in the world market. For whatever reasons, the United States has been supplying more dollars than foreigners have been willing to hold at previously higher rates of exchange.

See also **foreign exchange**.

fin

exchangeable debenture   Similar to a **convertible bond** or **convertible preferred stock** but exchangeable into the **common stock** of a different public corporation. Also refers to a **bond** that can be exchanged into another security of the issuing company—either debt for debt or debt for preferred or common stock.

FRAME OF REFERENCE

exchange rate

One trend has been clear in exchange rates—the decline of the U.S. dollar since the mid-1970s. The only blip came in the early 1980s when soaring U.S. interest rates were a magnet for foreign investors. In the severe drop of February 1994 to May 1995, the dollar slid 20 percent against the Japanese yen and 18 percent against the German mark.

Economists debate whether the dollar's decline is justified, but possible reasons include the ever-rising federal debt, more rapid inflation in the U.S. than elsewhere, and a failure of U.S. businesses to match the competitiveness of foreign rivals.

Is the dollar's decline a bad thing? It depends on whom you talk to. The cheaper dollar helps U.S. exporters, whose products become more attractive because of their lower prices in other currencies. But it makes it tougher for imported products and their buyers, who need to come up with more dollars to pay for them. Still, many argue that the cheap dollar is a drug keeping inefficient U.S. industries artificially high and will bring down the country's quality of life in the long run.

E

EXAMPLE | In 1993, Pennzoil issued debt in the form of two exchangeable debenture offerings that mature in 2003. The first bond, containing a 6-1/2 percent coupon rate, was exchangeable for 23.77 shares of Chevron common stock per $1,000 in principal. The second bond, which had a 4-3/4 percent coupon, was exchangeable for 17 shares of Chevron common stock per $1,000 in principal.

fin

exchangeable rate   **Interest rate** or **dividend** that changes periodically.

See also **adjustable rate**.

mgmt

executive compensation   Total pay package given to the top officers of a corporation.

Compensation can be divided into four categories:

1 **Base Salary**
   In many cases a relatively small portion of the total package.

2 **Bonuses**
   Usually tied in some way to the performance of the company. They are granted by the board of directors, which often establishes a formula based on such things as profits and **total return to shareholders**.

executive compensation

Quick Facts!

What happened at Walt Disney Company in 1993 made a lot of headlines. The company's profits dropped 63 percent to about $300 million, while the compensation of its chairman Michael Eisner rose more than 25-fold to $203 million. But base salary accounted for only $750,000 of Eisner's 1993 compensation. The rest came from stock options that had been granted nearly a decade earlier and were due to expire in 1994.

Under Eisner's stewardship beginning in 1984, Disney's stock price had increased more than 11-fold (from $3-11/16 to $42-5/8), and its market value had expanded by more than $22 billion, putting Eisner's $203 million payout into perspective. The value of the options had been based on the performance of the company, making his compensation a long-term reward for long-term results.

3 Stock Options

The right to buy shares in the future at a set price, usually the one prevailing when the option is granted. The **Securities and Exchange Commission (SEC)** counts the value of options as executive compensation during the year that they are exercised.

For example, you are the CEO of your company and several years back were granted options to buy 25,000 shares at $30 a share. Now, with the price at $50 a share, you exercise your options on 1,000 shares. So you pay $30,000 (1,000 shares x $30) for stock worth $50,000 (1,000 shares x $50). You can sell all or some of the 1,000 shares you bought; but even if you hold them, the $20,000 in value you obtained ($50,000 – $30,000) becomes part of your executive compensation for that year.

4 Severance Payments

Special compensation made available if the executive's employment has ended under certain conditions, like a **takeover**. The most lucrative of these have come to be known as **golden parachutes**.

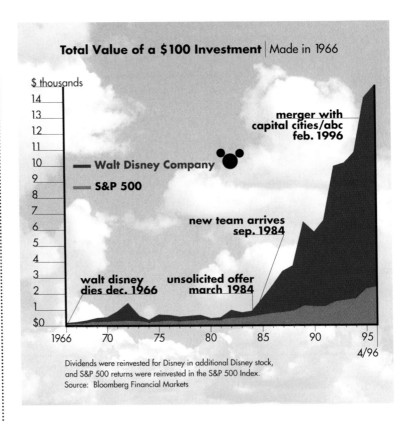

Total Value of a $100 Investment | Made in 1966

$ thousands

— **Walt Disney Company**
— **S&P 500**

merger with capital cities/abc feb. 1996

new team arrives sep. 1984

walt disney dies dec. 1966

unsolicited offer march 1984

1966   70   75   80   85   90   95
4/96

Dividends were reinvested for Disney in additional Disney stock, and S&P 500 returns were reinvested in the S&P 500 Index.
Source: Bloomberg Financial Markets

In a publicly held company, executive compensation is set by the board of directors, often acting on the recommendations of a compensation committee. According to *Forbes* magazine, the median compensation of CEOs at the 800 largest U.S. companies in 1994 was $1.3 million, with $993,000 of the figure coming from base salary and bonuses.

Packages, of course, vary widely by industry, company size, and other factors. Sometimes, the value of executive compensation rises markedly during a year when the company's profits dip. In many cases, that is because the stock price remained high and the executive exercised a large number of stock options. (See chart on the following page.)

The SEC requires publicly held companies to disclose in their **proxy statements** the compensation of the top executives. While the details disclosed have varied over the years, in 1993 the SEC called for a summary table giving the three-year history of pay in all the major categories for each senior executive and a statement by the board's compensation committee explaining how the pay level is determined. Also required is a table of stock options granted—those outstanding and those exercised during the year. And, for comparison, the SEC requires a graph showing the company's total return to shareholders over five years along with the total return for a stock index and a peer-industry group.

Concern over excessive compensation has led to changes in the tax code. With some exceptions, corporations cannot deduct compensation over $1 million a year to an executive unless the individual met performance goals set by a board committee that included at least two outside directors. The format of the pay package must be approved by a shareholder vote, and the compensation committee has to certify to shareholders that the terms have been met. The impact of the tax changes has been mostly symbolic because large pay packages traditionally have come primarily from performance-based options and bonuses. What has changed is the extent of the explanation given to shareholders in the proxy statement.

Some observers feel that basing compensation on profits and shareholder return keeps CEOs too focused on short-term goals.

EXAMPLE | You close your long-term research function, saving $10 million a year. That gives you an immediate profit boost and may please shareholders looking for a short-term rise in share price, but without research you are not likely to develop the new products to keep your company going five to ten years out.

executive compensation

---

mgmt   tech

executive information systems (EIS)   Systems designed to support top management decision making. A more advanced version of an EIS is an executive support system (ESS), which includes analytical and communications capabilities to support executive work.

fin

Eximbank   See **Export-Import Bank**.

executive compensation

Top-Paid Chief Executives

	1995 Salary and Bonus ($ thousands)	Long-term Compensation ($ thousands)	Total Pay ($ thousands)
1 Lawrence Coss Green Tree Financial	$65,580	—	$65,580
2 Sanford Weill Travelers Group	$5,607	$44,233	$49,840
3 John Welch, Jr. General Electric	$5,321	$16,741	$22,062
4 Gordon Binder Amgen	$1,513	$19,992	$21,505
5 James Donald DSC Communications	$5,595	$13,588	$19,183
6 Casey Cowell U.S. Robotics	$2,799	$15,770	$18,569
7 Floyd English Andrew Corp.	$1,739	$15,927	$17,666
8 Howard Solomon Forest Laboratories	$611	$16,416	$17,026
9 Stanley Gault Goodyear Tire & Rubber	$2,207	$14,343	$16,550
10 Edward Brennan Sears, Roebuck	$3,098	$13,252	$16,350

Source: *Business Week,* April 22, 1996

mgmt

expectancy theory Explanation for motivation developed by psychologist Victor Vroom.

Expectancy theory focuses on:

▶ The expectation that an act will be followed by a predictable result.

▶ The desirability of that result.

EXAMPLE | A cellular phone company promises each salesperson a 10 percent bonus if he or she signs up more than a set number of new accounts in a month. According to the expectancy theory, the employees would be very motivated to exceed the quota. There is a connection between sales performance and the bonus when the size of the bonus is attractive.

But if the reward for exceeding the sales quota was entry into a lottery for a pen-and-pencil set with the company logo on it, expectancy theory would predict low motivation. There is no direct link between an individual's sales performance and the bonus (you can make your numbers and not get the reward). And—let's face it—a pen-and-pencil set is nothing to write home about.

expectancy theory

fin **mgmt**

expected rate of return   Way of evaluating competing investments or portfolios based on the probability of future events.

Because it involves predictions, the expected rate of return is commonly used along with a calculation of standard deviation, which measures the average deviation from an expected result. The larger the deviation, the riskier the investment.

Expected value is calculated:

E

Expected Rate of Return

$$r_e = \Sigma r_j p_j$$

r_e Expected rate of return

r_j The return for the jth possible event

p_j The probability of the occurrence of event j

Σ The sum of

The formula can be restated:

$$r_1 p_1 + r_2 p_2 + r_3 p_3 + \ldots + r_j p_j = r_e$$

EXAMPLE | A $100,000 investment in security X has the following expected rates of return for different states of the economy:

	Return (r_j)	Probability (p_j)
Recession	−10%	30%
Normal	15%	50%
Growth	20%	20%

The expected return (r_e) of security X is:

$$(-10\%)(30\%) + (15\%)(50\%) + (20\%)(20\%) = 0.085, \text{ or } 8.5\% \text{ or}$$
$$-.03 + .075 + .04 = 0.085, \text{ or } 8.5\%$$

Security Y offers the following returns:

	Return (r_j)	Probability (p_j)
Recession	5%	30%
Normal	10%	50%
Growth	25%	20%

The expected return (r_e) of security Y is:

$$(5\%)(30\%) + (10\%)(50\%) + (25\%)(20\%) = 0.115, \text{ or } 11.5\%, \text{ or}$$
$$.015 + .05 + .05 = 0.115, \text{ or } 11.5\%$$

On the basis of expected return alone, security Y looks like the better choice. Of course, potential investors must also consider a number of other risks.

See also **alpha (α), beta (β), market risk,** and **nonmarket risk.**

expected rate of return

> *A nimble sixpence is better than a slow shilling.*
>
> —English Proverb

acct

expense Cost of goods and services that are used in a business's attempt to gain revenue.

mgmt

experience curve Describes improvements in **productivity** as workers gain experience.

See also **learning curve.**

expert system

tech

expert system Interactive computer application that helps users by simulating the reasoning of a human expert. It is a form of application of **artificial intelligence.**

EXAMPLE | Compaq Computer's customer service department once used an expert system to help handle incoming calls. Equipment problems were presented to the system, called SMART, which then retrieved the most similar problems in its database and their suggested solutions. SMART presented these to a customer service analyst for use in resolving the problem. Initial evaluations of the system showed an increase in resolving customer problems on the first call from 50 percent without SMART to 87 percent with SMART.

The main components of an expert system are:

▶ A **language interface**.

▶ An **inference engine** that controls reasoning and rules for all eventualities.

▶ A **database** with access to further rules and information.

`fin`

Export-Import Bank (Eximbank)   Bank established by Congress in 1945 to help U.S. companies compete in international trade.

The Eximbank's original aim was to compensate U.S. exporters for the subsidies that competitors received from their governments. It has grown into the largest source of export credit and guarantees for American goods sold abroad.

Through its **Foreign Credit Insurance Association (FCIA)**, the Eximbank also provides exporters and their lending institutions with insurance coverage against commercial and political risk. Eximbank's **City-State Agency Cooperation Program**, started in 1989, helps small and medium-sized businesses take advantage of the bank's services.

`mgmt` `strat` `econ`

externality   Benefit or cost to parties who are not directly involved in a specific transaction or course of action.

It is important to understand how externalities can affect your company. When deciding on a landscaping project, you might consider the possible improvement in community relations and what rising real estate values might mean for your plant.

Companies are held responsible for the full costs of many of the negative externalities associated with their activities. A company mining phosphate, for example, is responsible for the costs of any environmental damage. These kinds of externalities can result in **barriers to exit** because the costs of closing down are greater than the costs of continuing production.

`acct`

external reporting   Disclosures of public information to potential investors, creditors, government agencies, and so on.

See also **management accounting**.

`acct`

extraordinary item   Something that affects your **income statement** but is not part of your regular business and does not usually happen.

See also **cumulative effect of accounting change** and **special item**.

---

externality

A common example of a negative externality is air and water pollution. If your company discharges waste into a river, it increases costs to the people or companies who rely on the river for tourism, fishing, and drinking water. An example of a positive externality is the landscaping of the grounds surrounding your factory, which increases property values for your plant's neighbors.

E

extraordinary item
Quick Facts!

The $900 million that Exxon agreed to pay in civil damages for the Valdez spill was reported in their financial statements as an extraordinary item. The loss was charged against their earnings, thus reducing Exxon's profit for the year.

Electric Utilities

While electric arc lights were available in the late 1870s, they were noisy and short-lived, suitable only for street illumination. In 1879, Thomas A. Edison invented a long-lasting incandescent light bulb and, equally important, a complete lighting system—including generation equipment and transmission lines—to bring electric illumination to homes, offices, and factories.

George Westinghouse

Edison Electric Light Co., organized with the assistance of J.P. Morgan, opened its original system in New York in 1882, with Morgan's home the first to be wired. Edison's direct current could not be transmitted more than a few miles from the generator. George Westinghouse developed alternating current, which could be delivered over much longer distances. Westinghouse won the struggle of the systems, although some direct-current operations continued.

Edison was more interested in producing equipment than in organizing companies to generate and transmit power. From the beginning, Edison Electric was concerned primarily with manufacture, and Edison licensed those who wanted to organize companies that provided services. Soon Edison turned his attention to iron-ore processing and permitted others to take charge of Edison Electric. In 1892, Morgan brought together the Edison company with Thompson-Houston, a major producer of arc lighting equipment, to form General Electric. Edison withdrew from the industry, and his other interests in the field, controlled by the Thomas A. Edison Co., were merged with McGraw Corp. in 1957 to form McGraw Edison. The Edison name endures in the names of many operating companies.

Initially, the gas companies battled the electric utilities by developing better gas lights and lowering prices. But most of the gas companies either left the business or purchased electric

licenses and migrated to that industry. This shift is evidenced by the names of many modern utilities, which are "gas and light" companies.

With the victory of alternating current, it became evident that electricity was an undifferentiated product and that competition would be costly and wasteful. For this reason, there were demands that electricity be made a public utility, as was the case in many parts of the world.

Municipalities formed their own electric companies, a reaction against public fears of monopolies. By 1902, there were 2,805 privately operated and 847 municipal power companies. In time, the states would grant monopoly privileges in return for control of the companies through public service commissions, which had the power to establish rates and rules.

Electric power generation spread quickly; by 1929, 70 percent of American homes were wired. Electricity became significant in manufacturing, replacing steam power. This was one of the more important reasons for the economic progress made during that decade.

The industry's growth was made possible by large holding companies that came to dominate the industry through their ownerships of other holding companies, with operating companies at the bottom of a pyramid. J.P. Morgan & Co. organized United Corporation, whose largest holding was Commonwealth & Southern, itself a holding company. Others in the group were Niagara Hudson, Public Service of New Jersey, and Columbia Gas & Electric. United controlled firms that produced some 23 percent of the nation's electric power.

Celilo Substation in Dalles, Oregon

Contributing Editor, Michael S. Worms
Vice President, CS First Boston

Electric Bond and Share, formed by Chase National Bank, was second in size with 17 percent of power generation and distribution. The Insull Group, which was composed of two large holding companies, produced 11 percent of the nation's electricity and dominated the Midwest. Associated Gas & Electric and North American were two of the more aggressive holding companies. By 1930, holding companies controlled more than 70 percent of the nation's electric power generation.

The dominating positions of these holding companies attracted government attention during the New Deal and was one of the reasons President Franklin D. Roosevelt was able to gain support for the Tennessee Valley Authority, which brought public power to that part of the country. Other public utilities were organized as sentiment turned against the holding companies.

In 1935, Congress passed and Roosevelt signed the Public Utility Holding Company Act, which mandated the dismantling of the holding companies within three years. Although utilities executives fought back and managed to win some delays, hundreds of operating companies were made independent in the end. Some holding companies remained, but they were limited in scope and scale, and the pyramiding was eliminated.

By the end of the 1930s it appeared the electric-utility business was quite simple. The technology was in place, the utilities were regulated, and in the nature of things, slow, unexciting growth was expected. It was a cost-plus business, which is to say, the companies were permitted a specified return on investment, and this put a premium on negotiations and lobbying but not on efficiency.

The arrival of nuclear power altered this situation. Legislation passed in 1954 made possible the development of atomic power in electricity generation. Westinghouse created the first plant for Duquesne Light Co., and others followed. By the early 1960s it seemed that, given economies of scale and technological advances, atomic

power would replace coal, and then oil- and gas-generating facilities. Proponents of nuclear power liked to say that in time electricity would be so cheap it would not pay to meter it.

Argonne National Laboratory's experimental Breeder Reactor II at Idaho Falls

Despite opposition from antinuclear organizations, construction continued, and the first OPEC oil shock in 1973 gave new impetus to the movement toward atomic power. (Although no new plants were planned after 1974.) Then, in 1979, there was a mechanical failure at the Three Mile Island facility owned by a subsidiary of General Public Utilities, which seemed to doom this form of energy creation. Interest now turned to wind and solar power, but given technological and cost pressures, these initially showed little promise.

Wind turbines at Tehachapi, California

But rising energy prices in the 1970s prompted the government to prod the electric utilities into accepting changes in their industry. The Public Utility Regulatory Policies Act of 1978 (PURPA) encouraged the search for new power sources and the use of renewable energy sources. Specifically, PURPA required the companies to purchase power from these energy sources at prices higher than their own generating costs. At first, this was considered a minor modification, but soon companies that manufactured equipment established their own plants. These "qualifying facilities" under PURPA bypassed the utility by using their own generating units and then sold any excess energy back to the utility. Many firms—independent power producers (IPPs) and nonutility generators (NUGs)—began entering the market, with particular focus on California and New York.

As the changes developed, many companies reacted with a diversification strategy, entering into completely different lines of business. Houston Industries entered the finance area and purchased KBLCOM, a cable TV operation that was later sold for a large profit to Time Warner. Arizona Public Service became involved in land development and bought a savings-and-loan company, whose dismal record almost destroyed the company. These and other ventures into unrelated businesses were, for the most part, unsuccessful for the utility industry.

Then an even bigger transformation was signaled in 1989, when the Federal Energy Regulatory Commission (FERC) floated the idea that perhaps power plants and the operating companies, too, should be permitted to send electricity to any customer in the country.

In 1992 came passage of the Energy Policy Act, which gave the FERC broader powers and was geared to promote competition in the wholesale electricity market. Soon after, several states formulated their own plans to bring customer choice or competition to the retail customer. That the states were cooperating was not surprising. Grumblings about high rates from industrial customers had elevated to the point where some relocated to other states—taking their jobs and taxes with them—while others negotiated lower rates.

Photovoltaic power system at the Phoenix Airport

The competitive landscape of the power market was changed for good when, in 1994, California regulators proposed a new push toward "retail wheeling"—a system giving all consumers a choice of power providers. The new plan was intended to address the problem of California's relatively high electric rates. Although many consumer groups blamed the utilities, the utilities were largely trapped into their rate structures by expensive payments to small independents and high fixed costs related to nuclear plants. In response to the California commission's restructuring order, Pacific Gas & Electric (PG&E) proposed a program that would freeze prices for five years, with many customers allowed to make

Windfarms, Altamont Pass

Photovoltaic power system, Georgetown University

purchases from competitive suppliers in 1998. As part of this program and in conjunction with the commission's order, PG&E planned to sell some or all of its fossil-fuel generating plants and purchase much of its electricity from former competitors.

Going forward, generation in the future is expected to be priced at competitive market rates, and electric companies from outside a service area will be able to approach buyers with lower rates. Electric rates will not be allowed to fall to "free-market" rates right away, however. To protect and compensate utilities for "prudently made" investments—for example, generating plants that may become "stranded" (or uneconomic) in a competitive environment—customers choosing alternative energy sources will pay a transition charge for several years.

Anticipating these expected changes, each company reacted differently, although there were similarities in that all were trying to adjust to the new competitive environment. Some entered into mergers, such as Northern States Power's proposed combination with Wisconsin Energy and Potomac Electric's merger with Baltimore Gas & Electric. Others began diversifying overseas: U.S. utilities bought distribution companies in the U.K. and Australia or developed projects in higher-growth regions like Latin America and Asia.

The marketing of power had some unantici-

Solar Two Power Plant

pated consequences. If power could be bought and sold like any other commodity, why not set up procedures under which companies and speculators could take positions in power contracts, wagering on their rise or fall? As a result, power futures were admitted to trading on the New York Mercantile Exchange and soon became an active trading vehicle.

Shippingport Atomic Power Station

All of this came at a price. As recently as the 1980s, utilities were viewed as stodgy but safe operations. The companies paid generous dividends to boost the prices of their stocks, necessary because many would regularly sell new shares to raise funds for construction. As a result of these changes, this situation no longer exists. The eponymous "widows and orphans," who were steered into purchases of safe electrics paying generous dividends that were often boosted and never cut, found themselves owning shares of companies with uncertain future dividends.

Electric utilities were once a rapidly growing industry, but that period of expansion ended half a century ago. Barring any striking new technology—and there is none on the horizon—the greatest changes here will come from restructuring and economies realized by the new competitive environment.

Electronics

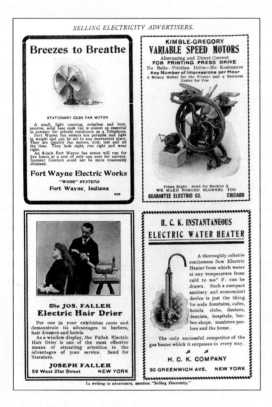

The grandfathers of the electronics industry were electricity and radio—Thomas A. Edison's investigations of electricity and the work of Lee De Forest, who invented the audion amplifier. By a narrower definition, the industry's origin could be traced to research into semiconductors during World War II.

After the war, a team of AT&T scientists, led by William Shockley, developed transistors as a substitute for and improvement on vacuum tubes. Several existing companies, among them Motorola, Philco, and Raytheon, worked on the devices. And some new companies, including Texas Instruments and Transitron, also entered the field. Texas Instruments, which developed the silicon transistor and miniature integrated circuits, quickly became the leader in electronics.

In 1955, Shockley established Shockley Semiconductor Laboratories in Palo Alto, California, selecting the site at the urging of Frederick Terman, a professor at nearby Stanford, who dreamed of making that school a West Coast version of Harvard-MIT. By

then, Terman had placed his engineering graduates at some of the nation's top firms in the East, but he wanted them to remain in the area. Terman's ambition was to bring together universities and electrical firms, both of which would be funded by government, all near Stanford. He succeeded beyond his dreams, and Terman might be called "the father of modern electronics."

Oscillator

Terman had made a good start. In 1939, two of his students, David Packard and William Hewlett, had founded Hewlett Packard and started selling audio oscillators to Walt Disney. Other companies came to Palo Alto after the war, including Varian Associates, Sylvania, and GE.

When several of Shockley's associates, led by Robert Noyce, squabbled with the CEO, they left to join Fairchild Camera and Instruments, which now entered the semiconductor business. Noyce was interested in integrated circuits, and soon Fairchild had devices of its own to compete with the Texas Instruments versions. But Fairchild could not hold together its fractious group of scientists, many of whom left to join other companies or organize new ones.

Several departed in 1959 to form Rheem Semiconductor, National Semiconductor, and Advanced Microdevices. Gordon Moore and Andrew Grove organized Intel to produce memory chips. In 1970 Intel developed a chip

Contributing Editor: Gunnar T. Miller
First Vice President, PaineWebber

that had a capacity of 1K (one kilobyte, which equals 1,024 bits of information). This chip, and those that followed, became the basis of the new industry.

Ted Hoff, a leading Intel designer, came up with the idea of placing an array of chips on a single platform, and so was born the microprocessor, sometimes called "a computer on a chip." The first of the breed, the 4004, was succeeded in 1974 by the 8080, which was used to create the first microcomputer.

By then, the Palo Alto area was known as Silicon Valley, and Stanford was one of the leading research universities in the world, its Applied Electronic Laboratory the equal of MIT's Lincoln. Moreover, the military-electronics-educational complex was firmly established as the heart of the industry. At the time, this union seemed unusual, but even more exotic affiliations were awaiting electronics, the building-block industry of the modern era.

The companies produced more powerful chips, microprocessors, and other electronic components at a rapid pace, as demand expanded exponentially. The 4004 had 2,300 transistors; the Pentium, which appeared in 1995, had five million transistors. All the while, as power increased, prices declined. In 1979, the cost of one million instructions per second (MIPs) was $1,080; by 1996 it had fallen to $5. Product performance doubled every 18 months or so, and prices declined 30 percent per year. A new $100 video game machine uses a higher-performance processor than the one that powered a 1976 multimillion-dollar Cray super-computer. Customers soon learned that the product life of chips and other electronic devices was extremely short.

All of this progress required large-scale financing, which, given the promise of the industry, was not too difficult to arrange. The small, new firms needed capital, and larger firms wanted to enter the field. So quite regularly small companies would agree either to be acquired or to sell interests to the large ones. Honeywell purchased Synertek. United Technologies acquired Mostek. IBM took a 20 percent stake in Intel in 1983 and could have expanded it at will to 30

percent, perhaps more, but sold its holdings instead.

European firms bought or took minority interests in Signetics, Litronix, Advanced Micro Devices, Intersil, and Fairchild Corp.. NEC Corp. acquired Electronic Arrays. Soon Silicon Valley was dotted with foreign-owned companies, and the American companies engaged in joint ventures with other American firms or with foreign ones.

As with all high-tech industries, the electronics industry has faced challenges from the Japanese. The Japanese challenge in chips came when the industry was moving from 4K to 16K of memory. Demand for the new chip was so great that the American companies could not meet all orders, so the Japanese made their move. Soon the Japanese were invading virtually all areas of electronics. By 1980, they had 40 percent of the market and were in strong positions to enter the next phase, the 64K market. The Japanese

took the lead in that market and seemed capable of doing the same in the forthcoming 256K area as well.

While the Japanese forged ahead in chips, the American companies retained strong positions in the higher-priced and even more important microprocessors. In addition, they were outperforming the rest of the world in custom chips and gate arrays.

Fearing the Japanese would do with computer electronics what they had succeeded in accomplishing with automobiles and consumer electronics, the American companies sought national alliances. In 1977 they established the Semiconductor Industry Association, which helped organize the Microelectronics and

Computer Technology Corp. and provided help against the Japanese, with the Defense Department Advanced Research Projects Agency (DARPA). DARPA funded several major programs, including Sematech (Semiconductor Manufacturing Technology), which attempted to restore semiconductor manufacturing capabilities; the Technology Reinvestment Program; and scores of smaller undertakings. In addition, in 1989 several computer and electronics companies united to form U.S. Memories, to challenge the Japanese in chips and other areas.

In 1986, Japan and the United States signed a semiconductor agreement designed to end dumping of Japanese chips on the American market and granting American access to the Japanese market. A year later the U.S. levied sanctions of $320 million on the Japanese for failing to live up to the terms of the agreement and imposed tariffs on some products.

By then, the chips were a commodity product, produced in high volume with low profits. Chip technology had become widespread, and companies in other countries entered the market with all of these government-sponsored programs in place. The American electronics industry emerged in the form Frederick Terman envisaged a quarter of a century earlier. Free enterprise remains, but the government and university components are extremely strong. America's top graduate schools attract students from all over the world, who are destined to work for American or consortium firms funded

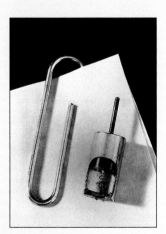

in part by the government. At Stanford and other major universities, corporate "parks" are situated on the campus, with professors and graduate students shuttling between the classrooms and laboratories.

More than any other industry, electronics is transnational, with American firms setting up installations throughout the world. More so than any other, electronics downplays or even ignores national, racial, religious, or gender differences. India and Israel are developing important electronics sectors, and so are several of the "Asian Tigers." By the early 1990s, the United States was importing more semiconductors from Southeast Asia than from Japan, and Korea-based Samsung became the world leader in this part of the market.

Many of the prominent figures at the American firms are foreign-born, so there is a blending of personnel that transcends nationalism. Intel's Grove was born in Hungary. Jean Hourni, a Swiss immigrant, developed the planar process that made miniaturization possible. An Israeli-American, Dov Frohman, invented programmable read-only memory. Federico Faggin, an Italian-American, coinvented gate technology. About one-third of Silicon Valley engineers are foreign-born, as is the case at other centers of electronics research. China is now attempting to attract their top scientists working abroad back to the mainland to help create an electronics industry of its own. "They're not interested in your clothes, your style, or when and how you work," said a researcher at Advanced Micro, whose personnel resembles the United Nations. "But they're sure interested in what you produce."

Pundits have spoken of how the age of silicon will replace that of petroleum. Perhaps so, if by that they mean the silicon-based electronics industry will be the fastest growing segment of the global economy for many years to come. But economic progress does not proceed uniformly. Half the people of the world have yet to make a telephone call, and less than 10 percent have flown in an airplane; the communications and travel industries, two of the world's fastest growing, devour enormous numbers of electronic components. Computers in their various forms are based on microelectronics. Worldwide computerization today is akin to the electrification of the developed world in the late 19th and early 20th centuries and doubtless will have as great an impact over time.

The electronics industry is largely technology driven, and so products from Intel, Motorola, NEC, Advanced Microdevices, Texas Instruments, Toshiba, Hitachi, and others in the field will determine the most significant changes. New consumer products based on electronic capabilities appear on the market at a staggering pace. Electronic products, with steadily declining prices, can control an individual's finances, monitor investments, and retrieve information; without electronics, there could be no "information superhighway."

Electronics already have revolutionized the automobile industry; semiconductors accounted for $200 to $300 per vehicle by the mid-1990s, and the amount is estimated to rise to $600 to $700 by the end of the century. Because unit costs are continually declining, this is more value than the price indicates. The military, which long had been a major source of demand for microelectronic products and a supplier of capital for research and development, is guided by political considerations. Forecasting demand from this sector is more difficult. But it seems clear the foreign electronics competition, while still substantial, is not as pressing as it was thought to be in the 1970s.

In 1992, the North American electronic components industry outgrew that of the Japanese for the first time since 1985. The lead widened as the decade wore on. This performance was the fruit of a U.S. government-industry-university collaboration, coupled with the problems experienced by the Japanese economy, and the rise of industries elsewhere in the world. In addition to all these factors, the openness of American society certainly plays an important role. At one time the unified, harmonious, and coordinated nature of "Japan Inc." seemed ideal for success in electronics, but it soon became evident that the more chaotic American business scene, guided by government in some areas but free in others, is better suited to this industry's requirements.

One of the more intriguing issues discussed within the industry is the possible alliance of electronics with biotechnology. There is talk of a "biochip," created of organic matter, which could lead to artificial life on a microprocessor or chip, as it were. Such machines (if they can be called that) could not only think, learn, and repair themselves but perform many tasks in ways superior to human endeavor. The future for electronics is exciting and unpredictable.

F

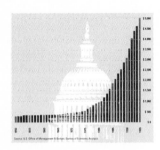

to

futures

FAC 2

FAC 2   A **Financial Accounting Standards Board (FASB)** ruling that defines materiality—something that must be included in a **financial statement**.

fin   **mgmt**

factoring   Selling your company's **accounts receivable** to another company for collection.

The accounts are sold at a discount from face value, taking into account the time value of money and the amount of bad debt that is expected. The seller gets immediate cash with no further responsibility for billing and collection. The purchaser, or factor, makes a profit as long as it has accurately predicted how successful collection will be.

The factor collects for its own account, not as an agent of the seller. So the factor has no recourse if the deal does not work out profitably. Factoring can be on either a notification basis, meaning the debtor is told to pay the factor directly, or a nonnotification basis, which means that payments continue to be channeled through the originating company.

acct

FAF   See **Financial Accounting Foundation**.

mktg

Fair Packaging and Labeling Act of 1966
See **consumer protection legislation**.

acct

FASB   See **Financial Accounting Standards Board**.

tech

fault tolerance   Ability of a computer system to continue operating satisfactorily even when it is incurring defects or faults. This is achieved by using backup systems and software routines that enable the computer to operate around the problem.

fin

FCIA   See **Foreign Credit Insurance Association**.

econ   **fin**

Fed   See **Federal Reserve System**.

factoring

fault tolerance

F

econ fin

federal debt Total amount owed by the U.S. government.

The federal debt has been growing every year since 1969. At year-end 1995, the total debt was approximately $5 trillion, or about 70 percent of the gross domestic product (GDP) for the year. Excluding amounts owed to the **Federal Reserve System (Fed)** and government bodies, the debt still approached 50 percent of GDP. While the amount is alarming to many economists, others consider it reasonable as long as the economy is sound. The federal debt should not be confused with the federal deficit. The federal debt is a cumulative number, whereas the deficit is simply the shortfall in any given year. More debt is added to cover the deficit each year.

federal debt

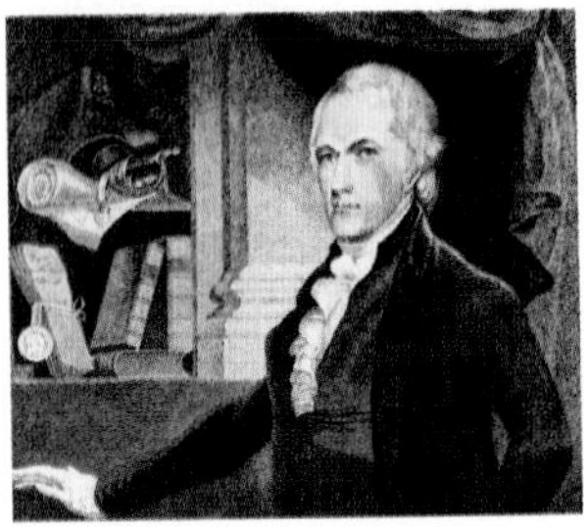

A national debt, if not excessive, will be to us a national blessing.

—Alexander Hamilton

econ fin

Federal Reserve System (Fed) The **central bank** of the United States.

The Fed is a nonprofit, government-created institution made up of the Board of Governors in Washington, D.C., 12 regional Federal Reserve Banks, their 25 branches, and the federal open-market committee, a major policymaking group. It is owned by its many

F

Federal Debt, 1950–1995 ($ Billions)

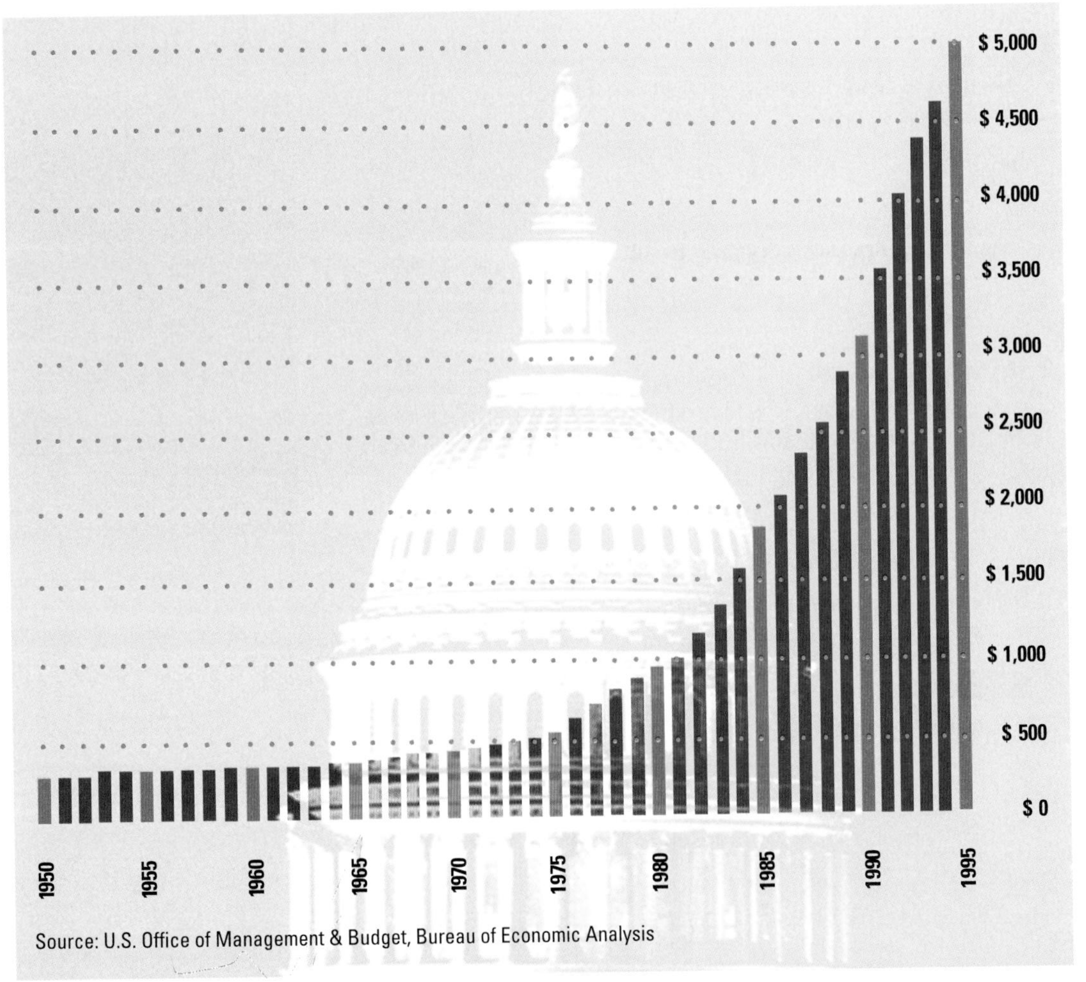

Source: U.S. Office of Management & Budget, Bureau of Economic Analysis

Federal Debt as Percentage of GDP, 1950–1995

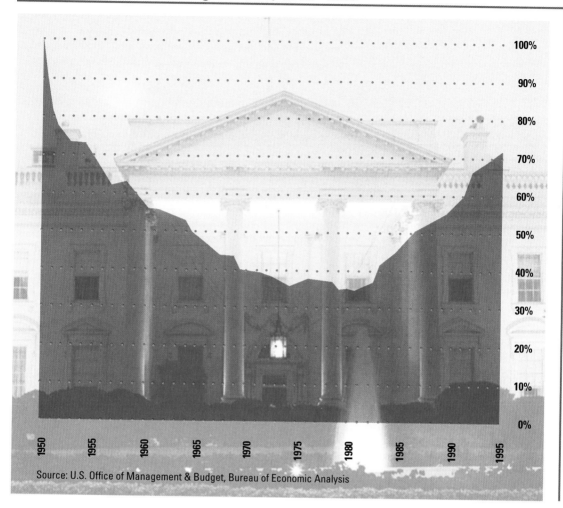

100%
90%
80%
70%
60%
50%
40%
30%
20%
10%
0%

1950 1955 1960 1965 1970 1975 1980 1985 1990 1995

Source: U.S. Office of Management & Budget, Bureau of Economic Analysis

member banks. All nationally chartered banks are required by law to belong to the Fed, and many state-chartered banks are also members.

The primary function of the Fed is to regulate the nation's money in a way that fosters price stability, economic growth, and moderate long-term **interest rates**. These objectives are, however, often at cross-purposes, so that the Fed must typically choose more of one and less of the others. Moreover, economists debate the ability of the Fed to promote goals other than price stability, and not surprisingly, they also disagree about which goals should be pursued.

The Fed has the ability to control the money supply by using three tools:

▶ **Buying and selling government securities on the open market.**
When the Fed buys securities, it boosts the banking system's reserves, putting more money into circulation. When it sells securities, it takes money out.

Federal Reserve System

In the 1830s, after the collapse of the second Bank of the United States, the country lacked an effective means of controlling the money supply. This predicament led to the creation of a central bank: By regulating the money supply, a central bank can raise or lower the cost of borrowing. Unlike other countries, which usually have one central state system, the United States relies on a multitiered system.

F

Federal Reserve System

Alan Greenspan, chairman of the Federal Reserve Board

F

Federal Trade Commission

The Federal Trade Commission building, Washington, D.C.

▶ **Adjusting the reserve requirement, the minimum fraction of a bank's deposits that it must hold in reserve.** Decreasing the reserve requirement enables banks to make more loans and increases the money supply. Increasing the reserve requirement means fewer loans and less money in circulation.

▶ **Changing the discount rate, the interest rate the Fed charges its member banks for borrowing.** A lower discount rate encourages borrowing and increases the money supply. A higher discount rate does the reverse.

The Fed also handles transfers of funds among banks, regulates the banking system, helps banks in trouble, and participates in negotiations with other governments on banking and economic issues.

> *Full dynamic estimates of individual budget initiatives should be our goal. Unfortunately, the analytical tools required to achieve it are deficient. In fact, the goal ultimately may be unreachable.*
>
> — **Alan Greenspan**, *Newsday*, January 11, 1995

See also **monetary policy** and **regional bank**.

mktg **mgmt**

Federal Trade Commission Act of 1914   Law setting up the Federal Trade Commission (FTC).

Congress gave the FTC the power to promote and enforce "free and fair competition in interstate commerce in the interest of the public through the prevention of price-fixing agreements, boycotts, combinations in restraint of trade, unfair acts of competition, and unfair and deceptive acts and practices."

acct

Financial Accounting Foundation (FAF)   Organization that appoints the members and funds the activities of the powerful **Financial Accounting Standards Board (FASB)**.

The FAF was founded in 1972 by the **American Institute of Certified Public Accountants (AICPA)**, the American Accounting Association, the National Association of Accountants (now the **Institute of Management Accountants**), the Financial Executives Institute, and the Financial Analysts Federation (now the Association for Investment Management and Research).

The FAF appoints the **Financial Accounting Standards Advisory Council**, which advises the FASB. In 1984, the FAF set up a similar structure for government accounting—the Governmental Accounting Standards Board and the Governmental Accounting Standards Advisory Council.

Financial Accounting Standards Advisory Council

Acts as an adviser to the **Financial Accounting Standards Board (FASB)**.

Financial Accounting Standards Board (FASB)

Organization that, since 1973, has been responsible primarily for setting the criteria for financial accounting.

The **Securities and Exchange Commission (SEC)**, the **American Institute of Certified Public Accountants (AICPA)**, and other groups accept the pronouncements of FASB (pronounced fas-bee) as establishing **generally accepted accounting principles (GAAP)**.

EXAMPLE | The FASB issued SFAC 2 in 1980. Among other things, it defines materiality, or when something is important enough that it has to be included in **financial statements**.

See also **materiality concept**.

financial audit   When an independent **certified public accountant (CPA)** examines a company's accounting records and procedures and gives a formal opinion on whether they comply with accounting standards and principles.

See also **audit**.

financial futures   A futures contract with a financial instrument behind it, like a certificate of deposit or a Treasury bond.

See also **derivatives** and **futures**.

financial leverage   Relationship of debt to **equity** in your company's **capital structure**—the greater the proportion of long-term debt, the greater the degree of **leverage**.

financial public relations   Division of public relations that deals with individual investors and financial professionals, like securities analysts and portfolio managers, also called investor relations.

Financial PR specialists work to maintain good channels of communication between their company and the investment community.

Financial Accounting Standards Board

EXAMPLE

In 1992, FASB issued SFAS 109—Accounting for Income Taxes. SFAS 109 changed some of the earlier standards for dealing with income taxes, such as allowing companies more opportunity to account now for future tax benefits.

This example is called a Statement of Financial Accounting Standards (SFAS). Another type of FASB pronouncement is the Statement of Financial Accounting Concepts (SFAC), which establishes or clarifies the conceptual framework of financial accounting and reporting.

F

acct

financial statements   Standard set of reports that document a company's financial status.

Produced at least once a year, they include an **income statement**, a **balance sheet**, a **cash flow statement**, and explanatory notes. Financial statements are included in the **annual reports** that companies provide to shareholders. The **Securities and Exchange Commission (SEC)** also requires publicly held companies to file annual **10-K** financial statements; interim quarterly reports are filed on form **10-Q**.

Financial statements are also submitted to credit-rating and credit-granting organizations, and are used in **underwriting**, among other things.

F

Balance Sheet
For the year ended December 31, 1996 ($ millions)

Assets		Liabilities and Shareholders' Equity	
Cash	$10	Accounts and notes payable	$18
Accounts receivable	25	Accrued liabilities	7
Inventory	28	Current portion, long-term debt	5
Current Assets	**$63**	**Current Liabilities**	**$30**
		Long-term debt	15
		Total Liabilities	**$45**
Fixed assets, net	15		
Other assets	5	**Shareholders' Equity**	
		Capital stock	20
		Retained earnings	18
		Total Shareholders' Equity	**$38**
Total Assets	**$83**	**Total Liabilities and Shareholders' Equity**	**$83**

financial statements

The balance sheet shows a company's financial position. It is also called a statement of financial position.

Income Statement

For the year ended December 31, 1996 ($ millions)

Sales	$ 100
Cost of goods sold	75
Gross profit	25
Selling, general, and administrative expenses	15
Net income from operations	10
Interest expense	2
Net income before taxes	8
Income taxes	4
Net income	$ 4

financial statements

The income statement is the summary of a company's revenues and expenses for an accounting period.

Cash Flow Statement

For the year ended December 31, 1996

Cash flows from operating activities ($ millions)	
Net income	$ 4
Adjustments to reconcile net income to net cash provided by operating activities:	
Depreciation	1
Changes in assets and liabilities:	
Accounts receivable	(2)
Inventory	(1)
Accounts and notes payable	2
Accrued liabilities	1
Net cash from operating activities	$ 5
Cash flows from investing activities	
Additions to fixed assets	(4)
Net cash used for investing activities	$ (4)
Cash flows from financing activities	
Repayments of long-term debt	(5)
Proceeds from sale of common stock	10
Net cash from financing activities	$ 5
Net increase in cash	$ 6
Cash at beginning of year	4
Cash at end of year	$ 10

F

The cash flow statement shows the cash coming in and going out over an accounting period.

acct

financing lease A lease that, in accounting, is treated as an installment purchase.

See also **capital lease**.

acct

finished goods inventory An **account** at a manufacturing firm that includes the costs associated with completed but unsold items on hand at the end of a reporting period.

See also **inventory**.

mgmt

FIRO See **fundamental interpersonal relations orientation**.

acct

first-in, first-out (FIFO) Way of accounting for goods in stock that assumes the first items bought were the first sold, then the next-oldest items in inventory were sold, and so on.

See also **inventory valuation**.

strat mktg mgmt

first mover Early entrant into a market.

A first mover can gain several advantages—like helping to establish industry standards; building relationships with customers, distributors, and suppliers that competitors might not be able to easily duplicate; and benefiting from being ahead of the competition on the **learning curve**. Taking advantage of any of these factors can help build a sustainable **competitive advantage**.

---

first mover

trap

While the benefits of moving first may seem attractive, they are sometimes fleeting. An aggressively competitive follower may feel that the first mover made entry into a new market easier by incurring all the development costs, solving the early problems, creating demand for the product, establishing distribution channels, and in some cases getting regulatory approval. A first mover may be reducing the costs and the risks of following into the market.

F

FRAME OF

REFERENCE

first mover

Fuji invented the recyclable camera, but Eastman Kodak Company followed with a full line of single-use cameras from panoramic to underwater, to specially packaged party and wedding packs. Kodak is now the U.S. leader by far in this fast-growing market, although it trails in Japan and is running neck and neck in the rest of the world.

Quick Facts!

first mover

First movers that capitalized on their competitive advantage are:

- McDonald's, fast-food hamburger restaurant.
- Lever Brothers, liquid laundry detergent (Wisk).
- Xerox, plain-paper copier.
- Procter & Gamble, disposable diapers (Pampers).
- Intel, microprocessor.
- Federal Express, affordable overnight delivery.
- Cable News Network, 24-hour televised news.
- MTV, continuous music videos.
- Chrysler Corporation, minivan.

EXAMPLE | In the 1980s, Mobil Chemical Company pioneered the coated packaging films now commonly used to wrap candy bars, potato chips, and other snack foods. But Mobil's high costs and slow-moving culture left a lot of room for smaller companies to follow into the market with lower costs. Mobil has had trouble maintaining the profitability of its packaging films.

econ   fin

fiscal policy
The exercise of government tax and spending policies to achieve economic goals, such as greater economic growth, increased **employment**, and stable prices.

Fiscal policy can influence the economy through its effects on either **aggregate demand** or **aggregate supply**.

Fiscal policy owes its popularity to British economist John Maynard Keynes. During the Great Depression of the 1930s, Keynes wrote *The General Theory of Employment, Interest, and Money*, in which he argued that the depression was due to a deficiency of aggregate demand. To boost demand, Keynes argued that governments could use fiscal policy in the form of deficit spending.

Many economists have contended that **budget deficits** would boost demand during times of economic downturns while budget surpluses would reduce demand during times of **inflation**. By following such policies over time, governments supposedly could smooth out the growth path of the economy.

Governments have eagerly obliged with deficit spending, but they have seldom produced budget surpluses. The last one in the United States, for example, was in 1969. Continual deficits in the federal budget increase the national debt and the future tax payments people will have to make to pay its interest and principal.

fiscal policy

The important thing for government is not to do things which individuals are doing already, and to do them a little better or a little worse; but to do those things which at present are not done at all.

—John Maynard Keynes,
The End of Laissez-Faire

fiscal policy

Economist, journalist, and financier John Maynard Keynes (1883–1946) is best remembered for his revolutionary economic theory on the causes of prolonged unemployment. His fame rests on a theory that recovery from a recession can best be achieved by a government-sponsored policy of full employment.

fiscal year

EXAMPLE

Education Alternatives, Inc.— a company that forms public-private partnerships with public schools, manages private schools, and provides consulting services in education—uses a fiscal year that ends June 30, coinciding more closely with the school year.

Economists have noted other problems with fiscal policy, too. One is that it takes time for government officials to realize what is happening in the economy. Then, it takes more time for Congress and the president to produce legislation to change taxes and spending accordingly. Still further time is required for the changes to have any effect—at which point, the original problem may have disappeared or been replaced by another problem calling for a fiscal policy that is just the reverse. In that case, the original attempt to fix the economy may unwittingly make it worse.

When both weak economies and inflation appeared in the 1970s, economists realized they had neglected aggregate supply while focusing their attention on aggregate demand and deficit spending. To use fiscal policy as a means of influencing aggregate supply, changes in marginal tax rates and government regulations, for example, were promoted as ways of altering producers' incentives and thereby affecting aggregate supply.

See also **Federal Reserve System (Fed)**, **monetarism**, and **supply-side economics**.

acct **fin** **mgmt**

fiscal year
The 12-month **accounting period** a company uses for financial reporting purposes.

Two-thirds of publicly traded U.S. companies use the calendar year, but it makes sense for some companies to use a different 12-month period. Retail stores, for example, use a fiscal year that runs through January, when the holiday season is behind them. Many other industries also have fiscal years that fit their businesses.

acct

fixed assets
Not likely to be converted into cash or used within a year.

See also **balance sheet**.

acct **mgmt** **econ**

fixed cost
A cost that tends to stay the same even though the level of business activity changes.

Insurance, rent, **depreciation** on equipment, and the payroll for salaried employees are all fixed costs. Since these remain about the same from month to month, per-unit fixed costs will fall as production rises.

EXAMPLE | You run a business assembling cellular phones. Your fixed costs (insurance, rent, and so on) total around $20,000 a month. If you produce 10,000 phones in a month, your fixed costs are $2 per unit ($20,000 ÷ 10,000 = $2). If you assemble 20,000 phones in a month, per-unit fixed costs drop to $1 ($20,000 ÷ 20,000 = $1).

See also **variable costs**.

fixed period review system   Reordering **inventory** at specific time intervals rather than as needed.

See also **periodic review inventory system**.

flexible manufacturing system   One that incorporates state-of-the-art technology to optimize every stage of a manufacturing process; such systems can manufacture variations of the same product on the same **assembly line**.

See also **automation**.

mgmt

flextime   Alternative scheduling approach that gives workers some options in setting hours.

With flextime, employees must work a set number of hours each workday, but they have some latitude in choosing their starting and ending times. There is a core time, usually six hours, when each employee must be present. Then there is a flexibility band before and after the core time.

See also **compressed workweek** and **job sharing**.

mktg

flighting   Approach to media planning and buying under which an advertiser places many print advertisements or broadcast commercials during a period of time, suspends the **advertising** for another period, then reinstates the advertising.

Typically, an advertiser using flighted media will repeat the cycle several times during a year. The theory behind flighting is for an advertiser to concentrate its limited advertising budget in certain periods so as to get maximum impact during those periods. Thus, while the advertising is running, the target audience is able to perceive the advertisements through the clutter of all other advertising. Many advertisers believe that if the advertising is suspended for a short enough period, the consumer will not even realize that he has not seen the product or service advertised for some time. By the time the consumer's recollection of the product or service starts to fade, the next cycle of advertising has begun, thus reinforcing the consumer's previous impressions.

float   (1) The portion of company shares that can be bought by the public.

A small float means the stock will be more volatile, since a large buy or sell order can have a dramatic impact on the share price. A large float means the stock will be less volatile, since the price cannot be as easily influenced by large transactions.

flextime
Quick Facts!

Employees at a company's headquarters work an eight-hour day with 30 minutes for lunch. Every worker must be at the office between 10 a.m. and 4 p.m.—the core time—but can add the other two hours before or after, or a combination of both. So the flexibility bands are from 8 a.m. to 10 a.m. and from 4 p.m. to 6 p.m. Employees may work from 8 to 4, from 10 to 6, or anything in between.

Businesses that offer flextime say it reduces absenteeism because people have more control over their hours. Since the facility is staffed over a longer period as workers' shift times overlap, flextime can reduce the need for overtime, too. Employers also say it increases productivity as well as employee autonomy and responsibility—factors that can boost job satisfaction. Flextime's major disadvantage is that it cannot be applied to every job. A receptionist, for example, must be on duty at certain established times.

F

The term also refers to bringing a new issue to market and to the portion of a new issue that remains unsold at a given time.

(2) In banking, the time that funds are in transition from one bank or one account to another.

Because of the float, after you write a check to your supplier, you may continue to earn interest until the payee deposits the check and your bank removes the money from your account. Your supplier's bank may get the funds the next day but withhold the money from his or her account for a specified number of days.

So the bank is then earning **interest** on the float. Your supplier's bank justifies this practice because it is still possible you did not have enough money in your account to cover the check. If that is the case, your bank will reclaim the money from your supplier's bank. Some states have regulations limiting the float that banks can impose on their depositors.

fin

floating rate **Interest rate** or **dividend** that changes periodically.

See also **adjustable rate**.

mktg   **mgmt**

focus group   People with similar interests who are brought together to discuss products and services.

Most focus groups include eight to twelve people. This form of qualitative **market research** is usually conducted over a one- to three-hour period to gain insight into feelings, attitudes, and behaviors. The biggest difference between focus groups and phone, mail, and other surveys is that the focus groups use discussions among the participants and a facilitator, or moderator.

A company might use focus groups when considering introducing or making changes in a product or advertising campaign. The main appeal is that focus groups explore attitudes in more depth, as the moderator probes for why participants feel certain ways and the group discussion expands on those feelings. The moderator can use props—like samples of product packaging or advertising—to enhance the discussion.

Focus groups are often held in rooms allowing observation, usually through a one-way mirror. The company conducting the research and the client requesting it observe the group from an adjoining room behind the mirror and record the proceedings on audiotape and possibly videotape. The research company will also prepare a report analyzing the group discussions.

EXAMPLE | Friendly Marketer is a large company that sells products all over the United States, spending a lot of money on **image advertising**. In print and TV campaigns, the company stresses its commitment to environmental issues and its humanitarian activities. New management at Friendly Marketer decides it is time to see if the ads are worth continuing.

---

focus group

trap |

Focus groups need a professional moderator to keep the results from being skewed by strong personalities among the participants. Because the sample of participants is too small, no quantitative data are produced, so a statistical analysis cannot be made. For this reason, it is smart to conduct several focus groups aimed at different types of participants, possibly in different parts of the country. In most cases you would want a phone or mail survey, too, to add some mathematical certainty, or projectability.

F

Focus groups take you where no survey has ever gone before—allowing extensive probing, brainstorming, and feedback to stimuli. Used creatively and cautiously, they can unveil a wealth of valuable insights.

—Bill Adams, President, Adams Research

Friendly hires XYZ Research Company to conduct a telephone survey and six focus groups. The telephone survey shows that many people are skeptical of the advertisements. The focus groups—conducted at various locations among union members, white-collar workers, government officials, users of Friendly Marketer's products, college teachers, and environmentalists—help Friendly understand what is wrong with the ads. Many types of focus-group participants clearly express that the ads are too self-serving; the company is mentioned too much. So Friendly decides to change the campaign to one that praises the good works of others, with the company name mentioned only once—at the end.

mktg **strat**

focus strategy
Tailoring your product for a narrow segment of the market.

You can do that by focusing on a geographic area where you have a distribution advantage or by differentiating your product.

EXAMPLE | With Lean Cuisine™, Stouffer's is aiming for people who are health conscious and want quality and convenience. Wrigley pitches its Freedent brand to people with dental work who like to chew gum but do not like for it to stick to their teeth. And speaking of teeth, Tom's of Maine's "natural toothpaste" leaves out artificial sweeteners, colors, and flavors (not to mention animal ingredients and preservatives) in an attempt to attract people whose concern for their oral hygiene extends beyond sparkling teeth.

mktg

font
Size and style of a typeface.

A font includes the letters of the alphabet, numbers, punctuation marks, and symbols. There are thousands of type styles; each one has a slightly different look and conveys its own message. The typeface you are now reading is called Sabon MT. Changing the font you use can make a dramatic difference in the impact of your text. For example, the following type across the top of a full-page magazine ad:

```
Year-End Inventory Sale
```

It may not seem very enticing in the font shown, which is Courier. You might generate more excitement with a livelier, bolder font like Univers Bold Condensed:

Year-End Inventory Sale

The unit of measurement for a typeface is called a point. Seventy-two points are roughly equal to an inch, and the type is measured vertically. In a 36-point typeface that you might see in an advertisement, for example, there is about a half-inch from the top of a letter like *h* to the bottom of a letter such as *g*. The typeface you are now reading is 10.5 points.

Font Styles

Example	Name of Font	Type Family of Font
Typography	Garamond	Old Style
Typography	Baskerville	Transitional
Typography	Egyptian	Slab Serif
Typography	Bodoni	Modern
Typography	Helvetica	Sans Serif

font

tip 👍

As the population ages, the size of the font becomes more important, because 70 percent of the population begins to experience a loss of elasticity in the eye after age 40.

trap 👎

Since type is measured vertically, the size alone does not tell you much about the amount of type that can fit in a given space. That is because some typefaces have much narrower characters than others.

F

Forbes 500

Forbes

---

mktg **mgmt**

Food and Drug Act of 1906 See **consumer protection legislation**.

mgmt **fin**

Forbes 500 Ranking of the 500 largest publicly owned companies in the United States published annually by *Forbes* magazine. The magazine ranks companies according to their assets, profits, sales, and market value of shares.

See also **Business Week 1000**, **Fortune 500**, and **Inc. 500**.

fin

forced conversion When an issuing company calls in a **convertible security**.

Despite the name, holders of the security are not forced to convert it to the underlying **common stock**. They can accept the issuer's call price or sell the security on the open market during the call's **notice period**. If the common stock price is higher than the call price, most people will take the conversion option.

mgmt **strat** **mktg** **fin**

forecasting Using current information to predict future trends in your company's sales, **market** potential, or prices.

Estimating future corporate income and expenses is part science, part art, and sometimes entirely fiction. But it is absolutely necessary if you ever want to borrow any money. Bankers and other lenders will expect a forecast that covers three to five years of income, cash flow, **assets**, and liabilities.

> *I believe that economists put decimal points in their forecasts to show they have a sense of humor.*
>
> —**William E. Simon**, U.S. Secretary of the Treasury, 1974–1977

Foreign Credit Insurance Association (FCIA)

Organization that offers insurance coverage against commercial and political risks for exporters and their lending institutions. Part of the **Export-Import Bank**.

foreign direct investment
Money a company invests in operations or businesses outside its home country.

This refers to investments like building a new plant, either alone or with a local partner. Buying shares in a foreign company, on the other hand, is called portfolio investment.

foreign exchange
Trading of various currencies in the international marketplace.

These currency exchanges arise when people trade goods and services, real **assets**, or financial assets like stocks and **bonds**. To implement such trades, people use the currencies themselves or short-term credit instruments such as bills of exchange.

A typical day sees more than a trillion dollar's worth of foreign exchange being transferred throughout the world, much of it occurring electronically, via computer.

foreign sales corporation (FSC)
Company incorporated outside the United States under the Tax Reform Act of 1984 to reduce taxes on U.S. export sales.

An FSC can cut a U.S. company's taxes on income from export sales by as much as 15 percent. The FSC must operate in a qualifying country and comply, along with its parent, with documentation requirements of the Internal Revenue Service. FSCs replaced Domestic International Sales Corporations (DISCs), which deferred taxes on foreign sales but did not actually reduce them.

The three general categories of FSCs are:

1 Large
These have very complex IRS reporting requirements.

2 Small
The requirements are much less complex, but the parent company must have annual export sales of $5 million or less.

3 Shared
Companies with annual export sales of less than $50,000 often find it too costly and complicated to establish their own FSCs, so a number of state and industry organizations have created shared FSCs, allowing any exporter to participate in the tax savings.

forced conversion

tip

If your company has convertible securities outstanding, the optimal time to call them is when the conversion price equals the underlying stock's market price. That is especially true if interest rates are low, so you can refinance your debt.

trap

The optimal call policy is largely theoretical for several reasons. Most important is that you have to give your security holders some notice—usually about a month—and neither the stock price nor interest rates can be predicted. In practice, most forced conversions come when the stock price goes way above the call price.

forecasting

tip

A forecast should not be completed and then stuck in the file cabinet. It must be tracked, as weeks and months roll on, to make sure it is in line with reality.

trap

*Most new businesses tend to overestimate **revenues** and underestimate expenditures, which could leave you dangerously undercapitalized somewhere down the line.*

FSC management companies located in all qualified foreign countries help smaller exporters with accounting and administrative tasks.

The qualified countries are Australia, Austria, Barbados, Belgium, Bermuda, Canada, Dominica, Egypt, Finland, Germany, Grenada, Iceland, Ireland, Jamaica, Malta, Morocco, the Netherlands, New Zealand, Norway, Pakistan, the Philippines, South Africa, South Korea, Sweden, and Trinidad and Tobago. Four U.S. possessions also qualify: American Samoa, Guam, the Northern Mariana Islands, and the U.S. Virgin Islands.

foreign exchange

acct

Form 3115 Businesses must use this to obtain approval from the Internal Revenue Service to change **accounting methods**. It has to be filed no later than the 180th day of the year for which you are requesting the change.

Form **3115**	**Application for Change in Accounting Method**	OMB No. 1545-0152
(Rev. November 1992) Department of the Treasury Internal Revenue Service	► See instructions specifically for "Automatic Changes in Accounting Method" and "When Not To File Form 3115". All applicants must complete pages 1 and 2.	Expires 11-30-95

Name of applicant (if joint return is filed, also give spouse's name) — Identifying number (see instructions)

Number, street, and room or suite no. (If a P.O. box, see page 2 of instructions.) — Applicant's area code and telephone number/Fax number ( ) ( )

City or town, state, and ZIP code — District Director's office having jurisdiction

Name of person to contact (If not applicant, power of attorney must be submitted.) — Contact person's telephone number/Fax number ( ) ( )

Check one of the following boxes:

☐ Individual ☐ Partnership
☐ Corporation ☐ S Corporation
☐ Cooperative (Sec. 1381) ☐ Insurance Co. (Sec. 816(a)) ☐ Insurance Co. (Sec. 831)
☐ Qualified Personal Service Corporation (Sec. 448(d)(2)) ☐ Other (specify) ► ....
☐ Exempt organization. Enter code section ►

Check the box(es) for other schedules that will be completed and attach only the completed schedule(s) to pages 1 and 2 of Form 3115.

☐ Schedule A–Change in Overall Method of Accounting
☐ Schedule B–Changes Within the LIFO Inventory Method
☐ Schedule C–Change in the Treatment of Long-Term Contracts, Inventories, or Other Section 263A Assets
☐ Schedule D–Miscellaneous Changes in Method of Accounting

1a Tax year of change begins (mo., day, yr.) ► .... and ends (mo., day, yr.) ► ....
b Enter the 180th day of the tax year ► .... If this date is earlier than the date signed by the applicant on page 2, see **Late Applications** in the instructions.
2a Enter the principal business activity designated on the latest filed income tax return ► ....
b Enter business activity code no. (if applicable) (see instructions) ► ....
3 Approval is requested to change (see instructions):
a ☐ Overall method of accounting from **present method** ► .... to new method ► ....
b ☐ The accounting treatment of (identify item) ► ....
from **present method** ► .... to new method ► ....
Attach a separate statement of all relevant facts, including a detailed description of present and proposed methods and an explanation of the legal basis (statutes, regulations, published rulings, etc.) for making this application.

	Yes	No
c If a change is requested on Item 3b above, check the present overall method of accounting that will not change: ☐ Accrual ☐ Cash ☐ Hybrid If "Hybrid" is checked, attach an explanation.		
d Number of tax years present method has been used by the applicant. (See Item 3d in the instructions.) ►		
e Is the present method a "Designated A" method as defined in section 3.07 of Rev. Proc. 92-20?		
f Is the present method a "Designated B" method as defined in section 3.09 of Rev. Proc. 92-20? . . . . If "Yes" to Item 3e or 3f, indicate the designating document		
g Is the present method a "Category A" method as defined in section 3.06 of Rev. Proc. 92-20?		
h Has the applicant entered into a transaction to which section 381(c)(4) or (5) applies during the tax year of change or is the applicant considering this type of transaction during the tax year of change? If "Yes," attach explanation . . .		
4a Is this the first tax year the applicant is required to change its method of accounting under section 263A, 447, 448, 460, or 585? If "Yes," state which section is applicable ►		
b Does the applicant produce or acquire property for resale subject to section 263A? . . . . If "Yes," Schedule C. Part III must be completed if the costs to be changed are subject to section 263A.		
5a Has the applicant or any member of the affiliated group been contacted by the IRS prior to submitting Form 3115 to schedule an examination of any of its Federal income tax returns, or is an examination in process (section 3.02 of Rev. Proc. 92-20)? If "Yes," indicate which window period under section 6 of Rev. Proc. 92-20 applies ►		
b If "Yes," has a copy of Form 3115 been sent to the district director? See section 10.06 of Rev. Proc. 92-20 . . .		
c Does the applicant have any Federal income tax returns under consideration by an appeals office or before any Federal court? See section 4 of Rev. Proc. 92-20		
d If "Yes," has the applicant attached a written agreement from the appeals officer or counsel for the government? . .		
6a In the last 6 years has the applicant applied for or changed its tax year, its overall method of accounting, or its accounting treatment of any item? If "Yes," attach a statement describing the changes and the year of change		
b If "Yes," has a ruling letter granting approval been received? Attach an explanation if no letter was received or if a letter was received but the change was not made. Members of an affiliated group, see Item 10e		
c Does the applicant, an affiliated corporation, or any other related corporation have pending any accounting method, tax year ruling, or technical advice request in the National Office?		
d If "Yes," indicate the name(s) of the corporation, type of request (method, tax year, etc.), and the specific issue involved in each request on an attached statement.		

For Paperwork Reduction Act Notice, see page 1 of the instructions. — Cat. No. 19280E — Form **3115** (Rev. 11-92)

mgmt fin

Fortune 500
List, published yearly by *Fortune* magazine, of the 500 largest public companies as measured by revenues.

From its inception in 1955 through 1994, the list included only what the magazine called "industrial" companies. In 1995—recognizing that a changing economy had boosted the importance of nonindustrial businesses like Wal-Mart and AT&T, which before had been on a separate list—*Fortune* began grouping all corporations on its Fortune 500 list.

See also **Business Week 1000**, **Forbes 500**, and **Inc. 500**.

mgmt fin

Fortune 1000
List, also published by *Fortune* magazine, includes industrial and financial service companies.

fin

forward contract
Contract to buy or sell a foreign currency, security, or **commodity** at its current price at a specified date.

EXAMPLE | In a year you will need at least 90,000 Japanese yen, but you fear that the dollar will drop sharply against the yen by then and you would like to lock in something close to today's rate. If the current exchange rate is, say, $1 = 90 yen, the 90,000 yen will cost you $1,000. You will pay 8 percent interest to borrow dollars for a year, and you can make 6 percent by lending yen for a year. Here is how your cash flow would look:

Forward Contract

	Now		1 Year Later	
	Dollars	Yen	Dollars	Yen
Borrow dollars at 8%	1,000		(1,080)	
Change dollars to yen	(1,000)	90,000		
Lend yen at 6%		(90,000)		95,400
Net cash flow	**0**	**0**	**(1,080)**	**95,400**

The net **cash flow** today is zero, but in one year you will pay $1,080 and receive 95,400 yen, for an effective exchange rate of $1 = 88.33 yen (95,400 ÷ 1,080 = 88.33). So you have engineered a forward contract to purchase Japanese yen in a year at a rate that is just slightly more expensive than today's rate. If your prediction was right and the value of the dollar has dropped so much that it would buy fewer than 88.33 yen, your forward contract was a smart deal.

Fortune 500

Just as British confectioners and haberdashers boast discreetly that they purvey this or that 'by appointment to Her Majesty,' so companies trumpet, often loudly, their presence on the Fortune 500.

—*Fortune* magazine, May 15, 1995

F

Quick Facts!

The top five companies on the 1995 Fortune 500 list, with revenues, are:

- General Motors, $155 billion
- Ford Motors, $128 billion
- Exxon, $113 billion
- Wal-Mart, $82.5 billion
- AT&T, $75 billion

franchise

International franchising has become a growth strategy of virtually all large U.S. franchisers. In the mid-1990s, for instance, restaurants outside the United States accounted for 40 percent of McDonald's sales and half of its operating income.

Little guys (franchisers with 50 to 100 franchisees) have been going global, too. Every type of company—from fast-food chains to water-leak detection outfits—is getting into the act.

franchise

There are five basic franchises.

1 **Product franchise**

2 **Manufacturing franchise**

3 **Trade-name franchise**

4 **Conversion franchise**

5 **Business format franchise**

F

`strat` `mgmt`

forward integration   Company's expansion on down the **distribution channel**.

This often ensures a **market** for the company's product and offers a new profit opportunity.

`fin`

forwards   Over-the-counter contracts calling for delivery of a specified amount of an underlying asset on a future date at a **spot price** or another negotiated price.

See also **derivatives**.

`mgmt`

401(k) plan   A defined benefit **pension plan** established in 1981.

`mgmt`

franchise   Rights granted a business to sell products and services to the buying public using somebody else's name, **trademark**, logo, and business systems.

Franchised sales increased 94 percent from 1985 to 1995, and franchising experts predict another 50 percent increase in the next decade. A *franchiser* is the party granting the rights; the *franchisee* is the party paying for the rights—usually a small business. The franchiser shows the franchisee how to organize and manage the business, train employees, and merchandise the products or services.

The franchisee is usually restricted in the types of products and services it may sell, how they are sold, and even when they are sold. A franchise is significantly different from a dealership or distributorship. Dealers and **distributors** (1) do not pay any fees or royalties to the manufacturer, (2) do not take the manufacturer's trademark or logo as their own, and (3) run their businesses as they see fit without any substantial restrictions from the manufacturer.

There are five basic types of franchises to choose from:

1 Product Franchise

Franchisees take on the identity of the manufacturer. They display the manufacturer's name and logo in their stores and in their **advertising**. The manufacturer gains a sales network without investing in stores and showrooms. The Singer Sewing Machine Company was one of the original product franchisers in the 1850s. Today, automobile dealerships and independently owned gas stations are typical product franchises.

2 Manufacturing Franchise

The least-used type, they perform work for a parent company. Coca-Cola and Pepsi bottling plants fit in this category.

3 Trade-Name Franchise

A company uses a franchiser's name without necessarily selling any of its products or services. Examples include Western Auto and Ben Franklin retail stores.

4 Conversion Franchise

Existing businesses join a chain of similar ventures operating under the umbrella of one franchiser. An example is Century 21 real estate offices. Many of its franchisees ran independent real estate offices before joining the franchise.

5 Business Format Franchise

The most popular type of franchise. The difference between this type of franchise and the product franchise is the large degree of control exercised by the business format franchiser. The franchisee gets a ready-made business that has enjoyed successes in other locations. A full set of instructions accompanies the initial fee the franchisee pays, like setting up the business, advertising and promoting it, obtaining building designs, and receiving lists of vendors and (sometimes) customer mailing lists. Most of what the franchisee does is closely regulated by the franchiser. Typical business format franchises are Barefoot Grass Lawn Service, Roto-Rooter, Franklin's Copy Service, McDonald's, and Management Recruiters International.

mktg

free on board (FOB)   Designates the point to which the price of an item includes shipping costs; at that point, the buyer assumes title to the merchandise and is responsible for all further costs. A piece of equipment marked "FOB Chicago," for example, means that the purchaser must cover any freight charges from Chicago to the final destination.

See also **distribution channel**.

---

franchise
Quick Facts!

Many companies are starting to repurchase some of their franchise locations to focus their operations. In 1994, Arby's Inc. bought back 33 of its franchised units in the Jacksonville and Orlando, Florida, markets. Arby's announced that the move would allow the company to consolidate their operations and marketing strategies in Florida, where the company is based. The acquisition also allowed Arby's to test new products and concepts more effectively.

F

freelance

**functional
organizational
design**

Treasury
Vice-President of
Finance
Controller
Vice-President of
Marketing
Sales
Advertising

F

`mktg` `mgmt`

freelance   Work done as an independent contractor without affiliation to the company.

The term is used primarily for people in creative disciplines—directors, film and video camera operators, graphic artists, illustrators, models, photographers, producers, writers, and the like. The advertising industry uses freelancers extensively, selecting individuals on a job-by-job basis.

`fin` `mgmt`

FSC   See **foreign sales corporation**.

`mgmt` `mktg`

FTC   See **Federal Trade Commission Act of 1914**.

`acct`

full-cost method   Approach to **costing** that takes into account **variable costs** as well as a share of **fixed costs**.

`mgmt` `strat`

functional organizational design   Structuring a company by the type of work done. This usually results in large, hierarchical groupings with power concentrated at the top.

The diagram on the opposite page shows how a large U.S. candy company might look with a functional design. All of the company's manufacturing and packaging operations report to the VP for manufacturing no matter where the facilities are or what is made. Likewise, all marketing functions, along with advertising and promotion, report to the VP for marketing.

In a static environment, a functional design is effective. But in a dynamic environment it can be problematic. Lower-level management may lack the authority to make necessary decisions, thereby overwhelming upper management with day-to-day operational issues. Consequently, the company will be less adept at responding to change.

In a dynamic environment, many companies have turned to **decentralization**, moving decision-making authority into more parts of the company. So our candy company might have a division devoted to chocolate bars, another to peanut-butter cups, and so on, with marketers and manufacturers reporting in together. And the functions might be decentralized further into geographic regions corresponding to parts of the country. That way, decisions can be made quickly by the managers with the most knowledge about their products and regions.

See also **matrix structure** and **organizational environment**.

Functional Organizational Design

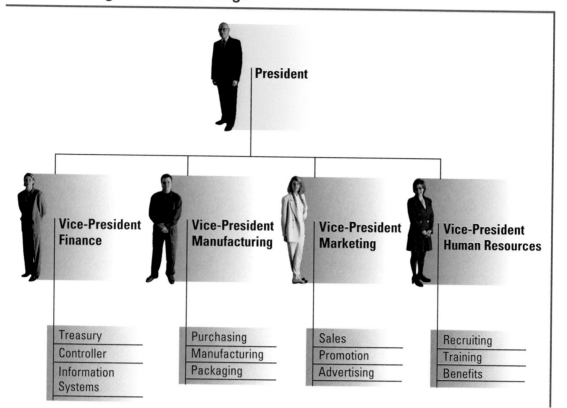

President

Vice-President Finance

Vice-President Manufacturing

Vice-President Marketing

Vice-President Human Resources

Treasury	Purchasing	Sales	Recruiting
Controller	Manufacturing	Promotion	Training
Information Systems	Packaging	Advertising	Benefits

F

---

mgmt

fundamental interpersonal relations orientation (FIRO) Way of studying how a person interacts with others.

Within the FIRO framework, there are three interpersonal needs:

1 **Inclusion/Interaction**
   This is measured as high (a great need to be included in group activities) or low (a need for more time alone).

2 **Affection/Friendship**
   Someone who seeks out close friendships would rate high. Those who prefer less-personal relationships are low on this scale.

3 **Control/Influence**
   People are rated as high if they need to control their environment and low if they do not need to be in charge.

future value

What an

investment will

grow to if it earns a

set rate of interest,

compounded

regularly, until a

specific date.

F

FIRO distinguishes between wanted behavior, which is how an individual wants others to act toward him or her, and *expressed behavior*, how the person acts toward others. FIRO can help you decide if employees are in their right niches. For example, people who score high on affection/friendship and low on control/influence may do well in customer service but have trouble in management positions.

fin

future value   What an investment will grow to if it earns a set rate of **interest**, compounded regularly, until a specific date.

Future value reflects both the interest on the initial sum and the interest compounded on the interest earned. Interest may be compounded annually, semiannually, quarterly, monthly, weekly, or even daily.

Published tables list the compounded value of $1 at various interest rates over various periods. A lot of business calculators and spreadsheet programs also do future-value calculations. The basic formula is:

Future Value	
FV_n	$= P(1 + r)^n$

FV_n The future value of an investment in n years

P Principal amount

r Interest rate

n Number of periods

EXAMPLE | You deposit $100,000 in a savings account that earns 5 percent annual interest. In 10 years, your investment will be worth:

$$\$100,000 \, (1.05)^{10} = \$162,889$$

fin

future value of an annuity   Value an investment will grow to if you make regular payments into it.

This assumes that you are earning a constant rate of interest. Calculating the future value of an **annuity** might be useful to a parent making regular payments into an account for a child's education. It is used in business to determine the future value of a fund receiving payments, like contributions to a **pension fund**.

Published tables give the future value of annuity payments, and many financial calculators and spreadsheet programs can do the calculations. The basic formula when annual payments are made at year-end can be written as:

Future Value of an Annuity

$$FV_a = A(1 + r)^{n-1} + A(1 + r)^{n-2} + A(1 + r)^{n-3} + \ldots + A(1 + r)^0$$

FV_a The future value of the annuity

A Annuity payments

r Interest rate

n Number of years in the annuity

When payments are made at the beginning of an annuity period rather than at the end, the investment is called an **annuity due**, and the future value will be larger. Here is the formula for calculating an annuity due:

Annuity Due

$$FV_a = (1 + r) \times [A(1 + r)^{n-1} + A(1 + r)^{n-2} + A(1 + r)^{n-3} + \ldots + A(1 + r)^0]$$

The effect of an annuity due is comparable to receiving an extra period of compound interest.

fin

futures Standardized contracts covering various items that are traded on organized exchanges and that lock in transactions at a certain price on a specific future date.

See also **derivatives**.

---

future value of an annuity

EXAMPLE

You are the pension manager for a company that puts $1 million at the end of every year into its pension fund. If you assume that the fund earns 8 percent interest and there are no withdrawals, at the end of five years it will be worth:

$1,000,000(1.08)^4 +
$1,000,000(1.08)^3 +
$1,000,000(1.08)^2 +
$1,000,000(1.08)^1 +
$1,000,000(1.08)^0 =
$5,866,601

Or if your company makes the annuity payment at the *start* of every year, the future value would be:

(1.08) x [$1,000,000(1.08)^4 +
$1,000,000(1.08)^3 +
$1,000,000(1.08)^2 +
$1,000,000(1.08)^1 +
$1,000,000(1.08)^0] =
$6,335,929

F

G

Star
High Market Share and Growing Strongly

Question Mark
Rapid Growth and Low Market Share

Cash Cow
High Market Share and Slow Growth

Dog
Low Market Share and Slow Growth

to

growth/market share matrix

GAAP

acct

GAAP   See **generally accepted accounting principles**.

acct

GAAS   See **generally accepted auditing standards**.

econ   **fin**   **mgmt**   **mktg**

GATT   See **General Agreement on Tariffs and Trade**.

econ   **fin**

GDP   See **gross domestic product**.

econ   **fin**   **mgmt**   **mktg**

General Agreement on Tariffs and Trade (GATT)

International treaty to advance world trade and economic growth via negotiation.

GATT was signed by 23 countries in 1947 and became effective in January 1948. Since then, there have been eight rounds of negotiation to advance the treaty. The most recent began in 1986 in Punta del Este, Uruguay, and became known as the **Uruguay Round** of GATT. The agreements growing out of the Uruguay Round were ratified by more than 100 countries and took effect in 1995. Key provisions were to:

▶ Reduce tariffs on many manufactured goods by more than a third.

▶ Protect **intellectual property**, a big help to the computer software, drug, and entertainment industries doing international business.

▶ Open markets for exports of services.

▶ Limit government ability to restrict agricultural trade.

▶ Establish rules for settling disputes.

▶ Create the **World Trade Organization (WTO)** to administer GATT and settle disputes.

It has been estimated that the Uruguay Round will add $1 trillion to the U.S. economy over the next 10 years and create perhaps two million jobs.

See also **copyright** and **patent**.

acct

general ledger   Basis for an accounting system—the location in which all of your active **accounts** are collected.

This is a book or a computer **database** that contains a full set of your accounts, such as cash, sales, and so on, each with its **debit** side

---

General Agreement on Tariffs and Trade

Quick Facts!

• As recently as the 1960s, almost one-half of all workers in the industrialized countries were involved in making (or helping to make) things.

• By the year 2000, however, no developed country will have more than one-sixth or one-eighth of its workforce in the traditional roles of making and moving goods.

• Already an estimated two-thirds of U.S. employees work in the services sector, and "knowledge" is becoming our most important "product."

—Peter F. Drucker, from *Post-Capitalist* Society

G

general ledger

ABC Corporation
General Ledger

4150-00-1050		Telephone Expense		
Date	Source	Dr	Cr	Balance
1/31/96	CD	$ 18		
Balance 1/31/96				$ 18
2/28/96	CD	$ 19		
Balance 2/28/96				$ 37
3/31/96	CD	$ 20		
Balance 3/31/96				$ 57

and its **credit** side. The ledger's function is to classify transactions so that all those affecting, say, cash are recorded in the cash account. It should be in balance at all times, with aggregate debits equaling aggregate credits.

See also **chart of accounts**, **journal entry**, and **trial balance**.

generally accepted accounting principles (GAAP)

Official criteria underlying financial reporting by U.S. companies.

At the broadest level, GAAP is based on "substantial authoritative support," with Accounting Research Bulletins, **Accounting Principles Board** Opinions, Statements of Financial Accounting Standards, and Financial Reporting Releases deemed to qualify as such. In the absence of any published rules, "substantial industry support" may be derived from industry practices, books, and treatises.

Since 1973, the **Financial Accounting Standards Board (FASB)** has been primarily responsible for promulgating GAAP, and it issues numbered standards at various times. Before FASB, the Accounting Principles Board issued opinions—APB Opinion No. 1 through APB Opinion No. 31.

EXAMPLE SFAS 16 set rules for two kinds of adjustments to previous years— how to correct a mistake and how to handle the tax benefits of preacquisition operating-loss carryforwards when buying a company. SFAS 87 told how to account for pension costs, while SFAS 106 established accounting standards for postretirement benefits other than pensions.

The audit opinion included in every publicly held company's annual report tells whether a company's financial statements are presented fairly (in all material respects) in conformity with GAAP.

generally accepted auditing standards (GAAS)

Guidelines for auditing **financial statements**.

The Auditing Standards Board of the **American Institute of Certified Public Accountants (AICPA)** issues numbered statements outlining acceptable practices.

EXAMPLE *Statement of Auditing Standards No. 58—Reports on Audited Financial Statements* gives the format for expressing the **audit** opinion, those three or four paragraphs signed by the auditor in the **annual report** of every **publicly held company**.

generic appeal Advertising approach promoting a type of product rather than a brand.

---

generic appeal

Breaking News

U.S. per-capita consumption of beef declined every year from 1985 through 1993. But the trend turned around in 1994, and generic-appeal advertising is believed to be part of the reason. The National Cattlemen's Beef Association sponsored a well-received campaign ("Beef. It's what's for dinner.") and also offered incentives to grocers who featured beef in their advertising.

From time to time industries, companies, or associations sponsor ads that promote the group's common interest. Often, they are trying to gain ground (or hold ground) against competition from a different type of product. Widespread generic appeals in recent years have been undertaken by the dairy industry ("drink milk, it's healthy") and the cotton industry ("buy garments made with comfortable cotton"). Sometimes generic appeals promote sources of goods or services instead of the specific type; "Made in the U.S.A." is a prime example.

strat **mgmt**

generic competitive strategies
Way of categorizing all business strategies as one of three types—**cost leadership**, **differentiation**, and **focus strategy**.

Competition occurs on the basis of either price, unique features, value, or appeal to a particular **market** segment.

mktg

generic product
Inexpensive, unbranded version of a common product, like paper plates, beer, or cereal.

By using inexpensive packaging and no advertising, and sometimes by avoiding costly ingredients, the producers of generic products can offer items at prices that are 30 to 50 percent lower than those of branded products. A store's **private label** might be considered a form of generic.

Low price is virtually the only reason consumers choose generics over branded products. When they were first introduced, generics were perceived by the public as inferior in quality (thanks largely to ad campaigns by big brand powerhouses). But today many generics are viewed as comparable. That is the key: Generics are most successful when consumers are convinced there is no loss in quality.

In the mid-1990s, generics accounted for a third of the $50 billion-a-year U.S. cigarette industry. Generics have also been a hit in canned fruits and vegetables, paper and plastic products, and soaps and detergents. A major surprise is the deep inroads generics have made in pharmaceuticals, where quality is of utmost concern. Branded drugs have become so expensive that consumers have adopted the practice of reading product labels to compare the active ingredients of brands and generics. Pharmacy and food chains have had great success selling these items.

Ironically, customers seem to be much more picky about pet products and soft drinks than medicines; they have been reluctant to switch to generics for these items.

See also **brand name**.

mktg **mgmt**

Geneva Phonograms Convention
See **Berne Convention**.

---

generic competitive strategies

t i p |

For most companies, the strategy evolves from individual actions taken over time to meet your customers' needs rather than from one big coup.

t r a p |

It is dangerous to pick a strategy and stick to it slavishly without listening carefully to your customers and their needs.

G

Different customers buy different kinds of value. You can't hope to be the best in all dimensions, so you choose your customers and narrow your value focus.... Leaders will not pursue a diffused business strategy, but must continually focus on running a tight ship where their business practices enhance the one special value that they can provide better than anyone else.

—Michael Treacy and Fred Wiersema, *The Discipline of Market Leaders*

BREAKING NEWS

global marketing

McDonald's, with over 16,000 restaurants worldwide, is marketing the globe with its golden arches. Burgers and fries served outside of the United States accounted for 54 percent of McDonald's income in 1995.

Levi Strauss & Co., which gets more than 35 percent of its operating income from abroad, is the world's leading marketer of branded apparel. It has built a strong competitive strategy by making sure that its name means high-quality jeans in any language. In June 1995 the company announced plans to enter the Indian market, estimated at $130 million a year, which has also lured Jordache, Pepe, Wrangler, and Lee. In India and South Africa, Levi Strauss works with local contractors that can meet its quality specifications.

G

globalization

tech

geographical information systems
Allows for graphical representation of special data like digitized maps by combining data with other text, graphics, symbols, and icons.

mktg **strat**

global marketing
Campaign for a standardized product that is structured to maintain consistent quality while being sensitive to cultural differences.

Each year the global market becomes more important to U.S. companies, whose exports have grown around 10 percent a year since 1985. By the year 2000, the world population will reach 6 billion, with less than five percent of it in the United States. Most of the other 95 percent will provide viable marketing opportunities for a Big Mac, a pair of Levi's, and many other U.S. products.

mgmt **strat** **fin** **econ**

globalization
(1) In management, the need to run a company in a way that takes advantage of worldwide opportunities and resources.

With the growing internationalization of business, to remain competitive many companies need to focus on building operations outside their home countries. But doing that successfully involves more than setting up shop in a new location. The company may have to adapt to various cultures and business **environments**. And senior managers may need to make a concerted effort to globalize their company.

EXAMPLE | Your U.S. company establishes offices in London, Singapore, and Tokyo. As you begin your operations there, you keep a watch for promising new local employees. Within a few years, you establish a program to develop those foreign nationals. You arrange assignments for them at the company's U.S. headquarters. Your goal is that some of these employees will rise to senior levels where their experience and insights will help guide projects in various foreign environments. You will also need to institute a program to make current managers sensitive to diversity issues as well.

(2) In finance, the joining of markets worldwide into a shared source of funds for both borrowers and lenders.

Globalization results from two trends:

1 Improvements in technology, which make instant transactions possible between companies in, say, the United States and Japan.

2 The growth in international trade, which results in increased international monetary flows.

With the mushrooming of both foreign banks having branches in the United States and U.S. banks doing business overseas, Americans can just step across Mainstreet, U.S.A., to finance their global transactions.

GNP   See **gross national product**.

going private   A company's purchase of all of its publicly held stock.

This converts the company from publicly owned to privately owned. Often, a family owning a large share of a company's stock buys the rest of the shares and takes the company private. Also, management sometimes identifies an investment group that may take a company private.

Going private may look attractive when the market price for a company's shares is way below their **book value**. The buyback then is a cheap acquisition of the company's assets. Another reason for going private is to remove the shares from the market so they cannot be bought in an unfriendly takeover.

See also **initial public offering (IPO)** and **leveraged buyout (LBO)**.

---

globalization

trap |

Until you have foreign nationals at the very top levels of your company, your employees abroad will remain cynical about the seriousness of your globalization efforts.

G

going private

Breaking News |

Wellington Leisure Products in Madison, Georgia, was owned by the Wellington family until the company went public in 1989. The family retained most of the stock. In 1993, the family decided to take the company private again and offered to buy back the 453,000 shares it did not already own. It completed the deal in early 1994, paying a total of $3.45 million.

G

mgmt

golden parachute
Lucrative benefits package given to a company's senior managers to compensate them if they lose their jobs after a merger or acquisition.

These became common in the 1980s along with the growing number of takeover attempts. Publicly held corporations with golden parachutes for senior executives must disclose them in their **proxy statements**.

See also **executive compensation**.

mgmt   **acct**

goodwill
(1) In general business, the value that comes from intangibles like your business's location, product quality, name recognition, and employees' skills.

This is an **asset** that a potential buyer of your business will consider, but it will not show up in your **financial statements** unless it meets the accounting definition that follows.

(2) In accounting, the amount you pay for a company you are acquiring in excess of the fair market value of the company's **assets** less **liabilities** assumed.

This applies only when a company is acquired under the purchase method of **consolidation**. The goodwill is an intangible asset on your **balance sheet** and will be amortized over its estimated useful life, but not over more than 40 years.

See also **amortization**.

acct

Government Accounting Standards Advisory Council and Government Accounting Standards Board
Both set up by the FAF in 1984 to advise on government accounting.

See also **Financial Accounting Foundation (FAF)**.

BREAKING NEWS

goodwill

In 1994, Eastman Kodak Company completed its purchase of a photofinishing company called Qualex. Kodak paid a total of some $310 million in cash and notes and assumed net liabilities (after deducting the market value of the assets) of around $35 million. It added about $345 million to the goodwill line on its balance sheet and began amortizing the asset on a straight-line basis over no more than 15 years.

mktg

government market   All U.S. federal, state, county, and municipal units buying goods and services.

Their purchases are usually for education, infrastructure (roads, water supplies), defense, common spaces such as parks and preserves, and public health and safety.

Governments commonly use one of two buying procedures:

1 **Competitive Bidding**

The government unit issues a bid request, commonly called a "request for proposal" (RFP). It contains specifications for the product; the quantity, terms, and condition of delivery; terms of the contract; and due date of the bid. Once bids are received and reviewed, the government unit will offer a contract to the lowest bidder that it determines can reliably meet the obligations of the contract.

2 **Negotiation**

The government unit predetermines that it will negotiate a potential contract with only a few companies. This process is usually employed for large or high-risk projects, such as building a bridge or cleaning up a nuclear waste site.

See also **consumer market** and **industrial market**.

tech

graphical user interface (GUI)   System of icons (little pictures) and pull-down menus used with a mouse, trackball, or other pointer to run computer applications.

The GUI (pronounced *gooey*) differs from character-based interfaces where the user needs to type in commands. GUIs were most closely associated with Apple Macintosh computers until operating systems like Windows were developed for IBM-compatible personal computers. Many people find that GUIs make computers more user-friendly.

mktg

green marketing   Producing and selling products and services that appeal to the environmentally conscious **market**.

A company might also use green marketing to differentiate itself from competitors. For example, since recycling is a major environmental concern, the maker of a new computer printer could emphasize that its printer cartridges are recyclable and offer a discount on a new cartridge when the old one is returned. (See related story on page 296.)

graphical user interface

G

green marketing

FRAME OF REFERENCE

green marketing

Aveda Corporation, makers of hair-care and other personal products, has gone so far as to consult medicine men and native elders as well as licensed medical professionals worldwide, looking for natural ingredients that work. And Aveda packages its products in recyclable containers. In running its daily business, Aveda also practices what it preaches. At its headquarters and manufacturing plant near Minneapolis, the cafeteria serves only organically grown foods, and all correspondence is written on recycled paper. Aveda also donates money to environmental causes.

`econ` `fin`

gross domestic product (GDP)   Chief measure of a nation's overall economic activity during a given period.

Gross domestic product measures goods and services produced by all resources located within a nation, even when those resources are

GDP Components, 1959–1994 ($ billions)

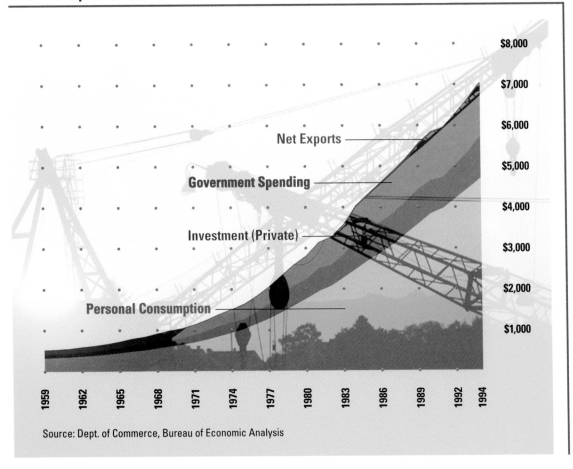

Net Exports

Government Spending

Investment (Private)

Personal Consumption

$8,000
$7,000
$6,000
$5,000
$4,000
$3,000
$2,000
$1,000

1959 1962 1965 1968 1971 1974 1977 1980 1983 1986 1989 1992 1994

Source: Dept. of Commerce, Bureau of Economic Analysis

owned by people in other nations. It is measured two ways: as the total market value of all so-called final goods and services produced, or as the total income received from those goods and services. Both measures are identical since the market value, or what is spent to purchase the final goods and services, must equal the money received for producing them. GDP also includes a nation's exports minus its imports.

Using GDP to evaluate changes in production over time requires statistical adjustments to remove the effects of **inflation**, which produces real GDP.

See also **gross national product (GNP)**.

U.S. Gross Domestic Product (in billions), 1994

Gross Domestic Product	$6,931.4
Personal Consumption	4,698.7
Durable Services	580.9
Non-Durable Goods	1,429.7
Services	2,688.1
Gross Private Domestic Investment	1,014.4
Nonresidential Structures	180.2
Producers Equipment	487.0
Residential	287.7
Change in Business Inventories	59.5
Net Exports of Goods and Services	(96.4)
Exports	722.0
Imports	818.4
Government Purchases of Goods and Services	1,314.7
National Defense	352.0
Non-defense	164.3
State and Local	798.4
Final Sales of Domestic Product	6,871.8
Gross Domestic Purchases	7,027.8

Source: *Economic Report of the President*

---

gross domestic product

Quick Facts!

The U.S. GDP is composed of four major components: personal consumption, investment, government spending, and net exports.

G

gross national product

econ **fin**

gross national product (GNP)   Measure of a nation's over-all economic activity over a period.

Until 1991, GNP was the primary measure used in the United States. Now that is the **gross domestic product (GDP),** which measures all goods and services produced by all resources located within a nation, even when those resources are owned by people in other nations. In contrast, GNP measures goods and services produced by all resources owned by a nation's citizens, whether located at home or abroad. Thus, production from foreign plants owned by U.S. citizens would be included in U.S. GNP but not in GDP. Production from a foreign-owned plant in the United States would be excluded from U.S. GNP but included in GDP. Real GNP is expressed on an annual basis and adjusted to remove the effects of **inflation**.

fin

gross proceeds   Total funds paid for an issue of securities or the sale of assets.

To arrive at **net proceeds**, you must deduct the costs of the transaction—such as an underwriter's fees and registration expenses.

acct **fin**

gross profit   Net sales minus cost of goods sold.

See also **profit margin**.

acct **fin**

gross profit margin   Ratio of gross profit to net sales.

See also **profit margin**.

mgmt

group   People joined together with a common goal.

The individuals do not need to be physically together or formally defined as a group. Three kinds of groups are central to managing any large organization, and employees often work in all three groups at the same time.

The group types are as follows:

1 **Functional Groups**
   Groups created within a company's structure that usually have clear lines of reporting. For example, an automaker will have a design department, engineering group, sales groups located in regions across the country, and more. The company determines their goals, leaders, performance requirements, and many of their procedures.

2 Task Groups

Groups put together to participate in a special function or one-time job. Most are temporary and dissolve once the job is done. Task groups may design a product that is new or different from the company's usual fare, or study a particular issue at a firm, such as the installation of a new computing system or a review of employee benefits. The work follows a schedule independent from the company's regular deadlines. Task groups may also diagnose and resolve particular problems. An industry association, for example, might establish a task group to recommend a new continuing education curriculum for its members.

3 Interest and Friendship Groups

Those that spring up on the basis of shared interests and activities. In an organization's accounting department, a friendship group may develop that goes jogging during lunchtime. Informal groups often form across functional or task groups in an organization; for example, workers from various departments in a company might convene to run a fundraiser for the local Red Cross.

For example, Jane Woods is an accountant in a large company's external-reporting unit. She is preparing the company's quarterly filing with the **Securities and Exchange Commission (SEC)** as she is also working on a task force to reduce the costs of the company's **annual report**. She participates in the weekend tennis group and has agreed to help organize a beach cleanup day.

group

There are three main types of groups: Functional, Task, and Interest and Friendship

G

Sometimes the goals of overlapping groups may conflict. If Jane in our example was also put on a task force to redesign the company's accounting functions, she might find herself questioning the external-reporting organization—and feeling disloyal to her coworkers there. Management needs to be aware of the various groups and their goals. To the extent possible, it also needs to work to bring the various groups' goals in line with the company's overall goals.

See also **fundamental interpersonal relations orientation (FIRO)** and **interdependence**.

mgmt

group norms   Standards of acceptable behavior.

All **groups** have norms: Actors say "break a leg" rather than "good luck" on opening night; in many offices, male workers wear jackets and ties, women wear skirts or dresses, and neither men nor women wear shorts or jeans; a driver waves to say thanks when allowed by another driver to enter a lane. A group could not exist without norms. They let group members know what to do and what not to do to feel included. (See related story on the following page.)

FRAME OF REFERENCE

group norms

A number of studies carried out by Western Electric in the 1920s and 1930s led to a recognition of how important group norms are. The exercises are known as the Hawthorne studies, because they were carried out at the company's Hawthorne Works in Cicero, Illinois. Researchers found that group pressure—workers' need for acceptance by other group members—and the security that goes along with it had much more influence on productivity than such things as light levels in the workplace, piecework incentive systems, job redesign, and scheduling changes.

G

group norms

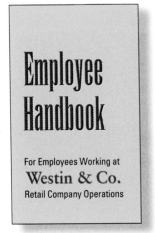

Employee Handbook

For Employees Working at
Westin & Co.
Retail Company Operations

Companies often prepare employee handbooks to help new employees understand and adapt to more formal group norms. Most norms, however, are informal.

groupware

Microsoft®

Some norms are written up in handbooks or other official communications of an organization. But the overwhelming majority of norms are informal. You do not need to be told not to sing when the worker at the next desk is adding up long columns of figures. Changes in fashion just happen without being announced. Because people like to feel included, group norms are very powerful in influencing behavior. If you can succeed in making a behavior (like being on time) widely accepted in your group, it may become a norm and reduce the need for other types of controls.

See also **fundamental interpersonal relations orientation (FIRO)**.

tech

groupware   Important tool for sharing data in a **client-server network**.

Examples include Lotus Notes and Microsoft Exchange. These programs work like the synapses of an electronic brain to help people collaborate and share knowledge without needing to meet. A user can summon the advice and expertise of others in the organization because everyone puts his or her contributions into **databases** that are available to all authorized users.

EXAMPLE | A task force at Microfutures Company, known for its desktop systems, needed to design a laptop computer. The engineers and customer-service people wanted a rugged, easily serviced laptop; the **marketers** argued for a design that would distinguish the product from the competition; the finance folks insisted that manufacturing costs be kept low. They were able to work together and iron out details on their **network** so that the laptop was developed in record time.

strat   **mgmt**

growth/market share matrix   Framework to help a manager of diversified companies see where they rank in **cash flow** and needs.

The matrix that follows was developed by The Boston Consulting Group to help managers maintain the right balance between businesses that generate cash and those that need funds to grow.

Companies fall into one of four categories:

1 Cash Cows

Those that have high **market share** and slow growth, so they generate more cash than they need or can reasonably use.

2 Stars

Those that have high market share and are growing strongly. Even if they are not generating enough cash to support their growth, you know they will yield good returns down the road.

3 Question Marks

Those that have rapid growth and low market share. These may be start-up companies, and the question is whether they will develop a strong enough market position to pay for their growth and yield an adequate return.

4 Dogs

Those that have low market share and slow growth. About half of all businesses fall into this category. Since the money they generate normally must be reinvested to keep them going, they are also called cash traps.

growth/market share matrix

t r a p |

Do not forget to feed your cash cow when it needs it. You may have to invest in technology, for example, to keep your cash cow competitive.

Growth/Market Share Matrix

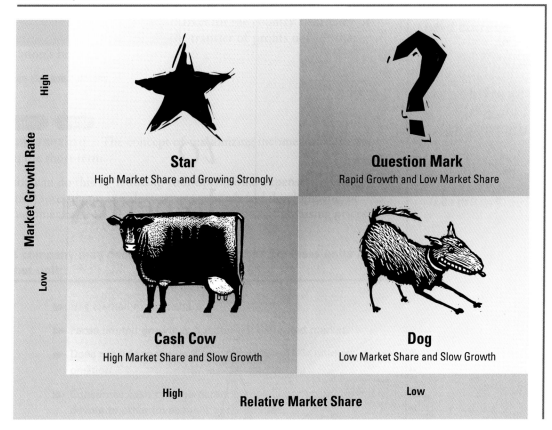

Market Growth Rate — High / Low

Star
High Market Share and Growing Strongly

Question Mark
Rapid Growth and Low Market Share

Cash Cow
High Market Share and Slow Growth

Dog
Low Market Share and Slow Growth

High / Low
Relative Market Share

Used by permission of The Boston Consulting Group.

high-performance organization

Quick Facts!

HPOs have a big appetite for workers with a good education or at least the ability to be trained. But many companies face poor educational systems in the communities around their facilities, and the United States is perceived as lagging overall, especially in math and the sciences. That is why companies like AT&T, Exxon, GE, IBM, and Pacific Telesis Group are donating more money and employee time to improving local school systems.

H

diversity. Since workers are well trained and highly autonomous, the company adapts easily and quickly to change in the marketplace. And even when no big changes occur, the company continuously improves, which makes it harder and harder for competitors to catch up. The HPO company can be called a learning organization because it adapts, improves, and grows from its experiences.

See also **continuous improvement**.

fin

high-yield bond
A **bond** that is ranked below investment-grade by the rating agencies. High-yield bonds are simply securitized loans for companies.

Only about 800 companies are classified as investment-grade. Therefore, more than 20,000 companies, each with at least $35 million in revenue, could be classified as non–investment grade, or "junk."

These classifications, however, can be very misleading from two key investment perspectives:

1 **Performance**

Total performance is difficult to measure in the bond market, but a review of the indices compiled by Salomon Brothers (a leading authority in the bond market) shows that, at least in the last 10 years, the high-yield sector outperformed both investment-grade and U.S. government bonds. (During the 10-year period through 1995, the Salomon Brothers High-Yield Composite Index returned 213 percent; the Broad Investment-Grade Bond Index[SM], 152 percent; and the World Government Bond Index[SM], 141 percent in local currency terms.)

BREAKING NEWS

high-performance organization

The National Association of Marketers (NAM), selecting a company in 1995 as a prime example of an HPO, settled on a small manufacturer called Universal Dynamics. With fewer than 230 employees and sales of about $30 million a year, the company makes machinery for the plastics industry.

Universal Dynamics achieved soaring **productivity** and improved profitability by using highly computerized manufacturing systems and a well-trained work-force. Employees, who do not need much formal education, are trained by coworkers on the factory floor in the specific skills needed.

With pay raises that average 10 percent a year, the workers are organized into teams having a lot of leeway to deal with operational problems. "We have no middle management basically. Everything's been pushed down to the factory floor," says Don Rainville, the company's president. There are just two supervisors for the 115 hourly workers.

Shortly after the NAM selected Universal Dynamics as a prime example of an HPO, the company's management success attracted a German plastics manufacturer looking for an acquisition. Mann & Hummel paid $13.2 million for Universal Dynamics, or almost 30 times its 1993 profits. The per-share price—$8—was more than five times what the stock had been trading at.

high-yield bond

High-yield securities have been around since the turn of the century—they were formerly called "high-opportunity" securities and oftentimes issued as **preferred stocks**. During the 1960s and 1970s, the high-yield market consisted primarily of companies that were in financial distress called "fallen angels." Many of America's greatest companies like Ford, Chrysler, Montgomery Ward, American Airlines, Chase Manhattan Bank, National Gypsum, U.S. Steel, ConEdison, even the city and state of New York, have been downgraded at one time or another and ranked non-investment grade, with their bonds trading at high yields.

Many of today's largest and most well-respected companies were built by raising capital with high-yield securities. Some examples include: Time-Warner, Inc., Turner Broadcasting, MCI Communications, Tele-Communications, Duracell, McCaw Cellular (now part of AT&T), Mirage Resorts, Healthtrust (now part of Columbia/HCA Healthcare), Medco Containment Services (now part of Merck), News Corp. (Twentieth-Century Fox).

2 **Risk/Reward Trade-off** Because of the higher coupons offered by high-yield bonds, any added risk is often more than compensated for. Even in the worst-case scenario—bankruptcy—bondholders have a high likelihood of being paid back, and with interest. The higher coupon provides the investor more "cushion" for exactly such a risk. For example, if the price of a bond with a 13 percent coupon dropped to as low as 70 cents on the dollar, it would still yield 8 percent over a five-year period—higher than the 6.25 percent offered on a 5-year T-Bill (as of February 1997).

Furthermore, the nickname "junk" seems ironic when we consider the importance of high-yield companies to the capital markets, and to the economy as a whole, particularly in the area of job creation. During the past twenty years, the majority of new jobs in the U.S. have been created by smaller, growth companies—which are categorized as high-yield in the bond markets. During the 1980s, for example, 36 million jobs were created, but the **Fortune 500** labor force actually lost 3 million jobs.

A market has developed for the [high-yield] bonds of emerging companies. This new market is, I believe, a big reason why America has produced so many new business pioneers in the last decade and why America has created so many new industries—cellular phones, cable television, the personal computer and our own (MCI) field of phone service.

—William McGowan, former
   Chairman and CEO, MCI
   Communications

EXAMPLE Although high-yield bonds garnered much attention during the 1980s, this type of instrument is no newcomer to the world of investments. The names enshrined in corporate history today were all start-ups at one time, and the debt these companies floated resembled "junk" because they had yet to prove their creditworthiness.

In 1910, for example, a start-up company with such an unpromising future that management could not sell stock placed $7 million in 6 percent "junk" bonds with the Guaranty Trust Company. Its balance sheet at the time showed $35,000 in cash and $200,000 in government bonds with which to collateralize loans.

The company survived to become known as one of the nation's best-managed firms. Its name: *International Business Machines*.

high-yield bond

Picking the Best Creditor

Even before Shakespeare penned the admonishment "neither a borrower nor a lender be," people understood that some loans do not get repaid. But which loans carry the greatest **risk** of default and which are the safest? To answer that question, broadly defined, you might start by identifying three kinds of borrowers in the world: countries, consumers, and corporations.

Countries

Country debt, otherwise known as sovereign debt, has long been perceived as relatively safe, with investors comforted by the idea of a bond backed by an entire government. This image was tarnished, to say the least, in the last round of write-offs taken by U.S. banks in the 1980s on Latin America (whose total loan defaults, led by Mexico, amounted to $251 billion by 1989). Of course, government defaults are nothing new. Some of the most sizeable defaults in history include Latin American countries in the 1820s and then again in the 1930s, Russia in 1911 at the end of the Czarist regime, and the Czechs after World War II.

Consumers

So what about consumer risk? Some believe that a built-in "safety factor" comes from the huge diversity of the consumer base, the idea being that a few consumer bankruptcies are less worrisome than that of a whole country or even a company. But this notion has been seriously challenged in past recessions, as high delinquency rates caught creditors by surprise. In one of the most spectacular examples of consumer default, the Texas S&Ls had over 20 percent delinquency rates on real estate loans in 1987. And if you've ever wondered why the interest rate on your credit card is so high, it's at least partially because lenders have to build in a cushion for the 2 to 5 percent delinquency rates that typically come with consumer debt.

Corporations

In terms of default history, company debt has fared better by most measures than either sovereign or consumer debt. To be sure, companies have defaulted—the default rate on corporate bonds (ironically mostly investment-grade) peaked in the 1930s at 3.2 percent, as might be expected. Two decades of prosperity following WWII sent the default rate down to .03 percent during the early 1960s, the lowest rate experienced during this century. But dramatic defaults in the transportation industry, railroads for the most part, put $1.3 billion of bonds into default by 1979—many of which had been rated AA and AAA. Trouble in REITs (Real Estate Investment Trusts) added another $380 million to the 1970s corporate defaults. Still, notwithstanding these more spectacular examples, corporate default rates are relatively tame. Moody's estimates that default rates have averaged less than one-tenth of 1 percent (.001) for investment-grade bonds during the past 25 years. High-yield bonds ranked above "B" (the bulk of the market) have averaged only a 1.7 percent default rate.

See also **bond ratings**, **going private**, **investment-grade bonds**, and **junk bonds**.

High-Yield Underwriting: Dollar Value and Number of Offerings

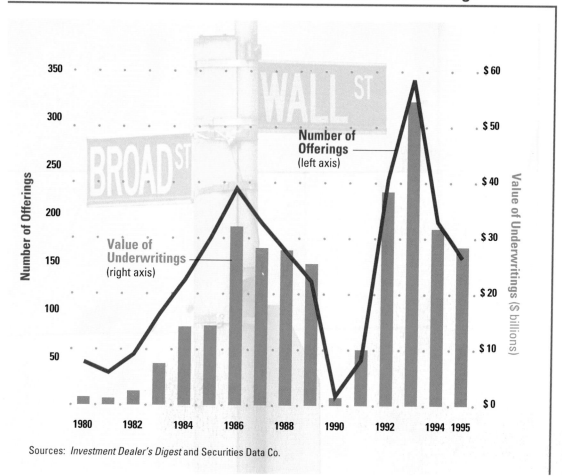

Sources: *Investment Dealer's Digest* and Securities Data Co.

The number and dollar amount of high-yield financings increased dramatically in the 1980s and 1990s. In 1980, there were only 45 high-yield underwritings, raising about $1.4 billion. By 1995, the number of underwritings had risen to 154, and the total dollar amount raised was $28 billion—a twentyfold increase over 15 years.

fin

holding-period return   Return on an investment during the time that it is held.

It includes both income from the investment and any profit or loss on its disposal—any capital gain or loss. Here is how you calculate it:

Holding Period Return	= (Income + Capital Gain or Loss)
	÷ Purchase Price

high-yield bond

Capital markets have built-in controls against overleveraging. Recent efforts by our regulators to override these built-in market mechanisms by destroying the junk bond market and by imposing additional direct controls over leveraged buying by banks will thus have the unintended consequences normally associated with such regulatory interventions. They will lower efficiency and raise cost.

—Merton H. Miller, Nobel Memorial Prize (Economic Sciences) Lecture, presented at the Royal Swedish Academy of Sciences in Stockholm, December 7, 1990.

home page

H

EXAMPLE You held two investments, Stock X and Stock Y, for a year.

	Stock X	Stock Y
Purchase price	$100	$100
Cash dividend	$16	$10
Selling price	$94	$110
Capital gain (loss)	($6)	$10

The holding-period return for each stock is:

Stock X: ($16 − $6) ÷ $100 = 0.10, or 10%

Stock Y: ($10 + $10) ÷ $100 = 0.20, or 20%

tech

home page   Initial screen of data for each organization on the **World Wide Web**.

See also **Internet**.

strat **mgmt**

horizontal integration   Company's expansion within its level of the production or **distribution channels**.

Often, it is a retail chain buying another retail chain or one manufacturer buying another. But the expansion does not have to be by acquisition. Wal-Mart's development of Sam's Wholesale Club is an example of horizontal integration; Boston Chicken becoming Boston Market and extending its menu to ham, meatloaf, and turkey is another. Horizontal integration can help a company attract a new segment of a market it is already in, broaden its product line, or enter related businesses. Over time, General Motors has accomplished all three objectives: Years ago it added models to attract more wealthy buyers, it broadened its base when it purchased Saab, and it entered the related field of financing when it started the GM Card credit card service.

See also **vertical integration**.

mktg **strat**

horizontal marketing strategy   Cooperative effort by two or more unrelated companies to take advantage of a **marketing** opportunity.

In the 1990s we have seen many examples as Chevron, Exxon, Mobil, and Texaco, among other gasoline marketers, joined forces with companies like Dunkin' Donuts, McDonald's, and Pizza Hut to sell donuts, hamburgers, or pizza at service stations. In addition to getting revenue from the food sales, the gasoline marketers hope to attract more gasoline business to their stations. The food franchisers are enhancing the convenience of their products.

housing starts

Number of new housing units workers have started building in a given period, usually a month.

Since residential construction accounts for roughly 3 percent of total U.S. **gross domestic product (GDP)**, this is an important economic indicator. In addition to housing starts (determined to have occurred when the foundation of the house or multifamily building is dug), other housing activities monitored by the Commerce Department include:

housing starts

► **Housing permits**—when new housing units are authorized by local governments.

► **Housing completions**—the end of construction.

► **New-home sales**—completion of the transaction.

New Private Housing Starts, Quarterly, 1975–1995 (millions)*

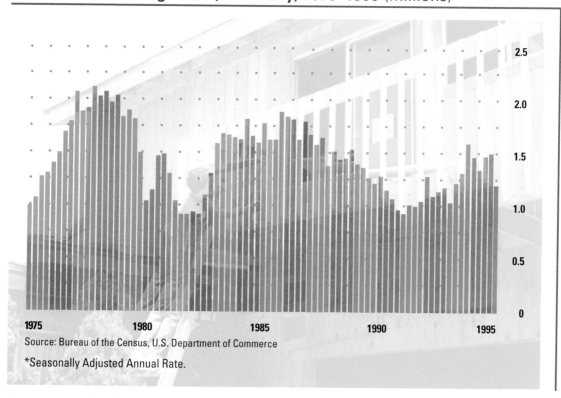

Source: Bureau of the Census, U.S. Department of Commerce

*Seasonally Adjusted Annual Rate.

As seen here, residential construction is highly cyclical because a new house is a major expenditure for a typical family and because the role played by mortgage interest rates is significant.

H

human-resource management

Quick Facts!

The importance of human-resource management was recognized by Bill Gates, founder and CEO of Microsoft Corporation, in a 1992 interview. Asked about the most important thing he had done the previous year, he replied, "I hired a lot of smart people."

H

humorous appeal

trap

If the advertising does not succeed in relating the product's benefit, it may work as entertainment but fail to sell. You do not want people laughing so hard that they do not remember the product.

---

mgmt

human-resource management   Way a company administers its relationship with employees.

A few old-fashioned, two-fisted managers who are uncomfortable spending much time on human-resource issues still exist. But many—probably most—of today's managers are even more uncomfortable leaving those issues to a personnel department.

The company that identifies the best prospective employees, recruits them, and keeps them motivated, engaged, and fully challenged has an enormous edge on its competition. Many executives consider their approach to human-resource management a key corporate strategy. Managers more and more view employees as a corporate asset and refer to them with phrases like human capital, social capital, intellectual capital, and even, in the case of a mining company, above-ground resources.

A company's internal plan for dealing with employees must fit in with the company's external strategy to meet the business environment. Microsoft's combative, competitive external stance, for example, is mirrored internally with a **corporate culture** of long hours, low base pay, and a philosophy of rewarding exceptional performance with lucrative **stock options**. More than 2,000 of its 16,000-plus employees have become millionaires thanks to the options.

Along with recruiting and compensation, key components of human-resource management are training, **performance appraisals**, career development, benefits, labor relations, and **employee discharges**.

mktg

humorous appeal   Use of humor in **advertising**.

When they are most successful, humorous ad campaigns capture the public's imagination, create excitement for the company, and become part of people's everyday language. The Energizer Bunny™ that keeps on going and going is a prime example. These ads have exceeded the life of an average commercial because of the creative talents that breathe new life into the commercials year after year.

mgmt

hygiene factors   Things like pay, working conditions, and fringe benefits that can make employees dissatisfied.

See also **motivation-hygiene theory**.

econ

hyperinflation   Extraordinarily strong **inflation**.

tech

hyperlink   Connection between **hypertext** and another set of computer data.

FRAME OF

REFERENCE

humorous appeal

Qantas Airways was a pioneer in humorous advertising in the United States. In 1965, as an obscure foreign airline competing for U.S. customers, Qantas turned to humor to boost the impact it could make with a tiny advertising budget. Helped by the Cunningham & Walsh advertising agency, Qantas developed the koala bear who complains "I hate Qantas" because of the tourists the airline brings to Australia. Once the irascible koala appeared in TV commercials, Qantas became a household word practically overnight and before long was bringing a lot more tourists to disturb the koala's peace. The koala remained an advertising symbol for Qantas until 1991.

tech

hypertext   In a document on your computer screen, highlighted words you can click on with your mouse to bring up a new set of data.

EXAMPLE | You are reading a definition of hypertext in a business-resource book on CD-ROM. One sentence reads: "Hypertext is widely used in the **World Wide Web** section of the **Internet**." By moving the on-screen pointer to the highlighted word (Internet) and clicking on your mouse, you will move immediately to the definition for it.

The hypertext may be in a different color, underlined, or boldfaced. Its tie to another set of data is known as a *hyperlink* or *hot button*. On the World Wide Web, the hyperlink may take you to information in another computer halfway around the world from the computer whose data you are reading.

H

Health Care and Pharmaceuticals

In its broadest definition, health care is one of the nation's largest industries. It would include medical care of all kinds, dental services, medical insurance, nursing homes, social services, and countless other related areas. Approximately 15 percent of Gross Domestic Product (GDP) is devoted to the treatment of illnesses, and regardless of political actions to hold down costs, the figure appears bound to rise as the population ages.

Institutions resembling hospitals existed in almost all societies. There were fewer than 100 of them in America during the early 19th century, and patients went there to die, not to recover. Typhoid fever and diphtheria were the two leading causes of death, and they usually did not call for hospitalization. There was no anesthesia, and sterilization was unknown. Life expectancy at birth was around 37 for men, 40 for women. More women died in childbirth than of cancer or heart attacks.

The situation began to change after the Civil War, when profit-making hospitals were established by doctors. In addition, there were "voluntary" institutions organized by religious and philanthropic groups. Finally, some municipalities opened hospitals as well. At first, the profit-making hospitals were more numerous, but the number of voluntaries grew more rapidly with passage of the Hill-Burton Act of 1946, which provided federal aid in their construction.

Government became a major force in medical treatments. The popularity of health insurance,

augmented by Medicare and Medicaid, prompted a revival of the profit-making sector, which by then was more commonly known as proprietary hospitals. In the late 1960s companies such as Hospital Corporation of America, Beverly Enterprises, and Humana, among many others, gobbled poorly performing hospitals or obtained contracts to manage them. By the mid-1980s close to a third of the nation's hospitals were investor-owned proprietaries, which boasted of economies of scale and even the advent of brand consciousness. It was no coincidence that HCA was cofounded by Jack Massey, one of whose earlier cocreations had been Kentucky Fried Chicken.

The need to effect economies impelled the hospital industry further in the 1990s. It also influenced delivery of services, with health maintenance organizations growing in popularity. When and if the federal government institutes a medical-care program in addition to Medicare and Medicaid, it doubtless will reverberate throughout the industry.

The origins of the modern drug industry are clouded, and even the vocabulary has changed over the years. Apothecaries were the key medical practitioners in colonial America. These individuals not only prepared drugs but prescribed them and often were considered doctors. The earliest apothecary shops in North America appeared in the mid-17th century. The apothecaries purchased drugs from merchants, who were known as druggists. But the druggists of that period were distinct from pharmacists, who appeared later.

The practice of medicine was a crude affair as late as the time of the American Revolution. There were 10 medical schools in the nation, but few of those who called themselves doctors attended any kind of school.

This was the age of patent medicines, the term referring to the fact that the formulas were protected by letters patent. These

Contributing Writer: Robert Sobel
Lawrence Stessin Distinguished Professor
of Business History, Hofstra University

medicines could be purchased from peddlers, dry goods stores, and grocery stores as well as apothecary shops. There were many patent medicines, but few were effective. One promised cures for all ailments: It was grain alcohol mixed with a variety of herbs. The likes of Wright's Vegetable Pills, Oman's Boneset Pills, Vegetine, and Hale's Honey of Horehound and Tar were popular nostrums. Coca-Cola, which appeared in 1886, was initially touted as a patent medicine to cure headaches, indigestion, and hangovers.

Patent medicines continued throughout the 19th century and into the 20th century. Sales

of Lydia Pinkham's Vegetable Compound came to $3 million annually as recently as the 1920s. The patent-medicine business thrives today, ranging from aspirin to cough medicines to reclassified "ethical" drugs, such as Tagamet, an antidote for indigestion.

Modern pharmacology may be traced to Edward Jenner, who vaccinated people against smallpox in 1796. Eventually, some of the companies that produced patent medicines switched to ethical drugs, available only through medical prescriptions. Among the early ethical houses that survive are E.R. Squibb & Sons, founded by a medical doctor in 1858, and Eli Lilly, formed in 1876.

Agitation to improve medicine resulted in the Pure Food and Drug Act of 1906 and the subsequent creation of the Food and Drug Administration. Medical-education reform was spearheaded by Abraham Flexner, and under his leadership questionable medical schools were closed. Those that remained had to be licensed, and standards were improved across

the board. It was at this juncture that medicine became a profession.

Along with this came continuous progress in the creation and use of drugs. The industry experienced a sharp change with the arrival of antibiotics in the 1940s, led by penicillin, strep-tomycin, neomycin, and the tetracyclines. The antibiotics were followed by tranquilizers, such as Librium, and amphetamines, like Dexadrine. New products now arrived in a rush. Jonas Salk and Albert Sabin produced vaccines for poliomyelitis. Syntex developed the birth control pill, and with it, dozens of other companies became major players in the industry.

By then the industry was led by such firms as Merck, Eli Lilly, Pfizer, and Upjohn. But the

Jonas Salk

pharmaceutical industry was on the verge of great transformation because of the growing use of drugs and new scientific development.

The creation of a new drug could result in startling modifications in treatments and billions of dollars in sales for the companies that controlled the patents. In the process, scientists became superstars. James Black joined Imperial Chemical Industries in 1958 and developed beta-blockers in the early 1960s, which were later perfected as Propranolol, released as Inderal, a drug used to treat a host of cardio-vascular, kidney, and psychological problems. It also helped win Black the Nobel Prize in 1988 and provided huge profits for ICI. Black soon left ICI for what then was Smith, Kline & French, where he developed Tagamet, whose sales were more than a billion dollars a year.

The movement continued and made its next major change in the late 1970s with the development of biotechnology, also known as genetic engineering. Based on discoveries regarding DNA, for which John Watson and Francis Crick won Nobel prizes in 1962, the development energized established companies and prompted the organization of many new ones.

Biotech also stirred philosophical debate, since the new science skirted the edge of the creation of life itself. In this sense, it blurred the distinction between biology and medicine. For example, in 1973 scientists Herbert Boyer and Stanley Cohen successfully implanted a frog's DNA into a common colon microbe. Several companies conducted research into artificial life forms that might be used to control oil spills. Did this mean companies could create and then destroy even primitive life forms at will?

In 1980 the Supreme Court finally ruled that companies had the right to control new life forms. But activists, concerned about the moral nature of the problem, persisted in opposition. When Myriad Genetics announced it had discovered a gene linked to breast cancer, the company was hailed for its breakthrough. But when Myriad tried to patent the gene, it encountered vocal opposition.

Even so, the court ruling prompted the formation of scores of ventures. By the mid-1980s, there were several hundred of these firms, most modestly capitalized and known only within the industry. But the rising costs of research, the need to plug away at multimillion dollar projects with no idea of when or where it would end, and the knowledge that competitors might develop a drug sooner took their toll on these small companies.

Funding was always a major problem since costs were high and often could lead to dead

ends, and the biotech firms were compelled to look for financial support. One company particularly adept at managing this process was Cetus Co., which was formed by Ronald Cape in 1971. Like most of the other biotech firms, Cetus raised funds for its pure research from private sources and then sold stock to the public. Then, when research proved promising, it entered into relationships with other, larger, better-funded companies. In this case, Cetus joined with W.R. Grace in 1984 to form a jointly owned company to be called Agracetus, which was to conduct research into producing genetically engineered rice, wheat, soybeans, and corn that would be able to resist infestation and disease.

By then, this kind of arrangement had become common. Cetus formed relationships with several companies, while other biotech firms obtained financing from venture capitalists like Kleiner, Perkins, Caulfield & Byers. But promise often was not translatable into financial success. In 1985 Cetus developed a drug known as Interleukin-2, which failed to win approval from the FDA; with this setback, the company faded.

Some of the biotechs became well known to the general public, only to undergo the same experience as Cetus. Genentech, which emerged as an industry leader, succeeded in synthesizing insulin and a growth hormone called Protropin, and was one of many companies involved in the development of Interferon, a promising antiviral protein that offered promise in fighting cancers.

Financial constraints were always a problem at Genentech. By 1986 the company had raised more than $75 million in two equity offerings and $106 million from three limited partnerships designed to fund investigations into specific products. Even so, like most of the other biotech firms, Genentech was obliged to seek a financial backer and in 1990 sold a 60 percent interest to Switzerland-based Roche Holdings for $2.1 billion.

Another firm, Biogen, was also interested in Interferon and in 1980 announced it had produced a genetically restructured bacteria to produce the drug. To raise funds, realize profits, and hedge its research in the face of challenges from other biotechs, Biogen entered into relationships with Schering Plough, SmithKline Beecham, and Merck.

The competition was intense and costly, and other biotechs simply sold themselves and disappeared. Genex, Cetus, Centocor, Integrated Genetics, Genetics Systems, and Hybritech were taken over by other, larger companies.

Biotech is an area in which American companies have a clear and large lead over their

foreign counterparts. Several Japanese companies made attempts to enter the field but failed to make much of a dent and instead purchased American companies or entered into joint ventures with them. For example, Kiren Pharmaceutical is involved with Amgen in developing a treatment for chemotherapy patients. Some British firms are conducting meaningful research, but none has come up with the kinds of developments seen in the United States. Switzerland has one of the most powerful drug industries in the world. But Roche elected to enter the field through Genentech and not on its own.

Amgen, one of the more successful biotechnology companies, was founded in 1980. It soon had two high-profile products, Epogen, a protein that stimulated the production of red blood cells, and Neupogen, a natural protein that sets off white-cell anti-infective activity. Like the others, Amgen entered into partnerships, in this case with Johnson & Johnson and Hoffman La Roche.

The larger drug companies were not immune to rising research and development costs. When discussion of rising health care costs and possible industry regulation reached its peak in

1992, the equity market value of the major pharmaceutical companies fell by a full $50 billion, or 22 percent, in one year. Many of the companies responded by "farming out" their research efforts to smaller R&D companies or by merging to share the risks involved with product development.

This experience has become a hallmark of biotech. It often becomes an all-or-nothing industry. Xoma, a promising Silicon Valley–based biotech, appeared to have the lead in creating methods for treating toxic shock syndrome and was well funded by Dillon Read. But its treatments came late to the market and were beaten by others. One false step and Xoma was on the ropes.

That the health care and the drug industries are two of the fastest growing in the nation has been clear for many years. Demography alone dictates this. By 2010 half the population will be older than 40, while the cohort of those 85 and older is growing at 3 percent a year. Paradoxically, the vigor and imagination of the drug industry will produce a longer-lived population, which will require more of these services than before.

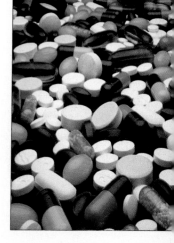

Yet such a future is by no means assured. This is an industry that constantly surprises even insiders. New drugs, more stress on preventive medicine, and better diagnostic care could result in a healthier, older population in need of different kinds of services than those now offered. More than most industries, health care in its many manifestations is as enigmatic as life itself.

I

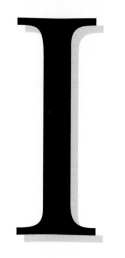

to

involuntary conversion

icons

tech

icons   Small pictures on a computer screen used to represent functions that can be selected, usually by a mouse or by touching the screen.

acct

IMA   See **Institute of Management Accountants**.

mktg   **mgmt**

image advertising   **Advertising** aimed at polishing the image of a company, product, or **brand name**.

The messages in image ads are not intended to generate immediate product sales. These ads lead consumers to regard the company in a positive light.

EXAMPLE | In Nike's "Just do it" campaign, the ads link the company and its brand name with famous athletes and a dynamic approach to life. Some potential customers are likely to find Nike an appealing organization to be associated with, even if it is only by wearing shoes with the company logo.

Sometimes, image advertising—which tends to be one of the most expensive forms of advertising—addresses a particular problem or seeks to change public perception about a product or service.

A number of companies have tried to identify themselves in advertising and other activities with environmental causes and programs that benefit the public in other ways. This type of advertising can be called cause-related advertising.

See also **cause-related marketing** and **green marketing**.

fin   **econ**

IMF   See **International Monetary Fund**.

mktg

in-house advertising agency   Part of its own client company, usually in the **marketing** division.

See also **advertising agency**.

mgmt   **fin**

Inc. 500   Listing of the 500 fastest-growing privately held companies in the United States as determined by *Inc.* magazine. The magazine's annual ranking is based on companies' sales growth over a five-year period.

See also **Business Week 1000**, **Forbes 500**, and **Fortune 500**.

---

image advertising

Quick Facts!

In 1984, after buying General Electric's small-appliance business for $300 million, Black & Decker reportedly budgeted another $100 million for a two-year image campaign showing that the company is not just power tools.

I

incentive plans

Incentive plans have made millionaires of some employees at growth companies with high-flying share prices. Home Depot reportedly pays its store managers a base salary of about $60,000 a year, but through stock options and bonuses more than 100 of them have a net worth in seven figures. Microsoft employees have done even better. Despite low base pay, thousands are millionaires, and three have become billionaires thanks to stock options.

I

mgmt

incentive plans
In management, rewards for performance. Also called **pay for performance** or **performance-based compensation**.

Incentive plans range from cash bonuses and **stock options** for senior executives who meet key financial goals to a weekend getaway for the customer-service rep who fields the most phone calls in a month. The common theme is that employees' pay, or at least some of it, is based on a measure of performance rather than time worked.

Large companies have used incentive plans for many years as a key part of **executive compensation**. In the 1990s, however, many companies have introduced broader incentive plans throughout their organizations in an attempt to focus their **corporate cultures** on performance. Incentive rewards based on measurable results began replacing the annual merit raise because many managers and compensation experts felt the old system failed to distinguish adequately between average and exceptional work. Annual salary increases fell on average from around 5.5 percent in 1990 to 4.0 percent in 1994, while the number of companies with performance-based systems grew from less than half to almost three-quarters.

EXAMPLE | Turner Bros. Trucking, an oil-field transportation company, began offering cash awards for safety in 1990. Within the next five years, the company had expanded the concept to all aspects of its business. It grants monthly awards of up to $200 to each member of the interdisciplinary teams accountable for Turner's operations. Each team is evaluated on five items: profit and loss, safety, training/customer relations, organizational development, and maintenance. Every team member gets $40 for each item rated favorably.

Mobil Corporation conducted a study for more than a year to come up with an overall compensation system tied more closely to performance. The system for employees at all levels includes **base pay** and **variable pay**. The variable component is determined by performance of the individual, his or her business unit, and the corporation as a whole. There is an additional premium for top-tier performers.

econ **strat**

income elasticity of demand
Economic measure of how responsive **demand** is to a change in income.

See also **elasticity**.

acct **fin**

income statement
Summary of a company's revenues and expenses for an **accounting period**. Also called **earnings report**, **profit and loss statement**, or **statement of operations**.

While the **balance sheet** examines the company at a fixed point in time, the income statement covers the period from one balance sheet date to the next. It explains, in broad terms, how the company arrived at its bottom line, or **net income**.

Let us look at the income statement for a large fictional corporation (in millions).

Income Statement

1	**Net Sales**	**$ 29,000**
2	Cost of Products Sold	17,000
3	Selling, General, and Administrative Expenses	9,000
4	**Operating Income**	**$ 3,000**
5	Interest Expense	(500)
6	Other Income (expense), Net	100
7	**Earnings Before Income Taxes**	**$ 2,600**
8	Income Taxes	(800)
9	**Net Earnings**	**$ 1,800**
	Average Shares Outstanding (in millions)	**600**
10	**Earnings per Share (EPS)**	**$ 3.00**

While the format for the income statement varies from company to company, the major categories are:

1 **Revenues**
On our sample statement, they are called net sales. This category is a summary of the sales your company made during the period net of returns, allowances, and discounts.

2 **Cost of Goods Sold**
What it cost to buy or make the merchandise you sold.

3 **Operating Expenses**
This goes by a variety of names, including **selling, general, and administrative expenses**. It is a summary of all expenses attributed to operating your business other than the cost of merchandise. It includes salaries and rent, selling and marketing expenses, **depreciation** and **amortization**, and general expenses like those for telecommunications, equipment repair, and so on.

income statement

While the format varies, major categories of income statements are:

- Revenues
- Cost of goods sold
- Operating expenses
- Operating income
- Interest Expense
- Other items
- Pretax earnings
- Income taxes
- Net income
- Earnings per share

I

FRAME OF

REFERENCE

income statement

You would think that calculating earnings per share should be a snap: Divide net income by common shares outstanding. But your shares outstanding are likely to vary over time. And if you have issued preferred stock, that also changes the picture. You have to subtract the preferred dividends from your net earnings. Then there are stock options, rights, and warrants to consider. That is why it took the Accounting Principles Board 35 pages to explain it all in its APB Opinion No. 15. But that was so complex that accountants complained, so they got an interpretation—more than 100 pages.

income statement

4 **Operating Income**
The earnings from your company's regular business activities.

5 **Interest Expense**
Interest you have paid out on money borrowed, most likely on bank loans or issued bonds.

6 **Other Items**
After you calculate your operating income, you deduct interest expenses and add interest income. You also add or subtract any other items not part of your regular business. In our example, other income (expense), *net*, represented $100 million in gains from financial transactions and the sale of several properties.

7 **Pretax Earnings**
Also called **earnings before income taxes**.

8 **Income Taxes**

9 **Net Income**
Also called **net earnings** or **net profit**. This is the bottom line. In some years, when you have had an **extraordinary item** like the sale of a major asset or an **accounting change**, net income may not represent the company's true earning power.

10 **Earnings per Share**
Net income after taxes divided by the weighted average number of common shares outstanding during the year. If your company has **convertible securities** outstanding, you may need to compute fully diluted earnings per share as well. That assumes conversion to common stock of everything that can be converted.

See also **cumulative effect of accounting change** and **special item**.

fin

increasing rate   **Interest rate** or dividend that changes periodically.

See also **adjustable rate**.

fin

increasing rate notes (IRNs) Securities with coupons that increase at predetermined rates, typically every quarter.

For example, an IRN might start out with a 6 percent coupon and increase to 6.5 percent (50 basis points) after the first quarter, then to 7 percent after the second quarter, and so on. Most IRNs will increase 50 basis points per quarter during the first year and by 25 basis points per quarter thereafter. They may also **float** at an increasing spread over **LIBOR**, with a "floor" attached to protect the holder from big drops in interest rates. IRNs are typically issued as bridge financing and are often callable at par within six months.

econ   **fin**   **mgmt**

incremental cost   (1) Effect on total cost, whether an increase or a decrease, of producing one more or one less unit.

See also **marginal cost**.

(2) The difference in cost between business alternatives.

incremental cost

EXAMPLE | If a newspaper can run color photography instead of just black-and-white, the first step in determining whether the option is worth the expense is to calculate the incremental cost.

	Color	B&W	Incremental Costs
Materials	$11,000	$9,000	$2,000
Labor	6,000	5,000	1,000
Total			$3,000

fin

indenture   Written agreement detailing terms of a **bond** and the rights and responsibilities of the issuer and the bondholder.

See also **debenture**.

mgmt   **econ**   **fin**

indexing   (1) Tying wages, taxes, other payments, or any dollar amount over time to an economic indicator like the **consumer price index (CPI)**.

If a labor contract, for example, has a provision to boost wages along with any sizable increase in the CPI over two years, the contract could be referred to as indexed for inflation. A provision like this is known as a **cost of living adjustment (COLA)**.

(2) Creation of a portfolio of securities designed to match the movement of a market index.

Common indexes are the **Dow Jones Industrial Average** or the **Standard & Poor's 500**. A number of mutual funds have been set up and maintained this way. They are called index funds. One reason they are so popular is that they have lower fees because they are easier to manage.

indexing

industrial goods

I

indirect cost   Production expense that cannot be readily attributed to a certain product—like **overhead** costs such as utilities and insurance—in contrast to direct costs like those for materials and labor.

industrial goods   Goods and services used to make a product and get it to the end customer.

Industrial goods fall into three categories:

1   **Raw Materials and Components**
These are incorporated entirely during manufacturing. Wheat for bread and wool for coats are raw materials; processors for computers and tires for new cars are components. Most raw materials are **commodities** sold primarily on price. Components are usually marketed on performance as well as price: You want to convince a manufacturer of cars or computers that the parts will install easily and work well.

2   **Capital Goods**
Factory buildings, tools, and office computers are examples of capital goods. They are not consumed entirely in the products they help make. Personal contact and service help sell these. In selling factory equipment, for example, you want your customer to trust you to help eliminate any problems installing and using the new unit.

3   **Services and Supplies**
These support production; they are not part of the product. Examples are pencils and coffee for the front office, and maintenance and cleaning services for the factory. Many services and supplies have straight rebuy arrangements—they are reordered regularly from the same supplier. A company supplying lubricating oil, for example, may monitor the oil's performance, recommend when it should be changed, and provide the oil when needed. Many of these items are standardized, so companies selling them usually emphasize price and service.

Trust is important in selling industrial goods, since the buyer's business may depend on the supplier's reliability.

industrial market   Everyone who buys goods or services except for the final consumer. Also called the producer market.

The industrial market has four types of buyers:

1 **Manufacturers**
Those who buy goods and services to make products of their own.

2 **Wholesalers**
Those who buy goods to sell to retail outlets.

3 **Institutional Consumers**
The large-volume purchasers like hospitals, hotels, nursing homes, and restaurants with their own clients. For instance, a huge institutional consumer is the U.S. Army when it buys rations for its troops.

4 **Retailers**
Outlets that offer the products they have acquired to the end user.

See also **consumer market** and **government market**.

industrial market

  econ   fin

industrial policy   Government actions to influence the development of particular industries.

Industrial policy often aims to replace market allocation of the nation's financial capital with government planning. Tax incentives, regional development programs, and subsidies for worker training or **research and development** are all ways that a government might carry out its industrial policy.

EXAMPLE | U.S. industrial policy encourages electric cars. There is a 10 percent federal tax credit (up to a total of $4,000) for the purchase of an electric car, and other tax breaks go to companies making the cars or building recharging stations. Also, various federal agencies grant direct subsidies for research and development of electric-car technology. And at least three states have enacted measures to mandate that a certain percentage of cars sold in those states must be electric.

Another form of industrial policy is so-called strategic trade, whereby a government restricts particular imports or subsidizes particular exports in an effort to promote development of specific industries.

Industrial policies enable the government to redirect a nation's scarce resources to certain industries. At the heart of the debate over industrial policy is whether the government or markets are better able to pick the industries with the best prospects for growth and so direct the nation's capital to its most productive uses.

See also **industrial goods** and **industrial market**.

industrial policy

econ

industrial production   What U.S. factories, mines, and utilities produce.

These are the goods in "goods and services," minus those produced in agriculture, fishing, and forestry. Detailed measurements of U.S. industrial output have been kept since the 1920s. It is one of the **coincident economic indicators**, because it very closely traces the behavior of the **business cycle**.

Industrial Production Index: Annual Percentage Change, Plotted with GDP

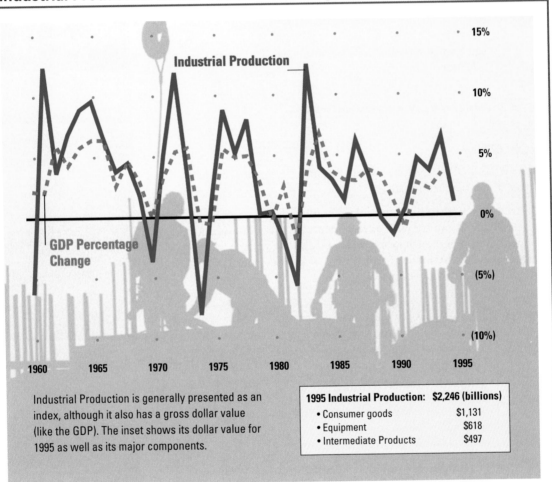

Industrial Production is generally presented as an index, although it also has a gross dollar value (like the GDP). The inset shows its dollar value for 1995 as well as its major components.

1995 Industrial Production: $2,246 (billions)	
• Consumer goods	$1,131
• Equipment	$618
• Intermediate Products	$497

strat

industry-attractiveness test   Way to scope out the strategic impact of entering a new industry.

One tool you can use to assess the industry is the five-forces model. The idea is that the new industry must be structurally attractive to your company. In other words, either the returns now available in that industry are at least as good as you could get in your industry, or your impact on the industry will improve the returns to acceptable levels.

EXAMPLE | When Westinghouse decided to buy CBS, it presumably believed it could do better by expanding its role in broadcasting than by increasing its investment in its other business segments.

See also **better-off test** and **cost-of-entry test**.

industry-
attractiveness test

`econ`

inflation | Sustained, generalized increase in the prices of goods and services, usually expressed as an annual percentage.

Inflation generally results when the money available to spend grows faster than do the goods and services available to buy. An inflation rate of up to approximately 2.5 percent is not considered a serious economic or social threat, but higher rates worry people.

Effects of Inflation: Prices over Time*

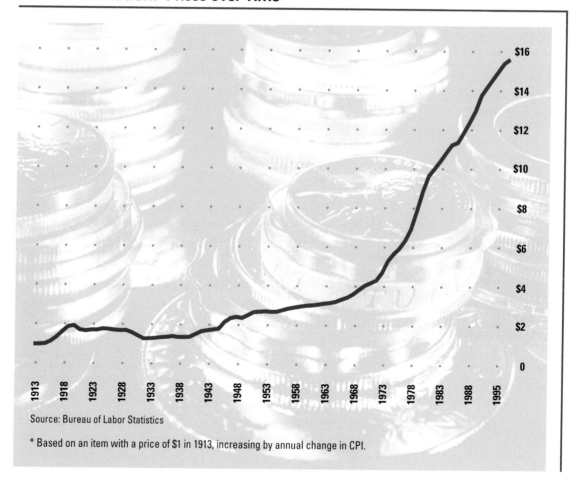

Source: Bureau of Labor Statistics

* Based on an item with a price of $1 in 1913, increasing by annual change in CPI.

Because inflation most often moves in small annual increments (the CPI has increased by an average of 3.5 percent during the time period shown here), its effects over time are often underestimated. Here, we illustrate its importance by charting the purchase price of an item based on inflation changes. This means that the same item that cost $1 in 1913 would cost you more than $15 in 1995.

informal organizational structure

In those very rare cases when inflation becomes so rapid that it is apparent on a day-to-day basis, it is called hyperinflation, which is a significant problem. In **hyperinflation**, people are reluctant to save their money because its value is so rapidly diminishing. Instead, they tend to buy **tangible assets** like real estate or gold.

The opposite of inflation is *deflation*, which is a decrease in the prices of goods and services. Deflation should not be confused with *disinflation*, which is when the rate of price increases slows down.

mgmt

informal organizational structure
Pattern of social relationships that emerge among coworkers over time.

An organization's informal structure usually deviates from its formal structure as social relationships bypass the organization chart.

EXAMPLE | You are the chief counsel of a large company. You report to the company's CEO. John Smith, a lawyer reporting to you, has frequent social contact with the CEO. They go to the same church, and their families are friendly. In meetings, you see that Smith is more relaxed and effective making presentations to the CEO than you are. Also, Smith can often get to see the CEO more quickly than you can.

Since you trust Smith's judgment, you see no point in trying to interfere. You encourage Smith to approach the CEO directly on matters Smith is working on but ask him to keep you fully informed. On occasion, when you need a fast decision from the CEO, you ask Smith to look for an opportunity to raise the matter informally.

As is clear from our example, the informal structure of an organization can be as important as its formal structure. During periods of change, the informal structure can be even more important as people turn to their friends for a sense of security. During periods of layoffs, for example, employees will often gather around the informal structure—a more powerful tool than most directives from top management. The informal structure is so strong, in fact, that many employees give the information it disseminates more credence than company pronouncements.

fin

initial public offering (IPO)
The first public sale of **common stock,** usually by a privately owned company that wants to go public.

After the IPO, the publicly held shares may be traded on a stock exchange or the **over-the-counter (OTC)** market. A company may go public when it needs more capital to support or expand operations. This is particularly true when market conditions make it more advantageous for a company to sell stock rather than borrow funds. Or a company may decide to go public when its private owners want to sell part of their stake.

See also **going private** and **investment banker**.

initial public offering

Netscape Communications Corporation, which makes software for cruising the **Internet**, came to market with a 5-million-share IPO on August 9, 1995. Snapped up by the public at $28 apiece, the shares were driven as high as $78 that first day before closing at $57, more than double the offering price—and this for a company that had yet to show a profit. The astonishing climb continued, with the shares reaching more than $170 in early December. Netscape, which did close out 1995 with a profitable fourth quarter, earning some $2.4 million, had a market capitalization of $5 billion.

NETSCAPE

™ Netscape Communications Corporation

inputs   What goes into making and delivering goods and services.

Production factors include such ingredients as capital, raw materials, labor, time, physical plant, and equipment.

mktg

insertion order   Instructions specifying a print ad's position and terms; usually a simple form filled out by an advertiser or its **advertising agency**.

The form indicates the dates when the ad should appear, where in the publication it should go (the inside front cover of a magazine, say, versus the front or back sections), the size of the ad, how it should be positioned on the page, and the price to be paid. Included with the insertion order is often a copy of the ad. Most publishers will not reserve space for the client until the order is received.

See also **advertising rates**.

fin

inside information   Proprietary details about the goings-on at a company that are made known to a few people but not the general public.

See also **insider trading**.

fin

insider trading   Making stock-market transactions based on private information that is unavailable to the public.

Insider trading may be unlawful, depending on the relationship between the individual who has the inside information and the companies involved in the insider trading.

initial public offering

trap

*One of the drawbacks to going public is the disclosure requirements of the **Securities and Exchange Commission (SEC)**.*

I

insider trading

EXAMPLE In the movie *The Big Chill*, the Kevin Kline character, who built a publicly traded running-shoe business, tells the William Hurt character that the company is about to be taken over. Hurt can triple his money by buying stock in the company. If Hurt buys the stock and makes a profit from the information, it is clearly illegal insider trading.

A lot of cases are not as clear-cut. It is generally agreed that directors, officers, key employees, and major shareholders are insiders who need to take special care not to trade in anticipation of news the public does not yet know. But during the work day, insiders may talk with financial printers, consultants, lawyers, and Wall Street professionals. And after hours, there is no limit to the kinds of people they may spread information to. A cab driver, a cop, a dentist, and the psychiatrist of an executive's spouse have all been charged in insider-trading cases. Sometimes the "insider" may not have any direct connection to the company at all.

EXAMPLE A *Wall Street Journal* reporter was convicted and a Kidder Peabody **broker** pleaded guilty in the early 1980s to securities fraud after it was learned that the reporter was selling the broker tips on what stocks would be touted in the paper's "Heard on the Street" column. A favorable mention in that column often boosts a stock's price, and the broker made more than $700,000 by trading around the information. The Supreme Court upheld the reporter's conviction, even though he by no means could be considered an insider in any of the companies whose stock was involved.

There is no question that insider trading exists, and much of it goes on without drawing criminal charges. Studies have shown that a stock's price will rise immediately before an announcement of a **dividend** increase or a big earnings improvement. Other studies have found that stocks do exceptionally well in the months after heavy insider purchases and poorly after big insider sales. Stock prices often rise markedly—and options get bought up—in the weeks before a takeover attempt or other major announcement.

EXAMPLE When Colt Industries announced in 1988 a plan to buy back much of its stock, the stock price rose $27 in a day, and people who had recently bought options in the company realized enormous profits. There had been heavy buying of the options in the days before the announcement, and an investigation showed that a lot of it came from one neighborhood. A lawyer with advance knowledge of the **buyback** announcement was convicted for tipping off 40 of his friends and neighbors.

Directors, officers, and major shareholders of publicly traded companies are required to report their trades in their company's stock to the **Securities and Exchange Commission (SEC)**, which publishes the information monthly. So the public can at least keep tabs on what insiders are doing.

insider trading

Shifting Boundaries

You are an insider and you buy stock in your company because you know that the new CEO is bright and talented. You are a portfolio manager who buys stock in a company because you like the general info you got at a meeting just for you and a few other institutional investors.

No one would see anything wrong with either of these actions, but they are both based on information and impressions unavailable to the general public. Drawing the line on illegal insider trading is not easy, and some people feel it is a waste of time. Henry Manne, dean of the George Mason University Law School, thinks that insider trading should be legal unless there is fraud involved, like stealing confidential information. Manne contends that allowing the people with the information to trade on it would keep stock prices closer to their true value and lessen the big price jumps when news is announced.

In 1988, President Reagan signed into law a bill toughening the penalties for insider trading. Individuals can be jailed for up to 10 years and fined as much as $1 million. Corporations and partnerships can be fined up to $2.5 million. The SEC can seek triple damages from securities companies, and the law paved the way for suits by people who sold while the insiders were buying, or vice versa.

But in this age of the **globalization** of securities markets, rules on insider trading vary greatly from country to country.

acct

Institute of Management Accountants (IMA)

Association of **accountants** in industry, public accounting, government, and teaching. Formerly called the National Association of Accountants.

You do not have to be a **certified public accountant (CPA)** to join the IMA, and membership is open to interested nonaccountants. The organization's focus is on **management accounting**.

The IMA offers continuing education and **ethics** counseling. Its Institute of Certified Management Accountants administers an examination for those seeking to become **certified management accountants (CMAs)**.

Founded in 1919, the IMA has almost 85,000 members and publishes a monthly magazine called *Management Accounting*.

mktg

institutional consumer

Large-volume purchaser within the **industrial market,** like a hospital or a hotel that has its own clients.

Institute of
Management
Accountants

INSTITUTE of
MANAGEMENT
ACCOUNTANTS
CERTIFIED MANAGEMENT ACCOUNTANT PROGRAM
CERTIFIED IN FINANCIAL MANAGEMENT PROGRAM

institutional investor

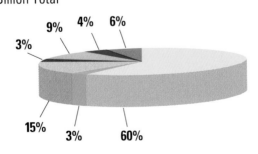

tip 👍

While the buying and selling decisions of institutions largely determine the price of many stocks, individual investors are considered more loyal and in for the long haul. So a large base of individual investors may add an element of stability to a stock's price.

fin

institutional investor   Organization pooling investment funds from multiple sources to trade securities in large volumes.

Examples include banks, insurance companies, mutual funds, pension plans, unions, and university endowment funds. As individual investors have turned more and more to institutions like mutual funds, the individual's influence on the market has shrunk. Institutions account for half to three-quarters of daily trading on the **New York Stock Exchange (NYSE)** and own around half the **common stock** of many of the largest U.S. corporations (General Motors, 45 percent; Exxon, 41 percent; General Electric, 55 percent; International Business Machines, 48 percent).

acct

intangible asset   An **asset** without physical substance, such as **patents**, **copyrights**, leases, and **goodwill**.

See also **tangible asset.**.

U.S. Equity Holdings, with Breakdown by Investor Category

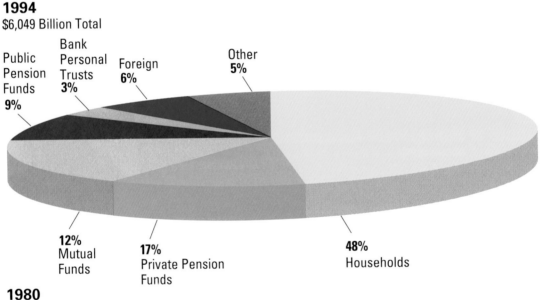

1994
$6,049 Billion Total

Public Pension Funds **9%**

Bank Personal Trusts **3%**

Foreign **6%**

Other **5%**

12% Mutual Funds

17% Private Pension Funds

48% Households

1980
$1,535 Billion Total

9%   **4%**   **6%**

3%

15%   **3%**   **60%**

Defining Institutional Investors: Shifting Categories?
Since 1980, households' piece of the investor "pie" seems to have shrunk – holding 48% of all equities (down from 60%). This shift is misleading, however, since many households now hold stocks through mutual funds, which now hold 12% of equities (up from 3%). Technically, this means more stocks are held by "institutional" investors, since mutual funds are considered institutional. Households, however, are still the end owners.

Source: Securities Industry Association

tech

integrated circuits   Basic operating units of a computer's memory or processors.

They are made of interconnected layers of etched semiconductor materials. They have off/on positions that direct the electrical current passing through them, thus storing and conveying **bits** of data.

tech

integrated services digital network (ISDN)   High-speed telephone link that allows the transmission of voice and data over the same wire.

ISDN transmits voice and data with a digitized signal four times faster than today's highest modem speeds. ISDN may also transmit video but requires a fiber-optic infrastructure for high resolution. Despite ISDN's promise, and the costly upgrading already performed by telephone companies in half of U.S. cities to accommodate the technology, experts believe that fiber-optic technology will displace ISDN as the technology for carrying voice, data, fax, cable TV, and video.

integrated circuits

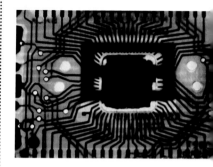

Integrated Services Digital Network (ISDN)

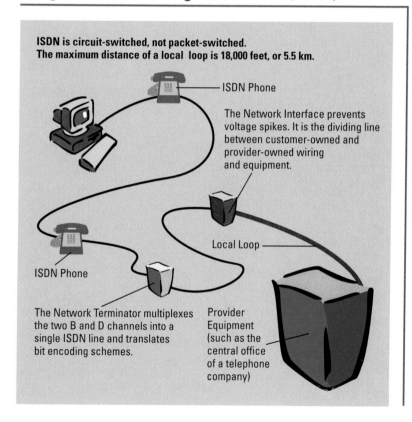

ISDN is circuit-switched, not packet-switched.
The maximum distance of a local loop is 18,000 feet, or 5.5 km.

ISDN Phone

The Network Interface prevents voltage spikes. It is the dividing line between customer-owned and provider-owned wiring and equipment.

Local Loop

ISDN Phone

The Network Terminator multiplexes the two B and D channels into a single ISDN line and translates bit encoding schemes.

Provider Equipment (such as the central office of a telephone company)

intellectual property

Poets often describe creativity as Promethean, referring to the mythical hero who brought fire to the earth. In the 1980s, the Promethean American creativity and entrepreneurship transformed economics and politics around the globe. From the convergence of computers and telecommunications, it created a new information economy and new foundation of national power.

—George Gilder, author and futurist, from *Portraits of the American Dream*

---

mgmt

intellectual property   Something created by original thought and owned by an organization or individual.

The primary examples are **copyright**, **patent**, and **trademark**.

---

tech

intelligent agents   Helpful computer tool for users based on **expert systems** technology. Agents can be embedded into computer-based information systems and can add a variety of support functions for a user.

EXAMPLE | Every time a manager logs in to his PC in the morning, he wants to know the opening price for certain stocks. Having noticed this for several days in a row, the intelligent agent offers to perform this function and automatically looks up the stocks for the manager, rather than requiring him to enter their codes.

---

fin   **econ**

Inter-American Development Bank   One of four major institutions whose primary objective is to help nonindustrialized countries by raising capital, providing technical assistance, and attracting investments.

See also **development bank**.

---

mgmt

interdependence   How **groups** count on one another to meet company objectives.

Three common types of interdependence are:

1 **Pooled**
The efforts of two or more groups working on their own that advance the company's aims. An automaker, for example, needs both a design group and a transportation department to create a new model and get it to market. But the groups are largely independent and distinct.

2 **Sequential**
One group relies on another, but the relationship is just one way. For example, our automaker's manufacturing division needs parts obtained by the purchasing department. If purchasing fails to order enough parts, production may come to a halt.

3 **Reciprocal**
Two or more groups have mutual inputs and outputs. The automaker's design, engineering, and manufacturing departments work closely on the development of a new model. Each produces ideas that are tested by the others and returned for more work. None of the groups could create the model without the others.

fin **econ**

interest rate The rate, expressed as an annual percentage, charged on borrowed money.

Interest rates are quoted on consumer and business loans, of course, but also on **bonds**, notes, bills, and credit cards.

Two lending rates play a big role in your cost to borrow money. The **discount rate**, which is what the **Federal Reserve System (Fed)** charges on loans to its member banks, sets a floor under lending rates. The **prime rate**, which is what banks charge their best, most creditworthy corporate customers, is a key determinant for other commercial and consumer loans.

When you get your loan, what the bank charges you is called the **nominal**, or stated, interest rate. But that can differ from the **actual rate** paid, also known as the **effective interest rate**.

Here is how a nominal rate can be the same as, or different from, the actual rate: If you borrow $1,000 at 10 percent for a year, and the interest is paid when the loan matures, you receive $1,000 at the start of the period and return it plus $100 interest at the end. You have paid an actual rate of 10 percent ($100 ÷ $1,000 = 0.1, or 10%)—the same as the nominal rate. But if you must pay the 10 percent, or $100, interest in advance, you get $900 at the start of the year and return $1,000 at the end, so the actual interest is 11.11 percent ($100 ÷ $900 = .1111, or 11.11%).

The **real interest rate** is the nominal rate minus **inflation**. The real rate is of particular interest to investors in fixed-rate instruments like bonds, notes, and bills because it gives them a way to see if the interest they are earning will keep them ahead of inflation-caused erosion in the value of their money.

See also **annual percentage rate (APR)**.

fin

interest-rate swaps When two parties agree to exchange periodic interest payments.

For example, traders might take responsibility for each other's loans because one company can get good terms on, say, a fixed-rate loan and another can do well on a floating rate. Or one company might trade long-term debt for another's short-term debt.

See also **derivatives**.

acct **mgmt**

internal audit When an auditor within a company investigates its procedures to make sure they meet corporate policies.

See also **audit**.

---

interdependence

tip

As a rule, senior management needs to spend very little time coordinating the work of groups whose interdependence is pooled but much more time on the other two categories.

Human life in common is only made possible when a majority comes together which is stronger than any separate individual and which remains united against all separate individuals.

—Sigmund Freud, *Civilization and Its Discontents*, 1930

I

interest rate

The

real interest rate

is the

nominal rate

minus inflation.

fin   **mgmt**

internal rate of return (IRR)   Measure of the income an investment will make over time, expressed as an **annual percentage rate**, or **discount rate**.

The IRR is the equivalent of the **interest rate** you could earn if you invested your money in a debt instrument at the same time that you made your investment in the project or business. Managers and financial planners often use IRR in evaluating a possible venture, such as expanding a plant or buying a company.

If you were deciding on a project, you might determine the **cost of capital**, the minimum return for an investment of similar risk, and then establish it as the minimum IRR that is acceptable for your company. If the expected IRR for your proposed project exceeds the minimum you set, it is a go.

The IRR is the discount rate where the **net present value (NPV)** of the investment is zero. NPV is the current worth in dollars of the activity's future **cash flow** after the initial investment has been recovered. (To find the formula for calculating NPV, see **net present value**.) Calculating IRR is basically a matter of trial and error, or many business calculators are programmed to do it.

EXAMPLE | You run a take-out pizza business and believe you could improve your return by buying a van and adding delivery service. You can buy the van for $15,000 and think you will use it for five years, then sell it for $5,000. After expenses, you estimate that your business will make another $3,500 a year from the delivery service. So your cash flow looks like this:

Scenario 1: Cash Flow, Years 1–5

Year #1	($11,500)	($3,500 income – $15,000 cost of van)
Year #2	$ 3,500	
Year #3	$ 3,500	
Year #4	$ 3,500	
Year #5	$ 8,500	($3,500 income + $5,000 proceeds of van)

Although you could make 7.5 percent in a risk-free investment like a U.S. Treasury bill over five years, you determine that investments with the added risks of the pizza delivery business earn at least twice that rate. So the cost of capital is 15 percent. Still, wanting to do better than the minimum, you decide that the IRR for the pizza van must be at least 18 percent or you will not buy it.

Using the figures above and a business calculator, you see that the IRR for your pizza van is 19.89 percent, so it is a go.

The results would be very different, however, if you could make only $3,000 a year after expenses from your delivery business. In that case, the cash flow would look like this:

Scenario 2: Cash Flow, Years 1–5

Year #1	($12,000)	($3,000 income – $15,000 cost of van)
Year #2	$ 3,000	
Year #3	$ 3,000	
Year #4	$ 3,000	
Year #5	$ 8,000	($3,000 income + $5,000 proceeds of van)

The IRR for the delivery van would be 12.97 percent, below both the cost of capital and your own minimum requirement.

International Banking Act   Law passed in 1978 that expanded the authority of the **Federal Reserve System (Fed)** to treat the American operations of foreign banks the same as those of U.S. banks.

See also **Edge Act**.

international bonds   Corporate **bonds** denominated in one country's currency but issued in another.

See also **Eurobonds**.

International Monetary Fund (IMF)   Multinational organization working to stabilize currencies, lower trade barriers, and help countries having financial problems.

Conceived at the Bretton Woods conference in 1944 and established in 1947 as part of the United Nations, the IMF is financed by its more than 100 member nations. When the IMF was formed, developed nations had their currencies pegged to the U.S. dollar. That method was largely abandoned in 1971, and since then most of the world's currencies have operated with floating exchange rates.

Although the IMF has little control over these exchange rates, it still exerts great influence. Member nations are encouraged to follow

---

internal rate of return

t i p |

An advantage of using the IRR is that it takes into consideration the value of money over time. Also, it avoids the accounting convention of depreciation, focusing entirely on cash flow.

t r a p |

By compounding the rate of return, IRR assumes that you can reinvest the money earned at the same percentage rate, which you probably cannot do. And the calculations will boggle even a good calculator when periods of positive cash flow are followed by periods of negative cash flow.

I

IMF rules of conduct that promote order in their currency dealings—that is, if they wish to continue receiving IMF funds. And when the IMF helps a developing nation pay off its debt or build its infrastructure, the IMF usually imposes strict guidelines designed to reduce **inflation**, cut imports, and raise exports. These are called structural adjustment policies.

International Monetary Market

CHICAGO MERCANTILE EXCHANGE®

fin

International Monetary Market (IMM) Division of the **Chicago Mercantile Exchange** that trades currency and interest-rate **futures**.

See also **derivatives**.

tech   **mktg**

Internet Huge online **network** of computers linked for the exchange of information, products, and ideas.

In June 1995, the estimate was that 30 million to 50 million people worldwide had access to the Internet, with the number doubling every 10 months. The Internet's roots date back to the early 1970s, when the U.S. Department of Defense set up links among the computers of academic, military, and scientific researchers working on defense projects. The U.S. National Science Foundation (NSF) took over coordination of the Internet in 1986, but its use was pretty much confined to the community of computer specialists until 1993.

That is when two related events caused an explosion in Internet activity: Commercial users were officially allowed onto the Net, and a software program called Mosaic introduced a **graphical user interface (GUI)** for the Net, making it much less intimidating.

Companies like Netcom Online Communications Services began providing access to anyone with a computer and a modem who was willing to pay a monthly fee. America Online, CompuServe, and Prodigy offered their users a gateway to much of what is available on the Internet. A user of, say, CompuServe not only has access to data made available on computers worldwide but can exchange **electronic mail (e-mail)** with all the Internet users, members of the other commercial services, and anyone else with a link to an e-mail distributor.

In 1995, the NSF turned over its role supporting the Internet to four private companies—Ameritech, Pacific Bell, Metropolitan Fiber Systems, and Sprint. An international organization called the **Internet Society** oversees the **protocols** for the net.

The Internet's most popular feature is the **World Wide Web**, where users can surf through screens of data offered by businesses, colleges, libraries, museums, political entities, and so on. As you are reading, you can click on a highlighted word or phrase to bring up more screens of information, which may have been obtained from yet another computer. Each organization offering data starts out with a **home page,** often with sophisticated graphics. Companies have been flooding onto the World Wide Web for publicity and to sell products.

Internet

trap

Many companies are establishing a presence on the World Wide Web, but things on the Web are still pretty haphazard and they can be slow. Moreover, if you want to sell products on the Web, you will have to do it in a way that assures your customers that their credit card numbers will not be intercepted by unauthorized individuals. A few companies are beginning to offer credit card–secure ways for conducting transactions.

I

Internet

- The most recent Nielsen survey (1995) concludes that 24 milllion Americans and Canadians age 16 and above have used the Internet in the past three months.

- 81 percent of Internet users and 74 percent of online service subscribers are under 44 years old.

- Men account for 66 percent of Internet usages; women for 34 percent.

- Netscape posted the fourth-biggest share price rise for a U.S. initial public offering. It was priced at $28 and closed on its first day of trading at $58.25.

The term *Internet advertising* is being used to mean a specific marketing strategy involving promotion of products and services on the Net. Consumers can "window shop," researching various products, or even place orders using computer interfaces. Companies should not depend, however, on consumers simply coming across an advertisement while casually surfing the Net. This medium lends itself to use by those investigating specific services and companies.

See also **hypertext**.

Internet Society   See **Internet**.

inventory   Finished items you hold for sale in the ordinary course of your business, raw materials and supplies that will be used in producing the finished goods, and goods that are in the process of being completed.

See also **inventory valuation**.

inventory

inventory turnover   Number of times during an **accounting period** that a company sells the value of its inventory. Also called **inventory turns**.

Turnover is calculated by dividing the cost of goods sold by the average inventory during the period. Average inventory is figured by adding beginning inventory and ending inventory, then dividing the sum by two.

EXAMPLE   In the Eastman Kodak Company's 1994 annual report, the **balance sheet** shows inventory at December 31, 1994, of $1,480,000,000 and at December 31, 1993, of $1,532,000,000, so the average inventory is

$1,506,000,000. Cost of goods sold on the 1994 **income statement** is $7,325,000,000. So the fraction becomes:

$$\$7,325,000,000 \div \$1,506,000,000 = 4.9$$

You can say that Kodak turned over its inventory 4.9 times in 1994.

inventory turnover

A high number shows you are moving your merchandise well and do not have your **working capital** tied up in inventory. But, as with other ratios, you need to put the number in the context of the industry: You would expect an inventory of bread products to turn over more often than an inventory of bulldozers.

`acct` `mgmt` `fin`

inventory turns   Number of times during an **accounting period** that a company sells the value of its **inventory**.

See also **inventory turnover**.

`acct`

inventory valuation   How you measure the cost of the goods you have in stock.

Like many other things in accounting, this is a lot more complicated than it may seem. You will use a method of **costing** to determine how much you paid for your goods. Then you need to figure out how much of your cost went into the goods you sold and how much is still in inventory. That is where the real fun starts. If your cost never changed, there would be no problem. You would know what each unit cost, whether it was sold or still in inventory. But the world does not work that way, so you need to select a method for valuing your **inventory**, such as **specific identification**; **weighted-average cost**; **first-in, first-out (FIFO)**; or **last-in, first-out (LIFO)**.

Here is how each would work if you started selling a high-quality fax machine in your office supply business on January 1, 1995, and the cost for the model rose during the year. Here is what your additions to inventory looked like:

Inventory Additions

January	15 units @ $290	=	$ 4,350
March	15 units @ $300	=	4,500
May	20 units @ $310	=	6,200
August	10 units @ $320	=	3,200
November	15 units @ $330	=	4,950
Total	**75 units**		**$ 23,200**

At the end of 1995, you had sold 55 machines and had 20 left. Now we will use each of the inventory valuation methods.

If you can trace each unit in inventory to its invoice, you can use the specific identification method. Then you will know how much you paid for the 20 fax machines in stock. Let us say that five are from the May purchase, five from August, and 10 from November.

As you can see, the fax machines in your inventory are valued at $6,450, and $16,750 ($23,200 − $6,450) went into the cost of goods sold.

inventory valuation

Specific Identification

May purchase	5 units @ $310	=	$1,550
August purchase	5 units @ $320	=	1,600
November purchase	10 units @ $330	=	3,300
Total	**20 units**		**$6,450**

In the weighted-average cost method, as the name implies, you take a weighted average, that is, total cost divided by total units. So the 20 units left in inventory are valued at $6,187 (20 x $309.33), and $17,013 ($23,200 − $6,187) went into the cost of goods sold.

Weighted-Average Cost

January	15 units @ $290	=	$4,350
March	15 units @ $300	=	4,500
May	20 units @ $310	=	6,200
August	10 units @ $320	=	3,200
November	15 units @ $330	=	4,950
Total	**75 units**		**$23,200**

$23,200 ÷ 75 = $309.33 (average cost)

First-in, first-out (FIFO) is calculated as though the first items you bought were the first sold, then the next-oldest items in inventory were sold, and so on. So the 20 machines still in inventory are valued as though they were the most recently purchased. Since there are 20, the November price goes for 15 of them and the August price for five.

Your total ending inventory is $6,550, and $16,650 ($23,200 – $6,550) went into the cost of goods sold.

First-in, First-out (FIFO)

November purchase	15 units @ $330	$4,950
August purchase	5 units @ $320	1,600
Total	**20 units**	**$6,550**

The flip side of FIFO—last-in, first-out (LIFO)—assumes that the last item you bought was sold first, then the next most recent item, and so on. So the items left in inventory are assumed to be the oldest. The January price would apply to 15 of the fax machines in inventory and the March price to the other five.

Now the total ending inventory is $5,850, and $17,350 ($23,200 – $5,850) went into the cost of goods sold.

Last-in, First-out (LIFO)

January purchase	15 units @ $290	$4,350
March purchase	5 units @ $300	1,500
Total	**20 units**	**$5,850**

Remember that these are all accounting methods. Except for the specific identification approach, they have nothing to do with how you manage your inventory. And specific pricing is practical only when you are selling a specific product in fairly small quantities—cars, for example.

See also **conservatism concept** and **consistency concept**.

FRAME OF REFERENCE
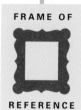

inventory valuation

Which is the best to use? The answer is a common one for accountants: It depends. Specific identification is the most accurate in many ways, but it is not practical for most businesses. The weighted-average method will smooth out the effect of price fluctuations. FIFO comes the closest to valuing your inventory at its replacement cost. LIFO, it is argued, makes the best match between your revenues and the cost of goods sold.

Between FIFO and LIFO, when your prices are rising, FIFO yields a higher net income. Your shareholders may like it, but so will the tax collector. When your prices are falling, LIFO produces more net income. But you cannot change every time there is a shift in your cost trend. Consistency dictates that you use the same accounting methods every year.

There is another accounting concept we need to mention here. If the market has collapsed and you cannot sell your inventory for what it cost you, conservatism requires you to use the lower of cost or market.

econ **fin**

investment
In economics, the flow of resources into capital, which in this sense means goods used to make more goods or services.

EXAMPLE | You start a corporation and sell 100,000 shares of stock for $10 each. You use the $1 million you have raised to buy a building, stock it with merchandise, and open a store. You may later channel profits back into the business to expand. You also may sell more stock or take out loans for the same reason. All of these steps would be additions to investment. But when a neighbor of yours buys shares of your business from your brother-in-law, that is not considered an investment in economic terms. Your neighbor and your brother-in-law simply exchanged one sort of wealth (stocks) for another (cash). No new capital was created.

investment

fin

investment banker
Middleman or agent between an organization issuing securities and the public.

In most cases the investment banker buys the securities from the issuer at a discount and sells them to investors and other dealers—the price difference is called the gross spread. This arrangement is called **underwriting** and often is carried out by a **syndicate** of investment bankers. If the securities are overpriced, or if the market falls before they are sold, the underwriters take the loss.

For certain securities, such as U.S. Treasury issues and municipal bonds, underwriters must be chosen by competitive bidding. For most other securities, the issuer negotiates an arrangement with an investment banker, who may then form a syndicate to spread the risk.

Investment bankers also advise clients on all aspects of issuing a new security or on other large capital transactions like **mergers** and **acquisitions**. They may be called on to handle the sale of **secondary offerings** or to act as finders, arranging the **private placement** of large blocks of a security.

EXAMPLE | By early 1984, Mattel was dangerously close to having its bank loans called when its electronics subsidiary incurred significant losses after a severe shakeout in the home video and computer market.

To strengthen its weakened financial condition, Mattel decided to restructure, with its first step to sell all of its nontoy businesses. They enlisted the help of investment banking firm Drexel Burnham Lambert, who took the lead in designing the company's recapitalization. Drexel helped Mattel obtain $231 million in long-term debt and equity from different investment groups, including venture capitalists, and financial institutions. These investments, together with an exchange of debt for new equity and a $100 million debt offering in 1985, dramatically strengthened the company, providing it with a stable base for long-term growth. Today, Mattel is the No. 1 toy manufacturer in the United States, with $3.6 billion in 1995 sales and 25,000 employees nationwide.

See also **best effort**.

FRAME OF REFERENCE

investment banker

Before Starbucks Corporation went public in 1992, it spent two years looking over 20 investment bankers. Then it selected Alex. Brown & Sons as lead underwriter. According to Orin Smith, president of Starbucks, the company grilled potential underwriters on their grasp of Starbucks' business, their experience taking companies public, their research standards, and the way they shared information with their sales force. Starbucks also considered the investment bankers' reputation among portfolio managers and their experience staying with client companies through acquisitions and **joint ventures** once the **initial public offering (IPO)** was over.

Starbucks followed Alex. Brown's advice to price the IPO 15 percent below where they expected it to trade the first day. Said Smith: "It's important to get a fair price, [but you] don't go into the IPO with the objective of getting the maximum. You want your investors to be happy in the long term because you may want to return to the market." The IPO of 2.1 million shares sold for $17 a share, and by the end of the day shares were trading at $21.50 on the **over-the-counter (OTC)** market. Starbucks undoubtedly had some happy investors.

Quick Facts!

investment-grade bonds

Investment-grade bonds are an important part of the economy, accounting for 96 percent of debt issued in 1995. But in 1988, Drexel Burnham Lambert commissioned a study that shed new light on the relative importance of the two sectors on the U.S. economy. The study's objective was to identify the number of "high-yield" versus "investment-grade" companies on a state-by-state basis.

In 1988, there were 758 U.S. corporations with investment-grade ratings, and 353 that were "estimated" to be investment grade for a total of 1,111 companies. By contrast, there were 21,103 "high-yield" companies with annual revenues of $35 million or more, which made up 95 percent of all companies in America.

mgmt

investment center   Area of a company handling the purchase of capital **assets** that will generate future profits.

See also **management control systems**.

fin

investment-grade bonds   Debt rated as Aaa through Baa3 by Moody's Investors Service and AAA through BBB– by Standard & Poor's.

See also **bond ratings**, **high-grade bonds**, and **high-yield bonds**.

acct   **fin**

involuntary conversion   Sudden loss of an **asset** that does not occur in the ordinary course of your business.

A building destroyed by fire qualifies as an involuntary conversion. So does land seized by a state highway department for use in the construction of a road. If you are compensated for your loss, the exchange is treated like any other transaction.

acct

IPO   See **initial public offering**.

fin   **mgmt**

IRR   See **internal rate of return**.

involuntary conversion

I

Insurance

Insurance is a large and complicated industry—or to be more precise, it is a collection of subindustries. Most people are familiar with life, casualty, property, and medical insurance. Americans are aware that Social Security, Medicare, and Medicaid are major government insurance programs and that bank deposits are insured. They may have mortgage and auto insurance. It is possible to insure virtually anything and anyone; Lloyds of London has built its reputation on unusual policies, like the one it wrote on Betty Grable's legs in 1949.

Insurance involves the pooling of resources by a group of individuals, who do so believing one or more may be struck by misfortune and that a portion of the funds gathered would be provided to them to alleviate distress. Insurance, then, is one product the holder hopes never to have to use.

Commercial insurance existed in Mesopotamia two millennia B.C. to safeguard transactions and secure crops. The Greeks and Romans—in fact, all ancient peoples—had insurance programs to protect against commercial failures, and the practice persisted into the modern period. Lloyds, which dates to 1688, was only one of many marine insurers, a necessity in a commercial age. Fire insurance became important in a world made of wood. There were commercial insurance companies in colonial America, and Benjamin Franklin helped found the Philadelphia Contributionship for Insuring Houses from Loss by Fire in 1768.

Insurance was considered necessary by most substantial businesses. The first fire insurers in the nation were stock companies, primarily because by selling stock they could start out with a reserve. But mutual companies, owned by their policyholders, became more popular after a disastrous fire in New York wiped out several stock companies, and policyholders concluded mutuals would be safer.

Some life-insurance companies appeared in the colonial period, such as Hand-in-Hand (1696) and the Society of Assurance for Widows and Orphans (1699), but life policies came late to the industry, reflecting the lower value assigned to life at the time. Insurers were keen observers of the scene, aware of the need to create products to meet changing circumstances and then dropping them when appropriate. Such remains the case today.

Benjamin Franklin assisted in the formation of several life-insurance companies, including the Presbyterian Minister's Fund (1759). By the end of the 18th century, there were 24 insurance companies in the U.S., most in fire and marine, and only one—the Insurance Company of North America—sold life policies.

Life-insurance companies appeared more frequently in the early 19th century. By 1855 there was more than $20 million of life insurance in force. But it was still a small industry, one reason being that life-insurance companies had a tendency to default and were not trusted. The failure of Ohio Life and Trust ignited the Panic of 1857 on Wall Street.

Another reason for the slow acceptance of life-insurance companies was no one knew much about life expectancy at the time. This deficiency was rectified by Elizur Wright, a Massachusetts polymath who became interested in the matter and prepared the first scientific actuary tables. Wright also lobbied for legislation requiring companies to employ his findings and maintain sufficient reserves. In 1858, Wright became Massachusetts Insurance Commissioner, and three years later his legislation was adopted.

The matter of reserves was of paramount importance. Following Wright's dicta, insurance companies were mandated by state laws to employ extremely conservative accounting practices to be certain they would have sufficient funds to pay claims. As a result, insurance companies became huge reservoirs of capital and so

---

Contributing Writer: Robert Sobel
Lawrence Stessin Distinguished Professor
of Business History, Hofstra University

were important forces in the investment arena as well as other areas of American life.

This new conservatism, which enabled the companies to better withstand the kind of pressures that forced Ohio Life into bankruptcy, provided impetus to the stock company concept. The organization of Equitable Life in 1859 was the first of these, and many more followed. By 1868, the amount of life insurance in force was larger than the national debt, and life insurance had become one of the most important financial businesses in the country, larger than banking and far larger than the equity markets.

Industrial-life policies, which originated prior to the Civil War as low-priced, low-benefit policies, sold initially for as little as three cents a week. Several major companies emerged from the industrial-policy business, among them Prudential, Metropolitan, and John Hancock. By the turn of the century, 19 companies specializing in this product had about $7 billion of policies, about five-sixths of all life insurance then in force.

As the insurance companies became larger and their reserves swelled, bankers vied for control of them, hoping to use their large treasuries as a source of financing for corporate creation. In 1905, a struggle developed for control of the Equitable Life Assurance Society, a company with 600,000 policyholders and assets of $400 million, with J.P. Morgan and E.H. Harriman both attempting to take command.

 THE
EQUITABLE

This led to a state investigation that brought about reforms in management, further shielded policyholders, and educated the public regarding the importance of life insurance and the financial power of the companies involved.

In the aftermath of the investigation, life insurance became more heavily regulated than before, and the trend continued through much of the century. This circumstance, combined with a major effort in advertising and sales and a growing awareness of the need to safeguard increasing family wealth, resulted in rapid expansion.

By 1920 there was $40 billion of life insurance in force, and the figure topped $100 billion on the eve of the Great Depression. Among the New Deal reforms was Social Security, enacted in 1935, which provided a new base on which many

Franklin D. Roosevelt signs New Deal

Americans constructed their life-insurance programs. During World War II, G.I. life insurance, which could be extended after discharge, provided another government prop. The arrival in the 1960s of Medicare and Medicaid, and other programs, further increased government participation.

In 1929, Baylor University Hospital offered schoolteachers 21 days of hospital care for $6 a year, a precursor to Blue Cross, an idea that spread throughout much of the country during the Great Depression. By 1938, 25 states had legalized not-for-profit hospital insurance plans, and by the end of World War II, 21 million Americans had this form of insurance.

This was not the only kind of plan to cover medical care. During World War II, Henry Kaiser provided health insurance for his shipyard workers, which developed out of a similar program he had introduced for his construction workers in 1938. There had been some earlier corporate programs, but none of them was popular or imitated. It was different with the Kaiser Permanente Medical Care Program, from which emerged the first true health maintenance organization, the ancestor of another form of health insurance.

Property, casualty, and auto-insurance companies had quite different experiences. These descendants of the old commercial business were strictly regulated, with rates established by state commissions. Competition was fierce, and returns on underwritings and investment could be devastated in bad years. Earnings on operations were low, which were compensated for by returns on the investment portfolio. The latter, in effect, subsidized the low rates offered customers.

As was the case with the life companies at the turn of the century, those large reserves attracted the attention of raiders in the 1930s and afterwards. In the 1960s, several major companies were acquired, in part, for their reserves. Leasco Data Processing acquired Reliance Insurance, and other takeovers followed. AVCO purchased Paul Revere, and Hartford Fire Insurance merged into ITT.

Despite the attention paid to property-insurance companies in the 1960s, even then it was evident that this segment of the industry offered relatively little in the form of innovation and importance. Rather, the life and health segments were destined to occupy center stage for the rest of the century and probably beyond.

The reasons for the growing importance of life and health coverage rested in demography and economics. Life expectancy at birth for Americans at the turn of the century was 46 years. It shot up sharply in the next half century, coming to 68 by 1950, and toward the end of the century had inched up to slightly more

than 75. When Social Security went into effect in the mid-1930s, life expectancy at birth was close to the retirement age of 65. Today's 65-year-old can expect, on average, to live another 18 years, and the over-65-year-olds are the most rapidly growing segment of the population.

They also are among the wealthiest, having worked and saved during the booming postwar years and having purchased homes for fractions of their current prices. Those who made investments lived through a period of generally rising stock prices, and this, too, proved a benefit. They also purchased life insurance, both ordinary and group, the latter often provided by employers. Total insurance purchases in 1950 came to $29 billion; by 1995, they were close to $2 trillion. In the same period, the amount in force went from $234 billion to $12 trillion.

In this span, through legislation and private initiatives, the industry received massive stimuli. In 1962, the Keogh Act provided tax benefits for self-employed individuals who saved for retirement, an indication the government would encourage workers to formulate their own plans. The individual retirement accounts arrived in 1974. Both Keoghs and IRAs supplemented the 401(k) plans offered by many employers. While all three were self-directed and could go into a variety of investments, substantial amounts were directed into insurance, especially annuities, insurance programs to provide income during retirement.

While the impetus toward life insurance continued, the industry itself was somnolent in the 1960s and early 1970s. By then it had to face a new kind of problem: The high inflation of the 1970s diminished the value of coverage. The annuity income, which was fixed, purchased less, and the death benefits no longer seemed so sizable.

In 1978, the Federal Trade Commission report on the industry came close to recommending the purchase of inexpensive term insurance, with the savings obtained used to purchase other investment vehicles, such as common stocks. The industry responded with the creation of variable policies, in which premiums and payouts varied. Single-payment deferred annuities became popular. As tax loopholes were closed in the 1980s, tax advisors encouraged older people to make cash gifts to heirs, who would use them to purchase insurance on the donor, so that when the donor died, the payouts would not be part of his or her estate and so not subject to estate taxes.

The dramatic growth of the industry has led to a huge presence in the securities markets: Total assets held by insurance companies amounted to nearly $3 trillion in 1996, or nearly 20 percent of all financial assets. The portfolios of insurance companies have been restricted in various ways throughout the years, giving them a reputation for favoring conservative investments like high-grade bonds. Still, they have proven to be significant players in the stock markets, and have also contributed greatly to the financing of smaller, "non–investment grade" companies.

By the 1990s, there had developed an intense national debate over health insurance. Total recorded expenditures for health care rose from $220 billion in 1980 to more than $800 billion in 1995, with some estimates placing it at $1 trillion if all aspects are taken into consideration. The costs of care rose sharply, as did those of health insurance. Health insurers faced squeezes, leading them to push policyholders into health maintenance organizations and to deny coverage to risky applicants. Citing the problems of the industry, political leaders demanded national solutions that might bypass the insurance companies. That life and health insurance would remain at the center of public debate for the indefinite future seemed quite evident. The health segment struggled to arrive at a compromise that would allow it to continue to offer insurance at affordable prices and sidestep attempts to introduce a form of single-payer plan now operational in Canada and other countries.

Clearly, such an industry-supported solution would involve heath maintenance organizations, hospital chains, and large insurers like Blue Cross and Blue Shield, which alone covered 65 million people. The "Blues" started to merge and seek partners; in 1996 some talked of selling themselves to HMOs. If and when this happens, the impact on the insurance industry will be profound.

The life segment of the industry also faces challenges. As life insurance has come to represent a better way of preparing for retirement than offering beneficiaries a payout on death, the companies have had to compete against stocks, bonds, and other investments. The life companies, like others in the industry, surely face considerable trials in the coming years.

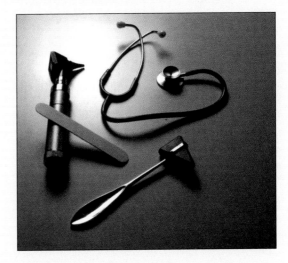

Investment and Commercial Banks

There were two basic banking functions during the 18th century—commercial and merchant—both of which can be traced to ancient times. Banks would accept deposits, make loans, and issue currency based on reserve assets. Commercial banking emerged from this foundation. The early banks also provided merchant banking services, investing their own funds in ventures. Investment banking later developed from merchant banking.

These merchant banks served clients by raising funds through the issuance of securities that were sold to investors. Acting as an investment banker, the bank had to devise a method of financing that would be acceptable to the client, who wanted the funds, and the investor, who would purchase the securities.

There are no records of these kinds of institutions in the early American colonies: Few colonists needed banking services, and those who did used the facilities of English banks. There were "land banks" in some colonies that issued notes secured by mortgages, and these notes functioned as one of many forms of currency. Still, the more conventional currencies were British pounds and foreign coins, such as Spanish dollars. America's three leading cities were the first to have commercial banks of

any importance. During the Revolution some Philadelphians formed the Bank of Pennsylvania, which issued currency to help finance the war, as did the New York–based Bank of North America and later the Bank of New York. The Massachusetts Bank was organized in Boston.

Alexander Hamilton

To provide a national currency, Secretary of the Treasury Alexander Hamilton obtained a charter for a Bank of the United States (BUS), which acted as a central bank, holding Treasury balances and issuing currency. The BUS was augmented by state and regional banks, most of which had only local sway. The BUS charter was not renewed in 1811, after which the state banks proliferated, as did failures and high transaction costs for the merchant class. Because of this, a second BUS was formed in 1816, which lasted until 1832.

Then followed a period of free banking, in which the local banks proved incapable of providing the kind of services needed by an expanding nation. Business interests required a central bank, which arrived with the 1860 election of Abraham Lincoln.

The new president asked for and Congress passed the National Bank Act, which required all banks to be chartered by the federal government and to redeem at face value notes issued by other chartered banks. More stable and effective than free banking, this new system was also flawed since the system was unable to

---

Contributing Writer: Robert Sobel
Lawrence Stessin Distinguished Professor
of Business History, Hofstra University

1791   1815   1913   1924

1791
First Bank of the United States opens its doors

1792
Organization of the New York Stock and Exchange Board

1812
First National City Bank, which became Citibank, chartered

1819
First financial panic in the United States results from real estate speculation

1896
Dow Jones Industrial Average first appears to track the direction of the market

1913
Death of J. P. Morgan; Federal Reserve System organized

1924
Organization of the Massachusetts Investment Trust, the first modern mutual fund

expand the currency in times of distress. In the absence of a "lender of last resort," the vacuum was filled by private investment bankers.

The first American investment banks were small operations that represented European banks in their American dealings. Prime, Ward & King worked with Baring Brothers, and Fitch Brothers had French banks as correspondents. The Rothschilds used several American banks and in time dispatched August Belmont to America to serve their interests. By the 1850s some of the investment banks had become more independent. Jay Cooke & Co., based in Philadelphia, was able to raise substantial sums for railroads and during the Civil War became a leading distributor of U.S. government bonds. But even Cooke could not have survived without foreign customers.

The continuing growth of the American economy after the Civil War led to the emergence of several major investment banks, among them Kuhn Loeb, J. & W. Seligman, and Goldman Sachs. J.P. Morgan & Co. was the best known and most powerful bank of the time. Morgan was the son of Junius Spencer Morgan, an American who had been a commanding power in London. His authority derived from an ability to bring together other banks to support his projects. Some of the commercial banks had investment banking

affiliates. National City Bank, led by James Stillman, was an influential force on Wall Street, and First National City, headed by George F. Baker, was an important Morgan ally. Morgan was well connected in London, which enabled him to tap major sources of financing there. Morgan helped create such firms as International Harvester, General Electric, and U.S. Steel. When the government faced bankruptcy in 1893, he raised funds in Europe to bail it out, and did the same again in 1907. To many Americans, Morgan was the very symbol of finance capitalism. Morgan died in 1913, but Wall Street and Washington had prepared a substitute, a force that might be able to act in case of another panic.

This was the Federal Reserve System, organized in 1913 as a new central bank, a "bank for banks." The "Fed" was composed of 12 regional banks and a central reserve board. All national banks had to join the Fed, and the state banks were encouraged to do so. Members maintained reserves at the Fed and could borrow from them when they wished. Even with the new central bank in place, the industry remained quite unregulated. While failures were relatively uncommon in the 1920s, depositors were uninsured and so stood to lose their funds should their banks fold. There were 976 such failures in 1926, a new record. In

1929		1970		1985			1995
1929 Stock market crash	**1933** Glass-Steagall Act separates investment and commercial banking	**1934** U.S. government creates the FSLIC	**1971** U.S. abandons the gold-bullion standard	**1980** Prime rate tops 20 percent, the highest level this century	**1985** The first Ginnie Maes are marketed successfully	**1987** Black Monday stock market crash	**1989** In the largest takeover of the 1980s, KKR takes RJR Nabisco private	**1995** Chase and Chemical Bank combine to form largest U.S. bank

In both examples, the change was motivated by the desire to serve customers more efficiently. But both also increased **job satisfaction** by giving employees larger roles. Job enrichment also often increases **job depth**: Workers have more control over the part of the process they will handle at any time.

See also **job enlargement** and **motivation-hygiene theory**.

---

mgmt

job involvement   How much an employee identifies with the job; how important the job is to the worker's sense of worth.

See also **job satisfaction**.

---

mgmt

job range   Number of tasks a worker does. Also called **job scope**.

For someone on an **assembly line,** job range is limited, providing little or no variety in his or her tasks. A chief executive has a much wider job range, going from making a speech to reviewing quarterly financial results, to being interviewed by securities analysts.

See also **job depth**.

---

mgmt

job satisfaction   Way a person feels about his or her job.

While pay counts as a reward, a lot of other things do, too. Two routes to nonmonetary rewards are:

1 **Job Involvement**
How much the employee identifies with the job; how important the job is to the worker's sense of worth.

2 **Organizational Commitment**
How much the worker identifies with the employer and its goals.

Not surprisingly, studies show that employees with high levels of job involvement and organizational commitment who are satisfied with their jobs take fewer sick days and are less likely to leave a company.

Measuring job satisfaction is often high in importance to management. It can be measured by a variety of **surveying** and interviewing techniques. A commonly used survey employs a 1-to-5 or 1-to-10 rating scale. Employees are asked how well they think their pay fits their job, how well their work is recognized and rewarded, how much their work ties in with organizational goals, and so on. Such

---

job satisfaction

There is no greater challenge than to have someone relying upon you; no greater satisfaction than to vindicate his expectation.

—Kingman Brewster, president of Yale, 1963–1977, and ambassador to Great Britain, 1977–1981

J

job satisfaction

A large corporation hired a surveying organization to devise and administer a survey of its employees worldwide. The survey was eight pages long and took about an hour for employees to fill out. The surveying company mailed it to every employee's home and promised that no individual's answers would be turned over to the corporation's management. The questions, mostly on a 1-to-5 rating scale, probed for various aspects of worker satisfaction.

Some parts of the survey were so detailed, though, that half of the employees chose not to return the survey, and many others answered the way they thought their bosses would want them to. Thus, the process itself should allow participants to express themselves candidly so that real improvements in the workplace can be implemented.

surveys are easy for management to administer, for employees to fill out, and for evaluators to score. Because they are so quantifiable, they allow for comparisons among departments and over time.

The big trap here, though, is worker honesty. Employees will not express their real feelings if they think the survey may not be confidential. Or, regardless of their feelings, they may give the answers they think will result in better pay and working conditions.

mgmt

job scope   How many tasks a worker performs.

See also **job range**.

mgmt

job sharing   Way of giving workers some flexibility in setting their hours.

This method of alternative scheduling allows two or more part-time employees to split one full-time position. For example, one dentist office receptionist might work from 9 a.m. to 1 p.m., while a second person works from 1 p.m. to 5 p.m. Or one person might work Monday, Wednesday, and Friday, with the other taking over on Tuesday and Thursday. Job sharing is less common than **flextime** or the **compressed work week** and has limited application. For example, it might work well for a receptionist position, but it would be tough to pull off for, say, the managing editor spot on a daily newspaper. However, job sharing does allow a company to hire skilled workers—such as women with young children, the handicapped, or retirees—who might be unable or unwilling to work a full shift.

job sharing

job shop

oper

job shop   Manufacturing operation that can make a wide variety of fabricated products to customer specifications.

Because of the customized nature of the process, the costs per unit can be a lot higher than they would be in an **assembly-line** operation. Job-shop manufacturing is used where quantities are relatively low and specifications, fabrication processes, or both are unique to each job.

See also **assembly line**.

mgmt   **strat**   **fin**

joint venture   Business enterprise developed by two or more unrelated companies.

One of the companies may act as manager of the venture, or each may supply a number of employees to fill some of the management positions.

Organizations form joint ventures for a number of strategic reasons, including:

1 **Spreading the Financial Risk**
A common example is when a number of companies join to develop an oil field, an enterprise whose cost can run into billions of dollars.

2 **Entering a New Market**
It often helps to have a local partner when you start doing business in a new country. A joint venture with a local company can overcome some of the cultural obstacles— as in Japan, for example. Sometimes, a country's laws require local ownership—as is the case in China outside of designated enterprise zones. You cannot do business there without a local partner.

3 **Taking Advantage of Complementary Skills**
A manufacturing company may join with one that has access to raw materials. They might also invite a marketing company into the venture. Or a company selling to specialty stores might joint-venture a product with a business that markets to companies such as Wal-Mart.

See also **coproduction**.

job shop

EXAMPLE

You want Lucite cubes in the shape of your company logo to give out as souvenirs at a plant dedication. You order 1,000 from a company that can produce just the required amount, to your specifications.

journal entry

acct

journal entry   Recording a business transaction in an accounting book or **ledger**. The entry usually consists of the **accounts** and the amounts to be debited and credited, the date, and an explanation.

See also **bookkeeping**.

BREAKING NEWS

joint venture

In 1989, Johnson & Johnson and Merck & Company, two of the largest companies in the pharmaceutical industry, formed a joint venture. Johnson & Johnson-Merck set out to take advantage of J&J's strength as a marketer of over-the-counter drugs and Merck's ability to develop new pharmaceutical products. In 1995, the joint venture introduced Pepcid AC, previously available only by prescription. It is billed as the first over-the-counter medication to prevent and relieve heartburn and works by blocking the secretion of acid in the stomach. Johnson & Johnson-Merck beat a number of competitors to the market with this new class of heartburn remedy.

---

acct

Journal of Accountancy   Publication that is a respected voice in the accounting industry.

See also **American Institute of Certified Public Accountants (AICPA)**.

mktg

Journal of Marketing   Publication of the **American Marketing Association (AMA)**.

fin

junk bond   A **bond** with a rating lower than investment grade.

The high-yield debt market dates back to the beginning of the securities market. Many of our nation's best known corporations were initially financed with junk bonds. Prior to 1920, U.S. Steel, General Motors, and Computing-Tabulating-Recording (which would later be known as IBM) all used high-yield debt to finance the expansion of their operations.

Until World War II, junk bonds accounted for 17 percent of all publicly issued straight corporate debt. The greatest increase occurred during the Depression due to the large number of companies that were downgraded from their original investment-grade ratings.

Spiralling inflation and increasing interest rates in the 1970s created a need for new financial products, which would provide investors with higher yields and companies with affordable, fixed-rated funding. The result was the birth of the new-issue junk bond market, which experienced its most explosive growth during the 1980s and continued to grow into the 1990s. According to the Securities Data Corporation, the high-yield market raised more than $50 billion in new underwritings for companies in its peak year 1993, up from about $1 billion in 1980.

See also **high-yield bond**.

junk bond

> *What we mean by junk bonds in a technical sense is below–investment grade securities. Almost all of the pricing of these securities depends not on who is selling them, (or) who is supporting them, but what is the firm or entity which is paying the interest and eventually the principal on those [bonds].*

> —Alan Greenspan, Federal Reserve Board Chairman, March 1, 1990

J

junk bond

During the 1980s, "junk bonds"—or **high-yield bonds**—were given a consistently bad rap by the media, the press, and regulators. Whether in articles written primarily about the securities industry or in pieces covering a variety of economic subjects, high-yield bonds have been blamed for everything from the S&L crisis to the recession.

But the general consensus seems to have come full circle in the 1990s, as more investors embrace the junk bond market (most now calling it high-yield). Why the new attitude? One important explanation is concern about job growth. Popular opinion now perceives small and growing companies as the engine of U.S. job creation, and high-yield bonds—as a critical source of capital for growth companies—have gained respect in turn. From an investment perspective, the superior returns of high-yield bonds have been a big draw. After hitting its low in 1990, the market has bounced back in a big way, with the Salomon Brothers High-Yield Bond Composite Index up 140 percent by the end of 1995. That compares with an 87 percent return for the S&P 500.

Investors have responded enthusiastically. The number of high-yield funds is up from 26 in 1989 to more than 100 at the end of 1995, now holding total assets of $58 billion. But there's more than just good performance behind this renewed interest. Investors are becoming aware of a number of misperceptions that have plagued the high-yield market since the 1980s.

Perhaps the greatest misperception about the high-yield market has to do with the S&L crisis in the late 1980s. While there were limited instances of S&Ls with mismanaged high-yield portfolios, high-yield bonds represented only about 1 percent of the assets of seized S&Ls—real estate loans accounted for more than half. What's more, only 5 percent of all of S&Ls ever invested in high-yield bonds. In fact, according to a General Accounting Office study released in February 1989, high-yield bonds were the second most profitable asset held by thrifts throughout the decade of the 1980s—second only to credit cards.

J

just-in-time inventory system

t r a p

During rapid or unexpected production fluctuations, JIT will leave you without a way to maintain supply to your customers. It also leaves you more vulnerable to strikes and temporary glitches.

*Of course, JIT systems push the responsibility for inventory control up the **distribution channel**. Suppliers need to increase their own efficiency or get stuck holding the inventory their customers do not want to hold.*

mgmt **oper** **strat**

just-in-time (JIT) inventory system   Getting materials from a supplier exactly when they are needed.

JIT is an approach designed to minimize **inventory** and increase product quality and plant productivity. If you can implement JIT, you will shift inventory cost to your suppliers and reduce your inventory investment. Your money will not be tied up in supplies sitting in a warehouse. The use of JIT has skyrocketed along with the popularity of computer systems that share data among businesses.

JIT systems originated in Japan, where they are often implemented using kanbans, or cards. It all started when companies supplying parts or raw materials to a manufacturer might ship their goods in containers with a card attached. When a factory worker opened the container to use the materials, he or she would send the card back to the supplier. That would let the supplier know when the next batch was needed.

BREAKING
NEWS

just-in-time inventory system

Wal-Mart can give Procter & Gamble access via computer to its district-by-district and store-by-store inventory and sales figures for Crest toothpaste. Then P&G is responsible for getting the right amount of the product to the right place at the right time.

In General Electric's various manufacturing businesses, it has billions tied up in inventories. In 1991, the company announced a goal of stepping up **inventory turnover** (the times per year inventory is replenished). Pressing suppliers for JIT arrangements, GE managed to bring inventory turns up from less than five in 1991 to more than nine in 1995. That brought the amount of GE's money tied up in inventory down from $6.7 billion at the start of 1991 to around $3.8 billion in 1995.

J

K

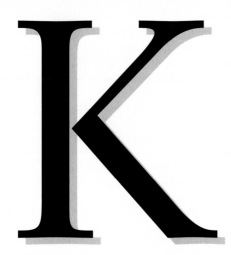

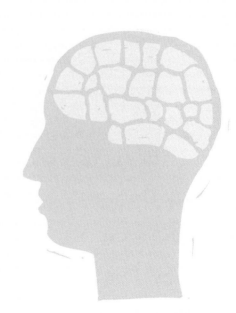

kaizen

to

knowledge
engineering

mgmt

kaizen   Japanese word for the philosophy of **continuous improvement**.

mgmt   **strat**   **mktg**

keiretsu   Informal but historically powerful Japanese business coalitions whose members join together for strategic advantages at home and in the global marketplace.

There are three main types of keiretsu:

1 Bank-Centered

Clusters of major companies with a bank at the core. The companies share financial risk and coordinate strategy for international investment. The big bank-centered keiretsu are Dai Ichi Kangyo, Fuyo, Mitsubishi, Sanwa (Securities (USA) Co. L.P.), and Sumitomo. Other types of keiretsu often have ties to a bank-centered keiretsu.

2 Supply-Centered

Clusters of vertically integrated companies that share a supply chain. A large manufacturer acts as a **channel captain**. These dominate in the automotive and electronics industries among others. The channel captains often strong-arm suppliers to yield to their time, cost, delivery, and price wishes. Examples of important supply-centered keiretsu are Canon, Nikon, and Toshiba.

3 Distribution

Relationships formed between wholesalers and retailers and a specific manufacturer channel captain. The manufacturers who dominate these keiretsu have given rebates to retailers who refuse to carry competing products and have cut back shipments to punish those who stray from the fold on prices. In 1991 the Japanese Fair Trade Commission tried to enforce

Supply-Centered Keiretsu

Bank # 1   **Bank # 2**   **Bank # 3**

Manufacturer
Communications System

Manufacturer
Air Conditioning
Electrical Parts

Auto-maker

Manufacturer
Audio System

Manufacturer
Transmissions

---

kaizen

Going, if not yet gone, are the 9 to 5 workdays, lifetime jobs, predictable, hierarchical relationships, corporate culture security blankets, and, for a large and growing sector of the workforce, the workplace itself.... Constant training, retraining, jobhopping, and even careerhopping, will become the norm.

—Mary O'Hara Devereaux
and Robert Johnasen,
*Global Work: Bridging
Distance, Culture and Time*

keiretsu

t r a p

A keiretsu can lead to competitive inefficiencies if it stifles innovative thinking or inhibits doing away with noncompetitive practices.

K

keiretsu

In 1993, when George Fisher donned the chairman's hat at Eastman Kodak Company, he also put on a Sherlock Holmes deerstalker. Fisher investigated why Kodak, which boasted a 70 percent share of the U.S. market and 40 percent in the rest of the world except Japan, could maintain only a measly 8 percent in that country.

Spending more than a million dollars, Kodak hired a top-notch team of trade lawyers who researched and produced a 250-page document charging that Japan's market was heavily rigged against foreign competition, in large part through the keiretsu. The document contended, among other things, that Fuji uses a complex system to keep tabs on whether wholesalers and retailers comply with its guidelines on prices. One component of the system is Fuji's use of market research firms that send out agents called Fuji Color Ladies and even postal workers to interrogate neighborhood retailers about their film prices.

keiretsu

Quick Facts!

There is one U.S. industry that has worked well with the keiretsu and is doing a booming business in Japan. That is the mail-order catalog business. More than 500 U.S. catalog operations register over $1 billion a year in sales to Japanese customers. It is the most lucrative foreign market for the industry. Some companies use their English catalogs, but others, like Eddie Bauer, provide Japanese product descriptions and ordering information.

K

Japan's Antimonopoly Law against some of these practices but with limited success. The distribution keiretsu of major automakers like Honda were a point of contention in 1995 when the U.S. government complained that the Japanese auto market was closed to imports. Another powerful distribution keiretsu is that of the Matsushita electronics powerhouse.

In the mid-1990s the keiretsu system was weakened somewhat because of several factors:

► Softening of the Japanese economy.

► Government pressure, spurred in part by complaints from international trading partners like the United States, who find that the keiretsu represent a strong **barrier to entry**.

► Liberalization of Japan's financial system, particularly the deregulation of lending rates, which encouraged competition among banks for loan customers.

mgmt

Keogh plan   Retirement plan for the self-employed.

See also **pension plans**.

mgmt   **strat**

key operating measure (KOM)   Statistical gauge of how well an organization is doing.

See also **key performance indicator**.

mgmt **strat**

key performance indicator (KPI)
Statistical measure of how well an organization is doing. Also called **key operating measure (KOM)**.

A KPI may measure a company's financial performance or how it is holding up against customer requirements.

EXAMPLE | The Chart House restaurant chain uses a computer application to track daily KPIs on such things as per-location revenues, customer counts, and labor costs. Monsanto has KPIs based on safety and efficiency measures for the trucking companies that transport its chemicals. Grand Rapids Spring & Wire Products has a **continuous improvement** program that involves cross-functional "minicompanies," each with its own set of KPIs revolving around customer satisfaction.

Mobil Corporation in 1994 and 1995 adopted a set of KPIs that includes such "hard" measures as per-share earnings and return on capital and a few "soft" ones dealing with worker satisfaction and progress toward **diversity**. Mobil announced in its 1994 annual report that future compensation levels would be based on the KPIs.

KPIs help focus an organization on its overriding goals and measure its progress in attaining them.

See also **metrics**.

tech

kilobyte
Unit of computer memory storage that equals 1,024 bytes.

See also **byte**.

tech

knowledge engineering
Process in which human knowledge is captured, usually through an interviewing process of one or more experts, and placed into computer systems so the knowledge can be used to solve complex problems normally requiring human expertise.

key performance indicator

t r a p |

It is tough to set fair KPIs for some staff jobs like accountants, lawyers, lobbyists, and planners. But other workers judged on KPIs may grow resentful if, say, the lobbyists escape being measured statistically.

knowledge engineering

K

L

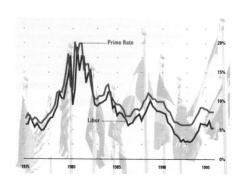

to

low-involvement products

labor force

labor force Total of those employed, those recently unemployed, and those looking for work.

See also **employment** and **unemployment rate**.

lagging economic indicators The seven components of an index that tell analysts where the economy has been in recent months.

The index components are:

▶ The average duration of **unemployment** (in weeks).

▶ A ratio of manufacturing and trade inventories to sales.

▶ A ratio of consumer installment credit to personal income.

▶ The average **prime rate**.

▶ The change in the **consumer price index (CPI)** for services.

▶ The total amount of commercial and industrial loans outstanding.

▶ The change in the index of labor cost per unit of output (manufacturing).

The index of lagging economic indicators is published monthly by the U.S. Commerce Department's Bureau of Economic Analysis.

See also **coincident economic indicators** and **leading economic indicators**.

LAN See **local area network**.

Lanham Act Law enacted in 1946 that sets forth the criteria under which a **trademark** can be registered. The Lanham Act also describes how to challenge a proposed registration and specifies the rights and obligations of the holder of a registration.

See also **brand**.

last-in, first-out (LIFO) Way of accounting for goods in stock that assumes the last item bought was sold first, then the next most recent item, and so on.

See also **inventory valuation**.

labor force

Quick Facts!

- Fewer than half the workforce of the industrial world will be holding conventional full-time jobs in organizations by the beginning of the 21st century. Those full-timers or insiders will be the new minority.

- Every year more and more people will be self-employed.

- Many more people will work temporary or part-time—either because that's the way they want it, or that's all that is available.

—John Handy,
The Age of Unreason

lagging economic indicators

latent market

Quick Facts!

In the 1970s, many beer drinkers in the United States complained that while loving the beverage, they hated the calories that went with it. Recognizing this latent market, companies like Anheuser-Busch, Coors, and Schlitz began to brew less-fattening beers. Today, almost every beer maker competes for its share of the light-beer market.

L

 mktg

latent demand   Potential customers of a product or service that is not yet available.

See also **latent market**.

mktg

latent market   Potential customers having a need or desire for a product that does not yet exist. Also called **latent demand**.

oper   **mktg**

lead time   In manufacturing, the time between placing an order and receipt of the finished product.

Lead time may include not just starting up your own factory but the time needed to get parts from your supplier.

EXAMPLE | Your printing plant receives an order for 500,000 full-color brochures printed on premium paper. The paper mill does not have that quantity on hand and has to manufacture and deliver it. In the meantime, you are doing the prepress work needed to prepare the job for printing. Once the paper arrives and the prepress work is completed, you may spend another half day or so getting the quality right on press before producing any acceptable brochures. Then the total order has to be printed and shipped. All together, several weeks of lead time may elapse between receiving the order, printing the first brochure, and getting the order to the customer.

Lead time varies according to the processes necessary to produce the goods. For example, manufacturing involving die casting or sheet-metal forming requires a relatively long lead time since it usually calls for extensive new tooling. On the other hand, products made mainly by machine and grinding processes can use existing tooling and thus need shorter lead times.

mgmt

leadership   Ability, through personality or organizational muscle, to influence others toward a goal.

Beyond that definition, it is hard to say much about leadership that will not be disputed. That is because countless theorists have come up with systems to describe types of leadership and characteristics of good leaders. But no theory of leadership has held up to testing over time. It could be that chemistry and circumstance mean more than any set of traits.

Some ways of looking at leadership:

▶ **Authoritarian vs. Democratic**
Authoritarian leaders tell others what to do and how to do it. Democratic leaders let others decide what to do and how to do it.

▶ **Task-Oriented vs. People-Oriented**

A task-oriented leader manages the work first and expects the employees to follow. A people-oriented leader thinks in terms of the employees and how they will get the job done.

▶ **Situational**

A situational leader varies his or her approach according to the needs of the job or the maturity level of the worker. This leader may teach one employee, coach another, and delegate to a third. In a more difficult business environment, she or he may switch to a more authoritarian style.

▶ **Charismatic**

Having a quality that followers identify as heroic or extraordinary. Charismatic leaders are seen as having a goal, strong personal commitment, and flair.

While it is difficult to prove that any leadership style is better than another, it is probably true that the needs of an organization at any time may determine which type of leadership will be most effective. In the 1990s, as companies strive to eliminate unnecessary work and unneeded levels of management, authoritarian managers are having a tough time. In a lean organization, there simply is not enough time for bosses to make all the decisions. So delegating, or empowerment, is a key characteristic of today's successful manager.

econ

leading economic indicators   The 11 parts of an index that usually change months before corresponding changes in overall economic activity.

leadership

The first responsibility of a leader is to define reality. The last is to say thank you. In between the two, the leader must become a servant and debtor. That sums up the progress of an artful leader.

—Max DePree, CEO of Herman Miller, in *Leadership Is an Art*

FRAME OF REFERENCE

leadership

Herbert Kelleher, CEO of Southwest Airlines, calls his leadership style "management by fooling around." An industry analyst said of him: "He keeps his employees motivated because he teaches them how to have fun. And that shows up in how the airline performs."

Kelleher has done a rap video promoting the airline and sometimes pitches in with mechanics, baggage handlers, and ticket agents, many of whom he knows by name. Says Kelleher: "I like to see them because they're fun to be with. I love their irreverence." At a company picnic, as 4,000 employees looked on, he wore a dress and bonnet and sang "Tea for Two."

Which just goes to show you it is hard to define what makes a good leader. Southwest's more than two decades of profitability help make it the fastest-growing airline in the United States.

David Woo

Herbert Kelleher

L

leading economic indicators

learning curve

tip

The learning curve is a useful phrase, but there is another curve that is more important in improving productivity. In the 1990s, the power of computer systems has been doubling every 18 months or so. It is through harnessing the power of this curve that today's big productivity improvements are being made.

L

learning organization

The goal of education is the advancement of knowledge and the dissemination of Truth.

—John F. Kennedy, address at Harvard University, 1956

The index components are:

- ► The average length of the work week of production workers.

- ► The number of new state unemployment-insurance claims.

- ► New orders for consumer goods, adjusted for **inflation**.

- ► An indicator of vendor performance based on the percentage of companies receiving slower deliveries from suppliers.

- ► Contracts and orders for plants and equipment.

- ► An index of permits for new private-housing units.

- ► The change in manufacturers' unfilled orders for **durable goods**.

- ► The change in certain materials prices that are considered economically sensitive.

- ► An index of stock prices.

- ► The **money supply**.

- ► An index of consumer expectations based on **surveying**.

Many of these indicators—housing permits, for example—represent commitments to future economic activity. The index of leading economic indicators is published monthly by the U.S. Commerce Department's Bureau of Economic Analysis.

See also **coincident economic indicators** and **lagging economic indicators**.

econ **mgmt**

learning curve   Changes in **productivity** caused by human experience. Also called **experience curve**.

Learning curves can be traced to the 1930s in the assembly of airplanes. The man-hours needed to put an airplane together decreased as production increased. For example, airframe manufacturers found that the fourth plane took 80 percent as many hours as the second plane, and the eighth took 80 percent as many hours as the fourth. Productivity improved by a steady 20 percent each time the cumulative output doubled.

You will see the biggest learning curve in labor-intensive efforts. More automated processes—manufacturing plastic packaging films, for example—show smaller productivity improvements because the human element is smaller. The improvement rate for automated processes might be around 10 percent every time cumulative output doubles. And the productivity will start leveling off faster for highly automated processes. That, of course, assumes that the equipment remains the same.

mgmt

learning organization   Company that uses its experiences to adapt, improve, and grow.

See also **high-performance organization (HPO)**.

Learning Curve

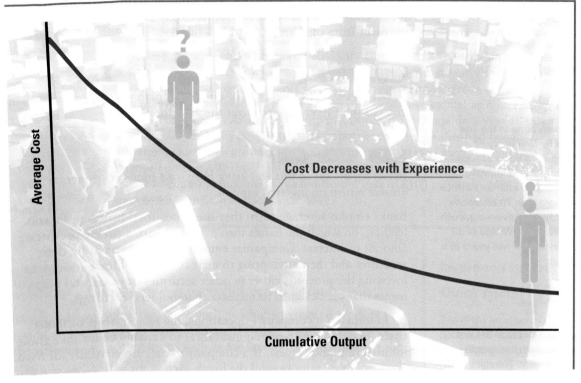

Average Cost

Cost Decreases with Experience

Cumulative Output

ledger   Book containing **accounts**, each of which usually has a separate page. Transactions are entered first in a journal, and then summaries are transferred to the ledger.

See also **bookkeeping** and **journal entry**.

legacy systems   Older information systems that have become antiquated, require heavy maintenance, and may be central to the operation of the business. They often need to be replaced by newer technology and software.

L

letter of credit (LC)   Bank document guaranteeing a customer's drafts up to a set amount within a stated period.

These are commonly required in international transactions. Essentially, an LC eliminates the seller's collection risk by substituting the bank's credit for the buyer's.

letter of credit

EXAMPLE   Your bicycle manufacturing business is exporting a shipment to a new customer in Costa Rica. You require your customer to arrange an LC. The customer's bank then sends you a letter promising that the bank will pay you when the goods are received.

management control systems

When you are setting up management control systems, remember the two most important factors:

Goal Congruence

Throughout your organization or section, do the objectives support the company's general strategies and goals? Managers work more efficiently when purposes parallel the company's overall plan. For instance, a plant manager concerned only with boosting production levels and decreasing costs might put off maintenance needed to protect future production.

Fairness

Devise an operating model that includes all the factors you can control and excludes the factors you cannot control.

management control systems

If a company has nothing going for it except one thing—good manage-ment—it will make the grade. If it has everything except good management, it will flop. That's the clear lesson of 50 action-packed years of U.S. business history (1917–1967).

—*Forbes*, 50th Anniversary Issue, September 15, 1967

There are four basic types of control systems, each of which contains its own set of objectives:

1 **Cost Center**
A section of a company where costs can be measured. Included are direct costs and often some part of the company's overall **fixed costs**. The packaging department of a factory is a simple example. Direct costs of the department's materials and labor are attributed to the manager, along with a part of the company's fixed costs, such as accounting services.

2 **Investment Center**
An area handling the purchase of capital **assets** that will gen-erate future profits. Under the manager's purview, the company's need for current profits is balanced with the need to garner investments that support the company's future goals. A cornerstone for judging a manager's success is his or her demonstrated **rate of return** on investment.

3 **Profit Center**
A company unit that is financially independent. Often man-aged as a separate business within the business.

4 **Revenue Center**
An area within a company that regulates revenue without controlling overall profits and/or costs. Usually, sales depart-ments are tagged as revenue centers, where the goal of a sales manager may be to broaden the margin of revenue despite the constraints of an expense budget.

See also **incentive plans**, **metrics**, and **performance appraisal**.

M

management discussion and analysis (MD&A)

Section of an **annual report** or a **10-K** where management comments formally on a company's financial results and its outlook.

This section is different from the letter from the boss and the operating review usually found in the front of annual reports. The MD&A is required under **generally accepted accounting principles (GAAP)** as well as by **Securities and Exchange Commission (SEC)** regulations.

management information system (MIS)   Way of organizing and presenting the operating and financial information needed for effective decision making.

Over the past four decades, these systems have changed dramatically. Originally, the MIS (then called data-processing systems) was a tool of the Finance and Accounting departments, where clerks kept billing, payroll, and other data. Output consisted of static monthly reports.

By the end of the 1960s, mainframe computers entered the picture, and newly established Data Processing Departments issued sales and operational reports broken out by department. Some managers got their reports via remote terminals.

FRAME OF

REFERENCE

management information system

Boston Market has used the most current MIS in every phase of its remarkable development. When Scott Beck, Saad Nadhir, and Jeffry Shearer set out to start a national retailing chain, they did not know what they were going to sell, but they did know how they would run the business. "We wanted to create a business where managers at the operating level had the expertise and knowledge to drive the company forward themselves," says Beck. "We, at the corporate level, would just be facilitators. Technology would be very important."

Beck and company have come through on their commitment to technology at every level of the corporation. Boston Market uses a proprietary system where store managers, staffers, and headquarters officials share data and communicate with each other as easily as if they were all in the same building. The company's Intellistore software helps managers in all phases of their tasks. Managers consult the system to determine what to buy, how much of each side dish to prepare, and how many workers to schedule at various times of the day. Headquarters executives get immediate data on how the stores are doing.

Using these tools, managers at every level are encouraged to collaborate on team projects like changing menus, solving distribution problems, and planning expansion—all on-line. Even complaints become part of the MIS: When a customer telephones in with a complaint, an operator immediately types it into a database. Complaints can be sorted by type, region, and individual store. The information is available at all levels in the company, from the CEO to regional management, to the staff at the store subject to the complaint.

M

The explosion of personal computer technology in the 1980s again transformed MIS. Data could be gathered, analyzed, and reported with hardly any time lag, and more control shifted to individual managers, who could determine the types of information they wanted.

But in the 1990s, networking, more powerful computers, and new trends in management changed the focus again. Today's MIS is controlled by individual managers but standardized across the organization. The standardization lets everyone talk the same language and benefit from continually updated data. The MIS is part of a package that also includes user-friendly software for word processing, spreadsheets, graphics, and access to giant **databases**, **electronic mail**, **bulletin boards**, and decision support systems.

mgmt

Management Review   Monthly publication of the **American Management Association (AMA)**.

tech   **mgmt**

management software   Specialized **expert system** that guides managers. Also called **MBA-ware**.

Its uses range from creating a business plan to writing employee manuals, from **forecasting** demand to assaying the use of human resources.

These programs come in various degrees of complexity:

▶ **Elementary Form**
The program provides templates the user fills in with the help of sample text and traditional word-processing and spreadsheet tools. The program might offer templates for employee appraisals, job descriptions, business plans, and the like. More advanced forms permit the user to adapt the program to a particular set of needs.

▶ **Complex Form**
You get advice from a number of experts. This type of program coaches you in business planning and answers hundreds of questions. Mathematical formulas may be built in to help analyze data or work flow.

For example, IntelligenceWare publishes software called Auto Intelligence that helps managers think through business problems step by step. A guided interview first establishes the basic terms and criteria used for decision making. The program generates questions to accelerate the transfer of information to the computer. As managers make a series of specific decisions via the computer, the program synthesizes the outcomes into an overall structure. The managers get to see the projected global impact of their individual decisions before they make them.

M

acct **mgmt**

managerial accounting
Branch of accounting directed at internal management operations.

See also **management accounting**.

mgmt

managing diversity
Attempt by companies to accommodate the lifestyles, work styles, values, and family needs of different groups without compromising the operations of the organization.

See also **diversity**.

oper

manufacturing manager
Person in charge of meeting a plant's budget and schedule.

See also **operations manager**.

oper **mgmt**

manufacturing resource planning (MRP-II)
Complex computer software that controls a wide range of manufacturing planning functions.

MRP-II grew out of an earlier computer system called MRP, which stood for **material requirements planning** and coordinated material flows to meet production schedules. MRP-II software packages go a step further by integrating materials management with financial issues like costing and payroll. A typical MRP-II system can accumulate actual costs by order and relate orders to labor requirements and payroll, thus enabling improved accounting and cash management and more accurate **costing**.

These systems also can gauge the implications of production schedules on resources like equipment and labor. By calculating the capacity requirements of a production schedule, MRP-II allows production planners to decide whether to move orders to reduce loads or to increase capacity to meet workloads by utilizing overtime, part-time workers, subcontractors, and so on.

fin

margin
Amount of money a brokerage firm customer may borrow to buy additional securities based on the market value of his or her other securities.

Margin is based on a percentage of the market value of those securities held in the customer's account. The required margin percentage is set by the Federal Reserve Board. If the balance in a margin account falls below the required minimum—which usually results from a price drop for a security bought on margin—the brokerage firm issues a **margin call**, meaning the customer must deposit more funds or face the liquidation of his or her securities.

margin

Before the 1929 stock market crash, there was no restriction on buying securities on credit. Many banks would lend 90 or 95 percent of the value of their clients' holdings. That meant a 5 percent decline could wipe out an investor. Many investors were ruined in the 1929 crash, and this was attributed in large part to the easy credit. In 1934, the Federal Reserve Board adopted Regulation T, which sets a more restrictive margin requirement (currently 50 percent).

trap | 👎

Remember—using margin to leverage your investment can increase your losses dramatically. With the $5 stock price drop in the example above, you lost $1,000 on your fully margined account, rather than the $500 you would have lost with no margin.

M

margin

"Reg T" (Regulation T as established by the Federal Reserve Board in 1934) currently requires that your margin balance be at least 50 percent of the market value of your account and 25 percent going forward. For example, say that you have $2,000 to invest and decide that a particular stock is a good buy at $20. Rather than simply buying 100 shares, you decide to leverage your investment using margin and purchase 200 shares. Your account would look like this:

Market Value of Stocks	$4,000	**($20 x 200 shares)**
Margin	$2,000	**(market value less amount borrowed)**
Amount Borrowed	$2,000	
Margin Percentage	50%	**(margin balance ÷ market value of stocks)**

This balance satisfies the minimum 50 percent requirement under Reg T, and the value of your investment has increased. Now, if your stock goes up $5, your profit is $1,000, rather than $500 (ignoring interest and transaction costs).

But what if the stock price drops? If it were to drop by $5, your account would look like this:

Market Value of Stocks	$3,000	**($15 x 200 shares)**
Margin	$1,000	**(market value less amount borrowed)**
Amount Borrowed	$2,000	
Margin Percentage	33.3%	

Your margin percentage is still above the 25 percent maintenance threshold. For you to receive a "margin call," the value of your securities would have to drop to $2,667, or about $13.34 per share.

Of course, this assumes that the margin requirements of your brokerage firm are the same as those of Reg T—they may in fact be higher. Reg T sets only minimum requirements.

M

fin

margin call   Demand for more money to back up a **margin** account so as to meet the minimum level required by the Federal Reserve Board. Failure to comply means the account may be liquidated.

See also **Regulation T**.

oper   **econ**   **mktg**   **acct**

marginal cost   Effect on total cost, whether an increase or a decrease, of producing one more or one less unit. Also known as **differential cost** or **incremental cost**.

Marginal Cost

Quantity	100,000	Cost	$150,000
Change in Quantity	10,000	Change in Cost	$5,000
Total Quantity	110,000	Total Cost	$155,000

$$\text{MC} = \text{Change in Total Cost} \div \text{Change in Quantity}$$
$$= \$5,000 \div 10,000$$
$$= \$0.50$$

EXAMPLE | If a printing company has an order for 100,000 copies of a full-color brochure, the cost—including paper, labor, press time, and an allowance for **fixed costs** like rent and insurance—is $150,000, or $1.50 per copy.

Since the fixed costs are already covered, and a lot of the other costs are in preparing for the press run, printing another 10,000 copies will add only $5,000 to the printer's total cost. The marginal cost for the extra copies is 50 cents a copy ($5,000 ÷ 10,000 copies). Marginal cost is the lowest advisable sales price for a product or service. The printing company knows it must charge at least 50 cents a copy for the additional production.

On a broader basis, a firm's *average variable cost* (AVC) is the critical "breakpoint" in deciding whether to continue production. For example, if our printing company has a marginal cost of $0.50 but an AVC of $0.60, then it should discontinue production for any sales price less than $0.60, even though the marginal cost is lower.

See also **contribution margin**, **economies of scale**, and **marginal revenue**.

marginal revenue Change in a company's total revenue if one more unit is sold.

It is calculated by subtracting total revenue before the sale from total revenue after the sale. Marginal revenue is simply the price of the product, as long as the unit price remains constant.

EXAMPLE | A vacuum cleaner company makes and sells vacuums for $350 each. The marginal revenue is $350 per unit as long as the company continues getting its price for each vacuum.

marginal revenue

trap

Marginal revenue can sometimes be a negative number. Say you sell imprinted pen and pencil sets. You charge $10 each for orders up to 100 and reduce the price to $9 for larger orders. Your revenue for selling 100 to a customer is $1,000 (100 x $10). For selling 101, the revenue is $909 (101 x $9). So the marginal revenue for the one extra set is minus $91 ($909–$1,000 = –$91).

M

In many cases, however, additional production can be sold only at a lower price. In such cases, it is important to compare marginal revenue and **marginal cost** before making a decision on whether to increase output. In general, every unit for which marginal revenue exceeds marginal cost should be produced.

See also **contribution margin**.

---

mktg **mgmt**

markdown   Amount deducted from an item's selling price.

The term markdown applies only if a piece of merchandise is subsequently priced below its original retail selling price.

See also **markup**.

---

market

tip |

You need to stay abreast of changes in your markets. If you sell groceries, for example, you have had to adjust to a higher proportion of working mothers. If you have not provided more options for quick preparation of meals, you have probably lost market share.

mktg **econ**

market   (1) In **marketing**, the people or organizations that want or need to purchase a product or service and have the authority to do so.

The nature of the product helps define the market. For example, the market for pleasure boats is made up of people who are old enough to run an engine and hold enough discretionary money or credit to invest in such an expensive item. The recreational value to the user may be more important than the actual price of the boat, whether it is high or low. However, consumers who would like a 50-foot motor yacht but cannot afford it are not part of the market.

See also **industrial market**.

(2) In economics, the institution through which buyers and sellers make their exchange, or the whole economic system where **supply** and **demand** interact for a certain good or service.

A livestock auction is a market for cattle. So is the network of farmers, brokers, and other organizations contracting for their sale. And in its broadest sense, the market for cattle includes all the breeders, farmers, truckers, distribution facilities, and so on, whose interactions determine the price.

---

fin

market capitalization   Current value of a company's **common stock**, determined by multiplying the market price per share by the total number of shares outstanding.

See also **market value**.

M

fin   **mktg**

market research
(1) In finance, extensive investigation and analysis of technical data concerning market price movements, corporate earnings forecasts, historical market reactions to various scenarios, the economic outlook—all aimed at trying to gauge the direction of stock, **bond**, and **commodities** prices.

(2) In marketing, a study that aims to define the size and scope of a company's potential **market** and determine how best to take advantage of it.

fin

market risk
Sensitivity of a stock's price to the things that affect all stocks—like shifts in the economy, interest rates, inflation, and general investor confidence. This is also known as **systematic risk**.

A stock's market risk is measured by its **beta (β)**.

See also **alpha (α), nonmarket risk,** and **market risk premium.**

fin

market risk premium
Return a stock pays, or should pay, to compensate investors for the **market risk**.

For the overall market, the premium is the difference between average annual returns for stocks and the **interest rate** for risk-free investments like Treasury bills. For an individual stock, the market risk premium can be calculated using the **capital asset pricing model (CAPM)**.

mktg

market segmentation
Dividing a large, multifaceted **market** into distinct parts that share a common association.

For example, if you are selling jeans, you may divide the market into seniors, men, women, young adults, college students, teenagers, children, and workers who wear jeans on the job. And you might segment further by geographic location, tailoring an approach, for instance, to the Southeastern U.S. young-adult market. Segmentation is a powerful tool to help marketers sell more and budget their promotional expenses wisely. You are not likely to sell sophisticated financial investments to a young, moderate-income market, for example; neither would an older, richer market be apt to buy rap-music CDs. You do not have to be a big manufacturer to rely on market segmentation.

A company will often create different versions of its basic product to meet needs and wants of customers within various segments, or submarkets. Even if it does not vary its product, a company will almost certainly develop a separate promotional program for each segment it targets. For example, most vitamin manufacturers market the same products to both young people and senior citizens but use different promotional campaigns.

---

market research

t r a p |

*Your competitors can mislead you about their sales in certain markets. Industry associations and government agencies may give you aggregate data on nationwide or worldwide sales, but getting information on a **product line** or market segment may be tough.*

market segmentation

t i p |

Segmenting the market can allow manufacturers to extend the life cycle of a product. It also allows marketers to spend wisely on advertising and promotion, allocating the biggest share to the most profitable segments.

t r a p |

The research needed to identify potential market segments can be costly. So can any manufacturing changes you might make to accommodate submarkets. And the new product you tailor to one segment may take sales from another. Your new line of jeans for industrial workers may appeal to teens, college students, and young adults, taking sales from those markets.

M

market share

tip |

You need to know your market share to understand how your company is doing. If your sales rose 15 percent, you might be pleased unless you knew the industry's rose 20 percent and your market share fell. Tracking services, like Selling Areas Marketing and A.C. Nielsen, may help.

trap |

Increasing market share is a worthy goal, but not if it comes at the expense of long-term profits. The airlines often fall into this trap—matching each other's slashed prices in highly advertised "fare wars." One airline may "win" by gaining the most passengers, but if they all lose money in the end, nobody wins.

M

The two main forms of segmentation are:

1 Descriptive Segmentation

Based on demographic and geographic factors—age, ethnic background, gender, marital status, income, education, and location. The U.S. Census Bureau and many research services provide descriptive information, including detailed breakdowns of demographic information by zip code. In the **industrial market**, the descriptive divisions focus on company size, industry, and location.

2 Behavioral Segmentation

Subdividing a market according to what motivates consumers to buy a product. Though the consumer may be looking for as many benefits as possible, the marketer using behavioral segmentation will focus on the main benefit. The buyer of Levi's jeans may be seeking durability, for example, while the buyer of Guess jeans wants status. Treating the durability-seekers and the status-seekers as separate market segments may help a company develop and refine its products and strategies.

As more and more companies tailor products and marketing strategies to smaller and smaller submarkets, the ways of segmenting markets are growing. In addition to descriptive and behavioral segmentation, there is *preference segmentation* (based on consumer preferences, like degree of sweetness in a soft drink), *psychographic segmentation* (based on consumers' values, attitudes, and interests), and *volume segmentation* (based on the amount consumers use).

For market segmentation to work, the following five conditions should apply:

1 The segment is identifiable and measurable and has distinct needs.

2 It contains enough potential customers to be profitable.

3 Customers within the segment are willing and able to buy the product.

4 Marketers can communicate effectively with the customers.

5 The segment does not change too rapidly.

EXAMPLE | A brokerage company vice president, Jane Smith, specializes in selling fixed-income securities, mostly corporate and municipal bonds. Most of her clients are successful businesspeople around retirement age. She regularly mails out letters offering her services to people in zip codes having a high proportion of affluent residents in their 50s and 60s. Her assistants also call people in certain telephone exchanges known to reach older, wealthier people.

See also **differentiated marketing**, **differentiation**, and **undifferentiated market**.

Different Segmentations of a Market

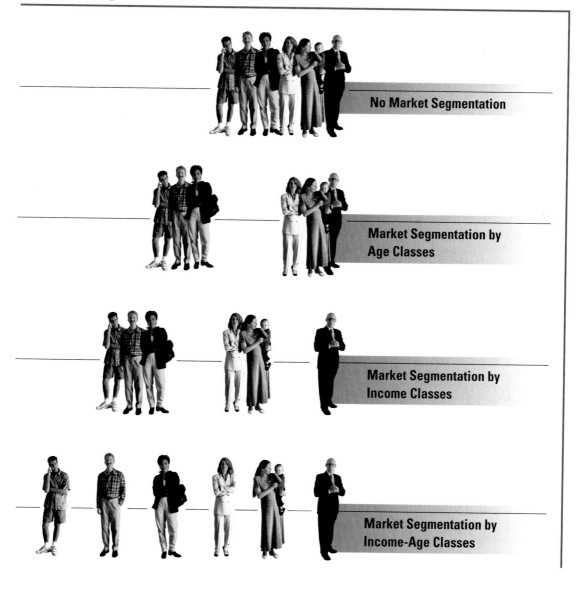

No Market Segmentation

Market Segmentation by Age Classes

Market Segmentation by Income Classes

Market Segmentation by Income-Age Classes

mktg

market share   Ratio of a company's sales to total sales in a given **market**.

Market share is calculated for a given period, often a year.

Market Share	=	One Company's Sales
	÷	Total Industry Sales

M

| Melex USA sold about 3,900 golf carts in the United States in 1994. Total U.S. golf-cart sales were 130,000. Melex's market share was

3,900 ÷130,000 = 0.03, or 3%

A company's market share may vary by region. Gasoline marketers in the 1980s and 1990s have focused their efforts in the geographic regions where they are strongest. So one brand may have a 20 per-cent market share in, say, New York state, a 4 percent market share in Texas, and no market share at all in Nevada.

fin

market value   Price at which a security, product, or service is traded.

If there are no recent trades to determine the market price, it is an estimate of what a willing buyer would pay a willing seller. The term is sometimes used for the total market price of a company's securities. **Market capitalization** is the current market price of one share of a company's **common stock** multiplied by the number of shares outstanding.

mktg

marketing   Planning and executing the strategy involved in moving a good or service from producer to consumer.

This philosophy, which focuses on satisfying the needs of customers, includes product, promotion, pricing, distribution, personal rela-tionship, and positioning, which completes the **marketing mix**. It affects almost everything a company does.

Marketing activities may include:

- ▶ An executive's decision to create a new product or service.
- ▶ A design department's effort to make a product more attractive.
- ▶ A grocer's display of a magazine at the **point of purchase (POP)**.
- ▶ A salesman's prospecting call on a customer.
- ▶ A doorman's warm greeting of a guest at a resort.

Marketing is a broader term than selling, which is trying to convince a customer to buy something. Marketing includes determining what customers want or need, or anticipating a latent need, and finding a way for your company to profitably meet the demand.

| You are setting up a home catering business. You conduct consumer research to determine the people or organizations in your area that have a need for your service. Then you contact potential customers

---

market value

tip

Market value, rather than book value, is often the more meaningful measure of an asset's worth. That makes intuitive sense—when was the last time a real estate broker listed a house by the owner's cost rather than market value? Similarly, when analyzing a company, many also believe that it makes more sense to focus on market value—which is based on the company's cur-rent share price—than the historical book value that appears on the balance sheet.

marketing

Marketing is what you do to bring someone to the table; selling is what you do to close the deal.

—Ginger Pine, senior vice president, Investments, Josephthal, Lyon and Ross

M

to learn more about the quantity and types of meals you may be able to market. You discover that an investment club buys an elegant dinner for its annual get-together, a manufacturing company wants inexpensive lunches for employees, a social club is looking for boxed meals to serve at its regular Saturday picnics. Armed with this information, you determine demand and tailor the types of dishes to meet expectations.

mktg **mgmt** **strat**

marketing control systems
Checks and balances to ensure that a company's **marketing** plan is consistent with the organization's objectives.

Through its marketing control systems, a company tracks its various activities, reviews and measures performance, and makes changes where needed.

mktg

marketing mix
Variety of approaches and techniques used by an organization to secure its goals in a particular **target market**.

Four major components make up the marketing mix:

1 **Product**

This can be a good, a service, or an idea. To be effective, a company must constantly strive to make sure its products are meeting customers' changing needs.

In 1995, after analyzing its sales figures, the Chevrolet division of General Motors came to the conclusion that its Caprice model was not attracting the family market it was designed to capture. So GM discontinued the model.

2 **Price**

A low price can be used as a marketing tool to gain entry into a saturated market. On the other hand, a higher price can be used to establish a quality image, which is called prestige pricing.

Southwest Airlines became the fastest-growing carrier in the United States in the mid-1990s by keeping costs—and fares—down, and by positioning itself as a low-cost, no-frills means of transportation. Continental, United, and USAir have all followed with cost-cutting programs. On the other hand, if Seagram dropped the price of Chivas Regal by 50 percent, it might lose those customers attracted to the elite image.

3 **Distribution**

Products must be available at the right time, in the right quantities, and at the right places. It is not easy to juggle distribution with the need to keep inventory, transportation, and storage costs down.

marketing

marketing mix

The marketing mix is made up of:

1 Product

2 Price

3 Distribution

4 Promotion

M

Adolph Coors Co. increased sales significantly when it expanded distribution into six Southeastern states. It widened its market by using an existing network of distributors from a rival brewer.

4 **Promotion**

The role of promotion, most visibly as advertising, is to get people to purchase a product. Depending on where a product is in its life cycle, promotion can be used to increase awareness, retain customers, or encourage customers to switch brands.

Apple Computer introduced the Macintosh by running a commercial during the broadcast of the 1984 Super Bowl that used a theme based on author George Orwell's *1984*. The commercial, which was run only once, is ranked among the top 10 most memorable commercials of all time.

Substituting the word *place* for *distribution*, these basics of marketing are known as the four Ps—product, price, place, and promotion. When a product, price, place, or promotion does not work well in the mix, marketers must go back to the drawing board to reconsider each of the four Ps and how they fit together. Maybe the product is okay but not the price; perhaps both are fine, but promotion was lacking; and so on.

marketing mix

EXAMPLE | One of the most successful models of arranging the marketing mix has been McDonald's. Ever since Ray Kroc began franchising the fast-food restaurants in the mid-1950s, the company has developed products and a pricing structure with wide appeal. Today, it maintains an effective distribution channel to more than 18,000 outlets worldwide that serve 30 million customers a day.

And McDonald's arranges what seems like an endless stream of promotions, often tied in to current movies popular with children. Any parent of a young child can tell you of McDonald's knack for promotional tie-ins involving drinking tumblers, trinkets, or posters with images that appeal to kids. McDonald's does extensive research before going systemwide with a new product, and a number of its products (pizza, for example) are available only in certain locations.

Marketing News

M

(mktg)

Marketing News   A publication of the **American Marketing Association**.

(mktg)

marketing orientation   Making the customers' wants and needs the primary focus of your business.

While many may use the term, companies with a true marketing orientation are more focused on satisfying their customers than their competitors are.

EXAMPLE | You are a toy manufacturer with an idea for a waterproof stuffed animal that small children can take into the bath with them. Before developing the item, you conduct quantitative research and focus groups involving parents and retail outlets to make sure there is a market. If these surveys indicate that such a market exists, you conduct additional surveys about product design to determine what size, color, price, and other features are most attractive to the parents, who will make the purchase. You also do **observational research** with small children to discover if the toy has any deficiencies and then incorporate any necessary improvements into the design and marketing of the toy.

See also **customer intimacy** and **market segmentation**.

mktg

marketing plan   Report that outlines your **marketing** strategy and plans for action.

Most marketing experts recommend writing a plan at least once a year and updating it monthly. Writing it forces you to focus on how well you are doing and whether you are paying attention to new and significant trends. It gives you an action plan, timetable, and budget you can share with employees and investors.

A marketing plan is particularly valuable when there is a change in personnel. The plan gives new employees a blueprint for what you are trying to accomplish and how you are going about it.

A typical marketing plan begins with an executive summary that briefly surveys the plan. It then presents an analysis of the current marketing situation—fundamental information on factors such as the state of the economy, the industry, the company, and the competition—and an analysis of the opportunity, which is an overview of the strengths, weaknesses, challenges, and opportunities of the product.

The plan then presents objectives reflecting market share, profits, and sales, and a marketing strategy, which is the approach to be taken, based on research, to reach those objectives. This is complemented by a plan of action, which specifies the ways in which the plan will be carried out.

Finally, the plan includes financial projections—a budget format that supports the plan—and control mechanisms for monitoring progress as the plan is carried out.

See also **marketing control systems**.

mktg **mgmt**

markup   Amount added to the cost of goods sold to produce a profit for the company.

marketing orientation

marketing plan

■ Executive Summary

■ Current Situation

■ Objectives

■ Approach

■ Plan of Action

■ Budget

M

Maslow's hierarchy of needs

By enjoying a five-course dinner with your friends at an expensive restaurant, you are simultaneously fulfilling physiological, social, and esteem needs.

Abraham Maslow

Most stores have a set percentage for each department and type of product. For example, Nordstrom's might set its markup on women's clothing at 55 percent, its markup on men's apparel at 40 percent, and its markup on high-quality jewelry at 100 percent. Boutiques and specialty stores like Ferragamo or Rykiel would likely have higher markups; discount stores like Kmart and Marshalls, lower ones.

See also **markdown**.

mgmt **mktg**

Maslow's hierarchy of needs
Theory of psychologist Abraham Maslow that analyzes the role of human needs in explaining people's motivations.

The theory centers on five levels of needs, ranked in the following order:

1 **Physiological**
Food, drink, shelter, and sex.

2 **Safety**
Security, protection, and order.

3 **Social**
Affection, belonging, and acceptance.

4 **Esteem**
Self-respect, prestige, reputation, and status.

5 **Self-Actualization**
Fulfillment.

Maslow's Hierarchy of Needs

Self-Actualization Needs

Esteem Needs

Social Needs

Safety Needs

Physiological Needs

M

According to Maslow, a person concentrates on the most basic level first. Once these needs have been substantially satisfied, he or she focuses on the next level, and so on. To understand how to motivate someone, marketers need to know what level the person is on so that the marketing strategy can be designed to fit the appropriate level. The theory recognizes that more than one need can be satisfied by the same action.

Maslow did not support his theory with research, and it has not held up to testing. It remains popular, though, probably because it seems so logical.

See also **ERG theory**.

mktg

mass market   Purchasers of goods and services for personal or family use.

See also **consumer market**.

mktg

mass marketing   Attempt to market a product or service to the widest range of consumers, without regard to individual tastes.

Mass marketing has become less common as manufacturers target products more and more to market segments. Companies that do practice mass marketing can use mass distribution and promotions emphasizing the broad uses of its product.

EXAMPLE | The WD-40® Company markets only one product (WD-40) as a maintenance and preventative good that will serve a broad spectrum of customers, including homeowners, mechanics, sports enthusiasts, and various office and factory workers. In its promotions, the company emphasizes the many uses of WD-40 in the home and in industry, recreation, and farming as a lubricant, a rust preventative, a water displacer, and cleaner. WD-40 distributes its product through more than 68 channels, including hardware, sporting goods, automotive, farm, grocery, drug, and mass merchandising stores.

fin

master limited partnership (MLP)   A public **limited partnership** that gives large numbers of investors a direct interest in a group of assets controlled by the project.

MLP units, which trade like stock, can be a liquid investment. But instead of the partnership paying taxes on its profits (like a corporation), each limited partner is responsible on his or her individual income tax for a proportional share of the MLP's profits. This means that although the investor avoids "double" taxes, since the MLP itself does not pay taxes, the investor may have to pay taxes on his proportional share of the MLP's income, even if the MLP does not distribute any cash.

mass marketing

tip |

Mass marketing, with its emphasis on one product, maximizes production efficiency and minimizes inventory costs.

trap |

A company that attempts to please everyone with one product may lose sales to companies appealing to the specific needs of customers within clearly defined market segments.

M

In the 1980s, many corporations converted to MLP status to take advantage of the elimination of double taxation. However, after the Tax Reform Act of 1987 eliminated a limited partner's right to deduct passive losses, most MLPs converted back to corporations. Today, few businesses operate as MLPs.

material requirements planning

tip

The successful implementation of an MRP system requires constant communication on the part of everyone involved in the production process. Accurate data must be fed constantly into the system and updated continually.

trap

The implementation of MRP can lead to discontent on the part of managers, who may feel constrained by a system that leaves them no room to informally make scheduling changes.

`oper`

master production schedule (MPS)   Manufacturing road map that extends several months into the future. Also called **master schedule**.

The MPS lays out the whole course—what will be produced, when, how, and in what quantity.

See also **aggregate plan** and **material requirements planning (MRP)**.

`oper`

master schedule   Manufacturing road map for the future.

See also **master production schedule (MPS)**.

`acct`

matching concept   Fundamental concept in accounting that links expenses with their associated revenues, or with the time periods in which benefit from the expenditures occurs.

EXAMPLE | You are a car dealer who purchases a car for $15,000 and sells it for $20,000. When you record the sale for $20,000, you must also record the cost of the sale by transferring $15,000 from inventory to cost of goods sold. In this manner, you are matching the sale of the vehicle with the cost of acquiring it.

Or you pay your salespeople a 5 percent commission on the tenth of every month for the previous month's sales. Jane Jones sold $100,000 in merchandise during December and earned a $5,000 commission, which she will receive in January. For accounting purposes, you show the $5,000 expense in December, when you got the benefit of the sales, even though you do not pay out the money until January. The matching concept fits neatly with the accrual **accounting method**.

The matching concept is also part of the reason for **depreciation**. Say you bought a pizza-delivery truck at the end of December 1995 and plan to use it in 1996 through 2000. You will depreciate it, recognizing part of the cost each year.

See also **adequate disclosure concept**, **conservatism concept**, **consistency concept**, and **materiality concept**.

`oper` `tech`

material requirements planning (MRP)   Computer-based system for planning and coordinating materials for production.

M

Using MRP, employees involved in every area of the manufacturing process continually feed data into the system. The computer stores information about production schedules, amounts of materials and supplies on hand, materials that have been ordered, parts in various stages of production, and orders that have been received. The main goal is to make sure the right amounts of materials are available at the right workstations exactly when they are needed without maintaining large inventories.

EXAMPLE | A maker of industrial cleaning supplies with 1,400 products, many based on a small group of base chemicals, would use MRP to substantially improve materials ordering and handling, reduce waste material, and raise the efficiency of production.

See also **just-in-time (JIT) inventory system**.

acct

materiality concept   Legal or accounting standard that determines the information that must be disclosed to investors.

Basically, the standard is whether the average investor would need to know the information to make an informed decision. In a **publicly held company**, you do not have to report everything you are doing, just items that will have a material impact on your results. The problem, of course, is defining what is considered material.

Materiality is relative. What might not be material to a company with $100 billion in revenues, might well be material to one with revenues of less that $100 million.

Materiality, like beauty, is in the eye of the beholder, and the beholder is the company until something goes wrong. Then the beholder is likely to be a court or government regulatory agency.

See also **adequate disclosure concept**, **conservatism concept**, **consistency concept**, and **matching concept**.

mgmt

matrix structure   Organizational arrangement for managing cross-functional projects in which an employee reports to two bosses. It was originally developed in the aerospace industry.

Although there's potential for conflict in matrix structures, they're not uncommon in situations where a particular technical or professional skill is used in various parts of a company. The dotted line relationships may be with either the boss of a project or a technical leader. A controller, for example, may report to a division president, handling that unit's financial issues, but the controller is also likely to have a dotted line relationship with the company's chief financial officer. In another organization, the controller would report to the chief financial officer and be assigned to the division president. (See chart on the following page.)

materiality concept

The magnitude of an omission or misstatement of accounting information that, in light of the surrounding circumstances, makes it probable that the judgement of a reasonable person relying upon the information would have been changed or influenced by the omission or misstatement.

—Financial Accounting Standards Board (FASB), 1980

M

Matrix Structure

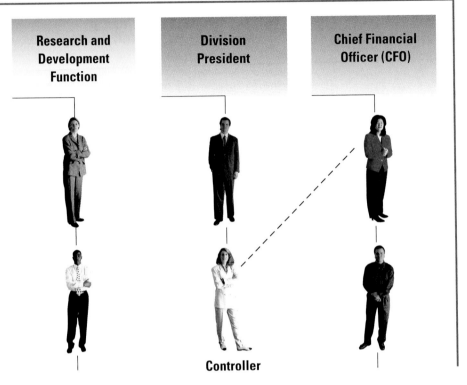

| Research and Development Function | Division President | Chief Financial Officer (CFO) |

Controller

matrix structure

tip

Making these relationships work requires lots of interpersonal skills and plenty of communication. The employee needs to keep both bosses informed about important issues, and both bosses need to consult often on how the employee is doing.

media buyer

tech mgmt

MBA-ware Specialized computer programs that guide managers.

See also **management software**.

mgmt

MBO See **management by objectives**.

acct fin mgmt

MD&A See **management discussion and analysis**.

mktg

media buyer Person serving companies by buying print **advertising** and/or broadcast commercial time for them.

Usually, media buyers are part of the integral services supplied by **advertising agencies**. Several large companies, however, specialize purely in planning and evaluating media coverage and buying time or print space.

EXAMPLE | You own a company that manufactures cookware. You are about to introduce a new line of pans safe to use in microwave ovens. Naturally, you want to spend your advertising dollars in the most effective way. So you hire a media buyer, who determines what print and broadcast outlets will be most efficient for your products. After studying your **marketing plan** and advertising budget, the media buyer, with your approval, places print ads in *Good Housekeeping* and *Family Circle* magazines. In addition, a commercial for your new product appears on a cooking show syndicated to local stations throughout the country.

fin

medium-term note (MTN)
Bond with a maturity between two and ten years. As the terms are generally understood, an MTN falls between a short-term bond (with a maturity of two years or shorter) and a **long bond** (with a maturity of 10 years or longer).

fin

megabank
Term used to describe a very large institution that conducts banking activities in a specific region of the United States. An example is NationsBank Corporation, headquartered in Charlotte, North Carolina, which had assets on March 31, 1996, of $194.4 billion.

See also **regional bank**.

tech

megabyte (MB)
Unit of computer memory storage. Although mega means one million, a megabyte equals 1,048,576 bytes. A typical floppy disk can hold 1.44 MB of data.

See also **byte**.

fin **mgmt**

merger/acquisition (M&A)
Two or more companies fusing into one.

Usually, one company buys another, and the acquired company gives up its independent existence; the surviving company assumes all **assets** and **liabilities**. Occasionally, a merger comes about without one company buying the other. Not all acquisitions come about in a friendly fashion. Sometimes a spurned suitor will launch a hostile bid for its desired partner.

EXAMPLE | In the spring of 1996, Western Resources Inc., a Kansas-based electric and gas utility, maneuvered to prevent a friendly merger between Kansas City Power & Light Company (KCPL) and Utilicorp United Inc. Thrice rejected by KCPL itself, Western Resources refused to accept the company's choice of Utilicorp and made a counteroffer to KCPL shareholders.

KCPL and Utilicorp responded by making their proposed deal more lucrative to KCPL stockholders. If they vote in favor of Western Resources, it will be the first hostile takeover in the electric utility industry.

Although M&A activity is commonly associated with **junk bonds**, the truth is that most **takeovers** and combinations have been financed by banks. The majority of M&As are simply combinations of large companies.

merger/acquisition
Quick Facts!

- After the Supreme Court's 1920 dismissal of the government's antitrust suit against U.S. Steel, businessmen concluded that antitrust enforcement was set for a period of laxity, and there ensued a great merger wave that would be repeated in good Thucydidean style in the 1960s.

- Between 1919 and 1930 more than 8,000 businesses in mining and manufacturing disappeared through combination or acquisitions.

- At the end of the decade an estimated 200 corporations owned nearly half the nation's corporate wealth.

- Of the 100 largest corporations, one-fifth were purely holding companies and only a handful were purely operating companies.

—Excerpted from *Forbes,* Sixtieth Anniversary Issue, September 15, 1977

M

EXAMPLE In 1993, The Price Company and Costco Wholesale Corporation merged into a holding company called Price/Costco, Inc. One share of common stock in the new company was issued for every share of Costco stock, and 2.13 shares of common stock in the new company were issued for every share of Price Company stock outstanding.

merger/acquisition

tip

*Horizontal mergers can create **economies of scale**, **efficiencies**, and a more diversified **product line**. Vertical mergers may cut the costs of obtaining and distributing needed materials and ensure their supply. Conglomerate mergers reduce business-cycle risk by diversification.*

trap

In both horizontal and vertical mergers, the company is increasing its exposure to the ups and downs associated with one business. In a conglomerate merger, a company buying another may learn that it lacks the management skill for the new industry.

M

...despite the debt incurred to finance takeovers and restructurings, for every dollar of increased indebtedness in the 1980s, non-financial corporations acquired 80 cents of financial assets plus $1.52 of tangible assets. This hardly seems to indicate that corporations are drowning in a sea of red ink, or that they lack sufficient resources to service their debt.

—Morgan Stanley economist John D. Paulus, in a *Wall Street Journal* op-ed, "The Non-debt Problem," July 19, 1990

There are three basic types of mergers and acquisitions:

1 Horizontal
The fusing of two or more companies involved in the same type of business. The Price/Costco merger is an example.

2 Vertical
A merging of two or more companies engaged in different stages of the same business. A company that manufactures nylon, for example, might buy a company that makes the chemical feedstocks needed.

3 Conglomerate
The combination of two or more companies whose products are not related. In these situations, even if one company buys the other, the management structures may remain separate because of the different natures of the businesses. The 1995 acquisition of CBS by Westinghouse is an example.

See also **tender offer**.

Top 10 Mergers and Acquisitions of All-Time

Year	Companies	Market Value ($ billions)
1989	RJR Nabisco / Kohlberg Kravis Roberts & Co. (KKR) (merger)	$25.0
1996	Bell Atlantic / Nynex Corp. (merger)	$22.7
1996	Walt Disney buys Cap Cities / ABC (cash & stock)	$19.0
1996*	SBC Communications agrees to buy Pacific Telesis	$16.7
1996	Wells Fargo buys First Interstate	$14.2
1990	Warner Communications / Time Inc. (merger)	$14.1
1988	Kraft Inc. / Philip Morris (merger)	$13.4
1984	Gulf Corp / Standard Oil of Ca. (merger)	$13.0
1996	Chase Manhattan / Chemical Banking (merger)	$13.0
1989	Squibb / Bristol-Myers Co. (merger)	$12.1

Source: Associated Press

*Announced in 1996.

oper **mgmt**

methods-time measurement (MTM)
System of recording and studying individual motions of equipment and people working in industrial settings, such as reach, pull, turn, and so on. Used to upgrade procedures to improve **efficiency**.

Modern MTM examines and measures videotaped motions, known as **micromovements**, performed by equipment and factory workers. Efficiency expert Harold Maynard developed the MTM model in 1947. The basic aim is to eliminate all waste in manufacturing by determining the least amount of time needed to complete a task and maintain quality. General Motors used MTM extensively in its European plants in the 1980s to increase production with fewer workers.

mgmt

metrics
Statistical measures of performance.

The metrics may reflect the work of an individual, a group, or an entire company. The current trend in management is toward quantifiable assessments like **key performance indicators (KPIs)**, so developing fair and accurate metrics is crucial to appraising work and determining compensation. A metric may be as simple as the number of invoices processed in a month or as complex as a computation of **return on shareholders' equity**.

econ

microeconomics
Study of the behavior and interactions of the individuals, households, businesses, and other decision-making units that make up the economy.

See also **macroeconomics**.

mktg

micromarkets
Smaller, more homogeneous units than **market segments**. Sometimes known as virtual marketing.

In identifying and pursuing micromarkets for your products, you will consider an already narrow market segment—say, people who fish—and narrow it further. Recognizing that there are many different types of fishermen—freshwater, saltwater, stream, lake, and so on—you will create products and design promotions based on the needs of each segment of the fishing market.

EXAMPLE | A major discount chain thinks its micromarket strategy gives it a competitive advantage. One store carries religious candles for the ethnic group in its neighborhood; another just a few miles away will not have the candles but will carry the baby-toting bicycle trailers popular among that area's affluent young couples.

See also **market segmentation**.

microeconomics

An economist is an expert who will know tomorrow why the things he predicted yesterday didn't happen today.

—Laurence J. Peter, author of *The Peter Principle*

M

oper **mgmt**

micromovements   Videotaped motions that are examined in an attempt to eliminate all waste in manufacturing.

See also **methods-time measurement (MTM)**.

microwave

tech

microwave   Portion of the electromagnetic spectrum used to transmit very high-frequency radio signals in a straight-line path between relay stations. Stations are spaced 25 to 35 miles apart due to the earth's curvature.

mktg

middlemen   Independent organizations between the producer and the **retailer** that are involved in the movement of goods and services.

See also **distribution channels**.

acct **fin**

minimum pension liability   **Balance-sheet** shortfall when the value of your company's pension-plan **assets** is lower than the **accumulated benefit obligation**.

When the assets in your **pension plan** do not cover the **present value** of the pensions your workers are eventually entitled to, you have a liability that must be included in your company's balance sheet.

Among companies showing a minimum pension liability in 1994 were Aluminum Company of America, American Pacific, CSX Corporation, Ford, General Motors, Goodyear Tire & Rubber, Fidelity Federal Bank, Rohr Inc., and Westinghouse.

tech

MIPS (million instructions per second)   Measure of computer processing power. The more MIPS that are processed, the more powerful the computer.

mgmt **tech**

MIS   See **management information system**.

mgmt

mission statement   Declaration of a company's core purpose.

M

Many companies have adopted mission statements in recent years. For example:

►**St. Paul Bancorp**
"The people of St. Paul Bancorp are committed to maximizing our stock's value, responding to customers' financial demands, and maintaining an active partnership with our neighborhoods that is characterized by sensitivity to their housing, credit, and savings needs. We believe our success is rooted in sound business practices and a corporate culture that recognizes and rewards employee achievement."

► **Century Telephone Enterprises**
"Century Telephone Enterprises, Inc. is committed to the provision of high-quality communications services at fair prices, strong growth and attractive returns for shareholders, competitive income and benefits for our family of employees, good community citizenship in our operating areas and the accomplishment of these goals within an environment of honesty and integrity."

► **Maytag**
"To improve the quality of home life by designing, building, **marketing** and servicing the best appliances in the world."

The main force driving mission statements is to help employees share a clear sense of what the company is striving for. It is not unusual for companies to spend months developing the statements. In addition to mission statements, companies have developed amplifications with names like values statement and **vision statement**. Many companies have spent considerable time and effort deciding what to call each of their statements, while in fact there seems to be little distinction among the different varieties. Here is the values statement for Research Inc.:

"We are committed to long-term, quality relationships for the mutual benefit of our customers, employees, vendors, representatives, shareholders and community."

mission statement

trap |

Broad and vague mission statements will get only a shrug from employees. You are wasting your time unless your words are specific, the statement is something employees can act on, and top management is committed to it.

M

`tech`

modem (modulator/demodulator)   Device that allows computers and terminals to communicate over phone lines.

Modems transform the **digital** pulses generated by a computer or terminal into **analog** signals for transmission and then convert the analog signals back to digital pulses understood by the receiving computer or terminal.

`acct`

modified accelerated cost recovery system (MACRS)   See **accelerated cost recovery system (ACRS)**.

monetarism

Milton Friedman

Quick Facts!

Milton Friedman, acknowledged as the father of modern monetarist economic theory, won the 1976 Nobel prize for his work. In promoting monetarist thought, he argued vehemently against the widely accepted Keynesian economic policies, which stressed government's role in shaping economic growth primarily through tools like taxation and budget spending.

Proponents of other theories argue that the monetarists' focus on the money supply is too limited, and point to the historically high interest rates in the early 1980s. Still, his work has influenced U.S. economic policy, particularly during the Reagan administration. He has also been credited with pushing other countries—including those in Latin America and Eastern Europe—toward freer markets.

M

econ

monetarism   School of economic thought holding that persistent **inflation** is largely the result of excessive increases in the **money supply**, and that government efforts to manipulate the money stock to promote economic stability are more likely to produce instability.

More specifically, monetarism—which is widely associated with the American economist and Nobel laureate Milton Friedman—is founded on at least three basic propositions:

1 Periods of persistent inflation are usually the result of sustained increases in the money supply that exceed the growth of real output.

2 Increases in an economy's anticipated inflation cause **interest rates** to rise and the **exchange rate** to fall.

3 Increases in the growth of the money stock produce temporary changes in real production but lasting changes in the rate of inflation.

Monetarists are usually skeptical of government's ability to use fiscal and monetary policies to improve an economy's performance. Instead, they tend to believe that government has the best chance of promoting economic stability by acting predictably and by avoiding efforts to steer the economy in one direction or the other.

See also **monetary policy**, **price controls**, and **supply-side economics**.

econ

monetary policy   In the United States, use of the **Federal Reserve System (Fed)** to regulate the **money supply** and thus influence the nation's economy.

The Fed implements monetary policy through open market operations, changes in bank reserve requirements, and changes in the **discount rate**.

See also **fiscal policy**, **monetarism**, **price controls**, and **supply-side economics**.

fin   econ

money center bank   A bank in a key financial center—like London, New York, or Tokyo—that has major national and international dealings.

Money center banks, also called money market banks, are major economic players because they handle large deposits from and loans to both governments and corporations, and they buy large quantities of securities. Through their policies and their interest rates, these banks are highly influential worldwide. The 11 acknowledged U.S. money center banks control almost a quarter of the **assets** of all U.S.-based banks.

See also **regional bank**.

money center bank

The largest U.S.-based money center banking companies in 1995 were:

- Citicorp, New York, with assets of $257 billion.

- BankAmerica Corporation, San Francisco, $232 billion.

- Chemical Banking Corporation, New York, $183 billion.

Worldwide, Citicorp ranked 28th-largest among money center banking companies. The biggest in the world is Germany's Deutsche Bank, AG, with assets of $502 billion. This was the first time since 1982 that a Japanese bank was not in the top spot, although Sanwa Bank, Ltd., came in second at $500 billion. The turnabout was only temporary, however, as Bank of Tokyo and Mitsubishi Bank joined forces in 1996 to create a gigantic, $711 billion institution.

When 1996 rankings of U.S. banks are published, they will show a different story as well. Citicorp lost its hold on the No. 1 ranking in the spring of 1996 when Chemical and Chase Manhattan completed their merger and created a new Chase with assets of more than $300 billion.

---

fin　**econ**

money markets　Where you can buy and sell debt securities with terms of less than one year.

These arenas for short-term lending and borrowing are really electronic markets similar to **over-the-counter (OTC) stock** markets. Short-term U.S. Treasury bills, certificates of deposit, and **commercial paper**, among other things, are traded on money markets.

econ

money supply　Total stock of money available, consisting in the United States of currency in circulation and various types of deposits at commercial banks, savings and loans, and other institutions.

According to the Federal Reserve, there are at least three measures of the money supply:

1 **M1**
Emphasizes money's role as a medium of exchange. It includes all the dollar bills and coins in circulation (outside of bank vaults), plus traveler's checks, demand deposits, and NOW accounts.

2 **M2**
Includes money's function as a store of value. It begins with M1 and then adds other savings accounts and time deposits. It also includes general-purpose money market mutual funds and other instruments. In 1995, M2 totaled $3.6 trillion.

3 **M3**
Includes M2 plus most additional forms of **savings**.

money supply
Quick Facts! |

Some economists believe an even broader definition is needed to gauge the money supply. They would include the credit available on bank credit cards. So if you have a $5,000 limit on your Visa card and owe $1,000, the other $4,000 would be considered part of the money supply, since it is easily available for you to spend.

The Fed's money supply figures, whose release was once anxiously awaited, have lost some of their significance as a premier economic indicator in recent years. This includes changes in people's savings habits, increased lending done outside the tradiional banking system, and the fact that the Fed no longer sets specific targets for money supply growth.

M

Money Supply Growth (M1 and M2), Annual Growth Rate, 1975–1995

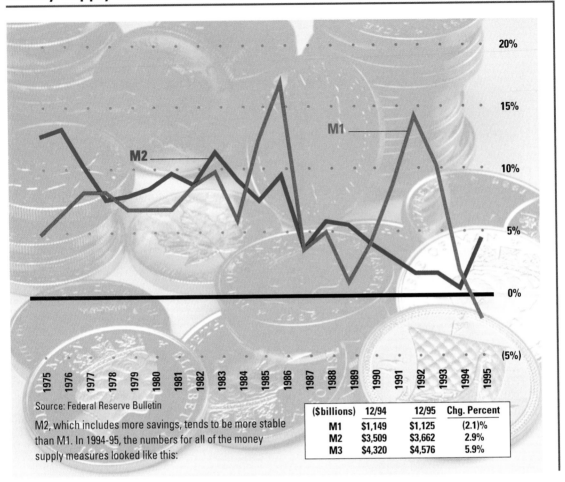

Source: Federal Reserve Bulletin

M2, which includes more savings, tends to be more stable than M1. In 1994-95, the numbers for all of the money supply measures looked like this:

($billions)	12/94	12/95	Chg. Percent
M1	$1,149	$1,125	(2.1)%
M2	$3,509	$3,662	2.9%
M3	$4,320	$4,576	5.9%

Both M2 and M3 tend to be more stable than M1. When banks are offering high interest rates on checking accounts, people shift funds from their money market and savings accounts to checking. That has no effect on M2 or M3, but M1 increases sharply.

mgmt

Monte Carlo simulation   Probability analysis using changing variables.

Because chance is involved, this method takes its name from the famous gambling resort town. Also called risk analysis when applied to business situations, it is used to study a situation with a random component, like projected sales for a product that has not yet been introduced.

EXAMPLE | You are concerned about how shifts in **exchange rates** between the U.S. dollar and the Mexican peso will affect your manufacturing business. You create a computer model that incorporates several variables. Some, like the **interest rates** in both countries, can be predicted with a degree of certainty. Others, like the possibility of a revolution or natural disaster, are a lot less predictable.

M

That is where the Monte Carlo simulation comes in. You assign probabilities to the various elements of the model. The probability of inflation continuing at the same level in the United States might be 50-50, while for Mexico it might be 40-60. Revolutions would get much longer odds. You use the model to help determine your capital budget and when and how much to hedge on currency rates.

The use of the risk-analysis method to help make business decisions was introduced by McKinsey & Company consultants and its retired director, David Hertz.

mktg

morning drive time   Hours between 7 A.M. and 10 A.M.—when many people are in their cars—that constitute prime radio **advertising** time.

See also **drive time**.

fin

mortgage-backed bond   Form of **asset-backed security** that is backed and paid off by homeowners' payments on mortgages.

The principal and interest payments from residential mortgages are transferred from the mortgage originators to intermediaries, usually quasi-governmental agencies like the Government National Mortgage Association (Ginnie Mae) or the Federal National Mortgage Association (Fannie Mae). These agencies pool and repackage the mortgages into securities that are then sold to investors. The investor receives a good **yield** with relative safety because the securities are guaranteed by the U.S. government.

mgmt

motivation-hygiene theory   Theory of worker motivation that has contributed to using **job enrichment** as a way to improve **job satisfaction**.

The concept grew out of psychologist Frederick Herzberg's 1959 book *The Motivation to Work*. Herzberg found that one set of factors (motivators) can make people feel good about their jobs while an entirely different set of things (hygiene factors) can make them dissatisfied. The motivators involve actual job experiences, or content. The hygiene factors are pay, working conditions, fringe benefits, and so on.

Before Herzberg's work, managers might think of a pay raise or better benefits to boost morale. In fact, these hygiene factors might prevent dissatisfaction, but they do not make people feel happy in their work. To really motivate people, according to Herzberg, you have to deal with the job content—challenge, opportunity, responsibility, recognition, personal growth, and so on.

Herzberg's theory has particular relevance in the 1990s as corporate downsizing and the quality movement create more opportunities for the **motivator** of job enrichment.

morning drive time

mortgage-backed bond

Quick Facts!

By giving mortgage lenders more liquidity, the mortgage-backed bond market helps to make more money available for home financing.

motivation-hygiene theory

M

Where much is expected from an individual, he may rise to the level of events and make that dream come true.

—Elbert Hubbard

mgmt

motivators Set of factors that can make people feel good about their jobs.

See also **motivation-hygiene theory**.

oper **tech**

MRP See **material requirements planning**.

econ **oper** **mgmt**

multifactor productivity Use of more than one element to measure the rate of production.

See also **productivity**.

multilevel marketing

Companies selling everything from long-distance to service health care products have adopted multilevel marketing.

mktg

multilevel marketing When salespeople make **commissions** on their own sales and the sales of others they recruit. Sometimes called pyramid marketing.

It offers the salespeople, who are independent contractors, the chance to build huge incomes if they can both sell the product and recruit and coach others who are successful. Companies selling everything from long-distance service to health care products have adopted multilevel marketing. Attracted by the possibility of substantial incomes, many people are recruited into selling this way. But, as with other forms of selling, many people fail and drop out. Some have sued the companies over claims of false promises and pressure to buy materials and supplies themselves from the companies.

Multilevel marketing should not be confused with illegal pyramid sales practices. These fraudulent schemes are built on nonexistent values and depend on money from new investors to pay "earnings" to previous entrants, whereas multilevel marketing involves moving valuable products or services to consumers. In addition, you cannot participate in a pyramid unless you join the program. And if illegal pyramids offer any product at all, it is usually worthless or nearly so and is just moved around among recruits. The emphasis here is on recruiting new salespeople, not on the product or services.

multitasking

tech

multitasking Having your computer get two or more things done at the same time.

Usually, in multitasking, a job like sending instructions to the printer will run in the background while you interact with the computer on something else, like entering and calculating numbers in a spreadsheet.

Assuming you have a reasonably recent computer, it is your operating system that gives you the ability to multitask. Your computer's processor can do only one thing at a time, but it does it very fast. Your operating system tells the processor how to switch between the jobs so both are done at what appears to be the same time.

M

Computers that actually have more than one processor are called parallel processors and are used mostly for high-powered computing functions, as in the space industry.

mgmt

Myers-Briggs Type Indicator (MBTI)®   Method for categorizing personality types.

Developed by the mother-daughter team of Katharine Briggs and Isabel Briggs Myers in the 1940s, the test is based on the theoretical work of Swiss psychologist Carl Jung. It contains 100 questions about how you feel or what you do in particular situations

The MBTI test characterizes people as:

▶ Extraverted or Introverted (E or I).

▶ Sensing or Intuition (S or N).

▶ Thinking or Feeling (T or F).

▶ Judging or Perceiving (J or P).

This makes for 16 possible combinations, and people familiar with the MBTI describe themselves or others as "an ENTP" or "an INTJ" and so on. An ENTP is resourceful and a quick learner but may skip routine work. An INTJ is a visionary with a passion for his or her ideas and perhaps a stubborn streak.

The MBTI is not intended to screen employees but to help people understand themselves and deal with others. Millions of people take the test each year in the United States. Among organizations that have used the MBTI are Apple Computer, General Electric, and the U.S. Army.

Myers-Briggs Type Indicator and *MBTI* are registered trademarks of Consulting Psychologist Press, Inc., Palo Alto, California.

mktg

mystery shopper   Person who conducts behind-the-scenes observational research to determine how consumers view a service or product.

One supermarket might send a mystery shopper to a competitor to check on prices and product positioning. A brand-name manufacturer also might use mystery shoppers to determine how its products, and its competitors', are being presented in the stores.

Myers-Briggs Type Indicator

Katharine Cook Briggs

Isabel Briggs Myers

Photos courtesy of the Center for Applications of Psychological Type.

M

mystery shopper

Motion Pictures and Video

Thomas A. Edison

Warner brothers, who started as exhibitors, formed their studio; and Marcus Loew, who owned a string of theaters, cobbled together what became Metro-Goldwyn-Mayer. In 1919, a group of performers and a director formed United Artists. In the 1920s, the silent movies turned out by these and other companies were the only rivals to the new medium of radio.

The first talking picture, "The Jazz Singer," was produced by Warner Bros. in 1927, and it revolutionized the industry. By the early 1930s, the older filmmakers had been joined by Twentieth Century Fox, RKO, Columbia, and several smaller companies. By then, too, the major firms had their own chains of theaters and so dominated both ends of the business. There were some independents, such as Walt Disney and Samuel Goldwyn, but the future seemed in the hands of the integrated companies. Artists were bound to them by ironclad contracts, and they worked as though on an assembly line. Independent theaters could exhibit the pictures but usually on a "block booking" basis, meaning they had to take what was offered. With this structure, the studio system entered its golden age.

While the concept of motion pictures occurred to Leonardo da Vinci in the 16th century, and a host of figures engaged in early photography considered the possibilities, the first successful devices that produced and projected motion pictures are usually attributed to Thomas A. Edison and his assistant William Dickson, with help from George Eastman, who created the celluloid roll film. In the early 1890s, Edison invented the Kinetoscope, which resembled a peep show, and, with associates, transformed it into a projector. The first films were shown in 1896, using what had become the Edison Vitascope.

Many companies were formed infringing on Edison's patents. In retaliation, he organized the Motion Picture Patents Co., through which he hoped to control the exhibitors and the distributors. But, just as computer software manufacturers would later triumph over hardware producers, early producers of films (software) prevailed over equipment manufacturers (hardware). Carl Laemmle, a distributor, developed the predecessor of Universal Pictures. Out of Adolph Zukor's efforts came Paramount; the

It was under this industrial model that Hollywood, the motion picture capital, turned out some of the finest films ever produced. Motion pictures, which seemed on the verge of failure during the early years of the Great Depression, were highly profitable by the end of World War

Contributing Editor: Harold L. Vogel
Managing Director, Cowen & Co.

1894 — 1910 — 1920 — 1930 — 1940

1894	1896	1919	1920s	1927	Early 1930s	1940
Thomas A. Edison invents the Kinetoscope	The first films are shown using the Edison Vitascope	Organization of United Artists	The first silent movies are shown	Warner Bros. produces the first talking picture, "The Jazz Singer"	Twentieth Century Fox, RKO, Columbia and several other production companies form	Courts rule that studios can no longer purchase theaters

II. Then the industry was struck by a double blow. From Washington came a political attack, and from television, a more serious contest for audience attention.

Government challenges to industry practices had begun in the 1930s. In 1940, the courts ruled that studios could no longer purchase theaters. In 1948, the Supreme Court upheld lower-court decisions on the illegality of certain trade practices. From that point forward, the studios could not force block booking on the independent exhibitors. Theatre owners could pick and choose those films they felt would appeal to their audiences. In 1951, in a test case brought against Paramount, the Supreme Court ordered the five major companies to divest themselves of their theaters. In this way, production was divorced from exhibition.

The powerful studios were dealt another blow by the end of the actor-contract system, in which artists had been bound to one studio at a time. Artists could form their own companies to produce films, perhaps engage the services of a studio, and then arrange for distribution.

By the late 1950s a substantial part of the motion picture industry was dominated by what later would be called "virtual corporations"—individuals and groups coming together to work on a project and then flying off in different directions when it was completed. Production companies proliferated: Morgan Creek, New Regency, and Polygram, among others. Burt Lancaster, Kirk Douglas, John Wayne, and other "bankable" stars organized their own companies.

Mary Pickford

The impact of these decisions on the industry was enormous. The studios no longer had an assured market for their productions. This spelled the end of the "B films," which were used to fill the second half of double features. The prime features became even more ornate to meet the challenge from television.

Perhaps the greatest threat to motion pictures was the invention that would change the entertainment industry forever—television. To many outside the industry, a marriage between motion pictures and television seemed not only sensible but inevitable. There seemed no reason why the motion-picture companies could not adjust to

1950   1980   1990   1996

Early 1950s
Universal, through its Screen Gems subsidiary, produces films for TV

1975
Sony introduces the Betamax videocassette player

1977
Panasonic introduces the VHS videocassette player

1985
Blockbuster Entertainment forms

1986
Video rental outlets number 19,000

1989
Warner Communications merges with Time Inc.

1994
DreamWorks SKG, a multifaceted entertainment studio, is formed

1996
Camcorder sales reach 3.5 million per year

the television environment. The studio heads saw it otherwise. In their view, television was an alternative to motion pictures, not a new outlet for their products. The studios refused to enter into production deals or permit their stars to appear on television. The television industry responded by producing their own stars and

Steven Spielberg

programs, most of them in New York. An entertainment war opened between Hollywood and New York. Believing their film libraries were worth little, the motion-picture leaders sold them to the television interests at low prices, and the old movies became television staples.

This divisive approach began to change in the early 1950s. Through its Screen Gems subsidiary, Universal produced films for television and then Warner Bros. fell in line. Other studios also entered the field. Meanwhile, thousands of theaters closed as television became a national mania.

In an attempt to retain audiences, the studios turned to wide-screen projection, such as CinemaScope and WarnerVision, and high-budget films that could be seen only in theaters. "An American in Paris," "The Greatest Show on Earth," and "Around the World in 80 Days" attracted large audiences.

These industry developments brought considerable change to the studios throughout the years and provided for some strange partnerships. General Tire & Rubber purchased RKO. Gulf+Western became the parent of Paramount. Kinney, which was involved in funeral

parlors and parking lots, purchased Warner Bros. in 1971 and became Warner Communications, only to merge with Time Inc. in 1989 to become Time Warner, now one of the industry giants. Transamerica, a financial services conglomerate, acquired United Artists. MCA, a former talent agency, entered film production by buying Universal, and it in turn was acquired by Matsushita. Coca-Cola purchased Columbia and then sold it to Sony. MGM and Twentieth Century Fox ended production and instead worked with independent producers. Quaker Oats, Mattel, Kellogg, and other non–movie companies backed the independents.

New start-ups were even more exciting. Dream Works was the most spectacular American start-up since the formation of U.S. Steel close to a century earlier. It was led by a trio of accomplished executives: Steven Spielberg, fresh from his successes with "Schindler's List" and "Jurassic Park"; David Geffen, one of the top figures in the popular-music field; and Jeffrey Katzenberg, formerly with Disney. At a time when talent was at a premium, Dream Works investors wagered billions on its future. The initial contributor, Capital Cities/ABC, provided $100 million in seed money, while Chemical Bank provided a $1 billion line of credit. Microsoft cofounder Paul Allen came in for $500 million. Samsung Electronics took a major equity position. HBO paid dearly for the right to its films. When negotiations were finalized, DreamWorks started life with a war chest of more than $2 billion.

Disney, led by Michael Eisner, acquired Capital Cities/ABC as part of its strategy to become a worldwide entertainment enterprise. Formerly specializing in children's cartoons, Disney seemed the powerhouse of the entertainment industry by the mid-1990s and even joined with McDonald's to promote videos and "Happy Meals."

Transnational arrangments were commonplace, and the trend toward internationalization accelerated. Shooting locations were dictated by financial as well as artistic factors. The forced demolition of the old industry created a new one even more vigorous and powerful to meet the challenge of television.

Alec Guinness, George Lucas

John Malone of Tele-Communications Inc. (TCI), whose empire spanned several industries and even the creation of new ones, emerged as one of the industry's leading figures. Malone's vision included the melding of motion pictures, television, and telecommunications, and the uniting of computers, television sets, and telephone services, including fax, databases, e-mail, and the Internet.

By then, the unification of motion pictures and television was complete as film producers included television releases as part of their contracts. Business arrangements were worked out between movies and television and cable. Columbia formed Tri-Star, which was a joint venture with CBS and HBO. Orion, organized by a group of former United Artists executives, had connections with several television interests.

The relationship between motion pictures and television had been further cemented by the introduction of the video cassette recorder (VCR.) Sony's Betamax was first introduced in 1975, and two years later, Panasonic came out with a similar machine using a different format. Although the initial VCRs cost well over $2,000, the prices fell rapidly as the battle between the two formats accelerated. The Panasonic version, which could play longer presentations and attracted a better film library, soon won the contest. The motion-picture industry appeared the real winner, though, because movies on cassette could bring in substantial revenues.

Advances for ballyhooed movies now included cassette rights, which made possible contracts that might have been rejected earlier. By the 1980s, half of the revenues for a promising film might derive from the sale of cassette and television rights. For those unwilling to purchase cassettes, small video stores appeared, renting them for overnight viewing. Initially, the selections offered were limited, but in the 1980s they expanded, as did the number of stores. There were 7,000 video-rental outlets in 1983 and 19,000 by 1986.

In 1985, Sandy Cook organized Blockbuster Entertainment with the intention of doing for cassettes what McDonald's Ray Kroc did for hamburgers. With large inventories and a powerful organization, Blockbuster opened outlets around the country. Wayne Huizinga, who had made a fortune in waste disposal, saw opportunities in this area too. Through stock purchases, he assumed command of Blockbuster. Then, believing the marriage between television, cable, and computers put the future of video rentals into question, Huizinga helped arrange a union of Blockbuster, Paramount, and cable giant Viacom.

While rethinking and restructuring roiled the motion-picture industry, yet another new technology appeared. The camcorder surfaced to

mixed reviews in the late 1980s and at first did not seem promising. The initial cameras were expensive, bulky, and difficult to operate. The camcorder recorded on tape, and those tapes were viewed directly on the television, as opposed to films viewed by projector. These drawbacks were overcome quickly, and by the mid-1990s they were selling at 3.5 million cameras a year. Armed with a camcorder, almost anyone could become a filmmaker. Film courses proliferated at universities, new schools of communications opened, and film festivals multiplied as the camcorder sparked a new revolution in news programs as well as in motion pictures.

N

NAFTA

to

numerical
control

NAFTA   See **North American Free Trade Agreement**.

fin

Nasdaq Stock Marketᔆᴹ   The world's first computerized stock market and second-largest market in the United States, based in Washington, D.C.

The Nasdaq today lists more than 5,300 companies, many of which are eligible to be listed on the **New York Stock Exchange (NYSE)** or the **American Stock Exchange (Amex)**. These include such giants as Microsoft, Intel, MCI, and Amgen. Nasdaq began operating in 1971 to handle start-up companies and others too small to meet the listing requirements of the NYSE and Amex. In 1995, Nasdaq traded more than 100 billion shares—more than any other stock market—although at a dollar volume of $2.4 trillion it still trails the NYSE.

Using sophisticated computer technology and high-speed data lines, Nasdaq links more than 530 broker/dealer firms across the country and around the world who make markets in Nasdaq stocks.

See also **National Association of Securities Dealers, Inc. (NASD)**.

Nasdaq Stock Marketᔆᴹ

NASDAQ

Nasdaq Dollar Volume, 1975–1995 ($ billions)

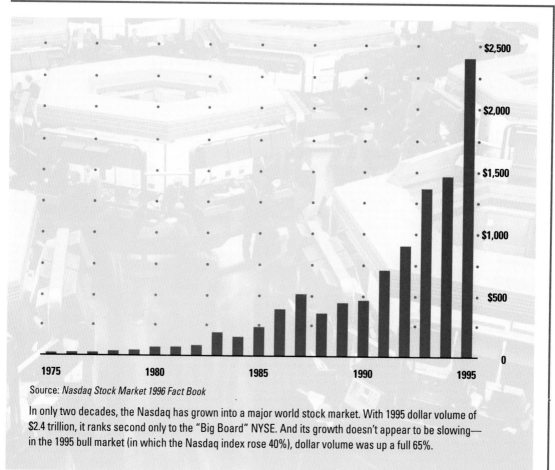

Source: *Nasdaq Stock Market 1996 Fact Book*

In only two decades, the Nasdaq has grown into a major world stock market. With 1995 dollar volume of $2.4 trillion, it ranks second only to the "Big Board" NYSE. And its growth doesn't appear to be slowing—in the 1995 bull market (in which the Nasdaq index rose 40%), dollar volume was up a full 65%.

Nasdaq Stock Market^{SM}

National Alliance of Business

National Association of Securities Dealers, Inc.

N

---

mgmt

National Alliance of Business (NAB)   Organization that works to build a quality workforce through education reform and enhanced job training.

The Washington, D.C.–based group brings together business and community leaders in programs that promote academic excellence, expand job-training opportunities, and develop industry-based skills standards. Its board of directors includes chief executives and other top officers from leading industries, key educators, and civic officials.

fin

National Association of Securities Dealers, Inc. (NASD)
Largest self-regulatory organization in the U.S. securities industry.

The NASD is the corporate parent of the **Nasdaq Stock Market** and the **National Association of Securities Dealers Regulation (NASD Regulation)**.

fin

National Association of Securities Dealers Regulation (NASD Regulation)   The independent regulatory subsidiary of the NASD that is responsible for oversight and regulation of the nation's more than 520,000 NASD-registered broker/dealers and 5,500 broker/dealer firms.

mktg **mgmt**

National Environmental Policy Act   See **consumer protection legislation**.

mktg **mgmt**

National Traffic and Motor Vehicle and Safety Act
See **consumer protection legislation**.

econ

natural monopoly   Industry characterized by **economies of scale** such that one firm can supply an entire market at a lower per-unit cost than could be achieved with multiple providers.

Examples are confined to utilities: Because the transmission of electrical power, natural gas, and local phone calls requires the existence of a single grid or network, duplicate investments of competitive providers would be wasteful and entail needlessly redundant capacity (although this may be changing for the local phone market). Since it is more efficient to have just one supplier in this circumstance, governments sometimes award exclusive franchises to a sole seller. And to prevent the seller from exploiting its monopoly position, a regulatory agency generally will regulate the rates of the natural monopolist.

See also **duopoly** and **oligopoly**.

net current assets   Current **assets** minus current **liabilities**.

See also **working capital**.

net income   Often referred to as *net earnings*, or **net profit**. For a company, it is the difference between **revenues** and **expenses**. It is typically an "after-tax" number, although "net income before taxes" is also a popular measure. **Dividends** are paid out of net income.

See also **earnings before interest and taxes** and **income statement**.

net present value (NPV)   Current worth of future amounts of money. Also called **discounted cash flow (DCF)**.

Net Present Value
$$NPV = P_0 + P_1 \div (1+r) + P_2 \div (1+r)^2 + P_3 \div (1+r)^3 + \ldots + P_n \div (1+r)^n$$

NPV	Net present value of the investment
$P_0 \, P_1 \ldots P_n$	Cash payments in periods 0 through n
r	Investors' required rate of return (the rate of return offered by a comparable investment)

You can use NPV in a number of ways, including:

▶ To calculate the benefits of a potential project or investment, including buying a business.

▶ To determine the price of a partnership or a minority interest when an investor´s interest is being bought.

▶ To compare the true cost of leasing equipment to outright purchase.

To arrive at the NPV, you need to find the opportunity cost of capital, or **discount rate**, you feel your investment should get.

net present value

tip |

*Advantages of the NPV approach are that it recognizes the value of money over time and avoids the accounting convention of **depreciation**, focusing entirely on **cash flow**.*

trap |

*Like **IRR** calculations, NPV is based on compound earnings. It assumes that you can reinvest the money earned at the same percentage rate, which you often cannot.*

N

net present value

EXAMPLE We will use the same situation that we used with **internal rate of return (IRR)**. You run a takeout pizza business and believe you could improve your return by buying a van and adding delivery service. You can buy the van for $15,000 and believe you will use it for five years and then sell it for $5,000. After expenses, you estimate that your business will make another $3,500 a year from the delivery service. So your cash flow looks like this:

Cash Flow: Years 1–5

Year #1	($11,500)	($3,500 income – $15,000 cost of van)
Year #2	$3,500	
Year #3	$3,500	
Year #4	$3,500	
Year #5	$8,500	($3,500 income + $5,000 proceeds of van)

You could make 7.5 percent by investing in a U.S. Treasury bill over five years, but you decide that the added risks of the pizza delivery business mean you should earn at least twice that rate. So you set the discount rate at 15 percent. With that discount rate, the NPV is $1,351. Even if you set the discount rate a bit higher, at 18 percent, you would still get a positive number, $494, for the pizza van's NPV.

As long as the number is positive, you are getting the return you want. But, of course, the higher the NPV, the better the deal. If you have also been thinking about expanding your restaurant but cannot take on both projects, you could compare the NPV for buying the van with the NPV at the same discount rate for the expansion.

fin

net proceeds Cash received from a loan, or from the sale of property or securities, after deducting the costs of the transaction.

See also **gross proceeds**.

acct

net profit The bottom line, or the amount remaining after deducting all costs from revenues.

See also **income statement** and **net income**.

acct **fin**

net profit margin Ratio of **net income** to net sales.

See also **profit margin**.

fin

net worth requirement

A **covenant** on a **bond** that requires a debtor to maintain a prescribed net worth. If the debtor fails to do so, the holders of the bond can declare a default and may have the right to demand immediate repayment.

See also **collapsed equity test**.

tech **mgmt**

network

System of linked computers along with **peripherals**, like printers.

The two commonly discussed types of networks are:

1 **Local Area Networks (LANs)**
Two to five hundred computers attached to each other by cables within the same building or geographic area.

2 **Wide Area Networks (WANs)**
These are larger and cover more geography, using dedicated telephone lines or radio waves.

The most common way for personal computers to work together is in a **client/server network** where one computer (the client) gets many of its applications and files from another (the server).

See also **local area network (LAN)** and **wide area network (WAN)**.

mktg

new-product development

Process of introducing a new product that involves extensive research, design, and manufacturing.

Though thousands of new products make their way into the marketplace yearly, their failure rate has been estimated from around 40 percent to as high as 90 percent. Even so, sometimes the risk of not developing a new product is even higher.

EXAMPLE | Those Characters from Cleveland (TCFC) is the creative and licensing division of American Greetings. TCFC scored tremendous hits with Hollie Hobbie, Care Bears, and Strawberry Shortcake. But for several years, the company introduced no new major characters. As a result, TCFC lost **market share** to competitors who did introduce new toys.

To regain its market share, TCFC developed a new stuffed fur animal called Popples and introduced it through a $10 million advertising campaign. The success of Popples helped the company recapture its position in the lucrative toy market.

network

Quick Facts!

- There has been more information produced in the last 30 years than during the previous 5,000.

- The information supply available to us doubles every five years.

—Richard Saul Wurman,
Information Anxiety

N

FRAME OF REFERENCE

niche marketing

The transformation of the cable industry in recent years has given new meaning to the idea of niche marketing. Cable companies now predict a day in which viewers have access to 500 channels, the majority of which would appeal to narrowly focused audiences. Already in 1995, an advertiser could appeal to viewers of the Golf channel, the History channel, or to Home and Garden Television. And this segmentation trend is just the tip of the niching iceberg: The Discovery Channel, for example, is targeting subniches, dividing their education-oriented programming into animal, science, and history categories.

Marketers are still grappling with implications of this kind of audience fragmentation and, of course, with how best to take advantage of it. Many experts see it as an opportunity—giving advertisers the ability to target their true consumers. Marketing theory holds that focused audiences offer higher efficiencies and contain less waste in terms of dollars. But others see the audience groups as simply becoming smaller rather than more focused—that an advertiser needs some kind of critical mass in a targeted audience, no matter how "pure" it may be.

news release

tip

Put your news releases into the style of the publications or broadcasters that you want to use them. If you can give an editor something to use without a lot of additional work, he or she will be more willing to use it.

trap

Remember that it is not a paid ad: You cannot control how, or even if, a news release will be used. As the saying goes in public relations, advertising is paid for, publicity is prayed for!

N

mgmt **mktg**

news release   Statement prepared for the news media. It is also called a **press release**.

You may use one to introduce or promote a product or service, to announce a major development within your company, to publicize the hiring of a well-known executive, or for any one of a number of other reasons. Press releases are usually written out for print media, and many companies distribute them electronically over the **PR Newswire**. Some companies also prepare sophisticated video and audio news releases for television and radio stations.

EXAMPLE | Mobil Corporation has promoted its pay-at-the-pump feature with press releases for newspapers and video news releases for TV stations. The video releases include interviews with motorists that can be inserted into news shows just as though they were created by the local station. Mobil's video news releases can be beamed to local TV stations via satellite.

mktg

niche marketing   Strategy focusing on a specialized segment of a market that is too small for major companies.

EXAMPLE | The watchmaker Swatch found its niche by producing timepieces but marketing them as trendy and affordable fashion accessories. Numerous buyers were enticed to purchase watches that complemented various outfits, regardless of whether they had one or several reliable watches at home already.

oper

nominal capacity   Output level at which a manufacturing plant was designed to run.

See also **design capacity**.

fin

nominal interest rate   The stated **interest rate** on a loan.

econ

nondurable good   A good, like food, clothing, gasoline, or heating fuel, which is consumed relatively quickly.

See also **personal consumption expenditures**.

fin

nonmarket risk   Potential price swings in one company's securities for reasons specific to that company. Also called **diversifiable risk**.

Nonmarket risk factors include anticipated growth in earnings per share, management effectiveness, labor relations, and so on. They contrast with **market risk** factors, which affect all securities. Market risk factors include shifts in the economy, interest rates, inflation, and general investor confidence.

A security's nonmarket risk is reflected by its **alpha (α)**. An investor can diversify his or her portfolio to minimize nonmarket risk, which is why it is also called **diversifiable risk**.

See also **beta (ß)**, **capital asset pricing model (CAPM)**, and **diversification**.

fin

normal distribution   In statistics, a division of data points that produces the bell-shaped curve. Also called Gaussian distribution, after Karl Friedrich Gauss (1777–1855), who identified the pattern of a bell curve.

In a normal distribution, most of the points on a graph are gathered around the center. They trail off rapidly—and more or less symmetrically—to each side. In general, the larger the sample, the more likely it is that the data will follow this pattern—and the closer it will come to total symmetry. For instance, the **Dow Jones Industrial Average (DJIA)** charts only 30 securities. As a result, it is less likely to follow the bell curve than the **Standard & Poor's (S&P)** 500 or broader indexes.

A company's **dividend** actions might be expected to follow a normal distribution over time, with a few very sharp increases or decreases in the rate, and the majority clustered between those extremes.

news release

niche marketing

Quick Facts!

The word niche is an import from France, where the verb nicher means to nest.

normal distribution

Karl Friedrich Gauss

N

O

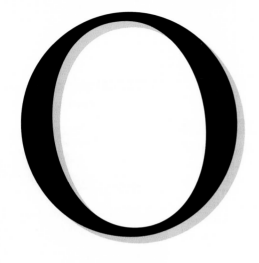

objectives

to

owner's
equity

mgmt **strat**

objectives Performance goals and how to meet them.

See **management by objectives (MBO)** and **strategic planning**.

mktg

observational research Collecting data by observing how consumers respond to a product.

EXAMPLE | Food companies learn from taste tests, but they also may lay out a table with a group of similar products, such as a variety of salsas, and ask consumers to try them and eat as much as they like. Through a one-way mirror, employees watch the people experiment. The researchers record data about things such as the tasters' facial expressions, which products the tasters avoid, and which ones they return to again and again.

See also **focus group** and **surveying**.

strat **mktg**

obsolescence When a product no longer serves its purpose.

In economic obsolescence, the product becomes inefficient to use because other products perform its function at lower cost. In physical obsolescence, the product becomes ineffective even though it has not worn out, as when standards have changed.

econ

OECD See **Organization for Economic Cooperation and Development**.

econ

OEEC See **Organization for European Economic Cooperation**.

fin

offshore financial center Place where banks conduct transactions in currencies other than the local one.

The term can apply to places like London, New York City, and Tokyo, where you can get loans and make deposits in a variety of currencies. But more often the term is used for **tax havens** like the Cayman Islands and the Channel Islands that offer inducements to encourage international banking. The Cayman Islands, for example, has one bank for every 50 citizens.

See also **Eurocurrency**.

observational research

offshore financial center

0

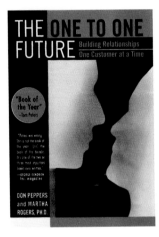

one-to-one marketing

econ

oligopoly   Industry characterized by just a few sellers.

Examples are household appliances, baby formula, and tobacco products. In these industries, the largest three or four sellers control more than 80 percent of the entire market. In industries where the market shares of the top sellers are large, the companies may recognize that price wars can be damaging for all players and thus avoid such contests. Price cooperation can easily replace price competition in oligopolistic markets.

See also **duopoly** and **natural monopoly**.

mktg

omnibus panel   Group of people participating in a variety of **marketing research** studies for a company.

EXAMPLE | A manufacturing and marketing company maintains a panel of consumers to try out and comment on new products as they are developed.

See also **longitudinal panel**.

mktg

one-to-one marketing   Tailoring a **product** or **service** to an individual consumer.

Following the 1993 publication of Don Peppers and Martha Rogers' manifesto *The One to One Future*, one-to-one **marketing** became a hot topic. But like many buzzwords that catch fire, it is not so much a new concept as a new wrinkle on an existing methodology. The practice of one-to-one marketing, albeit without the title, dates back to the beginning of commerce and has continued uninterrupted to the present day.

Even in the United States, the birthplace of **mass marketing**, some one-to-one marketing practices have remained unchanged since prerevolutionary days. There are tailor shops in New York City, for instance, where an individual can have a suit made to order, selecting everything from the bolt of cloth to the lapel size—as Alexander Hamilton or Aaron Burr did centuries ago.

Mass marketing took over on the basis of two strengths: **economies of scale** in manufacturing and exploitation of mass media. The former allows Filene's Basement to beat out a New York tailor on price; the latter enables Calvin Klein to sell more expensive suits than most people ever dream of. Some believe that computer technology will begin to eliminate those mass-market advantages and that one-to-one marketing will again reign supreme.

econ   **fin**   **strat**

OPEC   See **Organization of Petroleum Exporting Countries**.

oper **mgmt**

open board/open order   An order for products that have not been produced yet.

See also **backlog**.

acct **fin**

operating expenses   All costs that can be attributed to regular business activities.

See also **income statement**.

acct **fin**

operating income   Earnings from a company's regular business activities.

See also **income statement**.

acct **fin**

operating lease   A lease that essentially provides for the short-term use of equipment.

Under such a lease, the lessor usually handles all maintenance and servicing of the equipment, which usually can be returned to the lessor, or owner, if it is no longer needed. An operating lease meets none of the four conditions that would qualify it as a **capital lease**. It is not recorded on the lessee's **balance sheet** but may be disclosed in a footnote to the **financial statements**.

operating lease

fin **acct** **mgmt**

operating leverage   Relationship of a company's nonfinancial **fixed costs** to its **variable costs**.

See also **leverage**.

oper

operations   The process of taking **inputs**, such as raw materials, and producing **outputs**, or finished products. The operations function is the lifeblood of all companies.

EXAMPLE | The operations of Thermidor involve making stoves and refrigerators. The operations of Little, Brown and Company concern book production. The operations function of Lorimar is creating television programs, while that of Coopers & Lybrand is providing accounting services.

oper

operations manager   Person in charge of direction, coordination, and control of all plant operations so that budgets and schedules are met. May be called **manufacturing manager** or **plant manager**.

mktg

opinion leaders   Highly regarded individuals who can influence others because of their stature or position in society.

The term can be used broadly—as for celebrities and high-level government officials—or more narrowly, for those who influence a particular market. A common **marketing** strategy is to invest in winning over the opinion leaders in the hopes they will influence others.

EXAMPLE | We all see this on our trips to the dentist, who is regarded as an opinion leader for the dental-care-product market. He or she is likely to give us a new toothbrush or a sample of toothpaste, dental floss, or some other product. The manufacturers have spent much time and money on reaching the dentists and supplying them with give-aways. The idea, of course, is that you are likely to continue using that brand because the dentist endorsed it.

Another instance is when the American Bakers Association and the Wheat Foods Council embarked on a campaign to increase bread consumption in the United States. One of their key strategies was to influence opinion leaders, including professionals in the health and nutrition industries.

opportunity cost

strat   **econ**   **mgmt**

opportunity cost   Value of the best alternative given up by choosing one course of action over another.

Assessing opportunity cost offers decision makers a quantitative way to make informed choices between competing options.

EXAMPLE | A company makes $50,000 by leasing out its idle manufacturing equipment. An order comes in for 1,000 units, and the company is considering producing them. To do so, it will need to use the equipment it has been leasing out. An opportunity cost of making the 1,000 units is $50,000.

The same concept can be applied to money tied up in **accounts receivable**. If it takes three months for a company to collect $100,000 from a client, the opportunity cost of the tied-up money is the amount of interest that would have been earned if the money had been invested.

See also **cash management systems** and **cost of capital**.

fin

options   Contracts, available from organized exchanges and over the counter, that do not have to be exercised or offset.

See also **derivatives**, **put options**, and **call option**.

O

ordinary annuity   An **annuity** in which payments are made at the end of a specified period.

econ

Organization for Economic Cooperation and Development (OECD)   International forum organized to boost world trade and economic development.

It was set up in 1961, replacing the **Organization for European Economic Cooperation (OEEC)**. Its mission is to promote high growth, economic stability, international trade, and help for developing countries.

EXAMPLE | A 1994 OECD *Economic Outlook* predicted encouraging gains after several years of gloomy forecasts but warned about national budget deficits. The OECD reported that total public debt in member countries was rising above 70 percent of **gross domestic product (GDP)**. It called for budget cutting.

The OECD's member countries are Australia, Austria, Belgium, Canada, Denmark, Finland, France, Germany, Greece, Iceland, Ireland, Italy, Japan, Luxembourg, Mexico, the Netherlands, New Zealand, Norway, Portugal, Spain, Sweden, Switzerland, Turkey, the United Kingdom, and the United States.

econ

Organization for European Economic Cooperation (OEEC)   Forerunner to the **Organization for Economic Cooperation and Development (OECD)**.

econ   **fin**   **strat**

Organization of Petroleum Exporting Countries (OPEC)   International **cartel** of countries that coordinate their crude-oil output and prices.

Founded in Caracas, Venezuela, in 1961, OPEC is based in Vienna, Austria. Current members: Algeria, Ecuador, Gabon, Indonesia, Iran, Iraq, Kuwait, Libya, Nigeria, Qatar, Saudi Arabia, United Arab Emirates, and Venezuela.

OPEC's heyday began in the early 1970s, when its members held ranks on a brief embargo on oil shipments to the United States and the Netherlands. Feeling its muscle, OPEC was able to work as an effective cartel for about a decade. By the early 1980s, oil prices were around 20 times their 1970 levels.

But then things started to go wrong for OPEC. Motorists insisted on more fuel-efficient cars. Both individuals and businesses learned to conserve oil and switch to alternative fuels like natural gas and coal. Oil output grew from non-OPEC sources like Norway and the United Kingdom. And OPEC had trouble enforcing discipline on its members, who exceeded their quotas and lowered their prices.

Organization for Economic Cooperation and Development

0

Organization of Petroleum Exporting Countries

Since 1982, oil prices have generally stayed below half of their earlier highs, even though worldwide **demand** continues to grow moderately. OPEC goes on, but it has not been able to maintain anything like the kind of control it had on the market in the 1970s and early 1980s.

mktg **oper**

organizational buying   Purchasing by a company or other group that is part of the **industrial market**—that is everyone except the final consumer.

Since organizational buying involves high volumes and potentially large profits, the stakes are big for marketers. Those selling to organizations typically spend a lot of time identifying potential customers. Service is important, before and after the sale. If you are selling factory equipment, for example, you will provide specifications and technical advice before the sale, work almost frantically to ensure on-time delivery, and follow with continuing support during the start-up period.

Industrial marketers rely heavily on personal selling, often backed by a team supplying technical support. Industrial purchases are usually expensive and tailored to exact specifications. So buyers want to deal with people they trust to help with any problems and to negotiate fairly in any disputes. The smart marketer with an eye on repeat sales will do all he or she can to win and retain the customer's trust.

See also **behavioral response**, **market**, **marketing orientation**, **marketing plan**, and **market segmentation**.

mgmt

organizational commitment   Extent to which a worker identifies with the employer and its goals.

See also **job satisfaction**.

mgmt

organizational environment Those things that affect how a company is organized.

Two dimensions for evaluating the organizational environment are:

---

1 **Static-Dynamic**
Is the environment relatively constant over time, or is there a lot of change?

A manufacturer receiving regular orders and a steady stream of supplies operates in a static environment. It would be dynamic if orders changed often and supplies arrived sporadically.

2 **Simple-Complex**
Are there just a few decisions to make, all similar to each other, or many decisions of various types?

In the manufacturer's plant, the decisions revolve primarily around staffing levels and the length of shifts. We make those decisions based on the orders to fill and the availability of materials. So that is a simple environment. A product development operation, on the other hand, functions in a complex environment. It makes decisions about the size of potential markets, their needs, the design and engineering of new products, what set of attributes they should include, the availability of supplies, the price, and the **marketing** approach.

oper

original equipment manufacturer (OEM) Company that makes its own products with components from another manufacturer.

EXAMPLE | A manufacturer of flight simulators is an OEM that incorporates into its design the computers it buys from another company. Similarly, another OEM making portable electric generators buys the gasoline motors to power the generators from an outside company.

mktg

outdoor advertising Strategically placed ads in the open air that can be observed quickly by consumers.

The term usually refers to billboards but also includes everything from a display card on the trunk of a taxi to a poster in a shop window. These displays are used primarily to reinforce other advertising messages.

oper

outputs What your company produces. Your outputs can be goods or services.

---

organizational environment

t i p | 👍

*Overall, most companies today operate in a dynamic-complex environment. Managers face frequent change and a great deal of uncertainty. This environment calls for **decentralization**.*

outdoor advertising

0

FRAME OF REFERENCE

outdoor advertising

Anyone who has spent time in New York City is familiar with the posters for Broadway shows (and almost anything else) that seem to appear overnight pasted to any surface whose owner is not likely to complain. They tend to cover the many plywood construction walls lining Manhattan's streets. The phantoms who paste them around town are known as snipers. For many years, the sniping industry was cornered by a Lincoln Center stagehand who charged 50 cents per poster and prided himself on his fast, thorough, and surreptitious work.

outsourcing

Quick Facts

One of the big growth industries of the 1990s is the supply of contracting services to business.

oper **mgmt**

outsourcing   (1) Buying parts from outside suppliers for your manufacturing process. This is a common arrangement for computers and other electric appliances like stereos and televisions.

EXAMPLE | MicroAge assembles computer systems in a former warehouse in Tempe, Arizona. Nearly 600 companies supply MicroAge with monitors, motherboards, microprocessors, hard drives, keyboards, modems, and so on. The company moves more than 75 tons of equipment through its configuration center every day, assembling the components into the systems most desired by its customers. Because it outsources all the components, MicroAge has a great deal of flexibility to shift its emphasis to meet changing demand. If customers want more memory and a faster modem, it does not take MicroAge long to change components.

(2) Contracting out for services. Traditionally, companies have used contractors for such things as temporary help in a crunch or to run the headquarters cafeteria. But the phenomenon is growing as companies pare down their payrolls. Many have found that they can handle technical and logistical operations more efficiently by outsourcing them.

EXAMPLE | The nonprofit Shivers Cancer Center in Austin, Texas, in 1995 outsourced its billing, collection, and general accounting to Medaphis Corporation, a national company that specializes in management services to the medical industry. The purpose was to improve efficiency and to allow Shivers to focus its efforts on its primary business—caring for cancer patients and their families. Kash n' Karry Food Stores, based in Tampa, Florida, also outsourced a department that year. It closed its 45-person information services unit and hired GSI Outsourcing Corporation to upgrade and operate its computer functions, including cash-register scanners and systems that handle staffing and accounting.

Even on the home front, with today's two-income families, outsourcing is growing. Families, like businesses, are contracting out for services like child care, housecleaning, and yard work. The **opportunity cost** of doing the work yourself—the wages you would lose—makes outsourcing the efficient alternative.

See also **virtual organization**.

fin

over-the-counter (OTC) stocks   Shares in companies traded outside of organized stock markets like the **New York Stock Exchange (NYSE)** and the **American Stock Exchange (Amex)**.

acct

overhead   Indirect costs of running a business—such as expenses for power, heat, insurance, property taxes, and so on—that cannot be traced directly to an item or service that is sold.

See also **cost accounting**.

acct   **fin**

owner's equity   Item on a **balance sheet** expressing the value of the company's **assets** after **liabilities** are deducted. For a corporation, it is called **shareholders' equity**.

See also **accounting equation**.

over-the-counter stocks

overhead

0

payback period

penetrated market

tip

Companies that successfully penetrate a market and then develop a relationship with customers can expect to increase profitability over time.

fin | **acct**

payback period How long it takes for you to recover your investment in a project.

Although this is a meaningful number, it is not a very good measure of profitability. A project can have a short payback period and low profitability as well.

EXAMPLE | You are considering buying an office building that needs some work. The building and improvements will cost around $500,000. The work will take a year. You believe you could then sell the building, recover your investment, and make a profit of $30,000. So your payback period is a year. If you hold on to the building, though, you believe you could make $80,000 a year in rent. Then your payback period is more than six years. But, in the meantime, you would be making a good return on your money ($80,000 ÷ $500,000 = 16% annual return), and you would still have a building to sell.

See also **rule of 72**.

acct

PBO See **projected benefit obligation**.

mktg

penetrated market Customers who have already bought a product or service.

While in most industries marketers will not concentrate heavily on the penetrated market, they will pursue programs to build loyalty and encourage repeat sales. The frequent-flier programs of major airlines are an example of programs aimed at the penetrated market.

See also **potential market**.

mktg | **strat**

penetration pricing Setting a low price for a new product to build initial demand and capture **market share**.

Marketers use penetration pricing when they believe the extra sales volume will be large enough to balance out the lower **margin**.

EXAMPLE | You are opening a credit union in a new location. You find out what banks in the area are charging for installment loans and price yours at least half a percentage point lower than those of any of them.

See also **penetrated market**, **perceived-value pricing**, **pricing**, and **skimming**.

fin

penny stocks   High-risk stocks that generally sell for less than a dollar a share.

Penny stocks are traded between brokers in **over-the-counter (OTC)** markets. Because these companies typically have erratic results and a small number of shares outstanding, their stock prices can be highly volatile. Denver, Salt Lake City, and Vancouver, British Columbia, have traditionally been hot markets for penny stocks, often involving mining ventures.

See also **float** and **pink sheets**.

mktg

Pension Benefit Guaranty Corporation (PBGC)

Retirement-fund insurer established by the **Employee Retirement Income Security Act (ERISA)**.

See also **pension plans**.

mktg

pension fund   Sum of money set aside by companies, government bodies, unions, or other organizations to meet employee retirement obligations.

Pension funds are a major force in the U.S. capital markets. These **institutional investors** pour billions of dollars into the stock and **bond** markets annually, supporting companies through the purchase of equities and lending money by buying bonds.

See also **pension plans**.

mktg

pension plans   Ways of providing retirement income.

These are regulated for most nongovernment employees in the United States primarily by the **Employee Retirement Income Security Act (ERISA)**, enacted by Congress in 1974 and amended over the years.

There are two broad classifications of pension plans:

1 **Defined Benefit**
   At retirement, the employee gets specified payments based on a formula determined by his or her pay level and length of employment. There is no separate account for each employee, so the company meets its obligations by setting money aside in a pension fund. The government sets minimum funding requirements and requires insurance through the Pension Benefit Guaranty Corporation, established by ERISA. Also, accounting standards require certain disclosures about the funding.

---

penetration pricing

tip |

*If you believe your competitors are likely to drive your price down eventually anyway, consider striking first via penetration pricing. The strategy works particularly well if you have the facilities for **mass production** and can take advantage of **economies of scale**.*

trap |

*You will have to sell a lot more before reaching the **break-even** point and making a profit. And if competitors match your price, you may not be able to raise it later.*

P

performance bond

periodic review inventory system

Quick Facts!

The periodic system is appropriate when the cost of inventory tracking is high and the cost of running out low. Many retailers use this system.

P

---

mktg

performance-based compensation
Management plan that involves giving rewards for performance.

See also **incentive plans**.

fin

performance bond
Guarantee from a third party that one person or organization will meet its obligations to another.

Performance bonds are often required in construction projects, where a contractor will have to buy a surety bond from an insurance company to guarantee its work.

> **EXAMPLE** | You are the general contractor for the construction of a new office building. You require all your subcontractors to post performance bonds. When the plumbing contractor fails to perform the work properly and then goes out of business, you turn to the surety company for the funds you will need to fix it.

Other forms of performance bonds are issued by government agencies, banks, and individuals.

oper

periodic review inventory system
Reordering inventory at specific time intervals rather than as needed. Also called **fixed period review system**.

Under this system, the reorder point is fixed, but the quantity varies according to need. The alternative is to order a set quantity whenever inventories fall to a set level.

> **EXAMPLE** | In a supermarket, most department managers take stock once a week. For each product, they subtract the inventory on hand from the maximum level they should have in the store. That gives them a ballpark figure of what to order. They may add to the figure to cover expected sales in the days before the order arrives.

tech

peripheral
Any hardware device that is connected to a computer, such as a keyboard, monitor, mouse, optical scanner, printer, tape drive, and so on.

fin **acct**

perpetuity
An **annuity** that goes on indefinitely.

mktg

personal communications channels
Forms of one-on-one contact with customers. Sometimes called word of mouth.

Since personal contact gets results in influencing people, marketers will try to understand these channels in the **target markets** for their products.

There are three basic personal communications channels:

1 **Advocate Channels**
A sales staff directly contacting potential customers in a target market. Telemarketing is one example, but advocate channels can include any direct sales contact.

2 **Expert Channels**
Influential individuals with special knowledge about a product. A tennis pro, for example, might recommend a racket as one particularly suited for a student.

3 **Social Channels**
Family, friends, or neighbors suggesting a particular product.

Savvy marketers will try to reach all of these channels and make them work for the company's products.

econ

personal consumption expenditures Total consumer spending.

This classification typically accounts for between 60 and 65 percent of the **gross domestic product (GDP)**.

Personal Consumption (within 1994 GDP)

Gross Domestic Product	**$6,931**	
Personal Consumption	$4,699	
Durable Goods		$581
Nondurable Goods		$1,430
Services		$2,688
Gross Private Domestic Investment	$1,014	
Net Exports of Goods and Services	($96)	
Government Purchases of Goods and Services	$1,315	

Source: *Economic Report of the President*

Personal consumption is the largest component of GDP—68% of total U.S. output in 1994. The government then breaks consumption down into three major categories: durable goods, nondurable goods, and services. Services now make up more than half of the dollar value of U.S. consumption.

employer and then move on, you usually have to start over again in the new company's benefit plans. Of course, the popular **401(k) plans** for retirement offer some portability because they stay with you to administer pretty much as you please. But they cannot usually be rolled into your new employer's plan.

mktg **fin**

positioning   (1) In marketing, fixing an image of a product in a consumer's mind.

See also **product positioning**.

(2) In finance, when a broker buys a security for its own account, not just for trading or immediate resale purposes but to hold as a long-term investment.

mktg

potential market   Everyone who may be interested in a given product or service.

See also **penetrated market** and **served market**.

mktg

power   Ability to influence behavior or events.

Some kinds of power stem from **authority**, which is a right of control that has been given. Your company can give you the authority to reward or punish employees, for example, and that is a form of power. But no one can give you the power to change their behavior. That grows out of your **leadership** ability as much as any authority you may have to reward, punish, and determine working conditions.

Power, of course, can be abused in ways small and large. Subjecting your subordinate to an old, boring family story is a small way; requiring him or her to donate to a political campaign is a large one.

mktg **mgmt**

PR   See **public relations**.

P

FRAME OF

REFERENCE

potential market

Through its marketing research, Wrigley's identified a growing potential market for chewing gum in people who have recently quit smoking or need to refrain at work. Wrigley pitches many of its Wrigley's Spearmint gum ads to this potential market.

mktg

PR Newswire   Electronic means of distributing **press releases**. PR Newswire, which is based in New York but is owned by United News & Media in London, can send news releases to more than 2,500 print and broadcast newsrooms in the United States as well as to international locations. It operates 24 hours a day, seven days a week, and can be accessed by phone, fax, or computer modem.

See also **news release**.

mktg

preference segmentation   Dividing a **market** into distinct parts based on consumer preference.

See also **market segmentation**.

fin

preferred stock   Security that, like **common stock**, shows ownership in a corporation.

Both are forms of **capital stock**. Preferred stockholders, though, have priority over those who own common stock in terms of **dividend** payments and in any liquidation of the company. Dividends on preferred stock are usually paid in fixed amounts; however, **adjustable rate** preferred stock pays a varying amount based on changes in a specified interest rate such as the **prime rate**. Most preferred stock is cumulative, and unpaid dividends that have accumulated from year to year must be paid in full before common stockholders can receive

preferred stock

t r a p

Since preferred stock pays dividends in specified amounts, it seems like a bond paying interest. But dividends, unlike interest, are not tax deductible to the issuing corporation.

On the other hand, because preferred stock dividends are not guaranteed to the investor, a company may ship payments without going into default.

P

Price/Earnings Ratio: Computer Software vs. Steel

```
Hit 1 <PAGE> to view Column Choices
  B A S K E T    C O M P A R I S O N
S P C M S F    S&P COMPUTER SOFTWARE
Price    290.28 -4.39
T T-TICKER,N-NAME
```

Tickers	Today	Price	12 Mo EPS	Price /Earns
S&P COMPUTER SOFTWARE		290.28	6.34	45.80
1) ADSK UQ		22^1_4	1.63	13.65
2) AUD UN		40^1_4	1.52	26.39
3) CEN UN		46	1.54	29.87
4) CA UN		52^7_8	-.03	neg
5) CSC UN		71^1_4	2.57	27.72
6) FDC UN		79^1_8	-.11	neg
7) MSFT UQ		121^3_4	3.43	35.50
8) NOVL UQ		10^3_4	.45	23.89
9) ORCL UQ		38^5_8	.91	42.60
10) SMED UQ		56	1.78	31.46

```
Hit 1 <PAGE> to view Column Choices
  B A S K E T    C O M P A R I S O N
S P S T E L    S&P STEEL
Price    62.03 +.52
T T-TICKER,N-NAME
```

Tickers	Today	Price	12 Mo EPS	Price /Earns
S&P STEEL		62.03	3.79	16.37
1) AS UN		4^1_2	-.24	neg
2) BS UN		10^3_4	.47	22.87
3) IAD UN		18^1_8	1.76	10.30
4) NUE UN		48^5_8	2.80	17.37
5) X UN		26^1_4	2.48	10.58
6) WTHG UQ		19^1_8	1.01	18.94

Source: Bloomberg Financial Markets

Price/Earnings ratios for the companies in the S&P Computer Software index are generally higher than those of companies that make up the S&P Steel index.

price/earnings ratio

trap 👎

Certain industries should be viewed for their long-term potential, but P/E ratios look only to the near term. Companies that are extremely capital-intensive in their early years, such as those involved in cellular communications and cable TV, might best be analyzed according to cash flows rather than P/E ratios.

pricing

EXAMPLE

Toyota and Sharp research how potential buyers will react to various price levels for a proposed new product. Then the companies can design the product so that its costs stay within a range to support the targeted price.

P

TOYOTA

`econ` `mktg`

price elasticity of demand   How demand for a product or service changes in response to a change in price.

See also **elasticity**.

`mktg`

pricing   Process of determining how much to charge consumers in relation to what they will spend for the quality and value involved.

The pricing of a good or service depends on several internal factors—costs and **marketing** strategy, for example—and external factors like competition, **demand**, government regulations, and consumers' value judgments about the product.

Sometimes companies determine price, then plan their product and strategy around it.

Companies like Food Lion, Inc., the huge North Carolina–based supermarket chain, use a strategy called **everyday low pricing (EDLP)**, striving all the time to offer prices lower than those of its competitors. Other companies, either by choice or because of market conditions, zero in on other parts of the **marketing mix**—the product itself, its distribution, and its promotion.

See also **distribution channels**, **penetration pricing**, **perceived-value pricing**, and **skimming**.

primary data

mktg

primary data   Original information you get through direct research.

The term is used in **marketing** for such things as **surveying** and observational research. It differs from **secondary data**, which is obtained from the published work of others.

EXAMPLE | Your company is considering a new product for the scuba-diving market. After gathering secondary data from newsletters, magazines, trade associations, and other organizations, you find that there are more than three million divers in the United States. Since the size of the market is large enough to justify the next step, you start gathering primary data: You rent a list of subscribers to a scuba magazine and mail out a survey to determine the degree of interest in your product. You also conduct a series of **focus groups** among divers to probe deeper for exactly what features they want in your product and how much they would be willing to pay for them.

FRAME OF

REFERENCE

pricing

Marketers of gasoline have a low-margin product amid heavy competition. Pricing decisions are determined largely by **supply** and **demand**, so there is little price difference among major brands. Gasoline marketers put most of their effort into distribution, promotion, and service. They work to maintain an efficient network of refineries, distribution centers, and service stations; to enhance the look and feel of their stations; and to advertise the qualities of the gasolines and the service they offer (like letting you gas up and get out quickly).

P

EXAMPLE | The Stop & Shop supermarket chain carries its many private-label products under the company name to enhance its image as well as boost sales. Exxon, Mobil, and other leading refiners of lubricating oils sell some of their products to chains like Kmart and Wal-Mart for private-label sales.

See also **generic product**.

private placement

Quick Facts!

Unlike public issues, private placements are more prone to have **equity kickers** as an incentive to potential investors. For example, buyers of the 1986 subordinated debt offering for Budget Rent-A-Car received **warrants** representing 15 percent of the company's equity. Less than one year later, those warrants—which were exercisable at $1 per share—provided a 250 percent return when Budget sold **common stock** in an **IPO** at $14 per share.

fin

private placement   Sale of unregistered securities, including stocks and **bonds**, directly to an **institutional investor**.

To qualify as a private placement, an offering must be made to "accredited investors," or investors who are financially secure and sophisticated. These investors must agree to hold the securities for a prescribed period. Securities sold in a private placement do not trade and are usually illiquid.

Private placements do not have to be registered with the **Securities and Exchange Commission (SEC)**, but the investor can later register and sell the securities in a **secondary offering**.

fin

privately held company   A company that does not have publicly traded stock.

It can be a corporation, partnership, **limited partnership**, **joint venture**, proprietorship, or **limited liability corporation**. In the United States, privately held companies are normally not obligated to disclose their **financial statements** publicly. However, if a privately held company has sold **bonds** to the public, it would be required to disclose financial statements.

See also **publicly held company**.

acct

pro forma   In accounting, an unaudited financial statement involving assumptions, usually taking the form of projections.

P

BREAKING NEWS

private placement

Before the 1980s, private placements were often the most important source of financing for non–investment grade companies, many of them young, high-growth companies in need of capital. This was particularly true after security holders were given the right to publicly register securities with the SEC and sell them into the secondary market—a factor that greatly reduced the illiquidity of the market. During the 1980s, private placements became less important to the financing of young companies after the growth in the high-yield bond market gave them better access to capital.

EXAMPLE | American Medical Response, a medical services and transportation company based in Aurora, Colorado, bought a number of ambulance companies during 1994. In its annual report for that year, it included some pro forma data showing what its income would have been for 1994 and previous years with all the companies in place.

oper

producer's risk　　The risk that a producer may reject a good lot of a manufactured item because random sample testing shows a disproportionately large number of defects.

See also **acceptance sampling**.

mktg

product attributes　　Characteristics of a product.

When marketers consider a new product, they concentrate on attracting customers via specific characteristics. These characteristics can be natural to the product or an add-on.

EXAMPLE | Beer makers constantly advertise their products based on specific attributes. Brewers of light beer gear their commercials to women and the health-conscious market, and tout the number of calories in their brands. Drug companies market pain medication based on whether it will give you an upset stomach, or how fast it will relieve a headache.

See also **conjoint analysis** and **product positioning**.

mktg

product concept　　How marketers want consumers to perceive a product. A single product can lead to many product concepts.

EXAMPLE | A city taxi cab company can advertise its service to businessmen as the fastest way to the airport. At the same time, it can also advertise to housewives as safer than the subway and, with door-to-door pickup, more convenient than the bus.

mktg

product differentiation　　Setting a **brand** apart from the competition.

See also **differentiation**.

pro forma

product attributes

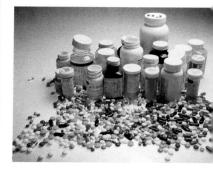

P

product line

tip

Any time you add one product, size up its impact on the sales of your others.

product mix

product positioning

mktg

product line   Company's products that are alike either in their characteristics or the way they are used.

Product lines vary in size from Procter & Gamble's potato crisps line of one, Pringles, on up to hundreds. The size of a product line is often called its depth.

EXAMPLE | Eastman Kodak Company has built **market share** by increasing the depth of its slide-projector product line, offering models with varying levels of complexity and price.

Companies with a good distribution system, in particular, may enhance profits by adding new product lines.

See also **product mix**.

acct

product-line costing   Accounting method that apportions all costs to specific lines or business segments.

See also **activity-based costing (ABC)**.

mktg

product mix   All the products offered by a particular company.

If a product mix includes many **product lines**, it is referred to as wide, or broad. If it contains only a few, it is considered narrow, or limited. The number of product lines is called the variety, while the depth within product lines is called the assortment. In the past two decades, major companies have tended toward diversifying their product mix by acquiring companies in different fields.

EXAMPLE | General Mills offers consumers a broad product mix organized into five major areas: ready-to-eat cereals, desserts and baking mixes, snack products, dinner and side dish products, and yogurt.

mktg

product positioning   Image of a product that the company wishes to fix in the consumer's mind.

Marketers use various techniques to position their products in a positive fashion for the **target market**.

EXAMPLE | Celestial Seasonings positions its teas as being made from rare and natural ingredients. It places extraordinary emphasis on the packaging of its products, adorning the boxes with scenes painted by specially commissioned artists. It also gives exotic names like Bengal Spice to its various blends. All of this product positioning gives Celestial Seasonings a cachet that its competitors find hard to match.

Product positioning is considered the most important element of the marketing strategy, because once an image is implanted in the consumer's mind, it is extremely difficult to reposition the product. Sometimes, though, unforeseen developments make repositioning necessary.

EXAMPLE | With women having fewer children, Johnson & Johnson had to reposition its baby shampoo as a product that women could use to maintain the softness of their hair. "If it's soft enough for your baby, it's soft enough for you!" women were told.

See also **product attributes**.

production function   The process that turns an **input** into an **output**—the recipe for making a good or service.

When a company increases one input but not another, it eventually encounters the law of diminishing returns, which states that when more of one input (such as labor) is used while the usage of at least one other input (such as equipment or space) remains fixed, output will expand but by successively smaller increments. Eventually, output may even cease to expand, despite continued increases in the use of the one factor.

EXAMPLE | A restaurant's popularity exceeds management's expectations. Management knows that, in the short run, all it can do is hire more servers and cooks; the restaurant's square footage can be increased only in the longer run. As more and more workers are hired, more and more patrons are indeed served. However, catering to more patrons in this way becomes successively more difficult. Space becomes the severely limiting factor. At some point, the servers may even have negative marginal **productivity**—that is, they begin to get in each other's way, making further expansions in employment self-defeating.

If a company increases all inputs simultaneously, it may get a proportionate return, or one disproportionately larger or smaller than the increase in input.

See also **economies of scale**.

productivity   Ratio of **output** to **input**, most commonly the output per worker hour.

output per worker hour = labor productivity

Other types of productivity are defined similarly; for example, energy productivity equals output divided by kilowatt hours.

production function

Production only fills a void that it has itself created.

—John Kenneth Galbraith,
The Affluent Society, 1958

productivity

Quick Facts!

Economists look at multifactor productivity on a nationwide and worldwide basis. Overall, while labor productivity is improving along with technological advancements, those advancements cost money. Multifactor productivity has not been improving.

P

One can also measure **multifactor productivity** in cases in which more than one type of input (say, labor and capital) is used. And when that involves different units of measurement (like labor hours and machines), it is examined in terms of percentage increases.

productivity

EXAMPLE

Ten workers assemble a total of 400 computers from components in an eight-hour day. There are 80 (10 workers x 8 hours) worker hours in a day. So the productivity is five units per hour (400 ÷ 80 = 5).

EXAMPLE | A farmer, William Brown, works 1,000 hours to produce 1,000 bushels of wheat (one bushel per hour). By upgrading his equipment, he produces 2,000 bushels with the same amount of labor (two bushels per hour). His labor productivity has improved by 100 percent.

The new equipment, though, increased his capital investment from $100,000 to $150,000, so capital productivity went from 0.01 (1,000 bushels ÷ $100,000 = 0.01) to 0.0133 (2,000 bushels ÷ $150,000 = 0.0133). That is a 33 percent improvement.

To arrive at multifactor productivity, Brown will look at both percentage improvements. If he assigns equal weight to his labor and his capital investment, the improvement in multifactor productivity will be an average of the two.

$$(100\% + 33\%) \div 2 = 66.5\%$$

Farmer Brown's improvement in multifactor productivity is 66.5 percent.

Profit Impact of Market Strategies

Quick Facts!

A company might use a PIMS database to answer questions such as:

- What is the "normal" profit level for a mail-order company after three years of business?

- What is a good benchmark for advertising/ revenue ratio?

- What has happened to other companies our size who've expanded into the international market?

Total factor productivity refers to those cases in which all inputs are used—labor, equipment, raw materials, and electricity.

In calculating multifactor and total factor productivity, all usages might also be converted to a common factor such as dollars, rather than using an arbitrary weighting, with market prices used to value inputs and outputs. In that case, the output measured in dollars would be divided by the dollar cost of all input factors being considered.

See also **efficiency**.

acct **fin**

profit and loss statement Shows how a company arrived at its bottom line for a specific **accounting period**.

See also **income statement**.

mktg

profit center Company entity with independent operating and financial reporting status.

See also **management control systems**.

strat **mktg** **mgmt**

Profit Impact of Market Strategies (PIMS) A **database** of information supplied by thousands of business units for use in **benchmarking**.

The PIMS database was originally developed in the early 1970s by Sidney Schoeffler and Robert D. Buzzell as part of an ongoing research project at the Marketing Science Institute. The database includes statistics on business performance as related to a company's structural and strategic characteristics, like **market share**, **research** and **development** spending, **advertising** costs, breadth of **product line**, quality, and **vertical integration**.

Among the uses for PIMS is to predict the profit impact of strategy changes or to assess how a company stacks up. PIMS found that the most important single factor in a company's performance was the quality of its goods and services as compared with that of the competition's.

profit margin
Net earnings divided by revenues. Also called **net profit margin** or **return on sales**.

EXAMPLE | In the earnings statement in Procter & Gamble's 1994 annual report, net sales are $30.3 billion, with net income of $2.2 billion.

$2.2 billion ÷ $30.3 billion = 0.073, or 7.3%

Procter & Gamble's profit margin is 7.3 percent.

Some analysts calculate a **gross profit margin**. That is **gross profit** divided by net sales. Gross profit is net sales minus cost of goods sold. For Procter & Gamble in 1994, cost of goods sold was $17.4 billion, so gross profit was $12.9 billion ($30.3 billion – $17.4 billion). Here is the gross profit ratio for P&G in 1994:

$12.9 billion ÷ $30.3 billion = 0.426, or 42.6%

profit sharing
A way to treat employees like financial partners by giving them a portion of the company's profits.

Profit sharing is used to provide an incentive for employees by directly tying the firm's success to their own. Often the percentage of profit is based not only on salary but on meeting individual targets—for example, keeping expenses down, building up the client base, or cutting the error rate in production.

Some profit-sharing plans give employees cash in the current year, while others pay out through retirement plans. In both cases, the amount offered is deductible by the employer—just like any other kind of compensation. But for retirement plans, the deduction is limited to 15 percent of payroll.

program evaluation and review technique (PERT)
A scheduling tool based on the relationships among the different phases of a complex project.

This analysis should provide an estimate of the time spent on each step of the project, which schedulers can then use to assess project deadlines.

---

profit margin

profit sharing

t i p |

Make sure you communicate completely with all employees so they can track the company's progress and know what they need to do to earn any bonus.

t r a p |

If the profit-sharing arrangement is seen as arbitrary, any goodwill generated will be fleeting.

Entrepreneurial companies should avoid elaborate profit-sharing programs in their early days. Follow the Kiss principle—keep it simple, stupid.

—Martha Priddy Patterson, director of employee benefits policy for KPMG

P

PERT is similar to the **critical path method (CPM)** for project control. In CPM, the most important sequential activities are charted as the critical path. Other activities then form subprojects, which may have critical paths of their own.

program evaluation and review technique

tip |

The success of these project management tools depends on honest and timely reporting of the current status of activities and obstacles to timely and successful completion. With good data, powerful computers and project management software permit the close tracking of even the most complicated projects.

acct

projected benefit obligation (PBO)
The **present value** of a company's future pension obligations, with assumptions about employees' future service and pay levels factored in.

See also **accumulated benefit obligation (ABO)**.

fin

promissory note
Legal document a borrower signs giving the loan principal, the **interest rate**, and the time and place for payments.

By borrowing money from a bank via promissory notes and repaying it, a company can establish a track record and eventually obtain a line of credit. Promissory notes, which may be short or long term, also give a company a way of dealing with an overdue **account**. Getting the customer to sign a promissory note means a formal acknowledgment of the debt and a firm commitment to a schedule of payment.

fin

prospectus
(1) Formal written document giving the facts about a new offering of securities.

In the prospectus, a company issuing stocks or **bonds** describes in detail what it plans to do with the money it is raising. It must lay out all the information an investor needs to make a decision before buying the securities. In a public offering, the prospectus is really part of the **S-1 filing**, or **registration statement**, the company must make with the **Securities and Exchange Commission (SEC)** to offer a security in interstate commerce.

A prospectus should include, among other things, the financial details of the offering at hand, as well as the financial standing and history of the company. Also included should be a discussion of the company's business, the use of proceeds of the offering, information about management, and any pending litigation or liabilities.

Ordinarily, after the filing with the SEC, the company must wait at least 20 days before offering the securities for sale (although this waiting period may vary depending on whether the SEC opts for a full review). During that time, a tentative preliminary prospectus can be distributed without pricing information or the issue date. That prospectus, which can be changed, is called a **red herring**, since portions are printed in red ink. Once the SEC has approved the registration statement, the full final prospectus is released to potential investors. After the SEC approval and the pricing of the offering by the underwriters and the issuing company, the securities are confirmed with the buyers or investors. When the entire issue has been sold out, it is "free to trade" in the open market.

P

(2) A prospectus may also be issued by a mutual fund, with information about its products and the overall company, to attract potential investors.

See also **underwriting** and **underwriting syndicate**.

PROSPECTUS

❶ 1,500,000 Shares

❷ Class A Common Stock

Of the 1,500,000 shares of Class A Common Stock offered hereby, 1,360,000 shares are being sold by Premiere Radio Networks, Inc. (the "Company") and 140,000 shares are being sold by the Selling Stockholders. See "Principal and Selling Stockholders." The Company will not receive any proceeds from the sale of shares by the Selling Stockholders. The Class A Common Stock is identical to, and votes together with, the Company's outstanding Common Stock, except each share of Class A Common Stock is entitled to one-tenth of a vote and each share of the Common Stock is entitled to one vote on each matter to be voted upon. See "Description of Capital Stock." The Company's Board of Directors has approved an amendment to the Company's Certificate of Incorporation, subject to stockholder approval, to provide that each share of Common Stock shall be entitled to ten votes per share and each share of Class A Common Stock shall be entitled to one vote per share, that each share of the Common Stock shall be convertible into one share of Class A Common Stock at the option of the holder at any time and that the Company may not treat the Common Stock and Class A Common Stock differently (except for voting rights) in any merger, reorganization, recapitalization or similar transaction or support a tender offer which attempts to do so and to increase the number of authorized shares of Common Stock and Class A Common Stock. Prior to this offering, there has been no public market for the Class A Common Stock. The public offering price has been determined with reference to the market price for the Common Stock. Immediately after this offering, the Company intends to declare a one-for-two stock dividend (the "Class A Dividend") to all holders of Common Stock and Class A Common Stock, payable 60 days after the date hereof in shares of Class A Common Stock. The Class A Dividend will be accounted for as a stock split. See "Underwriting."

The Class A Common Stock has been approved for quotation on the Nasdaq National Market ("NNM") under the trading symbol "PRNIA". The Common Stock of the Company is currently traded on the NNM under the trading symbol "PRNI". On January 25, 1996, the last sale price of the Common Stock as reported by the NNM was $18.25 **❹** per share.

See "Risk Factors" beginning on page 7 for a discussion of certain factors that should be considered by prospective purchasers of the Class A Common Stock.

THESE SECURITIES HAVE NOT BEEN APPROVED OR DISAPPROVED BY THE SECURITIES AND EXCHANGE COMMISSION OR ANY STATE SECURITIES COMMISSION NOR HAS THE SECURITIES AND EXCHANGE COMMISSION OR ANY STATE SECURITIES COMMISSION PASSED UPON THE ACCURACY OR ADEQUACY OF THIS PROSPECTUS. ANY REPRESENTATION TO THE CONTRARY IS A CRIMINAL OFFENSE.

	Price to Public	Underwriting Discount(1)	Proceeds to Company(2)	Proceeds to Selling Stockholders
Per Share........ ❺	$18.25	$1.095	$17.155	$17.155
Total (3)	$27,375,000	$1,642,500	$23,330,800	$2,401,700

(1) See "Underwriting" for information concerning indemnification of the Underwriters and other information.
(2) Before deducting expenses of the offering estimated at $719,000 payable by the Company.
(3) The Company and the Selling Stockholders have granted the Underwriters an option, exercisable within 30 ❻ days of the date hereof, to purchase up to 225,000 additional shares of Class A Common Stock for the purpose of covering over-allotments, if any. The first 72,000 shares subject to the exercise of such option shall be sold by certain of the Selling Stockholders, and the remaining shares subject to such exercise shall be sold by the Company. If the Underwriters exercise such option in full, the total Price to Public, Underwriting Discount, Proceeds to Company and Proceeds to Selling Stockholders will be $31,481,250, $1,888,875, $25,955,515 and $3,636,860, respectively. See "Underwriting."

The shares of Class A Common Stock are offered by the Underwriters when, as and if delivered to and accepted by them, subject to their right to withdraw, cancel or reject orders in whole or in part and subject to certain other conditions. It is expected that delivery of certificates representing the shares of Class A Common Stock will be made against payment on or about January 31, 1996 at the office of Oppenheimer & Co., Inc., Oppenheimer Tower, World Financial Center, New York, New York 10281.

Oppenheimer & Co., Inc.

Montgomery Securities

Dabney/Resnick, Inc.

The date of this Prospectus is January 25, 1996

---

tech

protocol   Procedure for starting, maintaining, and ending data connections.

Protocols define the precise methods of data exchange, including means of system control, formats, patterns of bits and data rates, and timing of signals.

---

prospectus

What should an investor look for in a prospectus? Remember that a prospectus is actually a legal document rather than a selling document. Some important items in this prospectus for a Premiere Radio Networks stock issuance include:

❶ Number of Shares
1.5 million.

❷ Class of Stock
Class "A" in this case (many companies have more than one class).

❸ Stock Exchange
The shares will trade on the Nasdaq.

❹ Stock Symbol
Ticker "PRNI."

❺ Share Price
The selling price of the shares is $18.25, yielding total proceeds of $27.375 million (1.5 million x $18.25). The underwriters' cut (listed at bottom)—in this case, $1.095 on each share, or $1.643 million. That leaves the company and selling shareholders with combined net proceeds of $23.33 million.

❻ Extra Issuance Option
Also known as the "greenshoe" clause. Most deals have an option to expand if demand calls for it, typically by 15 percent (225,000 shares in this case).

P

prototype

Car manufacturers may develop prototypes of new models they plan to produce in the future.

proxy statement

tip

The proxy statement vote is the one place where shareholders of large companies can formally register their opinions on important issues.

---

oper

prototype   Model or intermediate version of a product used during the testing process.

Traditionally, prototypes have included clay models, scaled-down versions of the final product, and full-size working models. Today, computer simulations have added a whole new dimension to the creation of prototypes. Through computer-aided design (CAD), a prototype of a final product or of any of its components can be designed faster and cheaper than ever before.

fin

proxy card   Shareholders use it to cast their votes on directors and other resolutions without attending the **annual meeting**.

See also **proxy statement**.

fin

proxy statement   A document sent to shareholders before a corporation's **annual meeting**.

The proxy statement accompanies a proxy card, where shareholders can mark their votes on issues to be decided at the meeting. The **Securities and Exchange Commission (SEC)** sets the rules for (1) what information must be in the proxy statement to help shareholders decide how to vote and (2) when the statements must be sent out.

Companies send the proxy material to shareholders of record, those people and institutions that hold stock in their own names. Financial institutions like brokerage houses that hold stock for others normally send out the proxy materials for a fee paid by the corporation.

A typical proxy statement includes:

▶ A letter of invitation from the board chairman and a notice from the secretary with details of the annual meeting.

▶ Information on the election of directors, their compensation, their committee assignments, brief biographical material, and a small photo of each.

▶ Disclosure of each director's stock ownership.

▶ Other issues proposed by management for a vote. These often include ratification of the independent auditors and approval of special compensation arrangements, like bonus plans for the top brass.

▶ Resolutions proposed by shareholders and opposed by the board. These usually involve social responsibility, like adopting a code for environmental performance, or corporate governance, like calls for **cumulative voting** or **staggered terms**.

P

▶ Data on compensation of the highest-paid executives and how it is determined.

▶ A graph depicting the common stock's performance.

▶ A supplement with the full text of any compensation plans being voted on.

See also **annual report** and **executive compensation**.

YOUR VOTE IS VERY IMPORTANT, REGARDLESS OF THE NUMBER OF SHARES THAT YOU OWN. PLEASE READ THE ATTACHED PROXY STATEMENT CAREFULLY, AND COMPLETE, SIGN AND DATE THE ENCLOSED PROXY CARD(S) AND PROMPTLY RETURN SUCH CARD(S) IN THE ENCLOSED ENVELOPE WHICH REQUIRES NO POSTAGE IF MAILED IN THE UNITED STATES.

PROXY STATEMENT
FOR THE ANNUAL MEETING OF STOCKHOLDERS TO BE HELD ON AUGUST 13, 1996
INTRODUCTION

The enclosed proxy ("Proxy") is solicited on behalf of the Board of Directors of Premiere Radio Networks, Inc., a Delaware corporation (the "Company"), for use at the Annual Meeting of Stockholders to be held on August 13, 1996 (the "Annual Meeting") or at any adjournment or adjournments thereof. The Annual Meeting will be held at 10:00 a.m., Los Angeles time, at the offices of Ernst & Young LLP, 1999 Avenue of the Stars, Suite 2100, Los Angeles, California 90067. These proxy solicitation materials were mailed on or about July 26, 1996, to all stockholders entitled to vote at the Annual Meeting.

Voting Rights and Voting of Proxies

The specific proposals to be considered and acted upon at the Annual Meeting are summarized in the accompanying Notice of Annual Meeting of Stockholders and are described in more detail in this Proxy Statement. On July 25, 1996, the record date for determination of stockholders entitled to notice of and to vote at the Annual Meeting, 3,533,100 shares of the Company's Common Stock, $0.01 par value per share (the "Common Stock"), and 4,013,273 shares of the Company's Class A Common Stock, $0.01 par value per share (the "Class A Common Stock"), were issued and outstanding. The presence, in person or by proxy, of the holders of a majority of the voting power of outstanding shares of the Company's Common Stock and Class A Common Stock constitutes a quorum for the transaction of business at the Annual Meeting. Each stockholder is entitled to one vote for each share of Common Stock and one-tenth of a vote for each share of Class A Common Stock held by such stockholder on July 25, 1996. The proxy card will be voted in the manner directed by the stockholder. If no instructions are marked on the proxy card, the shares represented thereby will be voted FOR each of the nominated directors and FOR each of proposals 2, 3, 4 and 5. Although management does not know of any other matters to be acted upon at the Annual Meeting, shares represented by valid proxies will be voted by the persons named on the proxy card in accordance with their best judgment with respect to any other matter(s) that may properly come before the Annual Meeting. As of the record date, directors and executive officers of the Company had the power to vote approximately 61.1% of the Common Stock and 26.9% of the Class A Common Stock, representing a combined voting power of 57.6%. All of the directors and executive officers have expressed the intent to vote in favor of all the proposals described below and, accordingly, the adoption of such proposals by stockholders at the Annual Meeting is assured.

Approval of the proposed amendment to the Company's Certificate of Incorporation will require the affirmative vote of a majority of the combined voting power of shares of the Common Stock and Class A Common Stock entitled to vote on such matter. Accordingly, abstentions and broker nonvotes will have the effect of a vote "AGAINST" such proposal. All other proposals will require the affirmative vote of a majority of the combined voting power of shares of the Common Stock and Class A Common stock represented at the Annual Meeting and entitled to vote on such matters. Abstentions as to such proposals will have the effect of a vote "AGAINST" such proposals and against any nominee for director. Broker nonvotes with respect to such proposals will not be counted for purposes of determining the number of shares represented and entitled to vote at the meeting, and will not represent a vote either "FOR" or "AGAINST" such proposals or any nominee for director, Accordingly, broker nonvotes as to these proposals will not have any effect on their passage or failure to pass.

Revocability of Proxies

You may revoke or change your Proxy at any time before the Annual Meeting by filing with the Secretary of the Company, at its principal executive offices, a notice of revocation or another signed Proxy with a later date, You may also revoke your Proxy by attending the Annual Meeting and voting in person (in which case your proxy shall be revoked automatically).

---

public domain

---

psychographic segmentation   Dividing a **market** according to consumers' preferences, values, and lifestyles.

See also **market segmentation**.

---

public domain   When literary, artistic, or musical work can be used by anyone and is not protected by **copyright**.

P

mktg   mgmt

public relations (PR)   Activities designed to build a positive image of a company or an individual.

public relations

tip

Designing the message and using public relations as the vehicle to disseminate information provides more credibility than advertising a product or service does.

trap

Despite your best efforts, you cannot be sure the media will convey your story or tell it the way you want it told. And it is a lot easier to measure your results with **advertising**.

PR departments usually focus on the company's overall image and other broad matters rather than promoting individual products, which falls to the **marketing** department. PR also plays an important role in crisis management.

PR pros talk about **publics**, tailoring their activities to the individual groups (publics) they are trying to reach. Examples of a company's publics are customers, potential customers, shareholders, potential shareholders, employees, potential employees, suppliers, government regulators, business journalists, and **opinion leaders**. PR may involve some **image** or **advocacy advertising** or an ad to promote an event, but much public relations is conducted in forums that are not bought—through press releases, speeches, interviews with print and broadcast media, and so on. When PR campaigns deal with products, it is often to counter negative images.

PR can be particularly important when a company is embroiled in a crisis. The firm's reaction, which wags like to call "damage control," can greatly affect its future.

EXAMPLE | In the 1989 Exxon Valdez oil spill in the Puget Sound, Exxon seemed to get off to a slow start in admitting its mistake to the public, and its image suffered for several years.

A classic example of successful crisis management was the handling of the Three Mile Island crisis in 1979, during which the Pennsylvania governor organized a crisis management team to manage the informational flow and to communicate with the public. The team was later credited with keeping the situation from becoming panicked.

FRAME OF

REFERENCE

P

public relations

In 1988, Upjohn introduced Rogaine, which regrows hair in people with hair loss. Within a couple of years, a lot of news articles criticized its high cost and low rate of success. With the help of the PR agency Manning Selvage & Lee, Upjohn began a campaign to enhance Rogaine's image.

Surveys showed that users who did have success with Rogaine were pleased with it. So Upjohn created the Rogaine Recognition Program for Personal Achievement. Using questionnaires and follow-up interviews, the company identified happy, hairy customers in each of 19 selected markets who were also successful in their personal or professional lives. Those individuals were then booked for extensive media interviews in their areas. Their enthusiasm for the product came across in the interviews and influenced others to try it.

FRAME OF REFERENCE

pull promotional strategy

Until recent years, the prescription drug industry directed virtually all of its promotional efforts at doctors and druggists, the two groups that make most of the decisions about which medication you will take. But in the 1990s, that pattern began to change, in part because patients seemed to grow more vocal about their medical care. Companies are advertising their prescription drugs directly to consumers who want help fighting things like allergy symptoms, seasickness, and the craving for a cigarette.

---

mktg

public service announcement   Advertisement aired free of charge on broadcast media to promote a public interest.

See also **Advertising Council, Inc. (ACI)**.

fin

publicly held company   Corporation whose common shares are traded on a public exchange.

Publicly held companies are subject to reporting requirements from regulatory agencies such as the **Securities and Exchange Commission (SEC)**. They must reveal detailed information about their business, finances, and operations.

See also **privately held company**.

mktg   **mgmt**

publics   Tailoring **public relations (PR)** activities to individual groups.

mktg

pull promotional strategy   Aiming a product's **marketing** approach right at the end user.

The idea is that the demand created among customers will pull the product from the **distribution channel**. In the contrasting approach, **push promotional strategy**, marketers focus their efforts on another level of the distribution channel, such as **retailers**, who then push the product. Most marketing efforts combine both strategies, but consumer-oriented companies like McDonald's and Procter & Gamble spend most heavily on the pull approach.

mktg

purchase-decision process   Steps a buyer goes through before and after a purchase.

---

public relations

In its marketing support function, public relations is used to achieve a number of objectives. The most important of these is to raise awareness, to inform and educate, to gain understanding, to build trust, to make friends, to give people reasons (and in some cases permission) to buy, and finally to create a climate of consumer acceptance.

—Thomas L. Harris, Thomas L. Harris & Company

pull promotional strategy

tip

The pull marketing strategy works best for easily differentiated products, inexpensive items, and those that appeal to a mass market.

P

purchase-decision process

P

The steps in the purchase-decision process include:

► Need recognition

► Information search

► Weighing alternatives

► Actual purchase decision

► After-purchase behavior

Since need recognition is the first step for the buyer, the marketer may start by identifying a need to solve a problem and the things that trigger the potential consumer's recognition of it. But all needs are not created equal, and the decision-making processes are different for **high-involvement products** and **low-involvement products**.

High-involvement products—like a new car or house—are most important to buyers and hold the most risk to budget, health, and other values if chosen unwisely. So in weighing alternatives and making the decision, buyers tend to do a lot of their own research. They may come prepared with detailed questions about the differences, for example, between a Plymouth Voyager, a Dodge Caravan, and a Ford Aerostar—three closely related car models with slightly different pricing. Marketers of high-involvement items need detailed and logical arguments to get people to buy their product instead of a competitor's.

Consumer decisions on low-involvement products like soap or hosiery involve much less research. Purchasers of these items gather data randomly and buy out of habit. Repetitive, attention-grabbing TV commercials are a good medium for reaching these customers. So are free samples and discount coupons.

In the final stage of the purchase-decision process, buyers evaluate the product on the basis of how well it met their expectations.

oper　**mktg**

purchasing　Department in a manufacturing company concerned with getting the goods and services needed to support production.

Purchasing employees need negotiating skills plus the stamina to follow up on things like timely delivery and quality standards. The field has grown to be highly specialized; purchasing managers need to be aware of advances in technology in the supplier community. A large and diversified company will have purchasing specialists for each part of the company.

EXAMPLE | A large chemical company may have one specialist who buys pipelines and tank trucks for transporting hazardous materials, another specialist who handles negotiations for processing units, and a third who buys chemical feedstocks and catalysts.

mktg

push promotional strategy

Aiming a product's **marketing** approach at a level of the **distribution channel** other than ultimate consumers.

With this strategy, the manufacturer concentrates on, say, retailers, who then push the product along. The contrasting approach is **pull promotional strategy**, where marketers focus their efforts on the final consumers, who then pull the product from its distribution channel. Of course, most marketing efforts combine both strategies.

fin

put option

Contract that gives the holder the right to sell an asset at a particular price before a certain date. Buyers of these are betting that the value of the underlying asset will fall.

See also **derivatives**.

push promotional strategy

tip

The push marketing strategy works best for durable goods, expensive items, and products with limited markets.

FRAME OF

REFERENCE

push promotional strategy

Sony Music Entertainment might create a music video and subsidize a road tour by the artist to reach the customers for a new CD. But the company will also advertise in publications read by music retailers and offer to pick up some of the retailers' costs for advertising featuring the CD. Publishers of books and computer software use a heavy dose of the push strategy. With thousands of books and programs on the market, the publishers compete hot and heavy for display space on the retailers' shelves, where most of the final buying decisions are made.

The push strategy is common also when the end user needs a lot of continuing support. A big manufacturer of pagers, like Motorola, for example, will focus its attention on paging companies, like PageNet, which then sell or rent the devices to end users.

P

Petroleum

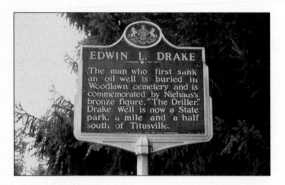

Part of the conventional wisdom regarding the petroleum industry is that prices rise and fall in relation to the arrival of new supplies to market. This is to say, when new discoveries are made, prices fall due to oversupply. When they fail to appear, prices rise. The petroleum industry has been market driven in the sense that here, more than in most fields, demand stimulates the search for new supplies and substitutes.

It was this way from the start. During the colonial period most Americans illuminated their homes with candles made of animal wax, while the wealthy had lamps that burned whale oil. The kerosene lamp, invented in the early 1850s, enabled many more Americans to use lamps. Initially, the kerosene was produced from the reduction of coal.

Seeking an even less expensive source, some innovators hit on petroleum, which in this period seeped from the ground and previously had been used primarily for lubricants and medicines. The demand for petroleum impelled Edwin Drake, an unemployed railroad conductor, to look for a less expensive source. Knowing that oil came from under the ground, Drake started digging near a spring of ground oil in Titusville, Pennsylvania, and on August 27, 1859, struck oil, which had to be pumped out of the ground. Others joined him in the area, and consequently the nation's growing need for kerosene was satisfied by petroleum.

Petroleum exploration and drilling were a boom-and-bust business. At first petroleum fetched $20 a barrel, but as large supplies came to market the price fell to 10 cents by 1861. This price was unattractive, so the drillers left, shortages developed, and the price was back to $7 in 1886, only to fall below $3 in 1879 when exploration resumed. John D. Rockefeller, who had been in the commission-store business, decided to enter the industry as a refiner.

Others could find the petroleum—worthless until refined—so they had to sell to individuals like Rockefeller, who in turn would market the kerosene to customers. After forming several companies, Rockefeller ultimately organized Standard Oil of Ohio in 1870, which soon became the largest petroleum enterprise in the world.

Standard had foreign competitors. The Nobel brothers of Sweden—Robert, Ludwig, and Alfred—developed Russia's Baku fields in the 1870s. Britain's Shell Transport & Trading was in Russia, too, marketing its product in the Far East. By 1888, America's share of world oil production was down to 53 percent because of foreign competition.

Standard Oil had domestic competition as well, but more important were political opponents. Reformers complained of its tactics in gobbling up or destroying rivals, and warrants for the arrest of Standard officers were outstanding in several states, including Texas.

The first American gusher came in at Spindletop near Beaumont, Texas, in 1901, leading to the formation of other companies, such as Gulf and the Texas Company (now Texaco), and the enrichment of some existing companies, including Sun. Shell T&T entered the lists, organizing an American Shell concern.

The Spindletop discovery was followed by additional finds in Texas, Louisiana, and other parts of the country. Within a few years, the California and the midcontinent oil fields far surpassed those in the East in production.

Contributing Writer: Robert Sobel
Lawrence Stessin Distinguished Professor
of Business History, Hofstra University

All of these finds came at the dawn of the automobile age and the arrival of electrification. Kerosene usage declined as demand for gasoline expanded rapidly. Refiners now attempted to squeeze every drop of gasoline possible from oil and downplayed kerosene as petroleum became one of the most important building blocks of industrial society.

In 1909 Standard Oil was dissolved under provisions of the antitrust laws, and out of the company came Standard Oil of New Jersey (today's Exxon), Standard Oil of New York (the ancestor of Socony Mobil, which later became Mobil), Standard Oil of California (or Socal, today's Chevron), and Standard Oil of Indiana (Amoco), along with more than 20 other companies. Competition within the industry intensified.

With demand increasing, new fields came online regularly in the first half of the 20th century. Mexico and then Venezuela proved to have large reserves, but the biggest finds were in the Middle East. In 1908, a major discovery was made in what we know today as Iran. That find resulted in the formation of Anglo-Persian Oil, the forerunner of British Petroleum. Another find occurred in Iraq, then under the control of the Ottoman Empire. It led to the organization of Turkish Petroleum, later taken over by Royal Dutch-Shell.

In 1921 the director of the U.S. Geological Survey declared that American oil reserves were declining rapidly, the first in a long line of such pronouncements. This led to the creation of the Federal Oil Conservation Board, which encouraged higher prices by restricting domestic output. American firms began to look overseas for oil.

In 1928 the leaders of SONJ, Royal Dutch-Shell, and Anglo-Persian met in Scotland to divide the world's oil markets (excluding the United States and the U.S.S.R.) into what was the first global oil cartel. But the other companies also moved ahead. Socal went into Bahrain and, with Texaco, into Saudi Arabia in the Caltex venture, which later became Arab-American Oil (Aramco). Later SONJ and Socony joined the consortium, which had so much oil no single company could handle it. Gulf, along with other firms, formed a partnership with Anglo-Iranian in Kuwait.

By the end of World War II the industry was dominated by the "seven sisters"—SONJ, Socony, Socal, Gulf, Texaco, British Petroleum, and Royal Dutch-Shell. Even though there was abundant oil, there was talk of shortages. In 1952 the Paley Commission forecasted a decline in American reserves and large-scale shortages by the 1970s. While this prediction appears prescient today, it also was before the significant Middle East discoveries, the Alaska finds, and North Sea oil.

Sporadically, those countries in which petroleum was found made increased financial demands on the American, British, and Dutch companies. Mexico went so far as to nationalize its holdings. Venezuela asked for better financial arrangements from the producers after 1935, and there and elsewhere the seven sisters were obliged to make higher royalty payments. When Iran's Mohammed Mossadegh attempted to nationalize that country's industry, he was overthrown by a CIA-managed coup in 1953 and succeeded by the Shah, who negotiated higher royalties.

The new Iranian deal inspired the creation of the Organization of Petroleum Exporting Countries (OPEC) in 1960. At first, OPEC had little power. This changed in 1971, when the industry was turned upside down.

In 1971 President Nixon divorced the dollar from gold, and it immediately plunged in relation to foreign currency. Since the OPEC countries sold their oil for dollars, this meant a diminution of those countries' revenues, and they began searching for ways to recoup their losses.

In October 1973, when the Yom Kippur War erupted in the Middle East, a barrel of Arabian light crude cost $3. During the war, OPEC embargoed oil deliveries to the United States in retaliation for its support of Israel and raised its price. By January 1974, a barrel of crude sold for $11.65, and the United States was tumbling into recession. There was a second "oil shock" in 1979, in the wake of cutbacks in production attending the Iranian Revolution. By decade's end, oil was selling in the mid-$30 range. These developments sparked an "energy crisis," which has concerned industrialized countries ever since.

Through it all, commentators spoke of the end of "the century of oil." Fearful the petroleum business would become less attractive, the oil companies attempted to diversify into other areas. In the 1970s Mobil purchased Marcor, the parent of Montgomery Ward and Container Corp. Mining companies seemed an attractive extension of the petroleum business, so Standard of California took over at Amax, Atlantic Richfield purchased Anaconda, and

Standard of Indiana acquired Cyprus Mines. Standard of Ohio capped it off in 1981 with the $1.7 billion purchase of Kennecott. Exxon purchased Reliance Electric, which was thought to have a promising energy-efficient engine in the works, and entered into the office machine industry. Each of these purchases proved disastrous. The companies foundered, and the prices of their stocks declined.

In 1983, the engineering firm of John Herold estimated that the shares of giant petroleum firms were selling for around 40 percent of their net worth. Why seek oil by drilling, which would cost $12 to $15 a barrel and provide little or no profit, when oil might be purchased by taking over a large company at $3 or $4 a barrel? One joke of the period held the cheapest place to find oil was on the floor of the New York Stock Exchange.

So the petroleum companies did a complete switch, going into the market to purchase other oil-rich firms. The takeovers began traditionally enough, when Shell purchased Belridge Oil for $3.6 billion in 1979. The following year, the Sun Company bought Texas Pacific from Seagram for $2.3 billion. DuPont purchased Continental Oil (now Conoco) for $7.2 billion. U.S. Steel purchased Marathon for $5.9 billion and Texas Oil and Gas for $3 billion. Texaco won Getty Oil for $10.1 billion. British Petroleum acquired Standard of Ohio for $8 billion. These deals were friendly and, despite their great size, conventional.

This friendly tone changed when several individuals, known collectively as "raiders," entered the scene. One of these, T. Boone Pickens, CEO of Mesa Petroleum, became the symbol of the takeover movement. Pickens went after Cities Service, Supron Energy, General American Oil, and Superior Oil, taking large positions and making offers to stockholders, only to be opposed by managements and failing to acquire the companies. But in the process, Pickens made huge profits, since the prices of these stocks invariably would rise. Pickens then went after bigger game—Gulf Oil, Phillips Petroleum, and Unocal, repeating the earlier pattern. The hostile takeover movement peaked in the mid-1980s, leaving an American industry that was more concentrated.

While many accused raiders, such as Pickens, of being ruthless, others considered them to be leaders of the shareholder rights movement that gained strength during that era. The takeovers notified entrenched company managements that underperformance would not be tolerated. Consequently, many of the companies that were bought out went on to become healthier entities.

All the while, the higher oil price stimulated conservation and exploration. The demand for petroleum in the United States fell from 6.9 billion barrels in 1978 to 5.6 billion in 1982. Drilling in non-OPEC areas turned up large reserves in such places as Mexico and Alaska. The North Sea became a major oil field, and Norway and Scotland garnered great wealth from their petroleum reserves.

By then, oil prices were falling. In 1983, OPEC lowered its price, and some members simply ignored the quotas. While the cartel still existed, its power had diminished.

In the 1990s, one no longer heard predictions that the world would run out of petroleum in the near future. Production actually rose in the first half of the decade. Exploration in Africa and Latin America turned up new reserves. The breakup of the Soviet Union promised to revitalize that region's oil industry. American, European, and Japanese capital poured into the former U.S.S.R. to help remedy an inefficient and wasteful situation; long-term investment in Kazakhstan alone will be more than $50 billion by 1997. China, whose oil production is half that of the former U.S.S.R., contains large unexplored regions, and the waters off the Asian mainland are quite promising. Technologies exist to extract petroleum from shale and tars, and will be employed once prices reach economical levels.

The search for alternate fuels, sparked by the oil crisis, also continued. The difficulties of nuclear energy doomed that industry, while coal posed the dual problems of pollution and safety. As a result, interest turned to natural gas, which was used as far back as the early 19th century, when it was extracted from coal. Natural gas often exists in oil wells, but initially the gas was allowed to escape since it was viewed as a useless by-product, incapable of being transported. This changed with the development of pipeline technology.

The use of natural gas leapt during the oil shocks, as customers switched from oil to gas for home heating. Legislation that controlled natural-gas prices was reconsidered. The Natural Gas Policy Act of 1978 boosted prices, and when all controls were released in 1983, it seemed prices would head higher still. But it was not to be. Although natural gas appears destined to become increasingly important, but for the foreseeable future the world will be reliant on oil.

Q

qualified opinion

to

Russell 2000 index

R

qualified opinion   Report by an **accountant** that notes some reservation about the examination of a company's **financial statements**. For example, an auditor's opinion might include a statement about a lawsuit that, if lost, would substantially change the financial condition of the company.

See also **audit**.

quality circle   Small group of employees who meet regularly to discuss quality issues.

Typically, a quality circle is eight to ten employees and supervisors who share an area of responsibility and concentrate on solving problems. Quality circles were developed in Japan in the early 1960s. They were introduced in the U.S. as part of the **total quality management (TQM)** movement of the 1980s. Ford and General Electric are examples of companies that have adopted quality circles.

fin

quality ratings   Security rankings—both debt and **equity**—that attempt to rank a company's potential **risk**.

See also **bond ratings**.

mktg

quantity discount   Price reduction based on how much you buy. At the **retail** level, an example would be shirts for $18 each or two for $35. In the **industrial market**, there are two types of quantity discounts:

1   **Noncumulative Discounts**
A manufacturer of CD players might offer retailers a 20 percent discount on orders of 20 to 50 machines and a 30 percent discount on orders of more than 50.

2   **Cumulative Discounts**
These are based on purchases over time and may be offered as rebates once a certain quantity is reached. United Parcel Service offers special rates for frequent shippers.

quick ratio   Measures a company's ability to pay what it owes over a roughly 30-day period. The formula used to calculate this ratio appears in the entry for **acid test ratio**.

quality circle

The focus is on problem solving. Workers discuss quality problems, investigate causes, and recommend solutions.

One cannot raise the bottom of a society without benefitting everyone above.

—Michael Harrington, *The Other America*, 1962

quality ratings

tip

Moody's and Standard & Poor's debt ratings are important to consider when analyzing a bond. Although much of the rating decision depends on historical financial information, current market price is a more timely indicator of a bond's risk because the marketplace reacts more swiftly to changes in credit outlook.

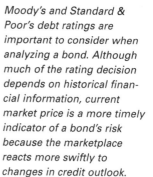

Q

random sampling

mktg

quota sampling Selecting people to be surveyed using deliberate rather than random choice.

See also **sampling**.

oper **mgmt** **mktg**

R&D See **research and development**.

mktg

random sampling Selecting people to be surveyed using a method whereby every member of the population has an equal chance of being chosen.

See also **sampling**.

fin

random walk theory The theory that prices in capital markets are unpredictable and are not instrumental in forecasting future prices.

The theory came from the idea that security price movements are an entirely "random walk." It discounts the value of technical analysis, which relies heavily on past prices through charting. Many people use the theory to point out that long-term investment is not really an art; rather, your best bet is to pick almost any good stock and stick with it. The random walk theory is essentially a less stringent form of the **efficient market theory**.

FRAME OF

REFERENCE

R

random walk theory

The random walk theory was first introduced in 1900 by Louis Bachelier, a French mathematician, and was further developed by Princeton economist Burton Malkiel in 1973 when he published *A Random Walk Down Wall Street*. Although the theory is still widely studied and respected, it has also received considerable skepticism during the past two decades. Critics often tell a story about the person who found a $20 bill on the street but didn't pick it up because he surmised that it couldn't actually be there or it would have been grabbed by someone else.

The idea behind the random walk bears some similarities to economist Adam Smith's famous theory of the "invisible hand" that guides the marketplace, developed in the 18th century. Simply put, Smith speculated that the competitive nature of an economy's individual components will lead to an efficient overall result. Economist David Birch uses the analogy of traffic during morning rush hour—at ground level, each driver is out for himself, measuring detours, switching lanes, and so on to get to a destination as quickly as possible; but from above, the traffic seems to be in utmost harmony, with streams of cars smoothly adjusting for detours and stalled vehicles, almost as if orchestrated by some master plan.

mktg

rate card   Price list of charges for **advertising** time or space.

See also **advertising rates**.

fin   **acct**

rate of return   (1) What an investment yields, expressed as a percentage.

(2) In accounting, the rate of return is expressed as:

Accounting Rate of Return		
ARR	=	Net Income ÷ Investment

See also **expected rate of return** and **internal rate of return (IRR)**.

mktg

reach   Number of individuals who see or hear an advertisement a minimum of one time during a set period.

This includes everyone who had access to the magazine or newspaper, who had the TV on when your commercial ran, who passed your billboard; it does not measure how many people noticed your ad. If at least four-fifths of your **target market** is exposed to your message, you are considered to have gotten wide reach.

See also **ad response** and **advertising**.

fin

real interest rate   Stated **interest rate** on a loan minus inflation.

tech

real-time processing   Online computer systems where there is no perceived delay between making an inquiry or initiating a transaction and receiving a response.

mktg

rebate   A **sales promotion** returning money to the customer after he or she buys something.

The use of rebates has been growing, especially to attract consumers to the high-price end of a product line.

EXAMPLE | You plan to spend $700 for a double bed with a headboard. When you get to the store, you find that you can buy a king-size bed for $825, with a $100 rebate from Sealy. You buy the bigger bed for a $25 dollar difference, and in the meantime, the retailer has increased his sales revenue by $125.

---

random walk theory

Among the evidence that seems to shed doubt on the idea of a "random walk" are the following "pricing anomalies," or groups of stocks that have been shown to consistently outperform other stocks in the market for various reasons:

- *Low-P/E stocks.* Stocks with low price/earnings ratios tend to outperform high-P/E stocks.

- *Underdogs.* Stocks that recently performed poorly tend to outperform those with better overall records.

- *January stocks.* Stocks have generally shown higher returns during January (explanations range from tax-related reasons to investor optimism). Also known as the *January effect.*

real-time processing

EXAMPLE

Airline reservations systems allow immediate adding, modification, or deleting of records.

R

rebate

Rebates have long been a common practice in the automobile industry to increase sales in slow times.

recapitalization

The right time for a company to finance is not when they need capital but when the market is most receptive to providing capital.

—Michael Milken

fin

recapitalization   Revision of a company's **capital structure**.

Examples are exchanging **common stocks** for **bonds** or bonds for common stocks. **Bankruptcy** or financial distress may be a reason. Cash-poor companies may try to reduce their debt payments by issuing equities to replace bonds or other debt. But healthy companies sometimes recapitalize as well. A company can reduce its taxes, for example, by replacing **preferred stock** with bonds whose interest payments are deductible. Another company might convert some debt to equities to improve its future borrowing power.

EXAMPLE | The effects of leverage and the motivation behind a recapitalization effort can be seen by comparing the basic financial information of the two companies below (in $ millions except ratios):

	Company A	Company B
EBITDA*	$200.0	$200.0
Long-Term Debt	$500.0	$800.0
Long-Term Debt Interest Rate	8.5%	15%
Interest Expense	$42.5	$120.0
Depreciation	$40.0	$60.0
Earnings Before Taxes	$117.5	$20.0
Taxes (assume 40 percent rate)	$47.0	$8.0
Net Profit	$70.5	$12.0

*Earnings before interest, taxes, depreciation, and amortization

Although the two companies have the same earnings before interest, taxes, depreciation and amortization—$200 million—they have very different debt structures. Company A carries long-term debt of $500 million at 8.5 percent, while Company B carries a much higher debt load of $800 million, on which it pays a higher rate of 15 percent. This difference in leverage significantly affects the financial outlook of the two companies. Indeed, because of the higher depreciation and interest paid by Company B, we see that it ends up with only $12 million in net profit, compared with Company A's income of $70.5 million.

R

FRAME OF REFERENCE

recapitalization

One of the most dramatic examples of a successful recapitalization has been the transformation of Warnaco, the apparel and department store leader. The company was taken private in a **leveraged buyout** (LBO) in 1986 by a management group led by president and CEO Linda J. Wachner. Wachner has been credited with restoring Warnaco to health, working specifically on **cash flow** and debt levels. In the five years between the LBO and the company's **initial public offering** in 1991, Warnaco's debt level dropped by 40 percent, interest expense was cut nearly in half, and operating cash flow nearly doubled.

econ

recession   An economic slump. While people argue about what exactly makes up a recession, the National Bureau of Economic Research defines it as a period of at least two consecutive quarters of decline in inflation-adjusted **gross domestic product (GDP)**. It is also characterized by rising **unemployment rates**.

Recession: Real GDP Growth Rate, Quarterly, 3/75–9/95

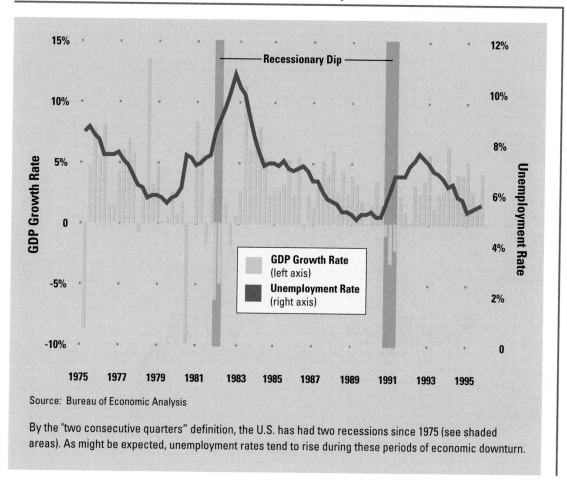

Source: Bureau of Economic Analysis

By the "two consecutive quarters" definition, the U.S. has had two recessions since 1975 (see shaded areas). As might be expected, unemployment rates tend to rise during these periods of economic downturn.

fin

red herring   Tentative, preliminary document about a new offering of securities, so called because of a statement on it, printed in red ink, advising that a registration statement for the issue has been filed with the Securities and Exchange Commission (SEC) but has not yet become effective. (See example on page 486.)

See also **prospectus**.

R

red herring

Shown at right is a sample red herring.

reference group

tip 👍

It is important to understand the difference between marketing to a group's physical age and to their psychological age, and to design advertising copy and visuals accordingly. Men who are 65 view themselves as 18 years younger. Women who are 65 view themselves as 15 years younger.

R

PRELIMINARY PROSPECTUS DATED APRIL 2, 1996

PROSPECTUS

SAVE MART
$500,000,000
SAVE MART Corporation
% Subordinated Debentures due April 1, 2021
(Interest Payable April 1 and October 1)

The Debentures are redeemable at any time on and after April 1, 2001 on no less than 15 days' notice at the option of SAVEMART, in whole or in part, at redemption prices declining from % of the principal amount initially to 100% of the principal amount on and after April 1, 2011, together with accrued interest, except that no such redemption may be made prior to April 1, 2006 from or in anticipation of money borrowed at an interest cost of less than % per annum.

Annual mandatory sinking fund payments sufficient to retire $30 million principal amount of Debentures commencing on April 1, 2006 are calculated to retire 90% of the issue prior to maturity. SAVEMART has the non-cumulative option to increase the sinking fund payment in any year by an amount not exceeding $30 million. SAVEMART may deliver Debentures in lieu of cash in making mandatory sinking fund payments.

The Debentures will be subordinated in right of payment to Senior Indebtedness (as defined). As of February 28, 1996, SAVEMART's Senior Indebtedness was approximately $500 million. The Indenture will not restrict SAVEMART from incurring additional Senior Indebtedness or restrict SAVEMART's subsidiaries from incurring indebtedness. See "Description of Debentures."

THESE SECURITIES HAVE NOT BEEN APPROVED OR DISAPPROVED BY THE SECURITIES AND EXCHANGE COMMISSION NOR HAS THE COMMISSION PASSED UPON THE ACCURACY OR ADEQUACY OF THIS PROSPECTUS. ANY REPRESENTATION TO THE CONTRARY IS A CRIMINAL OFFENSE.

	Price to Public(1)	Underwriting Discount(2)	Proceeds to Company(1)(3)
Per Debenture	%	%	%
Total	$	$	$

(1) Plus accrued interest, if any, from April 1, 1986.
(2) SAVEMART has agreed to indemnify the Underwriter against certain liabilities, including liabilities under the Securities Act of 1933.
(3) Before deducting expenses of SAVEMART estimated at $

A registration statement relating to these securities has been filed with the Securities and Exchange Commission but has not yet become effective. Information contained herein is subject to completion or amendment. These securities may not be sold nor may offers to buy be accepted prior to the time the registration statement becomes effective. This prospectus shall not constitute an offer to sell or the solicitation of an offer to buy nor shall there be any sale of these securities in any State in which such an offer, solicitation or sale would be unlawful prior to registration or qualification under the securities laws of any such State.

`oper` `mktg`

reduction to practice   Process by which the idea for a device reaches a tangible form.

See also **patent**.

`mgmt`

reengineering   Radical redesign of an organization's processes to achieve performance breakthroughs.

See also **business reengineering**.

`mktg`

reference group   Group of people that influences buying decisions.

Reference groups influence us through the standards and values we think they hold. Their influence is strongest for expensive items that stand out—a home, a car, or an office wardrobe.

Reference groups can be subdivided this way:

▶ **Membership Group**
A group you are part of, like a family or a union. These groups can be divided further into **primary groups** (your family, coworkers you see every day, and so on) and **secondary groups** (unions, health clubs, professional organizations, any other groups where you do not know everyone on a first-name basis).

▶ **Aspirational Group**
A group you would like to belong to, maybe a country club or a professional basketball team.

▶ **Dissociative Group**
A group you do not want to be associated with.

EXAMPLE | You are planning an advertising campaign for a car that is bought by many people 50 and older. You run ads in the magazine of the American Association of Retired Persons (AARP) and other publications with older readers. The ads all have photos of couples with gray hair happily using your car. The **copy** portrays the car as having the safety and comfort that make it the choice of retired people. You are aiming to appeal to AARP members, the happily retired (membership groups), and everyone who wants to be happily retired (an aspirational group).

See also **image advertising**, **opinion leaders**, and **purchasing-decision process**.

regional bank

The map below shows the locations of the 12 regional banks in the Federal Reserve System.

Federal Reserve Banks

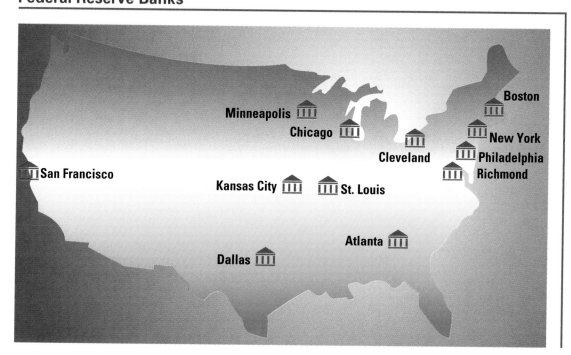

R

econ   fin

regional bank   (1) Each of the 12 Federal Reserve Banks. (See map on the previous page.)

(2) Bank that makes loans and collects deposits throughout a region of the United States. Many U.S. regional banks and bank holding companies have become so large they are known as **superregionals** or **megabanks**. An example is NationsBank Corporation, headquartered in Charlotte, North Carolina, with assets on June 30, 1996, of $192.3 billion.

Regional banks are influential but not on the national and international level of **money center banks**. NationsBank, for example, is the fifth-largest U.S. bank and is the largest energy lender in the world, but it is not considered a money center bank.

See also **Federal Reserve System (Fed)**.

mktg   mgmt   fin

regression analysis   Statistical technique for predicting how a **dependent variable**, the unknown, relates to one or more independent variables, the known.

regression analysis

When an accounting firm recruits recent graduates, it might predict a candidate's potential success (the dependent variable) by considering such factors (independent variables) as (1) score on the CPA exam; (2) grade point average; and (3) relevant work experience. The regression would show a positive relationship among high test scores, grades, work experience, and a successful recruit.

Regression Analysis: CPA Score vs. Potential Success

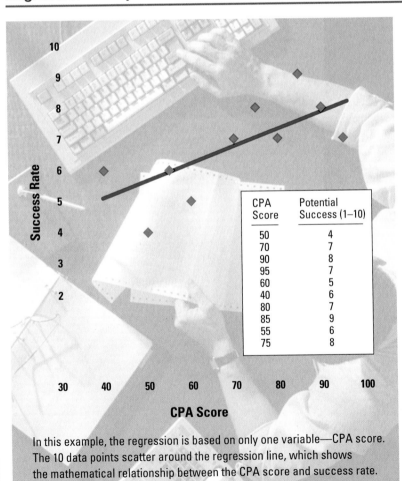

CPA Score	Potential Success (1–10)
50	4
70	7
90	8
95	7
60	5
40	6
80	7
85	9
55	6
75	8

In this example, the regression is based on only one variable—CPA score. The 10 data points scatter around the regression line, which shows the mathematical relationship between the CPA score and success rate.

Simple regression analysis involves the comparison of one known against one unknown; in multiple regression analysis, two or more knowns are cast against an unknown. When you have more than one unknown, you build a model.

fin

Regulation A   A **Securities and Exchange Commission (SEC)** provision based on the Securities Act of 1933, which lets small companies issue up to $1.5 million in securities to the public under somewhat relaxed registration and disclosure requirements. Also called the **small-issues exemption**.

fin

Regulation Q   Federal Reserve Board rule that formerly put a ceiling on how much interest savings institutions could pay on time and **savings** deposits. The Depository Institutions Deregulation and Monetary Control Act of 1980 gradually phased out Regulation Q.

fin

Regulation T   Pronouncement by the Federal Reserve Board, enacted in the 1930s, that determines the amount of credit brokers and dealers can extend to customers for the purchase of securities.

See also **margin** and **margin call**.

relationship marketing

mktg

relationship marketing   Strategy that focuses on building relationships and retaining customers over a long period.

It helps marketers show they care about their customers and goes a long way toward building repeat sales.

EXAMPLE | Monroe Litho prints high-quality annual reports, brochures, and other items needed by big companies like Kodak, Mobil, and Xerox. The Monroe salespeople, management, and technical staffs all develop relationships over time with the corporate clients who buy the printing.

Since the paper used is an important aspect of printing quality, Monroe's people also have long-term relationships with paper companies like Westvaco. It is not unusual for a Monroe salesperson, the corporate client, and a representative of the paper company to spend a day or two together at the printing plant to make sure the job gets off to a good start. Over time, these relationships build the client's trust in Monroe's ability to deliver quality printing.

R

oper   **mgmt**

reliability-centered maintenance   Getting the most from machines by letting the operators maintain them.

See also **total productive maintenance (TPM)**.

remanufacturing

repeat rate

Courtesy, The Gillette Company

EXAMPLE

You are introducing a new snack food, which should have a high repeat rate. After your first wave of advertising, sales were good, but the repeat rate was a big disappointment. It is clear that the advertising worked but the product did not. You decide to take it off the market and either reformulate or discontinue it.

R

---

oper

remanufacturing   Restoring used products to new condition.

It is not just repairing or rebuilding in that the result can be considered a new product. In oil refining, used lubricating oil is sometimes reprocessed for reuse, and that is called **rerefining**.

EXAMPLE | In July 1995, Boeing Helicopters began delivering 13 glass-cockpit Chinook choppers to the Royal Netherlands Air Force. Seven of the helicopters were remanufactured from models originally used in Canada.

mktg

repeat rate   Frequency with which a consumer buys a product during a specified period.

Bottles of Coca-Cola, for example, have a higher repeat rate than cans of Gillette Foamy shaving cream. Advertisers keep a close eye on the relationship between repeat rates and **advertising** when promoting many new products.

fin

repurchase agreement (repo)   Transaction, usually with Treasury issues, where the seller agrees to buy the security back at a set price.

The deal may set a date for the repurchase, or it may be an open repo. In effect, a repo is a form of low-risk, short-term loan to a bank or securities dealer. The duration is typically from overnight to a week or two.

EXAMPLE | Your company has $5 million it wants to hold for three days, so it executes a repurchase agreement with a bank. You give the bank the money, and the bank gives you Treasury bills. Three days later you get your money back plus $1,800, and the bank gets its T-bills. You have found a very safe way to earn what would amount to an annual interest rate of 4.4 percent by effectively "loaning" your money to the bank. The bank gets to keep the T-bills and the interest they earn, which is 5.5 percent. (See chart on following page.)

In a reverse repo the bank or securities dealer buys the securities and agrees to sell them back later. This provides short-term cash for the securities' owner.

The **Federal Reserve System (Fed)** often uses repurchase agreements to temporarily adjust the **money supply**.

Repurchase Agreement (Repo)

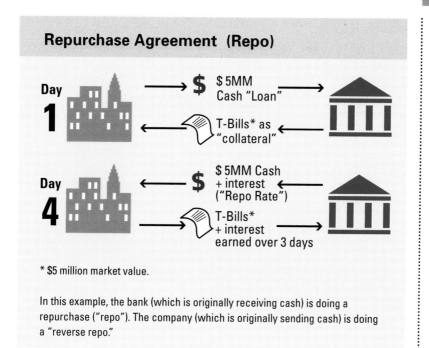

Day 1

$ 5MM Cash "Loan"

T-Bills* as "collateral"

Day 4

$ 5MM Cash + interest ("Repo Rate")

T-Bills* + interest earned over 3 days

* $5 million market value.

In this example, the bank (which is originally receiving cash) is doing a repurchase ("repo"). The company (which is originally sending cash) is doing a "reverse repo."

 oper

rerefining   Reprocessing used lubricating oil for reuse.

See also **remanufacturing**.

---

oper   **mgmt**   **mktg**

research and development (R&D)   Department that improves current products or comes up with new ones. It is a function that responds to market needs or new opportunities.

R&D is about as close as most companies get to top secret work, since competitors would love to know what you are up to. For that reason, among others, R&D is often carried out in independent laboratories isolated from manufacturing operations. The success of the new product, however, will depend in part on how easy it is to manufacture and service, so R&D includes input from the factory and customer-service reps at some point.

R&D budgets are often closely held secrets, particularly in high-tech companies. Since research may be started without any certainty that a product will emerge, or what it will look like if it does, any project's funding may be a source of hot debate.

EXAMPLE | In the mid-1980s, Sun Microsystems debated whether to continue development of a new computer chip called SPARC. After much discussion, it was decided not to continue with the project. But then the decision was reversed at the very top of the corporation. Because of the SPARC technology that resulted, Sun rode to world leadership in workstation-based computing.

---

research and development

Quick Facts!

With pressure in the 1990s to reduce health care costs, advocates have worried that large pharmaceuticals would begin cutting back on their R&D. The time and cost of bringing a new drug to market can be prohibitive, but drug companies have been creative in their response by entering into mergers to better spread the R&D risk and by teaming up with small biotechnology firms to tap into more innovative technologies.

R

491

mktg **mgmt**

research validity   Evaluation of a research project and its results.

There are two ways of looking at research validity:

1 **Internal**
The way the research was conducted. If you ask your customers a series of questions as they walk into your store, that will have less internal validity than a carefully designed survey.

2 **External**
Whether the research results can be transferred to a larger group. If you test consumer reaction to a new snow shovel at a store in Vermont, that will not tell you much about how a customer in Ohio is likely to react to it.

See also **A-B split**, **market segmentation**, **sampling**, **surveying**, and **variable**.

mktg

reseller market   Individuals and organizations that make a profit from buying goods and selling or renting them.

The reseller market is made up mostly of retailers and wholesalers and is a big part of the **industrial market**. A business can be considered a reseller even if most of its revenue comes from renting its product.

acct **fin** **econ**

reserve requirement   Minimum percentage of a bank's deposits that it must hold in reserve.

The requirement is set by the **Federal Reserve System (Fed)**. Cash in the vault and deposits at the Fed are the only things that qualify as reserves. As of 1995, the reserve requirement on transaction accounts is 3 percent of the first $52 million of net transaction balances and 10 percent of the rest. Time deposits require 0 percent.

See also **Federal Reserve System (Fed)**.

---

reseller market

EXAMPLE

Blockbuster Video has made itself a giant in the reseller market by buying videocassettes of motion pictures and then renting or selling them to viewers.

R

FRAME OF REFERENCE

reserve requirement

Reserve requirements affect the potential of the banking system to create transaction deposits. If the reserve requirement is 10 percent, for example, a bank that receives a $100 deposit may lend out $90 of that deposit. As the process continues, the banking system can expand the initial deposit of $100 into a maximum of $1,000 ($100 + $90 + $81 + $72.90 + … = $1,000). In contrast, with a 20 percent reserve requirement, the banking system would be able to expand the initial $100 deposit into a maximum of $500 ($100 + $80 + $64 + $51.20 + … = $500). Thus, higher reserve requirements should result in reduced money creation and, in turn, reduced economic activity.

Source: Federal Reserve Bank of New York

mktg

response rate   Percentage of replies received because of a **direct marketing** campaign.

The response rate is usually below 5 percent, and even 1 percent is considered good. Both **telemarketing** and personal selling usually get better results than less personal approaches, like mailed brochures with no follow-up.

EXAMPLE | A breakfast food company puts a card in cereal boxes offering a sample of a new brand to everyone who fills out the card and sends it in. The company inserts two million cards and gets 60,000 of them back. The response rate is:

$$60,000 \div 2,000,000 = 0.03, \text{ or } 3\%.$$

See also **ad response**.

response rate

mktg

retailer   One who sells products and services to the ultimate customer.

See also **retailing**.

mktg

retailing   Selling products and services to the ultimate customer.

Most retail transactions take place in stores, but techniques like **telemarketing** and **direct mail** also account for a significant amount.

retailing

Retail outlets vary a great deal in size and form of ownership:

▶ **Independent**
  Your local plumber or privately owned shoe store.

▶ **Corporate Chain**
  A big one is Federated Department Stores, which owns Bon Marché, Bloomingdale's, Burdines, Macy's East, Stern's, and other stores.

▶ **Consumer Cooperative**
  A retail outlet owned by consumers who manage and shop at it.

▶ **Trade Cooperative**
  A group of independent stores that join to act like a chain, or at least to gain better wholesale prices by buying in larger quantities.

▶ **Franchise**
  Individually owned outlets that operate under contract with a company that sets uniform standards. McDonald's and Baskin-Robbins ice cream are two examples.

Outlet types include:

■ **Independent**

■ **Corporate chain**

■ **Consumer coop**

■ **Trade coop**

■ **Franchise**

R

Other ways of setting apart types of retailers are:

▶ **Level of Service**
From self-service (like Sam's clubs) to limited service (Home Depot, Wal-Mart), to full service (Nordstrom's, Victoria's Secret).

▶ **Merchandise Line**
A store that sells a wide range of products is said to have *breadth* of **product line**. One that carries a large assortment of each type of product has *depth* of product line.

▶ **Method of Operation**
How goods and services are sold—in a store, over the phone, by catalogue, through a vending machine, via a computer, and so on.

`acct` `fin`

retained earnings   Earnings accumulated on a company's balance sheet after **dividends** have been paid out.

Retained earnings are a part of **shareholders' equity** on the balance sheet and may also be referred to as an "earned surplus." For example, if a company's net income were $5 million, and it paid out **dividends** of $1 million, that would leave $4 million to add to its retained earnings on the **balance sheet**, thus adding to the total value of shareholders' equity and the company's net worth.

`acct` `fin` `mgmt`

return on assets (ROA)   Measurement of how well your company is operating, expressed as a percentage. To arrive at this figure, you divide total average **assets** into **net income**.

ROA	= Net Income
	÷ Average Assets

EXAMPLE | McDonald's 1994 annual report shows net income of $1,224,400,000. Total assets were $12,035,200,000 on December 31, 1993, and $13,591,900,000 on December 31, 1994. Total average assets then are $12.8 billion.

$$(12,035,200.000 + 13,591,900,000) \div 2 = 12,813,550,000$$

And return on assets is 9.6 percent.

$$\$1,224,400,000 \div \$12,813,550,000 = 0.096, \text{ or } 9.6\%$$

return on assets

Measurement of how well your company is operating, expressed as a percentage.

R

return on investment (ROI)   How much you earn as a rate of return on your investment in a project. For the entire company, how much it earns each year, expressed as a percentage, on its total capital, that is, its **common** and **preferred stock**.

See also **return on shareholders' equity**.

return on sales   How **net income** stacks up to net sales.

See also **profit margin**.

return on shareholders' equity (ROE)   Ratio of net income to average **shareholders' equity** for the **accounting period**. This is one measure of a corporation's performance. To get average shareholders' equity, you add the number from the **balance sheet** at the start of the period to the one for the end of the period and divide by two.

ROE	= Net Income
	÷ Average Shareholder's Equity

EXAMPLE McDonald's 1994 annual report shows net income of $1,224,400,000. Shareholders' equity was $6,274,100,000 on December 31, 1993, and $6,885,400,000 on December 31, 1994. Average shareholders' equity then is $6.58 billion.

$6,274,100,000 + 6,885,400,000 = $13,159,500,000

$13,159,500,000 ÷ 2 = $6,579,750,000

And return on shareholders' equity is 18.6 percent.

$1,224,400,000 ÷ $6,579,750,000 = 0.186, or 18.6%

A variation on this measure singles out common shareholders' equity.

revenue center   Area within a company that regulates revenue without controlling overall profits and/or costs.

See also **management control systems**.

R

fin   acct   mgmt

revenues   Your company's sales in dollars. Revenues should be expressed net of all returns, allowances, and discounts.

See also **income statement**.

fin

reverse split   Method of reducing the number of a company's shares outstanding. A company exchanges one share of stock for a larger number of shares outstanding, so that while the total value of the stock remains the same, the per-share price increases because fewer shares are now outstanding.

EXAMPLE | Electron Corp. started with 10 million shares authorized at $5 par value. If they engaged in a one-for-two reverse split, it would end up with 5 million shares outstanding at a $10 par value. As with stock splits, the key thing to remember is that there is no change in the value of the company or in the value of your investment (assuming any dividend is split-adjusted). If you had originally owned 100 shares at $50 per share, you would end up with 50 shares at a $100 market value, still totaling $5,000.

See also **stock split**.

fin   strat

reverse takeover   An **acquisition** where the acquiring company is much smaller than the company it is buying.

Reverse takeovers are often **leveraged buyouts (LBOs)**: The acquiring company puts up very little cash, borrows heavily to finance the acquisition, and then uses the **assets** or the **cash flow** of the acquired company to repay the debt.

EXAMPLE | The Triangle Industries takeover of National Can in 1985 is a case of the minnow that swallowed the whale. Triangle, a small vending machine, wire, and cable company, had revenues of less than $300 million in 1984, plus about $130 million that had been raised from the sale of **junk bonds**. National Can's revenues at the time were $1.9 billion. But there were no other parties interested in National Can, and this provided Triangle with the opportunity for a **leveraged buyout**.

Triangle went on to purchase American Can and, in 1988, was acquired itself by a French company, Pechiney. All in all, the path of acquisitions was a very profitable one for Triangle's shareholders—$1,000 invested in Triangle in 1983 (before its buying spree began) would have been $59,520 by the time of the Pechiney buyout.

---

reverse split

Breaking News

Although a stock split or reverse split has no effect on a company's overall value, management may have other reasons for changing their share price. In February 1996, DBS Industries, a wireless technology company, announced a one-for-forty reverse split that raised their share price to $3—the cutoff to be listed on the Nasdaq exchange.

reverse takeover

Quick Facts!

The London-based Saatchi & Saatchi advertising agency climbed to the world's largest advertising group through reverse takeovers. In 1975, it rose from 13th to 5th in England by buying the publicly traded Garland-Compton.

fin

right   Short-term entitlement to buy shares of stock. Also called **subscription right**.

Rights normally have a life of a few weeks and usually give the holder the opportunity to buy the shares at a price lower than the current market price. If registered with the **Securities and Exchange Commission (SEC)**, the rights can be traded on the open market.

EXAMPLE | Newport Petroleum Corporation, a Canadian company, wanted to raise about $13 million (Canadian) in new capital in 1995. With its stock trading at around $2.50 a share, it issued one right for every share of stock outstanding. Four rights could be used to buy one new share at a price of $2.10. With about 25 million shares outstanding, that meant the company issued more than six million new shares to raise the money it needed.

The rights were traded on the Toronto Stock Exchange during the three weeks of their lives. Stockholders who did not want to buy the new shares could sell the rights, which were exercised by their final owner.

Issuing rights to current shareholders allows them to retain their proportional ownership in the company. Shareholders exercising their rights will not have their equity diluted.

See also **warrant**.

fin

risk premium   Higher return that an investment yields—or should yield—to compensate for increased risk. Risk can take many forms—from the risk that inflation will erode the long-term value of one's **assets** to the risk that a new, untested business venture will fail, to the risk that currency exchange fluctuations will affect the value of investments abroad.

See also **market risk** and **capital asset pricing model (CAPM)**.

mktg fin mgmt

Robinson-Patman Act of 1936   See **antitrust law**.

oper tech

robotics   Using a combination of computers and electromechanical devices instead of humans to perform manufacturing tasks.

Current uses include welding, riveting, painting, and packaging. Sankyo Seiki has installed more than 12,000 robot systems in a variety of small-parts manufacturing and medical applications. Together with Integrated Surgical Systems, Inc., of Sacramento, California, it has developed Robodoc to precisely drill into a patient's femur during hip-replacement surgery.

Motorola uses robotics in manufacturing its paging products, where there is a need for high precision in assembling small parts.

robotics

If there is technological advance without social advance, there is, almost automatically, an increase in human misery.

—Michael Harrington, *The Other America*, 1962

Quick Facts!

The first practical industrial robot was introduced during the 1960s. By 1982, there were approximately 32,000 robots being used in the United States. Today there are over 20,000,000.

—John Huey, "Waking Up to the New Economy," *Fortune*, June 27, 1994

R

S

S corporation

to

systematic
risk

fin

S corporation
Corporation taxed like a **partnership** or **sole proprietorship**.

Under subchapter S of the Internal Revenue Code, a domestic company with 35 or fewer shareholders can elect to have its corporate income treated as income of its shareholders. Thus, as with a partnership, the corporation pays no income tax; instead, shareholders include their proportionate share of the corporation's income or losses on their individual tax returns. The shareholders still enjoy the protection from liability they get from incorporation but avoid the double taxation that happens when a company pays taxes on its income and then the investor pays taxes on **dividends**. Unlike a regular corporation, an S corporation may not have any **subsidiaries** and all of the shareholders of an S corporation must be individuals.

fin

S-1 filing
The most comprehensive of the detailed disclosure statements that have to be filed with the **Securities and Exchange Commission (SEC)**, before a stock offering.

See also **prospectus**.

fin

sale/leaseback
Form of financing where a company raises funds by selling real property or equipment and then leasing it back.

The company retains the use of the **assets**, which stand as collateral for the funds. Businesses requiring a lot of machinery may enter sale/leaseback agreements. Hotel companies often use them as well—selling the hotel itself and leasing it back.

sale/leaseback

EXAMPLE | You buy a $5 million press for your printing company. Rather than arranging an installment loan to finance it, you sell it to a finance company, which leases it back to you. At the end of the 10-year lease, you have the right to buy the press back again at a predetermined price.

See also **capital lease**.

mktg

sales promotions
Strictly speaking, efforts aimed at getting people to purchase a product. **Advertising**, selling, and publicity are not included.

Because you sometimes hear the term used to include advertising and publicity, too, it pays to clarify what is meant. In the paragraphs that follow, we are using the term in its strict sense.

sales promotions

tip |

Sales promotions work best when they complement advertising.

S

You may aim sales promotions at one of three groups:

1 Your Sales Force

You might hold a kickoff rally at the start of your peak selling season. You would outline the key themes for the product and perhaps offer a free weekend at a resort for the top salesperson.

2 Other Companies in the Distribution Channel

Here is where, for example, you could offer **cooperative advertising** to retailers along with special posters and product displays for their stores. For a new product—say, an electronic organizer—you might give samples to **wholesalers**. They could then pass the devices out to their customers so the retail salespeople would have a chance to learn the benefits of the new product.

3 Final Consumers

You might use cents-off coupons, samples, contests, **rebates**, trading stamps, **warranties**, or in-store demonstrations of your products.

---

acct

salvage value

Estimate of what an **asset** can be sold for at the end of its useful life.

See also **depreciation**.

---

mktg

sampling

Selecting the people to be **surveyed**.

Marketers conducting research will choose individuals representative of the **target market**. The sample must be large enough so the results are likely to be valid for the whole population.

Types of sampling include:

► Random Sampling

A method where every member of the population has an equal chance of being chosen for the survey.

For example, you are the general manager of a local cable company that is considering a new all-sports network. You put the names of all your subscribers in a box, shake it up, and blindly pick 300 names. You give these subscribers free reception of the network for three months in return for their reactions.

► Stratified Sampling

You divide the population into groups based on selected criteria (like age and income level) and then make a random sampling of each group. The size of the sample for each segment is proportionate to that group's representation in the total population. This ensures that your total results will reflect the right **demographic** mix. And if the sample size of each group is large enough, you will get useful data on the segments.

---

sales promotions

EXAMPLE

Procter & Gamble advertises its Pampers disposable diapers in magazines read by expectant and new parents. It also supplies samples to obstetricians and maternity hospitals to give out along with booklets on infant care. And it arranges for supermarket shoppers buying other infant-care products to get cents-off coupons.

S

You are the campaign manager for a Senate candidate. You use a demographic profile of the state that breaks the population into segments based on gender, age, income level, race, and so on. You use that demographic mix for all your **surveying**.

▶ Area Sampling

This technique takes a geographic unit, breaks it into smaller areas, and then makes a random selection.

You are considering bringing your discount stores into the Phoenix metropolitan area. You want more information on the market and on where you might locate each store and how each should be stocked. You divide the region by zip code and then make a random selection within each zip code for a survey.

▶ Quota Sampling

This involves deliberate rather than random choice.

Speedy Eyeglasses hires you to conduct a survey in a shopping mall the chain is considering entering. Speedy wants you to stand in the mall and interview 100 men wearing glasses, 100 women wearing glasses, and 100 of each gender who are not wearing glasses. It is up to you where to stand and which people within each group to approach.

See also **A-B split**, **market segmentation**, and **surveying**.

econ

savings   Earnings that are not spent.

After taxes and other payments are subtracted from personal income, what is left is called disposable income, and in essence only two things can happen to it. The money will either be spent, thus becoming part of personal consumption expenditures, or be saved. Whether you stuffed the money into your mattress, ignored it as it sat in your checking account, earned interest by putting it in a savings account, bought stocks and bonds, or did almost anything with it short of giving it away, an economist would call it savings.

If you spend more than you earn, the savings will be a negative number, and that is called **dissavings**.

Besides personal savings, two other categories in the U.S. economy are business savings and government savings. Business savings consists of income received to replace capital goods that wear out and corporate profits that businesses retain instead of distributing to shareholders. Government savings occur only if tax receipts exceed spending, which is known as a budget surplus. During the last 15 years or so, total savings as a percentage of **gross domestic product (GDP)** have declined from about 18 percent to 12 percent, due to reduced personal savings and increased government dissavings. Business savings have remained fairly constant.

The total of all the savings in an economy provides an important source of **investment** funds for new plants, equipment, and technology.

savings

Quick Facts!

The savings rate, or the proportion of personal disposable income that goes into savings, in the United States is far lower than that for the rest of the industrialized world. For Japan, the savings rate is almost 20 percent; Germany, nearly 15 percent; Canada, France, and Italy, well over 5 percent. The U.S. savings rate? In 1994, it was just 3.1 percent.

A penny saved is a penny earned.

—Benjamin Franklin

S

secondary data

EXAMPLE

Your company is considering a new product for the scuba-diving market. First, you get what secondary data you can. You obtain newsletter and magazine articles that give estimates of the size of the market. You also approach the Diving Equipment Manufacturers Association, a trade group, and the agencies that train divers.

These sources agree that there are more than three million divers in the United States. Since that is a big enough market, you can go to the next stage, which is primary research—in this case a mail survey and a **focus group**—to gauge the interest in your product.

S

---

econ

savings rate   Proportion of personal disposable income that goes into savings.

See also **savings**.

mgmt

scientific management   Probably the first attempt at a modern management theory.

The term arose from Frederick Winslow Taylor's *Principles of Scientific Management*, published in 1911.

There are a couple of glaring problems with scientific management by today's standards. Two examples are the assumption that people tend to act in rational and predictable ways, and the belief that there is one right way to do any task. But the contribution of Taylor and others of his era was to recognize that management could be examined and improved. Until then, there were no clear statements of workplace responsibilities, few standards, no framework for management decisions, and an assumption of perpetual conflict between workers and management.

Scientific management used time and motion studies and tied compensation levels to meeting production goals.

acct   **fin**

SEC   See **Securities and Exchange Commission**.

mktg

secondary data   Information that is available from a source other than the original one.

This differs from **primary data**, which you gather through original research. You can obtain secondary data through published books and articles, government reports, trade associations, and so on.

See also **surveying**.

fin

secondary offering   Sale of a block of a company's previously issued securities. A secondary offering may be distinguished from an **inital public offering (IPO)** in which the company issues new shares to the public.

Such sales are usually made by large investors like corporations, institutions, or people affiliated with the company. Sometimes a company wanting to raise capital will sell a block of securities to a large investor through a **private placement**. Under **Rule 144**, a private placement investor must hold the securities for at least two years, after which they may be sold into the secondary market. All proceeds of a secondary offering go to the selling investor, not to the company whose stock is involved.

Section 936

In 1996, the U.S. Congress debated the elimination of the tax exemption. Proponents of the exemption argue that companies would move their operations from Puerto Rico to countries with cheaper labor if the United States removes this incentive, thus increasing Puerto Rico's 14 percent unemployment rate. Opponents of Section 936 call the loophole a giant $4.8 billion-a-year giveaway for a small group of large corporations, especially those in the U.S. pharmaceutical industry.

fin

Section 936
A section of the U.S. tax code giving incentives to companies with operations in Puerto Rico.

These organizations, known as *936 companies*, are exempt from U.S. income tax on money earned and remaining in Puerto Rico.

fin

secured debt
A debt obligation that is guaranteed by **assets** or other forms of collateral. Secured debt is differentiated from unsecured debt, or **debentures**, which are backed only by an **indenture**.

acct **fin**

Securities and Exchange Commission (SEC)
Federal agency created by the U.S. Congress to administer U.S. securities laws.

The *Securities Exchange Act of 1934* created the SEC to regulate securities markets, including the flow of information to investors and potential investors. The SEC historically has deferred to the **Financial Accounting Standards Board (FASB)** on the rules **accountants** must follow when preparing **financial statements**. But the SEC has a lot to say about exactly what information must be disclosed, when and how, and the contents of its required documents, like **annual reports**, **10-Ks**, and **prospectuses**.

fin

securitization
Way to spread risk by pooling debt instruments, then issuing new securities that are backed by the pool.

The term became popular in the 1970s to describe the mortgage-backed security business, which bundled mortgages and passed the income from homeowners' principal and interest payments through an intermediary, like a government agency or an investment bank, to investors in the pool. Other types of **accounts receivable**, like credit card debt, have now been securitized into **bonds** and notes as well. **Junk bonds** have been pooled and repackaged, creating a form of securitized commercial loan.

See also **asset-backed security**.

secondary offering

Just as with a primary offering, a secondary sale is handled by investment bankers working alone or in a syndicate.

Securities and Exchange Commission

S

segment reporting

Separating out some of the data in published **financial statements**, usually by industry grouping or geographic area of operation.

Financial Accounting Standards Board (FASB) standards set the rules for segment reporting, but companies have a lot of leeway in how to interpret them.

EXAMPLE | In the 1994 Procter & Gamble annual report, Note No. 10 deals with segment information. One table gives data on sales, profits, **assets**, **capital spending**, and **depreciation** for these product groups: laundry and cleaning, personal care, food and beverage, and pulp and chemicals. Another table gives figures for sales, profits, and assets for these geographic areas: United States, Europe, and the rest of the world lumped together as Canada, Asia, Latin America, and other. In both tables, there is also a "corporate" column that reflects mainly the handling of cash and investments along with corporate expenses.

You have to report by segment if:

► 10 percent or more of your revenue comes from one segment (however you define it).

► 10 percent or more of your operating profit comes from one segment.

► 10 percent of your assets can be identified as belonging to one segment.

At Procter & Gamble, one product line—disposable diapers—accounts for around 15 percent of sales, so the company mentions the line in Note No. 10, along with the table that includes the personal care category.

FRAME OF REFERENCE

segment reporting

The issue of segment reporting has long been a point of contention between companies and the investors and analysts who study them. Although the "10 percent rules" listed above provide some minimum standard of reporting, many companies resist giving investors any information beyond what is required, citing concerns about giving away competitive secrets. Adding to investor frustration is the fact that the segment reporting rules apply only to annual reports and not to quarterly filings. That means that interested parties may have to wait a year before finding out, for example, that a beverage company is having a disastrous year in a key growth market like China.

S

mgmt

self-directed work teams
Groups of workers who manage themselves with little or no direct supervision.

Team members work together on tasks like scheduling work, resolving conflicts, and ordering supplies. The team approach naturally grew out of the drive for **job enrichment** and employee **empowerment**. The idea is that the people closest to the day-to-day work are best suited to solve the problems that come up, helped along by the strength that comes from group discussion.

Studies have shown that at least half of the companies that launch self-directed work teams fail to meet their goals of improving productivity, decreasing costs, and increasing quality and employee morale. Proponents of the teams blame these statistics on lack of training, direction, or communication. Critics of the team approach say the groups cannot reach consensus quickly and that one team member will dominate the group, in effect becoming a boss.

> At our plant, all 130 employees take part. The paradox of teamwork is that we need to overcome some aspects of individualism—egos, styles, conflicts.... I have to overcome my own ego and the feeling no one else can do something as well as I can.... Today our plant is considered an industry leader thanks in great part to [our] high-involvement, quality-driven team environment.
>
> —**Jim Chartrand**, facility manager at International Paper Co.'s folding cartons plant in Richmond, Virginia, in *Training*, March 1994

mktg

self-liquidator
Item you sell at cost to build sales of a primary product.

EXAMPLE | A coffee company buys a large quantity of spill-proof mugs at $2.95 each. It offers the mugs at that price to customers who accompany their payment with a label from one of the company's coffees.

fin

sell-side analyst
Person who researches and recommends securities of various industries and who is employed by a company that then sells the securities to investors, such as a brokerage firm. (See list on the following page.)

See also **buy-side analyst**.

acct **fin**

selling, general, and administrative expenses
All costs other than production costs that can be attributed to business activities. S,G,&A—as these expenses are known—is sometimes referred to as **overhead**.

See also **income statement**.

---

self-directed work teams

t i p |

The self-directed teams that work best involve members with a variety of skills who work interactively with each other and are evaluated as a unit.

self-liquidator

S

sell-side analyst

Among the more highly anticipated events in the brokerage community is the analyst survey published each October in *Institutional Investor* magazine. Each year, the magazine polls the industry to compile its "All-Star" team of analysts in different industries. The listing shown here ranks the various brokerage firms by the total number of analysts that made the teams.

served market

S

Institutional Investor's All-American Research Team

Rank 1994	Rank 1995	Firm	Total Positions 1995
2	1	Merrill Lynch	45
3	2	Donaldson, Lufkin & Jenrette	36
1	3	Goldman Sachs	34
6	—	Morgan Stanley	34
8	5	Paine Webber	27
4	6	Salomon Brothers	24
7	7	CS First Boston	22
10	8	Prudential Securities	20
5	—	Smith Barney	20
11	10	Sanford C. Bernstein	18
15	11	Bear Stearns	15
16	12	Cowen & Co.	11
9	13	Lehman Brothers	9
13	—	Schroder Wertheim	9
17	15	Oppenheimer & Co.	7
14	16	Dean Witter Reynolds	5
—	17	J.P. Morgan	4
—	18	Alex. Brown & Co.	3
18	—	Montgomery Securities	3
18	20	Deutsche Morgan Grenfell	—
—	—	C.J. Lawrence	2
—	—	Gerard Klauer Mattison	2

© Institutional Investor, Inc.

fin

senior debt   Owed money that is first in line in claims on the borrower's **assets**.

Debt obligation that ranks below secured debt in event of default or liquidation but above **subordinated debt** and **preferred** and **common stock**. **Senior debt** usually includes loans from banks or insurance companies and any **bonds** or notes not clearly designated as junior or subordinated.

Senior debt has a number of variations: It may be fixed or **floating rate**, convertible or straight, long or short in maturity, or issued by a public or private company. It may pay its holders quarterly, semi-annually, or annually, and it may have features like a **call**, **sinking fund**, and special **covenants**. Because of its senior ranking, it may have more restrictive covenants than **subordinated debt** issues.

mktg

served market   Group of consumers whose similar needs or characteristics a company seeks to meet.

See also **target market**.

tech

server   Large computer holding the applications and files in a **client/server network**.

oper

service level   In operations, the availability of given items in **inventory**.

You will often hear the service level expressed as a percentage of time that the item is available. A 95 percent service level means that inventories are high enough that the item is on hand 95 percent of the time; it will be out of stock just 5 percent of the time. Many companies set service levels between 95 and 100 percent.

fin

settlement date   Date by which buyers and sellers in a securities trade must settle the transaction.

Buyers of securities deliver cash payment and accept the securities, while sellers deliver the securities and accept payment. For stocks and **bonds**, settlement is three business days after execution of the trade. For **options** and government securities, settlement is the next business day.

mgmt

sexual harassment   Unwelcome advances or other activities of a sexual nature.

In the past few years, remarks and activities such as reading *Playboy* magazine at work have also been considered to be sexual harassment in certain circumstances.

Title VII of the 1964 Civil Rights Act, which outlaws discrimination in the workplace, has been successfully used in court cases against sexual harassment since 1977. A number of states and municipalities also regulate against sexual harassment, and many large organizations have clear policies against it. But despite all this, complaints of sexual harassment increased sharply in the early and mid-1990s, in part because of the expanding definition of conduct that can be considered as harassment and in part because of a greater willingness among workers to file complaints.

According to the Equal Employment Opportunity Commission's definition, the two forms of sexual harassment are:

1 **Quid Pro Quo**
   When sexual conduct is a condition of employment or used as a basis for favorable treatment.

2 **Hostile Environment**
   Where sexual talk, actions, or objects create a hostile atmosphere or otherwise interfere with an individual's ability to work.

settlement date

sexual harassment

t i p |

A strong, well-communicated policy against sexual harassment, active training programs, and prompt action on complaints will help your company avoid lawsuits. It should also improve performance by enhancing trust and comfort in the workplace.

S

The laws regarding sexual harassment treat men, women, homosexuals, bisexuals, and heterosexuals the same. They apply to employer-employee, employee-employee, and employee-nonemployee situations. A company can be held liable if it fails to prevent sexual harassment.

acct

SFAC   See **Statement of Financial Accounting Concepts**.

acct

SFAS   See **Statement of Financial Accounting Standards**.

acct

SFAS 14   A **Financial Accounting Standards Board (FASB)** pronouncement that sets the rules for separating out some of the data in published **financial statements**, usually by industry grouping or geographic area of operation.

See also **segment reporting**.

acct

SFAS 16   Standard issued by the **Financial Accounting Standards Board (FASB)** that lays out how to correct a mistake made in a previous year's financial reports and how to handle the tax benefits of operating-loss carryforwards in an acquisition.

See also **generally accepted accounting principles (GAAP)**.

acct

SFAS 87   A **Financial Accounting Standards Board (FASB)** pronouncement on how to handle pension costs.

See also **generally accepted accounting principles (GAAP)**.

acct

SFAS 106   A **Financial Accounting Standards Board (FASB)** pronouncement on handling postretirement benefits other than pensions.

See also **accounting change**.

acct

SFAS 109   A **FASB** pronouncement that changed the standards for dealing with income taxes.

See also **Financial Accounting Standards Board (FASB)**.

mktg

share of voice   Percentage that one company spends on **advertising** out of a total given market. Marketers use share of voice as a way of measuring their effectiveness, comparing it with **market share**.

---

share of voice

EXAMPLE

You own a frozen foods company. You account for 15 percent of all the advertising in the U.S. frozen-pizza market. Your share of voice is 15 percent, but your frozen-pizza market share is only 10 percent. You may not be getting your money's worth out of your advertising. You might consider reducing the ad budget or hiring a new **advertising agency**. If your market share was higher than your share of voice, you would feel confident in your ad strategy and might boost the budget.

mgmt

shared services center   Group supplying **staff support** to various parts of a company.

In a shared services center, each employee is typically dedicated to one of the company's business units, which pays that person's salary.

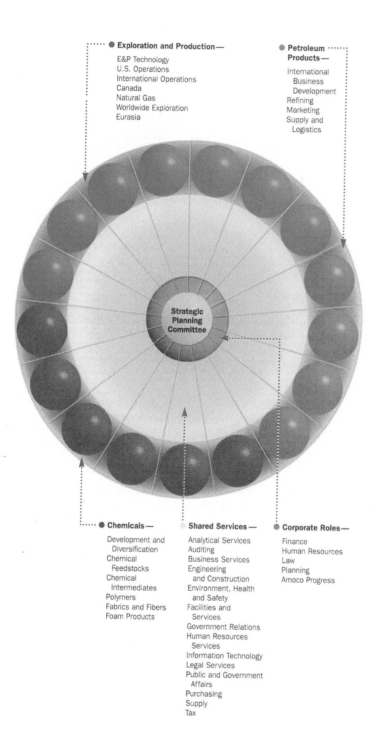

● **Exploration and Production—**
  E&P Technology
  U.S. Operations
  International Operations
  Canada
  Natural Gas
  Worldwide Exploration
  Eurasia

● **Petroleum Products—**
  International
   Business
   Development
  Refining
  Marketing
  Supply and
   Logistics

Strategic Planning Committee

● **Chemicals—**
  Development and
   Diversification
  Chemical
   Feedstocks
  Chemical
   Intermediates
  Polymers
  Fabrics and Fibers
  Foam Products

● **Shared Services—**
  Analytical Services
  Auditing
  Business Services
  Engineering
   and Construction
  Environment, Health
   and Safety
  Facilities and
   Services
  Government Relations
  Human Resources
   Services
  Information Technology
  Legal Services
  Public and Government
   Affairs
  Purchasing
  Supply
  Tax

● **Corporate Roles—**
  Finance
  Human Resources
  Law
  Planning
  Amoco Progress

shared services center

This diagram, taken from Amoco's annual report, shows their 17 business groups, which are all supported by a shared services center. (See related story on the following page.)

S

511

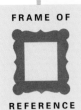

FRAME OF

REFERENCE

shared services center

Amoco, a major petroleum and chemicals company, reorganized in 1994 into 17 business groups, all supported by a shared services center made up of 14 departments: Analytical Services; Auditing; Business Services; Engineering and Construction; Environment, Health, and Safety; Facilities and Services; Government Relations; Human Resources Services; Information Technology; Legal Services; Public and Government Affairs; Purchasing; Supply; and Tax.

An accountant in the Business Services Department might serve one of the business groups—Natural Gas, for example—but report to the business services manager. That way all of Amoco's accounting is based on the same systems and procedures, and the number crunchers can easily shift from working with one business group to another.

acct fin

shareholders' equity Item on a **balance sheet** showing the value of the corporation's **assets** after **liabilities** are deducted. Also called stockholders' equity. For an unincorporated business, it is called **owner's equity**.

There are two major categories within shareholders' equity on a balance sheet:

1 **Paid-In Capital**
What investors paid for shares, both **common stock** and **preferred stock**. These are broken into **par value** and **additional paid-in capital,** or what investors paid above (or below) par value.

2 **Retained Earnings**
This is the company's accumulated earnings over the years after **dividends** have been paid.

Shown on the following page is the shareholders' equity section of American Medical Response's December 31, 1994, balance sheet. This shows, at least in theory, what the shareholders' claims would amount to if the company were liquidated. It is a theoretical number because real-world **supply** and **demand** would very likely put different values on the assets than accounting conventions do.

S

Shareholders' Equity

Preferred Stock	$.01 par value, 500,000 shares authorized, none issued	—
Common Stock	$.01 par value, 25,000,000 shares authorized, 14,765,633 shares issued and outstanding	$148,000
Additional Paid-in Capital		86,517,000
Retained Earnings		43,968,000
Total Shareholders' Equity		**$130,633,000**

The $86,665,000 the company got by selling its common stock is separated out into par value and paid-in capital. Similarly, if the company had issued any preferred stock, its par value would be listed in the first line, and the company would add the rest of the money it got into additional paid-in capital.

fin

shelf registration   Registering securities for public sale at a future date.

Under **Securities and Exchange Commission (SEC) Rule 415**, a company may file a registration statement as much as two years before it actually offers the securities. The registration must be updated quarterly, but it can be used quickly when the company decides that market conditions are right for making the public offering.

oper

shop floor control   System for monitoring work by accessing information directly from the factory floor.

S

shop floor control

shortage

tip

By keeping supplies low, marketers sometimes increase long-term demand for a popular product.

Shop floor control systems can be used to:

▶ Rank the priority of job lots on the floor.

▶ Track real-time changes in work-in-process inventories.

▶ Control machine capacity.

▶ Report order status to management.

▶ Measure **efficiency, productivity**, and utilization of the labor force or equipment.

At its simplest, shop floor control is just a matter of knowing what is going on and acting promptly on it. At its most complex, it involves sophisticated real-time computer monitoring.

fin

short sale   Selling borrowed stock.

Typically, stock is borrowed from a broker with the idea of replacing it later with stock bought at a lower price, thus producing a profit for the borrower. Of course, if the stock price rises in the interim instead of falling, the borrower takes a loss because the replacement securities are more expensive.

EXAMPLE | An investor expects that shares of ABC Corporation are going to decline. She tells her broker to sell short 1,000 shares of ABC at $20 a share. The broker loans the investor the 1,000 shares using stock held in another customer's **margin** account and completes the transaction. ABC's stock does indeed begin to drop. When it reaches $15 a share, the investor purchases 1,000 shares for $15,000, covers the short position with the broker, and makes a $5,000 profit.

Short sellers contrast with buyers who are bullish on a certain stock and thus go long; that is, they buy, sometimes on margin, in anticipation that the stock's price will rise and provide them with a quick profit.

See also **arbitrage**.

econ   **mktg**

shortage   When the **demand** for a good or service exceeds the **supply** at the current price.

In a shortage, consumers may face waiting periods until the price rises to its market-clearing level. Often, car buyers run into shortages when a new model is exceedingly popular.

S

EXAMPLE | When the Mazda Miata was introduced in 1989, the demand quickly outpaced the number of cars Mazda could deliver. As a result, car dealers put would-be buyers on waiting lists and often charged a premium as well.

See also **surplus**.

econ **mgmt**

shut-down point   Per-unit price so low it recovers only the **variable costs** (like materials and labor) involved in manufacturing a product.

When a company is losing money, it may keep operating as long as the price it gets pays the bills for the variable costs and recovers a portion of the **fixed costs** (such as rent and insurance). When the price falls to the shut-down point or below, the company might be better off closing its doors.

See also **contribution margin**.

fin

signaling effect   The academic theory that the price of a company's **common stock** tends to fall when the company announces that it will issue new shares and tends to rise when it announces a new debt issue.

The presumption is that management—which has better information than investors have—will sell its **equity** only when it is pessimistic about the future. If management is optimistic about the company's future, according to the theory, it will raise money by borrowing rather that give up any of the ownership in the company.

shortage

The Mazda Miata is an example of a product whose high demand created a shortage.

FRAME OF REFERENCE

signaling effect

Most studies testing the signaling effect concentrate on only short-term price effects a week or so around the share issuance announcement. A longer-term effect has yet to be proven. Chrysler, for example, engineered a high-profile share issuance in 1991 of more than 40 million shares (diluting shareholders by more than 15 percent). One could argue that the signaling effect held true initially, since the stock fell from $6-1/2 to $5 (down 23 percent) within two months. But the stock then staged a spectacular rally in subsequent years, rising to $16 by the end of 1992 and then to $26-5/8 by the end of 1993.

S

simple interest

EXAMPLE

The simple interest on $50,000 at an 8 percent annual rate borrowed for six months is:

> **$50,000 x .08 x .50 (6 months is half a year) = $2,000**

The interest payments on the six-month life of this loan come to $2,000.

sinking fund

Money

a company puts to redeem

aside bonds

or other

obligations prior

to maturity.

---

fin

simple interest   Calculation of interest paid on a loan or a deposit without compounding.

Simple interest is calculated like this:

Simple Interest Rate

$$I_s = P \times i \times n$$

I_s Simple interest rate

P Principal amount

i Interest rate per time period

n Number of time periods

See also **interest rate**.

oper   **mgmt**   **mktg**

single sourcing   Purchase of a product or a service from a single (or small group of) suppliers.

Influenced in part by the **just-in-time (JIT) inventory system**, many manufacturers have embraced single sourcing. They have found that the close relationship between buyer and seller can lead to a much smoother delivery process.

EXAMPLE   In 1993, the Tennessee Valley Authority (TVA) decided to shift to a single source for the lubricants it needs for its 28 hydroelectric dams, 11 fossil-fuels plants, four nuclear power generating stations, and two service centers. The TVA awarded the contract indefinitely to Mobil Corporation.

fin

sinking fund   Money a company puts aside to redeem **bonds** or other obligations prior to maturity.

The debt issuer puts a sum of cash into a separate custodial account that is then used to buy back the securities. The provisions of the sinking fund, which may be detailed in the **bond indenture**, enhance the safety of the investment since cash will be accumulated on a set schedule. This added degree of safety may allow the issuer to pay a lower **interest rate**.

S

In **private placement** bonds, a sinking-fund requirement is usually mandatory. Sometimes **preferred stock** is also issued with sinking-fund provisions.

For example, in our term sheet used to illustrate **convertible bonds** (see page 155), Comdisco's 8 percent convertible bonds had the following sinking-fund requirement: The company was required to retire 75 percent of the $250 million issue (or $187.5 million) prior to maturity. The retirements were to begin on May 1, 1993, with $18.75 million to be retired annually.

Because a sinking-fund requirement effectively shortens the maturity of some of the bonds, it is typically calculated into a **bond's valuation**. Rather than retire bonds to satisfy its sinking-fund requirements, an issuing company also has the right to buy them in the open market and put them into a custodial account against its sinking-fund requirement. This option may be attractive, for example, if its bonds are trading at a discount to par value. Alternatively, a company may choose this option as an investment if it has excess cash. This action is often interpreted as a signal of confidence on management's part— showing that the company would rather buy its own securities than make other investments.

mktg **strat**

skimming   Setting a high initial price to sell your product first to those willing to pay top dollar.

When that **demand** falls off, you boost your revenue by dropping the price to appeal to more price-conscious consumers. At that point, you are also likely to change the **marketing mix** to appeal to your new **target market** (the more price-conscious).

EXAMPLE | Your company develops a new video game machine with much more vivid graphics and sound than any of your competitors' products. You are reasonably certain that no other company will be able to come up with anything as good for a year or two. You set the initial price high and advertise mostly in magazines read by game fanatics. When sales drop off, you lower the price and begin a heavy schedule of TV **advertising**.

For the skimming strategy to work, a lot of people must be willing to pay the premium price, and competitors must be unable to jump in right away at a lower price.

See also **penetration pricing** and **pricing**.

fin

small-issues exemption   Another name for **Regulation A** of the **SEC**.

mktg

social marketing   Using marketing techniques to influence and change people's attitude and behavior toward social problems.

---

skimming

tip |

Skimming can help you recover the development cost of your product quickly. The high initial price may also enhance the product's image.

trap |

The high price might deter so many customers that your product never captures the market. It also might attract competitors.

S

social marketing

Ben & Jerry's ice cream company is often cited as the model of a company that "gives something back." The Vermont company donates a percentage of its profits to its nonprofit foundation, which is dedicated to improving the environment and promoting world peace. The company's advertising conveys all three of its goals: buy our ice cream, save the rain forests, and support positive social change.

soft landing

I don't believe in soft landings.... It conjures up the image of Neil Armstrong gently settling the rocket ship down on the moon, and then going out and taking a stroll. This is a $7 trillion economy. And it doesn't work that neatly. Any of the soft landings I've ever looked at have ended with a bang and not a whimper.

—Stephen Roach, Chief Economist, Morgan Stanley Group, Spring 1995

Soft landings exist and we'll have one.

—Everett Ehrlich, Undersecretary for Economic Affairs, U.S. Commerce Department, Spring 1995

econ **fin**

soft currency   Money that cannot be converted easily to the currency of another country.

It may be difficult to convert because a rapid fall in value has made outsiders mistrustful of holding it, or because it is offered only at an unrealistic **exchange rate**. The classic example of the latter type of soft currency was the ruble of the former Soviet Union. The Soviet government pegged the ruble at an arbitrary rate unrelated to its market power and not backed by gold.

Businesses and countries that deal in hard currencies, such as the American dollar or the British pound, are hesitant to keep assets in soft currencies. When doing business in a country with soft currency, a company may negotiate for at least some of its revenue in **hard currency**. The host country also may be trying to get more hard currency so it can make purchases in the international marketplace.

econ

soft landing   Swing of the nation's **business cycle**, after a period of high growth, that does not lead to a **recession** or high **inflation**.

This is an elusive concept, much talked about but seldom—if ever—achieved. Many economists define it as a sustained period with 2 to 2.5 percent annual growth in the **gross domestic product (GDP)**, and many will also tell you that it has never happened. The term tends to be used when the **Federal Reserve System (Fed)** raises interest rates to slow down a growth period.

tech **mgmt** **mktg**

software piracy   Illegally copying someone else's software onto the user's own medium.

See also **copyright**.

mgmt acct

sole proprietorship

Unincorporated business owned by one person.

Sole proprietors are liable for their company's debts and pay taxes as though they and their business are one entity.

fin

solvency

When a company can pay all its loans and other obligations as they come due.

Cash, short-term securities, inventory, and receivables all contribute to a company's solvency.

mgmt

span of control

Number of people a manager can effectively supervise.

The span of control applies only to direct reports; that is, each manager will have a span of control for workers reporting to them. You can end up with thousands of workers reporting to you, although your span of control is never likely to be more than a dozen or so.

Until recent years, management experts taught that the most effective span of control was five or six employees. But the trend today is to double those numbers. That is because of improved communications and information systems and because modern approaches call for increased **empowerment** and fewer layers of management.

acct fin

special item

Something that affects your income statement but is not part of your regular business and does not ordinarily happen. Also called **extraordinary item**.

Special items get a line of their own on the **income statement**. To be considered special items, they must be both unusual and infrequent.

EXAMPLE | In 1994, General Electric liquidated its Kidder, Peabody securities operation and sold off some of the assets. It reported a loss of almost $1.2 billion as a special item on its income statement.

acct

specific identification

Method for determining inventory value.

See also **inventory valuation**.

econ

spending multiplier

Ripple effect throughout the economy in response to an injection of spending.

Personal consumption expenditure, or consumer spending, is the largest category within the **gross domestic product (GDP)**, but its significance goes far beyond its size. That is because this spending

sole proprietorship

solvency

Solvency is entirely a matter of temptation and not of income.

—Logan Pearsall Smith, *Afterthoughts*, 1931

span of control

EXAMPLE

Nine senior executives report to Larry Fuller, CEO of Amoco Corporation. Together, the 10 of them make up the Strategic Planning Committee, which coordinates the company's 17 business units and its **shared services center**. Fuller's span of control is nine, but ultimately the 43,000 employees of Amoco all report to him.

S

generates income for the companies that produce the goods and services, and then that income fuels more rounds of spending and income.

spending multiplier

> **EXAMPLE** | Ace Corporation wants to move its headquarters from the New York City area to a suburb of Dallas. It hires an economics consulting company to estimate the multiplier effect—what the jobs created and the payroll spending will mean for other local businesses and for tax collections. Ace uses those numbers to help win tax concessions and other support from the local government.

fin **mgmt**

spin-off   (1) When a corporation divests itself of a division or **subsidiary** by setting it up as an independent company owned directly by the shareholders of the parent.

The **parent company** distributes shares in the new company to its shareholders on a proportional basis.

spin-off

> **EXAMPLE** | Eastman Kodak Company decided in 1993 to spin off its chemical company to sharpen its focus on its imaging business. At the start of 1994, stockholders got one share in the newly independent Eastman Chemical Company for every four shares of Kodak that they owned. The chairman and vice chairman of the new corporation had been the top executives in the chemical company when it was part of Kodak.

(2) Sale of part of a company to employees.

A company may spin off a subsidiary by selling it to the subsidiary's **Employee Stock Ownership Plan (ESOP)** in a **leveraged buyout (LBO)**.

fin **mktg**

spot market   Place where you pay cash for **commodities** and take immediate delivery.

See also **spot price**.

fin **mktg**

spot price   Current cash price on the free market.

The term is often used for **commodities** also traded under contract.

> **EXAMPLE** | A particular grade of crude oil has one price when bought by a refiner under contract with a producer, another price when traded for future delivery on a **derivatives** market, and a third price on the spot market. You are running a refining company and want to ensure a steady supply of crude oil. So you have contractual arrangements for about three-quarters of the crude you need. But you also take advantage of the spot market's lower prices by buying the rest from brokers in international oil-trading centers like Amsterdam and Singapore.

S

Spot Price

SPOT & FORWARD RATES				Source CMP Composite			
RATES FROM 8/ 5/96	MID RATES JPY/USD	SPREADS BID	ASK	MID RATES USD/JPY	SPREADS BID	ASK	VALUE DATES
SPOT	106.50	106.45	106.55	0.0093897 0.0093853	0.0093941		8/ 7/96
O/N	106.49	-1	0	0.0093910	8	17	8/ 5/96
T/N	106.49	-1	0	0.0093910	8	17	8/ 6/96
S/N	106.49	-1	0	0.0093910	8	17	8/ 8/96
1-WK	106.40	-10	-9	0.0093989	88	97	8/12/96
1-MO	106.03	-46	-46	0.0094313	415	416	9/ 5/96
2-MO	105.62	-89	-86	0.0094679	772	792	10/ 7/96
3-MO	105.18	-132	-131	0.0095080	1177	1188	11/ 5/96
4-MO	104.75	-176	-173	0.0095465	1548	1588	12/ 5/96
5-MO	104.31	-221	-217	0.0095868	1951	1991	1/ 6/97
6-MO	103.86	-267	-260	0.0096283	2356	2416	2/ 5/97
9-MO	102.73	-382	-371	0.0097343	3395	3496	5/ 5/97
1 YR	101.56	-499	-489	0.0098464	4514	4620	8/ 5/97
2 YR	97.30	-995	-845	0.0102775	8084	9686	8/ 5/98
3 YR	93.90	-1360	-1159	0.0106496	11465	13759	8/ 5/99
4 YR	90.90	-1660	-1459	0.0110011	14902	17355	8/ 7/ 0
5 YR	88.15	-1935	-1734	0.0113443	18254	20869	8/ 6/ 1
8/19/96	106.29	-21	-20	0.0094084	183	190	8/19/96
8/26/96	106.18	-31	-31	0.0094178	279	283	8/26/96

Source: Bloomberg Financial Markets

In this Bloomberg display of the U.S. dollar exchange rate with the Japanese yen, we see the difference that time frame makes in the "price" of a U.S. dollar. The spot price, for example, is 106.5 yen, while the price one year out is only 101 .6 yen. Going out further to five years, the exchange rate is only 88 Japanese yen.

---

mgmt

staff support   Workers who do not directly produce revenue.

People like accountants, lawyers, planners, and lobbyists are examples. In Michael Porter's concept of a **value chain**, these functions are called support activities.

Sometimes the distinction is hard to make. If you are the lawyer on a team negotiating a contract to start a venture in Russia, for example, your work certainly will have an impact on the bottom line.

mgmt

staggered terms   Electing a portion of the board every year. Also called **classification of directors**.

With staggered terms, directors usually are elected to three-year terms, with a third of the directors up for election at each annual meeting.

Staggered terms became popular for publicly traded corporations early in the 1980s as a defense against the possibility of hostile takeover attempts or proxy wars. If only a third of your board is up for reelection in any year, it is harder for a corporate raider to change the company's management and direction all at once. Companies with staggered terms—Kodak, Mobil, and Nynex are examples—believe that they ensure stability and continuity in management. Most large companies—among them AT&T, Exxon, General Electric, and General Motors—have remained with the traditional one-year terms.

A number of investor groups oppose staggered terms, believing that directors up for election every three years will be less responsive to

---

staff support

It is said that one machine can do the work of fifty ordinary men. No machine, however, can do the work of one extraordinary man.

—Tehyi Hsieh, *Chinese Epigrams: Inside and Out Proverbs*, 1948

staggered terms

We want to make sure the companies and their boards are accountable to the shareholders such as us. If the company is not performing, we want the board members to be accountable to that.

—Patrick Hill, CalPERS spokesperson

S

521

acct fin

statement of shareholders' equity

Breakdown of the components of **shareholders' equity** and how they have changed over the **accounting period**.

A corporation may include this table in its **annual report**.

acct

statement on auditing standards (SAS)

Numbered statement outlining an acceptable practice.

See also **generally accepted auditing standards (GAAS)**.

oper

statistical quality control (SQC)

Monitoring product samples to gauge quality.

See also **acceptance sampling**.

fin

stock dividend

Dividend payout in the form of stock rather than cash.

Stock dividends are used in "payment in kind" **preferred stocks**, or PIKs. A PIK preferred stock will pay dividends in additional preferred stock instead of cash. There may also be PIK bonds, which pay interest in the form of additional bonds. This structure can be onerous to the issuer and advantageous to the security holder.

PIK securities trade "flat" (that is, without accrued interest or dividends). Their price is expected to reflect accrued interest since the last payment. PIKs generally trade at higher **yields** than their cash-paying counterparts because of the lower perceived valuation of noncash payouts.

See also **stock split**.

fin

stock index

Any of a number of indicators used to measure stock-market price movements.

Stock market indicators include the following:

▶ The **Dow Jones Industrial Average (DJIA)** tracks the shares of 30 major corporations traded on the **New York Stock Exchange (NYSE)**. Dow Jones also maintains averages for transportation and utility stocks.

▶ The **Standard & Poor's** 500 tracks 500 widely held stocks.

▶ The New York Stock Exchange Composite Index measures the market value of all shares traded on the NYSE.

▶ The Nasdaq Composite Index measures the market value of all equity shares traded on the **Nasdaq Stock Market**.

---

stock dividend

tip

One advantage of PIKs and zero-coupon bonds is that interest payments are automatically compounded (reinvested) at the stated coupon rate, which is not the case with cash-paying securities. PIKs offer an added advantage over zero-coupon bonds—their payouts (in the form of more stock or bonds) can be sold for cash, which is more tangible than the accretion value of the interest in zero-coupon bonds.

stock index

Speculation is the romance of trade, and casts contempt upon all its sober realities. It renders the stock-jobber a magician, and the exchange a region of enchantment.

—Washington Irving, "A Time of Unexampled Prosperity," *Wolfert's Roost*, 1855

S

▶ The Amex Market Value Index measures the performance of more than 800 issues traded on the **American Stock Exchange (Amex)**.

Some investors and mutual funds build their portfolios on the basis of a market index, and many traded **derivatives** are based on an index.

fin **mgmt**

stock option   Right to buy or sell a stock at a particular price before a given date. Stock options are often included in the compensation packages offered to senior executives of public companies.

See also **derivatives**, **warrants**, and **executive compensation**.

fin

stock split   Increasing the number of a company's outstanding shares without changing **shareholders' equity**.

The immediate result is that the number of shares held by each shareholder increases, but the total values involved do not. If the company pays a **dividend**, it will be reduced in proportion to the split. In executing a stock split, the company reduces the **par value** of each share and probably needs to increase the number of authorized shares, so shareholder approval is required. A stock split can be in any proportion: two-for-one, three-for-one, three-for-two, and so on.

EXAMPLE | The board of directors and shareholders of Electron Corp. approved a two-for-one split for holders of its common stock, which took effect today. The par value had been $5, with 10 million shares authorized. With the split, the par value is $2.50, with 20 million shares authorized. There has been no change to shareholders' equity on the company's balance sheet. The dividend, previously $1 a share, is expected to be $0.50. Yesterday, Electron Corp.'s shares closed at $50 in over-the-counter (OTC) trading; today they opened at $25.

An investor who yesterday had 100 shares of Electron Corp., worth $5,000 and paying a total dividend of $100, today has 200 shares that are still worth $5,000 and pay $100.

Why declare a stock split if the overall values do not change? Many companies believe that a lower stock price is at least a psychological encouragement to investors. It also makes stock ownership more affordable to a larger number of people and increases **liquidity**. In addition, a split enables smaller shareholders to buy in lots of 100 shares and therefore may reduce their brokerage commissions.

Another way of increasing outstanding shares is by a **stock dividend**. This does not involve a change in the par value and is usually done on a smaller scale, so shareholder approval may not be needed. A company declaring a 10 percent stock dividend would issue another share to each holder of 10 shares. Although a stock dividend does involve some changes within shareholders' equity on the balance sheet, total shareholders' equity remains the same.

A **reverse split** works the other way. That is when a company reduces the number of shares outstanding. In a one-for-two reverse

stock split

Quick Facts!

Most companies around for any length of time have a history of stock splits. One share of General Electric obtained in 1892, when the company was formed, would be 768 shares today. A few companies, most notably Berkshire Hathaway, have a policy against stock splits. Shares in that company have traded at more than $30,000 each.

S

split, investors get one new share for two of the presplit ones, and the par value doubles. Again, there is no change to shareholders' equity or other total values. When a company's share price is low, it might consider a reverse split for psychological reasons and to reduce administrative costs.

storyboard

© Francisco Stohr

strategic business unit

> What is driving it is pressure in the marketplace to be fast and flexible. Strategic business units are, in a way, a hybrid. They let you hang on to a little of the hierarchy and enter into a more responsive approach.
>
> —David Calabria, president, Calabria and Co. consultants

mktg

storyboard   In **marketing**, a comic-strip-type depiction of the action in a TV commercial.

The illustrated panels show the sequence of the action, and the full script usually accompanies the illustrations. As the name indicates, everything is often arranged on a poster-like board for easy presentation.

Storyboards are usually prepared by an **advertising agency** to give clients a way to visualize and discuss a proposed commercial. Storyboards also give the producers of an ad a detailed blueprint to follow.

acct

straight-line method   Simplest method of **depreciation**, it spreads the cost of an **asset** in equal amounts over the asset's useful life.

See also **accelerated depreciation**.

strat   **mgmt**

strategic business unit (SBU)   Product lines or businesses that have been tied together inside a company because they share **markets**, competitors, or strategies.

Forming SBUs has been popular in the 1990s. They bring under one management various product groupings that had previously been administered separately. And their **staff support** services like accounting and technical development can be brought in, too.

EXAMPLE | In 1995, Mindscape, a rapidly growing developer and publisher of software, created SBUs to handle product development for each of the company's U.S. market segments—entertainment, home and kids, reference, and sports and games.

It is not uncommon for service or financial organizations to organize around SBUs.

EXAMPLE | In 1993, Empire Blue Cross and Blue Shield reorganized around five SBUs to improve service and streamline operations. The SBUs, which have since been replaced in yet another reorganization, were: group accounts with more than 1,000 participants, group accounts with 50 to 1,000 participants, individuals and small groups, managed care, and Medicare.

S

The key advantage of an SBU is the ability to run a strategically similar set of businesses under one management. This streamlines strategy formulation and eliminates a lot of redundant effort.

See also **value chain**.

strategic planning   Identifying the goals and programs to help a company achieve its mission.

Many large companies have strategic planning departments that work with business managers to develop assumptions about the environment and objectives for how the company can meet its goals in the context of those assumptions.

Strategic planning:

> ► Involves managers throughout the company.
>
> ► Requires sound underlying assumptions of external conditions expected during the lifetime of the plan.
>
> ► Focuses on long-term goals as well as short-term results.
>
> ► Reviews and distributes the company's resources, such as capital and equipment.
>
> ► Is concerned with the organization's external relationships and public-policy issues.

stratified sampling   Dividing a population into groups based on selected criteria before making a **random sampling** of each group.

See also **sampling**.

strike price   Point at which the **asset** underlying an **option** can be bought or sold.

See also **derivatives**.

subchapter S corporation   See **S corporation**.

fin

subordinated debt   Unsecured debt obligations that are junior in liquidation preference to senior secured and **secured debt**.

Because subordinated debt is further down in the capitalization ladder, it carries more risk than **senior debt**. This means that the **interest rate**, or yield, that a company must pay on subordinated debt is usually more expensive.

strategic planning

t r a p | 👎

Strategic planning often fails because it is based on extrapolations of current conditions, whereas change comes about in unexpected ways.

S

If a company is liquidated, **subordinated debt** does not get paid until the claims of holders of senior and secured debt have been settled. And there are hierarchies of subordinated debt. For example, a subordinated debenture ranks above a junior subordinated debenture. The ranking of a debt instrument such as a bond is set forth in the **indenture** and disclosed in its **prospectus**.

fin

subscription right
Authorization to buy newly issued **common stock** at a discount price.

See also **right**.

fin

subscription warrant
Security that lets its holder buy a certain number of a company's shares at a set price.

See also **warrant**.

acct **fin** **mgmt**

subsidiary
Company more than 50 percent owned by another.

See also **affiliated company** and **parent company**.

strat **mgmt** **econ**

sunk cost
Expenditures on a project that cannot be recovered regardless of any action you take now or later.

Since past costs cannot be changed, they are considered sunk: There is nothing you can do about them. You have to make further spending decisions based on the present and future.

EXAMPLE | Your company spent $10 million to set up shop selling your industrial chemicals in a new country. After five years, you still have not won over many customers from local competition. Since you are losing money and have little prospect of turning the situation around, your $10 million investment is irrelevant. You can sell some of your assets there for around $1 million, but you just have to walk away from the rest. You consider it a sunk cost.

tech

supercomputer
Fastest and most powerful computer available.

Supercomputers are used for highly complex and sophisticated computations—such as those involving fluid dynamics, physics, structural analysis, and chemistry. Applications like these require high-performance computing. Cray Research was the commercial pioneer of supercomputers and remains a worldwide leader.

EXAMPLE | Companies that explore for and produce crude oil use supercomputers to model reservoirs and figure out the most productive way to get the petroleum out.

Quick Facts!

Cray scientists David Slowinski and Paul Gage, testing a supercomputer, discovered the highest known prime number (one that cannot be divided evenly by any number other than itself or 1). The number has 258,716 digits and can be expressed as two multiplied by itself 859,433 times minus one.

superfund   Federal program that holds companies accountable for paying to clean up toxic waste.

Administered by the U.S. Environmental Protection Agency (EPA), superfund is a shorthand term for the **Comprehensive Environmental Response, Compensation, and Liability Act (CERCLA),** as amended in 1986.

Under CERCLA, if land is found to be contaminated, all the companies that owned the site or occupied it in the past may have to pay for the cleanup, even if they had nothing to do with the pollution. And they have what is called "joint and several liability," which means that the cleanup may be considered the sole responsibility of each of the participants.

EXAMPLE | If your company is one of 50 that may have contributed to a toxic waste site, you cannot figure that your share of the cleanup cost is 2 percent. If the other 49 companies cannot be found or are broke, your share is 100 percent.

fin

super-regional bank   Very large institution that conducts banking activities in a specific region of the United States.

See also **regional bank**.

mgmt   **oper**

supervisor   In a manufacturing plant, the first line of management, usually on the shop floor.

Workers are often promoted to this initial rung of the management ladder because of their thorough command of work operations. As they rise, their people skills become increasingly important.

See also **shop floor control**.

fin   **mgmt**

supplier credit   Financing extended through the seller to buyers of exported goods.

See also **trade credit**.

strat   **mgmt**

supplier power   The influence a supplier has over a buyer.

Powerful suppliers—such as Intel with its microprocessors—can really shrink the profitability of an industry by raising prices or reducing the quantity of goods available.

---

supercomputer

superfund

tip

If your company has any environmental risk, you need an experienced environmental lawyer or consultant to help you navigate through the maze of regulations. And do not buy, sell, or lease property without full environmental disclosures. Most lenders now require a review of the chain of title, review of EPA and other records for environmental incidents, aerial surveys, and site visits to look for obvious signs of contamination.

supervisor

tip

Supervisors are often good candidates for continued management training. You may be able to set up on-site courses taught by a local community college.

S

supplier power

supply

EXAMPLE

A freeze in Brazil will shrink the supply of coffee. A government quota on shoe imports will lessen the supply of shoes available to the consumer.

Supplier power tends to be high when:

▶ Supplies are controlled by a handful of companies, making the industry highly concentrated.

▶ Suppliers embrace **forward integration**, producing the same end-goods as the purchasers produce.

▶ There are few substitute products.

▶ The suppliers' products are well differentiated.

▶ It is costly for buyers to switch products.

▶ The purchasers' industry is not an important customer for the supplying industry.

See also **buyer power** and **differentiation**.

econ

supply   Amount of a product that companies are willing to sell.

Generally, at higher prices, sellers in a market want to sell more; at lower prices, they have less incentive to sell. This principle is known as the law of supply. Supply curves tend to be flatter in the longer run as companies have more time to adjust production to changed prices. Thus, a higher price will generate a larger supply over time once firms gear up capacity to take advantage of it.

Price, however, is not the only influence on suppliers. A major factor is the supplier's costs: If costs rise, supply will likely shrink; if costs fall, supply will expand. The cost and **productivity** of **inputs** determine mainly the seller's costs. For example, if wages rise for textile workers, the cost of making dresses will rise and the supply will fall. Alternatively, if the workers' productivity rises—say, because of technological progress—costs of making dresses will fall and supply will rise.

Acts of God and government can sometimes change supply, too.

See also **demand**, **shortage**, **supply elasticity**, and **surplus**.

econ   **strat**

supply elasticity   Measure of the responsiveness of producers to price changes.

See also **elasticity**.

S

econ

supply-side economics
School of economic thought that emphasizes a connection between government policies and **aggregate supply**.

More specifically, higher marginal tax rates and greater government regulation are thought to reduce incentives to work, save, and invest, thereby constraining the growth of **productivity** and aggregate supply. In particular, supply-siders have focused on marginal tax rates—or rates paid on additional (marginal) dollars of income—arguing that very high marginal rates constrict aggregate production and income. Lower incomes, in turn, generate smaller government revenues than originally anticipated from the higher tax rates.

Supply-side economics has helped to point up the effect of tax-rate changes on government revenues. Today, most economists recognize that higher marginal tax rates can, at the least, increase incentives to avoid paying taxes by using legal **tax shelters**. As a result, raising marginal tax rates will yield less additional income than originally anticipated.

Similarly, lower marginal tax rates can increase production and income and reduce incentives to use tax shelters. The higher reported incomes then partially offset the effects on government revenues of the lower tax rates. In cases of very high tax rates, some supply-siders argue that lower rates will actually increase government revenues because the higher incomes that result will more than offset the lower tax rates.

See also **fiscal policy, monetarism, monetary policy,** and **price controls**.

econ

surplus
What happens when the **supply** of a good or service exceeds the **demand** at the current price.

A surplus implies that there are at least some sellers stuck with items they would like to sell. So they are likely to cut prices to enable them to unload their excess inventories.

Surpluses sometimes happen as an overreaction to a period of **shortage**.

EXAMPLE | In 1992 and 1993, the cellular phone industry did not make enough phones to meet its fast-growing demand. Distributors reacted by overordering and producers by overproducing, so at the start of 1995 producers and distributors were swimming in cellular phones. Lots of below-cost deals were made until April, when inventory levels smoothed out.

mktg

surveying
Gathering information by using written or oral questions to determine consumer preferences and opinions.

Marketers use surveys to find out people's reactions to products, prices, **advertising**, and so on.

surplus

S

S

surveying

tip

People are reluctant to share personal views over the phone. In addition, they find evening calls extremely annoying. There are alternatives:

Personal interview. *It is expensive, but the interviewer has control over the individuals surveyed and can take the time to develop complex issues. The danger is that the subjects will say what they think the interviewer wants to hear.*

Focus group. *Eight to twelve people who hold a discussion with a facilitator. This allows for considerable depth, but the results cannot be projected with mathematical certainty.*

SWOT analysis

Some see private enterprise as a predatory target to be shot, others as a cow to be milked, but few are those who see it as a sturdy horse pulling the wagon.

—Winston Churchill

There are two common forms of surveying:

1 **Mail Survey**
The costs are moderate, but it takes considerable time to carry out. Moreover, the **sampling** may be skewed by the large number of people who fail to respond.

2 **Telephone Survey**
It can be timed to coincide with the introduction of a new ad campaign, and results can be compiled almost immediately.

See also **A-B split**.

`strat` `mgmt`

SWOT analysis Way of thinking about a company, summed up by a catchy acronym that stands for Strengths, Weaknesses, Opportunities, Threats.

► **Strengths**
They may be resources, skills, market position, **patents**, and so on. Strengths are also called **core competencies**. A high-tech company, for example, may have a strength in the creative minds of its young employees, who come up with proprietary technologies.

► **Weaknesses**
Company attributes that lead to poor performance. For example, outdated production methods or lack of modern technology can weaken a company's performance.

► **Opportunities**
External conditions that a company can use to improve its performance. For example, increasing societal awareness about saving the environment is an opportunity for paper companies that make products from recycled paper.

► **Threats**
External conditions that can adversely affect a company. Another war in the Middle East could once again pinch supply for U.S. oil companies.

`mgmt`

symbolic action Technique for developing a particular **corporate culture**, basically involving teaching by example.

`tech`

synchronous transmission Form of data transmission where blocks of characters are transmitted. The blocks are preceded by unique **bits**, and data transfer is controlled by a timing signal initiated by the sending device. Commonly used by communications satellites.

See also **asynchronous transmission**.

fin

syndicate   Group of **investment bankers** that join together to buy and resell a new issue of securities.

See also **underwriting syndicate**.

strat   **mgmt**

synergy   Term describing the boost in overall value that results from combining two or more businesses, activities, or processes.

The ideal is that, after the combination, the whole will be greater than the sum of the parts. Often a company uses the term in **annual reports** and other official communications to justify just about any company expansion, acquisition, or merger.

There are times, of course, when the whole actually is greater than the sum of the parts—when skills can be transferred among units or when different units can share a function.

EXAMPLE | Haggar Apparel Company and Dak, Inc., a Mexican marketing and manufacturing firm, formed a joint venture in Mexico. Dak provided low-cost labor and raw materials plus knowledge of the Mexican market. Haggar provided its clothing expertise and gave the exclusive right to Dak to make and distribute Haggar products in Mexico. Then there is Procter & Gamble, which uses a common sales force and distribution system for disposable diapers and paper towels.

fin

synthetic convertible   A **bond** with a set number of **warrants** attached.

See also **bond/warrant unit**.

fin

systematic risk   Sensitivity of a stock's price to things like shifts in the economy, **interest rates**, **inflation**, and general investor confidence.

See also **market risk**.

synergy

synthetic convertible

S

Steel

Andrew Carnegie

What telecommunications and electronics are to today's economy, steel was to the economy of the 19th century. In that period, steel—the elemental building block of the emerging industrial civilization—was a glamorous and exciting industry, its technologies rapidly evolving and its leaders, like Andrew Carnegie, celebrated and admired.

Fundamentally, steel making involves melting ore at high temperatures, withdrawing the molten metal, pouring it into shapes, and permitting it to cool. In the colonial period this was done in small installations, often operated by a few individuals, who used the modest amounts of iron they produced to turn out nails, horseshoes, and other items sold locally.

In the 19th century, this process was carried out in blast furnaces—towering cylinders lined with refractory bricks. The name derived from the blast of hot air and gases forced through the ore, coke, and limestone mix loaded into the furnace.

Open-hearth furnaces were introduced in the early 20th century. These were broad, shallow hearths in which pig iron and scrap were turned into steel, the heat coming from flames played over the surface. The resulting steel was superior to that produced in blast furnaces, an important consideration for automobile manufacturers and others demanding higher levels of performance from the metals they purchased.

By the late 1960s, open-hearth methods were being replaced by basic oxygen furnaces, which used molten pig iron from blast furnaces as raw material. Finally, electric-arc furnaces were used to produce alloys and stainless and tool steels. The electric-arc method used lower-cost machinery than that employed in continuous casting, enabling the operators to realize important economies.

In the 1830s, demand for steel increased to serve the growing railroad industry. Steel was imported from England as well, but after the 1870s, as the domestic industry expanded, American firms supplied an increasing amount of the needed shapes.

Toward the end of the century, as the railroad created national markets and investment bankers rearranged entire industries, the steel landscape changed rapidly. From 1898 to 1900 there were 20 amalgamations in steel, the largest being J. P. Morgan's Federal Steel. Taken together, they were capitalized at slightly more than $1 billion. Then, in 1901, Morgan bought out the Carnegie interests, wedded them to Federal Steel, National Tube, and National Steel, along with other companies, creating the largest steel company in the world. With the formation of U.S. Steel, the industry entered its national age.

While railroads continued to absorb large amounts of steel, even more was taken by construction, machinery, and automobiles. The canning industry was a large market for the metal as well (tin cans were really made of steel).

*Contributing Editor: Robert A. Hageman
Managing Director, Oppenheimer & Co.*

While U.S. Steel was by far the industry's largest company before World War II, it by no means was the only substantial one. Among the integrated companies—those involved in all aspects of steel-making—were Bethlehem, Youngstown Sheet & Tube, Wheeling, Inland, Republic, Jones & Laughlin, Steel & Tube, and a handful of others. In addition, there were

many specialty steel companies, such as Allegheny Ludlum, Armco, and Lukens.

Most of the steel companies specialized in several types of forms, such as structural shapes, sheet, hot-rolled bars, rails, pipe and tubes, and plates. Bethlehem, for example, provided sheet steel used in ship construction, while specialty producer Carpenter Technology turned out stainless steel for use in consumer durable and capital goods markets.

The American industry remained dominant in the first half of the century, but the situation started to change after World War II. The Europeans and Japanese rebuilt their facilities, employing the efficient basic-oxygen and con-

tinuous-casting methods—a way of casting steel into billets and slabs directly from its molten form—rather than the open-hearth furnaces saddling domestic companies. These modern mills were able to undersell American products on world markets. The U.S. share of output, which had reached 57 percent in 1947, fell below 30 percent by 1958. By then, imported steel had a quarter of the American market.

In this period the steel companies faced additional blows from substitutes. Steel cans were replaced by cans made of aluminum, and the lighter metal found many uses in products that previously had employed steel. Plastics, hardly known before the war, became quite common, and they, too, often replaced steel.

There were other problems. In the first half of the century America had cheap sources of iron ore. By midcentury many of these were depleted, so the companies had to go elsewhere for more expensive ore. Labor costs were high due to effective unionization, and since the Americans had to compete with proficient foreign firms, this proved a decided disadvantage.

The American industry was in disarray. Mills and foundries closed, workers were dismissed; from the more than 550,000 workers in 1960, the figure fell to 200,000 by 1990. Pittsburgh, once the center of steel production, had many miles of abandoned facilities. Once-strong companies disappeared. LTV purchased Jones & Laughlin and Republic Steel. National Steel became National Intergroup, sold off facilities to employees, and came under the control of Nippon Kokan, a Japanese firm. Another

Japanese company, Nisshin Steel, took an equity interest in Wheeling-Pittsburgh. NVF acquired Sharon Steel. U.S. Steel purchased Marathon Oil and Texas Oil and Gas, to become USX Corp.

As the old American steel industry deteriorated, a new one emerged to take its place. Those companies that remained converted to continuous-casting techniques, and by the mid-1990s the method accounted for almost 90 percent of all American steel production. At one time American companies scorned borrowing ideas and purchasing patents and machinery from foreigners. This ended, and as was the case with automobiles and other products, the American firms profited by learning how the Germans, Japanese, Belgians, and others achieved superior results.

To obtain breathing room while they retooled, the American companies sought government help in limiting imports. During the Nixon administration some restrictions were put into effect. Then the Carter administration instituted a "trigger price mechanism" aimed at Japanese producers, whereby dumping charges would be brought if foreign steel were sold at below what was believed to be the average Japanese level of costs. The policy was generally ineffective and may have aided European companies accused of dumping their steel in America at prices higher than those of the Japanese but lower than their costs. The American companies then went off on their own, bringing lawsuits against importers that threatened international relations until the Reagan administration negotiated voluntary guidelines limiting foreign steel to around 20 percent of the American market.

The rigorous industry atmosphere led to several failures. Wheeling-Pittsburgh filed for Chapter 11 bankruptcy in 1985, and LTV, which had purchased Republic Steel in 1984, followed in 1986. Most of the older companies survived, though industry production fell from more than 137 million tons in 1978 to fewer than 90 million tons in 1991.

While the glory days of the 1940s would never return, American facilities ranked among the most modern in the world. As for the labor situation, additional layoffs occurred while production increased; in the 1980s steel productivity doubled, imports declined, and exports increased.

In part, these showings were made possible by new companies that operated minimills, facilities capable of producing from 100,000 to 500,000 tons of steel a year. Minimills melted scrap in electric-arc furnaces to make simple carbon steel products, such as concrete reinforcing bars and ingots. Since the processes do not require ore and coke, facilities can be located near large amounts of available scrap. Thus, the minimills can be established close to markets rather than to ore supplies. Although radically dissimilar from small operations of the colonial period, the idea behind them was not too different. Both used local raw materials—outcroppings of ore 300 years ago, scrap today—to produce steel products for nearby customers.

This created problems of supply and demand: The price of scrap became crucial to the industry, while the opening or closing of a new facility or the awarding of a major construction contract could alter a company's outlook considerably. Finally, these new firms were not restricted by unions and so had flexible working conditions. By the mid-1990s, minimills were producing almost a third of American steel.

Nucor became the largest minimill operator, the fourth biggest American steel producer, and a pioneer in developing technologies and labor relations. F. Kenneth Iverson, its CEO, created an incentive and profit-sharing program other companies modified and adopted. Under his leadership, Nucor took the lead in importing European technologies and machinery. Entering the flat-rolled steel market, Nucor quickly became a leader in a product with widespread use in the manufacture of oil drums, siding, and decking. The company's success encouraged other minimills to enter the field, among them Gallatin Steel and Steel Dynamics.

Many of the minimills followed the Nucor model, though each was different in some ways. Oregon Steel could trace itself back to 1926, when, as Gilmore Steel, it produced steel for a market in the Northwest. There was a management-led buyout in 1984, and employees received a stake through the establishment of an Employee Stock Ownership Plan. The name was changed to Oregon Steel in 1987, and the company started on an expansion program that included the purchase of a pipe mill in California. In 1993, what originally had been Colorado Fuel and Iron, and had become CFI, was in bankruptcy. Once a prime supplier of rails to Western railroads, CFI had been unable to make the shift to new products and markets. Oregon Steel took CFI out of bankruptcy and modernized its facilities. Toward the end of the century, the company had close to a billion dollars in sales.

Bayou Steel was another local company, situated in La Place, Louisiana, on the outskirts of New Orleans, where it produced flats, wide-

flange beams, and other related products. The marketing area was local, but some steel was sent as far away as Canada and Mexico. It had two electric-arc furnaces in a plant put up by VoestAlpine, an Austrian steel company. Sales were less than $200 million annually. Once, before World War II, a steel company's blast furnaces could be easily seen, and steel facilities dominated their regions. People in New Orleans often were not even aware of Bayou Steel's existence.

The minimills have increased their workforces almost every year in the late 1980s and 1990s. Meanwhile, former Pittsburgh steelworks are vestiges of a time that has passed. The empty works remain a monument of sorts to the old industrial age. There was talk in the mid-1990s

of turning the many miles of abandoned buildings into a sort of industrial theme park, with the former workers as guides.

T

T-account

to

type II error

T-account Simplified rendition of an accounting **ledger** that is used to analyze or illustrate the effects of transactions on the various **accounts**.

It consists of two perpendicular lines that look like the letter "T." The account name appears above the horizontal line, and the **debits** and **credits** are on the left and right sides, respectively.

takeover When one company takes over controlling interest of another. A takeover can be friendly or hostile. A hostile takeover—one that is originally unsolicited by the target company—is often initiated through a public **tender offer** for the company's shares. A hostile takeover may eventually become a friendly one.

There were plenty of takeovers in 1995, as shown in the table below, but none provided the drama many have come to associate with the word. Of the top 10 deals listed below, four were **spin-offs** of divisions to shareholders by companies who wanted to focus on their core businesses. (See related story on the following page.)

See also **acquisition** and **merger**.

Top 10 Completed U.S. Target Deals, 1995

Date	Target	Acquirer	Market Value ($ billions)
Nov. 95	U.S. West Inc.–Dom. Cellular	AirTouch Communications	$13.5
July 95	Nynex Corp.–Cellular Phone	Bell Atlantic–Cellular Phones	$13.0
July 95	Allstate Corp. (Sears Roebuck)	Shareholders	$12.0
Nov. 95	U.S. West–U.S.-West Media Group	Shareholders	$ 9.3
Apr. 95	E.I. du Pont de Nemours and Co.	E.I. du Pont de Nemours and Co.*	$ 8.3
July 95	Marion Merrell Dow, Inc.	Hoechst AG	$ 7.1
Dec. 95	Scott Paper Co.	Kimberly-Clark Corp.	$ 6.8
Dec. 95	ITT Destinations Inc. (ITT Corp.)	Shareholders (ITT)	$ 5.9
Oct. 95	First Financial Management	First Data Corp.	$ 5.8
Dec. 95	ITT Hartford Group, Inc.	Shareholders	$ 5.7

Source: *Mergers and Acquisitions Report* (*Investment Dealers' Digest*)

*Du Pont bought back its own stock from major shareholder Seagram Co. Ltd.

T

FRAME OF REFERENCE

takeover

Takeovers and Their Consequences: Perception Versus Reality

After the number of high-profile takeovers that occurred in the 1980s, many investors and onlookers became concerned about their effects, fearing that takeovers—particularly hostile takeovers—led to layoffs, leverage, and dismembered companies. But the record shows this generalization to be misleading, at best. Many economists and regulators believe that takeovers result in more efficient companies, better returns for shareholders, and more jobs.

Perhaps the most important effect of hostile takeover has been its value in fighting the drain of entrenched management. Critics point to the rise in takeover defense as the tool of corporate managers who want to hang on to their jobs—not the reaction of a company trying to "protect" its shareholders. After all, a hostile takeover requires the approval of shareholders—most of whom are only too happy to receive a premium price for their shares. In 1987, when takeover controversy was at a peak, Federal Trade Commission Chairman Daniel Oliver argued this point to Congress, stating that "it is a misnomer to call such a takeover effort hostile; incumbent shareholders are usually happy to sell their shares at a premium to the acquiring firm."

tangible product

acct

tangible asset   An **asset** involving physical property, such as land, buildings, equipment, or inventory.

See also **intangible asset**.

acct   **fin**

tangible net worth   Owner's or **stockholders' equity** minus **intangible assets**.

mktg

tangible product   What the customer actually buys, something that can be touched, smelled, seen, or heard. It may be different from the **core product**.

The core product of Slim-Fast is hassle-free weight loss. The tangible product, however, is an attractively packaged, low-calorie drink in various flavors. The core product of a record album is enjoyable music. The tangible product is a CD, tape, or record, plus its packaging. If the album contains an insert with extensive background information on the artist, that is the **augmented product**.

mktg

target market   Group of consumers with similar needs or characteristics that appeal to a company and show profit potential. Also called the **served market**.

Though some companies sell to what is called an **undifferentiated market**—just about everybody in the universe—the overwhelming trend is toward **market segmentation**.

T

target market

Your neighborhood cafe is bringing in more than 75 percent of its revenue between 11 A.M. and 2 P.M. on weekdays. Profits have been steady but have not grown in a year, and one of the businesses whose workers eat at your cafe will soon be moving to a new area. You have been regarding the business lunch crowd as your primary target market, but maybe there is a new market waiting to be discovered.

You consider focusing on dinner service for either families or dating singles. You need to measure how large and profitable these potential dinner markets are before making expensive changes like adding menu offerings and redecorating your restaurant. You decide that the dating-singles crowd is too small in your neighborhood and decide to target families instead.

Once you identify your segment opportunities, you can decide which ones to go after by sizing up factors such as:

▶ The segment's size and growth potential. In doing this, you may decide that some markets are either too small or too big to meet your goals or fit your resources.

▶ The segment's potential for profitability.

▶ Your company's long-range goals.

Marketers often run a target market decision analysis on the whole market based on relevant characteristics—like age, residence, gender, and income. Then they choose a target that matches their resources and goals. Once you decide on a target, you have to think about what **position** you want your product or service to hold in your target consumers' minds. You can position on the basis of the characteristics of your product, how it is used, who uses it, and so on. The position you choose will determine the type of message you need to get across to your target.

See also **differentiated market**, **marketing mix**, **mass marketing**, **product positioning**, and **purchase-decision process**.

 fin

tax haven   Country offering low or no taxes for foreign companies and individuals.

The Cayman Islands, for example, have no income tax. One measure of the international business flowing through the Caymans is the more than 500 banks registered there—more than one for every 50 citizens. Other well-known tax havens include the Bahamas, Bermuda, the Channel Islands, Hong Kong, Liechtenstein, Luxembourg, Panama, and the Turks and Caicos Islands.

tax haven

T

541

technology transfer

> *Technology made large populations possible; large populations now make technology indispensable.*
>
> —Joseph Wood Krutch, in *Human Nature and the Human Condition*, 1959

telemarketing

tip |

You can improve your telemarketing success rate by first mailing brochures and letters letting people know that you will be calling. To reduce the stress of telemarketing, call qualified leads— like previous customers and/ or people who have actually asked for information.

T

oper **tech** **mgmt**

technical specialist   In a manufacturing plant, a professional concerned with materials conversion—or the way labor, machines, and raw materials come together in a series of operations to produce a product.

strat

technology transfer   Making expertise available to your trading partners or the countries where you are doing business.

This could involve the sharing of specifics like a **patent** or the design of a process, or it could refer to the experience that rubs off over time.

Technology transfer generally takes place in one of the following ways:

► A company sells or licenses its technology to another.

► In a countertrade arrangement, technical assistance or research is part of the package offered by a company.

► In a **joint venture**, each company benefits from the expertise of the other.

► When a multinational corporation does business in a developing nation, it transfers technology by hiring and training workers.

► A government agency in a developed nation funds technical assistance for a developing nation.

► Espionage.

mktg

telemarketing   Directly selling goods or services by telephone.

Telemarketers often place their calls during the evening—targeting people who are too busy at work to shop during the day. The technique has been used increasingly in recent years by nonprofit organizations.

EXAMPLE | The New York Philharmonic sells almost half of its new subscriptions, and 20 percent of total subscriptions, via the telephone. The organization's telemarketers help customers choose seat locations and dates of performance, and point them to future special events for which they might want to buy tickets.

Studies have shown that people who buy by phone tend to have a better-than-average education and a high-status job. Their family income is higher than that of families that buy almost all their goods in stores.

Many companies have established toll-free telephone "hot lines" that can be seen as an extension of telemarketing. The Scotts Company, for example, handles more than 350,000 consumer calls a year.

FRAME OF REFERENCE

telemarketing

A name practically synonomous with telemarketing is that of MCI Communications Corp. In the mid-1970s, MCI effectively used telemarketing to gain on industry giant AT&T in the battle for long-distance customers. In the mid-'80s, MCI led the way in automated tele-marketing by introducing computer equipment that dialed prospective customers' numbers, then transferred the calls to customer reps only if a human voice answered at the other end—an innovation that vastly improved the productivity of its sales force. Then, in the '90s, MCI's Friends & Family plan was hailed as a stroke of marketing genius: Besides being the first to offer discounts on frequently called numbers, MCI found an inexpensive way to attract new business by asking customers to provide a list of 12 prospects.

Scotts' telemarketers provide advice on how to use Scotts lawn-care products most effectively and, of course, where to buy them.

See also **cold calling** and **direct marketing**.

mktg

television rating   Percentage of households with at least one TV set tuned to a particular program.

If, for example, 19.2 percent of households with TVs are watching "Home Improvement," the program has a 19.2 rating. Nationally, one ratings point is equal to more than 950,000 homes. So when "Home Improvement" has a 19.2 rating, it might also have 32.3 **television share**, meaning almost a third of all TVs turned on at the time were tuned to that show.

Both ratings and share are used in determining the price of commercial time. Perhaps the best known of the ratings statistics are those released by Nielsen Media Research, which monitors the television-viewing habits of 4,000 families across the United States.

television share

mktg

television share   Percentage of TV sets in use that are tuned to a particular program.

See also **television rating**.

fin   **acct**

10-K   Annual filing that publicly traded corporations make with the **Securities and Exchange Commission (SEC)**.

Unlike the **annual report**, the 10-K need not be mailed to every shareholder, but it is made available on request. The SEC requires more information in the 10-K than in the annual report. In practice, companies usually put the supplementary data in the 10-K and include an index showing where other required information can be found in the annual report.

T

fin **acct**

10-Q Quarterly financial filing required by the **Securities and Exchange Commission (SEC)** that is similar to the **10-K** but less comprehensive.

fin

tender offer Public offer to buy a company's shares.

Tender offers are sometimes made by a company for some of its own shares, but more often they are part of a **takeover** attempt. An offer for another company's shares is called friendly when it is approved by the management of the target company, hostile when it is not. The bidder is usually referred to as the acquirer and the other company is the target. The acquiring company may offer to buy shares in the target company for a fixed price, for a specified number of shares in the acquiring company, or for a combination of the two. This price is virtually always above—and can be significantly above—the market price of the shares at the time the tender offer is announced.

The offer is made to all shareholders, although sometimes the bidder seeks less than 100 percent of the target company. If so, the bidder may accept a proportionate number of shares from each stockholder accepting the offer by the set date. Sometimes bidding wars develop between two or more suitors, or shareholders will hold out for a higher price. In those cases, if the bidder raises the price during the offer, the new price will be paid for all accepted shares, including those tendered earlier. Below is a shareholder form used in a tender offer.

See also **acquisition, leveraged buyout, merger/acquisition,** and **takeover.**

tender offer

The bidder is usually referred to as the acquirer, and the other company is the target.

| CUSIP number | Account no. | R.R. | Quan. |

| Offer expires: | Reply by: | Pro-ration date: |

We are enclosing material relating to this issue. Please indicate the action to be taken for the customer indicated above by checking one or more of the following letters.

A ☐ Exchange

B ☐ Tender _____ @ _____   *Indicate either B or K*

C ☐ Redeem

D ☐ Convert into _____ common shares

E ☐ Exchange under merger plan; Securities ( )   Cash ( )

F ☐ Subscribe for _____ shares

G ☐ Oversubscribe for _____ shares

H ☐ Rts. sold through order room: Trade date _____

I ☐ Exercise warrants

J ☐ Let warrants/rights expire

K ☐ Decline offer

BREAKING NEWS

tender offer

On April 4, 1995, two large paging companies announced a merger. As a first step, Arch Communications Group made a tender offer for more than a third of USA Mobile Communications shares. Arch offered $15.40 per share for up to 5.06 million common shares. Stockholders tendered more than 10 million shares by the May 5 expiration date. So each investor who tendered shares got that price for about half of the shares he or she tendered.

ARCH

---

fin **mgmt** **strat**

tender offer buyout
Form of **leveraged buyout (LBO)** that is completed through a **tender offer** rather than a **merger**.

mktg

test marketing
Getting consumer reaction to a product by introducing it first in limited areas representative of its full intended **market**.

Test marketing can minimize the risk of failure by subjecting each element of the **marketing mix**—product, price, distribution, and promotion—to a trial.

EXAMPLE | When Ocean Spray developed its liquid concentrate juice that needed no refrigeration, it test marketed the product in five major U.S. cities. The company found that the new product boosted sales 15 percent, so it launched the drink nationwide.

mgmt

360-degree appraisal
Approach to employee evaluation that involves peers, the employee, and customers.

See also **performance appraisal**.

oper **mgmt**

throughput
Number of product or service units that a company can produce in a set amount of time, such as 15 subcompact cars an hour on an assembly line or four muffler changes an hour at a repair shop. Also called **total processing time**.

econ **mktg** **strat**

time series analysis
Method used in predicting **demand** for a product or service.

See also **demand forecasting**.

---

test marketing
t r a p |

By test marketing a new product, you are tipping your hand to your competitors. They may then have a chance to launch similar products.

Ocean Spray

throughput

T

**tombstone
advertisement**

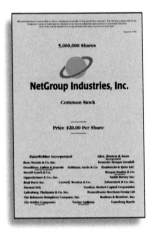

**total productive
maintenance**

fin

time value of money   Principle that a sum of money received today is worth more than the same sum received in the future because of its potental earning benefit.

See also **inflation** and **present value**.

fin

tombstone advertisement   Newspaper ad that **underwriters** place after floating a new securities offering.

The advertisement consists of a presentation of the securities sold and a listing of the members of the **underwriting syndicate** (in tombstone-like format).

See also **underwriting**.

oper   **mgmt**

total preventive maintenance   Maximizing the output of your equipment by letting those who operate the machines also maintain them.

See also **total productive maintenance (TPM)**.

oper   **mgmt**

total processing time   Number of product or service units that a company can produce in a set amount of time.

See also **throughput**.

oper   **mgmt**

total productive maintenance (TPM)   Getting the most from your machines by letting the people who operate them also maintain them. Also called **total preventive maintenance** and **reliability-centered maintenance**.

Developed since the mid-1970s by such Japanese companies as NEC, Nissan, and Toyota, TPM differs from the more traditional idea of using separate maintenance crews.

TPM also includes:

▶ Building maintenance around the need for high-quality output from the machines.

▶ Freeing up the maintenance staff from day-to-day chores to concentrate on the most-needed jobs.

▶ Predicting and planning for the maintenance needs of the equipment from the moment it is installed until it is removed.

American companies using TPM include DuPont, Ford, RJR's packaging operations, and the Timken Company.

T

EXAMPLE | The I.V. Systems Division of Baxter Healthcare uses TPM at its plant in North Cove, North Carolina. The 1.4 million-square-foot facility manufactures a variety of large-volume intravenous solutions and related products. Obviously, product quality is a priority.

All of its 2,400 employees are trained in TPM. Maintenance crews have not been eliminated, but they concentrate on major tasks and redesigning equipment to reduce the need for maintenance. The bottom line is that both equipment downtime and customer complaints are rare. In all of 1994, manufacturing delays caused by facility problems amounted to less than an hour. Out of 44,000 Department of Defense suppliers during Operation Desert Storm in 1991, the Baxter plant was one of just 15 recognized for outstanding customer service.

mgmt

total quality management (TQM)
Management philosophy dedicating the entire organization to a relentless quality-centered effort.

In TQM, quality means meeting or exceeding the requirements of one's customers. The customers can be the end users of the product, another department within the company, or even a supplier. TQM combines hard statistical tools like flow charts and process controls with soft features like teamwork and **empowerment**. It recognizes that involving everybody in maintaining and improving quality is a lot more efficient than paying a staff of quality-control inspectors.

The Japanese attribute much of their success in manufacturing to TQM techniques and named their top-quality prize after the American who in the 1950s taught them many of these methods, W. Edwards Deming, the father of TQM theory. He believed that management shortcomings—not careless workers—caused most product defects. And he taught that getting it right the first time beat out inspections after the fact. His system not only improved product quality but also cut back drastically on parts that must be scrapped or reworked, thereby cutting costs.

It was not until the early 1980s that Deming's methods came into vogue in the United States, where he consulted for a lot of top corporations, including Ford and Xerox. Until then, American manufacturers tended to see quality as expensive rather than as an efficient way to do business.

W. Edwards Deming, who continued to work until his death in 1993 at the age of 93, never accepted the term total quality management and, in fact, detested slogans.

In the 1980s and 1990s various consultants and corporations have come up with their own versions of Deming's approach, which is summarized in the 14 points below:

► *Create constancy of purpose.* This means, in part, taking a long-term view of the organization as an entity with a mission—to stay in business and provide jobs through employing quality techniques.

total quality management

Quality management therefore boils down to developing and operating work processes that are capable of consistently designing, producing, and delivering high-quality offerings. What, then, is total quality management? This is the business process itself. It is not something that you lay on top of what you do. It is what you do.

—David Kearns, former CEO, Xerox, in *Profits in the Dark: How Xerox Reinvented Itself and Beat Back the Japanese*

T

total quality management

t r a p

Though companies like Campbell Soup, Dow Chemical, Ford, New York Times, Procter & Gamble, and Xerox have used quality programs successfully, TQM in the 1990s is getting mixed reviews. Several surveys have concluded that most quality programs meet with failure or only partial success.

*Some reasons suggested for the failures: Senior management did not have the patience to stick with a quality program, which takes three to five years for results; rewards and performance evaluations did not support the program; and management failed to change the **corporate culture** to one where quality is key.*

T

▶ *Adopt the new philosophy.* The new philosophy does not accept mistakes and poor products but knows the value of high quality.

▶ *Stop depending on mass inspection.* Mass inspection means acceptance of a large number of defects, in effect paying workers to make defective products and rework them.

▶ *Stop awarding business to the lowest bidder.* The lowest-priced vendor may not be the one that provides quality goods and services. Deming suggested working regularly with a small number of vendors to bring their quality up.

▶ *Improve constantly and forever.* Quality is a never-ending process. This is similar to **continuous improvement**.

▶ *Institute training.* Workers too often are not well trained to do their job but learn bad habits from others who were never taught properly.

▶ *Institute leadership.* Leadership means helping people do a better job, as opposed to management, which is telling workers what to do and punishing them for failure.

▶ *Drive out fear.* Fear in the workplace prevents people from doing what is right but instead focuses them on avoiding punishment.

▶ *Break down barriers between staff areas.* This involves working toward the same goals instead of at cross-purposes.

▶ *Eliminate slogans and targets for the workforce.* Deming felt that slogans like "Think Quality" never did a thing to improve quality but instead insult workers who are hungry for better ways to do their jobs.

▶ *Eliminate numerical quotas.* Quotas do not measure quality but instead encourage high output and a large number of defects.

▶ *Remove barriers to pride of workmanship.* Workers want to produce great products and services, but too often the wrong equipment, lack of training, and poor supervision stand in the way.

▶ *Institute a vigorous program of education.* This means education in the new methods to improve quality—as opposed to training in specific job tasks.

▶ *Take action to build quality.* Top management must lead the change, understand the quality tools, and practice them.

fin

total return to shareholders   Calculation of the **dividend** received on a particular stock plus the change in its price. Also called total shareholder return.

It is often shown on a five-year basis, assuming that all dividends were reinvested in additional shares of the stock and making no allowance for income taxes. It may also be expressed as an annualized percentage.

EXAMPLE | If you had invested $100 in Eastman Kodak Company **common stock** on December 31, 1989, and reinvested all dividends in additional shares, your holdings would have been worth $182 at year-end 1994. That is like earning 12.7 percent a year. The same $100 invested in the **Standard & Poor's 500** stocks would have grown to $154, or 9.0 percent a year. Invested in the **Dow Jones Industrials**, the $100 would have reached a value of $162, growing at 10.1 percent a year.

The **Securities and Exchange Commission (SEC)** requires publicly traded corporations to include in their **proxy statements** a graph showing the company's total return to shareholders over five years and the total return for a stock index and a peer-industry group.

---

mgmt **mktg**

Toy Safety Act   See **consumer protection legislation**.

---

fin **mktg**

trade credit   (1) In international finance, the credit extended to those who purchase exports.

This may be a **supplier credit**, extended through the seller, or a **buyer credit**, arranged directly between the buyer and a third party, usually the **Export-Import Bank (Eximbank)** or a bank or agency in the buyer's home country. Supplier credit may also be backed by the Eximbank or a local organization.

(2) In domestic business, the credit allowed a customer by a vendor.

Sellers often offer a discount of 1 or 2 percent for payment within 10 days and demand payment in full within 30 days. Buyers of larger orders may get 60 days or longer. Trade credit is an important source of working capital for the buyer. If the buyer's credit rating is satisfactory, trade credit is usually offered without interest or collateral. A common trade credit agreement is 2/10, net 30, meaning the purchasing company gets a 2 percent discount by paying the bill in 10 days; otherwise, the full amount is due in 30 days.

EXAMPLE | Your company buys $200,000 in materials on 2/10, net 30 terms. If you pay within 10 days, the materials cost $196,000. Should you take the discount? You are giving up the use of $196,000 for 20 days in return for $4,000, or 2 percent. That is like getting that much interest over a 20-day period. In the course of a year, that would amount to more than 36 percent. You would do well to pay the money and get the discount, even if you have to borrow. The interest rate on the loan would certainly be less than what you make for paying within 10 days.

---

mktg

trademark   Any name, symbol, figure, letter, word, or mark a business uses to designate its product and distinguish it from others.

A trademark is property, and it must be registered with the U.S. Patent and Trademark Office. The 1946 **Lanham Act** sets forth the

total quality management

Institute leadership.

Create constancy of purpose.

Take action to build quality.

T

criteria under which a trademark can be registered. There are more than 700,000 registered trademarks in the United States.

Trademarks are essential to the concept of **branding**, which is the way marketers establish a presence for a product in the minds of consumers. Careful consideration should be given before changing a trademark associated with a successful product.

EXAMPLE | In 1972, the company then called Standard Oil Company of New Jersey (now part of British Petroleum) spent $100 million to change its U.S. brand name from Esso to Exxon, but it still uses Esso abroad.

As with **patents** and **copyrights**, trademarks have been the prey of unethical business people. In some countries it is easy for a citizen to register a trademark as his or her own, even if the trademark is the property of a company doing business in other countries. When the company tries to use the trademark in the country of the predator, it discovers that it cannot without buying the rights from the person who registered the mark there.

tech **mgmt**

transaction processing system Computer system that processes an organization's basic business transactions—such as billing, production scheduling, purchasing, and payroll. It provides much of the information used for management reporting and decision support systems.

mktg

transit advertising Advertisements appearing inside and outside of buses, bus stops, trains, and train stations. Transit advertising is highly visible, and consumers are likely to see it repeatedly.

See also **consumer market** and **reach**.

fin **econ** **acct**

treasury stock Issued shares that have been reacquired by a company, either through repurchase or donation. It is called treasury stock because it is held in the corporate treasury until it is resold or retired.

See also **capital stock**.

acct

trial balance List of all open **accounts** in a **ledger** and their balances. You can prepare a trial balance at any time, but it is one of the first things you do when you **close the books** at year-end. It proves that **debits** and **credits** are equal.

trademark

Virtually everywhere you turn, everything you watch or hear brings one face to face with many trademarks.... Statisticians report that every person in the U.S. is exposed to about 1,500 trademarks every day. When you think about about it, that figures out to 93 brand exposures per hour or 1.5 each minute, presuming you only sleep eight hours a night....

—Richard Wagner, communications manager, International Trademark Association

TM

T

EXAMPLE | Here is a one-month trial balance for a fictional gardening company we will call Lawnworks, Inc.

Lawnworks, Inc.
Trial Balance as of August 31

Account	Debit	Credit
Cash	$ 5,450	
Accounts receivable	0	
Inventory	550	
Prepaid expenses	750	
Equipment	7,200	
Accounts payable		$2,200
Notes payable		4,000
Paid-in capital		5,000
Sales revenues		12,200
Cost of sales	6,000	
Wage expense	3,000	
Utilities expense	450	
Totals	**$23,400**	**$23,400**

The trial balance for Lawnworks shows that the left-hand debit side and the right-hand credit side are equal for the period shown. It provides a summary that can be used in making later adjusting and closing entries before **financial statements** are prepared.

transit advertising

acct **mgmt**

turnover ratios Measures of **liquidity** that gauge how quickly certain **assets** can be "turned over" or converted into cash. Such calculations also indicate how efficient a company is at using its assets.

See also **accounts receivable turnover**, **asset turnover**, and **inventory turnover**.

oper

type I error When you reject a good lot of a manufactured item because random sample testing shows a disproportionately large number of defects.

See also **acceptance sampling**.

oper

type II error When you accept a bad lot of a manufactured item because random sample testing shows a disproportionately small number of defects.

See also **acceptance sampling**.

T

Telecommunications

Telecommunications, destined to be one of the world's largest industries in the 21st century, originated with the invention of the telegraph by Samuel F.B. Morse in the 1830s. Dozens of telegraph companies cropped up in the 1840s and early 1850s, and in 1856 a group of them came together to form Western Union, which completed the first transcontinental connection in 1861.

The telegraph not only established a new industry but set the pattern for future developments. For the first time, information could be dispatched instantaneously by mechanical

means. In the past, it was transmitted by man and beast, mostly along routes established for human transport. Now, information went wherever wires could be established. Further, the telegraph put other means of communication out of business. The Pony Express, only months in service, was eliminated in 1861. "The pony was fast," wrote one historian, "but he could not compete with lightning."

In time, the telegraph was displaced by the telephone. Alexander Graham Bell patented his technology in 1876, and commercial service began the following year. Soon the rival technologies of telegraph and telephone clashed.

Alexander Graham Bell

During this period, most business leaders considered themselves wedded to their technology, and the divisions between industries were quite clear. Western Union was a telegraph company and determined to defend its technology against interlopers. At that point, Western Union could have purchased the Bell interests for $100,000 but rejected the opportunity. It finally entered the field in force, employing Thomas A. Edison to develop technologies alternate to Bell's. But it was too late to displace Bell Telephone. The conflict was resolved in 1879 when Western Union agreed to abandon its foray into telephones in exchange for a 20 percent interest in Bell's rental receipts.

Telegraph would remain for another century, but as telephone connections grew, the telegraph became a supplemental means of communication and eventually all but disappeared. Unable to come to terms with technological change, Western Union faded.

Contributing Editors: Jack Grubman
    Managing Director, Salomon Brothers Inc.
    Sheri McMahon, Telecommunications team,
    Salomon Brothers Inc.

1837   1870   1880   1900

1837
Telegraph invented by Samuel F.B. Morse

1856
Western Union formed

1861
First transcontinental connection completed by Western Union; Pony Express put out of business

1876
Alexander Graham Bell patents telephone technology

1877
Commercial telephone service begins

1885
Bell Telephone incorporates as American Telephone & Telegraph

1921
Congress passes the Graham-Willis Act, which deems AT&T a natural monopoly

Led by Theodore Vail, Bell transformed into American Telephone & Telegraph (AT&T), which dominated long distance while licensing other companies to provide local service. Vail proved an outstanding manager, and under his leadership AT&T became the primary telecommunications company, gobbling up local companies, creating a superb research operation in Bell Laboratories, and acquiring Western Electric, which became its manufacturing arm. AT&T customers had to use Western Electric equipment and local operating companies had to cooperate with AT&T if they wanted to offer services outside of their areas. AT&T even threatened to acquire Western Union and dominate all aspects of telecommunications.

In 1913, to avoid antitrust prosecution, Vail agreed to divest AT&T of its Western Union shares and purchase no additional independent telephone companies without regulatory permission. AT&T further agreed not to enter related industries. The "Kingsbury Commitment," named after the AT&T executive who negotiated the arrangement, remained the basis for telecommunications policy for well over half a century. With this, AT&T became a "regulated public utility," accepting government regulation in return for the preservation of its dominant position.

The Kingsbury Commitment both helped and hurt AT&T. As part of this arrangement, AT&T offered low-cost local service that was subsidized, in part, by higher costs for long distance. This meant that long-distance customers were charged higher rates than economies might indicate, while local consumers received a better deal than they knew. It also meant that AT&T functioned in a uniform environment with fixed rules that enabled it to make long-term plans and improve services gradually.

Under this rubric, Americans enjoyed the best and most consistent telephone service in the world. But it also mandated that the many inventions that flowed out of Bell Labs, including transistors and other micro devices, software, solar-energy collectors, and numerous computer improvements, could not be produced and marketed. AT&T might well have become a major player in motion pictures and radio were it not for the constraints imposed in 1913. The Kingsbury Commitment did not halt technological progress, but for a while it blocked the emergence of the telecommunications industry while preserving the status of telephony.

Guglielmo Marconi

AT&T was aware of technological challenges to its position. One of those came from wireless, invented by Guglielmo Marconi in 1895. At first, the technology seemed supplemental to the telegraph, of particular use for contacting ships at sea. Radio Corporation of America, formed in 1919 from what originally was American Marconi, seemed poised to challenge Western Union and perhaps AT&T. But led by David Sarnoff, RCA instead entered into broadcasting, a completely separate industry, and the telecommunications possibilities of wireless were downplayed for the time being.

Radio's emergence increased federal regulation of the industry. Telecommunications was to be governed by the Communications Act of 1934,

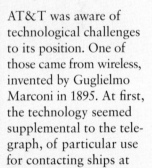

1960	1970	1980		1990	1996
1960 Entrepreneur Ted Carter develops Carterphone, which connects telephones to mobile radio transmitters	**1968** Microwave Communications incorporates	**1974** Justice Department files antitrust suit against AT&T	**1980** Sprint enters the long-distance market	**1982** AT&T agrees to divest itself of local operating companies, the "Baby Bells"	**1990** McCaw Cellular becomes wireless communication's largest player	**1996** President Clinton signs the Telecommunications Reform Act

which created the Federal Communications Commission to oversee the industry.

AT&T's quasi-monopoly started to crack in the 1960s in ways that would transform telecommunications forever. Carterphone developed a system to connect telephones to mobile radio transmitters. When AT&T threatened to disconnect customers who used the device, Carterphone sued and won FCC approval in 1968, ending AT&T's monopoly on telephonic equipment.

Microwave Communications Inc. (MCI) pre-

sented a major challenge to AT&T. In 1963, MCI asked FCC permission to furnish private-line service between Chicago and St. Louis. MCI's plan was to use microwave transmission, which was less expensive to create, operate, and maintain. Cost considerations, plus the absence of the need to subsidize local calls, enabled MCI to offer business customers substantially lower rates than those available from AT&T. Another company, Datran, asked for similar permission, and in the end, the FCC granted both requests.

Then the Justice Department filed an antitrust suit against AT&T in 1974. The suit was dropped in 1982 when AT&T agreed to divest itself of its local operating companies, then known as the "Baby Bells" and now also referred to as regional holding companies (RHCs) or regional Bell operating companies (RBOCs). This meant that AT&T was now freed from the constraints imposed by the Kingsbury Commitment. Thus the new era began, its outcome still unknown.

The major players in long distance were AT&T and MCI. Sprint was the third major player entering the field in the 1980s. They were joined by the wireless companies, which attempted to create a mobile telephonic system using cellular technology. Some of the Baby Bells were also quite interested in expansion but were restrained from entering long distance under the terms of the decree by which they were organized.

Wireless is one of the most glamorous and promising technologies in telecommunications. Its customer base is growing at the rate of 40 percent a year, with an expected 100 million users by 2004. Wireless is usually dated to 1946, when mobile-telephone service was attempted in St. Louis, but it really began with Marconi and citizen-band radio. In 1970, AT&T demonstrated an improved system in Chicago. Then in 1982, the FCC accepted applications for licenses in 30 cities with plans to permit two competing systems in each. Dozens of companies filed applications, and soon after, hundred of bidders appeared when 60 other cities were opened.

Established companies soon entered the wireless field. Sprint acquired Centel in 1993. Southwestern Bell purchased the cellular business of Metromedia and later changed its name to SBC, as though to indicate its new directions. BellSouth acquired the cellular business of Mobile Communications and entered into an alliance with MCI. (MCI had aquired Air Signal in its purchase of Western Union International in 1981 but sold it to McCaw in 1986.) More followed. The other regional holding companies—Bell Atlantic, NYNEX, U.S. West, Ameritech, and Pacific Telesis—also tried to find ways to enter into strategic alliances and mergers to expand their businesses.

McCaw Cellular Communications was the most important of the newcomers. Craig McCaw, who took over a family-controlled cable television company after his father's death in 1969, turned first to paging and then to acquisitions, the most important being MCI's national cellular rights, for which he paid $116 million, and control of LIN Broadcasting, which had valuable cellular properties and was valued at $6.3

billion. He cut back on his debt by selling 22 percent of his company to British Telecom, enabling that company to enter the American market.

In this way, McCaw Cellular became the industry's largest player. McCaw's ambition in the early 1990s was to displace AT&T as the premier provider of services. Given that cellular was being recognized as less expensive and more flexible than wired phones, his ambition did not seem entirely unreasonable. Indeed, McCaw suggested his biggest competition might well come from cable television companies planning to enter telephony.

Unlike Western Union more than a century before, AT&T understood the situation and reacted swiftly. Soon after McCaw partner British Telecom paid $4.3 billion for a 20 percent stake in MCI, AT&T astonished the industry by announcing it would purchase McCaw for $12.6 billion. Thus AT&T became not only the largest wired telecommunications company but the leading factor in wireless as well.

The arrival of new technologies in the 1990s spurred the creation of scores of start-up companies, which complicated the industries and blurred the divisions between telecommunications, cable television, computing software, and other industries. U.S. West formed an alliance with Time Warner, with plans for a union of cable television and telecommunications. Likewise, a venture between Southwestern Bell and Cox, a cable firm, failed to come about.

Pacific Telesis took a different route, divesting itself of its cellular operations and then announcing a union with SBC Communications to form the second largest telecommunications company in the nation. Pacific Telesis also indicated an intention to concentrate on the emerging personal communications services (PCS) market.

PCS, which uses a higher frequency band than cellular, initially served only local needs but in time could compete with cellular. Nextel, organized in 1987 as Fleet Call, provided what it called "specialized mobile radio" to several large communities and was one of the most important of the start-ups.

Clearly this was an industry in flux, and the outlines of what it will become by the turn of the century are by no means clear. The situation became even more fluid when, in 1996, President Clinton signed the Telecommunications Reform Act permitting the regional Bell companies to offer long-distance services outside of their areas. Soon after, Bell Atlantic and NYNEX announced plans for a merger, and SBC entered into a partnership with Pacific Telesis.

New technologies spawn even newer ones. It would not be surprising to see an expansion of the Internet into telephony. Craig McCaw, the most original telecommunications entrepreneur on the scene, had a plan of his own. After selling his McCaw Communications interest, he joined Microsoft's Bill Gates to organize Teledesic, which plans to launch and operate 840 satellites at a cost of $9 billion. This network would transmit telephone calls anywhere on earth. It would be akin to a telephonic version of the Internet and might bear a relationship to the Internet, similar to the one that once existed between the telegraph and the telephone.

The concept was McCaw's. More than a century ago, Alexander Graham Bell dreamed of such a system, and Thomas Alva Edison toyed with the idea as well. Princeton physics professor Gerard O'Neil organized Geostar, which was based on a similar concept. Motorola has plans for Iridium, a global telephone service based on 66 satellites, and other companies have similar concepts. This is not unusual; many major inventions have come out of intense competition between inventors struck by the same thought at the same time. If Teledesic, Iridium, or another newcomer becomes a reality, it could mean that every computer will connect with millions of other computers, that each person could have his or her own portable telephone and an individual number, and be able to contact anyone else in a flash—a vision that bears some resemblance to that of the individuals who marveled at the telegraph when it displaced the Pony Express in 1861.

Tobacco and Beverages

In the mid-1980s a securities analyst observed that Philip Morris, whose management was much admired and emulated, had hit on a winning formula: The company offers the safest versions of products many people consider dangerous. Philip Morris was the leader in filtered cigarettes, light beer, and noncola soft drinks. Using this objective, the company downplayed threats from nicotine and tars, weight problems, and caffeine. Marlboro, in all of its configurations, and Miller Lite were leaders in the field, while 7-Up was the best-selling noncola soft drink.

Cigarettes, beer, and soft drinks share a dubious distinction: All three have been made targets by groups claiming they are unwholesome products and, in the case of beer and cigarettes, have been the objects of attempted bans or distribution limitations. Likewise, the development of the three industries displays remarkable similarities: All began with a multitude of producers, which were winnowed down to a few major players. After this streamlining, the majors came out with many variants of their product along with even more minor brands, so customers were once again faced with abundant choices.

When the first explorers came to the Americas, they found tobacco being smoked and chewed by the natives. They brought the leaf home, where it proved very popular. But it was not yet in the form of cigarettes, whose use became common only in the post–Civil War period, when James Bonsack invented the rolling machine in 1881 and licensed it to James Buchanan Duke.

The time was right for cigarettes. The pace of American life was quickening, calling for fast smokes rather than leisurely cigars, while chewing tobacco, acceptable in an agrarian age, did not adapt to urban environments. In time, cigarettes would appeal to women as well.

At first there were many producers, but Duke's American Tobacco quickly dominated the industry. In 1911, the company ran afoul of the Anti-Trust Act and was dissolved. Out of "The Trust" came new companies, including American Tobacco, Liggett & Myers, Lorillard, and R.J. Reynolds, which dominated the growing field with a wide selection of brands. In addition, there were several minor firms, such as Philip Morris and Brown & Williamson. In 1913, Reynolds, the only tobacco company in the group that concentrated on cigarettes, introduced Camel, which quickly caught on. The others followed with their own entries— Lucky Strike from American, Chesterfield from Liggett & Myers, and Old Gold from Lorillard. For more than a generation, Luckies and Camels led the field, with the others as also-rans.

By the postwar period a major antismoking campaign had begun, sparked by a 1952 *Reader's Digest* article linking cigarettes to lung cancer. The companies responded by lowering nicotine levels, going to longer smokes, and creating and advertising filter brands. Philip Morris was most successful in this area. It was a small company up to that point, with several brands, one of which was Marlboro, then considered a high-priced English smoke. Marlboro was remade in the 1950s, placed in a hard, flip-top box, and given a major advertising push. Philip Morris offered Marlboro in several versions—king-sized, filtered, and mentholated, among others, and in a variety of packs. Brand proliferation ended, but those that survived came in assorted configurations, giving consumers a wider choice than ever before. By the late 1970s Marlboro in its many forms was the country's leading smoke.

Contributing Editor: Jennifer Solomon
Vice President, Salomon Brothers Inc.

Opponents of smoking continued the cigarette wars. They succeeded in having commercials banned from television and radio, and having warning statements printed on cigarette packs that pointed to the health risks of smoking. The tobacco companies reacted to harsh criticism with a three-pronged counterattack. The leaders diversified out of their bases, fearful that in time their product might be banned and that they would suffer the fates of the beer and liquor companies when Prohibition arrived.

American Tobacco changed its name to American Brands and acquired companies such as Jim Beam Distilling, Swingline, Franklin Life Insurance, Sunshine Biscuits, Master Lock, Wilson Jones, and many others. In the mid-1990s American Brands sold its tobacco unit and so left the business. Reynolds Tobacco became Reynolds Industries and, eventually, RJR Nabisco, after the acquisitions of energy companies, Del Monte, Heublein, Canada Dry, and most important, National Biscuit. Liggett & Myers became Liggett Group and was sold to Grand Metropolitan of Great Britain and then to New York investor Bennett LeBow. Brown & Williamson went into British American Tobacco (which became BAT Industries) and purchased cosmetic companies and department stores. Lorillard became part of Loew's.

Philip Morris, the industry leader, went into beer and soft drinks, though it later sold 7-Up, the soft drink company, to Hicks & Haas, which it merged with Dr. Pepper to form Dr. Pepper/7-Up. Philip Morris went on an expansion spree. It purchased General Foods, the nation's largest food company, and Kraft, the giant dairy and cheese company. By the late 1980s, while the future of cigarettes seemed in doubt, the survival of the companies that produced them was assured.

The second response was geographic diversification. While cigarette consumption stagnated in the United States, it was expanding overseas at a rapid rate, especially in the Orient. The major companies had always been represented in that part of the world, but now they moved in with factories and, where possible, advertising.

Finally, the companies responded vigorously to a continuing string of lawsuits with some impressive victories. In 1986, a federal appeals court decided that the warning labels on cigarette packs protected the industry against assertions that smokers were not adequately warned about dangers. But challenges continued to plague the industry, as shown when, two years later, another court ruled that it had engaged in a conspiracy to hide health hazards from the public.

The development of the beer-brewing industry was no less tumultuous. During the colonial period and into the 1890s most American beers

were of the heavy, English type, brewed and consumed locally. The large-scale German immigration of the late 1840s and the 1850s changed the situation. The Germans brought with them a lighter lager beer, which proved very popular. Soon lager breweries appeared in all parts of the country, starting in areas heavily occupied by Germans. Schlitz and Pabst were in Milwaukee and Anheuser-Busch, later best known for Budweiser, in St. Louis. At the turn of the century, there were more than 1,500 breweries in America.

Prohibition closed them down, but some companies survived by switching to such products as soft drinks, ice cream, and even electrical goods. Some breweries reopened in 1933 when Prohibition ended, but as before, they remained local. Then, during World War II, servicemen were introduced to beers brewed elsewhere. This, plus technological changes, enabled breweries to open satellite locations and go national. By the 1950s the "Big Three" nationally were Schlitz, Anheuser-Busch, and Pabst, and the total number of breweries fell to fewer than 400. Consumption increased, but 20 percent of the population drank 80 percent of the beer and were, by and large, young men.

In the early 1970s, the industry was transformed by the coming of low-calorie light beers. This transformation began when Phillip Morris purchased Miller and searched for ways to invigorate the company, which was best known for its premium beer. Miller had earlier purchased the rights to a low-calorie beer, which seemed unpromising. But in the mid-1970s Miller Lite went national and did surprisingly well. Applying elements of its Marlboro cigarette marketing strategy to Miller, Philip Morris eventually became second to Anheuser-Busch, whose market share for Budweiser had grown to half the American market. Many of the other brewers, including Anheuser-Busch, soon came out with their own versions of low-calorie beers, which captured a large share of the market.

At the same time a new national competitor appeared. Coors, which was brewed in a single facility in Colorado, made its mark, shaking up the industry further.

During this period, the second tier of brewers consolidated, hoping to survive through economies of scale. Stroh purchased Schlitz, Schaeffer, and other fading brands and regionals. Pabst acquired Olympia but was taken over by S&P, a holding company, which earlier had secured Falstaff. Heileman had a large number of smallish brands, such as Mickey's Malt, National Premium, Rainier, Weidemann, Warsteiner, Sterling, and others, including old standbys—Blatz, Carling, and Lone Star.

By the 1990s, the leading brewers had taken a cue from the cigarette manufacturers, offering their brands in several variations, including regular, light, draft, and such fads as dry, ice, and more. Some branched out into other areas; Anheuser Busch went into bakeries, snacks, bottled water, and wine, none of which is a

part of the company today. The brewers were more successful in forming partnerships with foreign companies and expanding into new markets made possible by the end of the Cold War and the prosperity of Asia. Likewise, foreign brands made a splash in the American market, among them Molson, Heineken, and Corona.

In a reaction against mass marketing and brewing, specialty brewers became popular, with Samuel Adams leading the pack. Toward the end of the century small breweries, selling beer from their adjoining outlets, gained in popularity. Thus, the brewing industry adjusted by going back to its roots, if only in a small way.

The major nonalcoholic sector of the beverage industry is soft drinks, which existed as far back as 1767, when Joseph Priestly made artificially carbonated water. Flavored "sodas" appeared in the 1830s, and in 1876, Charles Hires marketed his root beer as a medicine. Moxie Nerve Food and Dr. Pepper appeared soon after. In 1886, Coca-Cola was concocted, and Pepsi-Cola arrived in 1890. They, too, were originally considered medicinal. It was not until the new century that sodas came to be seen primarily as beverages.

In time, colas came to dominate the industry, with Coke and Pepsi perennial first and second. But there were scores of other colas, and even more beverages in other configurations, primarily fruit drinks. But soft drinks had a problem similar to the one that faced beer. Sodas were made with sugar and so were avoided by individuals hoping to control their weight. Then in 1961 Royal Crown started marketing its Diet Rite cola as a noncaloric drink made with artificial sweeteners and no caffeine. This transformed the industry in a way that resembled the arrival of filters in cigarettes and low-calorie brands in beers.

Coke and Pepsi continued their market wars during the 1980s and 1990s, and the two dominated the industry. Pepsi

sales were increasing more rapidly than those of Coke. Through a series of acquisitions, largely in restaurants (including Taco Bell and Pizza Hut), Pepsi surpassed Coke in sales (although they were still behind in profitability and market value). Taking this as a sign of the need for diversification, Coke purchased unrelated operations—Minute Maid orange juice, Maryland Club and Butter-Nut coffees and teas, and Hi-C fruit juice and powdered mixes. For a while Coke was involved in water treatment, wine, and shrimp farming, as well as the manufacturing of plastic cutlery, bags, and straws. It also owned Columbia Pictures. Roberto Goizueta

arrived at Coke in 1980 and became chairman the following year. He sold the nonbeverage operations, introduced new products, such as Diet Coke, and prepared an assault against Pepsi. In 1984, Goizueta announced a reformulated Coca-Cola. Coke's management was not prepared for the firestorm of criticism that fol-

lowed. Coke's telephone lines were jammed as irate consumers complained bitterly about changes in one of the nation's most familiar icons. Coke executives made the best of a bad situation. Five months after the reformulation they announced that both the old and the new would be available. The new would remain Coke, the old would return as Coke Classic.

This was the most dramatic example of brand expansion since the multiple Marlboros and Budweisers, and clear evidence of the direction in which the tobacco and beverage industries were heading. Time and again the dominant companies have defended their positions as industry giants and stand ready for new challenges.

U

to

utility

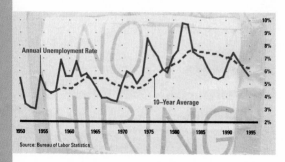

Annual Unemployment Rate

10-Year Average

10%
9%
8%
7%
6%
5%
4%
3%
2%

1950   1955   1960   1965   1970   1975   1980   1985   1990   1995

Source: Bureau of Labor Statistics

unconsolidated
subsidiary

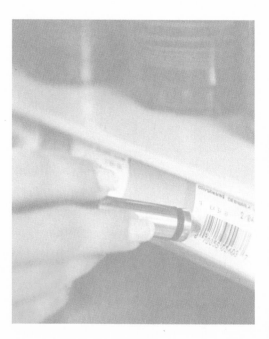

unconsolidated subsidiary   A **subsidiary** that issues its own **financial statements** apart from the **parent company**.

This happens, among other situations, when the parent is unable to exert effective control—such as when a subsidiary is in a foreign country and subject to control by that country—or when the parent and subsidiary are in incompatible industries, like banking and manufacturing. The parent will account for the unconsolidated unit using the **equity method**, recording its equity share of the subsidiary and its results on the parent company's books.

acct

underabsorption   Situation where a company's volume of business is lower than anticipated and the allocation of **overhead** to units of production does not cover actual costs.

EXAMPLE | The overhead costs of your car-repair service—rent, telephone, utilities, administrative salaries, and so on—are allocated to the various repair jobs performed by your mechanics at a predetermined per-hour rate intended to allow you to cover overhead. When business falls below expectations, your mechanics put in fewer allocable hours and you fail to totally offset these costs.

See also **cost accounting** and **costing**.

fin

underwriting   (1) In finance, an agreement by **investment bankers** to buy for resale a new issue of securities at a fixed price from the issuing company and/or existing securities from holders of unregistered stock also at a fixed price.

See also **best effort, secondary offering,** and **underwriting syndicate.**

(2) In insurance, underwriting refers to the assumption of risk in exchange for the premium.

fin

underwriting syndicate   Group of **investment bankers** that join to purchase an issue of securities from a corporation or government entity for resale to the public.

These syndicates are formed to spread the risk in larger offerings. One investment banker will act as lead underwriter or syndicate manager, finding other firms to take parts of the offering. The lead underwriter is also called the book runner because he keeps the book on the securities sold. In the biggest offerings, the lead underwriter may seek a second lead underwriter to help form the syndicate.

The underwriters, individually or as part of a syndicate, bear the risk that the securities will not be bought at the offering price. They may involve yet more brokerage companies as part of a selling

underwriting syndicate

Breaking News

One of the most successful—and most underpriced—**initial public offerings** ever was the August 1995 sale of common stock in Netscape Communications. Morgan Stanley and Hambrecht & Quist were the lead underwriters, and they recruited 26 more investment bankers into the syndicate. They quickly sold five million shares at the $28 offering price, which was already double their original estimate.

But even more indicative of just how far off the underwriters' estimates were in this case: When the market closed that day, Netscape's stock price had more than doubled again, to $57 a share.

™ Netscape Communications Corporation

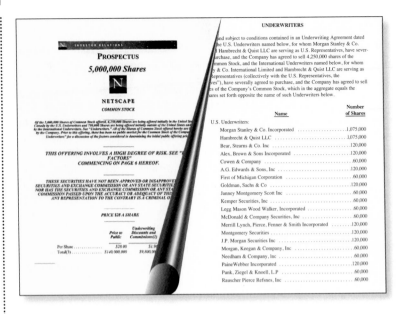

TM Netscape Communications Corporation

group. The underwriters are paid in the form of a discount on the offering price. That discount, or spread, varies widely based on the type of security and the size of the offering. The syndicate manager usually keeps 20 percent of the spread, the other syndicate members get 20 percent to 30 percent, and the selling group takes the rest.

In investment banking, underwriters syndicate public offerings much the same way banks syndicate a loan to spread the risk of larger offerings. One investment banker acts as a lead underwriter or syndicate manager. Sometimes there are comanagers of an offering who will share the risk equally with the syndicate manager but whose

FRAME OF
REFERENCE

underwriting

The Art of Pricing a Deal

Pricing a new security involves many variables. Whether it is an **IPO** or a secondary issue, **debt** or **equity**, there are some basic factors that must be considered. By the time a preliminary prospectus is filed with the **SEC**, the investment banking firm that is representing the company will have put together comparable data—price/earnings multiples, stock prices, volume traded, credit ratings, size of offerings, etc.—of companies in similar industries that have come to market recently or have securities outstanding.

With regard to **bonds**, there are other factors that need to be considered such as current **interest rates**, yield spreads (the differential between high-grade and high-yield bonds versus Treasury bonds), provisions regarding call protection, **sinking funds**, and **covenants**. Because this process is more of an art than a science, the investment banker must gauge the investors—some may want more favorable terms because they are under pressure to produce higher yields and dividends, or during volatile marketplaces, they may want **put** or **call provisions**, or shorter or longer maturities. Of course, as in all markets, **supply** and **demand** are key factors.

underwriting syndicate

How a Deal Unfolds

After a new issue has been filed with the **SEC**, a preliminary **prospectus** (also called a **red herring**) is circulated to a wide group of investors. After the SEC clears the registration statement for pricing, the syndicate manager and any comanagers evaluate their orders to see if there is enough interest in the deal and on what terms.

If the orders do not cover the size of the offering, the syndicate manager can postpone the deal and continue the marketing process until the orders come in or cut back the size of the issue. If the orders exceed the size of the issue, the company has the option of increasing the issue size if it believes it can utilize the excess funds. If the terms are acceptable to the issuing corporation, the deal can be priced, and the appropriate information is put into the final prospectus. The document is delivered to the SEC, and if everything is in order, the issue is declared effective.

The lead managers and the syndicate group must quickly verify the terms of the offering with potential investors, at which point the investors must reconfirm their indication of interest. The syndicate manager then must allocate the securities to the institutional investor, especially if the deal is oversubscribed, meaning there are more orders than there are securities. This can be a challenging situation because the salespeople obviously want access to enough securities for their best accounts while the syndicate manager has to do what is fair and equitable for the good of the transaction.

Once all of the orders have been confirmed the deal is free to trade, which means that the securities are now available for trading in the secondary market. Settlement date or date of funding for a new issue comes a few days after the deal goes effective with the SEC.

—Lorraine Spurge, syndicate manager, 1983–89, Drexel Burnham Lambert

---

responsibilities and compensation differ with respect to allocations, pricing, and overall marketing decisions. A lead manager may decide to further spread the risk by forming a syndicate that allows other firms to participate in the offering.

See also **underwriting**.

mktg

undifferentiated marketing   Targeting an entire **market**, not specific *segments*, for promotion and sales.

The classic example is Henry Ford's Model T—available in one style and color (black) for anyone with the money to buy it and the desire to drive. A more modern example is standard computer monitors. Though they are sold in a range of sizes and capabilities, their marketers usually think of all computer users with compatible equipment as the **target market**. For most goods and services, however, this type of marketing has become as outdated as the Model T.

See also **consumer market**, **differentiated marketing**, and **market segmentation**.

unemployment insurance

tip

How much tax an employer pays to the state may vary, depending on how many people he has fired in recent years. This is yet another reason to try to hire good people at the outset, instead of using the "Hire Them, Fire Them" method of personnel selection.

unemployment rate

We believe that if men
have the talent to invent
new machines that put
men out of work, they
have the talent to put
those men back to work.

—President John F. Kennedy,
September 27, 1962

mgmt

unemployment insurance Program that provides income to people who lose their jobs.

Unemployment insurance is a federal and state program financed by contributions from employers in 47 states. In Pennsylvania, Alaska, and New Jersey, employees also contribute. While the rates that employers pay vary from state to state, at the federal level it works out to a net rate equal to 0.8 percent of taxable wages.

econ

unemployment rate Percentage of the **labor force** that is out of work.

In the United States, the size of the labor force and the unemployment rate are measured by the Labor Department's Bureau of Labor Statistics based on data from a household survey. A sample of households representative of the United States population as a whole is asked:

► Whether household members 16 years or older were employed for the previous four weeks.

► Whether they left employment voluntarily or involuntarily during the previous four weeks.

► Whether they actively sought employment during the period.

Unemployment Rate, 1950–1995

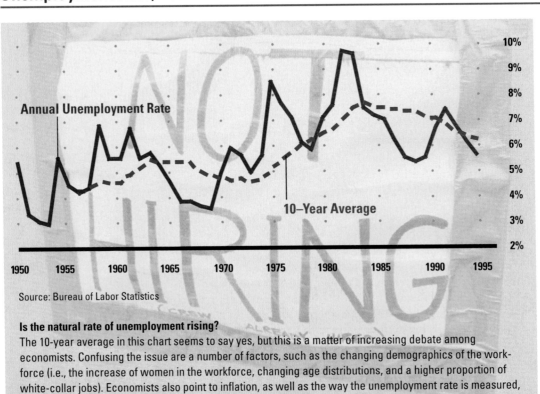

Source: Bureau of Labor Statistics

Is the natural rate of unemployment rising?
The 10-year average in this chart seems to say yes, but this is a matter of increasing debate among economists. Confusing the issue are a number of factors, such as the changing demographics of the workforce (i.e., the increase of women in the workforce, changing age distributions, and a higher proportion of white-collar jobs). Economists also point to inflation, as well as the way the unemployment rate is measured, as distorting factors in the debate.

The survey results are projected nationally. The labor force is the total of all three groups—those employed, those recently unemployed, and those looking for work. In the 1990s, the labor force has comprised about 66 percent of the total 16-years-and-older population. The unemployment rate is the percentage of the labor force that falls into the latter two categories—those who have recently lost jobs and those who have not recently lost them but have sought them.

Ways of grouping the unemployed include:

▶ **Job Losers**

Those who have been fired or laid off.

▶ **Job Leavers**

Those who resign because they are moving or because they are learning new skills. When this group grows, it often indicates confidence in the economy. Few leave jobs in times of economic uncertainty.

▶ **Reentrants**

Those returning to work after an absence. Women who interrupted their careers to raise families make up the majority of this group.

▶ **New Entrants**

Those seeking their first jobs.

Rising unemployment is one of the most important signs of an underperforming economy. It is one of the **lagging economic indicators**. After a **recession** starts, it may take a couple of months

unemployment rate

Quick Facts!

There are three basic forms of unemployment:

- *Frictional Unemployment.* Occurs when people change jobs and is generally considered to be temporary.

- *Structural Unemployment.* A long-term phenomenon resulting from declines in industries or other lasting changes in production processes.

- *Cyclical Unemployment.* Occurs because of the rise and fall in business cycles (in other words, fewer jobs available during a recession and more jobs during a recovery).

FRAME OF REFERENCE

unemployment rate

Where do jobs come from? For many years the prevailing opinion has been that small companies create the majority of jobs—a notion that gained wide acceptance in the 1980s after a well-known study by MIT researcher David Birch. His assertion that 88 percent of all jobs were from companies with fewer than 20 employees has been used repeatedly to emphasize the importance of small businesses to the U.S. economy. But Birch's study, along with the revered status of small businesses, has come under dispute in recent years.

Today, Birch backs away from the notion of small-versus-big disputes, saying that they're too simplistic. Rather, he prefers to categorize U.S. companies into three categories: (1) mice—companies that start and stay small, (2) gazelles—firms that start small but grow quickly, and (3) elephants—big companies likely to stay that way. Within those groupings, he points to gazelles as the real source of job growth, saying that they added five million jobs from 1990 to 1994, when total U.S. jobs grew by only 4.2 million. Examples of gazelles, according to Birch, are Intel, Microsoft, and Wal-Mart.

before the unemployment rate rises. More important, as the economy begins recovering from the recession, the unemployment rate may actually rise for a few months as reentrants and new entrants join the labor force, believing that jobs are opening up.

See also **employment**.

fin

unfunded/underfunded   Lack of money set aside to pay a future obligation.

If no money has been set aside, the obligation is unfunded. If there is a reserve, but its balance is not enough to cover the future costs, it is underfunded. The terms are often applied to **pension plans**.

acct   **mgmt**

uniform accounting system   Use of the same accounting and financial reporting system by all companies within a given industry. Uniform systems may be imposed by governments, as in the case of banks and other regulated financial institutions, or by associations, such as the American Hospital Association's requirement for hospitals.

acct

Uniform CPA Examination   Test given by state licensing bodies to those who want to be **certified public accountants (CPAs)**.

See also **American Institute of Certified Public Accountants (AICPA)**.

mgmt

unit cost   As the name implies, the cost of one unit of product or service, such as a labor rate per hour, a computing charge per contact minute, or a telephone rate per minute.

tech   **oper**   **mktg**

universal product code (UPC)   Type of **bar code**.

universal product code

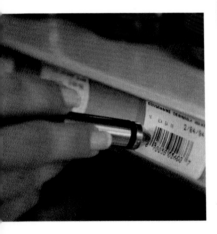

tech

UNIX   Group of operating systems conforming to specifications originally set by AT&T.

UNIX operating systems are particularly good at letting computers from different manufacturers talk to each other, so they are common in **networks** and on the **Internet**. Many techies have long favored UNIX, although it has been a bit formidable for the average computer user. In recent years a number of **graphical user interfaces (GUIs)** have been developed for it, making it much more friendly.

Users of the Internet, for example, no longer need to know UNIX's command structure but can point and click their way around the world.

U

unqualified opinion   Report by an **accountant** that says a company's **financial statements** fairly present its position and opertions in conformity with **generally accepted accounting principles (GAAP)**.

See also **audit** and **qualified opinion**.

unsecured   (1) Loan that is not collateralized and relies on the general creditworthiness of the borrowing entity or individual. Credit cards, for example, represent a type of unsecured borrowing.

(2) In corporate finance, an unsecured bond is one that is backed only by the integrity of the issuer and a document called an **indenture**.

See also **debenture**.

upstream   (1) Term that refers to earlier stages of the manufacturing process.

(2) May also refer to the financial flow from a subsidiary to a parent company.

See also **downstream** and **vertical integration**.

Uruguay Round   Negotiations begun in 1986 to advance the **General Agreement on Tariffs and Trade (GATT)**.

utility   Measure of a product's usefulness to the consumer.

There are four main types of utility:

1 **Form**
The actual product, delivery, and timing issues held constant.

2 **Time**
Making goods or services available when customers want them.

3 **Place**
Making goods or services available where customers want them.

4 **Ownership**
Transferring rights to goods or services.

While form utility is created by manufacturing processes, time, place, and ownership utilities are created by marketing.

---

utility

In marketing, the ability of a product to satisfy a customer's needs or wants.

U

V

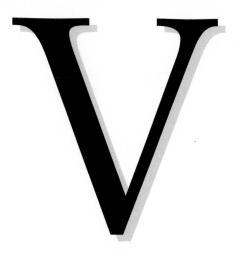

value added

to

volume

segmentation

value added   Increased worth resulting from enhancements or alterations made to a purchased product.

EXAMPLE | You buy an unpainted wooden bench for $100 and spend $10 to paint it, adding $10 to the bench's value. Or you purchase $100 worth of raw materials and manufacture a product with a total cost of $400. The $300 difference between the cost of materials and the final cost of the product would be value added.

econ

value-added tax (VAT)   Form of national sales tax common outside the United States.

It is added to the price each time a product changes hands during its manufacture and delivery to the customer, who picks up the final tab.

EXAMPLE | Here is how it usually works. Daisy Clothing Company makes dresses. The value Daisy adds to the product is the difference between its cost for materials and the price it charges its customer Trend Wholesale. The VAT is a percentage of that added value, and Daisy folds the tax into its price. Daisy also gets a rebate from the government for the VAT it paid as part of the price for its materials. Trend Wholesale will collect the tax on the value Trend adds and will get a rebate for the VAT included in the price it paid.

So Trend, Daisy, and the mill that supplied the materials all act as tax collectors. So does the retail store selling the dress. At the end of the process, the retail price includes all the VATs collected along the way. A provider of a service—accounting, for example—might collect a VAT on his or her entire fee.

The VAT is common in European countries and most of the other developed nations of the world. It differs from the type of sales tax collected in most U.S. states, whose taxes are levied at the retail level on the entire price. While a VAT may seem much more complicated to administer, one advantage is that there are more checks and balances against cheating—the tax is collected in stages throughout the process.

See also **consumption tax**.

strat   mgmt

value chain   Series of things a company does to make its product or service competitive.

The term was popularized in 1985 by Harvard Business School Professor Michael Porter in his book *Competitive Advantage*.

value chain

t i p |

*Whether **chain** or **constellation** is the right word, it is helpful to look at the value you add to your product or service with every component of your business.*

A value chain…shows how a product or service goes from raw material to goods on the shelf. The idea is to add as much value as possible as cheaply as possible, and—most important—to capture that value in your markup.

—Thomas A. Stewart, *Fortune*, June 12, 1995

V

Porter grouped value chain activities into two categories:

1 **Primary Activities**
These include inbound logistics like materials handling and operations, and outbound logistics like distribution, **marketing**, and service.

2 **Support Activities**
These involve things like accounting, **human-resource management**, purchasing, and technological development.

Generic Value Chain

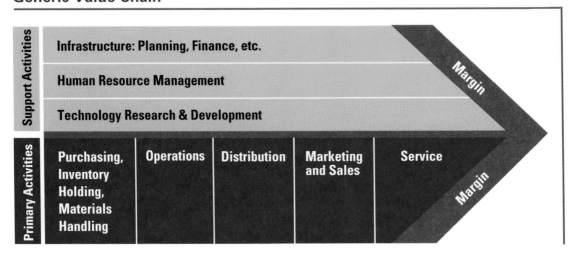

Support Activities	Infrastructure: Planning, Finance, etc.					Margin
	Human Resource Management					
	Technology Research & Development					
Primary Activities	Purchasing, Inventory Holding, Materials Handling	Operations	Distribution	Marketing and Sales	Service	Margin

value chain

Quick Facts!

Michael E. Porter of the Harvard Business School built his reputation as the foremost authority on the concept of competitive advantage. The premise outlined in his 1985 best-selling book *Competitive Advantage* is that economic performance rather than military might is the index of a nation's strength.

Each of the primary activities involves its own support activities, like **human-resource management**, which adds value to all of them. One way of looking at **strategic business units (SBUs)** is that they bring together the value chain associated with a group of products that logically fit together.

European management consultants Richard Normann and Rafael Ramirez argued in the mid-1990s that the idea of the value chain does not go far enough. In their concept of a **value constellation**, they explain that, with today's highly competitive business environment, companies need to do more than add value in their activities. To be successful, companies need to reinvent value in a sometimes complex web of relationships, Normann and Ramirez say. That web resembles a constellation more than a chain.

strat **mgmt**

value constellation   Term coined to describe the sometimes complex web of relationships needed to reinvent value in today's highly competitive business environment.

See also **value chain**.

value chain

European management consultants Normann and Ramirez cite IKEA as a company that has reinvented value in its industry. Doing so transformed the small Swedish mail-order furniture business into the biggest retailer of home furnishings in the world. IKEA found its value constellation by a number of innovations that enable it to supply simple, high-quality Scandinavian furniture at low cost:

- It forged a relationship with customers where they take on some of the in-store service and at-home furniture assembly in return for lower prices and plenty of support from IKEA. That support can include everything from child care to tape measures to a roof rack.

- IKEA has 30 buying offices worldwide to find suppliers able to deliver what it needs at low cost, then gives these suppliers technical help. The company works two to three years in advance to develop products and find the right suppliers for each part.

- IKEA's internal structure reflects the demands of its special relationships with both its customers and its suppliers. An example is its sophisticated worldwide warehouse and distribution system, which includes data relays from cash registers in IKEA's stores to the nearest warehouse as well as to company headquarters.

---

fin

Value Line Investment Survey
Investment advisory service that tracks the financial and stock market performance of 1,700 large companies.

Value Line ranks stocks for their safety as an investment and their "timeliness" as a purchase. Using complicated computer models, Value Line projects the expected price performance of the issues over the next 12 months and ranks them.

mgmt

values statement
Another name for a company's declaration of its core purpose.

See also **mission statement**.

mktg

variable
In market research, a factor that may be allowed to change or held constant.

An independent variable is one where the researcher controls the change. A **dependent variable** is one the researcher does not control directly.

variable

tip

In market research, as in other studies, the key is to isolate the independent variables. If you change just one at a time, you will get a clearer picture of what is responsible for changes to the dependent variables.

V

variable

See also **research validity**.

variable costing

Accounting approach that attributes only **variable costs** of manufacturing to the cost of goods produced.

See also **costing**.

variable costs

Those costs that tend to fluctuate in direct proportion to the level of business activity.

Supplies, parts, and the wages of hourly employees are all variable costs. While these change from month to month depending on the business volume, per-unit variable costs stay about the same.

EXAMPLE | You run a business assembling cellular phones. In January, when you assembled 10,000 phones, your variable costs (mostly parts and hourly labor) were $30,000, or $3 per phone ($30,000 ÷ 10,000 = $3). In February, you produced 20,000 phones, so your variable costs doubled to about $60,000, but your per-unit variable costs stayed around $3 ($60,000 ÷ 20,000 = $3).

See also **fixed cost** and **economies of scale**.

variable pricing

t r a p

Variable pricing can cause ill will when a customer discovers that other buyers paid a lot less for the same thing.

variable pricing

Selling similar goods or services to similar types of buyers at different prices.

EXAMPLE | You own a Pontiac dealership. James Green comes in looking for a Bonneville. He wants one right away, and you sell him one off the lot for $20,200. Later that day, Mary Brown is seeking a Bonneville with the same color and features as the one you sold Green. You do not have another like it in stock, but she orders one from you at $21,500.

See also **penetration pricing**, **perceived-value pricing**, **price discrimination**, and **pricing**.

variance

Difference between a budget estimate and actual results. Also, the difference between the actual cost and the standard cost of materials, labor, and **overhead**.

econ

VAT   See **value-added tax**.

fin

vendor financing   Credit extended to a company by its suppliers, usually less than 10 years in term.

Normally, vendor financing is **senior secured debt**, backed by equipment. In the event of a bankruptcy, because of its seniority in a company's capital structure, this type of security is paid off before **subordinated debt**, **preferred stock**, or **common stock**.

Vendor financing can be particularly effective when a company has numerous suppliers, who can be forced to compete not only on the products they provide but also on the credit terms they extend.

fin

venture capital   Funding for start-up companies and private **research-and-development (R&D)** projects. Also known as risk capital.

A number of private investors, investment companies, and **limited partnerships** provide venture capital. Because of the risks involved with start-up companies—whose failure rate estimates are as high as 80 percent—venture capitalists look for high rates of return, usually between 25 and 40 percent. But start-ups seldom generate enough cash flow to pay those returns, so the investors get shares in the new company as part of their return. They hope to get their profits by selling the shares when the company goes public.

strat   **mgmt**

vertical integration   Extent to which a company controls all the steps of a business. That can be everything from product design to procuring parts and supplies, to manufacturing, all the way to finalizing a deal with the end user.

Vertical integration is described as being downstream when it moves from manufacturing along the **distribution channel** toward the consumer. It is upstream when it moves toward control over the sources of supply, which can also be called **backward vertical integration**.

Decisions over the degree and direction of vertical integration involve both financial and strategic considerations. If the expansion does not fit your core competencies, it might very well be a failure.

EXAMPLE | In the 1980s, one example of vertical integration was the more than 80 retail stores that IBM maintained throughout the United States. But they detracted from the computer manufacturer's core business, and IBM sold them to Nynex in 1986.

---

vendor financing

t i p |

Vendor financing helps a vendor see a company as a partner as well as a customer. It gives the vendor greater interest in seeing a company succeed, and it often translates into additional attention and service.

t r a p |

Vendor financing can put the company in a weak position when negotiating prices with the same vendor.

venture capital

There are two times in a man's life when he should not speculate: when he can't afford it, and when he can.

—Mark Twain, "Pudd'nhead Wilson's New Calendar," *Following the Equator,* 1897

V

virtual corporation

mktg

vertical marketing system (VMS)   A **distribution channel** that acts as a coordinated system.

There are three kinds of VMS:

1 Corporate

When there is single ownership of the **marketing** channel.

Dow Jones & Company sells a variety of financial news ser-vices on the open market. However, it offers certain services only to people who subscribe to its own Dow Jones News Retrieval online system.

2 Administered

When a dominant member of the channel uses its brand power to achieve market leadership.

Sony, through the powerful brand reputation of its products, induces strong loyalty from its independently owned retail dealers.

3 Contractual

Based on formal agreements among members. This is the most common form of VMS, accounting for 40 percent of all retail sales. Typical of these is the franchise agreement.

More than 14,000, or 80 percent, of McDonald's outlets worldwide are operated by franchisees. They are indepen-dent businesses, but their contract requires them to operate according to McDonald's standards and buy their supplies from the company. The rest of McDonald's outlets, almost 4,000, are owned by the company or one of its subsidiaries, so they are examples of a corporate marketing system.

See also **horizontal marketing strategy**.

strat   **mgmt**

virtual corporation   Alliance of independent companies seek-ing to capitalize on today's rapidly changing business opportunities.

See also **virtual organization**.

strat   **mgmt**

virtual organization   (1) Network of independent companies brought together to capitalize on quickly changing opportunities.

Companies in a network like this will tend to have different but complementary skills. There may currently be a few relationships worthy of the term. When Wal-Mart opens its inventory system to suppliers who then are trusted to get products where they are needed when they are needed, you might call that relationship a virtual organization. But mostly the term is used for something that does not quite exist today and that might even be called a **virtual corpora-tion**. Today's alliances need longer periods of negotiation to form, involve fewer companies, and have longer lifespans and much broader business mandates than the theorized ideal.

The idea is for each company to bring its **core competencies** to the project. For instance, one company might specialize in product design, another in manufacturing, a third in marketing, and a fourth in service. By having each contribute its strongest skills, the partnerships could design, produce, and market a product or service faster than any of the members on their own. With global competition expanding, windows of opportunity for new products are shrinking, so winners and losers are often determined by who can get to market first.

For these collaborations to work, honesty and trust are crucial. Any one company's management will lose the kind of complete control over a project that it is used to. The temporary alliances will require supervision from a new breed of manager, who knows when to step in and when to step back.

Some rules for the virtual organization:

► **Define Goals**
Assess the opportunities in the marketplace, and be honest in determining what is in it for your company, as well as what the payoff can be for your partner.

► **Select Carefully**
Virtual relationships depend heavily on mutual trust. Pick your partners because they deliver on promises, can be trusted to act ethically, and offer strengths your organization needs.

► **Create Win-Win Deals**

► **Ante the Best**
To avoid the kinds of failures that can forever cloud your company's opinion of partnerships, make sure all virtual members are putting forward their best resources and brightest workers.

► **Create a Positive Virtual Work Environment**
Take steps to make sure there is a common system for all the partners to work together, be it a physical location or a seamless information network.

(2) Business that combines a core staff with a network of specialists retained on an as-needed basis and connected by telecommunications.

EXAMPLE | Since 1985, Ray Brown has run a virtual advertising and public relations agency in San Jose, California. The outfit joins a nucleus of marketers and administrative and support staff with a cadre of independent contractors who perform the task-specific work. Linked by telecommunications technology, they are brought into agency teams and, with those teams, interact directly with the client—unlike freelancers working for conventional agencies, which usually shield contractors from contact with clients.

---

virtual organization

trap |

The IRS auditors take a suspicious view of subcontracting and may think the arrangement is helping circumvent tax responsibilities. You have to be able to show that the freelancers control where and when they work. If you make these decisions for them, the IRS will call you their employer, and you will have to pay in more tax money.

More companies are waking up to the fact that alliances are critical to the future. Technologies are changing so fast that nobody can do it alone anymore.

—James R. Houghton, CEO, Corning, Inc.

V

FRAME OF

REFERENCE

virtual organization

When did the virtual tag get attached to business organizations? Jan Hopland, an executive at computer powerhouse Digital Equipment Corp., is credited with coining the phrase virtual organization in 1986. At the time, he was a Digital sponsor of a five-year "Management in the 1990s" research program at the Sloan School of Management at MIT to predict how management would change in the 1990s and the role information technology would play.

The term stemmed not from the virtual reality of computer games and simulations but from another computer term, virtual memory. Just as virtual memory makes a computer seem to have more capacity than it actually does, the virtual enterprise appears as a single organization with immense capabilities when it is really pieces cobbled together from many different companies.

Authors William H. Davidow and Michael S. Malone built on this concept in their far-ranging 1992 book *The Virtual Corporation*.

virtual reality

A flight simulator can create a visual environment in which a pilot actually perceives that she is taking off, flying, or landing an aircraft.

About half of the agency's work is done by the freelancers, who are well known at the agency, drawn from an informal network built up over the years. The freelancers, who use the agency's billing software, are given business cards identifying them as agency associates.

Brown says this approach has enabled his business to "grow without limitation," unencumbered by the burdens of expanding payroll, administration, and capital expenditure that come with more employees. In addition, it allows him to tap the experts needed for critical but often short-lived assignments.

See also **outsourcing.**

tech

virtual reality (VR)
World that exists only in **cyberspace** but is made to look and sound real to a human being wearing or using special gear.

A virtual reality computer delivers visual and aural stimuli to a person wearing a helmet equipped with graphics displays and speakers. Once you put the head-mounted display on, you hear sounds and see 3-D graphics that make it seem as if you are physically immersed in another world.

tech

virus
Code that a prankster or a saboteur has hidden somewhere—often in a program—that will duplicate itself if it manages to get into your computer.

If a virus does get into your computer, it likely will attach itself to a number of programs, including your operating system, until it is ready to activate itself. That is when you will find out if it is a prank, like Christmas greetings repeating themselves a few thousand times, or something more sinister, like everything on your hard drive being wiped out.

Viruses most often are spread via programs downloaded from the **Internet** or commercial services like America Online, CompuServe, and Prodigy. You can buy any one of a number of commercially available programs that check for signs of viruses and take preventive action if one is found.

To guard against a virus:

▶ Run an antivirus program periodically to check your entire hard drive.

▶ If you want to use software that was not bought in a sealed package, check it out with your antivirus program before doing anything with it.

▶ Run a check on all disks that are not coming out of a sealed package, even if they have only data on them.

▶ Back up your hard drive regularly.

If your employees use personal computers on the job, you need to instruct them all to follow those rules.

mgmt

vision statement   Another name for a company's declaration of its core purpose.

See also **mission statement**.

mktg

VMS   See **vertical marketing system**.

mktg

volume segmentation   Way of dividing a large **market** into distinct parts based on the amount of a product or service that consumers use.

See also **market segmentation**.

vision statement

> The vision statement for Mobil Corporation:
>
> To be a GREAT, global company. A company, built with pride by all our people, that sets the standard for excellence. A company that brings value to our customers, provides superior returns to our shareholders and respects the quality of life in every one of our communities.

V

W

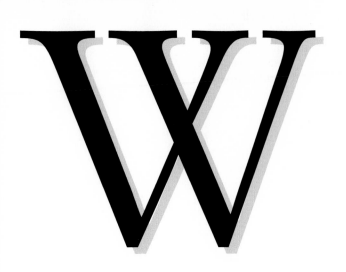

to

write up

wage
controls

econ

wage controls   Government attempt to establish the price for labor.

See also **price controls**.

tech

WAN   See **wide area network**.

tech

warm boot   Pressing a button or series of buttons to restart a computer without turning the power off.

See also **boot**.

fin

warrant   Security allowing its holder to buy a certain number of a company's common shares at a set price in the future; the price may escalate over time. Also called **subscription warrant**.

Warrants are usually issued in connection with the sale of other securities, such as a **bond** or **preferred stock**, to make them more attractive to buyers. For the investor, a warrant works like a **call option**, but any shares bought will come from the company issuing the warrant rather than from another investor. Warrants also usually have longer terms than options and occasionally have a perpetual life. They also raise money for a company, whereas an option purchased from another investor does not.

EXAMPLE | In a 1983 transaction by Drexel Burnham Lambert and Shearson Loeb Rhoades (now Lehman Bros.), MCI used warrants to complete what was then the largest nonutility corporate underwriting in U.S. history. The deal worked like this: Attached to each 10-year bond ($1,000 face value) were 72 warrants, which allowed the holder to buy MCI stock at $13.75 per share, a 31 percent premium over the then-current price of $10.50. The warrants had a separate price of $2.84, and they expired in five years—meaning that investors had five years for the stock price to rise above $13.75 and cash in. The five-year structure had a significant effect on the cost to MCI—a 10-year expiration would have cost the company another $1 billion.

In this case, MCI's stock price never reached the exercise price, but investors did receive a common stock trade-out when they expired, one for each 100 warrants that they held. Warrants may also trade on the open market prior to expiration, so investors could have made money during their five-year life by trading them.

See also **equity kicker, right,** and **stock option**.

---

wage controls

warm boot

warrant

tip | 👍

The higher cost of straight debt (versus convertible debt) can be offset by attaching a warrant that enables bondholders to participate in upward share price moves.

W

warranty

mgmt acct

warranty   Promise by a manufacturer or seller to repair or replace defective parts or products.

For accounting purposes, a company is required to estimate financial exposure related to warranties and make a provision for estimated **liabilities**. At the time the product is sold, the company would debit warranty expense and credit the estimated liability **account**.

Tape Cassette Player/Recorder/CD Player
Mini Disc DAT/Radio/Head Phones/
Speaker/MIC/Personals

Portable Audio

Limited Warranty

Electronics World INC. ("E-World") warrants this Product (including any accessories) against defects in material or workmanship as follows:

1. LABOR: For a period of 90 days from the date of purchase, if this Product is determined to be defective, E-World will repair the Product at no charge, or pay the labor charges to any E-World authorized service facility. After the Warranty Period, you must pay for all labor charges.

2. PARTS: In additions, E-World will supply, at no charges, new or rebuilt replacements in exchange for defective parts for a period of one (1) year. After 90 days from the date of purchase, labor for removal and installation is available from E-World authorized service facilities or an E-World Service Center at your expense.

To obtain warranty service, you must take the Product, or deliver the Product freight prepaid, in either its original packaging or packaging affording an equal degree of protection, to any authorized E-World service facility. This warranty does not cover customer instruction; installation, set up adjustments or signal reception problems.

This warranty does not cover cosmetic damage or damage due to acts of God, accident, misuse, abuse, negligence, commercial use or modification of, or to any part of the Product, including the antenna. This warranty does not cover damage due to improper operation or maintenance, connection to improper voltage supply, or attempted repair by anyone other than a facility authorized by E-World to service the Product. This warranty does not cover Products sold AS IS or WITH ALL FAULTS, or consumables (such as fuses or batteries). This warranty is valid only in the United States.

Proof of purchase in the form of a bill of sale or receipted invoice which is evidence that the unit is within the Warranty period must be presented to obtain warranty service.

This warranty is invalid if the factory applied serial number has been altered or removed from the Product.

REPAIR OR REPLACEMENT AS PROVIDED UNDER THIS WARRANTY IS THE EXCLUSIVE REMEDY OF THE CONSUMER. E-WORLD SHALL NOT BE LIABLE FOR ANY INCIDENTAL OR CONSEQUENTIAL DAMAGES FOR BREACH OF ANY EXPRESS OR IMPLIED WARRANTY ON THIS PRODUCT. EXCEPT TO THE EXTENT PROHIBITED BY APPLICABLE LAW, ANY IMPLIED WARRANTY OF MERCHANTABILITY OR FITNESS FOR A PARTICULAR PURPOSE ON THIS PRODUCT IS LIMITED IN DURATION TO THE DURATION OF THIS WARRANTY.

Some states do not allow the exclusion or limitation of incidental or consequential damages, or allow limitations on how long an implied warranty lasts, so the above limitations or exclusions may not apply to you. In addition, if you enter into a service contract with the E-World Partnership within 90 days of the date of sale, the limitation on how long an implied warranty lasts does not apply to you. This warranty gives you specific legal rights, and you may not have other rights which vary from state to state.

FOR FREQUENTLY CALLED TELEPHONE NUMBERS, PLEASE SEE REVERSE SIDE.

acct

weighted-average cost Method for determining inventory value.

See also **inventory valuation**.

mgmt

what-if analysis Commonly used with computer-based decision support systems, this exercise enables a decision maker to see what the effect would be of changing different variables in a decision-making process.

EXAMPLE | An executive might want to assess the impact of an increase in interest rates on the overall profitability of a new capital investment project. He might rework his numbers assuming a 2 percent interest rate, then go through the same exercise for a 3 percent rise, and so on.

what-if analysis

tech

wide area network (WAN) Large system of linked computers using dedicated telephone lines or radio waves.

See also **network**.

fin

Wilshire 5000 Equity Index Widely followed measure of price movements of approximately 6,500 stocks listed on the **New York Stock Exchange (NYSE)**, the **American Stock Exchange (Amex)**, and the **over-the-counter (OTC) market**.

Created in 1974, the Wilshire 5000 uses capitalization-weighted returns to gauge the performance of U.S.-based equity securities. Changes are measured against its base value as of December 31, 1980. Its capitalization is about 81 percent NYSE, 2 percent Amex, and 17 percent OTC.

acct

window dressing (1) Technique for making things look better than they are. Companies can create a distorted financial picture by anticipating **revenue**, deferring **expenses**, or inflating the value of **assets** like **inventory**.

(2) Or mutual fund managers may spruce up their portfolio before a reporting period—selling unpopular names or buying those considered to be in favor.

mktg **mgmt**

WIPO See **World Intellectual Property Organization**.

W

Wilshire 5000 Index

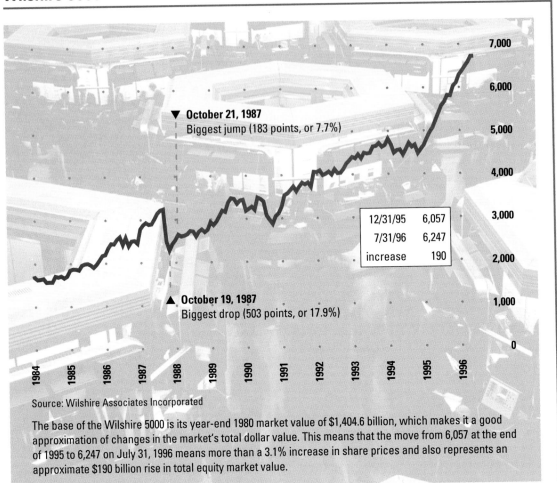

▼ **October 21, 1987**
Biggest jump (183 points, or 7.7%)

12/31/95	6,057
7/31/96	6,247
increase	190

▲ **October 19, 1987**
Biggest drop (503 points, or 17.9%)

(Vertical axis: 0, 1,000, 2,000, 3,000, 4,000, 5,000, 6,000, 7,000)

(Horizontal axis: 1984, 1985, 1986, 1987, 1988, 1989, 1990, 1991, 1992, 1993, 1994, 1995, 1996)

Source: Wilshire Associates Incorporated

The base of the Wilshire 5000 is its year-end 1980 market value of $1,404.6 billion, which makes it a good approximation of changes in the market's total dollar value. This means that the move from 6,057 at the end of 1995 to 6,247 on July 31, 1996 means more than a 3.1% increase in share prices and also represents an approximate $190 billion rise in total equity market value.

work in process

EXAMPLE

A toy company that manufactures yo-yos decides to create one that glows in the dark. It first orders raw materials—light-sensitive plastic spheres, metal shafts, string. When the plastic arrives, it is sent to a cutting and molding line, where it becomes work in process. Metal shafts being inserted into two plastic halves of the yo-yo and string being wound around the inserted shafts also constitute work in process.

oper **acct**

work in process   Information or materials in a company that are being developed into a product, report, or other salable good.

In accounting terms, work in process is one of three elements of **inventory** for manufacturing firms, along with raw materials and finished goods.

mgmt **fin**

workout   (1) In management, empowering mechanism that aims to identify and remedy an organization's problems.

General Electric's workout process began in 1989 with something resembling an off-site town meeting where the rank-and-file got together with bosses to discuss their work. Today, it is an accepted and continuing forum for uncovering difficulties, exploring ways to right a problematic situation, and taking concrete action. The process now includes not only GE employees but suppliers and customers as well. In fact, CEO Jack Welch uses workout to implement his **boundaryless** model that encourages employees to bypass traditional barriers to exchange information and ideas with those outside the company.

See also **empowerment**.

W

FRAME OF

REFERENCE

workout

Debt service workouts sometimes have to be negotiated with entire countries. One of the most dramatic examples in recent history is the Brady Plan, proposed in 1989 by U.S. Treasury Secretary Nicholas Brady in response to the Latin American debt crisis of the late 1980s. A number of U.S. banks were facing huge **write-offs** as a result of the insolvency of Latin American countries, with Mexico leading the pack with nearly $50 billion in money owed.

Under this grand-scale workout, the banks swapped the outstanding debt for the new Brady bonds as well as for equity in industrial projects. Since the plan actually cut the principal amount owed by the Latin American countries, the U.S. banks were understandably unhappy but were persuaded to go along rather than face a default on the entire amount. The new debt was backed by the World Bank and the International Monetary Fund, providing an extra level of comfort. Brady bonds still trade in the market today.

(2) In finance, it is a situation where a lender works with a distressed company to avoid **bankruptcy** after a default. It usually involves a restructuring of finances so as to lower the debt-service burden.

See also **Chapter 7**, **Chapter 11**, and **recapitalization**.

workout

---

acct   **fin**

working capital   Your current **assets** minus your current **liabilities**. Also called **net current assets**.

This is used by lenders and analysts as a measure of a company's ability to operate its business and pay its bills. Loan agreements often mandate that the company keep a certain level of working capital. But the number is significant only in relation to other variables, like the company's sales and industry standards.

Sources of working capital in a typical business arise from an increase in long-term borrowing, the sale of stock, the sale of **fixed assets**, and **net income** from operations adjusted for **depreciation** and other noncash items. Conversely, uses include the repayment of long-term debt, the **buyback** of **treasury stock**, the purchase of fixed assets, and the coverage of operating losses.

---

fin   **mgmt**   **strat**

working capital productivity   Financial measure that shows improvement in efficiency. Sometimes called **working capital ratio**.

The relationship between this measure and process improvement was first noted by management consultant George Stalk working in Japan. The formula on page 584 shows how to calculate working capital productivity:

W

write off

EXAMPLE
Coin Bill Validator, Inc., wrote down the value of its inventory by $1.1 million in the quarter ended March 31, 1996, to reflect the growing obsolescence of one of its product lines. The Hauppauge Company, New York, which makes paper currency validation systems used in the gaming industry, plans to discontinue the product altogether by the end of the year. Why? It has come up with a new bill-validator that will put the old one out of business.

acct

write off To transfer the entire remaining balance of an **asset** account to an expense **account**, such as when a piece of equipment is retired from service and has no further use.

EXAMPLE | Hollywood Park, Inc., had to write off its investment in Sunflower Racing because the Kansas City subsidiary could not stem the tide of red ink. Riverboat gambling on the nearby Missouri River was already pulling away gaming patrons when a vote in the Kansas legislature killed Sunflower Racing's hopes of luring gamblers back by adding slot machines at the greyhound and thoroughbred track. In May 1996, a few days after Hollywood Park said it had written off its $11.3 million investment in Sunflower, the beleaguered subsidiary filed for **Chapter 11** bankruptcy.

FRAME OF REFERENCE

write off

Automaker General Motors (GM) has had ample experience with write-offs—too often a part of the capital-intensive and cyclical auto industry. One of the earliest examples was when GM wrote off $100 million in losses in 1920. Although the company managed to avoid bankruptcy, the stock price dropped substantially, wiping out the personal fortune of the company's president, William Durant, in a few short months.

GM's write-offs have continued to be a part of the company's history. Perhaps most spectacular was the $24 billion charge taken in 1992, primarily because of an accounting change for retiree health care costs. Taken against the company's shareholders equity of $31 billion, that charge wiped out nearly 80 percent of the company's net worth. But the market's reaction to the announcement was mixed: Was this an example of a company "wiping the slate clean" or of one whose ongoing existence was at issue?

GM's stock performance reflected a more positive opinion, at least in the short run. The company's stock rose dramatically in the months after the write-off but fell again by the end of the year. Over time, GM stock has outperformed the market—up 83 percent from 1991 through 1995 versus 47 percent for the S&P 500.

acct

write up   To increase the value of an **asset** without expending funds, such as in a business valuation where assets purchased are recorded at fair value.

econ   **fin**   **mgmt**   **mktg**

WTO   See **World Trade Organization**.

tech

WWW   See **World Wide Web**.

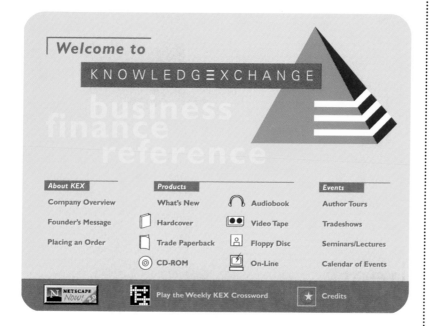

world wide web

The *Knowledge Exchange Business Encyclopedia* can be found online at http:// www.kex.com or in the E-Library at http://www. elibrary.com

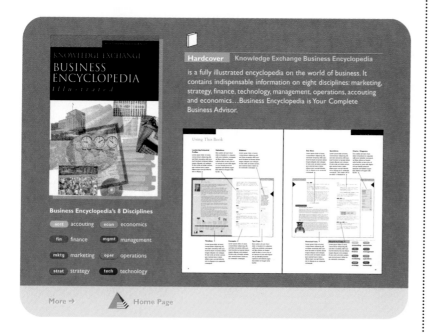

X

Y

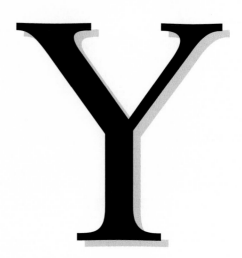

yellow sheets

Z

to

zero-coupon
bonds

fin

X   In a newspaper listing, an indicator that a stock has gone ex-dividend—the time period between when a **dividend** is announced and when it is paid. This means that the seller of the stock will receive the dividends. A stock's price will often increase by the amount of the dividend as the ex-dividend date approaches, then drop immediately afterward.

fin

yellow sheets   Daily publication that lists the bid and asked prices of **over-the-counter (OTC)** corporate **bonds**.

The publication, named for the color of the paper it is printed on, also provides the names of the firms that make a market in these OTC bonds. The yellow sheets are published by the National Quotation Bureau.

See also **pink sheets**.

fin

yield   Actual, as opposed to nominal, **rate of return** on an investment.

See also **internal rate of return (IRR)** and **bond yield**.

fin

yield curve   For **bonds**, a graph showing the relationship of **yield** measured against time to maturity.

Bond investors use yield curves to help them determine trends and plan their buying and selling strategies. **Interest rate** yields are plotted on the vertical axis and time on the horizontal, producing a normal yield curve that is upwardly sloping. Since yields typically increase as they move out in time, the yield curve bends upward as time to maturity lengthens. A normal yield curve is created when short-term rates are lower than long-term rates.

In rare circumstances, when long-term rates fall below short-term rates, the yield curve is inverted, sloping downward as they move out

yellow sheets

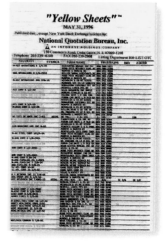

Quick Facts!

Prior to the 1980s, when the corporate bond market gained recognition, the yellow sheets facilitated an active and wide market for traders of corporate bonds. This market allowed hundreds of investment firms to act as market makers in the bonds of thousands of companies, both **investment-grade** and **high-yield**.

Quick Facts!

yield curve

An inverted curve occurred in early 1981 as the presidency (along with "stagflation") passed from Jimmy Carter to Ronald Reagan. In December 1980, short-term Treasury bill rates were 16.55 percent, compared with 11.89 percent for long-term bonds, marking the country's steepest-ever yield-curve inversion. By February 1981, the inversion had narrowed to three percentage points, with short-term yields falling to about 15 percent and long-term yields climbing slightly to around 12 percent.

T-bill

XYZ

Yield Curve

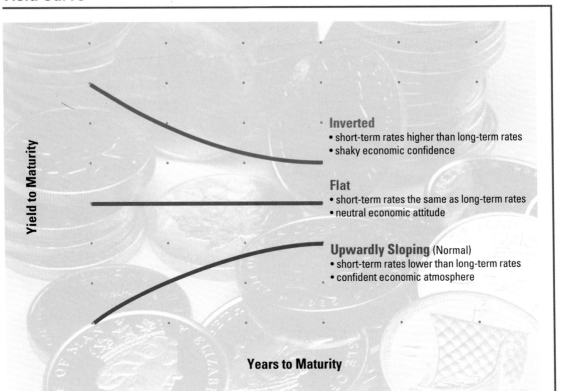

Yield to Maturity

Inverted
- short-term rates higher than long-term rates
- shaky economic confidence

Flat
- short-term rates the same as long-term rates
- neutral economic attitude

Upwardly Sloping (Normal)
- short-term rates lower than long-term rates
- confident economic atmosphere

Years to Maturity

yield curve

in time. An inverted curve is usually indicative of an unstable financial situation and a lack of confidence in the economy.

A flat yield curve occurs when short- and long-term rates are approximately the same. Since predicting the shape of the yield curve is a risky business, many bond investors hedge their bets, dispersing their buys over short-, medium-, and long-term bonds and rolling them over when **market** conditions are deemed right.

fin

yield to maturity (YTM)   Calculation of overall return on a **bond** that takes into account its current market price, **par value**, coupon interest rate, and time to maturity. YTM can be approximately determined using a bond yield table, but since calculating a bond's yield to maturity is complex and involves trial and error, it is usually done by using a progammable calculator equipped for bond mathematics calculations. Essentially, the yield to maturity is the **discount rate** in a **present value** calculation where the present value is the bond's current price. The future **cash flows** are both the bond's interest payments and its value at maturity.

See also **bond yield**.

FRAME OF

REFERENCE

zero-coupon bonds

Ted Turner has used zero-coupon bonds a number of times to finance the growth of his cable network empire, Turner Broadcasting System (TBS). The earliest and most newsworthy example involved the purchase of MGM/UA in 1986 for approximately $1.5 billion. Although critics accused Turner of over-paying for the company, he remained focused on MGM's film library, realizing that it would be a valuable programming resource for his cable stations.

To finance the acquisition, Turner's investment bankers, Drexel Burnham Lambert, structured an offering of $1.4 billion in debt, including $440 million in zero-coupon notes—although because of the zero-coupon deep discount, these notes netted about $247 million to Turner. The notes were split into four even tranches of $110 million, with maturity dates from 1989 to 1992, and varying yields to maturity between 13 and 14 percent. Turner continued to include zero-coupon bonds in future financings, issuing $200 million in 1989 as part of a restructuring, and another $200 million in 1992 to fund more acquisitions. Turner continued to grow TBS and in 1996 merged with Time Warner, making it the largest media and entertainment company in the world.

---

zero-based budgeting   Way of determining budgets for corporations that requires justification for all planned expenditures, not just those that differ from existing ones. It contrasts with incremental budgeting where current outlays provide the base to which new items are added and adjustments are made for **inflation** or other expected increases and decreases in costs or **revenues**.

fin

zero-coupon bonds   Debt security that pays no cash interest until maturity. Known as zeroes.

Zero-coupon bonds, which may also be convertible, are sold at deep **discounts**, and investors receive face value when the bond matures. Zeroes may be sold by a company, or a brokerage house may create them by separating out the interest stream and selling it as another security.

Zero-coupon bonds can be particularly attractive to investors who believe that **interest rates** will decline, since the absence of interest payments takes away the reinvestment risk inherent in other bonds.

zero-coupon bonds

tip |

Current U.S. tax treatment allows an issuing corporation to deduct annual interest expense even though it does not actually make any payouts until the bond matures.

trap |

The IRS considers the difference between the purchase price and the face value (or the "original issue discount") to be interest that is accrued each year over the life of the security. So holders must pay taxes annually as if they had received interest payments.

XYZ

Leadership Profiles

Mark Twain once wrote that "History does not repeat itself. But it rhymes."

To fully appreciate the whirlwind of economic, social, and technological changes we are experiencing today, a historical perspective can be

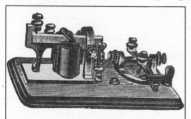

enlightening. How the Internet will change our lives can be compared with the impact of the telegraph and telephone in the 19th century. In order to fully grasp the the implications of the current competitive environment, juxtapose today's global marketplace with that of a century ago when a nationalized economy replaced the local and regional ones.

As entire economies, social structures, industries, and companies are built, there is usually one person who stands out to make a difference. That has been as true throughout history as it is today. In the 50 Leadership Profiles that unfold in this section, we have matched 25 significant businesspeople of today with their counterparts from yesterday. While business problems and practices have changed dramatically, the manner in which people respond to these challenges has not. Business leaders have always been faced with the responsibility of bringing together the factors of production—land, labor, and capital—and combining them with knowledge, vision, and acumen.

One business analyst remarked that it is the function of the businessman to make people happy, by which he meant to satisfy their needs and desires. In the second half of the 19th century, meatpackers like Gustavus Swift labored to find ways of transporting inexpensive beef from the West to the East and to explore new methods of using what formerly had been waste products. Swift succeeded, improving the nation's diet and lowering costs for consumers. He was also successful in creating a brand-name product out of a commodity. Swift sold a better prod

uct at a lower price—and that has always been a formula for success.

In more recent times, with consumers becoming increasingly health and weight conscious, there has been a pronounced shift from beef products to chicken. By the end of the 1980s, for the first time ever, American's consumption of chicken exceeded that of beef on a per capita basis. This change occurred not only because of diet but cost as well. Chicken had been considered a luxury food by the nation's urban dwellers. By recognizing the need for healthier diets at lower costs, Don Tyson was able to do for the chicken industry what Gustavus Swift had done for beef.

Next consider the case of Charles Dow, one of the most important figures in business information. A century ago when our society was

Charles Dow

emerging as an industrial power, Dow identified the urgent need for up-to-date information. At the time, businesspeople and investors had to rely on news provided by general newspapers and weekly sheets that were often outdated. Dow saw a gap in the market and filled it by organizing the Dow Jones News Service.

What Dow created for the mechanical age, Michael Bloomberg did for the information age. Bloomberg figured out how to move business data and information with lightning speed by putting terminals on investors' and traders' desks. He later created Bloomberg Business News, which provides multimedia information—print, radio, television, and an online service.

New products and services lead the way to new industries and companies. One of the nation's most celebrated figures, Benjamin Franklin is known for his contributions to the creation of the new nation and his many scientific discoveries. But Franklin was more than that; he was also a superb businessman. In the colonial period, newspapers placed commercial notices on their front pages. Franklin was well aware that to deliver news quickly, we first needed to improve our mail service. He had always advocated better communication systems, and no one person in our early years was more important in this regard. Benjamin Franklin became the first Postmaster General under the Continental Congress in 1775, and was responsible for the Constitutional clause mandating that the U.S. government create a national postal service in 1787.

Now fast forward to 1973. Fred Smith, founder of Federal Express, had a similar dream. Both men saw the need for a rapid delivery system for letters and packages. For Franklin the challenge was simply to deliver the mail from New York to Boston in less than three days. Smith had a far more ambitious plan—to deliver packages anywhere overnight. With help from modern technology, Federal Express has been able to keep its promise of delivering packages around the globe, "absolutely, positively overnight." Ben Franklin would have been proud.

Perhaps the most significant Wall Street figure of the 20th century, Charles Merrill recognized that the individual investor wanted the buying and holding of securities to be more accessible. This was a revolutionary idea particularly after World War II because the generation of young people were brought up fundamentally distrusting the securities markets. By totally revamping the image of brokerage firms, Charles Merrill's greatest dream came true when he built a broad base of securities investors. But the world in which he established Merrill Lynch & Company is a far cry from the capital markets we know today. Merrill courted and advised investors with expert guidance. This concept developed into what commonly was known as the mutual fund industry. Today the leader in

this industry is Fidelity Management and Research, and the individual behind the driving force of Fidelity is Edward C. Johnson 2d.

Such vision and determination is manifested in virtually every American industry. The soil for entrepreneurship is rich and fertile in the United States, yet such imagination is still extraordinary. Each new generation brings forth someone who will develop an improved version of an earlier model. And it has been advances in technology that made these changes possible.

In the following Leadership Profiles, you will

Charles Merrill

experience the stories of 50 notable individuals who have forever transformed the business landscape—yesterday and today. While the businesspeople of the past performed magnificently in their times, new forces in society demand new products and services. The visionaries who have met these new demands in our time are those we perceive as true leaders.

As John F. Kennedy said, "The American, by nature, is optimistic. He is experimental, an inventor, and builder who builds best when called upon to build greatly."

Andrew Carnegie

1835–1919

In his time, Andrew Carnegie was considered by some to be the very embodiment of the American dream. Carnegie arrived in America from Scotland with his family in 1848. The 13-year-old boy found work as a bobbin boy in a

textile mill, earning $1.20 a week. He went on to become a messenger for O'Reilly's Telegraph in Pittsburgh. By 1851 Carnegie had become a full-time telegrapher, sending and receiving messages for businessmen, who were the prime users of the medium at the time. From reading the telegrams, he received an invaluable education in business, along with an appreciation of what America had to offer. "In Scotland I would have been a poor weaver all my days, but here, I can surely do something better. If I don't, it will be my own fault, for anyone can get along in this country."

In 1852, Carnegie had another stroke of good fortune. Tom Scott, head of the western division of the Pennsylvania Railroad, offered Carnegie a post as secretary and assistant, which he accepted. Now he was making $35 a month but, more important, learning about the railroad industry from a master. Carnegie accompanied Scott when the older man became assistant secretary of war during the Civil War. After the war, Scott offered Carnegie the post of superintendent of the railroad, but he rejected this plum, preferring instead to go off on his own.

Carnegie invested in several companies, among them Keystone Bridge, which he knew was about to receive major contracts from the Pennsylvania Railroad. Then, in 1872, he made another career change. Selling almost all of his investments, Carnegie entered the steel business by financing a modern plant in Pittsburgh, a city whose location, due to markets and access to raw materials, was nearly perfect.

Once again, Carnegie had made a wise move at a propitious time. Demand for steel for railroads and construction was booming. He earlier had remarked, "Watch the costs and the profits will take care of themselves." Carnegie applied that maxim to the steel business. Seeing that there was little integration of different processes, Carnegie rationalized steel production by placing all procedures in a single plant. He insisted his managers account carefully for expenditures, and in this way and others, he lowered the price of steel manufacturing sharply. In 1872, Carnegie was able to produce steel for $56 a ton; by 1900, he was down to $11.50. Along the way, he undercut his competitors in the market and grew rapidly.

In 1901, Carnegie sold his steel company to J.P. Morgan for $492 million. Morgan used it to form the foundation for U.S. Steel. Carnegie turned to a new occupation—disposing of his fortune. His motto at the time was, "The man who dies rich, dies disgraced." Before his death in 1919, he had disposed of $350 million.

Carnegie was as deliberate in making donations as he had been in creating a steel empire. He did not believe in charity, which he considered demeaning to the receiver, but rather philanthropy, bequests to deserving institutions and individuals. Among these were the Carnegie Foundation, the Carnegie Endowment for International Peace, and the Carnegie Institutes of Pittsburgh. Before he died, Carnegie had erected 2,505 libraries in the United States, although the recipient localities bought the books.

In our time, Walter Annenberg comes closest to Carnegie in business audacity and originality but even more so in his philanthropic work. Like Carnegie, Annenberg is most careful in selecting recipients. Carnegie once remarked that disposing of great wealth can be more difficult than acquiring it.

1908–present

Walter H. Annenberg

While establishing himself as one of the most successful publishers in American history, Walter Annenberg was also a diplomat, political activist, and art collector. In recent years, however, all of this has been eclipsed by his activities in philanthropy. In this regard, Annenberg has become a contemporary version of Andrew Carnegie, who also amassed a huge fortune and distributed it to carefully chosen organizations.

Annenberg's father, Moses Annenberg, immigrated to America in 1885. After working at a wide variety of jobs, the elder Annenberg entered the William Randolph Hearst organization, where he demonstrated a talent for newspaper promotion. By 1920 he had become circulation manager for all the Hearst publications. On his own he purchased two important horse racing newspapers, the *Racing Forum* and the *Morning Telegraph*. In 1936 he bought *The Philadelphia Inquirer*, one of the nation's oldest newspapers. Soon after, he organized Triangle Publications as a holding company for his newspaper properties.

Upon his father's death in 1942, Walter Annenberg, who had been running Triangle, took over completely. He began adding to Triangle's list of publications. While serving as editor and publisher of the *Philadelphia Inquirer*, Annenberg founded *Seventeen* magazine in 1944 to fill a need he saw among teenage girls. It was an instant success.

In 1945 Annenberg purchased WFIL, one of Philadelphia's leading radio stations, and other radio and television stations soon followed. This division of Triangle grew to include six AM and six FM radio stations as well as six television stations. Annenberg's foresight in the growth of television led him to establish *TV Guide* in 1953, which became the standard for the medium. By 1968, it was selling at the rate of 14 million copies per week. He went on to purchase additional newspapers, making him one of the nation's most powerful media figures.

A man with a deep interest in education, Annenberg was instrumental in the development of televised educational programs. He won several awards for his pioneering vision in broadcasting, including the Alfred I.

DuPont Award for educational programming, and the Ralph Lowell Medal for outstanding contribution to public television. He founded The Annenberg School for Communication at The University of Pennsylvania in 1958 and The Annenberg School for Communication at the University of Southern California in 1971.

Annenberg supported Richard Nixon in the 1968 presidential election, and the following year was named Ambassador to the United Kingdom. At that point, Annenberg sold several of his newspapers to Knight Newspapers for $55 million. He had hoped to retire as Ambassador after Nixon's reelection, but remained in that post until 1974.

Through the years Annenberg amassed an impressive collection of art, now estimated to be worth in excess of $1 billion, which will be donated to the Metropolitan Museum of Art. Annenberg also made many philanthropic contributions through the Annenberg Foundation and the Philadelphia Inquirer Charities. He has made major donations to the Mount Sinai School of Medicine in New York.

In 1988 Annenberg sold Triangle to Rupert Murdoch for $3.2 billion. Shortly thereafter, he donated $365 million to a number of schools—Harvard University, Peddie School (the college-prep school he attended), the University of Southern California, and the University of Pennsylvania, among others. Annenberg's most ambitious project is the Annenberg Challenge, which will provide some $500 million to the nation's public schools.

Like Andrew Carnegie, he believes that "giving is a mark of citizenship." On his desk in Philadelphia, Annenberg placed a plaque that sums up his approach to life. It contains a quotation from Winston Churchill: "Look not for reward from others, but hope you have done your best."

Gabrielle (Coco) Chanel   1883–1971

The words "fashion designer" are inadequate to describe the effect Coco Chanel had on haute couture and women in general. Hailed as the most influential designer of the 20th century, she set a standard of simple elegance that continues to influence the world more than nine decades after she got her start. From her humble beginnings—born in a poorhouse, orphaned at age seven—Mademoiselle Chanel became the undisputed queen of Paris fashion.

In 1905, when the 22-year-old designer opened her first shop, a millinery business, there were few career choices for women other than wife or courtesan. Wanting to be independent, Coco hit upon the novel idea of work. From the outset, she resolved to "rid women of their frills, from head to toe, for each frill discarded makes her look younger." Society women loved her designs, and demand for Chanel hats mushroomed. Her first clothing collection in 1914 was a success as well, but it was not until after World War I that the "Chanel look" really took off.

The end of the conflict that so devastated Europe ushered in the 20th century. The need for something new and original suffused society. No age could have been more perfect for Chanel, whose objective was to revolutionize the feminine costume, to redraw the female silhouette. She once said that "the corset is nothing more than a survival of the Middle Ages chastity belt," and women could not have agreed more. They were ready to be liberated by Chanel's practical way of dressing. She freed women to move, to have fun. Among her clothing innovations were knitted "sport" dresses, short evening dresses, and the ubiquitous "little black dress," which symbolizes the lasting impact of the Chanel mystique.

In 1922, Chanel decided to move into fragrances, a daring step since perfumes then belonged exclusively to the perfumeries. However, Chanel had a highly developed sense of smell. She hated the flowery, overbearing scents that had emerged primarily as cover-ups amid the rather primitive hygienic standards prevailing until after the war. Coco wanted to give women a "natural" scent. Working with a renowned chemist, she developed the first of the modern perfumes, Chanel No. 5, so named because it was the fifth of 10 samples offered to Chanel. The fact that Chanel No. 5 is still one of the most popular fragrances in the world, nearly three quarters of a century after its creation, is testimony to the genius of mademoiselle's "nose."

Chanel employed nearly 4,000 women by 1935 and had sold 28,000 dresses in Europe, the Near East, and the Americas. She surprised the world when she abruptly closed the House of Chanel just after the outbreak of World War II in 1939, which was the beginning of a 15-year exile. Her return in 1954 was considered a fiasco in France, but she took America by storm. At that time, she introduced the much-copied Chanel suit, which became a prestige item in the United States. By the time of her last collection in August 1970, Coco Chanel once again stood at the top of the fashion world.

1908–present

Estee Lauder

The name Estee Lauder, like that of Coco Chanel, is recognized around the world as exemplifying quality in a world of glamour and beauty. And that is so largely because of the drive and merchandising genius of one woman, whose company still flourishes today.

Born Josephine Esther Mentzer in the New York City borough of Queens, this dynamic entrepreneur built a small beauty service into an international cosmetics empire. Under the brand names Estee Lauder, Clinique, Origins, Prescriptives, Bobbi Brown (one of her newest acquisitions), and Aramis for men, the company markets some 700 skin-care, makeup, and fragrance products, capturing an astonishing 40 percent of all U.S. department and specialty-store cosmetics sales. Total sales in 1995 reached nearly $2.9 billion.

Estee, whose birth date has been variously reported as 1908 or 1910, started by selling skin creams, beauty products, and simple fragrances made by her uncle, who was a chemist. A beautiful young woman noted for her flawless complexion, Estee had a knack for establishing rapport with customers. She has been quoted as saying that she "was always interested in people being beautiful—the hair, the face." Her company bio states that as a young girl she dreamed of becoming a skin doctor.

Estee and her husband Joseph established their own company in 1946, marketing four products. The big break came after Estee gave away her lipsticks at a benefit luncheon at the Waldorf-Astoria. Women who had attended the luncheon sought to purchase her products at Saks, convincing that famous department store that there was, indeed, demand for Estee Lauder. The Saks account, in turn, gave Lauder the cachet she needed to expand nationally.

From the start, Estee targeted upscale stores as the proper marketplace for her products. And everything she did from advertising to packaging was done to appeal to the distinctively classy customer. One of Estee's most successful advertising ideas was to use only one model to personify the Lauder look, and that model symbolized Estee's vision of the gracious good life. Her marketing innovations included the "gift with purchase" idea, now a standard in the industry. After the introduction of her Youth Dew bath-oil fragrance vaulted her to fame, she cleverly used it to lure customers into trying her skin-treatment products.

Known as a "creative tyrant," Estee demanded quality. A typical fragrance contains a complex blend of many flowers, fruit essences, oils, animal materials, and chemicals in varying amounts. When one of Estee's new scents was about to debut, she pulled all the stock out of stores at the last minute after finding that one ingredient was missing. When told by a frustrated Lauder executive that nobody would know the difference, Estee replied, "But I'll know the difference!"

Leonard Lauder, Estee and Joe's elder son, took over as president of the company in 1972, becoming CEO in 1983 and chairman in 1995. Estee retains the title of founding chairman. Ending 49 years of private ownership, the company floated an initial public offering in 1995 that raised $365 million. The family still controls more than 86 percent of the stock.

Lee De Forest

Radio was not the product of a single inventor but dozens of them, ranging from Guglielmo Marconi's wireless to Thomas Edison's inventions in the area of sound, to contributions by England's Reginald Fessenden, Germany's Heinrich Hertz, and Alexander Popov of Russia. Lee De Forest belongs in this company: His audion tube transformed a technology based on sending the Morse code into one based on transmitting the human voice.

Thus, just as Andrew Grove set the stage for the development of the computer, Lee De Forest made possible the development of radio and then television.

After earning his Ph.D. at Yale, De Forest held a variety of jobs, including one at AT&T's Western Electric subsidiary in Chicago. There he experimented with perfecting mechanisms invented by Marconi. Brilliant, arrogant, and always confident of his ability, De Forest became convinced he could do it better. He worked at the Armour Institute of Technology from 1900 to 1902, leaving to organize De Forest Wireless Telegraph, which installed high-powered equipment at several naval bases. That company earned De Forest one of the several fortunes that he made and lost.

De Forest invented several radio antennae that expanded the range of telegraph signals. Then, in 1905, came the audion amplifier, a three-electrode vacuum tube that enabled wireless operators to transmit words as well as telegraph signals. De Forest thought his invention would replace wired telephones with wireless ones: "Unwittingly, then, had I discovered an Invisible Empire of the Air," he wrote in his diary. He then formed De Forest Radio Telegraph to capitalize on this invention.

Seven years later, De Forest perfected the oscillating audion, the key invention that earned him the title of "father of radio broadcasting." But 1912 was also marked by moves that, in hindsight, De Forest must have regretted: He sold some of his patents to AT&T for a pittance although AT&T did eventually pay the inventor $400,000 for others. The bottom line, however, was that De Forest had relinquished his rights to an invention that would be worth billions of dollars.

De Forest continued to experiment, although none of his later inventions proved to be as consequential as the audion tube. In the mid-1920s, he developed a method of wedding sound to film, making him one of the originators of talking movies. He called the process Phonofilm. Others created superior technologies, however, and De Forest was left with little to show for his efforts other than several lost lawsuits.

Seemingly spending as much time in court as in the laboratory, De Forest sued many radio and telephone companies for infringement of patents. He also suffered financial reverses, including the bankruptcy of Lee De Forest Inc., a company he had established in 1934. De Forest persisted in his creative efforts, working often simultaneously on radar, television, and telephone enhancements, and even diathermy machines. At his death in 1961, he held more than 300 patents.

While De Forest ranged the scientific landscape, Andrew Grove has been content to remain within a single locus of activity. Yet the two men shared an attribute that is immeasurable in its importance: Each invented a device that created a new industry and made possible a cultural transformation.

1936 — present

Andrew Grove

The microprocessor chip did for personal computers what Lee de Forest's audion tube did for radios. While Andrew Grove did not invent the microprocessor, he led in its development. He is the cofounder and CEO of Intel, the largest chip manufacturer in the world.

Born Andras Grof in Budapest, Hungary, in 1936, Grove fled to the United States in 1957, earning an engineering degree from New York's City College. In search of a warmer climate, Grove moved to the University of California at Berkeley for graduate work. With a 1963 doctorate in hand, he took a job with a start-up company called Fairchild Semiconductor.

When two senior managers at Fairchild, Gordon Moore and Robert Noyce, decided to start Intel in 1968, Grove went along expecting to be named director of engineering. He was instead named director of operations. Grove became president and chief operating officer in 1979 and took the helm of the company eight years later.

Semiconductor chips are the smaller-than-a-postage-stamp integrated circuits that make personal computers possible. The microprocessor—or heart—of the PC is made of these chips that do the job it used to take roomfuls of computer equipment to carry out. Under Grove's leadership, Intel has taken an aggressive path in developing and marketing these chips. Although it was making most of the microprocessors for PCs and compatible computers when Grove took over, many clone manufacturers ate into its market share with low-priced knockoffs. Grove's answer was the highly successful "Intel Inside" marketing campaign, aimed at getting consumers to demand name-brand chips and rewarding manufacturers for publicizing their use of Intel. When Grove became CEO, the promotional budget targeting the consumer market was essentially nonexistent. Now it exceeds $100 million a year, and Intel's name recognition ranks just ahead of that of NutraSweet.

Marketing is not Grove's only stroke of brilliance. The company is driven by research and development, staying ahead of the competition by working on several chip designs at once. By the time the clone manufacturers turn one chip into a commodity product, Intel has rolled out the next design, making the earlier chip obsolete.

Also, more and more of Intel's ventures are aimed at sidestepping computer manufacturers and speaking directly to consumers. For instance, Intel is working on technologies to deliver Internet access over cable-TV at speeds far greater than those of any telephone-line modem. This will allow full-motion video, intense color graphics, and audio to load into computers at acceptable speeds.

Grove's management style is open and informal. He welcomes what he calls "constructive confrontation." Intel has become a regular on *Fortune* magazine's list of most-admired companies. Grove's strategies are paying off with rapid growth. Revenues jumped 600 percent from 1987 to 1995, and industry analysts expect sales of $50 billion by the year 2000.

Charles H. Dow

1851–1902

The importance of news is nowhere more obvious than in the area of business and finance, where events often are acted on almost instantaneously. Although business journalism is quite old—Benjamin Franklin's print shop published maritime and other trade news in the 1700s—its true beginnings date to the late 19th century and Charles Dow.

The company that bears his name, Dow Jones & Company, publishes the *Wall Street Journal* and *Barron's*, two of the world's leading financial publications. But Dow didn't start *Barron's*, and the *Wall Street Journal* of his

time was a skimpy news sheet that bore little resemblance to today's national newspaper. Dow's legacy lies in the idea behind the publications and his introduction of the Dow Jones Industrial Average, the most widely watched barometer of the U.S. stock market.

Charles Dow appeared on Wall Street in 1880 as a financial writer and editorialist for the *New York Mail and Express* and the Kiernan News Agency. He previously had worked at several New England newspapers and as a reporter of silver-mining activities in Colorado. He had a reputation as a quiet but reliable reporter who could turn routine financial reporting into expert financial analysis.

In 1882, he joined with two other Kiernan employees, Edward D. Jones and Charles M. Bergstresser, to form Dow Jones. (Bergstresser was made a silent partner, having been persuaded that his name was too long to fit the corporate title.) According to one company legend, the founders had some trepidation, believing their knowledge of finance was meager. They asked railroad tycoon Collis Huntington for advice. "Go ahead,"

Huntington supposedly said. "Nobody else knows anything about the stock market."

Dow and Jones initially put out handwritten news bulletins that runners delivered to Wall Street clients at various times during the day. In 1883, they started printing the *Customers' Afternoon Letter*, a two-page financial bulletin that, in 1889, became the *Wall Street Journal*. By then, the newspaper had two employees, including its first out-of-town reporter, Clarence Barron, who covered the Boston markets.

Prominent from the *Journal's* early years was Dow's innovative index of common stocks. First devised in 1894 using 11 stocks, mostly railroads, that were considered representative of the market, the first industrial average appeared on May 26, 1896, comprising 12 issues. Dow's initial intentions were modest: to take the temperature of the markets, and use that information to gauge the blossoming industrial economy.

Dow Jones grew, and in 1897 it purchased the Kiernan News Agency when the proprietor retired. Kiernan was not only the financial district's most important news service, it also owned Printing Telegraph News, which manufactured tickers. The Dow Jones News Service, or "the broad tape," was soon launched.

By 1902, Jones was weary of the business and Bergstresser wanted to seek opportunities elsewhere. Dow, who was ill, knew he could not run the service alone given the state of his health, so the partners sold the company to Clarence Barron. Dow remained at the newspaper until his death that April.

Michael Bloomberg

1942–present

Taking a page from Charles Dow, Michael Bloomberg created a multimedia news enterprise based on finance and helped along by the information revolution and the public's seemingly insatiable appetite for business news.

The 1980s and 1990s witnessed enormous growth in mutual funds and 401(k) pension plans, as well as the phenomenon of repeated mortgage refinancings to take advantage of changing interest rates. Businessmen like Jack Welch, Michael Milken, Lee Iacocca, and Bill Gates became front-page news and household names. As economic news took on increasing importance, Bloomberg capitalized on these changes and plunged enthusiastically into the fray against Dow's offspring at Dow Jones & Company and other well-established competitors.

Known for his aggressive and demanding style, Bloomberg has built a cutting-edge organization that includes Bloomberg Business News, Bloomberg Information Television, *Bloomberg Magazine*, Bloomberg News Radio, and various Bloomberg newsletters. Underpinning the entire empire is the terminal—actually some 60,000 of them—that supplies information to brokers and investment managers around the world, and that is known simply as "the Bloomberg."

Bloomberg
FINANCIAL MARKETS
COMMODITIES
NEWS

Michael Bloomberg, who was born in 1942, was a successful trader and partner at Salomon Brothers in the 1970s but was forced out in 1981 after repeated clashes with management. With $20 million in cash and stock from his years at Salomon, and the knowledge gleaned from trading and time spent running Salomon's technology department, Bloomberg decided to launch an information and trading system.

The terminal he developed was an innovative piece of equipment that did much more than just report stock and bond prices. Initially aimed

at the global bond market, Bloomberg's software allowed users to analyze their investments and evaluate them under different risk scenarios. Furthermore, he provided vast amounts of data, including current prices from Treasury and corporate bond dealers, historical price data on thousands of securities, and breaking news and statistics on 15,000 companies.

But Bloomberg had plans to be more than just a niche player. He had expanded his service's coverage of the equities market, mortgage-backed securities, and other areas, but he wanted to go head-to-head against larger rivals like Reuters, Quotron, and Dow Jones. He turned to *Wall Street Journal* reporter Matthew Winkler to help him build a news service, and in 1990, Bloomberg Business News was born. Defying the odds against a start-up's success, particularly in an era of retrenchment for many news organizations, Bloomberg Business News has thrived and prospered.

The company is privately owned, and precise figures on its size are hard to come by. However, 1995 revenues were estimated at around $600 million, with 30 percent owned by the Merrill Lynch investment bank and the rest held by Michael Bloomberg. Yet, despite its expansion, Bloomberg still prides himself on running the business like a much smaller firm. Neither he nor anyone else has a private office, there aren't any secretaries, and no one has a corporate title. How long he can maintain this unconventional, small-shop style is anyone's guess. But one thing is certain, Michael Bloomberg is still growing: 1996 brought news of expansion into yet another venue, book publishing.

Thomas A. Edison   1847–1931

His contemporaries called him "the most useful American," and he is known to us as the "wizard of Menlo Park." Based on his amazing string of inventions— many among the most important ever developed—these designations cannot be disputed.

Edison, who left school at age 12, sold newspapers and sundries on trains before becoming a telegrapher. He quit that job in 1869 to become a full-time inventor. Edison established his Menlo Park, New Jersey, facility in 1876, which was an "invention factory" manned by a powerful team of scientists that Edison kept in the background, preferring not to share the spotlight. In this regard, Edison differed from the equally brilliant Robert Noyce, the Silicon Valley great of our time who invented the integrated circuit. Noyce set an egalitarian tone that became a hallmark of high-tech Silicon Valley.

The funds for Menlo Park came from sales of Edison's improved stock ticker and some telephone patents, activities that showed the

The Armature

ingenious inventor was also a shrewd businessman with an eye for commercial value.

Modern electric lighting was his most famous and far-reaching invention—or to be more precise, system. The invention itself was the simplest part and might have been discovered by others who were working on the idea. After perfecting his incandescent light in 1879, Edison had to come up with the infrastructure to get it accepted.

He had to convince people that the electric light could replace gas lights, which were simple, safe, and inexpensive. So he advertised electricity as though it were an improvement over gas, describing his "lamps" in terms of candle-

power, setting them at the same intensity as gas light, and charging customers for "burners" just as the gas companies did.

He organized Edison Electric Light and sold a one-sixth share to a group of investors that included J.P. Morgan, the Vanderbilts, and Western Union. He then designed a central power station, planned to run wires to homes taking the service, and set up a lamp factory. Next, he formed Edison Electric Illuminating and applied to New York City for the right to electrify some of its street lamps. Stiff opposi-

tion came from gas interests, including John D. Rockefeller, but Edison plowed on, and his Pearl Street station began operating in 1880. Morgan's home was the first to be electrified.

The inventor encouraged others to form illuminating companies in other cities and provided some 250 patents in return for large blocks of stock in the new firms. This not only helped spread the new technology but earned Edison and his backers huge fortunes.

Edison went on to invent the phonograph, the motion picture projector, electric motors, storage batteries, multiple telegraph transmissions, and the mimeograph machine, among many other things. He produced a patentable device at the rate of one every two weeks during his adult life. When he died at age 84, his final efforts included trying to extract a rubber-like product from sunflowers.

1927–1990

Robert N. Noyce

Acclaimed as the founding father of the semiconductor industry, legendary figure Robert Noyce helped usher in the age of the computer with his invention of the integrated circuit. Although never a household name, Noyce—like Thomas Edison before him—forever changed the way the world lives, making possible space travel, microcomputers, digital watches, pocket calculators, and robots.

Inventor, scientist, and businessman, Noyce founded two of the electronics firms, Fairchild Semiconductor and Intel Corporation, that were responsible for landmark discoveries in the Silicon Valley world of high technology. At Fairchild, Noyce built multiple transistors on a single chip of silicon, and the microchip was born. Unbeknownst to Noyce, a young Texas Instruments engineer, Jack Kilby, had invented a similar device made of germanium, and both Noyce and Kilby are listed as "coinventors" of the semiconductor chip. But Noyce's silicon-integrated circuit was more efficient and easier to produce, and so became the industry standard.

In 1968, Noyce and another of the Fairchild founders, Gordon Moore, left their brainchild to set up Intel (short for integrated electronics). They wanted to explore the area of computer memory and to find a more efficient means of storing data. The ceramic cores then in use could store only one piece of information on each core at any one time. What they came up with was a silicon-polysilicon chip that contained 4,000 transistors and did the work of a thousand ceramic cores. Called the "1103 memory chip," it quickly replaced ceramic cores.

Shortly after that breakthrough, one of Intel's young engineers discovered the microprocessor, a revolutionary invention that allowed a single chip to hold the circuitry for both information storage and processing. One chip could be programmed to perform a multitude of tasks.

With back-to-back successes, Intel's stock price shot ahead and the company grew rapidly. Within four years of its founding, Intel's revenues were nearly $25 million, and they grew to $854 million by 1980. In 1995, revenues totaled $16.2 billion.

Brilliant, innovative, and with a breadth of interests that included snow skiing, scuba diving, flying his own plane, and directing a madrigal singing group, Noyce cited the values instilled in his Iowa youth—called the "first principles"—as the basis for his accomplishments: "Work hard, save your money, get an education, try to get ahead."

The third of four sons of a Congregational minister, Noyce got his undergraduate degree at Grinnell College in Iowa and was one of the first people to study the newly developed transistor. After earning a Ph.D. at MIT, Noyce worked for a short time at Philco before accepting an offer from Nobel laureate William Shockley, one of the inventors of the transistor, to join a team of young Ph.D.s who were working to develop better transistors. But this working environment was not without its problems, so Noyce and seven of his colleagues left to start their own business—Fairchild Semiconductor.

At his death at age 62, Noyce was heading up Sematech, a government-industry consortium established to advance U.S. competitiveness in the semiconductor industry.

Benjamin Franklin   1706–1790

Sometimes called "the American Leonardo," Benjamin Franklin was the most distinguished American of his time. Were it not for his age, Franklin might have become the nation's first president. His numerous accomplishments

ranged from pioneering experiments involving electricity to helping write the Constitution, to skillful service as a diplomat, to innovations in journalism and printing. And not so incidentally, Franklin helped remake the postal service during the colonial period.

In 1737, Franklin—who had long been aware of the importance of inexpensive, reliable, and rapid communication—was named postmaster general for the Philadelphia area. "I accepted it readily," he later wrote, "and found it to great advantage; for though the salary was small, it facilitated the correspondence that improved my newspaper." The post enabled Franklin to send his newspapers through the mail for free using his personal frank, but he also insisted on low rates for other newspapers as well.

Franklin became copostmaster for all the colonies in 1753 and immediately embarked on a tour to witness operations firsthand. Within months, he had instituted reforms and new services: Where mail between towns previously had been delivered only twice during the winter months, Franklin instituted weekly delivery. Another change enabled mail to travel from New York to Philadelphia by night, and the New York-to-Boston run was reduced from six weeks to three. Franklin and copostmaster William Hunter of Virginia provided a businesslike system and cracked down on dishonest and inefficient postal operations.

Postal service was disrupted in 1766 by events leading up to the American Revolution, with the Sons of Liberty rightly concluding that communications between British forces would be difficult without it. Franklin had made the post office profitable to the British government for the first time, but London became wary of Franklin's activities and dismissed him for political reasons in 1773. The service declined thereafter, due largely to continued interferences during the revolutionary period.

In 1775, the Continental Congress recommended establishment of a postal service, making Franklin the new nation's first postmaster general. He did not hold the post for long, though, becoming commissioner to France the following year. The office then passed to his son-in-law, Richard Bache.

Franklin's contributions to the postal system were not yet finished, however. At the Constitutional Convention in 1787, a somewhat frail Benjamin Franklin helped frame the document that, in Article I, Section 8, gave the government the right "to establish Post Office and post roads."

Few men can be compared to Franklin in overall achievements. But in understanding the importance of rapid communication, Fred Smith followed Franklin's example by reinventing the mail for our time with his creation of Federal Express and overnight delivery.

Frederick W. Smith

1944–present

More than two centuries after Ben Franklin revolutionized postal service by instituting weekly delivery of the mail, Fred Smith came up with the radical idea of promising to get a package there "absolutely, positively" overnight.

Smith was a Yale undergraduate in 1965 when he wrote an economics term paper proposing the concept that would eventually blossom into the Federal Express Corporation. Recognizing that the changing U.S. economy was becoming more service-oriented and technology-dominated, Smith posited that there was a market for overnight, door-to-door delivery of documents and small packages. With $40 million from investors, $8 million from family sources, and bank financing that brought the total to more than $90 million—the largest start-up ever funded by venture capital—Smith opened for business on April 17, 1973.

Initially, FedEx served 25 cities, and the first night's shipment consisted of only 186 packages. Now, a little more than two decades later, the Memphis-based company boasts the world's largest fleet of cargo planes, which deliver 2.5 million items to 193 countries daily. In 1983, FedEx went down in the record books as the first corporation ever to reach $1 billion in sales within its first decade of operation. Its 1995 sales totaled some $9.39 billion.

Frederick Wallace Smith was born in 1944, the son of an outgoing Southern businessman who managed to make a fortune during the Depression. After graduating from Yale with a degree in economics and political science in 1966, Smith served two tours of duty as a Marine in Vietnam. He received the Silver Star, a Bronze Star, and two Purple Hearts. The experience of war impelled Smith to embark

on his business career. "I got so sick of destruction…that I came back determined to do something constructive," he confided in an interview with *Forbes* magazine. Besides CEO Smith's vision and innovation, various factors have been cited as contributing to FedEx's astonishing success:

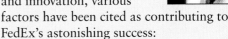

- Public perception that the U.S. Postal Service was unreliable provided the right psychological climate for a new alternative.

- Rapid growth in air-passenger traffic made package operations less important to the commercial airlines.

- A 1974 strike at UPS hobbled the competition.

Moreover, FedEx has been highly visible right from the start. Its orange and purple corporate colors and its motto—"The World On Time"—are easily recognized by many Americans, thanks to its memorable and amusing advertising campaigns. One well-known spot featured a fast-talking character speaking nonstop, literally, in a one-minute commercial. Telling its story with humor has been a hallmark of FedEx.

Another hallmark is FedEx's reputation as a "people company." When it was named one of the top 10 U.S. companies in the 1985 edition of *The 100 Best Companies to Work for in America,* FedEx was cited for its personnel policies, including no layoffs, top wages, profit sharing, a five-step grievance procedure, and unusual benefits. In addition, FedEx has instituted employee programs to reinforce and reward top performance. It was, in part, the employee contributions that allowed FedEx to be the first service company to win the Malcolm Baldridge National Quality Award in 1990—a testament to its high customer service ratings.

Amadeo Peter Giannini   1870–1949

A.P. Giannini was born in California, the son of Italian immigrants. When he was six years old, his father died, and his mother married Lorenzo Scatena, a teamster. The family moved to San Francisco, where Giannini attended school until the age of 15, when he quit to join his stepfather, who had become a commission agent in the fruit and vegetable business. Giannini showed such business acumen he was made a partner at age 19.

In 1892, Giannini married Clorinda Cuneo, the daughter of a wealthy businessman. When his father-in-law died in 1902, Giannini took over management of the family properties, which included a minority interest in the Columbus Savings and Loan Society. He became a member of the board, but when they refused to

serve the farmers and small businessmen he knew from his days in the commission business, he quit to start his own bank. The Bank of Italy was founded in 1904 to "serve the little fellow." It was capitalized at $300,000, divided into 3,000 shares at $100 each. Giannini limited ownership to 100 shares per person so the shares could be distributed as widely as possible.

The turning point for Giannini came with the 1906 San Francisco earthquake and fire. While the larger banks had to close down, Giannini erected a makeshift desk on a pier and made loans to anyone who wanted to rebuild. With

this, the legend of A.P. Giannini began. He was barely touched by the financial panic of 1907, because he had the foresight to store gold.

In 1909, he started opening branches in other parts of California, beginning with San Jose, concentrating on the same small depositors and borrowers that had made the San Francisco bank so successful. In 1921 he organized a subsidiary, the Liberty Bank, and three years later Giannini acquired the Los Angeles-based Bank of America, which already had 21 branches. Both were eventually merged with Bank of Italy, which by 1927 had 289 branches in 185 California towns and cities, with capital of $750 million. By then it was the largest bank west of the Hudson and the third largest in the country. It played a major role in financing California agriculture and was one of the earliest lenders to the motion-picture industry. "Building California" became the bank's motto.

Giannini turned his attention eastward, acquiring banks in New York and a controlling interest in banks in other states. He saw nationwide branch banking as the best way to strengthen the banking system and bring a wide variety of banking services to more people.

Giannini had organized a holding company, BankItaly Corporation, into which he placed all of his financial interests. In 1928, to reflect his expansive vision, he created a new holding company called Transamerica. In 1930, the Bank of Italy itself was renamed Bank of America.

Giannini retired as president of Bank of America in 1936 but remained its leader the rest of his life. It continued to grow and in 1945 became the largest bank in the world. More than half a century later, BankAmerica Corporation remains a strong institution with an international presence, and Giannini's dream

of interstate banking is finally a reality. A.P. Giannini revolutionized banking by putting capital in the hands of working people and thereby raising democracy in America to a new and greater level.

1939–present

Charles Schwab

The modern history of the securities broker-age business began when the Securities and Exchange Commission decided to deregulate commissions paid to brokers. It was done grad-ually, starting in 1974, and on May 1, 1975, commissions became fully negotiated. Old-line firms, and newer ones prepared to discount commissions, eyed each other carefully, waiting for an indication of what to expect. Merrill Lynch started it off surprisingly by raising commissions 10 percent, indicating it believed customers were prepared to pay for full service, including research reports and "hand holding" by registered representatives.

The response backfired. Almost immediately, scores of discount operations sprang up, clear-ing through member firms and offering discounts of more than 50 percent off the old posted rates. Many of these early discounters folded after a few months or so. Charles Schwab was one of the few who managed to jump ahead of the pack.

Schwab was a Stanford graduate who, on leav-ing school, managed First Commander Corp., a California-based brokerage firm, which in time was renamed Charles Schwab & Co. When May Day arrived in 1975, Schwab cut his commissions sharply and competed vigorously for business. Through skillful advertising and promotion, he was quite successful.

Charles Schwab
Helping Investors Help Themselves®

Schwab took his company public in 1987, and in 1983 sold it for $53 million in stock to BankAmerica Corporation. By then, Schwab was the largest discounter by far, with more than 400,000 customers. The marriage was rocky, so Schwab repurchased the company in 1987 for $280 million, went public again, and continued to prosper. By the mid-1990s, Schwab had more than 3.4 million active accounts and over 40 percent of the discount business.

Like Charles Merrill before him, Schwab is a visionary, possessed with an ability to develop programs to satisfy customer needs. But there were differences in approaches and goals, not

surprising considering these men operated in dif-fering market environments. Merrill geared his actions to investors who needed to be introduced to the markets in a period of relatively low technology; Schwab targeted more experienced investors who did not require the services of advi-sors. Utilizing his strong cash flow to automate operations, he employed the latest technology in his efforts.

In 1982, Schwab inaugurated a 24-hour, 7-day-a-week order entry for customers, and seven years later made transactions possible through Telebroker, an automated telephone touchpad entry system, with customers receiving further discounts for using the service. StreetSmart for Windows™, introduced in 1993, made it possi-ble for investors to make purchases and sales through their computers.

Perhaps his biggest innovation was OneSource, instituted in 1992, by which customers could purchase hundreds of mutual funds through Schwab, with no transaction fees for no-loads (Schwab received revenue from the funds them-selves). Customers could transfer between fund families with ease, at no additional charge, which made transactions and transfer much simpler.

Schwab also cut costs, eliminating fees for divi-dend reinvestment on more than 4,000 stocks. To cap things off, he bought Mayer & Schweitzer, which accounted for 6 percent of all Nasdaq trades. He purchased seats on the Pacific Coast Stock Exchange, opened a London brokerage office, and purchased a brokerage firm there, becoming the U.K's largest discounter. In the process, Schwab demonstrated an originality and energy not seen in brokerage for decades.

Schwab may be compared with A.P. Giannini, founder of what became BankAmerica, the man credited with bringing banking services to the masses almost a century ago. Interestingly, the temporary marriage of Schwab with BankAmerica brought under the same corpo-rate umbrella two of the most innovative firms in 20th century banking.

William Randolph Hearst   1863–1951

At the peak of his power and fame, William Randolph Hearst commanded a media empire that included newspapers in key cities, magazines, a news service, radio stations, and motion-picture interests. Frustrated in his attempts to gain political power through elec-

tive office, he was nevertheless feared and courted by those who did hold office. For more than half a century, Hearst defined media power, and another half century would pass before his counterpart would appear in the person of Rupert Murdoch.

Hearst was to the manor born. His father George was a California-based geologist who made a fortune in mining and then turned to politics and journalism. After an indifferent college career, William entered the newspaper business, first as an apprentice at Joseph Pulitzer's *New York World*, and then as editor and publisher of one of his father's papers, the *San Francisco Examiner*. Drawing on his own proclivities and the Pulitzer experience, Hearst turned the *Examiner* into a crusading newspaper, relying on sensationalism to expand

circulation. He initiated campaigns against the railroads that dominated California politics and came to be considered a radical reformer.

In 1895, Hearst's mother purchased the *New York Morning Journal* and William promptly transformed it into a New York version of the *Examiner* and began a circulation war with Pulitzer. Hearst's sensationalism, dubbed "yellow journalism" because of popular cartoon characters of the time, climaxed with a crusade to go to war with Spain. When the war came in 1898, it was called "Mr. Hearst's War."

After the war, Hearst turned to fashioning a political career, geared initially toward a bid for the Democratic vice-presidential nomination. Toward this end, he purchased or organized newspapers in other parts of the country, having concluded that control of the media would translate into political power.

In 1902, Hearst unsuccessfully sought the governorship of New York, after which he was elected to a seat in the U.S. House of Representatives. He served two terms with no significant accomplishment. An effort to secure the Democratic presidential nomination in 1904 failed, as did a run the following year for the New York mayoralty. A second bid for the governorship also ended in defeat. A subsequent feud with Democratic Governor Al Smith finished Hearst's political career.

Even so, by the 1920s, Hearst was considered one of the nation's most powerful opinion shapers, having fashioned a major media empire. To the newspapers and radio stations, he added film companies, in part to boost the career of his mistress Marion Davies.

Hearst's interests suffered during the Great Depression, and he had to sell off some of his properties. He increasingly withdrew to his fabled mansion at San Simeon, California, becoming a shadowy figure. In 1941, he tried to block release of the Orson Welles film "Citizen Kane," which purportedly was based on his life.

1931–present

Rupert Murdoch

He is sometimes compared to media tycoon William Randolph Hearst, particularly because his newspapers thrive on being brash and controversial. Also like Hearst, Murdoch has a lifelong passion for journalism.

From its beginnings in Australia, Murdoch's News Corporation Ltd. has expanded to include holdings in the United States, Great Britain, New Zealand, Hong Kong, Latin America, and Germany. Today its entrepreneurial leader continues his quest for opportunities around the globe—particularly in Asia and Europe. Without a doubt, Murdoch is well on his way to attaining his vision of a global communications company. But perhaps even more impressive than the breadth of Murdoch's global vision is his depth.

A shrewd businessman, known for taking enormous personal risks, Murdoch is constantly venturing into new businesses. News Corp. is the world's largest newspaper publisher, with 100 Australian newspapers, various independent papers in New Zealand, the *New York Post* in the United States, *The Times of London*, and three other U.K. papers. But dwarfing those investments are News Corp.'s ownerships in Twentieth Century Fox Film Corporation, Fox Broadcasting Company, Fox Television Stations Inc., Star TV (a pan-Asian satellite television network), a Latin American cable channel, a television network in Australia, British Sky Broadcasting (a digital television satellite broadcast service), *TV Guide*,

HarperCollins Publishers (books), Ansett Transport (air transport), and Australian Newsprint Mills, among other things. In the mid-1980s, Murdoch made history when he purchased Metromedia Broadcasting and turned it into the fourth network—Fox Broadcasting Company—alongside NBC, ABC, and CBS.

The Oxford-educated Murdoch, who was born in Australia in 1931, built his multibillion-dollar industry virtually from scratch. He inherited two Adelaide newspapers from his father Sir Keith Murdoch in 1952 and started up *The Australian*, the country's first national daily, in 1964. From there he moved into the British market, buying *News of the World*, a London Sunday paper, in 1968 and *The Sun* in 1969. *The Sun*, a London-based tabloid, proved to be one of Murdoch's greatest print successes, albeit a controversial one. The first British paper to print nudity, *The Sun*'s circulation soared to more than 4 million from about 950,000 under Murdoch's ownership.

Considered to be one of the most powerful men in the world, he is admired and feared. Still, Murdoch is not without his charms and has been described by one British media official as "a great seducer." A staunch conservative, he has successfully cultivated political connections here and abroad.

MCI Communications Chairman Bert Roberts, who entered into a $2 billion interactive-technology deal with Murdoch in 1995, said of the media mogul: "I would be the first to tell you that he knows what he's doing, and we are going to look to him for expertise."

Conrad Hilton

1887–1979

Although some hoteliers before him had owned more than one property, Conrad Hilton pioneered the concept of owning a chain of hotels. Several chains now jockey for position in the marketplace, but no one disputes that Hilton was first in the industry.

Returning from service in France in World War I, Hilton wanted to resume his banking career. He

had his eye on a bank in Cisco, Texas. When negotiations dragged on, Hilton decided to use his money to buy the 50-room Mobley Hotel instead. Finding the business to his liking, he sought other properties and that same year, 1919, bought the Hotel Melba in Fort Worth. The following year, he acquired the Waldorf in Dallas. By 1923, Hilton owned five Texas hotels with a total of 520 rooms and a value of around $250,000. He continued to buy, sell, and build hotels, and was the largest hotel operator in the region by the end of the decade.

The advent of the Great Depression pushed Hilton to the brink of disaster. He lost some of his properties, closed down entire floors in others, and removed telephones to save whatever money he could. He even took a job at the rival Affiliated National Hotels to earn enough money to get by.

The turning point came in the late 1930s as the economy began to improve and property values remained low. Hilton started buying distressed hotels on the West Coast, the first of which

was San Francisco's Sir Francis Drake. In the early 1940s, he moved into New York, purchasing the Roosevelt and then picking up the famed Plaza for $7.4 million. Hilton now had a motto: "Across the Nation."

By then, Hilton had learned to adjust to changing environments—and for a while, no one was better at it. Later in the decade, he obtained his first foreign holdings, starting out in Mexico and then moving on to Europe. In 1949, Hilton formed Hilton International Company, signaling his intention to concentrate more on foreign operations. As a result, he was well situated to capitalize on the postwar tourism and business boom. His motto now became: "World Peace Through International Trade and Travel," and "Across the Nation" was replaced by "Around the World."

In 1949, Hilton capped his expansion spree by purchasing operating control of New York's Waldorf-Astoria for $3 million, eventually acquiring total ownership of that crown jewel in the 1970s. He was known as the "No. 1 innkeeper," and Hilton's success was attributed partly to his "minimax" formula—minimize cost, maximize hospitality. Although mass purchases of equipment and food produced economies, Hilton spurned the idea of redecorating the hotels in a common pattern, insisting that each maintain the individuality that gave it its prestige in the first place.

Recognizing new trends, the hotelier organized Hilton Credit in 1958 to operate Carte Blanche credit card operations. However, Carte Blanche was mismanaged and never amounted to much. Moreover, Hilton was unprepared to capitalize on the new age of air travel and interstate highways, missing out on the motel boom. At Conrad's death in 1979, his son Barron Hilton took over as the company's chairman.

1932–present   J. Willard Marriott, Jr.

From a nine-stool root beer stand to one of the world's leading hotel operators—that's the Marriott International story in a nutshell. Bill Marriott, son of the company founder, has been at the helm during the phenomenal growth of the past three decades.

When Bill took over as president in 1964, Marriott consisted of four hotels, 45 Hot Shoppes restaurants, and an airline-catering operation that produced total sales of $85 million. By the time he assumed the chief executive post in 1972, the expansion of the hotel operation was well under way, and the company was concentrating primarily on business travelers. Today, Marriott

has more than 1,000 domestic and international hotels and sales exceeding $8.96 billion, and offers the broadest spectrum of products in the lodging industry. In 1995, it swept into the luxury end of the hospitality business by acquiring a 49 percent interest in Ritz-Carlton.

Bill Marriott was born in 1932 into a strict Mormon family that valued hard work. "My father couldn't stand to see me idle," Marriott once told *People* magazine. Consequently, he started learning the family business early on, first by working summers in the company's architectural department, then as a food-service employee while he was still in college, and as a manager of the company's first hotel, the

Twin Bridges in Washington, D.C. He moved up through various executive positions within the company before taking over as president.

Marriott International has been recognized as one of the country's best-managed companies, and much of its success can be attributed to Bill. He believes in developing well-trained managers and recruits from the leading hotel-management training schools. One of his prime concerns is that his people respond quickly and cordially to customers' wants and needs. "You can build the best hotel in the world, but if you haven't got friendly people in the front desk, the customer is not going to come back," he has said. Moreover, he insists that every employee work to maintain the company's good name and reputation: "We hold no patents; all we have is our name."

Besides its traditional lodging operations, which range from economy to luxury accommodations, the company has also gotten into the vacation ownership business. Time-share has blossomed under the Marriott banner to encompass Hawaiian as well as international opportunities, catering to an upscale clientele. The company uses its reputation for quality to great advantage in marketing this once-stigmatized vacation product. Food service and facilities management as well as retirement-community operations round out the Marriott businesses.

Although Bill Marriott passed his 64th birthday in 1996, this acknowledged workaholic gives no indication of slowing down. The company's 1995 letter to shareholders, in addition to announcing record net income of $247 million, outlined plans for additional growth in all segments, including a plan to add another 120,000 hotel rooms by the turn of the century.

William Levitt   1907–1994

No figure is more closely associated with the building boom that followed World War II than William Levitt. He revolutionized the housing industry as epitomized by Levittown, New York. Even now, 40 years after its completion, foreign visitors trek to Long Island to see this miracle of the age.

Levitt's father and brother drifted into the housing business during the 1920s, and William joined them soon after in a company known as Levitt  & Sons. In the late 1920s and early 1930s, the family built 600 houses on Long Island in four years. In 1934, it started Strathmore-at-Manhasset, a 200-house development that was considered daring for the Depression era. The development was a success, and in the next seven years the Levitts put up more than 2,000 additional homes, becoming the leader in that region. When World War II came along, William served with the Seabees, but not before assisting in the construction of a 1,660-unit development for the military in Norfolk, Virginia.

After the war, William wanted to put his experience to use on a massive housing project geared primarily toward returning veterans. He quietly amassed 7.3 square miles of land in the Island Trees area of Nassau County on Long Island, not far from the Queens border. Then, using a design drawn by his brother Alfred, he put up 17,500 nearly identical, 800-square-foot homes. Levitt accomplished this feat over a four-year period (1947–51) by employing on-site mass-production techniques developed in the auto industry. After the foundation slab was poured and settled, workers organized in teams would put up the prefabricated sections of a house in little more than a week, then move on to the next one. Each worker had his own task to perform; one did nothing but bolt washing machines to the floors of the houses.

"What it amounted to was a reversal of the Detroit assembly line," Levitt said. "There, the car moved while the workers stayed at their stations. In the case of our homes, it was the workers who moved, doing the same job at different locations. To the best of my knowledge, no one had ever done that before." The original owners picked up on the analogy, referring to their houses as the "1948 Cape Cods."

The buyers of these "Levitts" often were the first in their families to own homes. Levitt had achieved economies by making large-scale purchases from manufacturers, so the initial models rented for $65 a month, with an option to buy for $6,990. Later, the price was raised to $7,990; after 1949, they could only be purchased. Levitt went on to produce other Levittowns in New Jersey and Maryland.

In 1968 Levitt sold Levitt & Sons to ITT Corp. for $92 million in stock and for a while was quite wealthy. He soon lost much of this in other ventures and had to sell his yacht and other luxuries. In 1981 Levitt was charged with having taken money from a charitable foundation he had established and was forced to repay $5 million. Levitt died a ruined and broken man. Yet he has his monument in the Levittowns he constructed as well as other projects. No homebuilder of the 20th century has had a greater impact than he. Even today, visitors to America ask to see several sights in the New York metropolitan area, among them the Empire State Building, the United Nations—and Levittown.

William Levitt was an opportunist of the first rank, the most famous of a large breed that followed. Eli Broad, the head of Kaufman and Broad, carries on in the Levitt tradition today, constructing well-made homes for middle-class Americans, making them the best-housed people in the world.

1933–present

Eli Broad

Following in the footsteps of William Levitt of a generation before, Eli Broad devised a simple formula: Put up basic, low-priced homes for first-time buyers. From that simple blueprint flowed spectacular success, making the company Broad founded the largest home builder in the western United States.

After graduating from Michigan State University with a degree in accounting and becoming Michigan's youngest CPA at age 20, Broad decided that there were opportunities to be found in home building. So he borrowed $25,000 from his in-laws, formed a partnership with builder Donald

Kaufman in 1957, and began making the American dream a reality for thousands of Michiganders. On the first weekend of business, Detroit-based Kaufman and Broad sold $250,000 worth of homes; by the end of the first year of operations, the company had revenues of $1.7 million.

Rapid expansion followed, and in 1962 the company went public. It became the first home-builder to be listed on the American Stock Exchange in 1962, then moved on to take that same title on the New York Stock Exchange in 1969.

Meanwhile, the company left Detroit and moved into the California market, building its first homes in Orange County in 1963. California was in the midst of a boom, and Kaufman and Broad boomed right along with it. The company acquired several smaller firms, becoming one of the leading U.S. home-builders while still in its first decade of operations. It added a mortgage subsidiary in 1965 and branched out to other parts of the country, putting up homes in New York, San Francisco, and Chicago. Kaufman and Broad soon moved into the international market as well and is now one of the leading builders of apartments and condominiums in the Paris metropolitan area. It also has home-building operations in Canada and Mexico.

In the early 1970s, as the company's revenues passed $100 million, Broad became bored with his success and withdrew from day-to-day management to spend time traveling with his family. When California real estate soured in 1973, he quickly took back the reins and went to work revitalizing the company. In 1989, Kaufman and Broad was spun off to shareholders, and its insurance subsidiary—today known as SunAmerica, Inc.—was established as an independent financial services company. Broad was named chairman, president, and CEO of the firm, which holds assets of $36 billion as of June 1996. Broad is betting that those aging baby boomers to whom he once sold houses are now worrying about retirement, and he is aggressively marketing fixed and variable annuities to fill their needs.

Broad, who was born in 1933, has amassed a fortune that *Forbes* magazine estimated at $800 million in 1995. But he is known for his budget-minded demeanor and acknowledges that "no one ever accused me of overpaying." However, he does allow himself one great extravagance: Broad owns a spectacular collection of contemporary art that includes works by Roy Lichtenstein, Jasper Johns, and Robert Rauschenberg. Taking his passion for art beyond personal collecting, he chaired the creation of the Los Angeles Museum of Contemporary Art in 1980.

Marcus Loew 1870–1927

History is replete with stories of individuals who sought one objective and wound up with another. The ability to take advantage of opportunities with flexibility and vision—as Sumner Redstone did at Viacom—often leads to success. At the dawn of the motion-picture age, a befuddled striver who hoped to invest in real estate wound up as a major show-business tycoon.

Marcus Loew worked as a salesman for a New York furrier, saving all he could with the desire to purchase a property that would provide him with additional income. Joining with a friend, Herman Baer, he purchased a small tenement. He hoped it would be the first in a string that would make him a real estate manager.

But Loew had other interests as well. He loved the theater, a fondness he shared with Adolph Zukor. Zukor, in a casual discussion, mentioned the profits to be made by owning nickelodeons, and Loew, in turn, spoke to Baer and an actor friend, David Warfield. The men decided to form a company, People's Vaudeville, which opened a peep show on 23rd Street in 1904. From there, People's expanded into movie theaters and then vaudeville bookings, taking a new name each time—first Loew's Consolidated and then Loew's Theatrical Enterprises.

Around this time, several motion-picture studios appeared, but Loew was not interested. His theaters were booming and vaudeville was in good shape, so why switch? In 1919, he restructured his holdings into Loew's Inc., which was capitalized at $17.5 million, equal to more than $200 million in today's dollars. Modest and unpretentious, Marcus Loew was exhibiting a quiet genius for business, achieving success beyond his wildest dreams.

But Loew was beginning to realize that content was an important part of the equation in the theater business. And although he controlled a huge string of theaters and ran one of the leading vaudeville circuits in the country, Loew had trouble finding the kind of quality pictures he wanted for his audiences.

In 1920, he picked up a failing company, Metro Pictures, with the idea of assuring an affordable supply of films for his enterprises. Metro's president was Richard Rowland, a Pittsburgh exhibitor, and its secretary was Louis B. Mayer, who also owned a chain of eastern theaters. Metro had a few hits but nothing like the 50 to 75 quality films Loew had hoped for each year. So in 1924, Goldwyn Pictures, with its extensive Culver City production facilities, was added, followed the next year with Mayer's producing organization.

Loew, an opportunist in the finest sense of the word, had succeeded in establishing Metro-Goldwyn-Mayer, the greatest of the Hollywood studios and a name that came to be synonymous with the golden age of movies. With Louis B. Mayer at its head, MGM dominated Hollywood during the 1930s and 1940s.

After Loew died, humorist Will Rogers said of him: "He would have been successful in a legitimate business." Marcus Loew might not have appreciated that humor, however. Although he always considered films as an adjunct to his true business—theaters—nevertheless, he did consider show business to be legitimate. For him, business always took precedence over the show.

1936–present

Sumner M. Redstone

Starting with his family's chain of a dozen drive-in movie theaters, Sumner Redstone, chairman and CEO of Viacom Inc., has built a global entertainment empire that produced revenues of more than $11 billion in 1995 and that includes theaters, cable programming operations, movie and television production studios, book publishing, and video and music retailing.

Redstone presides over cable operations that encompass MTV, VH1, Nick at Nite, The Movie Channel, Showtime, and Nickelodeon, the world's largest producer of children's programming. Viacom's stable of production and syndication successes includes names like "Entertainment Tonight," "Frasier," the "Star Trek" series, and "Cheers." Redstone vaulted the company into world-class status in 1994 with his $10 billion takeover of Paramount Communications Inc. and subsequent acquisition of Blockbuster Entertainment Corp.

The unassuming Redstone, whose personal wealth has been estimated at $4 billion, began life in Boston in 1923, the elder son of a struggling businessman who sold linoleum during the Depression. His father Michael Rothstein (the family name was later changed) also worked as a liquor wholesaler and eventually came to own the Latin Quarter and Club Mayfair nightclubs in Boston. In 1934, Rothstein opened his first drive-in movie theater on Long Island, a novel idea at the time.

Meanwhile, young Sumner grew up in a family atmosphere that demanded perfection. He enrolled at the prestigious Boston Latin School, noted for its highly disciplined academic achievers, where he won numerous honors and graduated with the highest grade-point average in the school's history. He enrolled in Harvard at age 17, completing his bachelor's degree in only two and a half years. "Harvard was like going to kindergarten after Boston Latin," Redstone once told *Time* magazine.

Military service in World War II, a return to Harvard for a law degree, and six years of life as a lawyer preceded Redstone's decision to enter the business world in 1954. He expanded the family drive-in business into National Amusements, Inc., which owns and operates

more than 1,000 screens in the U.S. and the U.K. Along the way, he personally litigated a suit that forced the movie studios to give drive-ins equal access to first-run films. He also came up with the trademarked idea of multiplex theaters.

In the late 1970s and early 1980s, Redstone made millions, investing in the stocks of movie studios, and then he began buying shares of Viacom International Inc. Just as he had correctly foreseen in the mid-1960s that indoor theaters would eclipse drive-ins, Redstone realized that cable television and the use of VCRs would change global viewing habits, and he wanted to be a part of that play. In 1987, he initiated a takeover offer for Viacom. A bitter fight with Viacom management ensued, but Redstone prevailed in a $3.4 billion leveraged buyout that gave him 83 percent of the company's stock.

The tenacity that has marked Redstone's business career served him well in 1979 when he survived a hotel fire by clinging to a third-floor ledge with one hand until help arrived. Severely burned and requiring 60 hours of surgery to repair the damage, Redstone was not expected to walk again. He spent a year recovering, returned to work with renewed energy, and not only walks but jogs daily and is an avid tennis player.

Louis B. Mayer   1885–1957

Of all the motion-picture studios during Hollywood's golden age of the 1930s and 1940s, none was more acclaimed than Metro-Goldwyn-Mayer under Louis B. Mayer. Called the "Czar of Hollywood," Mayer had a talent for organization and an intuitive knack for recognizing star material.

Mayer was a Jewish immigrant from Minsk, Russia, who arrived in America as a child. He had limited formal schooling and worked as

a junk dealer for a while before purchasing a nickelodeon in Massachusetts. Before long, he had a string of them. He also entered film production, turning out several well-regarded motion pictures.

After a series of transactions by Marcus Loew that created MGM in the mid-1920s, Mayer agreed to take over the Loew's Inc. production arm, and a new kind of studio emerged. Up to then, studios operated on instinct and even whim. Mayer transformed MGM into a film factory, where directors directed, writers wrote, and actors acted, all under the leadership of a taskmaster who combined concern for the balance sheet with an interest in public tastes.

Dancer Ray Bolger once remarked, "They thought people like you would go into a grocery store and say, 'Give me four comics and three toe dancers. I want 19 character actors and I want some unique personalities.'"

When MGM acquired Irving Thalberg as head of production in 1923, it gained a coexecutive who could transform Mayer's wishes into strategy and tactics. Thalberg also had an unerring sense of taste—which Mayer lacked—and a concern for financial considerations that earned him much admiration and a measure of Mayer's envy. The combination worked well. MGM outperformed most studios during the silent era and became the clear leader when sound arrived. Also the most ambitious studio, it had, by 1934, 23 sound stages on 117 acres, which included an artificial lake, a park, a jungle, and the world's largest film laboratory.

Recognizing his limitations, Mayer rarely read scripts, knowing others had a better feel for judging them. He was content to select excellent managers and leave them to manage. Yet he had his finger on the pulse of the studio, personally attending to a mass of details and often consulting on a host of trivial matters. He insisted on "uplift" and happy endings in MGM films and above all patriotism. "We are in the business of making beautiful pictures of beautiful people," he once remarked. "Anyone who doesn't acknowledge that doesn't belong in the business." Mayer's favorite series was "The Hardy Family," starring Mickey Rooney, which portrayed small-town life as Mayer imagined it to be.

Mayer repeatedly clashed with the Loew's interests in New York. After World War II, with the threat of television looming, the struggle over budgets and content led to battles. In 1951, Mayer was forced to resign as production chief and was replaced by Dore Schary. Mayer tried to make pictures on his own but had no success. When Mayer died, the rabbi at his funeral said, "This is the end of a volume, not a chapter."

1942–present

Michael D. Eisner

Brought in to rescue the Walt Disney Company in 1984, Michael Eisner has achieved spectacular success. Since he took over as chairman and chief executive, Disney's profits have increased eightfold, and it has become a major movie studio. And in the process of "reanimating" Disney, Eisner himself has become a highly visible symbol of the company he loves. In fact, people who know Eisner well say they cannot imagine him anywhere else.

In the spring of 1984, when Disney was floundering, Michael Eisner was considered one of the hottest properties in Hollywood. Hailed for the successes he achieved in his eight years as president of Paramount Pictures—years in which Paramount moved from last place to first among the six major studios—Eisner could virtually write his own ticket. Many people were surprised when he left Paramount for the struggling Disney. Eisner, however, was eager to take the job because he felt that his abilities meshed perfectly with the Disney tradition. His reverence for Walt Disney, his love of children's programming, and his desire to produce family entertainment made Eisner the right choice. His creativity, his energy, and his highly competitive nature made him the right person to take on the challenges posed by a poorly performing company.

With astounding speed, Eisner was able to right the Disney ship. Within months, the company that had been stagnant since the death of Walt Disney in 1966 came to life. Film successes—both live-action and animated—television hits, large-scale syndication of Disney's vast video library, and moves to increase theme-park revenues all combined to boost net earnings by more than 75 percent at the end of Eisner's first year, with the company's profits doubling within two years.

Like another dominant force who preceded him in Hollywood—MGM's Louis B. Mayer—no detail is too small to escape Michael Eisner's attention. And Eisner's tastes affect every area of the vast empire, from carpeting for new hotels to scripts for animated films, to construction designs for building projects.

Born in 1942 to an affluent family in New York, Eisner attended prestigious private schools before going on to Denison University in Ohio, where he majored in English and theater. After graduating in 1964, Eisner moved to Paris with the intention of becoming a writer, but he stayed only ten days. Returning to New York, he took a clerk's job at NBC, then moved on to CBS, and finally to ABC, where he achieved huge success in programming. Said to have an almost instinctive feel for what audiences want to see, Eisner was the driving force behind dramatic improvements at ABC.

Disney has had setbacks during Eisner's reign, but even the maligned EuroDisney, which opened in 1992, seems to have benefitted from his touch. Renamed Disneyland Paris, it stemmed its tide of red ink by turning a profit in 1995. And critics who had faulted Eisner for being unduly conservative and risk-averse were left speechless by his $19 billion acquisition of Capital Cities/ABC in 1996. With its vast and reputable operations, and its formidable marketing skills, Michael Eisner's Disney would seem to be in little danger of reverting to a "Sleeping Beauty."

Charles Merrill

1885–1956

Just as Edward Johnson saw the potential in growth-stock investing, Charles Merrill recognized the rewards that lay in catering to the small investor. His spectacular success in bringing Wall Street to Main Street not only changed the face of investing but resulted in the creation of the world's largest brokerage house by assets under management.

Merrill, who studied at Amherst College and briefly attended law school at the University of Michigan, came to Wall Street after a summer stint as a semiprofessional baseball player in Florida. He served an apprenticeship at George H. Burr & Company before striking out on his own to form Charles E. Merrill & Company in 1914. When his friend Edmund C. Lynch joined him a short time later, the firm became Merrill, Lynch & Company. In the early years, it handled mainly underwritings for the just-emerging chain-store industry, bringing out stock issues for S.S. Kresge (the forerunner of Kmart), J.C. Penney, and Safeway Stores, among others.

Merrill Lynch

After the October 1929 market crash—which Merrill had presciently prepared for—he understood that Wall Street's wounds would not heal quickly, so he decided to retrench, withdrawing from the retail business. In 1930, he transferred his brokerage clients and employees to E.A. Pierce & Company and invested $5 million in that house. His "retirement" ended in 1940 when he was asked to resume active participation at the struggling firm.

Merrill was well aware that the public still viewed Wall Street with a jaundiced eye, believing that most stockbrokers were dishonest. He concluded, however, that he could make a go of building "a department store of finance." In 1941, he absorbed Fenner & Beane. The new Merrill Lynch, Pierce, Fenner & Beane was a

substantial operation, and in fact became the world's largest brokerage house, with 71 partners, offices in 93 cities, and memberships on 28 securities and commodities exchanges.

Merrill's task was to convince the broad middle class to purchase common stocks. He knew small investors started with little, but in time, if the experience was salutary, they might become more substantial investors. In effect, he hoped to do for brokerage what the chain stores had done for retailing: Make smaller profits per client but lure many more of them to his operation. "Our business is people and their money," he said. "We must draw the new capital required for industrial might and growth not from among a few large investors, but from the savings of thousands of people of moderate incomes."

Research operations were beefed up. Reports and advisories were offered free of charge to interested individuals at a time when other brokerages imposed fees on just about every service rendered—monthly statements, holding clients, securities, clipping coupons on bonds. Merrill waived charges on these activities. And right from the start, Merrill Lynch published an annual report, the first ever for a brokerage firm.

Merrill made brokerage efficient, trouble-free, and trustworthy. "When people came to Merrill Lynch in those days, they never thought about going anywhere else," remarked William A. Schreyer, a future Merrill Lynch CEO who arrived in this period. The approach worked. The firm's gross income surged from $9 million in 1941, its first full year of operation, to $45.7 million in 1950, and then to $82 million in 1956, the year Merrill died.

1898–1984   Edward C. Johnson 2d

Acknowledged as one of the chief creators of the modern mutual-fund industry, Edward Johnson helped lay the foundation for a revolution in America's investing habits—perhaps to a larger extent than he ever imagined. What drove his success was his understanding that investors basically wanted to benefit from the healthy growth of America by taking part in a pooled investment that would produce better-than-average results.

When Johnson founded the Fidelity Management & Research Company in 1946, his radical ideas on investing were considered almost scandalous by the traditional old-line management firms. Prudent investment at the time meant trustee oversight of fixed-income securities and blue-chip stocks, with little if any growth.

Fifty years later, mutual-fund investing ranks as the prime method of saving money for America's aging baby boomers, with inflows into equity mutual funds surpassing all other forms of personal savings. And the Fidelity family of funds sits atop the industry as the recognized giant, managing an estimated $400 billion of assets for 10 million investors.

Edward Johnson came from a Boston family of merchants with Puritan roots. He graduated from Milton Academy and Harvard College, attended Harvard Buiness School for one year, and graduated from Harvard Law in 1924. Johnson then joined a well-known law firm. His work at the firm, as well as his association with his father in the management of family trust funds, stimulated Johnson's interest in the investment business. Excited by the possibilities of this world—"You were what you were, not because you were a friend of somebody, but for yourself," Johnson once said—he left the law firm in 1939 to become in-house counsel at a small mutual fund.

In 1943, Johnson found his vehicle for success, the ailing Fidelity Fund, which had only $3 million under management. He put his investment philosophy to work, buying common stocks that were a notch or two below the blue chips and seeking out special situations. The company's results were stunning, especially during the go-go market of the 1960s. The market

went into a slump in the 1970s, taking mutual funds down with it, but Fidelity continued to prosper by expanding into money-market funds and other ventures. By the time Johnson retired in 1974, Fidelity had a stable of 17 funds with nearly $3 billion in assets.

Long intrigued by Eastern philosophy and religions, Johnson often turned to Buddhism for his ideas and inspiration. But his investing sense was well grounded in a comprehensive knowledge of investment principles and the tools of the trade, and he made extensive use of a variety of charted materials. He could call to mind a precedent for virtually any unusual occurrence in the market. His son Edward C. (Ned) Johnson III, who succeeded him at the helm of the family business, said of his father: "People enjoyed listening to him. They had confidence in what he said, and so they had confidence in the funds."

J. Pierpont Morgan   1837–1913

The day after his death, the *Wall Street Journal* wrote, "There will be no successor to Morgan." The paper was right. J.P. Morgan is considered the most powerful private banker in American history and is likely to remain so. There have been influential bankers since, including Henry Kravis, a founder of Kohlberg, Kravis, Roberts & Company, but none has matched Morgan's level of influence.

He was born in Hartford, Connecticut, to a banking family whose base was in London. After serving an apprenticeship, he formed the partnership of Dabney, Morgan & Company in 1864, which rose to some prominence due largely to its London connections. Participating in syndicates, Morgan excelled at placing bonds and stocks with his London customers. He soon formed an alliance with Anthony Drexel of Philadelphia, out of which came Drexel, Morgan & Company. (It would be reorganized in 1895 as J.P. Morgan & Company, with branches in Paris and London.) After selling 200,000 shares of New York Central common for William Vanderbilt in 1879 without disturbing the market, Morgan's reputation for "placement power" reached a new high.

The financier spent much of his time in the 1890s arranging railroad deals and by the end of the decade was busily reorganizing most of the nation's major lines. In 1895, he used his London connections to place $100 million of U.S. government bonds at a time when the Treasury was unable to do so. Thus, his reputation surpassed that of the government itself.

Morgan helped finance and reshape some of the most important industries in the nation—railroads, telegraph, telephone, electric power, banking, and insurance. His work laid the foundation for the enormous growth of America's power in the 20th century. By 1890, the United States surpassed Great Britain in the production of iron and steel, and was operating more miles of railroad track than all of Europe and Russia combined.

In 1901, Morgan put together a complex merger that produced U.S. Steel, the largest corporation of its time. But he seemed to falter after that accomplishment. He failed to perceive the promise of automobiles, several of his railroads encountered difficulties, and his International Mercantile Marine was a failure. But he did have one more moment of glory: Wall Street was struck by a panic in 1907 and the government was unable to stop it. Morgan called the city's major bankers to a conference, created a rescue fund, and used it to stop runs on key banks.

Fearing what might happen during the next panic if Morgan were not there to assist, Congress in 1908 passed the Aldrich-Vreeland Act to provide for the temporary issuance of currency in times of distress. Would this be enough? All realized that no regulatory body could match the great banker's reputation and ability to command financial resources. In an appearance before a congressional committee in 1912, Morgan was asked if credit was based on money and property. He replied that it was not; rather, a person's trust and integrity determined their worth.

1944–present

Henry R. Kravis

Anthony Savignano

Investment banker Henry Kravis epitomizes the financiers who made the term "leveraged buyout" synonymous with the go-go 1980s. As a founding partner of Kohlberg, Kravis, Roberts & Company (KKR), Kravis is a master at the art of using limited partnerships to buy, streamline, and then sell off undervalued companies, making huge profits in the process. Although he operates in a drastically different environment from that dominated by J.P. Morgan in the 19th century, Kravis, nevertheless, has reshaped and revitalized many companies just as Morgan did.

Simultaneously viewed as hero and antihero, Kravis engineered the biggest buyout of them all, the $25 billion takeover of RJR Nabisco Inc. in 1988. In an intensely bitter, five-week bidding war with the Shearson Lehman Hutton brokerage firm, Kravis managed to outwit his adversaries by giving the impression that he was about to withdraw from the competition for the tobacco and food giant. After lulling the Shearson-led group into complacency, Kravis sprung a sweetened bid that, with some fine-tuning, eventually won acceptance from the committee in charge of auctioning the company.

But for the limited partners in the 1988 buyout fund—largely pension funds and other institutional investors—the victory proved to be a disappointing one when all was said and done. KKR acquired RJR Nabisco for $5.62 a share on an adjusted cost basis, and when the last of the shares were sold six years later, they fetched about $5.73 apiece. That is not to say that KKR itself fared poorly in the deal. Admittedly, its own $126 million investment did not appreciate much either, but the firm garnered nearly $500 million in transaction, advisory, and other fees.

RJR Nabisco is but one of a host of leveraged buyouts completed by Kravis, many of which have been highly profitable. In fact, *Wall Street Journal* reporter George Anders, writing in his 1992 book *Merchants of Debt: KKR and the Mortgaging of American Business*, estimated that leveraged buyouts have generated more than $7 billion in investment gains.

Typically, after taking over an undervalued and inefficiently run company, Kravis and his team will impose a stringent cost-cutting program, usually with significant layoffs, and then will use the increased cash flow to service the debt taken on in the buyout. Parts of the company are sold off to pay down debt and recoup the initial investment. The resultant lean core business is then either spun off to management or another buyer, or returned to the marketplace through a public stock offering.

Kravis was born in 1944 in Tulsa, Oklahoma, the son of a petroleum engineer and owner of a geological survey business. After attending a Massachusetts prep school and earning an economics degree from Claremont Men's College in California, he landed a summer job at Bear Stearns in New York. Later, with an M.B.A. from Columbia in his pocket, he officially joined that brokerage firm, working for Jerome Kohlberg, Jr., a corporate finance manager who pioneered the leveraged buyout technique— then called "bootstrap" acquisition.

When Kohlberg left Bear Stearns in 1976, Kravis went with him, and Kohlberg, Kravis, Roberts & Company was born. But Kohlberg resigned in a policy dispute in 1987, wanting the firm to continue in its traditional role of a white knight rescuing companies from unwanted suitors, while Kravis wanted to expand the firm and pursue other avenues.

Robert Moses

1881–1981

Robert Moses was the powerful force behind some of the most important public construction projects of the 20th century. Moses probably held more appointed public offices than any other figure in American history, but he failed in his few attempts to win voter approval. He crisscrossed the New York metropolitan area with 481 miles of highways but, ironically, never bothered to learn how to drive a car himself.

After graduating with distinction from Yale in 1911, Moses attended Oxford University, where he received a second B.A. degree and an M.A. He earned a Ph.D. from Columbia University in 1914. By then, he was working for New York's Bureau of Municipal Research, and during  World War I, he served on the U.S. Shipping Board. But Moses' true public career began in 1919 when New York Governor Al Smith named him to several posts involving construction of public facilities; there his reputation grew.

Moses declined a fusion nomination for the New York mayoralty but still craved a political career. He ran for governor of New York as a Republican in 1934, losing by a huge margin. He was urged to run again for public office and occasionally nibbled at the bait but always withdrew before the main contest began.

After Mayor Fiorello LaGuardia named Moses as Parks Commissioner in 1934—a post he would hold for 26 years—he started in earnest as a builder. Seeking to tie the city together with highways, Moses constructed the Grand Central Parkway, the Henry Hudson Parkway, the Belt Parkway, and the Cross Bay Parkway Bridge. He increased the number of city playgrounds from 117 to more than 600. Later in the decade, he worked on the East River Drive, the Whitestone Parkway, the renovation of Central Park, and scores of other projects. As chairman of the Jones Beach State Parkway Authority, Moses built Jones Beach and then constructed the Northern and Southern State Parkways to bring people there. Other accomplishments included the Triborough Bridge, the Verrazano Narrows Bridge, and the Niagara and St. Lawrence power projects. Moses made possible two world's fairs in New York and transformed what had been a dump into a major park. All of these projects, and more, were completed over a 44-year span, ending in 1968.

In the process, however, the "master builder" bulldozed neighborhoods and was criticized for being more concerned with edifices than with human values. His opponents asserted that the Cross Bronx Expressway, which sliced through established neighborhoods, played a large part in the subsequent decline of that borough.

During the time of his public service, Moses occupied many offices, including head of the State Parks Council and chairman of the Triborough Bridge and Tunnel Authority. He pioneered in the establishment of public authorities, semiautonomous entities that raised money by issuing bonds and operated with little political interference. Thus freed from control by others, Moses was able to weather criticisms.

1914–present

Trammell Crow

He is a familiar figure in Dallas but not particularly well known in the rest of the country. A shy man who keeps a low profile, Trammell Crow is one of the most spectacular builders and real estate men in the nation, an innovator who has remade the skylines of Dallas, Atlanta, and San Francisco, and who has overseas projects as well. Trammell Crow has done for the private sector since World War II what Robert Moses did for the public sector during and after the Great Depression.

Crow Residential is one of the largest developers of housing in the nation, with special interest in mixed-use properties that combine residential and commercial operations. The Dallas Market Center, a string of exhibition and convention buildings, is the largest of its kind in the world. Adjoining it is the Anatole Hotel, with an atrium as large as four football fields. Crow has sold rice plantations to Japanese investors and provides house-cleaning services for other developers. On top of all this, he has more warehouse space than the U.S. Postal Service.

Crow was born in 1914 into a large, religious family that today would be considered poor. Having come of age during the Depression, he had limited ambitions. At first, he wanted to be a bank teller and then an accountant. He entered the Navy during World War II and in 1942 married Margaret Doggett, the daughter of a prosperous Dallas merchant.

After his discharge from the Navy, Crow tried his hand at several jobs, ultimately opting to work for the Doggett Grain Company, which was housed in an undistinguished six-story building. The company rented part of the building, giving Crow the chance to learn something about real estate. In 1948, he started renting space in warehouses and then considered building them.

The budding builder entered into agreements with the Stemmons brothers, John and Story, to construct warehouses on land they owned adjacent to downtown Dallas. Operating on borrowed money, Crow built the first of dozens

of warehouses. Most had positive cash flow from the start. Encouraged, Crow saw himself as the warehouse king of Dallas. However, he had developed other ambitions as well.

Crow started work on office buildings and then the Market Center in Dallas, after which he entered into partnerships in Atlanta to construct hotels and more office buildings. In 1968, he formed Crow, Pope & Carter, the first of his residential operations. By then, he had developed a unique management theory: He formed partnerships with his agents, giving them financial stakes in their efforts. In the process, many of them became millionaires.

Things fell apart in the 1970s, however. Facing near bankruptcy due to overextension, Crow barely survived but emerged with slimmer and better-managed operations. Gradually, Trammell Crow withdrew from the business, having established a young management team to take the reins of the nation's largest real estate empire.

William Paley   1901–1990

Early on in the radio and television industry, Bill Paley recognized—like Bill Gates did with software and computers—that program content and talent were the key elements, not the boxes that delivered them. With that guiding vision, he turned the Columbia Broadcasting System into the industry's dominant force.

Paley came from a well-to-do Chicago family whose fortunes were based on the Congress Cigar Company. After graduating from the

Wharton School in 1922, Paley entered the family business. As an officer there, he signed an advertising contract with a newly established radio station and soon became preoccupied with the infant medium. "My imagination went wild in contemplating the possibilities of it," he later recalled.

In 1928, Paley purchased a budding network called United Independent Broadcasters, changed its name to Columbia Broadcasting, and started expanding. Within two years, he had increased the number of affiliates across the country to 70.

Taking an active interest in programming right from the start, Paley launched the "Columbia School of the Air" in 1930, which set the tone for educational shows, and began broadcasting the New York Philharmonic's Sunday concerts that same year. As part of his emphasis on music, Paley formed Columbia Concert Corp., which became one of the largest musical-artist booking agencies of its time. CBS also took over Columbia Records, turning it into a principal recording studio. Paley later developed "The Columbia Workshop," generally considered the best dramatic series of the 1930s.

By this time, CBS was competing with RCA and often besting the larger network. This was especially true in news, where Paley assembled a staff that included Edward R. Murrow, William Shirer, Eric Sevareid, and Howard K. Smith—generally conceded to be the premier news-gathering team during World War II. Paley himself served in the Office of War Information during the conflict.

Following the war, Paley turned over day-to-day operations to others and concentrated on strategy, especially in the area of television. Here he struggled to overcome the RCA lead. Paley lost the battle over color TV to RCA, whose system eventually won acceptance, and his venture into TV-receiver production was a dismal failure.

But where Paley's star shone bright was, once again, in programming. Under his guidance, CBS became the undisputed leader in television programming. As he had done in radio, Paley worked for a balance in mass entertainment, offering public service, cultural, and dramatic fare along with soap operas, game shows, and comedy and adventure series. The network boasted figures such as Walter Cronkite in news and hit shows like "I Love Lucy," "The Jackie Gleason Show," "All in the Family," and "M*A*S*H."

In building his stable of talent, Paley never shrank from raiding the competition. He signed NBC stars like Jack Benny, Fred Allen, Edgar Bergen and Charlie McCarthy, and George Burns and Gracie Allen. When an enraged David Sarnoff, who headed NBC's parent RCA, phoned Paley to complain, Paley replied with no embarrassment that he went after the stars because "I needed them."

1955–present   William F. Gates III

W hat Bill Gates saw before anyone else was that content—in the form of software—would determine the future of computing. The co-founder and chairman of Microsoft, Gates was largely responsible for establishing MS-DOS and Windows as the primary international operating systems for personal computers. Then he built that advantage into a leadership position in applications programs.

Gates, born in 1955, started his first company while an eighth-grader at a private school in Seattle. By the time he was 31, he had become the youngest billionaire in the history of the United States. Gates's growing fascination with

what computers could do for mainstream society pushed him to drop out of Harvard during his sophomore year in 1975 to found Microsoft with his boyhood friend Paul Allen. They wound up in the driver's seat of an industry that has reshaped the way people work, shop, bank, watch television, learn, and communicate with each other—an industry that may, some futurists theorize, even change patterns of thought and perception.

The fledgling company's first big break came when IBM went shopping for an operating system in 1981. Gates didn't have one, but he knew of someone who did. He bought the rights to QDOS (Quick and Dirty Operating System) for $50,000, revamped it, named it MS-DOS (for Microsoft Disk Operating System), and cut a deal with Big Blue—with one key caveat: Microsoft could sell its operating system to other computer companies as well. As IBM manufactured and sold millions of personal computers, dozens of clones flooded the market, and MS-DOS was the operating system on 90 percent of them, making it the best-selling software of all time.

Companies that made DOS-based software, like WordPerfect and Lotus, rode to riches on the crest of the tidal wave Gates set in motion. Eventually, as Gates developed new versions of DOS and later Windows, Microsoft's word-processing, spreadsheet, and other applications began edging out the competition.

Gates's grasp of the technical aspects of his trade is complemented by an astute business eye and a rigorous competitive drive. That is what sets him apart from the other computer wizards who surfaced in the 1970s and early 1980s only to fade. He is that rare multifaceted genius who can actually communicate his vision to others.

Microsoft may have no debt and several billion dollars in the bank, but Gates refuses to relax. He believes that the Internet and the personal computer will deliver content and technology to more and more consumers around the world. To that end, he is pushing Microsoft to develop interactive content and to build Net capability into virtually every product. Gates has bought up the rights to the voices of popular cartoon characters and digitized files of famous paintings and the Bettman Archives, the largest privately held photograph collection in the United States.

Microsoft®

John D. Rockefeller

1839–1⟩

An acknowledged titan of American business, John D. Rockefeller turned Standard Oil into the country's premier petroleum company just as the United States was changing into an industrial nation. And Rockefeller, understanding that this gigantic enterprise could not be run by an individual—no matter how talented and energetic—assembled a superlative management team that was widely imitated.

John D. was one of four Rockefeller children who grew up in New York, later migrating to Ohio. After learning his trade in the Cleveland commission house of Hewitt & Tuttle, he made his first fortune as a partner in the commission firm of Rockefeller & Andrews.

During the war, Rockefeller's attention was drawn to the petroleum discoveries in Pennsylvania. He quickly realized that the big money to be made in this product lay not in the business of production but in the area of refining. In 1863, with Maurice Clark and Samuel Andrews, an expert in refining, Rockefeller erected the Excelsior Oil Works, a small refinery in Ohio. Two years later, he bought out Clark's interest in the refinery. He later wrote, "That was the day that determined my career."

Over the next two years, Rockefeller purchased 50 refineries in Cleveland and another 80 in Pittsburgh. He also purchased stands of timber whose lumber was used to fashion barrels, warehouses, and the fleets necessary to transport the refined petroleum products, mostly kerosene. His was the first integrated operation of its kind in the industry.

Rockefeller was known for his uncanny ability to spot gifted young businessmen. In 1867, he brought in Henry Flagler, a Cleveland businessman, to form Rockefeller, Andrews & Flagler. Flagler provided needed capital and a knowledge of railroading, elements vital to the transport of petroleum products. Stephen Harkness, Flagler's cousin, also joined the company, contributing capital and managerial skills. From this nucleus came Standard Oil of Ohio, organized in 1870 and within a decade the industry leader.

There seemed no end to the flow of talent into the Standard Oil empire—from purchasing and marketing specialists to field commanders in Pittsburgh and Philadelphia, to chemists and attorneys. This remarkable team did not go unnoticed by other notable businessmen. William Vanderbilt once said, "These men are smarter than I am a great deal. They are very enterprising . . . I never came into contact with any class of men so smart and able."

Rockefeller never seemed to mind the credit given his employees and associates, perhaps because he was clearly the leader. John D. Archbold, who handled affairs at the home office, once remarked that Rockefeller could see further than any of his executives "and then see around the corner."

1936–present   John F. Welch, Jr.

The son of a railroad conductor, Jack Welch restructured General Electric into the conglomerate we know today that boasts $70 billion in revenue, $6.6 billion in profits, and a reputation as one of the nation's best-managed companies. Executives around the world have emulated his innovative management methods.

When Welch replaced Reginald H. Jones as CEO of GE in 1981 at the age of 45, the company hardly seemed in need of fixing. It generated $25 billion in sales and $1.5 billion in profits and enjoyed the kind of name recognition second only to brands like Coca-Cola and Ford. But Welch *did* think the company needed change. What he saw was a company bogged down by layers of bureaucracy just as global competitors (especially those in Japan) were becoming more nimble.

It took other American companies another decade to implement the kinds of adjustments GE made under Welch's guidance. Since 1981 he has phased out layers of management, consolidated 350 business units into a dozen autonomous businesses that report directly to him, and moved the company away from housewares and televisions and into broadcasting and capital-services businesses. In the process, he reduced the company's workforce by nearly half.

Critics called him "Neutron Jack" during the restructuring for the perception that he destroyed workers and left the buildings standing. But Welch maintains that the tough steps were necessary to build a stronger company, and the company's performance has proven him to be right.

One of his hallmarks is the clarity with which he communicates his vision of a boundaryless company where every employee is an energized player meeting ever-expanding "stretch" goals and "de-complicating" everything GE does. In fact, GE was one of the first companies to adopt the 360-degree appraisal, which has subordinates and peers contributing opinions along with bosses in evaluating middle managers.

Welch is determined that GE will be first in every one of its businesses. Those who cannot make the grade are shed. In 1994 Welch acted decisively to sell Kidder, Peabody in the face of weak margins and SEC violations.

Welch's managers have become attractive candidates to head up other companies in need of a vision. Lawrence Bossidy left the No. 2 job at GE in 1991 to breathe new life into Allied Signal. Stanley Gault left GE after 31 years for Rubbermaid, where he served as chairman and CEO until 1991. He has been chairman and CEO of Goodyear since then.

When Welch underwent triple-bypass surgery in 1995, questions were raised about who would succeed him. Although no one has been publicly identified as Welch's successor, the company says it certainly does have a succession plan and contends its only problem is in having "too many excellent leaders from which to choose." In the meantime, Welch says he has every intention of staying on the job until the year 2000, when he turns 65. Maybe by then, corporate America will be ready for the next trendsetters.

David Sarnoff   1 8 9 1 – 1 9 7 1

David Sarnoff catapulted to fame on April 14, 1912, when, as a telegraph operator at the Marconi office in New York, he relayed news of the sinking of the *S.S. Titanic*. But Sarnoff's real and lasting fame was to come as a progenitor of modern entertainment communications.

Sarnoff was present at the birth of the wireless industry and became a manager at Radio Corporation of America (RCA), which took over Marconi interests in 1919. Engrossed with wireless, Sarnoff had innovative ideas for the new technology. In a 1916 memo he wrote: "I have in mind a plan of development which would make radio a household utility in the same sense as the piano or phonograph. The idea is to bring music into the house by wireless." Although he called his idea a "radio music box," he added that the programs could also include drama, news, lectures, sports, and speeches. Sarnoff had grasped the potential of the new medium.

He was named president of RCA in 1930, but he had become the leader there even before that. During the 1920s and 1930s he fashioned an entertainment conglomerate that was the most glamorous company of the time. RCA developed two networks, the Red and the Blue, and its National Broadcasting Company unit had the most stations and—for a while at least—the lead in programming. Sarnoff negotiated the acquisition of the Victor Talking Machine company and, in 1928, purchased a string of motion-picture houses, Radio Keith Orpheum (RKO), to which he added a studio. Subsequently, he acquired two large music publishers and started a talent agency.

Sarnoff envisioned a complete, self-contained entertainment company with artists appearing on NBC programs heard on RCA radios, making motion pictures at RKO studios to be exhibited at RKO theaters equipped with RCA sound systems, recording music published by the RCA companies and played on a Victrola, all the while represented by an RCA agent.

Early on, however, Sarnoff's vision extended beyond the established world of radio and film. In a 1923 memo he called television "the technical name for seeing instead of hearing by radio." Later cited by the Television Broadcasters Association as "the father of American television," Sarnoff made RCA a leader in television just as it was in radio. RCA produced receivers and NBC developed programs, some of which were drawn from films and radio. Although rival William Paley of CBS led the way in developing color television, the RCA version came out on top in 1953.

Color television was to be Sarnoff's last great victory. Although he passed executive authority to his son Robert in 1966, he clung to the chairmanship until 1969, a period during which the company declined. Its lead in radio and television receivers was lost to others, and CBS was recognized as the premier television network. Even so, setbacks in corporate fortunes could not tarnish the achievements of the man who led the way in bringing the world within everyone's reach.

1941–present

John C. Malone

Known as the "King of Cable" and arguably the most powerful figure in the industry, John Charles Custer Malone is a man whose influence reaches beyond the industry he helped create.

As chief executive officer of Tele-Communications, Inc. (TCI), Malone guides the world's largest cable company. With nearly 14 million subscribers in 49 states and investments in various other cable providers, TCI has a link to one of every four homes connected to cable. Not bad for an operation that teetered on the edge of bankruptcy in the 1970s.

Moreover, Malone's penchant for deal-making has placed him at the center of a dynamic industry. TCI has significant stakes in many of the major cable networks and wields great influence over programming. Among its holdings are interests in TNT, CNN, Black Entertainment Television, the Discovery Channel, and The Learning Channel. And in 1995, Malone entered into a joint partnership with Rupert Murdoch and two Latin American broadcasters to create a 150-channel satellite television service. Finally, and also in 1995, TCI made a move toward the telephone industry when it announced a joint venture with Sprint, Cox Communications, and ComCast to build a mobile-phone network.

An engineer by training, Malone sports an impressive list of academic credentials, including two undergraduate degrees from Yale, master's degrees from both New York University and Johns Hopkins, and a Ph.D. in operations research from Johns Hopkins. He is said to have an almost photographic memory and is extremely gifted with numbers.

Malone, who was born in 1941, got his start in the cable business in the early 1970s when he was promoted to president of the Jerrold Electronics subsidiary of General Instrument Corporation. His performance at Jerrold, a maker of equipment for cable television systems, led to offers from Steven Ross, chairman of Warner Communications Inc., to head up its cable division, and from cattle rancher Bob John Magness, whose small, Denver-based TCI served Western communities.

Foreseeing unwanted personnel problems at Warner and because his wife did not want to remain in the East, Malone accepted the Magness offer, even though it meant taking a 50 percent pay cut to $60,000 a year. Installed in 1973 as president and CEO of the nearly bankrupt TCI, he embarked on a cost-cutting, revenue-producing journey that within five years had propelled TCI to a point where it had a cash flow of $31.5 million—and was growing. In 1995, TCI racked up $5 billion in revenue.

There is no disputing that Malone is one of the giants in the media world, nor that he understands the increasingly complex role that technology plays. He is determined to be a major player on the information superhighway, where television, telecommunications, and computers are uniting to redraw the playing field.

Gustavus Swift

1839–1903

Two centuries ago, more than 90 percent of American males worked as farmers; by 1900, that figure had fallen to 42 percent. Today, just 3 percent of the population not only feeds America but gives it major export items.

The most important factor in this transformation is the increased productivity of U.S. food producers—and in the area of meat production, no one is as important as Gustavus Swift. A pioneer whose goal was to bring "whole-

some, fresh, and inexpensive meat to the American people," Swift turned meat production and processing into a national industry.

When Swift was born on Cape Cod, Massachusetts, beef cattle were raised and slaughtered locally, then sold door-to-door. Swift left school at age 14 to work for his brother, a local butcher, but within two years he was off on his own, dealing in cattle and eventually opening several butcher shops.

Knowing that cattle were less expensive in the West, he thought about ways of bringing them to the higher-priced Eastern market. He extended his operations to Albany, New York, and then to Chicago, where cattle were loaded onto rail cars and shipped East. Swift realized this was a needlessly costly process: Not only did the cattle have to be fed along the way but many died in transit. A more cost-effective procedure, he reasoned, would be to butcher the cattle in Chicago and then ship the beef to the East. It was Swift's innovation to use refrigeration to keep the products fresh.

At the time, several butchers and mechanics were exploring the feasibility of air-cooled freight cars, but these cars could be used only in the winter. As early as 1871, a Chicago butcher, G. H. Hammond, experimented with air-cooled cars, and three years later, another Chicago butcher, Morris & Company, sent refrigerated meat to Boston.

Swift, who bought the Morris operation in 1875, tried using insulated cars that had ice packed under the roofs, with a drainage system that allowed the water to escape. Ice was purchased along the route, and cold storage rooms were established in cities so that the beef products could be safely stored until they were sold to local butchers.

Swift demonstrated fine organizational and sales skills in running his vast enterprise and became the first to offer branded meat products. That move stirred opposition, but Swift was not deterred. In time, he formed more than 100 partnerships with local butchers.

His search to save money in the processing phase led him to develop overhead conveyors to move the beef from butcher to butcher to speed up operations. This "disassembly line" was to inspire Henry Ford's automobile assembly line. Swift, who also entered the hog-slaughtering business, eventually found uses for all parts of the animal and became the industry leader in meat by-products.

1930–present

Donald J. Tyson

Borrowing from American political lore, poultry king Don Tyson's slogan might very well be "a Tyson chicken in every pot." It's been said that half the people in America eat Tyson Foods chicken every week. Many of those undoubtedly partake at fast-food outlets: Tyson supplies most of the major chains, including Kentucky Fried Chicken and McDonald's.

Besides its preeminent domestic position, the Springdale, Arkansas, firm ships chickens to 43 countries. In Japan, it provides 70 percent of the imported chicken. And although chicken may be the biggest egg in its basket, it's not the only one: The company also produces beef, pork, and Cornish game hens, in addition to selling seafood and Mexican food products.

Senior chairman Don Tyson, who stepped aside as chairman on his 65th birthday in 1995 (after 50 years in the chicken business), helped create an industry that has every right to crow: What once was considered a luxury saved for Sunday dinner now costs less than half what it did 30 years ago, adjusted for inflation. Using genetic selection and statistical analysis, poultry processors can grow chickens faster with less feed, which results in less-expensive chicken.

Don Tyson's father John founded the business in 1935. Having figured out a way to provide feed and water in a trailer so that he could transport live poultry over greater distances, the Arkansas farmer bought 500 Arkansas chickens and sold them in Chicago. In 1947, when Tyson incorporated the business as Tyson Feed & Hatchery, he was already raising the chickens himself, but production took on greater importance as the 1950s progressed. The first processing plant, which came on stream in 1958, featured an ice-packing system that expanded the company's marketing reach.

Don began working at the company when he was just 14 and left the University of Arkansas his senior year to join the business full-time. He became manager in 1960, then took over the company in 1967 after John was killed in a car-train accident. Under Don's stewardship, Tyson Foods Inc. (the company went public under that name in 1963) grew rapidly to become the country's largest chicken producer, reaching a sales volume of $1 billion in 1985. It acquired several other poultry producers along the way, including major competitor Holly Farms in 1989.

Don, like all Tyson executives, wears a khaki shirt and pants with his first name stitched on the breast pocket. He explains that money isn't made in the office but out in the field, and Tyson executives need to dress appropriately. As he told *Forbes* magazine, he's just a "hometown guy."

Theodore Vail   1 8 4 5 – 1 9 2 0

Although he was not involved with telephone technology, Theodore Vail was the man most responsible for the creation of the telecommunications industry and its dominant company, American Telephone & Telegraph.

In 1878, just about everyone realized the importance of the telephone, but what shape the new industry would take was uncertain.

The Bell Telephone Company, a subsidiary of National Telephone Company and based on Alexander Graham Bell's patents, was being challenged by the American Speaking Telegraph Company, which was backed by the formidable Western Union using rival patents.

Gardiner Hubbard, a lawyer and member of the U.S. Railway Commission, was National Telephone Company's president but was eager to step aside in favor of a better-qualified candidate. He found one in Theodore Vail, the 33-year-old general superintendent of the U.S. Railway Service. Vail was named general manager of Bell Telephone and given a mandate to beat back challenges and create a structure for a national telephone company.

Vail met with the American Speaking Telegraph leadership and, after some discussion, agreed to purchase its 56,000 telephones in 26 cities in return for 20 percent of Bell's licensing fees. He then set about fashioning the strategy for expansion. He began by licensing five producers to manufacture equipment for Bell to meet anticipated demand. Soon after, he entered into a cross-licensing agreement with Western Electric and started purchasing that company's shares to have an in-house supplier.

In 1880, National Telephone Company was rechartered as American Bell and empowered to issue licenses to local operating companies—with the proviso that they had to give 35 to 50 percent of their shares to American Bell, along with a fee of $20 per telephone per year. American Bell then set about purchasing these independent franchises. Believing that the more telephones a customer could reach, the more desirable the service would become, Vail concentrated on connecting cities with long-distance lines. When he announced his objective of enabling Americans to speak easily with others across the country, that task seemed impossible. But Vail's strategy was effective. By 1885, American Bell franchises had 155,000 telephones in service and revenues exceeding $10 million. Franchisee payments, which had been just $11,000 in 1881, rose to $597,000, more than $10 billon in today's dollars. The long-distance company was restructured as American Telephone & Telegraph (AT&T), and Vail was named president. He did not remain in the post for long, however: Frustrated by bitter corporate infighting, Vail resigned in 1887.

The company foundered in his absence and was taken over by the J.P. Morgan interests. Vail returned to AT&T's board in 1901 and became its president again in 1907. By this time, there was talk of antitrust prosecution, which Vail avoided through an arrangement with the government. Under the deal, AT&T was to divest itself of the Western Union shares it had acquired and was not to purchase additional franchises. In return, the government agreed to treat AT&T as a natural monopoly. It remained so until 1984 when technological change—which had made the company possible in the first place—dictated a new shape for telephony and ushered in the generation that would see Craig McCaw emulate Vail's success in the realm of cellular communication.

Craig O. McCaw

1949–present

A visionary who recognized the potential of the cellular telephone, McCaw has parlayed his beginnings with a 2,000-subscriber cable-TV system in Centralia, Washington, into his position today as one of the most important names in telecommunications. Following the sale of his McCaw Cellular Communications Inc. to AT&T in 1994 for $11.5 billion, McCaw took control of Nextel Communications Inc., with an eye toward developing its national digital-wireless network.

McCaw, born in 1949, is a reserved, publicity-shy, self-made billionaire. The second of four sons of John Elroy McCaw, a reckless entrepreneur who bought and sold radio and television stations and cable-TV systems, Craig McCaw got his start when his father died in 1969, leaving behind an empire that had to be liquidated to pay off huge debts. All that remained was one cable company, which McCaw ran from his dorm room while a history major at Stanford. Using that dorm room as the base of his business operations, McCaw's early attempts at expansion didn't go quite as planned—he failed in his bid to take over the university's vending machine business. Nevertheless, from that inauspicious start, McCaw built the company that became the nation's cellular phone leader.

In 1983, propelled by AT&T projections for the cellular market—projections that, incidentally, would turn out to be so low as to be laughable—McCaw won licenses in six of the top 30 U.S. markets. He further used those AT&T numbers to finagle bank financing to buy up cellular licenses around the country. McCaw then employed a strategy of buying, selling, and swapping his licenses to move toward creating a seamless cellular network.

Having built the original cable business into one with 434,000 subscribers, McCaw sold it in 1987 for $755 million and promptly bet the pot on cellular. With the nerve to take on a huge debt—including $1.25 billion raised with the help of Michael Milken between 1986 and 1988—McCaw went on a huge buying spree, a leveraged gamble that scared a lot of people who didn't grasp what McCaw understood so well: Every license he bought could easily be

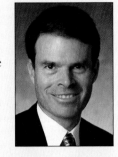

sold to the Baby Bells, whose belated recognition of cellular's potential had allowed McCaw to gain the upper hand.

Just how great was McCaw's foresight? When he started acquiring cellular licenses in 1983, they could be purchased for about $4.50 per POP—that is, per potential customer. By the time McCaw negotiated his deal with AT&T a decade later, cellular was valued at $200 to $300 per POP.

Now McCaw has turned his attentions to Nextel, planning to invest more than $1 billion to develop that company's national digital-wireless network. He is also focusing on a revolutionary new telecommunications concept—a venture named Teledesic—this time with backing from none other than Bill Gates. Within ten years, McCaw plans to build an "information skyway"—a system of 840 satellites that will surround the earth and free information from the confines of cable. His critics call the idea crazy, but McCaw once again looks forward to proving them wrong.

Aaron Montgomery Ward   1843–1913

Realizing that people who lived far from large stores wanted to make the same kinds of purchases as their city cousins, Aaron Montgomery Ward hit on the idea of sending out a mail-order catalog. Ward's "wish book" became a staple of rural America, and his approach spawned the modern-day mail-order business that led directly to the mail-order computer industry created by Michael Dell.

Why would any sensible individual buy goods sight unseen from someone many miles away, to be delivered by mail? Ward guaranteed satisfaction and promptly returned payments when customers rejected his products. He concentrated on building a reputation for honesty more than profits. By acquiring the former, he achieved the latter. And as a result, he built the first great mail-order enterprise.

As a boy in the Midwest, Ward drifted from job to job. Landing a position in a general store at the age of 19, he discovered that he liked merchandising. Other sales jobs followed. Most of these were in urban areas, but working as a traveling salesman led him to an important revelation: Country people were often unhappy with the meager selections available at their small general stores. Ward's answer to the problem was sales by mail.

In 1872, Ward and two acquaintances scraped together $1,600 to open operations in a small Chicago shipping room. With a minuscule stock of dry goods, they published the world's first general merchandise mail-order "catalog," a one-page affair featuring inexpensive goods. The firm was called Montgomery Ward & Company. A year later, Ward's longtime friend and brother-in-law George R. Thorne joined the firm as an equal partner.

By spurning what he termed "high-priced salesmen" and avoiding the middleman, Ward claimed that his customers could save from 40 to 100 percent. The mail-order merchandiser quickly acquired a reputation for honesty, which led to a contract to supply the retail stores of the National Grange, a large farmers collective. That, in turn, gave him additional exposure and distinction as a "friend of the farmers." Ward understood the value of this status and advertised his young company as "The Original Grange Supply House."

Next, Ward expanded both his catalog and his range of operations, with each enlargement of offerings spurring sales. By the fall of 1884, the catalog had grown to 238 pages. By then, rivals

had been attracted to the business, and one of them, Sears Roebuck, succeeded handily by imitating Ward's policies and operations. Despite the competition, Ward's business continued to expand dramatically. In 1900, the company earned $8 million.

Economists have observed that trust significantly lowers transaction costs and that this has long been a hallmark of the American economy. Aaron Montgomery Ward exemplified that concept and based an industry on it.

1965–present

Michael Dell

Using the sales tool developed by Aaron Montgomery Ward for general merchandise, Michael Dell created the catalog mail-order computer industry.

Dell was only 19 years old in 1984 when he started PCs Limited—soon renamed Dell Computer—in his dorm room with $1,000. It made sense for him: As a 12-year-old, he made $2,000 selling stamps by mail order, and in high school he sold newspaper subscriptions. But Dell wasn't just your ordinary paperboy. By targeting newlyweds with a two-week free trial, he made enough money to pay cash for a new BMW—at age 17.

Initially, Dell Computer bought IBM PCs from dealers who hadn't satisfied IBM's quotas and were stuck with excess inventory. Dell then souped them up with graphics accelerators and hard drives, and sold them at a tidy profit. Almost immediately, the business brought in $50,000 per month.

Dell's parents weren't thrilled with their son's success, however, because his studies were suffering. By this time, Dell—who had investigated getting a General Equivalency Diploma at age 8 to get high school out of the way—was much more interested in his company than in finishing college. But he agreed to run the business full-time over summer vacation and return to school if it wasn't successful. He rented a one-room office, sketched out his first ad on a pizza box, and generated an astonishing $180,000 in revenue the first month, $265,000 the second.

Nine months into the game, with sales of $6 million, Dell decided to manufacture his own computers instead of reselling IBMs. He gathered

three people around a six-foot table to build them. Then came the innovations that propelled Dell to $2 billion in sales within four years and put the young company on the Fortune 500 list. Generating the ideas he implemented, Dell:

- Set up national toll-free telephone numbers instead of a dealer network, thus slashing costs and prices.

- Offered complete customization even on single-unit orders and shipped out the finished products quickly.

- Took on No. 2 PC manufacturer Compaq with an aggressive advertising campaign.

- Provided high levels of customer service.

- Offered a 30-day, money-back guarantee.

- Gave phone reps detailed and accurate databases of information that helped them deal with specific customers.

Forbes magazine noted Dell's innovations in marketing and compared him to Ray Kroc of McDonald's. Customer service was key for Dell too, and the company never tried to be the price leader, though its prices were far lower than IBM's and Compaq's. Rather, the company aimed to be the value leader.

Like Ward before him, Dell knew his biggest task was to build a special kind of trust so his customers would be comfortable buying through direct mail. His mail-order computer company was made viable through air freight carriers—and by eliminating the middlemen—just like Ward did nearly a century before.

Thomas J. Watson, Sr.

1847–1956

Amaster salesman, Thomas Watson saw the potential for punched-card tabulating machines as early as 1914. He built International Business Machines into the world leader in data-processing equipment. Along with his son Thomas, Jr. (1914–1993), he later led IBM to the first big successes with mainframe computers. Indeed, the Watsons made IBM synonymous with mainframe computing just as Steven Jobs led Apple to represent desktop personal computing. But IBM's dominance lasted much longer.

Thomas, Sr., known as "T.J.," grew up poor in Painted Post, New York, but discovered sales as his road to success. He sold organs and household appliances before joining National Cash

Register, where he rose to the No. 2 spot. Fired by NCR in 1913, he vowed to build a bigger company, and he did. He became president of the Computing-Tabulating-Recording Company, which sold punched-card tabulating machines, time clocks, and scales.

Watson understood that C-T-R's cards and tabulators held the key to growth. He sold the new technology to insurance companies and railroads, making C-T-R a market leader. Through aggressive national and international marketing of the tabulating machine, he tripled revenues to almost $15 million in just six years. Watson changed the name to International Business Machines in 1924, and the company outsold all its competitors in tabulators, time clocks, and electric typewriters through 1950.

In 1944, IBM researchers had a hand in developing the first computer, the Harvard Mark I, but the usually farsighted Watson saw little market potential for the new machines at first. Only after Remington Rand's UNIVAC began replacing IBM tabulating machines in 1951

did Watson jump on the bandwagon, in part because of the advocacy of his son, then an IBM vice president. Through superior research and development and fieldwork by his impressive "Big Blue" sales force, Watson quickly won back market share to dominate this emerging field.

While T.J. and Steven Jobs both excelled in their ability to see value in new technology, they used very different management styles. Watson ran a tight ship, the way a stern but fair father runs a family. His guiding principles were loyalty, unity, and idealism, and he was fond of slogans to direct the workforce. Some of his favorites were: "Make things happen," "Beat your best," and—especially—"Think!"

The younger Watson became president of IBM in 1952 and took over as chairman and CEO when his father died in 1956. He retired in 1971, before IBM made the mistake of waiting too long to capitalize on a new technology—the personal computer championed by Steven Jobs.

Steven P. Jobs

1955–present

Like Thomas Watson, Sr., at IBM, Steven Jobs—the cofounder of Apple Computer—identified the potential for a new hardware technology and showed how to exploit it. Making the personal computer attractive to nontechnical people, Jobs became a driving force in the industry. He left Apple in 1985 and now heads NeXT Software Inc. and Pixar films.

Always colorful, never predictable, Jobs is the single most important reason that most personal computers today run a graphical user interface (GUI) like those on the Macintosh operating system and Microsoft Windows.

Born in 1955, Jobs had a summer job at Hewlett-Packard while still in high school. He entered college but dropped out after the first year. In 1974, he took a job designing video games for Atari. A year later, along with engineer Stephen Wozniak—a friend from high school and Hewlett-Packard—Jobs started building his first computer, the Apple I. He designed it in his bedroom and built the prototype in his garage.

Though the Apple I could not do very much, it began a long tradition of product innovation, featuring a video interface connected to a monitor or TV set and a built-in ROM (Read Only Memory) that allowed the computer—rather than the person running it—to load programs. Jobs and Wozniak sold only a few hundred, mostly to hobbyists.

The vastly improved Apple II hit the market in 1977, dominating the personal computer field until IBM introduced the PC in 1981. VisiCalc, the first spreadsheet for a personal computer, was written for the Apple II, as were some early word-processing and database programs. Writers, educators, bookkeepers, and inventory managers started seeing computing as something valuable—and affordable. The Apple II brought in revenues of $139 million in its first three years.

As a visitor to Xerox's Palo Alto Research Center (PARC) in 1979, Jobs saw an innovation that Xerox apparently had no plans to market. At the time, computers were controlled by typed commands. But at PARC, Jobs saw a GUI and a mouse, which inspired him to create an "appliance computer" that would be accessible even to those who were leery of the new machines. That led to the original Apple Macintosh, released in early 1984.

Having difficulty managing Apple's growth, Jobs was forced to step down. He founded NeXT almost immediately, then, in 1986, bought Pixar, a film animation company, for $10 million. The firm released such products as RenderMan (used to create the dinosaur skins in Jurassic Park), Typistry (a 3-D typography generator), and a computer animation production system. Jobs scored a major success with Disney's 1995 release of Pixar's "Toy Story"—the first full-length feature film done entirely in computer animation.

Meanwhile, NeXT, of which Jobs is chairman and chief executive officer, has been developing software (WebObjects and OPENSTEP) for customized applications on both the World Wide Web and the Enterprise Web server.

Frederick Weyerhaeuser　　　1834–1914

The first Europeans who arrived in North America were amazed at the vast expanses of woodland they found. One wrote that a squirrel could jump onto a tree in what is now New Jersey and travel branch to branch all the way to the Mississippi River without alighting once. It was still that way in 1852 when Frederic Weyerhaeuser arrived in America at age 18 and, like so many German immigrants, headed West. His fortune lay in the agricultural bounty of this new land, just as John Simplot discovered in the century that followed.

Weyerhaeuser worked for a while as a brewer's apprentice before drifting into the lumber business in Illinois. Because the economy was bad and money was scarce, "I went around among the farmers exchanging lumber for horses, oxen, eggs, anything they had," Weyerhaeuser later said. "This country produce I traded to the raftsmen for logs or to the merchants for stoves, tinware, and logging kits." Weyerhaeuser built a mill, purchased logs, turned them into lumber, and then built houses and shops for sale. By the time of the Civil War, he was already a wealthy man.

He continued to expand his operations after the war, organizing the Mississippi River Boom and Logging Company in 1872, a consortium that dominated logging and sawmill operations in an area larger than France. In time, Weyerhaeuser concentrated on Douglas firs and Idaho ponderosa pines, and became the most significant figure in the land-development business since John Jacob Astor.

Relocating to St. Paul, Minnesota, in 1891, Weyerhaeuser became friendly with James Hill, the master of the Great Northern Railroad, which was the largest landholder in the Northwest. Hill was trying to settle the area in the hope that farmers and others would provide business for his railroad. Lumbering clearly was one area that could be capitalized on, so Hill and Weyerhaeuser formed an alliance.

Although Weyerhaeuser had nibbled at land in the region earlier, he now plunged into Northwest lumber in a big way. In 1900, he led a syndicate that purchased 900,000 acres of unexplored timberland from the Northern Pacific, the largest single purchase of timber up to that time. Since the only way the lumber could get to market was via the rails, Hill profited enormously from the deal.

Many criticized Weyerhaeuser for this move, arguing that the unexplored land could never be profitably utilized. But he plunged on, purchasing more land and organizing the Weyerhaeuser Timber Company, then and now the biggest force in the industry. By the time of his death in 1914, Weyerhaeuser owned nearly 2 million acres of timberland in the Pacific Northwest, purchased at an average cost of $8.80 an acre.

The gamble on what was called "the inland empire" paid off handsomely. In 1900, the West Coast produced 3 billion board feet of lumber; by 1914, the figure had risen to 7 billion board feet while lumber prices had doubled.

John R. Simplot

J ust "an old potato farmer" is the way John R. "Jack" Simplot fashions himself, but that folksy epithet does not begin to describe the billionaire industrialist who made a fortune selling frozen french fries to McDonald's and other fast-food chains.

His firm J.R. Simplot Company has estimated annual sales of $2.5 billion and is one of the largest private businesses in the United States. Agribusiness is the heart of his empire, but Simplot's 22 percent stake in Idaho computer chip maker Micron Technology Inc. has drawn considerable interest the past few years.

Born in 1904, Jack Simplot's tale reads like the script for a soap opera. An eighth-grade dropout who moved out of his father's house after an argument, the combative 14-year-old set himself up as a hog farmer in 1923. During one particularly hard winter, grain to feed the hogs was hard to come by. So young Jack devised a method of producing hog slop out of potato scraps and wild horse meat. The result: Jack Simplot took fat hogs to market the following spring—and money to the bank—while other farmers had little to show for their winter's work. Simplot used his earnings from hogs to buy his first potato field.

But J.R. Simplot Company really took off when Jack started processing other farmers' production. During World War II, he produced dehydrated potatoes and onions before discovering a process to freeze potatoes that could be used in french fries. When the fast-food industry exploded onto the American scene during the 1950s and 1960s, Simplot's business grew right along with it.

Jack Simplot retired as chairman of the company in 1994, turning over day-to-day operations to three of his children and a grandchild. He continues to be a highly visible part of the Boise, Idaho, landscape, however, driving to work every day in his white Lincoln Continental with the MR SPUD license plates.

He also plays a significant role in Micron, which he helped launch in 1980 with a $1 million investment. Deciding to back a pair of local businessmen who wanted to try making semiconductors in Idaho, which most people thought was a

crazy idea, Simplot gambled and won—big. Micron evolved into one of the world's most efficient makers of memory chips, becoming a prime American challenger to the huge Japanese and South Korean electronics companies.

The crusty old potato farmer took to the semiconductor business with gusto. Known as a tireless promoter of the company's products, he has also backed up his words with cash, continuing to increase his Micron holdings over the years. At one point, he even offered to cover any losses sustained by J.R. Simplot employees who had purchased Micron shares and then suffered price declines. His faith in the company has not gone unrewarded: In early 1996, the 22 percent of Micron shares he controls were valued at $1.8 billion.

Adolph Zukor

1873 – 1976

With a self-effacing manner, Adolph Zukor was a pioneer of the burgeoning entertainment industry. He created the first feature-length movie and built Paramount Pictures into a Hollywood powerhouse.

Born in Hungary, Zukor immigrated in 1888 to the United States, where he worked as a furrier.

In 1900, he invested in a kinetoscope arcade and soon recognized the potential in screening motion pictures before large audiences rather than having them watch flickering images in peep shows. Zukor became the arcade king of the East Coast, then expanded into motion-picture theaters. He eventually merged his enterprises with a vaudeville circuit owned by Marcus Loew, another former furrier.

Zukor wanted to control all aspects of the industry. He realized that owning a chain of theaters was only part of the equation: He needed to dominate a source of supply of feature films, which meant control of a studio as well. Accordingly, he organized Famous Players as a production company that would supply "product" for his theaters. By 1913, Famous Players was the leading force in the field, producing 30 films that year.

The company started by filming plays and familiar novels. In time, however, Zukor commissioned original screenplays. He entered into an arrangement with impresario David Belasco under which Mary Pickford appeared in "A Good Little Devil." Then, in 1914, Pickford was seen in "Tess of the Storm Country," which established her as the screen's first star.

That year, Zukor contracted with a distribution company, Paramount Pictures, to supply it with a picture per week. He then merged with a production company headed by Jesse Lasky to form Famous Players-Lasky. Gaining control of Paramount in 1917, Zukor eventually merged it with Famous Players-Lasky. During the period of silent films, Paramount dominated the industry, employing such directors as Cecil B. DeMille and featuring the talents of Pickford, Rudolph Valentino, and Gloria Swanson. It introduced the first big Western film, "The Covered Wagon," in 1923.

Paramount was crippled, however, by overexpansion on the eve of the Great Depression and the financial shock of having to convert to talking pictures. The company was forced into bankruptcy in 1933.

Zukor came close to losing control of Paramount, but he managed to hang on by playing one faction against another. The company emerged from bankruptcy in 1935 with Zukor as chairman of the board. His period of greatest influence was over, but he remained an industry icon and mentor. As such, he urged cooperation with television to broaden the scope of what was becoming the "entertainment industry."

1938–present

Ted Turner

Mark Hill

Well known as an entrepreneur, philan- thropist, and celebrity, Ted Turner pioneered several highly successful television phenomena, including the first superstation, TBS, and the first all-news channel, Cable News Network (CNN), as the chairman and president of Turner Broadcasting System, Inc. A world-class sailor and legendary deal-maker, Turner has never been afraid to take risks. Many of his ven- tures have proved him a visionary.

Born Robert Edward Turner III in 1938 and raised in Savannah, Georgia, Turner joined his father's billboard company in 1960. The com- pany had gone bankrupt and the young Turner turned it around. He entered broadcasting with the 1970 purchase of an independent UHF channel. After renaming the station WTBS, Turner realized he could use satellites to reach cable stations coast to coast and turned his broadcast outlet into a model of superstation success. In 1976, Turner bought the Atlanta Braves baseball team and a year later the Atlanta Hawks basketball team.

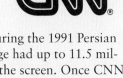

The TBS experience led Turner in 1980 to found CNN—a pioneer in live, on-the-scene, full-time coverage of the news. During the 1991 Persian Gulf war, CNN's coverage had up to 11.5 mil- lion Americans glued to the screen. Once CNN was well established, Turner also started Turner Network Television, Headline News, and the Cartoon Network—as well as a movie studio, Turner Pictures.

In 1985, Turner bought MGM/UA Entertainment, then sold parts of it, retaining primarily MGM's film and television libraries. That enabled TBS to show MGM's vast store of movies without paying licensing fees. In 1994 and 1995, Turner completed the acquisitions of New Line Cinema and Castle Rock Entertainment to ensure an ongoing supply of movies.

Turner is nothing if not diverse. He is the largest bison rancher in the United States, with four ranches that total about as much acreage as Rhode Island. As a sailor, Turner has won the America's Cup and other high-profile races.

Turner's 1985 attempt to take over CBS failed, but in 1995 he agreed to merge Turner Broadcasting into Time Warner, the world's largest media and entertainment company. The deal marks another remarkable achievement for Turner. The $7 billion transaction makes him the largest shareholder and vice chairman of the new company's vast entertainment empire. Time Warner now spans nearly every aspect of the entertainment industry, including Warner Bros. studios and TV, the Warner Music Group, cable (HBO, CNN, TNT), publishing (*Time*, *People*, *Fortune*, and Warner Books), merchandising (Warner Bros. Stores), and even theme parks (Six Flags).

The American Dream

In a healthy society, free enterprise is the source of growth, prosperity and progress. Why is this so? How does free enterprise fulfill society's needs? My experience as a businessman suggests the answer. After starting Inner City Broadcasting Corp. in 1972, I quickly learned that in our business, success comes to those who provide something people need or want. I listened to our customers and provided programming and entertainment they enjoyed.

Using this formula, I was able to build Inner City into a successful enterprise. One of our radio stations has been the most-listened-to station in New York City. The other station pioneered programming that many others adopted. We also produce "It's Showtime at the Apollo," a nationally syndicated music, dance and comedy television show.

The business lessons I learned while building Inner City taught me something about free enterprise. I realized in a fundamental way, my company was no different from any other, that business succeeds only if it serves people's needs.

This section describes how the persistence and spirit of a diverse group of people allowed them to realize their dreams and create businesses from which we all benefit. Our neighbor is employed by one, our grandfather relies on

another, and society benefits from the tax dollars generated by all. It is business, not politics, that weaves the stronger fabric of American life.

Herein lies a secret of our free-enterprise system. Ours is a society in which most people are employees or owners of private businesses. As we have seen, however, the success of an enterprise is tied directly to its ability to serve others. Therefore, successful companies are those that enrich our daily lives and promote the well-being of our communities.

The reverse is also true. Prosperous communities promote prosperous businesses.

Companies depend on the customers, skilled workers and suppliers that a healthy community nurtures. They also depend on other businesses for essential services such as communications, data processing and financing. Each of these fields has been transformed in recent years, and the companies here— including my own—could not function without them.

These interdependent relationships between companies and communities are a hallmark of our society. They enrich our lives, give expression to our ideas and values and are a source of our nation's strength and prosperity.

People who fight for change in every corner of the world are placing their faith in our way of life, confident it will allow them, like us, to build better lives for themselves, their families and their communities. Watching their struggle should give us all a better appreciation of the American dream and the free-enterprise system that makes it possible.

PERCY SUTTON
Chairman Emeritus,
Inner City Broadcasting

Warnaco Inc.

Linda Wachner is chairman, president and chief executive officer of Warnaco Inc., a major force in the apparel industry. Its menswear labels include Calvin Klein Men's Underwear and Accessories and Chaps by Ralph Lauren. Its women's intimate apparel brands include Warner's, Calvin Klein, Olga, Lejaby, Valentino, Intimo, Bodyslimmers by Nancy Ganz, and Fruit of the Loom.

After graduating high school at age 16 and working her way through college, Wachner had a meteoric rise in the apparel business. At 28, she became the first female vice president in the 100-year history of Warner's.

A few years later, at 33, she was recruited to be president of the U.S. Division of Max Factor. In 1982, she became president and chief executive of the company worldwide. She left three years later and began a search that led to the April 1986 purchase of Warnaco, the parent company of the Warner's division where she had started a decade earlier.

What makes Wachner special? A cornerstone of her style is thorough knowledge of the consumer. Early in her career, she visited sales floors during lunches and evenings, quizzing customers about why they buy, and asking clerks what is moving. This led Wachner to shock the intimate apparel industry by taking bras out of boxes from behind retail counters and displaying them on hangers. Allowing women to browse was a big change and a big success. She has brought this same style to Warnaco, where one responsibility of middle managers is to spot the latest trends around the world.

The company pays attention to incentives. Key executives can double their salaries by meeting goals for earnings, cash flow, distribution of products, and innovation.

"I'm having a wonderful time," says Wachner, who rarely stops to think that for millions of women, she embodies the American dream.

Hovnanian Enterprises, Inc.

Kevork Hovnanian, an Armenian Christian living in Iraq, was part owner of a large road construction firm in his home country but lost everything during the 1959 revolution. Almost penniless, he fled to America with his wife and children. He joined his three brothers, who were living in New Jersey. They scraped together $20,000 and started a construction company. Several years later Hovnanian formed his own home-building firm.

About the time he arrived in the United States, land and housing prices were beginning to soar. Hovnanian believed he could keep homes within reach of middle-income buyers by applying mass production techniques to the construction of condominiums and townhouses. "People should have a reasonable opportunity to live in decent housing," he says.

Hovnanian Enterprises, Inc.'s basic products are two-bedroom, two-bath, garden-style homes and townhouses, built in multi-unit sets on a single concrete pad. The first homes were less than 1,000 square feet. Today they average around 1,600.

From the start, the company concentrated on newlyweds, growing families, and other first-time buyers. Thirty years and 30,000 homes later, it is one of the nation's top home builders, with annual revenues of more than $800 million and more than 1,000 employees. Based in New Jersey, where it is the leading home builder, the company has also branched into

other states across the country, including Florida and California; and also has develo ments in Poland.

The company's founder feels so strongly a keeping new homes within the reach of av age Americans that he personally sets pric This strategy, coupled with quality workm ship, has created a challenge for the compa deciding who may buy. The "Grand Openi of Hovnanian communities often draw hug crowds eager to buy one of the homes. On the company even tried a lottery in a 20,000-seat arena.

The firm has moved into mid-city areas, con structing townhouses and garden-style home in Jersey City and in the Newark, N.J., neigh borhood that was torn by race riots in the 1960s. Says Hovnanian's son Ara, president o the company, "The problem with most marke is that both homeowners and developers have set their sights on excessively high prices. We can price moderately and still make a fair profit."

In realizing his own dream, Kevork Hovnania has made it possible for thousands of others t realize their dream of home ownership.

Comdisco, Incorporated

In 1968, Ken Pontikes was a salesman at International Business Machines Corp. He had a comfortable life, but it wasn't enough for someone with his energy and spirit. He quit and, after a year at a smaller firm, started his own company with $5,000.

With technology changing rapidly, many corporations did not want to buy entire computer systems or bear the expense of upgrading existing ones. Pontikes believed there was a huge market in leasing computer equipment.

Thirty years later, Comdisco, Inc., is the nation's largest independent lessor and remarketer of high-technology equipment. Its sales exceeded $2.4 billion in 1996, and it has expanded into a global concern, with offices in Canada, Europe, and the Pacific Rim.

Founder Ken Pontikes died in 1994, but his family maintains active participation in the business, with his brother William and son Nicholas still in top management. Comdisco has also expanded to other businesses and now leases equipment in the telephone, health care, and semiconductor industries.

The company believes that its job doesn't stop at installing and maintaining equipment—it must also solve problems. That's why it provides sophisticated planning for customers who need help financing their leases. It also runs the world's largest service for recovering computer data. When a terrorist bomb forced the evacuation of one customer's offices in New York's World Trade Center in 1993, Comdisco teams worked throughout the night to recover critical functions and recreate their worldwide business systems. The customer was up and running—even handling 7,500 calls—on the first business day after the blast.

Ken Pontikes' motto, "Growth through strength and profits through discipline," is a good formula for any manager who shares the dream of becoming an entrepreneur.

Hasbro, Inc.

T he Hasbro story began three generations ago with Henry Hassenfield and his two brothers. They were immigrant merchants from Poland who settled in Pawtucket, R.I., in 1923. They made pencil boxes and hat liners. During World War II, they turned the boxes into children's doctor kits, their first toys.

In 1943, Henry's sons, Merrill and Harold, took over. Soon they added crayons, paint sets, and nurse kits to the company's line. In 1952, they introduced Mr. Potato Head, the first toy ever advertised on television. More than 50 million Mr. and Mrs. Potato Heads have been sold, and sales continued at a million a year. In 1964, the company introduced G.I. Joe, it's all-time greatest hit. Hasbro is also one of two licensees to produce Star Wars toys for Lucasfilm Ltd. That market is expected to generate $500 million in 1997.

Merrill's son, Stephen, took over in 1979 when Hasbro was American's sixth-largest toy company. Under his management, the company became No. 1 in the industry by the mid-1980s and was the leader of roughly 800 firms that were introducing over 5,000 new products a year. Stephen transformed the company and industry by moving from dependence on a few products, popular primarily at Christmas, to a broad, reasonably priced line selling year-round. Hasbro acquired Milton Bradley in 1984, and took a place among the Fortune 500. Beginning in 1989, Hasbro began a major acquisition trend, acquiring such properties as Coleco

Industries' Cabbage Patch doll line, Tonka, and Japanese toymaker Nomura Toys. The company is looking forward to new frontiers: In 1995, Hasbro signed a deal with the popular Nickelodeon cable channel to produce toys under the Nickelodeon brand name. The market value of Hasbro's stock tops $3.65 billion.

Stephen's brother, Alan, now runs the company. When asked what the family cares about most, he says, "Remember that we are a family that lives by the tradition of giving back to the community, particularly to help children."

Barnes & Noble, Inc.

Imagine taking a job in a bookstore to work your way through college and within a few short years owning the world's largest retailing chain of bookstores. Then imagine that you transform book retailing by pioneering just about every major innovation in bookselling for the past thirty years. Len Riggio did just that in his pursuit of the American dream.

Len started his bookselling career while attending New York University as an engineering student in the early 1960s. Working as a clerk in the university bookstore, he became convinced that he could do a better job serving students, so he decided to open a competing store of his own. Within a couple of years, Len's Student Book Exchange in Greenwich Village became one of New York's finest independent bookstores, known for its staff, selection, and service.

In 1971, Len's thriving business acquired the flagship Barnes & Noble Bookstore on Fifth Avenue and 18th Street in Manhattan, which had virtually gone into bankruptcy. In a few years he returned the institution to its former glory, and this began the modern Barnes & Noble.

Over the following years Len introduced many revolutionary concepts to the book industry. Barnes & Noble was the first to discount books, advertise on television, and open book superstores—combining wide selection, distinctive ambiance, knowledgeable booksellers, and exciting community events.

"One of the most rewarding accomplishments of our company is bringing books to communities through-

out the country, which previously had no easy access to them. People who once had to travel 60 miles to their nearest bookstore are now able to find a source for books minutes from their own homes," according to Riggio.

Today, Barnes & Noble, Inc. is the world's largest bookseller. In addition to the more than 400 Barnes & Noble stores, the company owns B. Dalton Bookseller, which operates more than 600 bookstores in regional shopping centers. Barnes & Noble also publishes its own books for sale exclusively through its stores and direct mail catalog. In 1997 the company began selling books online through a web site offering more than one million titles at deep discounts.

American Shared Hospital Services

Early on, the parents of Ernest Bates instilled in their son a belief in integrity, hard work, and self-reliance. Bates' father had a limited education. His mother had been a school teacher in Virginia but found no teaching jobs open to her in the small upstate New York community where Bates was born. Both worked hard. Bates' father had several small businesses. His mother became a domestic and later took a job with the phone company.

Their values and Bates' own lively mind carried this young man from one achievement to the next. He was elected president of a high school class that included only three blacks and later became the first black accepted into the liberal arts school of Johns Hopkins University in Baltimore. His mother wanted him to be either a preacher or a physician. He became a neurosurgeon and eventually a trustee of John Hopkins.

In the late 1970s, Bates invested in a new venture for saving lives. Many hospitals could not afford a million dollars or more for such advanced diagnostic equipment as CT Scanners and Magnetic Resonance Imagers (MRI). The idea was to make the equipment mobile, dividing the time and cost among many hospitals. Soon, however, the project was on the ropes, and Bates stepped in to run it. He even once made payroll out of his own pocket.

Under his management, the service grew. Today, American Shared Hospital Services provides diagnostic equipment to more than 220 hospitals and clinics in more than 22 states, in places as diverse as Chicago and rural Oklahoma. It operates nearly 30 MRIs and approximately 20 CT scanners and other medical diagnostic imaging units.

The availability of such equipment has changed medical treatment for patients and their doctors. At each hospital, company technicians set up equipment under the direction of a physician from the hospital. The doctor directs procedures, interprets results, and maintains responsibility for patients.

The Saturday Evening Post reported on a man who suffered severe back pain. His doctor prescribed pain killers, which didn't work, and X-rays found nothing. Finally, he sent the patient to a medical center served by an MRI unit. Within an hour, the imager had located a bone infection in the lower back that threatened the man's life. Once discovered, the disorder was easily treated. The man's life was saved and the back pain was gone.

In 1996, revenues for American Shared totaled $37 million, and the company continues to push into new frontiers. Bates is moving the company into the operating room, with plans to revolutionize the surgical equipment market. His primary focus is on the new gamma knife, which can treat many critical conditions without surgery. Just as he has demonstrated in the past, Bates will lead the industry in new directions.

Movado Group, Inc.

In 1960, 29-year-old Gedalio Grinberg fled Castro's tyranny. He arrived in Miami hoping to return to a liberated Cuba. But it was not to be. The next year he moved to New York, took a room at the YMCA, and started a business with a family he'd worked with in his former homeland.

In Cuba, Grinberg sold high-fashion watches, but marketing $1,000 timepieces to Americans accustomed to inexpensive watches seemed impossible. Still, he and his partner bought the North American rights to Piaget, a small, little known Swiss watch company with just $165,000 in sales. By 1966, they had built a $1 million enterprise.

In 1967, Grinberg bought out his partner, who was older and had become ill, and formed North American Watch. That year, he purchased the North American distribution rights to Corum watches, famous for Gold Coin timepieces. In 1969, he acquired Concord, makers of the thinnest watches in the world, and in 1982, Movado, which has a design in the permanent collection of New York's Museum of Modern Art.

Gedalio Grinberg is still the CEO of the company, with his son Efraim serving as president. The company changed its name to Movado Group, Inc., in 1996 (meaning "always in motion" in the universal language of Esperanto), to reflect its international scope. The company has also signed a 10-year exclusive agreement with Coach, the leading American leather maker, to design, manufacture, and distribute fine watches on a worldwide basis.

From just a few hundred watches in 1961, Movado now sells more than 500,000 a year—some for over $500,000—and has more than 650 employees. In 1996, the company's sales exceeded $200 million.

U.S. Gross Domestic Product (GDP) and Gross National Product (GNP)

Gross Domestic Product (Constant 1992 $)

Period	Quarterly (Annualized)	Growth	Annual	Growth
1959	$1,904.9		$2,212.3	—
	1,937.5	1.7%		
	2,225.6	14.9		
	2,225.8	0.0		
1960	2,283.3	2.6	2,261.7	2.2%
	2,268.5	(0.6)		
	2,265.8	(0.1)		
	2,229.1	(1.6)		
1961	2,245.6	0.7	2,309.8	2.1
	2,286.1	1.8		
	2,328.2	1.8		
	2,379.4	2.2		
1962	2,420.4	1.7	2,449.1	6.0
	2,440.0	0.8		
	2,465.2	1.0		
	2,470.7	0.2		
1963	2,502.3	1.3	2,554.0	4.3
	2,532.9	1.2		
	2,581.4	1.9		
	2,599.7	0.7		
1964	2,661.8	2.4	2,702.9	5.8
	2,692.5	1.2		
	2,723.9	1.2		
	2,733.6	0.4		
1965	2,800.8	2.5	2,874.8	6.4
	2,844.2	1.5		
	2,889.2	1.6		
	2,965.2	2.6		
1966	3,034.4	2.3	3,060.2	6.4
	3,046.2	0.4		
	3,067.6	0.7		
	3,092.6	0.8		
1967	3,119.7	0.9	3,140.2	2.6
	3,122.3	0.1		
	3,147.3	0.8		
	3,171.6	0.8		
1968	3,230.2	1.8	3,288.6	4.7
	3,286.6	1.7		

Gross National Product (Constant 1992 $)

Period	Quarterly (Annualized)	Growth	Annual	Growth
1959	$1,915.1		$2,224.3	—
	1,947.7	1.7%		
	2,237.7	14.9		
	2,238.7	0.0		
1960	2,295.7	2.5	2,274.8	2.3%
	2,281.2	(0.6)		
	2,279.1	(0.1)		
	2,243.4	(1.6)		
1961	2,260.7	0.8	2,324.6	2.2
	2,300.3	1.8		
	2,342.8	1.8		
	2,394.3	2.2		
1962	2,435.3	1.7	2,465.9	6.1
	2,456.4	0.9		
	2,481.8	1.0		
	2,489.9	0.3		
1963	2,520.4	1.2	2,572.0	4.3
	2,550.4	1.2		
	2,599.1	1.9		
	2,618.0	0.7		
1964	2,681.9	2.4	2,722.3	5.8
	2,711.7	1.1		
	2,743.8	1.2		
	2,751.9	0.3		
1965	2,821.9	2.5	2,895.2	6.4
	2,866.1	1.6		
	2,909.4	1.5		
	2,983.3	2.5		
1966	3,053.1	2.3	3,078.9	6.3
	3,065.0	0.4		
	3,085.8	0.7		
	3,111.7	0.8		
1967	3,138.5	0.9	3,159.4	2.6
	3,140.5	0.1		
	3,167.5	0.9		
	3,191.1	0.7		
1968	3,250.2	1.9	3,309.2	4.7
	3,307.2	1.8		

Gross Domestic Product
(Constant 1992 $)

Period	Quarterly (Annualized)	Growth	Annual	Growth
1968	$3,311.1	0.7%		
	3,326.3	0.5		
1969	3,376.9	1.5	$3,388.0	3.0%
	3,385.2	0.2		
	3,404.3	0.6		
	3,385.6	(0.5)		
1970	3,378.1	(0.2)	3,388.2	0.0
	3,382.1	0.1		
	3,412.9	0.9		
	3,379.6	(1.0)		
1971	3,471.5	2.7	3,500.1	3.3
	3,491.3	0.6		
	3,514.0	0.7		
	3,523.6	0.3		
1972	3,593.9	2.0	3,690.3	5.4
	3,676.3	2.3		
	3,713.8	1.0		
	3,777.2	1.7		
1973	3,876.9	2.6	3,902.3	5.7
	3,903.3	0.7		
	3,892.8	(0.3)		
	3,936.2	1.1		
1974	3,903.0	(0.8)	3,888.2	(0.4)
	3,920.4	0.4		
	3,878.4	(1.1)		
	3,850.9	(0.7)		
1975	3,793.6	(1.5)	3,865.1	(0.6)
	3,825.6	0.8		
	3,897.0	1.9		
	3,944.2	1.2		
1976	4,039.1	2.4	4,081.1	5.6
	4,068.9	0.7		
	4,087.7	0.5		
	4,128.4	1.0		
1977	4,181.8	1.3	4,279.3	4.9
	4,268.0	2.1		
	4,336.3	1.6		
	4,331.0	(0.1)		

Gross National Product
(Constant 1992 $)

Period	Quarterly (Annualized)	Growth	Annual	Growth
1968	$3,332.3	0.8%		
	3,347.3	0.5		
1969	3,397.9	1.5	$3,407.8	3.0%
	3,405.3	0.2		
	3,423.3	0.5		
	3,404.6	(0.5)		
1970	3,397.7	(0.2)	3,407.7	0.0
	3,402.4	0.1		
	3,432.9	0.9		
	3,397.7	(1.0)		
1971	3,493.5	2.8	3,522.2	3.4
	3,514.7	0.6		
	3,534.9	0.6		
	3,545.8	0.3		
1972	3,617.2	2.0	3,714.3	5.5
	3,699.1	2.3		
	3,738.9	1.1		
	3,802.1	1.7		
1973	3,906.1	2.7	3,936.0	6.0
	3,934.7	0.7		
	3,930.0	(0.1)		
	3,973.5	1.1		
1974	3,947.3	(0.7)	3,927.1	(0.2)
	3,962.1	0.4		
	3,916.1	(1.2)		
	3,882.9	(0.8)		
1975	3,820.0	(1.6)	3,894.5	(0.8)
	3,852.3	0.8		
	3,926.2	1.9		
	3,979.6	1.4		
1976	4,073.3	2.4	4,116.9	5.7
	4,104.7	0.8		
	4,124.0	0.5		
	4,165.6	1.0		
1977	4,224.8	1.4	4,320.2	4.9
	4,310.1	2.0		
	4,378.0	1.6		
	4,367.7	(0.2)		

(continued)

Gross Domestic Product
(Constant 1992 $)

Period	Quarterly (Annualized)	Growth	Annual	Growth
1978	$4,340.8	0.2%	$4,493.7	5.0%
	4,501.3	3.7		
	4,540.5	0.9		
	4,592.3	1.1		
1979	4,597.7	0.1	4,624.0	2.9
	4,608.6	0.2		
	4,638.8	0.7		
	4,651.0	0.3		
1980	4,674.3	0.5	4,611.9	(0.3)
	4,562.6	(2.4)		
	4,559.6	(0.1)		
	4,651.1	2.0		
1981	4,741.3	1.9	4,724.9	2.5
	4,701.3	(0.8)		
	4,758.4	1.2		
	4,698.6	(1.3)		
1982	4,618.9	(1.7)	4,623.6	(2.1)
	4,637.4	0.4		
	4,615.3	(0.5)		
	4,622.8	0.2		
1983	4,669.8	1.0	4,810.0	4.0
	4,771.3	2.2		
	4,855.5	1.8		
	4,943.6	1.8		
1984	5,053.4	2.2	5,138.2	6.8
	5,129.8	1.5		
	5,167.0	0.7		
	5,202.7	0.7		
1985	5,261.3	1.1	5,329.5	3.7
	5,290.8	0.6		
	5,367.0	1.4		
	5,398.9	0.6		
1986	5,465.4	1.2	5,489.9	3.0
	5,469.6	0.1		
	5,497.6	0.5		
	5,527.0	0.5		

Gross National Product
(Constant 1992 $)

Period	Quarterly (Annualized)	Growth	Annual	Growth
1978	$4,383.9	0.4%	$4,534.4	5.0%
	4,536.6	3.5		
	4,579.5	0.9		
	4,637.7	1.3		
1979	4,644.6	0.1	4,680.8	3.2
	4,661.6	0.4		
	4,702.6	0.9		
	4,714.3	0.2		
1980	4,738.3	0.5	4,667.7	(0.3)
	4,621.6	(2.5)		
	4,615.1	(0.1)		
	4,695.9	1.8		
1981	4,789.9	2.0	4,774.1	2.3
	4,747.1	(0.9)		
	4,806.8	1.3		
	4,752.8	(1.1)		
1982	4,661.5	(1.9)	4,665.4	(2.3)
	4,685.6	0.5		
	4,654.4	(0.7)		
	4,660.2	0.1		
1983	4,707.0	1.0	4,851.2	4.0
	4,812.1	2.2		
	4,897.8	1.8		
	4,987.8	1.8		
1984	5,092.4	2.1	5,176.1	6.7
	5,169.3	1.5		
	5,206.2	0.7		
	5,236.6	0.6		
1985	5,284.3	0.9	5,352.7	3.4
	5,317.8	0.6		
	5,385.9	1.3		
	5,422.8	0.7		
1986	5,485.7	1.2	5,503.4	2.8
	5,482.7	(0.1)		
	5,511.7	0.5		
	5,533.3	0.4		

Gross Domestic Product
(Constant 1992 $)

Period	Quarterly (Annualized)	Growth	Annual	Growth
1987	$5,561.4	0.6%	$5,648.4	2.9%
	5,616.8	1.0		
	5,666.0	0.9		
	5,749.4	1.5		
1988	5,782.9	0.6	5,862.9	3.8
	5,841.7	1.0		
	5,876.5	0.6		
	5,950.7	1.3		
1989	6,008.7	1.0	6,060.4	3.4
	6,053.4	0.7		
	6,086.2	0.5		
	6,093.0	0.1		
1990	6,154.1	1.0	6,138.7	1.3
	6,174.4	0.3		
	6,145.2	(0.5)		
	6,081.0	(1.0)		
1991	6,047.9	(0.5)	6,079.0	(1.0)
	6,074.1	0.4		
	6,089.3	0.3		
	6,104.4	0.2		
1992	6,175.3	1.2	6,244.4	2.7
	6,214.2	0.6		
	6,260.9	0.8		
	6,327.3	1.1		
1993	6,327.0	0.0	6,383.8	2.2
	6,353.7	0.4		
	6,390.4	0.6		
	6,463.9	1.2		
1994	6,504.6	0.6	6,604.2	3.5
	6,581.5	1.2		
	6,639.5	0.9		
	6,691.3	0.8		
1995	6,701.6	0.2		
	6,709.4	0.1		
	6,763.2	0.8		

Gross National Product
(Constant 1992 $)

Period	Quarterly (Annualized)	Growth	Annual	Growth
1987	$5,568.2	0.6%	$5,657.2	2.8%
	5,627.5	1.1		
	5,674.7	0.8		
	5,758.5	1.5		
1988	5,799.9	0.7	5,876.2	3.9
	5,855.1	1.0		
	5,887.3	0.5		
	5,962.8	1.3		
1989	6,020.8	1.0	6,074.0	3.4
	6,063.5	0.7		
	6,099.9	0.6		
	6,111.7	0.2		
1990	6,174.3	1.0	6,159.4	1.4
	6,190.8	0.3		
	6,158.8	(0.5)		
	6,113.4	(0.7)		
1991	6,074.8	(0.6)	6,094.4	(1.1)
	6,085.8	0.2		
	6,098.3	0.2		
	6,118.7	0.3		
1992	6,191.6	1.2	6,255.5	2.6
	6,225.1	0.5		
	6,270.4	0.7		
	6,334.8	1.0		
1993	6,342.7	0.1	6,393.7	2.2
	6,362.9	0.3		
	6,404.0	0.6		
	6,465.1	1.0		
1994	6,506.2	0.6	6,596.6	3.2
	6,573.9	1.0		
	6,631.1	0.9		
	6,675.4	0.7		
1995	6,695.7	0.3		
	6,701.2	0.1		
	6,749.5	0.7		

Sources: U.S. Department of Commerce, Bureau of Economic Analysis

Gross Domestic Product by Country: 1980 to 1994

Country	Amount ($ US billions)						Per Capita ($ US)					
	1980	**1985**	**1990**	**1992**	**1993**	**1994**	**1980**	**1985**	**1990**	**1992**	**1993**	**1994**
OECD (Total)	$7,373	$10,798	$15,041	$16,838	$17,260	$18,130	$8,501	$11,963	$16,003	$17,604	$17,890	$18,646
OECD Europe	3,087	4,368	6,106	6,921	6,917	7,232	7,517	10,391	14,130	15,808	15,694	16,321
European Union	2,870	4,035	5,620	6,368	6,328	6,645	8,079	11,244	15,427	17,307	17,116	17,914
Australia	128	194	272	289	306	328	8,678	12,303	15,941	16,541	17,332	18,382
Austria	67	93	128	148	153	162	8,850	12,278	16,623	18,827	19,167	20,210
Belgium	87	118	163	190	195	204	8,820	11,933	16,318	18,953	19,323	20,166
Canada	246	370	509	536	559	597	10,020	14,262	18,304	18,782	19,314	20,401
Denmark	45	67	85	94	99	107	8,746	12,997	16,548	18,241	19,154	20,546
Finland	38	57	81	76	79	83	8,004	11,682	16,193	15,083	15,646	16,208
France	507	712	984	1,107	1,078	1,112	9,414	12,872	17,347	19,294	18,690	19,201
Germany	658	921	1,269	1,509	1,500	1,602	8,410	11,870	15,991	18,721	18,479	19,675
Greece	51	71	92	109	112	118	5,283	7,131	9,133	10,537	10,783	11,315
Iceland	2	3	4	5	5	5	9,495	13,104	17,267	18,348	18,696	19,271
Ireland	18	27	39	48	49	54	5,291	7,501	11,245	13,416	13,791	15,212
Italy	478	666	923	1,045	1,011	1,068	8,464	11,756	16,274	18,377	17,709	18,681
Japan	936	1,463	2,174	2,485	2,528	2,594	8,011	12,112	17,596	19,986	20,279	20,756
Luxembourg	4	6	9	10	11	12	10,852	15,855	22,929	26,752	28,135	29,454
Mexico	244	349	446	621	637	673	3,499	4,479	5,180	6,939	6,987	7,239
Netherlands	124	172	239	269	271	286	8,750	11,839	15,958	17,693	17,743	18,589
New Zealand	24	37	45	49	53	57	7,711	11,185	13,484	14,307	15,206	16,248
Norway	38	58	74	88	92	95	9,205	13,898	17,497	20,612	21,328	21,968
Portugal	44	60	92	113	117	122	4,548	6,035	9,371	11,407	11,796	12,335
Spain	219	308	458	522	521	532	5,868	8,018	11,787	13,374	13,323	13,581
Sweden	77	109	146	149	147	153	9,250	13,057	17,004	17,205	16,823	17,422
Switzerland	75	104	143	159	161	167	11,720	15,969	21,283	23,088	23,183	23,942
Turkey	102	169	264	300	331	319	2,284	3,327	4,660	5,143	5,562	5,271
United Kingdom	453	649	912	980	986	1,030	8,039	11,449	15,874	16,890	16,943	17,650
United States	2,708	4,017	5,490	5,937	6,260	6,650	11,892	16,844	21,966	23,246	24,252	25,512

Source: Organization for Economic Cooperation and Development (OECD).

*Reflects the amount of currency needed to buy equal amounts of goods and services.

| | Constant (1990) Price Levels and Exchange | | | | | | | |
| Amount ($ US billions) | | | | | | Annual Growth Rate | | |
1980	1985	1990	1992	1993	1994	1992	1993	1994
$12,764	$14,361	$16,800	$17,240	$17,423	$17,921	1.6%	1.1%	2.9%
5,714	6,200	7,229	7,386	7,357	7,548	1.1	(0.4)	2.6
5,344	5,776	6,730	6,871	6,828	7,019	1.0	(0.6)	2.8
214	251	295	297	308	323	2.5	3.8	5.0
128	137	158	166	167	172	2.0	0.4	3.0
159	166	192	200	197	201	1.8	(1.6)	2.2
427	493	568	562	575	601	0.8	2.3	4.6
106	120	129	132	134	140	0.8	1.5	4.4
99	114	135	121	119	124	(3.6)	(1.2)	4.1
957	1,031	1,195	1,221	1,203	1,235	1.3	(1.5)	2.7
1,321	1,421	1,640	1,724	1,704	1,753	2.2	(1.2)	2.9
70	75	82	85	84	85	0.4	(0.9)	1.5
5	5	6	6	6	6	(3.2)	1.0	2.8
32	36	45	48	49	53	3.9	3.1	6.7
880	943	1,095	1,116	1,103	1,127	0.7	(1.2)	2.2
1,960	2,354	2,932	3,091	3,084	3,100	1.1	(0.2)	0.5
7	8	10	11	11	11	1.9	n.a.	3.3
207	228	244	260	262	271	2.8	0.6	3.5
229	243	284	296	297	305	2.0	0.2	2.7
36	42	44	44	47	49	3.0	5.4	6.1
91	107	115	123	125	132	3.3	2.1	5.7
50	52	67	69	69	69	1.1	(1.2)	0.8
366	395	492	506	501	511	0.7	(1.2)	2.1
188	205	230	224	218	223	(1.4)	(2.6)	2.2
184	197	226	225	223	226	(0.3)	(0.8)	1.2
91	115	151	161	174	165	6.0	8.0	(5.5)
752	828	976	951	972	1,010	(0.5)	2.2	3.8
4,205	4,793	5,490	5,600	5,791	6,027	2.5	3.4	4.1

Federal Budget: Receipts, Outlays, and Deficit

($ billions)

Year	Receipts	Outlays	Deficit	On-Budget Deficit*
1940	$6.5	$9.5	($2.9)	($3.5)
1941	8.7	13.7	(4.9)	(5.6)
1942	14.6	35.1	(20.5)	(21.3)
1943	24.0	78.6	(54.6)	(55.6)
1944	43.7	91.3	(47.6)	(48.7)
1945	45.2	92.7	(47.6)	(48.7)
1946	39.3	55.2	(15.9)	(17.0)
1947	38.5	34.5	4.0	2.9
1948	41.6	29.8	11.8	10.5
1949	39.4	38.8	0.6	(0.7)
1950	39.4	42.6	(3.1)	(4.7)
1951	51.6	45.5	6.1	4.3
1952	66.2	67.7	(1.5)	(3.4)
1953	69.6	76.1	(6.5)	(8.3)
1954	69.7	70.9	(1.2)	(2.8)
1955	65.5	68.4	(3.0)	(4.1)
1956	74.6	70.6	3.9	2.5
1957	80.0	76.6	3.4	2.6
1958	79.6	82.4	(2.8)	(3.3)
1959	79.2	92.1	(12.8)	(12.1)
1960	92.5	92.2	0.3	0.5
1961	94.4	97.7	(3.3)	(3.8)
1962	99.7	106.8	(7.1)	(5.9)
1963	106.6	111.3	(4.8)	(4.0)
1964	112.6	118.5	(5.9)	(6.5)
1965	116.8	118.2	(1.4)	(1.6)
1966	130.8	134.5	(3.7)	(3.1)
1967	148.8	157.5	(8.6)	(12.6)
1968	153.0	178.1	(25.2)	(27.7)
1969	186.9	183.6	3.2	(0.5)

Sources: Department of Commerce, Department of the Treasury, and U.S. Office of Management and Budget

*The Federal Budget Act of 1985 moved the Social Security surplus off-budget, which reduces the reported deficit number. The on-budget deficit does not include this surplus and so it is larger.

Year	Receipts	Outlays	Deficit	On–Budget Deficit*
1970	$192.8	$195.6	($2.8)	($8.7)
1971	187.1	210.2	(23.0)	(26.1)
1972	207.3	230.7	(23.4)	(26.4)
1973	230.8	245.7	(14.9)	(15.4)
1974	263.2	269.4	(6.1)	(8.0)
1975	279.1	332.3	(53.2)	(55.3)
1976	298.1	371.8	(73.7)	(70.5)
1977	355.6	409.2	(53.7)	(49.8)
1978	399.6	458.7	(59.2)	(54.9)
1979	463.3	504.0	(40.7)	(38.7)
1980	517.1	590.9	(73.8)	(72.7)
1981	599.3	678.2	(79.0)	(74.0)
1982	617.8	745.8	(128.0)	(120.1)
1983	600.6	808.4	(207.8)	(208.0)
1984	666.5	851.8	(185.4)	(185.7)
1985	734.1	946.4	(212.3)	(221.7)
1986	769.1	990.3	(221.2)	(238.0)
1987	854.1	1,003.9	(149.8)	(169.3)
1988	909.0	1,064.1	(155.2)	(194.0)
1989	990.7	1,143.2	(152.5)	(205.2)
1990	1,031.3	1,252.7	(221.4)	(278.0)
1991	1,054.3	1,323.4	(269.2)	(321.4)
1992	1,090.5	1,380.9	(290.4)	(340.5)
1993	1,153.5	1,408.7	(255.1)	(300.5)
1994	1,257.7	1,460.9	(203.2)	(258.8)
1995	1,346.4	1,538.9	(192.5)	(226.2)

U.S. Balance of Payments:
Current and Capital Account Balances*

($ millions)

Year	Current Account Balance	Capital Account Balance
1970	$2,330	($2,330)
1971	(1,435)	1,435
1972	(5,797)	5,797
1973	7,138	(7,138)
1974	1,958	(1,958)
1975	18,114	(18,114)
1976	4,293	(4,293)
1977	(14,347)	14,347
1978	(15,143)	15,143
1979	(290)	290
1980	2,316	(2,316)
1981	5,031	(5,031)
1982	(11,438)	11,438
1983	43,989)	43,989
1984	(98,948)	98,948
1985	(124,247)	124,247
1986	(152,086)	152,086
1987	(167,394)	167,394
1988	(128,438)	128,438
1989	(105,573)	105,573
1990	(94,657)	94,657
1991	(9,512)	9,512
1992	(62,582)	62,582
1993	(99,936)	99,936
1994	(148,399)	148,399
1995	(148,153)	148,153

Source: U.S. Department of Commerce

*The current and capital accounts offset
each other by definition.

U.S. Gross Federal Debt

Fiscal Year*	Federal Debt ($ billions)	Fiscal Year*	Federal Debt ($ billions)
1940	$51	1968	$370
1941	58	1969	367
1942	79	1970	383
1943	143	1971	410
1944	204	1972	436
1945	260	1973	466
1946	271	1974	484
1947	257	1975	542
1948	252	1976	629
1949	253	1977	706
1950	257	1978	777
1951	255	1979	829
1952	259	1980	909
1953	266	1981	995
1954	271	1982	1,137
1955	274	1983	1,372
1956	273	1984	1,565
1957	272	1985	1,818
1958	280	1986	2,121
1959	288	1987	2,346
1960	291	1988	2,601
1961	293	1989	2,868
1962	303	1990	3,207
1963	311	1991	3,598
1964	317	1992	4,002
1965	323	1993	4,351
1966	329	1994	4,644
1967	341	1995	4,962
		1996	5,153

Sources: U.S. Department of Commerce, Bureau of the Census, and U.S. Office of Management and Budget

*Through 1976, the fiscal year ends on June 30. From 1977 forward, the fiscal year ends on September 30.

Key Interest Rates

Quarter Ending	Discount Rate	Prime Rate
Mar-75	6.25%	7.93%
Jun-75	6.00	7.07
Sep-75	6.00	7.88
Dec-75	6.00	7.26
Mar-76	5.50	6.75
Jun-76	5.50	7.20
Sep-76	5.50	7.00
Dec-76	5.25	6.35
Mar-77	5.25	6.25
Jun-77	5.25	6.75
Sep-77	5.75	7.13
Dec-77	6.00	7.75
Mar-78	6.50	8.00
Jun-78	7.25	8.63
Sep-78	8.00	9.41
Dec-78	9.50	11.55
Mar-79	9.50	11.75
Jun-79	9.50	11.65
Sep-79	11.00	12.90
Dec-79	12.00	15.30
Mar-80	13.00	18.31
Jun-80	11.00	12.63
Sep-80	11.00	12.23
Dec-80	13.00	20.35
Mar-81	13.00	18.05
Jun-81	14.00	20.03
Sep-81	14.00	20.08
Dec-81	12.00	15.75
Mar-82	12.00	16.50
Jun-82	12.00	16.50

Quarter Ending	Discount Rate	Prime Rate
Sep-82	10.00%	13.50%
Dec-82	8.50	11.50
Mar-83	8.50	10.50
Jun-83	8.50	10.50
Sep-83	8.50	11.00
Dec-83	8.50	11.00
Mar-84	8.50	11.21
Jun-84	9.00	12.60
Sep-84	9.00	12.97
Dec-84	8.50	11.06
Mar-85	8.00	10.50
Jun-85	7.50	9.78
Sep-85	7.50	9.50
Dec-85	7.50	9.50
Mar-86	7.00	9.10
Jun-86	6.50	8.50
Sep-86	5.50	7.50
Dec-86	5.50	7.50
Mar-87	5.50	7.50
Jun-87	5.50	8.25
Sep-87	6.00	8.70
Dec-87	6.00	8.75
Mar-88	6.00	8.50
Jun-88	6.00	9.00
Sep-88	6.50	10.00
Dec-88	6.50	10.50
Mar-89	7.00	11.50
Jun-89	7.00	11.07
Sep-89	7.00	10.50
Dec-89	7.00	10.50

Source: *Federal Reserve Bulletin*

Quarter Ending	Discount Rate	Prime Rate
Mar-90	7.00%	10.00%
Jun-90	7.00	10.00
Sep-90	7.00	10.00
Dec-90	6.50	10.00
Mar-91	6.00	9.00
Jun-91	5.50	8.50
Sep-91	5.00	8.20
Dec-91	4.50	7.21
Mar-92	3.50	6.50
Jun-92	3.50	6.50
Sep-92	3.00	6.25
Dec-92	3.00	6.00
Mar-93	3.00	6.00
Jun-93	3.00	6.00
Sep-93	3.00	6.00
Dec-93	3.00	6.00
Mar-94	3.00	6.13
Jun-94	3.50	6.75
Sep-94	4.00	7.50
Dec-94	4.75	8.13
Mar-95	5.25	9.00
Jun-95	5.25	9.00
Sep-95	5.25	8.75
Dec-95	5.25	8.65
Mar-96	5.00	8.25
Jun-96	5.00	8.25

U.S. Trade Balance

($ millions)

Year	Trade Balance	Imports	Exports
1960	$4,546	$15,020	$19,566
1961	5,461	14,769	20,230
1962	4,637	16,385	21,022
1963	5,249	17,151	22,400
1964	7,013	18,598	25,611
1965	5,255	21,284	26,539
1966	3,736	25,617	29,353
1967	4,083	26,928	31,011
1968	1,000	33,092	34,092
1969	1,278	36,011	37,289
1970	2,793	39,936	42,729
1971	(1,923)	45,529	43,606
1972	(6,371)	55,585	49,214
1973	1,425	69,434	70,859
1974	(5,399)	103,394	97,995
1975	8,367	99,330	107,697
1976	(9,237)	124,458	115,221
1977	(30,318)	151,534	121,216
1978	(32,614)	176,074	143,460
1979	(28,676)	210,322	181,646
1980	(24,325)	245,009	220,684
1981	(27,533)	261,008	233,475
1982	(31,629)	243,953	212,324
1983	(57,490)	258,152	200,662
1984	(107,949)	325,590	217,641
1985	(132,894)	346,160	213,266
1986	(138,279)	365,437	227,158
1987	(152,119)	406,241	254,122
1988	(118,526)	440,952	322,426
1989	(109,399)	473,210	363,811
1990	(101,029)	494,841	393,812
1991	(66,250)	488,173	421,923
1992	(84,501)	532,664	448,163
1993	(115,568)	580,659	465,091
1994	(150,629)	663,255	512,626
1995	(158,703)	743,445	584,742

Source: U.S. Bureau of the Census

Money Supply, Annual Growth

Year Ending	M1 ($ billions)	Annual % growth	M2 ($ billions)	Annual % growth	M3 ($ billions)	Annual % growth
1960	$140.7	0.5%	$312.4	4.9%	$315.2	5.2%
1961	145.2	3.2	335.5	7.4	340.8	8.1
1962	147.8	1.8	362.7	8.1	371.3	8.9
1963	153.3	3.7	393.3	8.4	405.9	9.3
1964	160.3	4.6	424.8	8.0	442.4	9.0
1965	167.9	4.7	459.2	8.1	482.1	9.0
1966	172.0	2.4	480.2	4.6	505.4	4.8
1967	183.3	6.6	524.8	9.3	557.9	10.4
1968	197.4	7.7	566.9	8.0	607.2	8.8
1969	203.9	3.3	587.9	3.7	615.9	1.4
1970	214.4	5.1	626.6	6.6	677.2	10.0
1971	228.3	6.5	710.3	13.4	776.0	14.6
1972	249.2	9.2	802.3	13.0	886.0	14.2
1973	262.8	5.5	855.5	6.6	985.0	11.2
1974	274.3	4.4	902.5	5.5	1,070.1	8.6
1975	287.5	4.8	1,017.0	12.7	1,172.1	9.5
1976	306.3	6.5	1,152.7	13.3	1,311.9	11.9
1977	331.3	8.2	1,271.5	10.3	1,472.5	12.2
1978	358.4	8.2	1,368.0	7.6	1,646.8	11.8
1979	382.8	6.8	1,475.7	7.9	1,806.5	9.7
1980	408.8	6.8	1,601.0	8.5	1,992.2	10.3
1981	436.5	6.8	1,756.0	9.7	2,240.7	12.5
1982	474.5	8.7	1,910.9	8.8	2,442.3	9.0
1983	521.1	9.8	2,127.9	11.4	2,685.0	9.9
1984	552.1	5.9	2,324.6	9.2	2,979.7	11.0
1985	619.8	12.3	2,497.8	7.5	3,198.0	7.3
1986	724.4	16.9	2,734.6	9.5	3,486.4	9.0
1987	749.8	3.5	2,834.4	3.6	3,673.3	5.4
1988	786.9	4.9	2,997.9	5.8	3,912.4	6.5
1989	794.2	0.9	3,164.0	5.5	4,065.5	3.9
1990	825.8	4.0	3,290.4	4.0	4,124.1	1.4
1991	897.2	8.6	3,383.7	2.8	4,178.4	1.3
1992	1,024.4	14.2	3,438.7	1.6	4,187.3	0.2
1993	1,128.6	10.2	3,494.1	1.6	4,249.6	1.5
1994	1,148.7	1.8	3,509.4	0.4	4,319.1	1.6
1995	1,124.9	(2.1)	3,662.6	4.4	4,570.5	5.8

Source: U.S. Bureau of the Census

Consumer Price Index

Year	CPI	% Change Annual	Value of a 1950 $ in Future*	Value of a 1995 $ in Past*
1949	23.6			
1950	25.0	5.93%	$1.00	$6.15
1951	26.5	6.00	0.94	5.80
1952	26.7	0.75	0.94	5.76
1953	26.9	0.75	0.93	5.71
1954	26.8	0.37	0.93	5.74
1955	26.9	0.37	0.93	5.71
1956	27.6	2.60	0.91	5.57
1957	28.5	3.26	0.88	5.39
1958	29.0	1.75	0.86	5.30
1959	29.4	1.38	0.85	5.23
1960	29.8	1.36	0.84	5.16
1961	30.0	0.67	0.83	5.12
1962	30.4	1.33	0.82	5.06
1963	30.9	1.64	0.81	4.97
1964	31.3	1.29	0.80	4.91
1965	31.8	1.60	0.79	4.83
1966	32.9	3.46	0.76	4.67
1967	34.0	3.34	0.74	4.52
1968	35.6	4.71	0.70	4.32
1969	37.7	5.90	0.66	4.08
1970	39.8	5.57	0.63	3.86
1971	41.1	3.27	0.61	3.74
1972	42.5	3.41	0.59	3.62

Source: Bureau of Labor Statistics

Note: Seasonally adjusted, 1982–1984 = 100

*Based on annual changes in CPI.

Year	CPI	% Change Annual	Value of a 1950 $ in Future*	Value of a 1995 $ in Past*
1973	46.3	8.94%	$0.54	$3.32
1974	51.9	12.10	0.48	2.96
1975	55.6	7.13	0.45	2.76
1976	58.4	5.04	0.43	2.63
1977	62.3	6.68	0.40	2.47
1978	67.9	8.99	0.37	2.26
1979	76.9	13.25	0.33	2.00
1980	86.4	12.35	0.29	1.78
1981	94.1	8.91	0.27	1.63
1982	97.7	3.83	0.26	1.57
1983	101.4	3.79	0.25	1.52
1984	105.5	4.04	0.24	1.46
1985	109.5	3.79	0.23	1.40
1986	110.8	1.19	0.23	1.39
1987	115.7	4.42	0.22	1.33
1988	120.8	4.41	0.21	1.27
1989	126.4	4.64	0.20	1.22
1990	134.3	6.25	0.19	1.14
1991	138.3	2.98	0.18	1.11
1992	142.4	2.96	0.18	1.08
1993	146.3	2.74	0.17	1.05
1994	150.1	2.60	0.17	1.02
11/95	153.7	2.40	0.16	1.00

U.S. Stock Market Indices

Quarter Ending	S&P 500*	DJIA†	Nasdaq	Wilshire 5000	Russell 2000#
Mar-75	83.4	768.2	75.7	730.3	
Jun-75	95.2	879.0	87.0	840.2	
Sep-75	83.9	793.9	74.3	734.6	
Dec-75	90.2	858.7	77.6	784.2	
Mar-76	102.8	999.5	90.6	903.5	
Jun-76	104.3	1,002.8	90.3	914.8	
Sep-76	105.2	990.2	91.3	920.7	
Dec-76	107.5	1,004.7	97.9	954.2	
Mar-77	98.4	919.1	94.1	888.8	
Jun-77	100.5	916.3	99.7	919.2	
Sep-77	96.5	847.1	100.9	887.5	
Dec-77	95.1	831.2	105.1	887.6	
Mar-78	89.2	757.4	106.2	847.8	
Jun-78	95.5	819.0	120.3	917.9	
Sep-78	102.5	865.8	132.9	996.1	
Dec-78	96.1	805.0	118.0	922.8	40.5
Mar-79	101.6	862.2	131.8	997.6	46.9
Jun-79	102.9	842.0	138.1	1,028.3	49.6
Sep-79	109.3	878.6	150.0	1,101.8	54.7
Dec-79	107.9	838.7	151.1	1,100.7	55.9
Mar-80	102.1	785.8	131.0	1,026.0	48.3
Jun-80	114.2	867.9	157.8	1,165.1	57.5
Sep-80	125.5	932.4	187.8	1,300.9	69.9
Dec-80	135.8	964.0	202.3	1,404.6	74.8
Mar-81	136.0	1,003.9	210.2	1,415.0	80.3
Jun-81	131.3	976.9	215.8	1,391.4	82.6
Sep-81	116.2	850.0	180.0	1,208.4	67.6
Dec-81	122.6	875.0	195.8	1,286.2	73.7
Mar-82	111.9	822.8	175.7	1,153.7	66.2

Sources: Bloomberg Financial Markets, Datastream, Wilshire Associates Inc.

* Standard & Poor's 500 Index quarterly, Mar-75–Jun-96.
† Dow Jones Industrial Average quarterly, Mar-75–Jun-96.
# The Russell 2000 begins on Dec-78 and was developed with a base value of 135 as of Dec-86.

Quarter Ending	S&P 500*	DJIA†	Nasdaq	Wilshire 5000	Russell 2000#
Jun-82	109.6	811.9	171.3	1,125.1	64.7
Sep-82	120.4	896.3	187.7	1,235.8	70.8
Dec-82	140.6	1,046.6	232.4	1,451.6	88.9
Mar-83	153.0	1,130.0	270.8	1,600.1	103.8
Jun-83	168.1	1,222.0	318.7	1,791.7	124.2
Sep-83	166.1	1,233.1	296.7	1,757.9	117.4
Dec-83	164.9	1,258.6	278.6	1,723.6	112.3
Mar-84	159.2	1,164.9	250.8	1,634.0	104.1
Jun-84	153.2	1,132.4	239.7	1,571.3	100.3
Sep-84	166.1	1,206.7	249.9	1,698.1	105.2
Dec-84	167.2	1,211.6	247.4	1,702.0	101.5
Mar-85	180.7	1,266.8	279.2	1,859.8	114.9
Jun-85	191.9	1,335.5	296.2	1,977.8	118.4
Sep-85	182.1	1,328.6	280.3	1,871.2	112.7
Dec-85	211.3	1,546.7	324.9	2,164.7	129.9
Mar-86	238.9	1,818.6	374.7	2,455.2	147.6
Jun-86	250.8	1,892.7	405.5	2,577.7	154.2
Sep-86	231.3	1,767.6	350.7	2,360.5	134.7
Dec-86	242.2	1,896.0	348.8	2,434.9	135.0
Mar-87	291.7	2,304.7	430.1	2,929.7	166.8
Jun-87	304.0	2,418.5	424.7	3,004.9	164.8
Sep-87	321.8	2,596.3	444.3	3,171.0	170.8
Dec-87	247.1	1,938.8	330.5	2,417.1	120.4
Mar-88	258.9	1,988.1	374.6	2,584.0	142.2
Jun-88	273.5	2,141.7	394.7	2,729.6	151.3
Sep-88	271.9	2,112.7	387.7	2,706.7	149.1
Dec-88	277.7	2,168.6	381.4	2,738.4	147.4
Mar-89	294.9	2,293.6	406.7	2,915.1	157.9
Jun-89	318.0	2,440.1	435.3	3,137.0	167.4

(continued)

Quarter Ending	S&P 500*	DJIA†	Nasdaq	Wilshire 5000	Russell 2000#
Sep-89	349.2	2,692.8	472.9	3,426.7	178.2
Dec-89	353.4	2,753.2	454.8	3,419.9	168.3
Mar-90	339.9	2,707.2	435.5	3,273.5	163.6
Jun-90	358.0	2,880.7	462.3	3,424.4	169.1
Sep-90	306.1	2,452.5	344.5	2,879.0	126.7
Dec-90	330.2	2,633.7	373.8	3,101.4	132.2
Mar-91	375.2	2,913.9	482.3	3,583.7	171.0
Jun-91	371.2	2,906.8	475.9	3,545.5	167.6
Sep-91	387.9	3,016.8	526.9	3,744.0	180.2
Dec-91	417.1	3,168.8	586.3	4,014.1	189.9
Mar-92	403.7	3,235.5	603.8	3,961.6	203.7
Jun-92	408.1	3,318.5	563.6	3,930.3	188.6
Sep-92	417.8	3,271.7	583.3	4,024.4	192.9
Dec-92	435.7	3,301.1	677.0	3,289.7	221.0
Mar-93	451.7	3,435.1	690.1	4,444.3	229.2
Jun-93	450.5	3,516.1	704.0	4,449.6	233.4
Sep-93	458.9	3,555.1	762.8	4,601.8	253.0
Dec-93	466.5	3,754.1	776.8	4,657.8	258.6
Mar-94	445.8	3,636.0	743.5	4,457.7	251.1
Jun-94	444.3	3,625.0	706.0	4,395.2	240.3
Sep-94	462.7	3,843.2	764.3	4,605.8	256.1
Dec-94	459.3	3,834.4	752.0	4,540.6	250.4
Mar-95	500.7	4,157.7	817.2	4,920.4	260.8
Jun-95	544.8	4,556.1	933.5	5,348.8	283.6
Sep-95	584.4	4,789.1	1,043.5	5,806.6	310.4
Dec-95	615.9	5,117.1	1,052.1	6,057.2	316.0
Mar-96	645.5	5,587.1	1,101.4	6,365.9	330.8
Jun-96	670.6	5,654.6	1,185.0	6,612.8	346.6

Sources: Bloomberg Financial Markets, Datastream, Wilshire Associates Inc.

* Standard & Poor's 500 Index quarterly, Mar-75–Jun-96.
† Dow Jones Industrial Average quarterly, Mar-75–Jun-96.
# The Russell 2000 begins on Dec-78 and was developed with a base value of 135 as of Dec-86.

Employment and Unemployment by Country: 1980 to 1994

	U.S.	Australia	Canada	France	Germany	Italy	Japan	Netherlands	Sweden	U.K.
Civilian Labor Force (millions):										
1980	106.9	6.7	12.0	22.9	27.3	21.1	55.7	5.9	4.3	26.5
1985	115.5	7.3	13.1	23.6	28.0	21.8	58.8	6.2	4.4	27.2
1990	125.8	8.4	14.3	24.3	29.4	22.7	63.0	6.8	4.6	28.5
1992	128.1	8.6	14.5	24.6	30.0	22.9	65.0	7.0	4.5	28.4
1993	129.2	8.6	14.7	24.7	30.0	22.8	65.5	7.1	4.4	28.3
1994	131.1	8.8	14.8	25.0	29.8	22.6	65.8	7.3	4.4	28.3
Labor Force Participation Rate (percentage):*										
1980	63.8	62.1	64.6	57.5	54.7	48.2	62.6	55.4	66.9	62.5
1985	64.8	61.6	65.8	56.8	54.7	47.2	62.3	55.5	66.9	62.1
1990	66.5	64.6	67.3	55.6	55.3	47.2	62.6	56.8	67.4	63.7
1992	66.4	63.9	65.9	55.9	55.1	47.5	63.4	57.9	65.7	62.9
1993	66.3	63.6	65.5	55.7	54.2	48.1	63.3	58.4	64.5	62.8
1994	66.6	63.9	65.3	56.0	53.7	47.5	63.1	59.6	63.9	62.6
Civilian Employment (millions):										
1980	99.3	6.3	11.1	21.4	26.5	20.2	54.6	5.5	4.2	24.7
1985	107.2	6.7	11.7	21.2	26.0	20.5	57.3	5.6	4.3	24.2
1 990	118.8	7.9	13.2	22.1	28.0	21.1	61.7	6.3	4.5	26.6
1992	118.5	7.6	12.8	22.0	28.7	21.2	63.6	6.5	4.3	25.5
1993	120.3	7.7	13.0	21.8	28.2	20.4	63.8	6.5	4.0	25.3
1994	123.1	7.9	13.3	21.8	27.9	20.1	63.9	6.6	4.0	25.6
Employment/Population Ratio (percentage):										
1980	59.2	58.3	59.7	53.8	53.1	46.1	61.3	52.1	65.6	58.1
1985	60.1	56.5	58.9	50.9	50.7	44.4	60.6	50.1	65.0	55.1
1990	62.8	60.1	61.9	50.5	52.6	43.9	61.3	52.5	66.1	59.2
1992	61.5	57.0	58.4	50.0	52.6	44.0	62.0	53.8	62.0	56.5
1993	61.7	56.6	58.2	49.1	51.1	43.1	61.7	53.2	58.5	56.2
1994	62.5	57.7	58.5	48.9	50.2	42.1	61.3	53.8	57.7	56.5
Unemployment Rate (percentage):										
1980	7.1	6.1	7.5	6.5	2.8	4.4	2.0	6.0	2.0	7.0
1985	7.2	8.3	10.5	10.5	7.2	6.0	2.6	9.6	2.8	11.2
1990	5.6	6.9	8.1	9.1	5.0	7.0	2.1	7.5	1.8	7.0
1992	7.5	10.8	11.3	10.5	4.6	7.3	2.2	7.2	5.6	10.1
1993	6.9	10.9	11.2	11.9	5.7	10.2	2.5	8.8	9.3	10.5
1994	6.1	9.7	10.4	12.7	6.5	11.3	2.9	9.6	9.6	9.6
Under 25	12.5	17.3	16.5	27.8	n.a.	32.4	5.5	n.a.	23.0	16.2
Teenagers	17.6	23.0	18.9	26.4	n.a.	37.0	7.7	n.a.	25.0	18.6
20 to 24	9.7	13.8	15.0	28.0	n.a.	30.8	5.0	n.a.	22.4	14.9
25 yrs. old	4.8	7.6	9.2	10.9	n.a.	7.8	2.5	n.a.	7.8	8.3

Source: U.S. Bureau of Labor Statistics

*Civilian labor force as a percentage of the civilian working-age population.

Compensation Costs by Country: 1980 to 1994

Hourly Costs for Production Workers, Indexed (United States = 100)

Area or Country	1980	1990	1991	1992	1993	1994
United States	100	100	100	100	100	100
Total	67	83	86	88	86	88
OECD*	77	94	97	99	96	99
Europe	102	118	117	123	112	115
Asian newly-industrializing economies	12	25	28	30	31	34
Canada	88	106	110	105	98	92
Mexico	22	11	12	14	15	15
Australia	86	88	87	81	75	80
Hong Kong	15	21	23	24	26	28
Israel	38	57	56	56	53	53
Japan	56	86	94	101	114	125
Korea, South	10	25	30	32	33	37
New Zealand	54	56	54	49	48	52
Singapore	15	25	28	31	31	37
Sri Lanka	2	2	3	2	3	n.a.
Taiwan	10	26	28	32	31	32
Austria	90	119	116	126	122	127
Belgium	133	129	127	138	129	134
Denmark	110	120	117	124	114	120
Finland	83	141	136	123	99	110
France	91	102	98	105	97	100
Germany	125	147	146	157	154	160
Greece	38	45	44	46	41	n.a.
Ireland	60	79	78	83	73	n.a.
Italy	83	119	119	121	96	95
Luxembourg	121	110	108	117	111	n.a.
Netherlands	122	123	117	126	119	122
Norway	117	144	139	143	121	122
Portugal	21	25	27	32	27	27
Spain	60	76	78	83	69	67
Sweden	127	140	142	152	106	110
Switzerland	112	140	139	144	135	145
United Kingdom	77	85	88	89	76	86

Source: U.S. Bureau of Labor Statistics

Note: Compensation costs include all pay made directly to the worker—pay for time worked and not worked (e.g., leave, except sick leave), other direct pay, employer expenditures for legally required insurance programs and contractual and private benefit plans, and for some countries, other labor taxes.

*Canada, Mexico, Australia, Japan, New Zealand, and the European countries.

U.S. Median Money Income of Households by State: 1985, 1990, 1995

(Current $)

	1995		1990		1985	
	Median Income	Rank	Median Income	Rank	Median Income	Rank
United States	3		$29,943		$23,618	
Alabama	25,991	48	23,357	46	18,333	45
Alaska	47,954	1	39,298	2	34,782	1
Arizona	30,863	35	29,224	26	23,877	18
Arkansas	25,814	50	22,786	47	17,451	48
California	37,009	12	33,290	9	26,981	9
Colorado	40,706	6	30,733	18	28,182	8
Connecticut	40,243	7	38,870	4	31,090	2
Delaware	34,928	22	30,804	17	22,980	24
District of Columbia	30,748	36	27,392	33	21,076	37
Florida	29,745	39	26,685	37	21,343	33
Georgia	34,099	25	27,561	30	21,049	38
Hawaii	42,851	3	38,921	3	28,961	5
Idaho	32,676	31	25,305	39	20,761	40
Illinois	38,071	10	32,542	10	24,870	14
Indiana	33,385	28	26,928	36	22,675	27
Iowa	35,519	19	27,288	35	20,927	39
Kansas	30,341	37	29,917	23	22,788	26
Kentucky	29,810	38	24,780	42	17,361	49
Louisiana	27,949	44	22,405	49	21,179	36
Maine	33,858	26	27,464	32	20,519	41
Maryland	41,041	4	38,857	5	30,136	4
Massachusetts	38,574	9	36,247	7	28,207	7
Michigan	36,426	14	29,937	22	24,242	16
Minnesota	37,933	11	31,465	15	23,856	19
Mississippi	26,538	46	20,178	51	16,413	50
Missouri	34,825	23	27,332	34	21,939	29
Montana	27,757	45	23,375	45	20,236	43
Nebraska	32,929	30	27,482	31	21,799	31
Nevada	36,084	17	32,023	12	23,274	22
New Hampshire	39,171	8	40,805	1	26,403	10
New Jersey	43,924	2	38,734	6	30,980	3
New Mexico	25,991	49	25,039	41	20,423	42
New York	33,028	29	31,591	14	23,639	21
North Carolina	31,979	33	26,329	38	21,451	32
North Dakota	29,089	41	25,264	40	21,205	34
Ohio	34,941	21	30,013	21	25,174	13
Oklahoma	26,311	47	24,384	44	21,205	35
Oregon	36,374	15	29,281	25	21,894	30
Pennsylvania	34,524	24	29,005	27	22,877	25
Rhode Island	35,359	20	31,968	13	24,625	15
South Carolina	29,071	42	28,735	28	20,036	44
South Dakota	29,578	40	24,571	43	18,142	46
Tennessee	29,015	43	22,592	48	17,778	47
Texas	32,039	32	28,228	29	23,743	20
Utah	36,480	13	30,142	20	25,238	12
Vermont	33,824	27	31,098	16	26,000	11
Virginia	36,222	16	35,073	8	28,429	6
Washington	35,568	18	32,112	11	24,000	17
West Virginia	24,880	51	22,137	50	15,983	51
Wisconsin	40,955	5	30,711	19	23,246	23
Wyoming	31,529	34	29,460	24	22,081	28

Source: U.S. Bureau of the Census

U.S. Mean Income and Share of Aggregate Income Received by Each Fifth and Top 5% of Households

(Current $)

	Lowest Fifth		Second Fifth		Third Fifth	
Year	Mean Income	Share of Income	Mean Income	Share of Income	Mean Income	Share of Income
1995	$8,350	3.7%	$20,397	9.1%	$34,106	15.2%
1994	7,762	3.6	19,224	8.9	32,385	15.0
1993	7,412	3.6	18,656	9.0	31,272	15.1
1992	7,288	3.8	18,181	9.4	30,631	15.8
1991	7,263	3.8	18,149	9.6	30,147	15.9
1990	7,195	3.9	18,030	9.6	29,781	15.9
1989	7,021	3.8	17,401	9.5	28,925	15.8
1988	6,504	3.8	16,317	9.6	27,291	16.0
1987	6,167	3.8	15,584	9.6	26,055	16.1
1986	5,944	3.9	14,961	9.7	24,979	16.2
1985	5,797	4.0	14,330	9.7	23,735	16.3
1984	5,606	4.1	13,634	9.9	22,547	16.4
1983	5,239	4.1	12,796	10.0	21,105	16.5
1982	5,003	4.1	12,238	10.1	20,195	16.6
1981	4,836	4.2	11,589	10.2	19,141	16.8
1980	4,483	4.3	10,819	10.3	17,807	16.9
1979	4,114	4.2	10,021	10.3	16,495	16.9
1978	3,807	4.3	9,112	10.3	15,010	16.9
1977	3,513	4.4	8,291	10.3	13,671	17.0
1976	3,278	4.4	7,780	10.4	12,762	17.1
1975	3,034	4.4	7,204	10.5	11,787	17.1
1974	2,911	4.4	6,973	10.6	11,206	17.1
1973	2,568	4.2	6,366	10.5	10,402	17.1
1972	2,316	4.1	5,898	10.5	9,625	17.1
1971	2,126	4.1	5,529	10.6	8,965	17.3
1970	2,029	4.1	5,395	10.8	8,688	17.4
1969	1,957	4.1	5,216	10.9	8,335	17.5
1968	1,832	4.2	4,842	11.1	7,679	17.5
1967	1,626	4.0	4,433	10.8	7,078	17.3

Sources: U.S. Bureau of the Census, U.S. Department of Commerce

Example: In 1995, those households with an income in the lowest fifth percentile in the U.S. had a mean income of $8,350 and earned 3.7% of total U.S. income. Those households in the highest fifth percentile had a mean income of $109,411 and earned 48.7% of total U.S. income.

Fourth Fifth		Highest Fifth		Top 5 Percent	
Mean Income	Share of Income	Mean Income	Share of Income	Mean Income	Share of Income
$52,429	23.3%	$109,411	48.7%	$188,828	21.0%
50,395	23.4	105,945	49.1	183,044	21.2
48,599	23.5	101,253	48.9	173,784	21.0
47,021	24.2	91,110	46.9	144,608	18.6
45,957	24.2	88,130	46.5	137,532	18.1
44,901	24.0	87,137	46.6	138,756	18.6
43,753	24.0	85,529	46.8	138,185	18.9
41,254	24.3	78,759	46.3	124,215	18.3
39,383	24.3	74,897	46.2	118,000	18.2
37,622	24.5	70,340	45.7	107,444	17.5
35,694	24.6	65,841	45.3	98,946	17.0
33,944	24.7	61,648	44.9	90,629	16.5
31,667	24.7	57,303	44.7	83,943	16.4
30,026	24.7	54,164	44.5	78,945	16.2
28,512	25.0	49,942	43.8	71,095	15.6
26,219	24.9	46,053	43.7	66,617	15.8
24,193	24.7	42,990	44.0	64,197	16.4
21,980	24.8	38,791	43.7	57,625	16.2
20,018	24.8	35,091	43.6	51,792	16.1
18,521	24.8	32,320	43.3	47,805	16.0
17,117	24.8	29,809	43.2	43,940	15.9
16,181	24.7	28,259	43.1	41,669	15.9
14,954	24.6	26,521	43.6	40,417	16.6
13,817	24.5	24,806	43.9	38,447	17.0
12,745	24.5	22,583	43.5	34,637	16.7
12,247	24.5	21,684	43.3	33,283	16.6
11,674	24.5	20,520	43.0	31,586	16.6
10,713	24.4	18,762	42.8	29,048	16.6
9,903	24.2	17,946	43.8	28,605	17.5

Economic Indicators

	Coincident Indicator Index*	Annual % Change	Industrial Production Index*	Annual % Change	Leading Indicator Index*	Annual % Change	Lagging Indicator Index*	Annual % Change
1948	33.2		23.6		69.9		51.4	
1949	32.3	(2.7)%	22.3	(5.5)%	71.9	2.9%	53.8	4.7%
1950	34.7	7.4	25.8	15.7	76.9	7.0	55.2	2.6
1951	36.9	6.3	28.0	8.5	72.8	(5.3)	61.6	11.6
1952	38.1	3.3	29.1	3.9	75.0	3.0	65.4	6.2
1953	39.9	4.7	31.6	8.6	71.2	(5.1)	69.6	6.4
1954	38.9	(2.5)	29.9	(5.4)	76.0	6.7	68.0	(2.3)
1955	41.4	6.4	33.7	12.7	78.6	3.4	68.8	1.2
1956	43.0	3.9	35.1	4.2	77.2	(1.8)	75.7	10.0
1957	43.5	1.2	35.6	1.4	73.2	(5.2)	78.3	3.4
1958	42.2	(3.0)	33.3	(6.5)	77.8	6.3	76.2	(2.7)
1959	44.8	6.2	37.3	12.0	78.8	1.3	77.7	2.0
1960	45.7	2.0	38.1	2.1	77.0	(2.3)	80.2	3.2
1961	46.0	0.7	38.4	0.8	80.9	5.1	78.7	(1.9)
1962	48.2	4.8	41.6	8.3	81.4	0.6	79.4	0.9
1963	49.8	3.3	44.0	5.8	83.3	2.3	80.5	1.4
1964	52.2	4.8	47.0	6.8	86.2	3.5	81.9	1.7
1965	55.3	5.9	51.7	10.0	88.2	2.3	84.0	2.6
1966	58.5	5.8	56.3	8.9	85.7	(2.8)	88.2	5.0
1967	60.3	3.1	57.5	2.1	88.2	2.9	89.9	1.9
1968	62.9	4.3	60.7	5.6	89.7	1.7	91.2	1.4
1969	65.4	4.0	63.5	4.6	87.4	(2.6)	94.4	3.5
1970	65.4	0.0	61.4	(3.3)	85.7	(1.9)	95.2	0.8
1971	66.3	1.4	62.2	1.3	89.8	4.8	91.7	(3.7)
1972	70.1	5.7	68.3	9.8	93.9	4.6	89.9	(2.0)

Source: *Survey of Current Business*, U.S. Dept of Commerce

*1987 = 100.

	Coincident Indicator Index*	Annual % Change	Industrial Production Index*	Annual % Change	Leading Indicator Index*	Annual % Change	Lagging Indicator Index*	Annual % Change
1973	74.0	5.6%	73.8	8.1%	91.9	(2.1)%	93.7	4.2%
1974	74.2	0.3	72.7	(1.5)	82.0	(10.8)	98.0	4.6
1975	71.5	(3.6)	66.3	(8.8)	88.2	7.6	93.7	(4.4)
1976	75.1	5.0	72.4	9.2	91.8	4.1	90.0	(3.9)
1977	78.8	4.9	78.2	8.0	92.9	1.2	91.0	1.1
1978	83.2	5.6	82.6	5.6	93.6	0.8	94.2	3.5
1979	86.0	3.4	85.7	3.8	90.0	(3.8)	98.2	4.2
1980	85.6	(0.5)	84.1	(1.9)	90.1	0.1	99.0	0.8
1981	86.8	1.4	85.7	1.9	86.6	(3.9)	97.2	(1.8)
1982	84.9	(2.2)	81.9	(4.4)	89.0	2.8	95.5	(1.7)
1983	86.5	1.9	84.9	3.7	95.8	7.6	91.3	(4.4)
1984	92.2	6.6	92.8	9.3	94.2	(1.7)	95.8	4.9
1985	95.0	3.0	94.4	1.7	96.4	2.3	98.9	3.2
1986	97.2	2.3	95.3	1.0	99.2	2.9	100.2	1.3
1987	100.0	2.9	100.0	4.9	99.6	0.4	100.0	(0.2)
1988	103.5	3.5	104.4	4.4	100.5	0.9	102.1	2.1
1989	105.8	2.2	106.0	1.5	99.4	(1.1)	104.6	2.4
1990	106.7	0.9	106.0	0.0	96.5	(2.9)	104.8	0.2
1991	105.3	(1.3)	104.2	(1.7)	97.2	0.7	102.1	(2.6)
1992	106.9	1.5	107.7	3.4	99.2	2.1	97.2	(4.8)
1993	109.7	2.6	111.5	3.5	100.3	1.1	96.4	(0.8)
1994	114.2	4.1	118.1	5.9	102.6	2.3	97.4	1.0
1995	n.a.		121.9		100.9		n.a.	

Compound Interest: Present Value

The formula is:

$$PV = \frac{FV}{(1+i)^n}$$

Interest Rate (i)	Number of Years (n)										
	1	2	3	4	5	6	7	8	9	10	11
1%	$990	$980	$971	$961	$951	$942	$933	$923	$914	$905	$896
2%	980	961	942	924	906	888	871	853	837	820	804
3%	971	943	915	888	863	837	813	789	766	744	722
4%	962	925	889	855	822	790	760	731	703	676	650
5%	952	907	864	823	784	746	711	677	645	614	585
6%	943	890	840	792	747	705	665	627	592	558	527
7%	935	873	816	763	713	666	623	582	544	508	475
8%	926	857	794	735	681	630	583	540	500	463	429
9%	917	842	772	708	650	596	547	502	460	422	388
10%	909	826	751	683	621	564	513	467	424	386	350
11%	901	812	731	659	593	535	482	434	391	352	317
12%	893	797	712	636	567	507	452	404	361	322	287
13%	885	783	693	613	543	480	425	376	333	295	261
14%	877	769	675	592	519	456	400	351	308	270	237
15%	870	756	658	572	497	432	376	327	284	247	215
16%	862	743	641	552	476	410	354	305	263	227	195
17%	855	731	624	534	456	390	333	285	243	208	178
18%	847	718	609	516	437	370	314	266	225	191	162
19%	840	706	593	499	419	352	296	249	209	176	148
20%	833	695	579	482	402	335	279	233	194	162	135
21%	826	683	564	467	385	319	263	218	180	149	123
22%	820	672	551	451	370	303	249	204	167	137	112
23%	813	661	537	437	355	289	235	191	155	126	103
24%	806	650	524	423	341	275	222	179	144	116	94
25%	800	640	512	410	328	262	210	168	134	107	86
26%	794	630	500	397	315	250	198	157	125	99	79
27%	787	620	488	384	303	238	188	148	116	92	72
28%	781	610	477	373	291	227	178	139	108	85	66
29%	775	601	466	361	280	217	168	130	101	78	61
30%	769	592	455	350	269	207	159	123	94	73	56

Note: Assumes $1,000 future value and annual compounding. For other future values, use table values as multiple factors divided by 1,000.

Example: If you were receiving $1,000 in 20 years, assuming a 6% compounding interest rate, the present value of your future cash receipt would be $312. If you were receiving $500, the present value would be $156 ($500 x 0.312).

					Number of Years (n)							
12	**13**	**14**	**15**	**16**	**17**	**18**	**19**	**20**	**25**	**30**	**50**	**100**
$887	$879	$870	$861	$853	$844	$836	$828	$820	$780	$742	$608	$370
788	773	758	743	728	714	700	686	673	610	552	372	138
701	681	661	642	623	605	587	570	554	478	412	228	52
625	601	577	555	534	513	494	475	456	375	308	141	20
557	530	505	481	458	436	416	396	377	295	231	87	8
497	469	442	417	394	371	350	331	312	233	174	54	3
444	415	388	362	339	317	296	277	258	184	131	34	1
397	368	340	315	292	270	250	232	215	146	99	21	.45
356	326	299	275	252	231	212	194	178	116	75	13	.18
319	290	263	239	218	198	180	164	149	92	57	9	.07
286	258	232	209	188	170	153	138	124	74	44	5	.03
257	229	205	183	163	146	130	116	104	59	33	3	.01
231	204	181	160	142	125	111	98	87	47	26	2	.00
208	182	160	140	123	108	95	83	73	38	20	1	.00
187	163	141	123	107	93	81	70	61	30	15	.92	.00
168	145	125	108	93	80	69	60	51	24	12	.60	.00
152	130	111	95	82	69	59	51	43	20	9	.39	.00
137	116	99	84	71	60	51	43	37	16	7	.25	.00
124	104	88	74	62	52	44	37	31	13	5	.17	.00
112	93	78	65	54	45	37	31	26	10	4	.11	.00
102	84	69	58	47	39	32	27	22	9	3	.07	.00
92	75	62	51	42	34	28	23	19	7	3	.05	.00
83	68	55	45	36	30	24	20	16	6	2	.03	.00
76	61	49	40	32	26	21	17	14	5	2	.02	.00
69	55	44	35	28	23	18	14	12	4	1	.01	.00
62	50	39	31	25	20	16	12	10	3	.97	.01	.00
57	45	35	28	22	17	14	11	8	3	.77	.01	.00
52	40	32	25	19	15	12	9	7	2	.61	.00	.00
47	37	28	22	17	13	10	8	6	2	.48	.00	.00
43	33	25	20	15	12	9	7	5	1	.38	.00	.00

Compound Interest: Future Value

The formula is:

$$FV = PV(1+i)^n$$

Interest	Number of Years (n)										
Rate (i)	1	2	3	4	5	6	7	8	9	10	11
1%	$1,010	$1,020	$1,030	$1,041	$1,051	$1,062	$1,072	$1,083	$1,094	$1,105	$1,116
2%	1,020	1,040	1,061	1,082	1,104	1,126	1,149	1,172	1,195	1,219	1,243
3%	1,030	1,061	1,093	1,126	1,159	1,194	1,230	1,267	1,305	1,344	1,384
4%	1,040	1,082	1,125	1,170	1,217	1,265	1,316	1,369	1,423	1,480	1,539
5%	1,050	1,103	1,158	1,216	1,276	1,340	1,407	1,477	1,551	1,629	1,710
6%	1,060	1,124	1,191	1,262	1,338	1,419	1,504	1,594	1,689	1,791	1,898
7%	1,070	1,145	1,225	1,311	1,403	1,501	1,606	1,718	1,838	1,967	2,105
8%	1,080	1,166	1,260	1,360	1,469	1,587	1,714	1,851	1,999	2,159	2,332
9%	1,090	1,188	1,295	1,412	1,539	1,677	1,828	1,993	2,172	2,367	2,580
10%	1,100	1,210	1,331	1,464	1,611	1,772	1,949	2,144	2,358	2,594	2,853
11%	1,110	1,232	1,368	1,518	1,685	1,870	2,076	2,305	2,558	2,839	3,152
12%	1,120	1,254	1,405	1,574	1,762	1,974	2,211	2,476	2,773	3,106	3,479
13%	1,130	1,277	1,443	1,630	1,842	2,082	2,353	2,658	3,004	3,395	3,836
14%	1,140	1,300	1,482	1,689	1,925	2,195	2,502	2,853	3,252	3,707	4,226
15%	1,150	1,323	1,521	1,749	2,011	2,313	2,660	3,059	3,518	4,046	4,652
16%	1,160	1,346	1,561	1,811	2,100	2,436	2,826	3,278	3,803	4,411	5,117
17%	1,170	1,369	1,602	1,874	2,192	2,565	3,001	3,511	4,108	4,807	5,624
18%	1,180	1,392	1,643	1,939	2,288	2,700	3,185	3,759	4,435	5,234	6,176
19%	1,190	1,416	1,685	2,005	2,386	2,840	3,379	4,021	4,785	5,695	6,777
20%	1,200	1,440	1,728	2,074	2,488	2,986	3,583	4,300	5,160	6,192	7,430
21%	1,210	1,464	1,772	2,144	2,594	3,138	3,797	4,595	5,560	6,727	8,140
22%	1,220	1,488	1,816	2,215	2,703	3,297	4,023	4,908	5,987	7,305	8,912
23%	1,230	1,513	1,861	2,289	2,815	3,463	4,259	5,239	6,444	7,926	9,749
24%	1,240	1,538	1,907	2,364	2,932	3,635	4,508	5,590	6,931	8,594	10,657
25%	1,250	1,563	1,953	2,441	3,052	3,815	4,768	5,960	7,451	9,313	11,642
26%	1,260	1,588	2,000	2,520	3,176	4,002	5,042	6,353	8,005	10,086	12,708
27%	1,270	1,613	2,048	2,601	3,304	4,196	5,329	6,768	8,595	10,915	13,862
28%	1,280	1,638	2,097	2,684	3,436	4,398	5,629	7,206	9,223	11,806	15,112
29%	1,290	1,664	2,147	2,769	3,572	4,608	5,945	7,669	9,893	12,761	16,462
30%	1,300	1,690	2,197	2,856	3,713	4,827	6,275	8,157	10,604	13,786	17,922

Note: Assumes $1,000 present value and annual compounding. For other present values, use table values as multiple factors, divided by 1,000.

Example: If you were to deposit $1,000 in a savings account with a 6% interest rate, compounding annually, at the end of 5 years, you would have $1,338. If your original deposit amount was $500, your end amount would be $669 ($500 x 1,338).

					Number of Years (n)						
12	13	14	15	16	17	18	19	20	25	30	50
$1,127	$1,138	$1,149	$1,161	$1,173	$1,184	$1,196	$1,208	$1,220	$1,282	$1,348	$1,645
1,268	1,294	1,319	1,346	1,373	1,400	1,428	1,457	1,486	1,641	1,811	2,692
1,426	1,469	1,513	1,558	1,605	1,653	1,702	1,754	1,806	2,094	2,427	4,384
1,601	1,665	1,732	1,801	1,873	1,948	2,026	2,107	2,191	2,666	3,243	7,107
1,796	1,886	1,980	2,079	2,183	2,292	2,407	2,527	2,653	3,386	4,322	11,467
2,012	2,133	2,261	2,397	2,540	2,693	2,854	3,026	3,207	4,292	5,743	18,420
2,252	2,410	2,579	2,759	2,952	3,159	3,380	3,617	3,870	5,427	7,612	29,457
2,518	2,720	2,937	3,172	3,426	3,700	3,996	4,316	4,661	6,848	10,063	46,902
2,813	3,066	3,342	3,642	3,970	4,328	4,717	5,142	5,604	8,623	13,268	74,358
3,138	3,452	3,797	4,177	4,595	5,054	5,560	6,116	6,727	10,835	17,449	117,391
3,498	3,883	4,310	4,785	5,311	5,895	6,544	7,263	8,062	13,585	22,892	184,565
3,896	4,363	4,887	5,474	6,130	6,866	7,690	8,613	9,646	17,000	29,960	289,002
4,335	4,898	5,535	6,254	7,067	7,986	9,024	10,197	11,523	21,231	39,116	450,736
4,818	5,492	6,261	7,138	8,137	9,276	10,575	12,056	13,743	26,462	50,950	700,233
5,350	6,153	7,076	8,137	9,358	10,761	12,375	14,232	16,367	32,919	66,212	1,083,657
5,936	6,886	7,988	9,266	10,748	12,468	14,463	16,777	19,461	40,874	85,850	1,670,704
6,580	7,699	9,007	10,539	12,330	14,426	16,879	19,748	23,106	50,658	111,065	2,566,215
7,288	8,599	10,147	11,974	14,129	16,672	19,673	23,214	27,393	62,669	143,371	3,927,357
8,064	9,596	11,420	13,590	16,172	19,244	22,901	27,252	32,429	77,388	184,675	5,988,914
8,916	10,699	12,839	15,407	18,488	22,186	26,623	31,948	38,338	95,396	237,376	9,100,438
9,850	11,918	14,421	17,449	21,114	25,548	30,913	37,404	45,259	117,391	304,482	13,780,612
10,872	13,264	16,182	19,742	24,086	29,384	35,849	43,736	53,358	144,210	389,758	20,796,561
11,991	14,749	18,141	22,314	27,446	33,759	41,523	51,074	62,821	176,859	497,913	31,279,195
13,215	16,386	20,319	25,196	31,243	38,741	48,039	59,568	73,864	216,542	634,820	46,890,435
14,552	18,190	22,737	28,422	35,527	44,409	55,511	69,389	86,736	264,698	807,794	70,064,923
16,012	20,175	25,421	32,030	40,358	50,851	64,072	80,731	101,721	323,045	1,025,927	104,358,362
17,605	22,359	28,396	36,062	45,799	58,165	73,870	93,815	119,145	393,634	1,300,504	154,948,026
19,343	24,759	31,691	40,565	51,923	66,461	85,071	108,890	139,380	478,905	1,645,505	229,349,862
21,236	27,395	35,339	45,587	58,808	75,862	97,862	126,242	162,852	581,759	2,078,219	338,442,984
23,298	30,288	39,374	51,186	66,542	86,504	112,455	146,192	190,050	705,641	2,619,996	497,929,223

Foreign Exchange Rates

Foreign Currency per U.S. Dollar

Quarter Ending	Japanese Yen	British Pound	German D-Mark	French Franc
Mar-75	294.0	0.417	2.35	4.21
Jun-75	295.7	0.455	2.35	4.04
Sep-75	302.9	0.489	2.65	4.50
Dec-75	305.2	0.494	2.62	4.50
Mar-76	299.6	0.522	2.54	4.70
Jun-76	297.9	0.560	2.58	4.74
Sep-76	286.9	0.602	2.44	4.90
Dec-76	293.1	0.588	2.36	5.00
Mar-77	277.6	0.581	2.39	5.00
Jun-77	267.6	0.581	2.34	4.90
Sep-77	263.7	0.572	2.31	4.90
Dec-77	240.0	0.522	2.10	4.70
Mar-78	229.9	0.538	2.00	4.55
Jun-78	203.7	0.538	2.07	4.51
Sep-78	189.2	0.505	1.94	4.33
Dec-78	194.3	0.490	1.82	4.17
Mar-79	209.6	0.485	1.87	4.30
Jun-79	217.8	0.459	1.74	4.27
Sep-79	224.5	0.454	1.74	4.10
Dec-79	240.3	0.451	1.73	4.02
Mar-80	245.0	0.463	1.95	4.50
Jun-80	219.9	0.424	1.76	4.09
Sep-80	210.9	0.419	1.81	4.20
Dec-80	203.1	0.419	1.97	4.54
Mar-81	211.3	0.448	2.11	5.00
Jun-81	226.8	0.518	2.39	5.72
Sep-81	232.3	0.556	2.32	5.56
Dec-81	219.8	0.522	2.24	5.69
Mar-82	248.2	0.561	2.41	6.28
Jun-82	255.0	0.576	2.45	6.83

Source: Bloomberg Financial Markets

U.S. Dollar per Foreign Currency

Quarter Ending	Japanese Yen	British Pound	German D-Mark	French Franc
Mar-75	0.0034	2.40	0.426	0.238
Jun-75	0.0034	2.20	0.425	0.248
Sep-75	0.0033	2.04	0.377	0.222
Dec-75	0.0033	2.02	0.382	0.222
Mar-76	0.0033	1.92	0.394	0.213
Jun-76	0.0034	1.79	0.388	0.211
Sep-76	0.0035	1.66	0.410	0.204
Dec-76	0.0034	1.70	0.735	0.200
Mar-77	0.0036	1.72	0.418	0.200
Jun-77	0.0037	1.72	0.427	0.204
Sep-77	0.0038	1.75	0.433	0.204
Dec-77	0.0042	1.92	0.477	0.213
Mar-78	0.0043	1.86	0.500	0.220
Jun-78	0.0049	1.86	0.483	0.222
Sep-78	0.0053	1.98	0.515	0.231
Dec-78	0.0051	2.04	0.549	0.240
Mar-79	0.0048	2.06	0.535	0.233
Jun-79	0.0046	2.18	0.575	0.234
Sep-79	0.0045	2.20	0.575	0.244
Dec-79	0.0042	2.22	0.578	0.249
Mar-80	0.0041	2.16	0.513	0.222
Jun-80	0.0045	2.36	0.568	0.244
Sep-80	0.0047	2.39	0.552	0.238
Dec-80	0.0049	2.39	0.508	0.220
Mar-81	0.0047	2.23	0.474	0.200
Jun-81	0.0044	1.93	0.418	0.175
Sep-81	0.0043	1.80	0.431	0.180
Dec-81	0.0045	1.92	0.446	0.176
Mar-82	0.0040	1.78	0.415	0.159
Jun-82	0.0039	1.74	0.408	0.146

(continued)

Foreign Currency per U.S. Dollar

Quarter Ending	Japanese Yen	British Pound	German D-Mark	French Franc
Sep-82	268.3	0.590	2.52	7.14
Dec-82	234.7	0.618	2.38	6.74
Mar-83	239.0	0.675	2.43	7.28
Jun-83	239.3	0.652	2.54	7.63
Sep-83	235.7	0.667	2.63	8.00
Dec-83	231.7	0.690	2.73	8.34
Mar-84	224.8	0.695	2.60	7.99
Jun-84	237.3	0.736	2.78	8.54
Sep-84	246.9	0.810	3.07	9.42
Dec-84	261.6	0.864	3.16	9.65
Mar-85	261.0	0.809	3.08	9.41
Jun-85	248.4	0.763	3.03	9.25
Sep-85	216.5	0.709	2.68	8.17
Dec-85	200.3	0.690	2.45	7.51
Mar-86	177.6	0.680	2.35	7.21
Jun-86	163.8	0.654	2.20	7.02
Sep-86	154.4	0.690	2.03	6.64
Dec-86	158.3	0.676	1.92	6.38
Mar-87	145.7	0.622	1.80	6.00
Jun-87	146.8	0.620	1.83	6.09
Sep-87	146.5	0.615	1.74	6.17
Dec-87	121.3	0.529	1.57	5.33
Mar-88	124.1	0.529	1.66	5.61
Jun-88	133.5	0.585	1.82	6.13
Sep-88	133.9	0.592	1.87	6.37
Dec-88	125.1	0.552	1.77	6.06
Mar-89	132.8	0.529	1.90	6.40
Jun-89	144.0	0.645	1.95	6.64
Sep-89	139.6	0.617	1.78	6.35
Dec-89	143.8	0.621	1.69	5.77

Source: Bloomberg Financial Markets

U.S. Dollar per Foreign Currency

Quarter Ending	Japanese Yen	British Pound	German D-Mark	French Franc
Sep-82	0.0037	1.69	0.397	0.140
Dec-82	0.0043	1.62	0.421	0.148
Mar-83	0.0042	1.48	0.412	0.137
Jun-83	0.0042	1.53	0.394	0.131
Sep-83	0.0042	1.50	0.380	0.125
Dec-83	0.0043	1.45	0.366	0.120
Mar-84	0.0044	1.44	0.385	0.125
Jun-84	0.0042	1.36	0.360	0.117
Sep-84	0.0041	1.23	0.326	0.106
Dec-84	0.0038	1.16	0.317	0.104
Mar-85	0.0038	1.24	0.325	0.106
Jun-85	0.0040	1.31	0.330	0.108
Sep-85	0.0046	1.41	0.373	0.122
Dec-85	0.0050	1.45	0.408	0.133
Mar-86	0.0056	1.47	0.426	0.139
Jun-86	0.0061	1.53	0.455	0.142
Sep-86	0.0065	1.45	0.493	0.151
Dec-86	0.0063	1.48	0.520	0.157
Mar-87	0.0069	1.61	0.555	0.167
Jun-87	0.0068	1.61	0.548	0.164
Sep-87	0.0068	1.62	0.574	0.162
Dec-87	0.0082	1.89	0.637	0.188
Mar-88	0.0081	1.89	0.604	0.178
Jun-88	0.0075	1.71	0.550	0.163
Sep-88	0.0075	1.69	0.534	0.157
Dec-88	0.0080	1.81	0.565	0.165
Mar-89	0.0075	1.89	0.526	0.156
Jun-89	0.0069	1.55	0.512	0.151
Sep-89	0.0072	1.62	0.562	0.157
Dec-89	0.0070	1.61	0.592	0.173

(continued)

Foreign Currency per U.S. Dollar

Quarter Ending	Japanese Yen	British Pound	German D-Mark	French Franc
Mar-90	157.8	0.606	1.69	5.69
Jun-90	152.4	0.571	1.67	5.59
Sep-90	138.3	0.532	1.47	5.24
Dec-90	135.8	0.518	1.50	5.10
Mar-91	140.6	0.571	1.70	5.76
Jun-91	137.9	0.617	1.71	6.15
Sep-91	132.8	0.563	1.66	5.66
Dec-91	124.9	0.535	1.52	5.20
Mar-92	132.9	0.575	1.65	5.58
Jun-92	125.9	0.526	1.52	5.13
Sep-92	120.1	0.562	1.41	4.80
Dec-92	124.9	0.662	1.62	5.53
Mar-93	114.9	0.662	1.61	5.46
Jun-93	107.3	0.671	1.71	5.75
Sep-93	106.3	0.667	1.63	5.70
Dec-93	111.9	0.677	1.74	5.92
Mar-94	102.8	0.676	1.67	5.72
Jun-94	98.4	0.649	1.59	5.44
Sep-94	99.2	0.633	1.55	5.29
Dec-94	99.6	0.641	1.55	5.34
Mar-95	86.6	0.617	1.37	4.80
Jun-95	84.6	0.625	1.38	4.84
Sep-95	99.7	0.633	1.43	4.90
Dec-95	103.5	0.645	1.44	4.90
Mar-96	107.3	0.655	1.48	5.03
Jun-96	109.7	0.644	1.52	5.16

Source: Bloomberg Financial Markets

U.S. Dollar per Foreign Currency

Quarter Ending	Japanese Yen	British Pound	German D-Mark	French Franc
Mar-90	0.0063	1.65	0.592	0.176
Jun-90	0.0066	1.75	0.600	0.179
Sep-90	0.0072	1.88	0.680	0.191
Dec-90	0.0074	1.93	0.667	0.196
Mar-91	0.0071	1.75	0.588	0.174
Jun-91	0.0073	1.62	0.583	0.163
Sep-91	0.0075	1.78	0.602	0.177
Dec-91	0.0080	1.87	0.658	0.192
Mar-92	0.0075	1.74	0.606	0.179
Jun-92	0.0079	1.90	0.656	0.195
Sep-92	0.0083	1.78	0.708	0.208
Dec-92	0.0080	1.51	0.617	0.181
Mar-93	0.0087	1.51	0.621	0.183
Jun-93	0.0093	1.49	0.585	0.174
Sep-93	0.0094	1.50	0.613	0.175
Dec-93	0.0089	1.48	0.575	0.169
Mar-94	0.0097	1.48	0.599	0.175
Jun-94	0.0102	1.54	0.629	0.184
Sep-94	0.0101	1.58	0.645	0.189
Dec-94	0.0100	1.56	0.645	0.187
Mar-95	0.0116	1.62	0.730	0.208
Jun-95	0.0118	1.60	0.725	0.207
Sep-95	0.0100	1.58	0.699	0.204
Dec-95	0.0097	1.55	0.694	0.204
Mar-96	0.0093	1.53	0.676	0.199
Jun-96	0.0091	1.55	0.658	0.194

Black Scholes Model

Formula:

$$C = P\,N\,(d1) - Se^{-rt}\,N(d2)$$

Assuming valuation of a call option of a stock, where:

C = Value of call option
P = Current price of stock
S = Strike price of option
e = natural log e
r = risk-free interest rate (continuous compounding)
t = time to expiration expressed as percentage of a year
σ = annual standard deviation of stock's return (volatility)

$$d1 = \frac{[\ln(p/S)] + rt + .5\sigma\sqrt{t}}{\sigma\sqrt{t}}$$

$$d2 = d1 - [\sigma\sqrt{t}]$$

N(d) = cumulative probablility distribution for d, assuming normal distribution.

Example: Consider a call option on IBM stock, with a $150 strike price, expiring in 3 months, or .25 years. The current IBM share price is $135, and the standard deviation is estimated at .40. The current T-bill rate is 5% and is used as a risk-free proxy.

P = $135
S = $150
r = 5%
t = .25

$$d1 = \frac{[\ln(135/150)] + .05\,(.25)}{.40\,\sqrt{.25}} + .5\,(.4)\,\sqrt{.25}$$

= -0.36

N(d1)= 0.359 {from normal distribution tables}

$$d2 = -.36 - [.4\sqrt{.25}]$$
$$= -0.56$$

N(d2)= 0.288 {from normal distribution tables}

C = $135(.359) - $150e^ - .013(.288)
= $48.5 - $42.64
= $5.86

Key Assumptions:

1. Underlying security pays no dividends.
2. The option is marketable (i.e., there is continuous trading activity).
3. The risk-free rate is constant over the life of the option.
4. The option is European (i.e., it cannot be exercised before the expiration date, as can American options.)
5. The underlying security's probability distribution is log-normal.

Discipline Index

Terms in the *Business Encyclopedia: Master Reference* cover the eight disciplines described below. Each term is indexed by discipline on the following pages.

acct   **Accounting** is the identification, measurement, and interpretation of a business's financial information to facilitate informed judgments by decision makers. It is an integral part of every management function.

econ   **Economics** looks at how societies distribute, exchange, and consume the goods and services that are produced using the limited resources available. The effects of supply and demand on prices, wages, profits, and employment are analyzed.

fin   **Finance** concerns the flow of money and credit that is the lifeblood of business, government, and individual investment. That flow of money and credit is in turn facilitated by the purchase and sale of legal instruments such as stocks, bonds, and loans by financial institutions.

mgmt   **Management** combines the complexity of organizing and administering a business with the aim of most efficiently achieving the owner's goals. It deals with planning, implementation of strategy, analysis of results, and revisions of processes, and extends to every level of the company.

mktg   **Marketing** involves planning and executing the strategy needed for a business to move a good or service from producer to consumer. A broader term than just selling, it focuses on determining what customers want or need, and finding a way to profitably satisfy that demand.

oper   **Operations** encompasses all the steps involved in taking raw materials or other inputs and changing them into finished products.

strat   **Strategy** is management's course of action for achieving the owner's objectives. To formulate a viable strategy, management must take into account the present and projected capabilities of the business while keeping a clear eye on potential problems and options for contingencies.

tech   **Technology** embodies the machines, materials, processes, and knowledge used in the application of scientific discoveries to the production of goods and services. Some of the technological advances that have profoundly affected business in recent years involve computers, communications, and synthetic substances.

acct

accounting

mgmt

(continued)

mktg

marketing

mktg

(continued)

mktg

(continued)

strat

(continued)

reverse takeover
skimming
strategic business unit
  (SBU)
strategic planning
sunk cost
supplier power
supply elasticity
SWOT analysis
synergy
technology transfer
tender offer buyout
time series analysis
upstream
value chain
value constellation
vertical integration
virtual corporation
virtual organization
working capital
  productivity
working capital ratio

tech

technology

analog
artificial intelligence
assembly language
assembly line
asynchronous
  transmission
automated storage/
  retrieval system
  (AS/RS)
automatic guided vehicle
  system (AGVS)
automatic merchandising
automation
autonomation
bandwidth
bar code
beta-tester
bit (binary digit)

boot
broadband channel
bug
bulletin board system
  (BBS)
bus
byte
CD-ROM (compact
  disk–read only
  memory)
character-based interface
client/server network
computer-integrated
  manufacturing (CIM)
cycle counting
data encryption
database
database management
  system (DBMS)
digital
electronic bulletin board
electronic conferencing
electronic mail (e-mail)
e-mail
executive information
  systems (EIS)
expert system
fault tolerance
flexible manufacturing
  system
geographical information
  systems
graphical user interface
  (GUI)
groupware
high-level languages
home page
hyperlink
hypertext
icons
integrated circuits
integrated services digital
  network (ISDN)
intelligent agents

Internet
Internet Society
kilobyte
knowledge engineering
legacy systems
local area network (LAN)
machine language
machine vision
mainframe
management information
  system (MIS)
management software
material requirements
  planning (MRP)
MBA-ware
megabyte (MB)
microwave
MIPS (million instructions
  per second)
modem (modulator/
  demodulator)
multitasking
network
parallel processors
peripheral
printer server
protocol
real-time processing
robotics
server
software piracy
supercomputer
synchronous transmission
technical specialist
transaction processing
  system
universal product code
UNIX
virtual reality (VR)
virus
warm boot
wide area network (WAN)
workstation
World Wide Web (WWW)

General Index

A

AAA
See American Academy of Advertising

AAAA
See American Association of Advertising Agencies

AAF
See American Advertising Federation

ABC
See activity-based costing (ABC); American Broadcasting Company (ABC); Capital Cities/ABC

abnormal cost, 1

ABO
See accumulated benefit obligation (ABO)

absorption costing, 1, 167–168
See also costing *versus* direct costing, *168*

A-B split, 1

accelerated cost recovery system (ACRS), 2–4, 194

accelerated depreciation, 2–4

acceptance quality level (AQL), 5

acceptance sampling, 4–5

accountants, 6–7, 146–147

accountant's responsibility, 7

account executive (AE), 6

accounting changes, 7–8
cumulative effect of, 171–172

accounting control, 8

accounting equation, *8,* 8–9, 70, 73

accounting methods, 9–10
changing, 280

accounting period, 10, 11, 274

Accounting Principles Board (APB), 10, 290

accounting rate of return, *483*

accounts, 5–6
closing the books, 137

accounts payable, 10

accounts receivable, 10–11, 53
opportunity cost and, 432
selling, 265

accounts receivable turnover, 11

accrual accounting, 9

accrual accounting method, 398

accrual basis, 11

accrued expenses, 11, 12

accrued liabilities, 11

accumulated benefit obligation (ABO), 12

accumulated depreciation, 12

ACI
See Advertising Council, Inc.

acid test ratio, *12,* 12–13, 174

ACRS
See accelerated cost recovery system (ACRS)

action research, 13–14

activity-based costing (ABC), 15

actor-contract system, 413

actual interest rate, 15

actuarial method, 37

actuary, 15

ADA
See Americans with Disabilities Act

Adams, Bill, 276

Adams, Samuel, 558

additional paid-in capital, 17

ADEA
See Age Discrimination in Employment Act

adequate disclosure concept, 17

ADI
See area of dominant influence (ADI)

adjustable rates, 17–18, *18*

adjusting journal entry, 18

administered VMS, 574

administrative expenses, 19
See also selling, general, and administrative expenses

Adolph Coors Co., 394, 558

ADR
See American Depository Receipt

ad response, 16

ADT Security, *175*

Advanced Microdevices, 260–263

adverse opinion report, 50

advertising, 6, 16, 19–20, 472
Internet, 339
size/space, 33
use of humor in, 312, 313

Advertising Age, 21

advertising agencies, 21, 45, 400, 526

Advertising Council, Inc. (ACI), 21–22

advertising expenditures, estimated, *20*

advertising frequency, 22

advertising rates, 22–23
newspaper, 140

advertorials
See advocacy advertising

advocacy advertising, 24

advocate channels, 449

Adweek, 24

AE
See account executive (AE)

aerospace industry, 54–57
See also aviation industry; specific companies
cost-plus pricing in, 166

AES Corporation, 237

affiliated company, 24–25, 241

Affiliated National Hotels, 612

affinity card, 25

affirmative action, 26

afternoon drive time, 26

Age Discrimination in Employment Act (ADEA), 26–28, 232

agent, 28

aggregate demand, *28,* 28–29

aggregate plan, 29

aggregate supply, 30, 531

Agracetus, 316

AGVS
See automatic guided vehicle system

List of Illustrations

Credits

Knowledge Exchange wishes to thank the following organizations for providing materials included in this volume.

A Chronology of Business

ABB Inc.
Apple Computer, Inc.
ARPA
Bettmann Archive
Boeing Company
Charles William Bush
Compaq Computer Corporation
Dow Jones & Company, Inc.
Federal Express Corporation
Great Atlantic & Pacific Tea Company, Inc.
Intel Corporation
International Business Machines Corporation
Library of Congress
McDonald's Corporation
Microsoft Corporation
Naval Historical Foundation
New United Motor Manufacturing Inc.
Oracle Corporation
PhotoDisc, Inc. ©1996
Time Warner Inc.
U.S. Department of Commerce, National Institute of Standards and Technology
U.S. Department of the Interior, National Park Service, Edison National Historic Site
The Wharton School, University of Pennsylvania

Leadership Profiles

Apple Computer, Inc.
Bank of America
Bettmann Archive
Bloomberg L.P.
Charles William Bush
Charles Schwab Corporation
Dell Computer Corporation
Dow Jones & Company, Inc.
Eagle River, Inc.
Federal Express Corporation
Fidelity Investments
Ron Galella Ltd.
General Electric Company
Hilton Hotels Corporation
Intel Corporation
International Business Machines Corporation
J. R. Simplot Company
Levittown Library

Library of Congress
Marriott International
Merrill Lynch & Co., Inc.
Microsoft Corporation
Mirage Resorts
Montgomery Ward
NeXT, Inc.
Paramount Pictures
SunAmerica, Inc.
Tele-Communications, Inc.
Trammell Crow
Turner Broadcasting System, Inc.
Tyson Foods, Inc.
U.S. Department of the Interior, National Park Service, Edison National Historic Site
Weyerhaeuser

Main Text and Industry Profiles

Advertising Age, Crain Communications Inc.
Advertising Council Inc.
Adweek, Billboard Publications Inc.
AES Corporation
AGV Products, Inc.
American Advertising Federation
American Airlines
American Association of Advertising Agencies, Inc.
American Honda Motor Co., Inc.
American Institute of Certified Public Accountants
American Marketing Association
American Petroleum Institute
American Stock Exchange
Amoco Corporation
Annette Del Zoppo Photography
Apple Computer, Inc.
Arch Communications Group, Inc.
Baltimore Sun Company
Bank of America
Bell Atlantic
Ben & Jerry's
Bettmann Archive
Black & Decker
Boeing Company
Business Week, The McGraw-Hill Companies
Celestial Seasonings, Inc.
Center for Applications of Psychological Type
Chicago Mercantile Exchange

Chrysler Corporation

CompuServe Incorporated

Cray Research, Inc.

Dannon Company, Inc.

Dell Computer Corporation

Dow Jones & Company, Inc.

Dun & Bradstreet Information Services

Eastman Kodak Company

Education Alternatives, Inc.

Eli Lilly & Co.

Equitable Archives

Federal Communications Commission

Federal Express Corporation

Federal Reserve Board

Federal Trade Commission

Forbes magazine, Forbes Inc.

Ford Motor Company

Fortune is a registered trademark of Time Inc. All rights reserved.

Milton Friedman

General Electric Company

General Mills, Inc.

General Motors

Gillette Company

Great Atlantic and Pacific Tea Company, Inc.

Hagley Museum and Library

IKEA

Institute of Management Accountants

Institutional Investor, Inc. Copyrighted material is reprinted with permission from the October 1995 issue, New York.

Intel Corporation

International Business Machines Corporation

John Hancock

Levi Strauss & Co.

Library of Congress

Logitech

Lotus Development Corporation

M. Hanks Gallery

Mazak Corporation

Mazda Motors of America

McDonald's Corporation

MCI Communications Corporation

MetLife

Microsoft Corporation

Mirage Resorts

Motorola Inc.

NASA Ames Research Center

NASD Regulation, Inc.

Nasdaq Stock Market, Inc.

National Alliance of Business

National Archives

National Association of Securities Dealers, Inc.

National Cattlemen's Beef Association

National Quotation Bureau, Inc.

NEC Technologies, Inc.

Netscape and the Netscape Communications logo are trademarks of Netscape Communications Corporation.

New United Motor Manufacturing Inc.

Nikon Inc.

Ocean Spray Cranberries, Inc.

The One to One Future, by Don Peppers and Martha Rogers, Ph.D. Used by permission of Doubleday, a division of Bantam Doubleday Dell Publishing Group, Inc.

PhotoDisc, Inc. ©1996

Premiere Radio Networks, Inc.

Procter & Gamble Company

Quantas Airways

Royal Crown Company, Inc.

Sean O'Donnell Photography

Securities and Exchange Commission

Sikorsky Aircraft Corporation

Social Security Administration

Southwest Airlines

Starbucks Coffee Co.

Francisco Stohr

Sussman/Prejza & Company, Inc.

Toronto Stock Exchange

Toyota Motor Sales, U.S.A., Inc.

Turner Broadcasting System, Inc.

United Airlines

U.S. Department of Commerce, National Institute of Standards and Technology

U.S. Department of Energy

The Waterman Group

WD-40 Company

Westinghouse Historical Collection

Whirlpool Corporation

Wm. Wrigley Jr. Company

Xerox Corporation

INTRODUCING

Knowledge Exchange
Business Solutions System

As part of Knowledge Exchange's commitment to producing and disseminating the most useful and beneficial business knowledge available, we are proud to launch our new Business Solutions System. In order to provide a full range of products, this System will include practical, comprehensive, full-color, illustrated encyclopedias, dictionaries, and industry and trade books that cover all aspects of eight critical business disciplines.

Included in the Business Solutions System are backlist titles under the categories of Reference Essentials, Management Consultant, Entrepreneurial Advisor, and Industry Expert.

Lorraine Spurge
Editor in Chief
The Knowledge Exchange Editorial Board

Founder, president, and CEO of Knowledge Exchange, Ms. Spurge is the editor in chief of the complete Business Solutions System. She is also the author of several books including *Failure Is Not an Option: How MCI Invented Competition in Telecommunications*.

REFERENCE ESSENTIALS SERIES

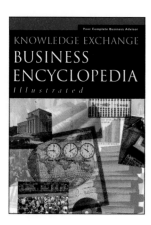

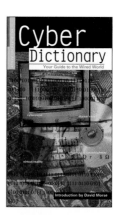

**Knowledge Exchange
Business Encyclopedia**

Your Complete Business Advisor

Lorraine Spurge, Editor in Chief

ISBN: 1-888232-05-6
750 pages 7 1/2 x 10 1/2
Business/Reference
$45.00 FPT hardcover (In Canada: $54.00)
Rights: World

The ultimate business tool and the ultimate business gift, this illustrated reference book provides a wealth of information and advice on eight critical disciplines: accounting, economics, finance, marketing, management, operations, strategy, and technology.

**Knowledge Exchange
Management Encyclopedia**

Your Complete Business Advisor

Lorraine Spurge, Editor in Chief

ISBN: 1-888232-32-3
448 pages 7 1/2 x 10 1/2
Business/Reference
$28.00 FPT hardcover (In Canada: $34.95)
Rights: World

Volume two of the Business Encyclopedia series, this book is an essential management tool providing in-depth information on hundreds of key management terms, techniques, and practices—and practical advice on how to apply them to your business.

CyberDictionary

Your Guide to the Wired World

**Edited and Introduced by
David Morse**

ISBN: 1-888232-04-8
336 pages 5 1/4 x 9 1/4
Reference/Computer
$17.95 FPT softcover (In Canada: $21.95)
Rights: World

In clear, concise language, *CyberDictionary* makes sense of the wide-open frontier of cyberspace with information useful to the novice and the cyber-pro alike.

INDUSTRY EXPERT SERIES: HEALTH CARE

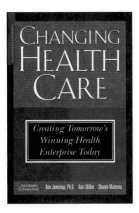

Changing Health Care

Creating Tomorrow's Winning Health Enterprise Today

Ken Jennings, Ph.D., Kurt Miller, and Sharyn Materna of Andersen Consulting

ISBN: 1-888232-18-8
336 pages   6 1/4 x 9 1/4
Business/Health Care
$24.95 FPT hardcover (In Canada: $29.95)
Rights: World

One of the major health care tasks is to deliver more value to consumers through better and expanded products and services. *Changing Health Care* outlines the strategies that all health care organizations must adopt if they want to regain their competitive edge.

The authors propose eight winning strategies designed to keep health care providers on the cutting edge—Keep Ahead of Consumers; Keep the Promise; Cut to the Moment of Value; Mind the Cycle of Life; Capitalize on Knowledge: Ride the Technology Wave; Give Your Best, Virtualize the Rest; and Mine the Riches of Outcomes.

Changing Health Care is an incisive wake-up call to the health care industry. It challenges health care providers to join the reengineering revolution reshaping American business—or face ruin.

Prescription for the Future

How the Technology Revolution Is Changing the Pulse of Global Health Care

Gwendolyn B. Moore, David A. Rey, and John D. Rollins of Andersen Consulting

ISBN: 1-888232-10-2
200 pages   6 1/4 x 9 1/4
Business/Health Care
$24.95 FPT hardcover (In Canada: $29.95)
Rights: World
Audiobook
ISBN: 1-888232-11-0
$12.00 (In Canada: $15.00)
60 minutes/Read by the authors

Authored by leading experts from the world's largest consulting firm, *Prescription for the Future* profiles an industry undergoing transformation and offers insights into the challenges facing the health care industry as it employs new technologies. This book directly addresses the concerns of managers and professionals in the health care industry regarding rapidly advancing information technology, which creates both new freedoms and new problems.

MANAGEMENT CONSULTANT SERIES

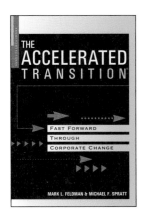

The Accelerated Transition®

Fast Forward Through Corporate Change

Mark L. Feldman, Ph.D. and Michael F. Spratt, Ph.D.

ISBN: 1-888232-28-5
225 pages   6 1/4 x 9 1/4
Business/Management
$22.95 FPT hardcover (In Canada: $28.95)
Rights: World

After the deal is done, many mergers fail. Why? Because the companies are poor matches and managers are unable to integrate disparate corporate cultures, thus causing management to be unsuccessful at achieving the goals that motivated the merger in the first place. The result? Company after company plunges into organizational upheaval and becomes unable to realize potential rewards.

Authored by America's top consultants on implementing corporate mergers, Mark L. Feldman, Ph.D., and Michael F. Spratt, Ph.D., *The Accelerated Transition*® provides critical lessons on how to turn major reorganizations into truly productive makeovers. Most important are intensive planning and speedy execution (once a merger closes, a transition should take about 100 days).

MANAGEMENT CONSULTANT SERIES

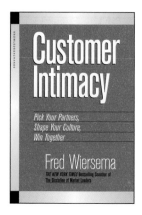

Customer Intimacy

Pick Your Partners, Shape Your Culture, Win Together

Fred Wiersema

ISBN: 1-888232-00-5
240 pages 6 1/4 x 9 1/4
Business/Marketing
$22.95 FPT hardcover (In Canada: $27.95)
Rights: World

Audiobook
ISBN: 1-888232-01-3
$14.00 (In Canada: $17.00)
90 minutes/Read by the author

One in three market-leading companies attains prominence today by making the most of what author Fred Wiersema calls "customer intimacy." This engaging book reveals why the most successful businesses are those that build close win-win relationships with their customers.

Richly illustrated with examples of some of the best-known and most successful customer-intimate businesses, **Customer Intimacy** is for companies wondering what to do next after having exhausted the potential of quality thinking, lean management, and business reengineering.

Fad-Free Management

The Six Principles That Drive Successful Companies and Their Leaders

Richard Hamermesh

ISBN: 1-888232-20-X
208 pages 6 1/4 x 9 1/4
Business/Management
$24.95 FPT hardcover (In Canada: $29.95)
Rights: World

The business place has become saturated with quick fixes that promise faster, better products and happier, more loyal employees. Unfortunately, however, these fads often waste time and energy. In this new book, Richard Hamermesh argues against this trend and stresses the necessity of getting back to basics.

Readers of **Fad-Free Management** will reap the benefits of the knowledge Hamermesh gained as a professor at the world-renowned Harvard Business School.

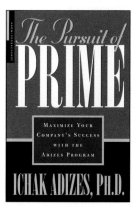

The Pursuit of Prime

Maximize Your Company's Success with the Adizes Program

Ichak Adizes, Ph.D.

ISBN: 1-888232-22-6
304 pages 6 1/4 x 9 1/4
Business/Management
$24.95 FPT hardcover (In Canada: $29.95)
Rights: World

Companies, like people, follow definite growth stages—infancy, childhood, adolescence, and *prime*. It is in this last state of development that both humans and companies are at their best. In **The Pursuit of Prime,** Ichak Adizes, Ph.D., provides a step-by-step guide for helping businesses reach this pinnacle of corporate life.

The Pursuit of Prime provides case studies of successful companies such as Bank of America and the Body Shop and enumerates the bad habits, philosophies, and myths that prevent companies from being attuned to their life cycles and thereby prosperous.

The Tao of Coaching

Boost Your Effectiveness by Inspiring Those Around You

Max Landsberg

ISBN: 1-888232-34-X
200 pages 6 1/4 x 9 1/4
Business/Management
$22.95 FPT hardcover
Rights: U.S.

Get the most out of your human capital—your employees—by transforming them into all-star managers and team players. Ideally, managers should be coaches who enhance the performance and learning abilities of others. They must provide feedback, motivation, and a master game plan.

In **The Tao of Coaching** Max Landsberg shares his belief that managers must possess a broad repertoire of management styles. The coaching skills managers can acquire from reading this book will allow them to diagnose different employee styles and use appropriate means to bring out the best in all individuals they work with.

Failure Is Not an Option

How MCI Invented Competition in Telecommunications

Lorraine Spurge

ISBN: 1-888232-08-0
272 pages 6 1/4 x 9 1/4
Business/Finance
$22.95 FPT hardcover (In Canada: $27.95)
Rights: World

Note: In KEX's Winter 1996 catalog, this book was entitled *Failure is Not an Option: A Profile of MCI.*

Educational and entertaining, **Failure is Not an Option** profiles MCI's stirring history from its meager beginnings to its present success, offering an enlightening view of the financial, management, and marketing issues the company faced. Readers will experience the tension and suspense as MCI fights for survival, takes on AT&T (then the mightiest corporation in the world), shakes up federal regulatory agencies, races to raise desperately needed capital, and ultimately alters forever the American business landscape.

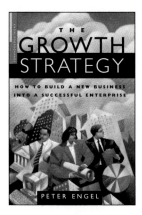

The Growth Strategy

How to Build a New Business Into a Successful Enterprise

Peter Engel

ISBN: 1-888232-30-7
240 pages 6 1/4 x 9 /1/4
Business/Entrepreneur
$22.95 FPT hardcover (In Canada: $28.95)
Rights: World

The Growth Strategy is a step-by-step guide on how entrepreneurs can help their companies make the transition from the start-up phase to a professionally managed business.

This book will show entrepreneurs in the midst of this transition how to:

- Develop a strong business from an entrepreneurial venture
- Create a valuable business that can be sold at a profit or taken public
- Grow beyond niche markets

The Growth Strategy profiles dozens of well-known companies such as Procter & Gamble, Federal Express, and Compaq, and demonstrates how they were transformed into successes through the power of aggressive growth.

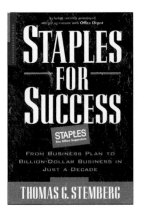

Staples for Success

From Business Plan to Billion-Dollar Business in Just a Decade

Thomas G. Stemberg

ISBN: 1-888232-24-2
192 pages 6 1/4 x 9 1/4
Business
$22.95 FPT hardcover (In Canada: $27.95)
Rights: World

Audiobook
ISBN: 1-888232-25-0
$12.00 (In Canada: $15.00)
60 minutes/Read by Campbell Scott

This engaging story details Staples' birth and subsequent transformation into office-superstore giant. Stemberg's hard work and commitment to excellence turned a radically simple idea into the $11 billion office-superstore industry we know today. The Staples story stands as a guide to forward thinking and successful management from genesis to innovation to large-scale, almost limitless growth.

Staples for Success is a must-read for every entrepreneur and anyone who believes in a great idea.

The World On Time

The 11 Management Principles That Made FedEx an Overnight Sensation

James C. Wetherbe

ISBN: 1-888232-06-4
200 pages 6 1/4 x 9 1/4
Business/Management
$22.95 FPT hardcover (In Canada: $27.95)
Rights: World

Audiobook
ISBN: 1-888232-07-2
$12.00 (In Canada: $15.00)
90 minutes/Read by the author

The World On Time is the inspirational story of how Federal Express became a leader in the overnight-delivery industry.

James C. Wetherbe, a preeminent business consultant and academic, provides a richly detailed, intimate portrait of Federal Express. Readers will learn how eleven innovative management strategies employed by Federal Express have set the standard for the way companies manage time and information, plan logistics, and serve customers.

Like the *Knowledge Exchange Business Encyclopedia,* the next five volumes in the in-depth Reference Essentials series—*Management, Marketing, Corporate Finance, Personal Finance & Investment,* and *Entrepreneurism*—are easy-to-use, comprehensive reference books. Each specialized encyclopedia presents tools and techniques unique to its discipline and is illustrated with lustrous, full-color graphics.

▲ Access thousands of essential business terms and in-depth definitions

▲ Track the evolution of global industries

▲ Discover innovative businesspeople–past and present

▲ Learn from hundreds of mini case studies, tips, and insights from renowned experts

▲ Utilize numerous formulas and custom-designed charts and graphs

▲ Get free online access to up-to-date information

Your Complete Business Advisor

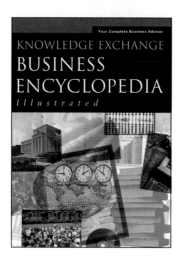

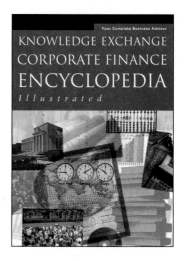

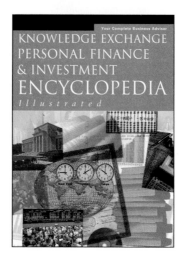

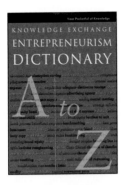

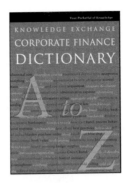

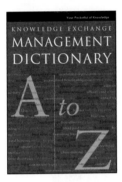

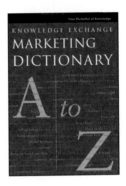

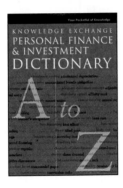

**Your Pocketful
of Knowledge**

Another facet of the Reference Essentials Series is the *Knowledge Exchange Dictionaries*. These easy-to-carry dictionaries are designed to provide concise and easily accessible definitions to hundreds of terms in specialized topics including

- ▲ *Entrepreneurism*
- ▲ *Corporate Finance*
- ▲ *Management*
- ▲ *Marketing*
- ▲ *Personal Finance and Investment*

Each user-friendly, illustrated dictionary expands on hundreds of basic definitions with numerous examples, tips, traps, and other special elements adapted from the *Business Encyclopedia* series.

A Brief History of Business

A short, lavishly illustrated history of business is contained in this companion to *A Chronology of Business* poster. This book focuses on the interchange of three major areas—technology, business organization, and banking—and shows how breakthroughs in these areas helped determine the various directions that business took. Additionally, it outlines how the nature of these changes has accelerated during the past two centuries. Written by Robert Sobel. Editor in Chief: Lorraine Spurge.

$24.95
(Available October 1997)

A Chronology of Business Poster

I'd like to purchase the following products:

Number of copies

_____ **Knowledge Exchange Business Encyclopedia**

_____ **Knowledge Exchange Management Encyclopedia**

_____ **Changing Health Care**

_____ **Customer Intimacy**
_____ *Also available as an audiobook*

_____ **CyberDictionary**

_____ **Fad-Free Management**

_____ **The Growth Strategy**

_____ **Prescription for the Future**
_____ *Also available as an audiobook*

_____ **Staples for Success**
_____ *Also available as an audiobook*

_____ **The Pursuit of Prime**

_____ **The Tao of Coaching**

_____ **The World On Time**
_____ *Also available as an audiobook*

_____ **A Chronology of Business Poster**

_____ **Knowledge Exchange Business Encyclopedia Canvas Tote Bag**
(See last page.)

Free Business • Reference • Finance Tote with Purchase of Three Books!*

Name_____ E-mail _____

Company_____ Title _____

Address _____

City/State/Zip _____

Telephone _____ Fax _____

Form of Payment:

❏ Check (payable to **Knowledge Exchange, LLC**)   ❏ Credit card

Card # _____ Exp. Date _____ Card Type_____

Cardholder's Signature: _____

Tell us more about yourself:

Occupation	**Where do you buy business books?**	**How many business books do you buy a year?**	**Age Group**
❏ Management	❏ Bookstore	❏ 0–3	❏ 18–24
❏ Marketing	❏ Mail Order	❏ 4–10	❏ 25–34
❏ Finance	❏ Warehouse Store	❏ 11–15	❏ 35–49
❏ Administrative	❏ Other	❏ 16 or more	❏ 50–over
❏ Sales			
❏ Other			

Knowledge Exchange products are available wherever books are sold.
To order by fax, photocopy this page and fax to 714.261.6137
or call toll-free to order with your credit card.

Telephone 1-888-394-5996 or Fax 1-714-261-6137

*Offer expires April 31, 1998 or while supplies last.
Shipping and handling is $4.95 for the first book, $1 for each additional book, $2 additional for each *Business Encyclopedia*.
Shipping is via Priority Mail. California residents please add 8.25% sales tax.

bnormal cost absorption costing accelerated depreciation acceptance sampling account executive acc
t adjusting journal entry administrative expense advertis   agency affinity card affirmative
smission attest average collection period baby bond bac   backorder bad debt expense bal
ehavioral response benchmarking best effort best practices beta-tester bill of lading blanket purchase
rming brand equity brand licensing budget surplus bundling bus business cycle business reengineering
se demand clearinghouse coaching cognitive dissonance cold calling cold canvassing column inch co
onver   rice conversion ratio convertible bond convertible preferred stock convertib
fficie   ng coupon rate covenant creative concept Michael Dell demand note demog
ent   diffusion process digital dilution direct mail direc   marketing disc
ome dotted-line relationship Dow Jones Industrial Average downstream d   time due dilige
nomic indexes economy of scope Edge Act effective interest rate efficiency efficient market theory e
ployee stock ownership plan empowerment events marketing everyday low pricing exchange rate expo
eserve System financial audit financial futures financial leverage finished goods inventory first move
estment foreign exchange forward contract freelance full-cost method functional organizational desig
eneric competitive strategies generic product geographical information systems global marketing glo
gross domestic product gross national product gross proceeds Andrew Grove harvesting high-yield b
acentive plans increasing rate   incremental cost indenture indexing indirect cost
sset integrated circuits intelli   agents international bonds Internet inventory tu
measure kilobyte knowledge   engineering labor force lagging economic indica
ion ledger legacy systems leve   aged buyout liability licensing lien liquidity list
Merrill Lynch machine language machine vision macroeconomics mainframe makegood management
trol systems marketing mix marketing plan mass marketing master limited partnership matching co
ission statement modem modified accelerated cost recovery system monetarism money markets mo
urdoch mystery shopper National Environmental Policy Act natural monopoly net current assets N
normal distribution North American Free Trade Agreement numerical control (NC) objectives obse
ders opportunity cost options ordinary annuity organizational buy   organizational comm
m allowances performance appraisal performance bond personal c   ption expenditures
enses   present value press release pretesting price contro   icing primary data
tivity   profit and loss statement profit center profit marg   omissory note pro
t purchasing push promotional strategy put option qualified opinion quality circle quantity discou
nterest rate rebate recapitalization recession red herring reduction to practice reference group region
turing repeat rate repurchase agreement rerefining return on investment return on sales revenues ro
ampling saving saving rate Charles Schwab scientific management self-directed work teams skimm
sampling subscription warrant subsidiary sunk cost surveying symbolic action synchronous transm
r buyout throughput time series analysis tota   preventive maintenance total processing
ndifferentiated marketing uniform accounting   system unit cost unqualified opinion
ion virtual corporation wage controls Thomas Watson Sr. weighted-average cost window dressing

A B C
H
I J
G
N
P
O
U
V
T